AF262979

Knife-Woman

Knife-Woman

———

THE LIFE OF LOUISE BOURGEOIS

Marie-Laure Bernadac

Translated by Lauren Elkin

Yale University Press | New Haven and London

Originally published in French as *Louise Bourgeois: Femme-couteau*.
© Flammarion, Paris, 2019.

Published with assistance from the Nancy Batson Nisbet Rash Publication Fund.

Published with assistance from Le Centre national du livre.

This work received support for excellence in publication and translation
from Albertine Translation, a program created by Villa Albertine
and funded by FACE Foundation.

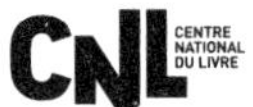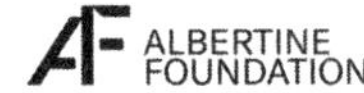

yalebooks.com/art

Designed by Jeff Wincapaw
Cover designed by Jeff Wincapaw
Set in Freight type by Jeff Wincapaw
Printed in the United States of America by Sheridan

Library of Congress Control Number: 2025936906
ISBN 978-0-300-26830-0
ebook ISBN 978-0-300-28623-6

A catalogue record for this book is available from the British Library.

Authorized Representative in the EU: Easy Access System Europe, Mustamäe tee 50,
10621 Tallinn, Estonia, gpsr.requests@easproject.com

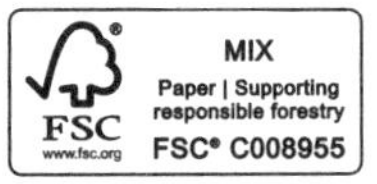

10 9 8 7 6 5 4 3 2 1

For Agathe and Théodora

CONTENTS

———

ACKNOWLEDGMENTS

This work would not have seen the light of day without precious support from The Easton Foundation.

I especially want to thank Jerry Gorovoy, who trusted me and who answered all of my many questions throughout the research process.

I would never have completed this work without the invaluable, essential, and amiable help of Maggie Wright, director of the foundation and the Louise Bourgeois Archive. Her concern for detail and exactitude as well as her complete knowledge of the archive's holdings and her perennial availability were essential contributions to this book and helped me avoid many mistakes. I want to thank Mira Brunner as well, who checked so many citations, and for the English edition I am deeply grateful to Sewon Kang of The Easton Foundation.

My thanks must extend as well to Louise Bourgeois's studio: the indispensable Wendy Williams, whom I met back in 1993, and who enthusiastically directed the studio until 2018; Richard Bruce, to whom I constantly turned for photographs; Beth Higgins and Johee Kim, for the audio and visual archives. All were constantly present and ready to respond to my requests.

I am very grateful as well to Jean-Louis and Alain Bourgeois, Louise's sons, as well as to Jessica and Claire Bourgeois, whose precious testimony enriched my sense of Louise.

This book owes a great deal to the amiable advice of Robert Storr, whose long years of work on Louise and monumental publication on her were important guides for me. Likewise, Philip Larratt-Smith's research on the psychoanalytic writings were a revelation, and helped me to better understand the artist's personality. And I must also mention Deborah Wye, whose catalogue raisonné of Louise Bourgeois's prints and books is an inexhaustible source of precious information on the artist's art and life, and Paulo Herkenhoff, whose numerous interviews with Louise were incredibly useful.

I also wish to thank those who, in one way or another, whether through sharing memories or advice, contributed to the writing of this book: Pietro Cicognani, Suzan Cooper, Paul Gardner, Joyce Kozloff, Max Kozloff, Chris Kraus, Rosalind Krauss, Sylvère Lotringer, Mark Setteducati; Nathalie Berghege, Jean Frémon, Xavier Girard, Shirley Jaffe, Hélène Leloup, Patrice Marandel, Isabelle Monod-Fontaine, Jean-Michel Place and his family, Caroline Poncet, Antoine Poncet, Nadine Pouillon, Mâkhi Xenakis, Henri Zerner; Marie-Claude Beaud, Marie de Brugerolles, Ramuntcho Matta, Daniel Milman, Nadine Satiat, Gérard Wajcman; and Arielle Bernadac and Bernard Marcadé for their brilliant readings of the manuscript.

Last, I want to thank Laure Adler, editorial director, who from the very beginning supported me and encouraged me in this vast project, and my editors, whose critical eyes on the manuscript were very useful: Julie Rouart, who immediately shared her enthusiasm for the project; and Manon Clercelet, Marion Doublet, Sylvie Bellu, and Aline Carpentier, who were patient enough to proofread and correct the manuscript with such skill.

I am so grateful to the institutions housing the archives I consulted, especially the Bibliothèque Kandinsky and its director, Didier Schulman, where Dominique Bozo's archives are kept; the Institut de la Mémoire et de l'Edition contemporaine and its director, Nathalie Léger, for Roman Cieslewicz's archives; as well as the Archives Nationale and its director, Pascale Riviale, for the École du Louvre archives. Finally, my thanks to the MoMA archives, for the 1982 exhibition, and the Archives of American Art for the Robert Goldwater correspondence.

Infinite thanks to my translator, Lauren Elkin, for her patience, care, style, and sensibility. This book owes so much to her, as well as to my excellent editor, Katherine Boller.
—Marie-Laure Bernadac

———

Louise Bourgeois wrote her diaries in both French and English and sometimes alternated between the two in the same entry—or the same sentence. If not specified, it should be assumed that the entries quoted were in French; otherwise, I have indicated in the notes if they were written in English or a mix of the two. The psychoanalytic writings quoted here (and in Philip Larratt-Smith's *Return of the Repressed,* cited throughout) were translated into English by Richard Sieburth and Françoise Gramet.

Bourgeois's English could be idiosyncratic—it was not her mother tongue, after all—but her French could be as well, and I have sought to preserve that in my translations of her writings. Moreover, she employed an eccentric approach to punctuation; we have kept most of her own here, except where it inhibited comprehension.

I would like to express my extreme gratitude to Marie-Laure Bernadac, who was a pleasure to work with and an inexhaustible source of knowledge about Bourgeois, her work, and her time. Thank you as well to Sewon Kang and Maggie Wright of The Easton Foundation for their tireless work on this manuscript, making sure each writing was as Bourgeois had written it, each fact true as far as anyone knows, and each page reference of the many books and catalogues written about Bourgeois's work correctly corresponding to the English edition. It was a major undertaking, and this book benefited immeasurably from their care and attention. I am so deeply grateful. And grateful, as well, to everyone at Yale for their patience and support as we took the time we needed to get this right.

—Lauren Elkin

——

Holy Louise!

On May 31, 2010, I went, as I do every morning, to my office in the Mollien Pavilion of the Louvre. I turned on my computer, checked my email, and immediately opened one from Wendy Williams, the director of the Louise Bourgeois Studio. It read: "Just a quick note to tell you that Louise passed away this morning. We thought she would live forever . . . ."

Passed away: I didn't immediately understand what she meant. I reread the email more closely and then I understood. Louise Bourgeois was dead! I couldn't believe it. For me, for all those who loved her, she was immortal; how could she suddenly disappear, leave us, *abandon* us?

I called her close friends, who had received the same message. They were in tears. All the radio stations wanted interviews. What to say? How to speak of the stupefaction and sadness at the loss of one of the great artists of the second half of the last century, whose work had been such an important turning point in contemporary aesthetics? Then came the inevitable flood of posthumous tributes on the front pages of the French and American newspapers. Many mentioned her spiders, or the organic, sexual works which had influenced an entire generation of artists. Others emphasized the way her creative practice was driven by the powerful reactivation of the past, and the profoundly autobiographical nature of her work, drawing on her childhood trauma. But in the end, everyone agreed that she was a pioneering feminist who created a visual language for multiple experiences which took into account many different aspects of femininity. "Louise in seventh heaven,"[1] "Art has lost its queen,"[2] "Louise reigned over the end of the century,"[3] "Louise Bourgeois, Franco-American artist,"[4] ran the headlines in the French newspapers.

Finally, in September 2010, an official tribute was held at the Museum of Modern Art in New York. One after another, curators and art historians spoke. We heard from two great American artists, Richard Serra and Jenny Holzer, whose minimalist work seemed the polar opposite of Louise's oeuvre. Nevertheless, they admired her. "I feel closeness to the expression of violence in her sculpture and to the acerbity of her writing, and I admire her demonic intelligence," said Serra.[5] Holzer's remarks were more personal: "My visits with Louise stay vivid. She was unfailingly generous with advice, with attention, and with surprising gifts. But I was more than a little afraid of her. She didn't suffer fools and was highly intelligent, so I was leery of being fool fodder."[6]

I listened attentively to their valuable comments; everyone was very moved. Louise's oldest living son, Jean-Louis Bourgeois, didn't speak until much later; his remarks were brief and of a more personal nature. He was barely audible.

I was very sad. What was it that I'd lost? A grandmother, a mother, a wife, a friend, a sister, a granddaughter? All of that at once? But especially, primarily, a great artist—unique, irreplaceable, "indispensable."

To fill this enormous void, I could see only one solution: to write her biography. To tell, in another form, the stories that she herself never stopped telling. Through writing I could resuscitate her. Of course, we still have her work—so present, so overwhelming—but I wanted to know what was really hiding behind her ironic, mischievous gaze. What had her life been like as a little girl, a young woman, an adult? Who was this strong but delicate person, with her keen sense of humor, who escaped all categories and classifications?

We know that late in life Louise Bourgeois talked a great deal about her "traumatic" childhood, the discord between her parents and in her family; but what part of this story became fictionalized as it was told—how was the past reinvented in these narratives? What relationship was there between her life, her personality, and her art? Would a biography even be able to answer these questions?

I knew her work well enough, having organized several exhibitions of it;[7] I had met the artist herself many times, and I liked her very much. I was most familiar with her writings and interviews because I had published some of them.[8] But after her death, when her extensive archive was made available to a small group of researchers, I had to start over from scratch.

Like many people of her generation, Louise kept everything. She threw away nothing—not papers, not clothing. To throw something out was, for her, a complete waste and even a sign of death. Her clothes, like her writings (letters, diaries, poetic or psychoanalytic texts) were her relics, her souvenirs, her muses, and the raw material of her creative practice; as such their value was inestimable.

She began keeping a diary when she was eleven years old and maintained this journaling practice until her death. But she also held onto letters—from her father, mother, sister, brother, and all her friends from school—as well as her school notebooks, inventories from her parents' business, Aux Vieilles Tapisseries, the account books and invoices from the gallery she ran in her father's shop. But above all, Louise was a compulsive writer. She wrote endlessly about her feelings, her thoughts, her moods, her emotions, her rages, her angry outbursts—everything, absolutely everything. And during a long-term analysis, the bulk of which took place in the 1950s and 1960s, she kept track of her dreams, what she said or planned to say to her psychoanalyst, Henry Lowenfeld, and what the analysis helped her to understand.

This mania for conservation reminds me of Pablo Picasso,[9] who also kept everything, arguing that he couldn't throw away anything that had done him the honor of appearing to him and "because one day there will be a science, which we will perhaps call 'the science of man,' which will attempt to penetrate deeper into mankind through a study of the creative man. . . . I often think of this science, and I hope to retain for posterity as full a documentation as possible. . . . That is why I date everything I make."[10] Louise, who greatly admired Picasso, was equally interested in the "behavioral sciences": "museums should see," she wrote, "that the field they have not explored is the inward vista" which might help us better "to understand *why* we do what we do."[11]

Her archive is held at The Easton Foundation, which she established in the late 1980s. On her death in 2010, her friend and assistant, Jerry Gorovoy, located the foundation in the building next door to Louise's home, at 349 West Twentieth Street. Louise acquired the house, which belonged to the famous costume designer William Ivey Long, in 2009, specifically for the foundation. Jerry became its president. "The houses separated but the 2 together," she wrote on a drawing made during a sleepless night in 1994.[12] This notion of dual houses side by side yet distinct from one another illustrates the double structure of her personality, given that for her the house is the body. These houses are also a couple, touching on another of her favorite themes. But the idea of duality also informs my approach to this book, which combines contemporary testimony and later reflections; the moment as it is lived and the memory as it is recalled.

When I did research at The Easton Foundation, I slept there, in the house, which has been completely restored and is quite comfortable and which has the same layout as Louise's old house in parallel.[13] The archives are kept on the parlor floor; the garden level holds some sculptures, photographs, and exhibition announcements, as well as some handwritten documents in glass vitrines. Her garden in the backyard has become a display space for a sculpture of two large, interlocking spiders—*Spider Couple* (2003). The kitchen is on the second floor, along with a bedroom, a terrace, and some overflow of Bourgeois's extensive library. At the very top is an additional bedroom and a much-used office.

The houses new and old are connected by two doors—one on the second floor and one on the garden level—leading from the one that preserves memory and the past to the one in which Louise lived out her everyday life. It is very moving to pass between worlds and times in this way. Nothing, or near nothing, has changed; the house looks more or less as it did when Louise lived there. In the back parlor, where Louise received guests, there are flyers, invitations, and photographs pinned to the wall, and her books are as she left them. Her clothes are still hanging in the closets. The little wooden table, positioned in front of the nook that served as a kitchen, is still there, covered in pencils and brushes. The garden-level studio is clean and tidy but full of old plaster casts, the antique printing press that she used for her printmaking, and a number of bins containing bits of fabric. Artists' houses have a heart and a soul. Louise's, preserved as it was when she lived there, with signs of her presence everywhere, has a particularly powerful energy; it is like a den, an animal's burrow. A bohemian, disorganized atmosphere reigns, with names and phone numbers scribbled directly on the walls, newspapers piling up on shelves, an overflowing stack of faxes—this faithful reconstitution requires that we bridge the divide between different temporalities, different eras; it is one that is unfamiliar to us, with its own preserved scent. A time which is past but still active, both painful and pleasurable to revisit. It was through these emotions, and this feeling of spanning the gap between memory and its activation in the present, that Louise would begin a new project.

I had never written a biography before. I immersed myself in reading her correspondence and innumerable private writings and tried to weave these biographical threads together with her work, her statements and texts, and the historical context while trying to remain as close as possible to Louise's own voice, to her expressions, her inimitable tone, and to real events. That is, assuming a diary—with its compendium of dates, places, and people met—can truly reflect the personality of its author. I also met with a number of people who knew her well and worked with her.

As I read these texts, some written in English, others in French or in a funny mix of the two, her own *franglais,* I discovered a woman who was more complex and difficult to pin down than I had thought—a multifaceted individual, with a corrosive sense of humor, deeply eccentric, fundamentally original and singular, and at the same time quite vulnerable. How could a person with such profound psychic disturbance, suffering from serious anxiety and depression, create such an audacious, innovative, spectacular oeuvre?

To write the biography of Louise Bourgeois is not simply a question of telling the story of a great artist—her training, her influences, her encounters, her doubts, and her success—but to evoke a life which cut right across the twentieth century. Louise was born in 1911 and died in 2010; she lived through two world wars, studied, traveled, experienced exile, married a famous art historian, had three children, and then found recognition late in life, becoming an icon for a whole generation. Her life demonstrates the difficulty of being both a woman and an artist, a wife and a mother, but above all, of simply being an artist: the constant doubt, the lack of self-confidence, the extreme sensitivity, the unrelenting suffering. Louise managed to make her feelings material, to sculpt them, transferring them from her body to another. Her work also incarnates the complexity of female sexuality and attests to a constantly divided way of being in the world.

. . .

Biography is not hagiography, and Louise, who saw herself as a woman without secrets, did not hesitate to write about her fits of rage, her violence, and her aggression, which could sometimes verge into sadism and cruelty.

Reading her diaries, we discover that she could be jealous, manipulative, depressive, lacking in self-confidence, often devastated by fear and terror. Her fear took many forms: it was principally of abandonment but also of creative impotence, the difficulty of communicating with other people, and especially an inability to value herself, although she unceasingly sought to please and be loved.

Louise often saw herself as an "empty house." Her work as an artist was for her a way of filling the void. Art truly served a therapeutic function and was "a guarantee of sanity."[14]

As an artist, she had a privileged, direct access to her "volcanic unconscious."[15] Rarely has an artist gone so far in her attempts to know herself, in exploring complex feelings of love and family, in the description of paralyzing neuroses. Art is therapy, she declared, but for her—like psychoanalysis—it was also a religion. Louise had access to three religions, and she associated them closely with one another.

She was extremely cultured, a great reader, a lover of music and nature, curious about everything, sensitive to political events, generous, engaged, handy around the house, a friend to dogs and cats. She loved young people, especially men, but also fragile women. She was a good mother and also a bad one, but a mother nevertheless.

Her depressive tendencies led her to begin analysis, though she would never admit having done it; this experience saved her and helped her get back to sculpting in the 1960s.

She worked constantly with paradox, often saying one thing and its complete opposite, as a matter of course. Hers was a contradictory personality, double, at once rational and chaotic.

She is the knife-woman par excellence, the sculptor who cuts, slices, snips, but also the embodiment of ambivalence: masculine and feminine, protection and menace, tenderness and violence, fragility and force.

Though a biography may aim for neutrality, it will always be subjective, and in the case of Louise Bourgeois inevitably empathetic. It is therefore no accident if, in spite of my best intentions, I found numerous similarities between her life and mine—shared affinities, places, and memories. This familiarity is on one hand useful, more easily affording access to the emotions of my subject, but could also be illusory, leading to inappropriate projections. I therefore strove for distance and objectivity. This isn't a portrait of "my" Louise but one, I hope, of "our" Louise.

This book was patiently written and woven, like a gigantic tapestry, made of numerous interlacing threads: the voices of Louise and those who were close to her, analysis of her work, testimonies. Like Penelope's weaving, it is never finished. Sometimes an image takes shape, a portrait, but one that is always in movement, blurred, ambivalent, incomplete, as if Louise went on refusing to be neatly slotted into someone else's plan. And so I'm leaving the tapestry unfinished, so that other, more profound studies may take shape.

CHAPTER 1

The "Mystery" of Childhood

All my work in the past fifty years, all my subjects, have found their inspiration in my childhood. My childhood has never lost its magic, it has never lost its mystery, and it has never lost its drama.

What exactly is the "mystery" of Louise Bourgeois's magical, dramatic childhood, which would haunt all of her work, and which she endlessly revisited later in life? For Louise, as for many artists, those early years remained an infinite territory of repressed, tremulous, secret memories, which upon being recovered—almost "erotically"—provide an inexhaustible source of emotion and cast the mold for the work to come. Louise was apparently happy as a child, according to the diaries she kept starting from the age of eleven. It was only much later, when she underwent analysis, and then in the 1980s, when her work was finally recognized, that she revisited her past and saw it differently.

Birth was for her the first separation, the first abandonment: "the abandonment. I want revenge I want tears, for having been born. I want apologies, I want blood, I want to do [to] others what has been done to me. To be born is to be ejected; to be abandoned, from there comes the fury."[1] "I mean who is born on Christmas Day?" she asked, sardonically, many years later.[2] On December 25, 1911, at ten o'clock in the morning, Louise Joséphine Bourgeois was born in Paris. She was the third child born to Joséphine Valérie Fauriaux (1879–1932) and Louis Isadore Bourgeois (1884–1951), after another child who died, and Henriette, who was born in 1904.[3] "When I was born, they abandoned me flat," she later wrote. "I was born on Christmas Day; my mother was very apologetic and the doctor said: 'Madame Bourgeois, really you are ruining my festivity.' [. . .] I was a pain in the ass when I was born. To all these people, they had their oysters and champagne and there I came."[4] It was an unusual time to be born, one that, since it was Christmas, heralded another kind of incarnation. But it was especially unexpected given that the baby was another little girl, whereas Louis Bourgeois desperately wanted a son. "So a daughter is a disappointment, everybody knows that. If you bring a daughter into this world, you have to be forgiven. The way my mother was forgiven for bringing not one but three daughters in a row into this world and I was the third one, right."[5] To console her husband and help him get over his "disappointment," Joséphine decided to name the little girl after her father, Louis, because she looked like him[6] but also, the artist said, "because Mother was a feminist and a socialist; her ideal was Louise Michel, the French Rosa Luxemburg. All the women in her family were feminists and socialists—and ferociously so!"[7]

Her maternal grandparents, the Fauriaux family, were originally from Aubusson, a city whose weaving industry was founded in the sixteenth century by migrants from Belgium, attracted by the chemical composition of the tannin-rich Creuse River, which permitted dye to take well. Louise's grandmother ran the Maison Fauriaux, a Parisian gallery at 212, boulevard Saint-Germain, which restored and sold tapestries from Beauvais, Gobelins, and Aubusson. "My mother's mother, she was hardworking. She worked like a slave and she was not unhappy. She was a tapestry woman, in Aubusson."[8] Her grandfather was a granite cutter. Louise often spoke about her grandparents' artisanal, traditional origins and of her memories of Aubusson. "I was brought up in Aubusson, my mother having been born and brought up there.[9] Aubusson is in a part of France—a very poor part of the country— where there is nothing but granite, as in Brittany, which is famous for its lace; the same combination of stone and needlework in both. The women wove and the men cut stone in the quarries."[10] Sewing on one side, sculpture on the other. Louise's art came directly from this double maternal inheritance: to repair, restore, carve, cut.

Louise's maternal grandmother, Henriette Marie-Louise Lepetit Fauriaux, whose second husband was a man named Monsieur Bathelot—whence her nickname, Granny Bathelot (Mémé Bathelot)—and whom Louise particularly loved, had three children. The eldest, Alex, her favorite, was an architect and a tapestry designer; the second son, Émile, was good friends with Louis Bourgeois, with whom he shared a passion for gliding: "My father and Émile went gliding. My mother tagged along with them when they rode their bicycles out to the flying fields."[11] Then there was Joséphine.

Joséphine was five years older than Louis—an age difference which did not please her parents, who were wary of this young man, however charming. In her *Album* (1994), there is a picture of Louis in a carriage with Joséphine and his future brother-in-law, who seems to be saying to him: "You are just a kid. Look here, kid, you're nineteen, why don't you mind your own business, you don't need our sister, she's an older woman—going on twenty-four. Just get lost."[12] "But this was not my mother's idea. She loved my father. So as I said, they eloped. They just left."[13]

Very much infatuated with each other, Joséphine and Louis decided to live together immediately. Henriette, Louise's elder sister, was born March 11, 1904, a year before her parents' marriage—a fairly rare occurrence and not a very accepted one at that time—which was celebrated at Clamart on March 4, 1905. Two photographs document the wedding: one shows the young couple surrounded by members of their two families, the other with their arms around each other. Louis is dressed soberly in a long black coat and a white shirt; Joséphine is wearing a light-colored silk dress, with a white lace shawl. He is handsome, with light eyes, a small mustache, and sensual lips—a good-looking, charming young man, with an almost childlike air. She is a sturdy, pretty young woman with dark hair in crimped waves, parted severely around her face and pulled back into a bun—her even, well-structured features reveal a great force of character and solid good sense. "He was as emotional and unreasonable as my mother was patient and reasonable," Louise said.[14]

Louis Bourgeois, Louise's father, was born in Paris on December 8, 1884, at 18, rue Beccaria, in the 12th arrondissement. His father was Jacques Désiré Bourgeois (1854–1929), a clothing manufacturer, and his mother, Marie-Albertine Lemarié (1853–1931), was a seamstress. Marie-Albertine was initially married to François Eugène Jean, a wine merchant in Montchauvet, with whom she had a son, Eugène (1872–1929). She left her husband to live with Jacques Désiré in Paris; they had two children out of wedlock, Louis and Désiré, both recognized by their father. Eugène was therefore Louis's half-brother. After François Jean's death, Jacques Désiré and Marie-Albertine were legally married in 1903. It seems that Louis never spoke of his illegitimate birth. His birth certificate bears the name of his father, Jacques Désiré Bourgeois, but he could not be given the name of his mother's husband, François Jean.[15] From the outset, there was a secret in the family. Was Louise aware of this situation? It doesn't seem as if she was, although she makes a mysterious allusion in one of her diaries: "The secret was copied from your father and *l'avare* [miserly] grandfather—also their not being married + elopement."[16] However, this could refer to her grandparents' or her own parents' marriage.

Louis studied to be a landscape architect. "His profession was landscape architect, but he never got a single cent out of it. Our garden was filled with the decorative lead statues he brought back from his travels in France, Spain, and Italy. [. . .] This is how he found the first tapestry: he saw a horse in a barn, covered with part of an old tapestry, and he brought the scrap back to my mother."[17] Louis's parents lived in Clamart, a small town in the Hauts-de-Seine, to the southwest of Paris.[18] The young couple visited every Sunday. Numerous photographs show the whole family sitting together in the garden—grandparents, uncles, aunts, and all the cousins. The way there led past the Château de Sceaux and its huge metal gate topped with two stone statues: "This is Sceaux, which is sitting in between Choisy-le-Roi and Clamart. My family is buried there. We were familiar with the Château de Sceaux, because we saw it all the time." This is how Louise annotates this old photograph, which she included in *Album*: "This picture is very important for me. What is special about this is that it is a kind of symbol of the nostalgia and distance of childhood. It has a kind of decrepit splendor, which is faraway behind this ironwork. The two figures on the high posts preside over reality in their forbidding way and they establish a very real distance between today and the past. And how we see the past."[19]

Louis's half-brother Eugène Jean married Alzire Héloïse Descaves, with whom he had five children: Lucien (1898–1939), who died at the beginning of the Second World War,[20] Raymond (who also died in the war), Marcel, Jacques,[21] and Suzanne. Désiré, Louis's beloved brother, died at the front on September 21, 1914. After his death, Louis Bourgeois took in his widow, Madeleine Eugénie Flandrin, and their two sons, Jacques and Maurice, were raised alongside his own three children. Louise took this rather badly, calling it an "invasion": "So it is the story of an invasion," she said later, though she had a great fondness, and even a bit of a crush on her cousin Jacques.[22]

He drew very well, and was admitted—aged only sixteen—to the École des beaux-arts, and graduated with a diploma in architecture. He married Chantal Lemoine and had two children: Claire Bourgeois Le Maigre (a painter, who lived in Montchauvet[23] and sometimes wrote to Louise) and Édouard Bourgeois. Maurice married a woman called Jeanne, with whom he had a daughter. Louise always remained in touch with her cousins, as her letters during and after the war attest.

Louise Joséphine was born at 174, boulevard Saint-Germain, in Paris, in a beautiful stone building next to the Café de Flore. Henriette, her older sister, was six years old, and her little brother, Pierre, wasn't born until 1913. Louise very quickly became her parents' favorite, adored for her intelligence, her beauty, and her "abilities."[24] Henriette suffered from a physical handicap (the result of a bone condition in her leg, which made it misshapen, as can be seen in photographs; she limped slightly all her life).[25] She married Georges Bonnotte in 1927. They lived in Clamart, and then in Antony (boulevard Gabriel-Péri) and eventually inherited the house in Montchauvet. The Bonnottes had no children. Pierre quickly ran into serious trouble: a bad student at the Lycée Montaigne, unable to find stable employment, and suffering from mental illness for which he was institutionalized in 1945, he spent the rest of his life in a psychiatric hospital in Villejuif. Louise was the middle child, a difficult sibling position, a source of jealousy on both sides: of the older sister as well as the eagerly wanted younger brother, who doubly stole her place as the boy and the baby of the family. She wrote in English, late in life: "The cost of Parents' fixation (one of the cost[s]) is your total inability to deal with siblings. My intense jealousy is a sibling hatred"[26] and "ferocious jealousy against the brother and sister."[27]

After working for a while with his in-laws, in 1910 Louis Bourgeois took over the family business and started his own, with a metallic sign and headed notepaper: "Aux Vieilles Tapisseries. *Panneaux et Fauteuils en Tapisserie Ancienne*,"[28] headquartered at 174, boulevard Saint-Germain.[29] The Bourgeois family rented an apartment on the fourth floor of the building next door, 172, boulevard Saint-Germain, above the Café de Flore—a handsome apartment, with wood paneling, marble fireplaces, and antique furniture and lighting fixtures, as well as wardrobes full of tapestries.

Choisy-le-Roi

In 1912, in hope of expanding their business, Louis and Joséphine decided to rent a large nineteenth-century house in Choisy-le-Roi. Number 4, avenue de Villeneuve-Saint-Georges took up four floors and included a workshop that could accommodate up to twenty-five workers; it also had a garden overlooking the Seine. The town of Choisy-le-Roi, to the southeast of Paris, frequently flooded, once quite severely in 1912. Louise, who would always live near a river, was forever haunted by the idea of a flood.

Louis Bourgeois, who had previously looked after the antiques and secondhand sales, decided to develop a workshop for restoring tapestries. He traveled all throughout France looking for tapestries and furniture to restore, as well as sculptures for the garden. "There was a *grenier*, an attic with exposed beams. It was very large and very beautiful. My father had a passion for fine furniture. All the *sièges de bois* [wooden chairs] were hanging up there. It was very pure. [. . .] You would look up and see these armchairs hanging in very good order. The floor was bare. It was quite impressive. This is the origin of a lot of hanging pieces."[30] Louise revived this memory in a piece called *Passage dangereux* (1997), in which seventeen chairs are suspended in the last room of a long wire cage.

The first photographs of Louise were taken at Choisy; there we see her as a baby sitting on her mother's lap in the garden. The whole family often gathered together for Sunday lunch, with grandparents, uncles, aunts, and cousins, everyone dressed up except for Louis, who sometimes stayed in his pajamas, embarrassing his daughter: "everybody is proper and well-dressed—except him."[31]

Then there is a photograph of Louise alone, standing on a chair, staring down the camera with her light eyes and direct gaze. She stands up straight like a queen, bundled up in a pretty white coat, dainty boots on her feet and a cloche hat on her head. She was a cosseted little thing, idolized even, as many photographs of the period attest, often showing her nestled in her mother's arms. When she was five years old, her father photographed her in the garden, with the house behind her. It is a low-angled shot, her eyes are closed, and she looks rigid and annoyed—no doubt by the camera. Both arms are plastered to her embroidered blouse.

The family liked to give each other nicknames; Henriette became Rico, and Louise had several: Louison, Louisette, Lison, or Lisette, but above all they called her the "pink diamond." "Kiss our little pink diamond. Is she not the most beautiful and luminous thing in the world?" wrote Joséphine in 1929.[32] Louise had blue eyes, delicate features, light hair often pulled back with a flower barrette. She looked just like her father. "My mother for very kind of low reasons loved me, basically because I looked like her husband."[33] "I recognize you, sir, your daughter looks so much like you that there's no use explaining that you've come on her behalf," said a Parisian bookseller, years later.[34] Whereas Henriette, the elder daughter with the less desirable physique, more resembled her mother, dark and round.

Although Louise lived there for only six years, this childhood home played a fundamental, formative role in her life. When the artist learned that it had been torn down and replaced by the Théâtre Paul Éluard in 1972, she created two works in its memory: *Cell (Choisy)* (1990–93), in which a pink marble model of the house is threatened by a guillotine—"the past is guillotined by the present"—and then *Les bienvenus* (1995), two aluminum sculptures suspended from trees in the small garden in front of the town hall, a traditional greeting place for newlyweds.[35]

The First World War

The trauma of abandonment began when my father enlisted in World War I and has remained active ever since.
When my father left me 1915 I wanted a Penis to replace him.

The First World War was one of Louise's earliest memories.[36] In 1914, Louis and Désiré Bourgeois were called up to fight. Louis was first sent to La Flèche, where he attended classes at the military school. It was wrenching for Joséphine, who tried to follow him wherever he was sent, bringing along her younger daughter. Photographs depict the three family members: the father in a soldier's uniform, the mother adoring and protective, and little Louise perched on a bench between the two. Louis was wounded in October 1916 and hospitalized in Chartres. Joséphine visited him there, always accompanied by Louise. "My mother got hysterical as soon as he was gone. She proceeded to follow him from camp to camp and she dragged me along."[37] In the photographs taken at Chartres, Louise is wearing a beautiful velvet coat with gold buttons, with a little hat on her head. She is only five years old.

Why did Joséphine take the little girl with her from city to city, to hospitals filled with the war wounded, far from the security of home, leaving her two other children to the care of their grandmother? Joséphine was already showing signs of a symbiotic relationship with Louise, who had rapidly become a pawn in the game of power and one-upmanship between her parents. In his letters, her father always included kisses first for "our dear Louison," and then Henriette and Pierre. "I was the wonderful little girl of two wonderful Papa and Maman—we were the three of us in a hostile world."[38]

Louise later remembered the soldiers who returned from the front: "There were whole trains filled with people wounded at the front and you would hear them in the night."[39] The massacre of the Great War, being taken hostage by her mother, and the lovemaking she witnessed at a very young age were the sources of her earliest traumas.[40]

Louise also described her mother's jealousy of the nurses. "We traveled during the war, my mother and I. To follow my father—She would get quite hysterical when she had no letter from him (daily letter). We had our photo taken, the three of us, when he was taken (wounded) to the hospital, she got hysterical because the Ladies of the Red Cross in Chartres thought he was a poor dear and so handsome and quite weak."[41] Once he had recovered, Louis Bourgeois was sent back off to war: "I always remember Maman crying when Papa went back after he was wounded for the second time," she wrote to her friend Colette Richarme in January 1940, when her husband was called up to fight.[42]

Her earliest memories of childhood were thus bound up with her father's suffering and hospital visits with her mother, as well as with the sight of those who had been wounded and mutilated in the First World War. The theme of amputation and prosthetics eventually became a motif in her work in the 1990s, but images of disabled people returned to her as early as 1937–38, when she worked at the Louvre; in the cafeteria she encountered the numerous disabled veterans who worked there as caretakers.[43] "To get a job in a museum in those days you had to be amputated; if you were wounded in the war you were entitled to a job. All of them were crippled in some way.

It made a very big impression on me—I couldn't take it, again I couldn't take it."[44] Perhaps this was the memory that inspired her painting *Regrettable Incident in the Louvre Palace* (1947).

Louis and Joséphine Bourgeois seem to have been very close and very much in love during this period, at least judging from the letters Louis wrote in January 1917, when he was at the barracks at Nogent-le-Rotrou: "Darling, everything is fine, your dear husband thinks he is on a business trip. Take good care of yourself so I can find you in good health [on] Sunday and send me your temperature every day. I kiss you before going to bed with all my strength. Your adoring husband."[45] "Your little husband forever."[46]

Joséphine fell ill in 1917; she caught the Spanish flu, and her complications turned into emphysema, from which she never truly recovered. Hence Louis's worry over her health: "My little darling, It was so difficult for me to leave our Choisy this morning, especially knowing you were ill [. . .]. I would like for you to take your temperature every morning and evening and send me the reading in the mail. [. . .] I kiss you with all my heart, hold our little Louison tightly to your chest for me and kiss the two other little darlings."[47]

Louis wrote nearly every day to Joséphine, detailing his health problems and describing his schedule. Compared with other soldiers at the front, he seems to have been well fed and well cared for;[48] he had a tooth out, avoided having to do exhausting chores, and worried regularly about his wife: Did she have coal? Was she feeling better? He thanked her for the packages and provisions she managed to get to him.[49] During the war, Joséphine moved with the children to Aubusson to stay with her parents, where all four of them remained until December 1918. She, too, wrote regularly to her husband, in terms that were very affectionate and above all anxious to talk about the future: "My husband, my only thought[s] are you, and after that how to arrange our tapestry, that you could open a nice shop [. . .]. I adore you my darling husband and I kiss you with all my power."[50] She describes also creating a workshop with many workers: "what bothers me is that we will have to feed them, to have them in the house. Choisy is big, granted [. . .]. You will have plenty to sell darling husband."[51]

During the summer of 1914, the Bourgeois family went to the Normandy coast for a brief trip to Trouville. Louise still remembered it in 1957: "I was afraid of the waves in Trouville and we were there before the war! I was 2 years old [. . .] my mother did not go into the water so that I went into the sea with my father."[52] And Louis mentioned it again in a letter of 1945: "I feel as if I can still see you at Trouville in 1914. Do you remember what a little band of rascals you were, with Madeleine's children?"[53] Then in December 1918, after the war was over, Louis, finding Aubusson to be "quite depressing," brought his wife and children to Paris. But Joséphine's health remained fragile. "After that, maybe their sex life was not quite the same, not as it had been. It was then that my father looked at other women, looked. His behavior became very, very childish. Immature. Not childish, but immature. After the war, the First World War, he was desperately trying to find peace, and women were his way of doing so."[54]

Antony

In 1917, Joséphine and Louis Bourgeois decided to leave Choisy-le-Roi due to the lack of tannin in the Seine, which is necessary for dyeing tapestries. In May 1919 they bought a large house at 13, avenue d'Orléans (which became avenue de la Division-Leclerc after the Second World War) in Antony, on the banks of the Bièvre, a river which unlike the Seine was very rich in tannins. This new house was the perfect playground for the children, who ran wild in the garden or on the portico between the chestnut trees. Louise, the little tomboy, climbed trees and wore her father's short trousers. Louis Bourgeois brought all kinds of farm animals: rabbits, pigs, a goat, a donkey, chickens, guinea fowl, pigeons.[55] They had a dog, Pyrame, to which Louise became very attached. When he died she was devastated, especially by the casual way her father buried him in the garden, in a shallow grave that created a little bump in the earth. In a piece of writing from 1927, she describes her love of dogs—sweet, faithful, affectionate—and her loathing of cats, whom she describes as hypocritical, selfish, incapable of love: "What spiteful animals cats are, I hate them! [. . .] Their propensity for deception is a vice that runs in their blood."[56] This declaration is all the more astonishing when we consider the profound attachment she developed later in life to her two cats, Tyger and Champfleurette, and the presence of cats in several of her prints. Sadie, she said, had the face of a cat.[57]

The soil was fertile by the river, enabling the family to grow a garden with a great number of plants. "What grew well was boxwoods. When it rains, they smell so sweet. And there were hawthorns, pink and white. And tamaris. There were the asparagus beds [. . .]. Masses of peonies. Fruit trees, pear and apple, grew in espaliers using and hiding the stone walls."[58]

> Each of us, my sister, my brother, and I, had a garden and we tried to make the most of it, learning the art of cutting trees, espaliering pears and apples. They were formal gardens, with roses in certain areas marked off by boxwood. I was hardworking, interested in that garden. And I had a passion for rock collecting. [. . .] But that garden had another importance for me. We had a tent at the bottom of it, and sometimes we would sleep there. Often we took our meals there. [. . .] Dinner was served late, and night would surprise us as we were eating. Then you could look back and see the light of the kitchen, only far away through the trees. And then our father would often say, "Now, I don't want to have children who are afraid, so you are going to go to the kitchen and bring the salt shaker." So my brother and I would run, terrified.[59]

The childhood in Antony that Bourgeois describes, with its joys and its terrors, seems a privileged and happy one. The children were given a good deal of freedom, in the context of an affectionate, warm, and ever-present family. Louise's life was punctuated by visits to her mother's workshop, her father's frequent absences, games with her cousins, especially with her cousin Jacques or her little brother, Pierre, and family meals on Sundays.

After first attending the Collège Sévigné in 1917, and then the École de la Rue Saint-Benoît in Paris from 1920 to 1921, Louise, along with Henriette and Pierre, was sent to the local school in Antony. She carefully preserved her numerous notebooks and report cards, which demonstrate that she was at that time a gifted and hardworking student. In October 1921, she started at the Lycée Fénelon, in the heart of the Latin Quarter, and divided her time between the apartment at 174, boulevard Saint-Germain, not far from the school, and the house in Antony. But it was a long ride from Antony to Porte d'Orléans—around twenty-five to thirty minutes by train. She did it either by car, driven by André, a young weaver, or with her governess, Sadie, when she was around; but most often, she went by tram, then took the train from the Luxembourg station, with her brother, Pierre. Louise later recalled the noise made by a steam locomotive called La Tubize, which ran past her window and whose white steam filled up the house.[60] It ran on a track called

L'Arpajonnais, created in 1893, which linked the Porte d'Orléans to Antony and then to Arpajon. But in 1901, this track was replaced with an electric one, and from then on La Tubize, which brought fruit and vegetables to Les Halles in the center of Paris, ran only at night.

Louise's diaries from this era detail her comings and goings between Paris and Antony: running in the morning so as not to miss the train (she often arrived late), her lunches, either in Paris with her father or in Antony with her mother, who stayed with the workers. The Bourgeois family employed a maid at that time, Suzanne Lamoine, who was engaged to marry a man called Georges; she came from Vitry-le-François, and Louise often went there to visit her. "Maids were everywhere enveloping our lives as children like a dirty towel," she wrote around 1960.[61]

When Louise was a child, Antony was the heart of an agricultural region that was particularly strong in the production of raspberries and lettuce. Then, "suddenly this changed into a heavily trafficked area. Land was at a premium, so the river was filled in, covered over by the highway. I hadn't seen the house we lived in for fifteen years. When we came back, the children and I, we looked for the river, and it was gone. The public wash house stood. And the poplars my father had planted were still there as witness."[62]

In *Ode à la Bièvre* (2002), a fabric book with texts and collages made from old clothing and textiles, she drew once more on her memories of Antony: "There were boxwoods. And honeysuckle that smelled so sweet in the rain." The river, so crucial for treating tapestries, also drew the children to it: they loved to go out in their rowboat and fish.

Joséphine's Atelier

The tapestry restoration workshop is the backdrop of all of Bourgeois's memories, the maternal material that structured and enfolded her artistic apprenticeship. Without this environment of thread and needles, of seamstresses, spinners, and weaving, we cannot understand her work.

Throughout her life Louise would revisit the role played by her mother's atelier, omnipresent from earliest childhood. In article from 1969 called "The Fabric of Construction," a review of the *Wall Hangings* exhibition at the Museum of Modern Art in New York, she mentions that at one time damaged tapestries were used as blankets for animals and says that as a child she used to hide behind them, thinking of them as sculptures. "My personal association with tapestry is [. . .] highly sculptural in terms of the three-dimensionality."[63] "My father brought them all torn up to the house and they were put back in shape according to my mother's standard of quality. She took over completely, did everything. It was a lot of work. Tapestry was the family tradition, the family business. The idea of tapestry was in my family for generations. There was just nothing else."[64]

> My mother had helped her mother in the atelier, but she had never left home and had no business sense. All she lived for was the dyeing of the wool and the repair. My mother [. . .] decided that she would repair only the old tapestries made before 1830. Before that date, the tapestries were woven on the warp of wool, but after that, they were woven on a warp of cotton. Gobelins made the cotton ones, and my mother said they were ruining tapestry by making it that way and by using chemical, not natural, dyes. [. . .]
>
> The wool, when it comes from the animal, smells a mile away. First, the grease had to be removed through alkaline baths. Then the spinner prepared the wool by hand, twisting it, lifting the wool from the pile, twisting it with her fingers into a spiral-shaped spindle. There would still be grease in the wool, so the thread, now looped into skeins about two feet long, was bathed in vats of ammonia outside near the river (if grease is left in, moths eat the wool). Then it would be rinsed in the river, because of the tannin.
>
> In the dyeing, the important thing was the fire. We had to have a gas stove with a series of burners with vats of the different dye baths at different temperatures sitting on them. You had to leave the skeins for a certain length of time in the dyes to get the desired density of color. Each of the skeins, held on two sticks, went into progressively darker dye baths. The skein would be held in the dye for one minute, two minutes, then it would be lifted out and moved along on the sticks. Sometimes the dye would be boiling; we used a thermometer to know its exact temperature. The important thing was to leave the skein untangled. The dyed skeins would be put on wooden rollers across the bridge or on the trees to dry. When they did at last dry, the wool was finally rolled into balls.[65]

The balls, spindles, skeins, wool braided or hung on trees, the washhouse—all these images, anchored deeply in Bourgeois's memory, reemerged in her sculptures of the 1990s. "My mother revolted against the chemical dyes by demonstrating that they were not fast [. . .]. She used natural colors [. . .] our ingredients came from the *herboriste* who strictly sold herbs for health and beauty. There was cochineal, a purplish red made from the bodies of little red female insects, and indigo, which was a fast color. Gaude, the name of the yellow dyeing agent, was not stable, so that the verdure, the landscape, which is supposed to be green, faded to blue. The underside is green, spinach green, but the front of the tapestries is that lovely blue."[66] On a trip to the Basque country, Joséphine discovered a breed of black sheep whose wool kept its color though they stood in the sun for long periods, so she bought their wool in great quantities.

> Little by little, it would turn out, one could say, this used to be an Aubusson, a Gobelins Metrounnaire, an Arras. My mother had shelves where she kept the tapestries folded up, arranged like books in a library by subject.[67] [. . .] To bring them [the cut-up tapestries] back together, we put them through a process called *rentrayage*: remake, reweave across the cut, rather like invisible weaving. The most infinite care was needed [. . .]. This was done in our home, where we lived.
>
> First the tapestry had to be cleaned off in the Bièvre with a special unadulterated blue soap from Marseille. On the riverbank was the public washhouse where the women came to do their laundry. There were rocks lining the bank that they would use as a washboard. [. . .] The wet wool would be so heavy that men would have to help the women as they held the tapestry in the water. Then it would be spread out to dry in the open air, reverse side exposed to the sun. Once dry, the tapestry would be laid down and nailed in place on top of a large table, and the women would start the reweaving. A woman could accomplish about fourteen inches of this work in a day. When my mother would at last say a piece was finished, it would be taken off the loom. A little oil lamp with a flame turned low would be passed across the surface of the repaired areas to burn off the fuzz from the new wool. That was always the way you could tell a tapestry was really wool, by the smell.[68]

This long description of the kind of work that went on in the atelier shows the extent of the knowledge Bourgeois acquired at a young age, regarding weaving and dyeing techniques but also, as we'll see later, of art history and mythology. Alongside the between twenty-five and thirty workers in her mother's atelier—women from modest backgrounds, with names like Jeanne, Germaine, Berthe, and Marcelle, who knew how to sew, repair, and weave—young Louise rapidly developed a solid training in both art and craft.

This atelier was her first apprenticeship as an artist. She began by drawing the missing parts of the designs, particularly the figures' feet; because the tapestries sometimes hung to the floor, this was the area that was often most damaged. Louise describes how when she was around twelve years old, Monsieur Gounaud, the Gobelins designer who regularly came to the atelier, was absent, and she filled in so well for him that her mother asked her to draw the feet. Legs and feet would remain a recurrent motif in her work. "I became an expert at drawing feet. [. . .] I was very satisfied with the feet I drew for my mother. It was a great victory. And it also taught me that art is interesting, and that it can be useful. [. . .] It can restore. So it gave me great pleasure. [. . .] That is how my art got started."[69] Tapestry as a material returns very late in her career, with *Spider* (1997), a gigantic arachnid crouched over a wire cage in which hang scraps of old tapestries, and then again in a series of "head" and "pillar" sculptures (2001-2), which are covered in stitched-together pieces. Louise would later explain in a film, with a glint of mischief in her eye, that her mother cut out the cupids' genitals and other explicit parts and replaced them with flowers or fruits, because the puritanical American collectors couldn't bear to see sexual organs on tapestries. Joséphine kept these woven bits of genitals clumped together in a box.[70]

Lison's Diary, 1923

When she was eleven years old, Louise began to keep a diary, a habit she would sustain all her life. Hundreds of writings filled her closets—notebooks, notepads, and loose sheets of paper, agendas big and small, meticulously preserved, dated, and archived. Her first diary was rediscovered by accident many decades after the fact. Around the time that I was organizing a joint exhibition between the Centre Pompidou and the Musée d'art moderne de la Ville de Paris in 1995, with all the media coverage that went with it, I received a telephone call from a man who said he had bought a PLM calendar book at a flea market dated 1923 and signed both "Louise Bourgeois" and "Lison Bourgeois" (her nickname).[71] He had bought it for his daughter, also called Louise, and wondered if by any chance the diary might happen to belong to Louise Bourgeois. After an examination of the document and the writing, and a consultation with the artist herself, it was declared that it was indeed her earliest childhood diary, forgotten on a train that took her from Paris to the Côte d'Azur.

This diary, found many years later and returned to the artist, is particularly moving. Reading it, we can tell that she was a sensitive, hard-working young person, who did everything she could to please her parents. Her narrative of the year begins on January 1, as she left Cannes, and concludes on December 31 with this phrase: Happy New Year to everyone who reads my diary from 1923.[72] It is as if she already had no secrets, as if she knew, with some kind of awareness of the future, that one day all her writings, even the most private ones, would be read.

In this notebook Louise demonstrates her attachment to Sadie (the English au pair who joined the family in November 1922), writing to her every week and worrying when she is sad.[73] From the very first notebook she describes the almost excessive love she has for her parents, the concerns that have already surfaced about her mother's health, the importance of school and then lycée, and her friends (for example, Madeleine Rheims and Reine Sylvestre). Over the course of the diary, it becomes clear that her father lavished her with presents and beautiful clothing. Young Louise painted, drew, practiced her English, studied the piano—she played every day and, it seems, quite happily for long periods of time. She also spent a great deal of time reading: *Don Quixote*, *Bécassine*, *La semaine de Suzette*, La Fontaine's *Fables*, *The Count of Monte Cristo*.[74]

Some of her phrasing demonstrates a poetic, lyrical sensibility: "we had a delightful trip, filled, for me, with beautiful pink and blue dreams."[75] The landscape of the Midi and the scent of the orange trees filled her with excitement, and she was particularly moved by the sound of the "trickling of water": "livid and leaping about [. . .] now that I have returned home to Paris, in the middle of all the noise, I think when I am alone of the charms of the stream running through the forest."[76] The allure of water can be found in her *Insomnia Drawings* (1994–95) and in numerous texts in which she describes the "sound of the singing water," the rivers of her childhood, the

Creuse, the Seine, the Bièvre—*la rivière gentille* (gentle river)—and finally the Hudson River in New York.[77]

The diary reveals a singularly precocious, independent young girl,[78] strong and delicate at the same time, with a great deal of awareness about herself, the complexity of her emotions, and the difficulties she had in her relationships: "The people who will read this diary will certainly think that this child is too nervous she has nothing else to do but sleep play eat, but not at all I have things to think about to reflect upon mysteries to dig up all these worries are not important to you but for me it isn't the same."[79] Nothing was ever the same for Louise, who developed an unusual personality and was already prone to angry outbursts: "I break everything smash everything because I can't find my notebook."[80]

A Romantic Friendship

Louise's second diary covers the years 1926–27.[81] Written between the ages of fourteen and fifteen years old, when she was at the Lycée Fénelon in Paris, it mainly focuses on her crush on a girl in her class, Simone Pourroy, and the feelings of jealousy and guilt she experienced toward her two best friends, Cécile and Paulette, whom she neglected a little. "I want to be everything for Simone. [. . .] I want her to be jealous of me, I want her to continue loving me absolutely, like last Wednesday. I know she adores me, and me I have exactly the same passion for her, but I don't want her to see it any longer."[82] From her earliest adolescent romantic relationships, we can detect a certain sadistic tendency: "I could hurt her a little myself." "I love to be cruel with the ones I love I always felt this need to be mean."[83] Her relationship with Simone went through many periods of crisis, passing from hatred to love: "She might be hurt, furious, but she only loves me more for it," Louise noted after an argument with Simone over a secret she refused to tell.[84]

Lovers express their feelings through gifts—roses, jewelry, handkerchiefs—through kisses, meetings, invitations. Louise nicknamed Simone "Brune-rose" (brown-haired rose). Her days were shaped by their meetings: "We were walking hand in hand, sharing in the same love, our hearts were brimming."[85] And when Simone wasn't there, Louise was in despair, and felt a violent urge to scratch the girls who sat near her in class.[86] The two young girls told each other about their first boyfriends: that is how we learn that Louise received a love letter from a boy when she was in Cannes in 1924. She showed it to her mother; because the boy lived in Syria, she knew she would never see him again.

Her parents were worried when she dropped Paulette, who had nevertheless given her a beautiful bracelet, and asked her: "why have you fallen out with her?" "oh, because I stopped liking her," said Louise.[87] "Cécile said to Maman: 'Louisette thinks herself a little God that everybody has to adore.'"[88] Louis was aware of his daughter's uncompromising, passionate nature: "a real woman in the making!!!" he said of her.[89] Louise could prove manipulative in her friendships. She made sure to maintain Paulette's faithful friendship, although she had betrayed her, because it could prove useful: "Since then I have made up with P. [Paulette], she's a very good little girl who really trusts me (she is perhaps wrong to do so). [. . .] I will be very happy to have a little place in Paulette's heart."[90]

The young ladies of the Lycée Fénelon talked about literature, music, and religion: "I want to know, if you will tell me, which is your religion," Ginette asked her. "I am a free thinker [. . .] I have a religion of my own [. . .] I am against religion [. . .]. This pretty little fairy tale for idiots as Papa says."[91]

This early allusion to religion is very significant. Born into a family of atheists, Louise became religious around this time, discovering the comfort of prayer and finding in it an ideal that was up to her high standards. She prayed to God regularly, falling asleep joyfully after praying, and had herself baptized in 1935. "I grew up with socialism + anticlericalism, and *manger du curé*. [. . .] It was familiar and seemed normal—for artists to be political seems a matter of course."[92] Moreover, the diary reveals further aspects of her symbiotic relationship with her parents, who spoiled her in the extreme. Louis often gave her money—which allowed her to purchase her first tapestry—and bought her pretty clothes. This went on for years. Later, he would bring her dresses from the great designers (Chanel, Poiret, Sonia Delaunay), no doubt a way to seek forgiveness for having been an irresponsible and oft-absent father. (He similarly looked after young Sadie's wardrobe.)

This excessive, quasi-incestuous love weighed heavily on young Louise, though she made no reference to it in her diaries of the period.

Louis even went so far as to interfere with her teachers. When the prizes were handed out at school, he turned on the charm: "It is a lucky thing to have a big, strong father who can, in one go, knock all the audacity and spite out of the teachers."[93]

Louise's grades were decent for someone who didn't work very hard. When Louise was fourteen, she even came in first in her class.

Travels

Come summer, the Bourgeois family usually went to the coast of Normandy: Cabourg, Houlgate, Villers, Deauville in 1923 and 1924, Trouville in 1928. Louise wrote about these holidays in her school notebooks—"I hopped up and down and jumped for joy at the thought that we were going to go swimming in the ocean"[94]—and she remembered this well enough that she mentioned it when she wrote to her father in the 1940s.[95] Several photographs show family members wearing swimsuits on a Normandy beach, with its famous striped canvas beach huts. Before that, they would go to Mont-Dore, a spa resort in Auvergne, which had been recommended for Joséphine, whose health required numerous stays in spa towns: La Bourboule, Saint-Honoré-les-Bains. She first went for therapy in 1919, taking only Henriette with her, then in 1920 with Louise and the others. Photographs attest to the donkey rides they took in the mountains.

In a school notebook dating from 1926–27, Louise wrote a short essay about this trip to Mont-Dore,[96] mentioning the chapel and the *trou de Lancy*, as well as the lake.[97] A few pictures also document this trip: dressed in a pretty jersey dress with big stripes and a belt, wearing a beret, the young girl stands proudly, slightly feral, in the mountainous landscape.[98]

One image is particularly well known, as Louise included it in her work later on:[99] it shows her guiding her father along a hiking trail as he pretends to be unable to see. She echoed this photograph in her sculpture *The Blind Leading the Blind* (1947–49), which is also a reference to the statue of Oedipus and Antigone found in the entryway to the Lycée Fénelon:[100] Louise never forgot it; she could never get over the idea that such a sculpture reigned over the entrance hall of a girls' school.

Other photographs document automobile trips in the family's Chrysler, to Rambouillet (1931) or Fontainebleau (1930). The Bourgeois family also went skiing in Chamonix in 1929 and then Interlaken, in Switzerland, although Louise later said she didn't like the snow.

Sadie

In 1922, a young woman named Sadie Gordon Richmond began to spend regular periods of time with the family to teach the children English—Louis, who was an avid Anglophile, wanted the children to speak the language perfectly—as well as to look after Joséphine when her husband was away. "Sadie was the unhappy teenage English girl—eighteen or twenty—who thinks about going to the Riviera and being paid. She has no money and she goes there *au pair*: she became part of the family," Louise later said, sarcastically.[101] But at the time, she felt a great deal of affection for young Sadie, her elder by only six years. In any case, she wrote regularly to Sadie when she went back to England. There is no trace in Louise's diaries and letters of this period of the relationship Louise's father was carrying on with the young Englishwoman. Louis, whom his daughter would later describe as macho, fickle, and a womanizer, was not often home: "my father developed habits of finding other women attractive. My mother endured these escapades, and he invariably came back."[102] This childhood trauma, she later said, was responsible for her psychological fragility, for the hairline crack in her psyche. "She was introduced into the family as a teacher for Pierre and myself. And she slept with my father. [. . .] The story of Sadie is to me almost as important as the story of my mother in my life. The motivation for the work is a negative reaction against her. [. . .] I thought she was going to like me. Instead of which, she betrayed me. [. . .] I was betrayed not only by my father, dammit [*sic*], but by [my mother] too. It was a double betrayal."[103] A double, even a triple betrayal. Her father was cheating not only on her mother but on her as well, in the same way that Sadie had.

It was not, however, until much later that Louise realized how hypocritical and unhealthy this situation was, through an analysis she began in 1952. Only in this period did her hostile feelings toward Sadie and her father become clear. When Sadie left the house in 1929, Louise wasn't yet angry with her: "When Sadie was pushed out if I felt the wish to kill her how could I wish to castrate her—."[104]

Some family photos were nevertheless explicit as to the role that Sadie had assumed in the family. In Nice, on the promenade des Anglais, it seems as if Louis and Sadie are a couple and Louise and Pierre their children; in another, we see Sadie looking young and triumphant on the back of a motorcycle. In a letter from 1926, Louis Bourgeois asks Sadie to come and look after Joséphine when he is away, which makes her reflect:

Your letter with your new project thoroughly amazed me. It is not a thing one can decide on the spot. [. . .] You told me in your letter that you were traveling these days and that it would be nice if I could stay with Madame during your travel. So if this would help you, I will arrive next Saturday the 30th for 8 to 15 days and during this time we will talk about the future; what do you think? [. . .] If [you say] yes, I will arrive Saturday at six o'clock at Saint-Lazare. [. . .] I am yours truly, Sadie.[105]

Louise's First Trip to England, 1926

Louise went to Great Britain twice to work on her English: in July 1926, she traveled to stay with a woman named Mrs. Worte, as part of an exchange with a young English girl of her age, who previously spent several weeks in France. Then, in the summer of 1929, she stayed with some friends of her father's, the Ashtons, and with Sadie Gordon Richmond's family. She described these two trips, especially the latter, with great precision in her diaries.

Sadie had put herself in charge of organizing them. Paging through the diary we can see that in those years, Louise had very friendly, affectionate, even ardent feelings toward her. "Sadie arrives today [. . .] what pleasure! what joy . . . but what is bothersome is that she's bringing with her the little English girl who is going to replace me. She is fifteen years old."[106] With the young English girl, on the other hand, Louise was downright sarcastic, calling her a "little gray package": "This is the portrait of my replacement. I am somewhat disappointed. 1) she doesn't know one word of French [. . .] 2) she is indolent and sleepy like a little teapot 3) she is sad and cries all the time."[107] Here we recognize Louise's very particular vocabulary and sense of humor.

At this time she regularly wrote in her diary. Out of fear that her landlady, Mrs. Worte, might read it, she invented a bizarre alphabet with illegible letters. Then she left it in a drawer for six months. When she returned to it in January 1927, she noted: "if you read this diary one day don't imagine the young person who is writing it has ever committed anything bad on the contrary, and I swear on everything I cherish most that out of everything I did while alone everything I thought could have been seen and communicated to Papa."[108] Always "Papa": judge, god, and master. These private confessions once again reveal the symbiotic nature of the relationship between Louise and her parents. It upset her when they didn't look after her. Her father sulked if she didn't kiss him every morning. "Papa is mad at me but if he knew how much I love him and how much I am sad to see him like this he would certainly forgive the oversight [. . .] that I committed by not giving him a kiss this morning."[109] Her mother sometimes found him too self-centered and reproached him for it. Louise, however, did what she could to control his anger and to please him.

In 1926, Joséphine went to Pau for two months for a treatment. "I suffered being separated from my dear maman, she always has been my guardian angel."[110] These two separations were cruelly difficult for Louise: "My mother left me behind two winters. winter of 26–27 when she went to Pau."[111]

A passionate, spirited teenager who loved intensely, Louise also believed in God and the benefits of prayer. "I reflected, I thought, my mind my heart have seen the light. I believed, I loved God. [. . .] The short prayer that I said every morning gave me courage and hope. I loved, I loved too much. Who? everybody, in God, I wanted to expand these waves of love that were submersing me."[112] At that time she was experiencing a true crisis of faith: "who took me out of nothingness, who took me out of the black hole to place me into full daylight, flashing on me a blinding and divine light, It is God!! I believe and I am happy. My hope lies in God, only he brings no disillusion."[113]

Louise wanted to be good, to give, to love. But she was able to analyze her defects with great lucidity: she was quick to anger, prideful, authoritarian, jealous, greedy, selfish.

She was, otherwise, a joyful young person, who loved trees, the countryside, nature, gardens. "To be able, for an instant, to inhale the gentle breath of happiness as it passes, as if it were the perfume of flowers! [. . .] Alone before the immensity of heaven, alone with nature, alone with herself, and before God. Her initial melancholy had given way to a delicious feeling of peace, to an internal joy."[114]

But as soon as she arrived at secondary school, the demons returned. Love could so quickly turn to hate. Louise always wanted to appear superior and to be right. "I came off [. . .] as a little savage. I suffered from that reputation," she wrote in an essay in 1927.[115] She nevertheless possessed a strong desire for honesty and never wanted to betray her word. What she most valued, during this time, was forthrightness.

The 1929 Trip

During the summer of 1929, Louise returned to England from July 18 to August 3. She stayed with the Ashtons, friends of her father, and then with Sadie's parents. She went in an airplane with Louis; a photograph shows the two of them posing before a small aircraft, with Pierre. This second trip she similarly described in great detail in her diary, beginning with the excitement of traveling by plane, what was at that time still rare, a novelty.[116] The noise of the engine, the dials, the wings, the pilots, and, especially, the view from up high: "metaphor of the countryside, squares or painted material white braids the towns and their symmetry forest, seine [*sic*]. The sea divine impression."[117] Louise notes that she goes to church on Sundays: "Everything is sung in English [. . .] what is missing is the majesty of our churches."[118]

She visited museums, going first to the Wallace Collection: "I stop in front of every painting. This has been a very good lesson. [. . .] There were also pieces of living room furniture, 2 of which were very beautiful, designed by Oudry and signed by Jacob."[119] Then she went to Hampton Court, where "the paintings do not interest them so I go there alone which I much prefer. I revisit the tapestries, the pictures."[120] But her critical faculties were intact: "we go to a flower and vegetable exhibition, it is entertaining to see how much the British are interested in things that nobody would bother looking at in France."[121] In a more personal register, she criticized a young friend for not being kinder to her mother.[122] Because for Louise, "[Maman] is my truth in life I would suffer without her."[123]

Mother and daughter kept up a regular correspondence during these two weeks, which indicates the force of their love, their mutual attachment, but above all their great emotional codependence. Joséphine had trouble living without Louise—she felt isolated in the big house, even if Pierre sometimes came to look after her, as well as Aunt Madeleine or Joséphine's mother: "[I don't like to] be separated from you. If you knew this big emptiness around me."[124] She worried about her health, alone and far away. However, she recognized that Louise was a woman now. She tried to reassure her daughter, explaining that she was doing all she could to recover, or at least to feel a little better, and that despite her weakness she was getting back to work a bit on the tapestries. Through these letters, we can surmise that before her departure Louise had been tired and no doubt slightly depressed. Joséphine therefore hoped that this trip and this distance would be good for her—"My little girl needs change"[125]—and that she would come back rested: "Have you found the emotional respite we desired, I hope so."[126]

She counted the days: "Only a few hours separate us and it feels like months. [...] I'll call [on] 'Madame Reason' if she wants to come to me. I'll let myself believe that ten days isn't a very long time [...] I await your telegram."[127] "Darling girl, I will be so happy to see you come back. The days pass and it's evening and in the morning I don't see your blue eyes to start my day. [...] I kiss you till your cheeks are blue."[128] "I adore you my sweet girl, till Friday. I think of you all day long."[129] "I kiss you my beautiful little queen on your two beautiful blue eyes, so pure."[130]

Joséphine was nevertheless very proud of her daughter, who was working, drawing, and perfecting her English. "When you return, I will be so happy to work on the tapestries [together] [...]. You must not neglect them. [...] I love you with all my strength."[131]

The Lycée Fénelon: "This Prison I Adore"

Louise Bourgeois loved her high school: "My sweetest love outside of Antony."[132] She was proud to study there because it was an excellent school for girls, "a school of long tradition and high scholastic standing."[133] She liked to study, to learn, to understand; she had passionate relationships with her friends, which vacillated between love, hate, and jealousy. She was moreover a child of the Latin Quarter, very attached to the specific atmosphere of the triangle formed by Saint-Germain-des-Prés, Saint-Michel, and Luxembourg.

She started at the Lycée Fénelon on October 3, 1921, and stayed until

July 13, 1927. Her parents effectively decided to take her out in her next to last year so she could train in the art of tapestry-making—not sewing but the artistic, technical, and commercial sides of the business. "My mother was of delicate health and she considered that I ought to become established in her profession as soon as possible. [. . .] my parents took me out of school when I was fifteen (two years before the 'Bachot' degree)."[134] Leaving school in this way was intolerable. "I was the first for the whole school, right? At that point my parents said: 'no more school. You know enough. Come and do business.'"[135] In leaving high school, not only was she leaving a reassuring world—the spiritual and intellectual life she needed and her dear friends who helped her escape her family's oppressive affection—but all this additional free time confined her to the role of her mother's nursemaid.

She was already impatient with the long summer holidays: "No more school: these three words keep buzzing in my ears. Two and a half months without classes, the courtyard, and this little café [. . .] to never see my lycée again [. . .] my heart is sad. [. . .] I hope the approaching holidays won't be a nightmare [. . .] closing me up within the enormous walls of this prison I adore." Later, when she was no longer enrolled there, she returned, alone and nostalgic, in October 1929: "I go to my lycée."[136] "I feel like it belongs to me. Nobody is overjoyed to see me, but I possess it, it speaks to me in a way that the others can't understand. When I come to visit our two souls listen to one another. The others live with but don't hear the poetry that emerges from the heavy cloistering walls."[137]

Louise kept several class photographs from her years at the Lycée Fénelon. On one, she has blotted out her face because she didn't like her new haircut. On another, she poked out the eyes and heart of her friend Annie Segalen. She retained a strong memory of her classmates and kept all their letters. Their names evoke childhood and France, and they frequently recur in her later diaries and writings: Madeleine Rheims, Cécile Chasse, Paulette Mauduit (who became Paulette Place, the mother of the editor Jean-Michel Place), Simone Pourroy, Annie Segalen (the daughter of Victor Segalen), who lived in Bourg-la-Reine. Since Pierre went to the Lycée Lakanal in Sceaux, Annie and Louise saw each other often. They regularly met in the 1950s when Louise visited Paris.

Later on, Mâkhi Xenakis[138] sent Louise photographs of the Lycée Fénelon, in particular the famous statue of Oedipus and Antigone that presided over the stairway at the entrance to the school. Louise also kept her notebooks from when she was eight to fifteen: writing, arithmetic then algebra and geometry, French history, music class, natural history (with numerous sketches of animals), sewing with different stitches, swatches of fabric, and classes in pattern making—even her rough draft notebooks. In an essay from 1922 or 1923 on the utility of sewing, she writes that she doesn't enjoy this activity, which she finds too calm for her taste, though she did recognize its usefulness—"[since] I won't always have Maman or a big sister beside me."[139] Some of her notebooks have detailed little sketches, and even a rebus.

At this time, studying at the Lycée Fénelon was a privilege. Louise was a devoted, brilliant student. Reading her homework from when she was fourteen or fifteen, it becomes very clear that she had an advanced knowledge of classical literary culture—the tragedies of Racine and Corneille, for instance—as well as philosophy: Voltaire, Montaigne, Montesquieu, not to mention a perfect mastery of French and English. However, in an essay on Molière's satire *The Learned Ladies,*[140] she had a precocious way of mocking pedants and the pretentiousness they displayed by calling themselves authors.

Despite being forced to stop attending school between 1927 and 1930, Louise returned to Fénelon for several months[141] and passed her philosophy *baccalauréat* on June 28, 1932; she received her official diploma on October 29. In 1931, she took courses at the Lycée universel de Nice in order to prepare the first part of the exam; she kept her practice essays. She was at that time an excellent student of mathematics and physics, as her math teacher, Rahissa Frenkel, confirmed.[142]

In July 1932, her mother wrote to her while she was on a Baltic Sea cruise: "You passed, look at how beautiful life is. [. . .] We are thinking of you and speak only of you."[143] Passing the *bac* was a great triumph for Louise, in the eyes of her family and friends. Very few young women obtained their baccalauréat in those days.

Self-Education

During her high school years, Louise read a great deal and developed her own discipline. "[I]n the tramway, one wonderful hour of reading, I am reading Sainte-Beuve who interests me a great deal and above all yesterday

L'Éloquence de Mirabeau, Isnard et Vergneaux [*sic*] fascinate me [. . .] the more profound the material, the more absorbed I am in it."[144] She received letters from her friends who also passed the bac: "Cécile announces that she obtained her baccalaureate as did Rosine and Berthe. I am very happy about it but Paulette didn't pass [. . .] she isn't writing anymore. Why? [. . .] If she doesn't get her diploma in October it will be a poor start for her, her mother will want to marry her off. [. . .] I wasn't aware of my deep attachment to her. I will go look for her one of these days."[145]

Louise tried very hard to compensate for missing school with the satisfactions of self-education.

> I have learned all sorts of things in two years and although I left secondary school the books are not off limits. [. . .] I think that to learn this way one would have to be extremely intelligent and above all one would have to be analytical, not encumbered by that knowledge, and not to parade it on a silver platter, throwing it in everyone's faces and treating other people as if they were inferior. What I reproach these students for is their pedantry, they only learn in order to amaze and shine. It's so beautiful to learn, but to study for oneself, to learn to understand oneself, to comprehend the movements of one's spirit, which other people capture in their books—that is, to try to discern truth from falsity, and to understand a little bit at a time the difficulties of life. So few are capable of doing this, and misuse that sacred education, vulgarizing it, using it to be, for the most part, vain, pretentious women.[146]

We can already see the main outlines of Louise's personality: disdain for pedantry, critique of social appearances, a refusal of superficiality, the sacredness of learning. Louise was demanding and very cultured, but she created this culture for herself, in much the same way she would forge her own artistic path through different schools of study. This independence is a testament to the strength of her character, to her precocious open-mindedness and undeniable maturity. Later on in the diary of 1929, she described her qualities in comparison to those of her friends from school. On the positive side, she insisted on the experience she acquired: she developed a nose for business, became accustomed to overseeing personnel (workers and servants) and interacting with merchants, and acquired a deep knowledge of the métier (dyeing, the jobs of the different workers, fabrics, stitches, an understanding of the processes put in place by Joséphine, the artistic component, composition). "Drawing, artistry, balance and rhythm, the art and above all the appreciation of a job well done is a question of feeling but also of looking and factoring in precisely good common sense and an analytical mind. For it to be beautiful, a work of art must first of all be healthy. These ideas of a soul and spirit I shall develop later as I grow up therefore as my feelings my vibrations and my thoughts become sharper."[147] Fully aware of her skills, Louise seemed ready to become an artist.

The Côte d'Azur

From 1922 to 1932, Joséphine and Louise spent the winter from December or January until late March in the south, sometimes joined by Louis, Pierre, Sadie, Joséphine's mother, or aunt Madeleine. The climate was gentler there, and better for Joséphine's health, since she had fallen ill with emphysema. The Côte d'Azur had been stylish since the late nineteenth century and was particularly popular since the First World War with foreigners, especially with British tourists. The promenade des Anglais in Nice became the gathering place for a well-off clientele, often artistically inclined, who enjoyed displaying themselves there.

During the winter of 1922, the Bourgeois family stayed at the Hôtel des Anges in Le Cannet, a luxurious hotel that was also the site of the father's debauchery—which Louise remembered much later. "My father never belonged to the house. Felt at the hotel des anges with the three girls. And the mannequin in his bed."[148] She also remembered the scent in the air: "the big eucalyptus on Carnot Avenue [. . .]. It is the smell of the eucalyptus at 475 Dean that reminded me [of] the hotel des anges."[149]

Next they rented the Villa Marcel on avenue Carnot, and starting in 1929, the Villa Pompéiana on avenue de Picardie, in Cimiez, not far from Nice. From 1931 to 1932, Louise was enrolled in a baccalauréat program at the Lycée universel de Nice run by Rahissa Frenkel; she also took classes in drawing and piano, and perfected her English at the Berlitz school. She passed the first half of the bac by correspondence, with help from Frenkel, who became a friend. She saw her again Paris in 1934, but Frenkel would be deported during the war.

Mother and daughter took the train from the Gare de Lyon, while Louis drove down in the family car. Louise was enthusiastic about what she discovered during these trips: the luxurious vegetation of the Mediterranean, with its palm trees and orange trees and southern smells; she liked to swim in the sea and go for long walks in the neighboring villages. In her letters to friends and to her brother, she expresses amazement at the local patois, the southern accent, the Provençal markets, and Carnaval.

In a school notebook, she drew a view of the Midi with its palm trees and wrote a short essay on the Mediterranean landscape, where she described mimosas, lemon trees, cacti, roses, and Grasse carnations.[150] She later described a trip to visit Pierre Bonnard, who lived closed by.

Several photographs provide an image of these vacations in the south: one shows Louise looking pensive as she sits on a stool in the garden, wearing a white lace dress, her hair in two long braids. One shows her dressed in a kimono; in another she poses on the promenade des Anglais with Louis, Sadie, and Pierre; in still another she is with Joséphine, who is wrapped up in a large dark coat and restitching a tapestry. Despite having been brought so far from Paris, her high school, and her friends, she seems to be fully enjoying these trips, even though they had been made in order to bolster her mother's health. She visited Menton, Vence, and Saint-Paul-de-Vence with her father. She sometimes mentions in her diary how much pleasure she takes in swimming in the sea, in the mildness of the climate, and the beauty of the landscape: "I am happy, I sing sweet warm [missing word] that the night scatters around [...] my happiness is pure. This crazy ride through the night between ocean and rocks brings me back 6 years earlier on the way to Aix [en Provence], when I sang [the song] l'étoile du berger."[151]

Joséphine's Illness: Diary, 1928–1929

Louise left on Monday, December 24, 1928, for Nice; the Villa Pompéiana had been rented for four years. From the train she saw the red rocks and jagged boulders of the Massif de l'Estérel, Fréjus, and Saint-Raphaël. That winter, she continued to take drawing classes: "I draw a face of Christ which is good, the teacher is satisfied."[152] She drew constantly, did her own self-portrait, copied Donatello's "beautiful unknown woman,"[153] the "lady of Nuremberg,"[154] and tried out different media: watercolor, gouache, pencil.

Louise's father took her to the casino to entertain her, gave her a watch and then a superb blue leather coat. Most importantly, he gave her an easel and a box of paints.

In a letter to her friend Cécile Chasse dated in January 1929, she explained that their return had been delayed by her mother's health. She talked about her drawings and charcoals and made particular reference to her anatomy class: "I go and draw nerves, muscles, and flayed skin."[155] These anatomy notebooks, which she carefully kept, attest to the precision of her line. Louise and Cécile also talked about what they were reading: "Voltaire and Montesquieu [. . .] it will interest you a lot."[156] Cécile talked about the Prix Goncourt of 1929, which had gone to a bad imitation of Jules Verne or Jack London.[157]

Sadie and Louis went to the casino alone to see Mrs. Boeler and celebrate Epiphany: "and the three of us have dinner at our small table, Maman, Pierre, and me."[158] In February 1929 we learn of the death of her mother's father. Louise took charge of dyeing the clothing black for the mourning period. She regularly wrote to her friends, to her grandmother, to Henriette, to Sadie, to her father, and to her friend Cécile. "I started keeping my diary again, which I'm writing as a sequence of letters (which I keep in my drawer) addressed to different people, according to the feelings I want to translate there."[159]

Louise's days pass according to the rhythm of her mother's health: "[Maman is sick], I play nurse [. . .] give her several Gardenals, [she has a fever], I wash her linens."[160] The whole beginning of the 1929 diary minutely describes the medical details and symptoms of Joséphine's illness, the care Louise dispensed to her, the visits from doctors, the worry and the weight of her daily activities: "Maman is deeply sad, she cries all the time [. . .] no way to cheer her up. [. . .] She has a violent spell as if she was going to have a spitting episode [. . .]. [She] fainted for a few minutes."[161] Louise took care of bathing her and giving her injections, administered quinine and Gardenal, applied the *ventouses* (little glass vials that are heated and applied to the skin), mustard poultices, and a treatment called a Rigollot.[162] Several doctors regularly visited Joséphine's bedside, as she was often confined there: Dr. Baudraut as well as Dr. Oelnitz,[163] who seemed less worried and thought that there was nothing wrong with her lungs, that she was, rather, suffering from menopause-related difficulties, which is why she was prescribed

Gardenal. Nevertheless, she had "a loose cough, she spits green stuff but this morning there were blood stains in her spit."[164]

Louise took it all in hand: the atelier, paying the workers, cleaning, looking after the mail, the shopping, the cooking.

"Travail," "Devoir," "Vertu" (Labor, Duty, Virtue): not only did she write these three words on the cover of the diary she started on June 13, 1929[165] (which she finished the following September) but they also appeared as three initials, TDV, which return during analysis in 1952: "I wanted to go away and save other people from evil. *Travail devoir vertu* [Labor Duty Virtue], T.D.V. It lasted for years. I was 16 years old."[166]

For those two months, she wrote in her diary every day, recording every detail of what had happened, between caring for her mother, her drawing and piano classes, working in the atelier, meals, housekeeping, reading, dreaming.

"I am happy only when I am with Maman."[167] Forty years later, she would note: "The peace I felt with Maman when she was ill is a peace I have never felt with anybody else, because it appeased a [feeling of] guilt."[168]

This diary is particularly difficult to read because Louise included everything to do with her mother's illness, including the different diagnoses she received from Drs. Baudraut and Médeville, who were regularly called upon during her most acute attacks and periods of faintness. "I went from doctor to doctor to try to claw my mother back from the jaws of death," she wrote later.[169] It seems that Joséphine was suffering from both a damaged lung—"a fracture [at] top left of the right lung"—and complications of menopause.[170] "Pain and generalized spasms are a nervous phenomenon related to epilepsy [. . .] and these attacks are a result of the complicated intoxication of menopause-related difficulties."[171] "We have bought a medical dictionary I consult it for a longue [*sic*] time about the menopause and asthma."[172]

Louise also described the diet her mother had to follow (milk, vegetable bouillon) as well as the treatments that she was prescribed: Gardenal, quinine, sucking candies for her cough, inhalations. She took her temperature every day, kept an eye on her bowel movements, gave her injections, and worried frequently. Given that at one moment the doctors suspected a nascent case of tuberculosis, the phlegm Joséphine coughed up was sent for analysis, but the results were good. Louise's mood was entirely bound up in her mother's state of health, oscillating between extreme concern and total joy at learning she could come down to dinner or that she had slept well.

But the diary also tells us much about Louise's personality at the age of seventeen, when she had left lycée and was drawing more and more for herself. Labor: she worked very hard, from the moment she got up at 6:30 a.m.—distressed if she woke later than that—into the evening: drew in the garden, took piano lessons, worked in the atelier, kept house, cooked, washed. Duty: she took care of her mother, playing nursemaid. Virtue: Louise had a strong moral sense. She was keenly aware of her responsibilities, defended the poor against the rich, was happy when she learned things and cultivated herself. "What a good day, I have learn[ed] a great deal and I love life when I learn, when I grow up increase morally and intellectually [...] to live is virtue and beauty."[173] She read Maeterlinck and a biography of Jules Laforgue, and her father gave her a copy of *My Friend's Book* by Anatole France.

Her feelings toward her parents were as strong as ever; she loved them more than anything: "I am persuaded that I love mother more than she does [me]."[174] "[T]he older I get, the better I understand [them and] the more I love them," she wrote in her 1928–29 diary.[175] Her father was tender and attentive and lavished her with presents. When he bought the family a Citroën automobile, she used it to get to Paris more easily and to take her mother out so they wouldn't have to depend on Sadie. Louise drew a lot on her own but continued to take drawing lessons in the rue Madame. She went swimming in the Molitor pool, did errands at the Bon Marché or at the shops at the Louvre, and went walking in her beloved Paris, especially the Tuileries: "I think it is my favorite spot in Paris—beautiful statues, flowers, wonderful view all along to the Champs-Elysées."[176]

This very dense diary was largely written in English, no doubt to keep up the level of proficiency she had acquired during her stay in England. It's clear she'd already developed a political conscience: "We hear TSF about The Hague & the conference which is now nearly finished. I like politic[s] and I have followed all the conference on the papers."[177] She is referring to the conference of August 1929 at The Hague during which Aristide Briand, the minister of foreign affairs, proposed a plan for a European Union, a short-lived proposal but one that raised a number of questions in the press.

Why did Louise, at only seventeen years old, take on the role of nurse-maid to her mother? The only explanation is their close bond. Louise precociously played the role of father and mother to her, all the while remaining blind to her own father's irresponsibility and infidelities. Louis's absences were always justified by a trip or by work—and she was always overjoyed when he arrived in Paris in time for dinner. This difficult period during her mother's illness was an enriching one for Louise, who grew in maturity, setting her apart from other girls her age. She understood much later that she suffered greatly from this arrangement.[178] "Your anger comes from the fact that your father never appreciated what you had done for your mother when she was sick—true—he never appreciated it and never said thank you, neither did Henriette—true—but they never asked you to do it."[179]

It was during the course of her later analysis that Louise became aware of the ambiguities in this relationship: "overdoing the care of my mother showed a hatred motivation."[180]

Only her maternal grandmother, Mémé Bathelot, recognized what she had done for Joséphine: "to know that you are happy is an immense joy for me you really deserve it," she wrote to her on January 12, 1939; "you were so good to your mother."[181]

The Death of the Mother

Joséphine Valérie Bourgeois died September 14, 1932, after years of suffering and illness. Louise was twenty years old. There is no trace of her death in her diaries, writings, or correspondence; it seems to have been fairly sudden. During the summer of 1932, she had gone traveling in Scandinavia and Russia, which would suggest that her mother's state of health was not much cause for concern. Every year on her calendar, Louise noted the anniversary of this death and returned several times in her later writings to this tragic period of mourning and her suicide attempt. When her father mocked her tears and grief, Louise threw herself in the Bièvre, and he had to fish her out and save her. This near-suicide returns regularly in her memories. "In the scene at the river when I attempted suicide I felt the phrase 'you are using blackmail now' as a sexual assault. [. . .] I flew to the river, dived in, and got under the bridge. He ran and jumped in pulled me out. To my agonizing shame in front of Yvonne and Germaine I had no pants on. He drowned me then under reproaches that his own children wanted him to catch a pneumonia."[182]

Louise would have done anything for her mother to get better; she even took an oath of virginity—or at least promised not to marry—if Joséphine were to recover. "If she survives until dawn—I swear to never get married."[183] Or she swore to become Catholic: "she is so bad that at that moment I swear that I will make me a Catholic before [I am] 21 years old."[184] As early as 1929, she foresaw her death: "I have thought that when I will not have mother I will have to married [*sic*] an older man. [. . .] I will need someone to console and love me like mother otherwise I will become neurasthenic."[185] This is the role that her future husband, Robert Goldwater, would play; she often compared him to her mother.

At Joséphine's funeral, Louise refused to march behind the coffin with the women. "I stay by my father's side. I have paid dearly for this. I do not like one woman in the world."[186] Finally she remembered her uncle Alex and her father in the dining room: "I throw myself on the coffin—and then I sleep in Maman's bed. At the same time 1) I take her place without taking anything from her, 2) I identify with her, and I am entitled to her privileges vis-à-vis the others I inherit them."[187] Louise took her mother's place—and finally had her father all to herself.

What is certain, and later references to her mother confirm this, is that this early grief was the great trauma of her youth; but it also triggered her freedom and independence: "When my mother died in 1932, this rage to understand took me over."[188] Louise would later recognize that after her mother's death, which delivered her from her protracted suffering, she herself felt a deep sense of relief.[189]

Picking Up the Threads

Between 1929 and 1932, Louise continued to work at the atelier, sketching in the missing parts of the tapestries while also studying classical life-drawing. In her 1929 diaries she described her various projects: "During drawing class I work on my Condé bust, it is too difficult for me and I toil without decent results."[190]

"[T]apestry of Audenarde we finished cutting. [. . .] I draw our beautiful Gothic [lady] in the workshop, a missing character the legs of Orpheus and a background charact[er]. I spend the afternoon on it. [. . .] I practice my piano a little [and] look for the topic of the tapestry in my mythology book."[191]

"I [. . .] go [. . .] to my drawing class [. . .] work for a half hour alone in the classroom, I draw a Greek head and sketch a model. [. . .] Papa sells our cochineal tapestry with a fleur de lys [*sic*] coat of arms. We have lunch at La Coupole. [. . .] I practice my piano for an hour."[192]

"Two heads of the Diane of [Gabii] which are not bad."[193]

"Very interesting [drawing] lesson study of the Lady of Nuremberg which I had done in Nice. [. . .] I draw Louise Brogniart, the small bust by Houdon, not bad."[194] She also drew a little Bacchus: "Painting in the morning. [. . .] I show what I have done at my drawing lessons to Mr. Gounod [. . .] he explains to me in perspective that when a line is in front of you, you see it straight for instance my house that I have painted this morning. He judges Jacques's painting v[ery] good and I am proud of him."[195]

These diaries, kept on a daily basis (and often in idiosyncratic English), are a treasure trove of information on Louise's life as the seventeen-year-old girl she was then, splitting her time between artistic and commercial activities. She very often took note of what the tapestries cost, furniture to be reupholstered, and clients' names. We also learn that she continued to practice piano regularly: "Saturday, at 8 a.m., I am at the piano, which I practice for an hour. [Handel's *Passacaille*] piece involving various difficult études."[196] Louise writes about her piano teacher, a modern young woman in whom she eagerly confided: "I speak with my teacher about marriage and artists. She is really clever and free of language with me."[197]

Music was her other passion, after drawing: "Every time I play again after a few days I love it always more. It makes me better and spreads out my nerves when they are crisped."[198] After the emotions of the eye, those of the ear.

"A Completely Luxurious Life"

It is somewhat difficult to define the social milieu in which Louise grew up.[199] A socialist, anticlerical one, to be sure: "Louise Michel [and] Rosa Luxembourg were sources of inspiration to my mother, and Zola could do no wrong for my fath[er] grandfather + Proudhon."[200]

But it was also a world of shopkeepers and artisans: her parents ran a small company employing somewhere around twenty-five people in the Antony atelier; her father also ran an important gallery of tapestries and antiques on the boulevard Saint-Germain and was a recognized expert in his field. Louise said that they were very independent and happy with their situation: "they were not social climbers, they were perfectly satisfied with their status [. . .] there was no outlandish ambition in my family. There was no rat race, you see. They wanted to be independent."[201]

Nevertheless, they were quite well off: the family had a chauffeur and several cars (a Chrysler, then a Citroën C4), wintered on the Côte d'Azur and summered in Normandy, and sometimes went skiing in Switzerland. Moreover, they had good taste and dressed elegantly—Joséphine and Louise owned several dresses from prominent designers—and whatever they bought was always of the finest quality. It could be, as described by Julia Kristeva, "old France sloughing the old to become enlightened bourgeoisie, optimistic acolytes of Rousseau"[202] but was, however, more artisanal than artistic or intellectual; Louis was very absorbed in his trips and his clients, and Joséphine by the atelier, although she also played the piano. As people who worked very hard, they believed an artist must prove himself useful: "my father hated those pretentious people who want to be artists. He would say to me: never talk to me about artists—they are parasites."[203] Always eager to learn, Louise was the most cultured of the three Bourgeois children. However, Louis apparently did not approve of her studies; her father wanted her to become an antique dealer, and to learn several languages.[204]

Louise spent time around the students in Saint-Germain-des-Prés and Saint-Michel, which she liked very much, just as she liked the green suburb where she lived. Reading her diaries and her correspondence from this period, we come to understand that she found the familial setting oppressive and upsetting, with children and parents codependent on one another in a promiscuous physicality that Louise later complained about and gave an account of in *Seven in Bed* (2001): "most of my sculptures are made of people nestling against each other."[205]

We can also surmise—and Louise would confirm it—that she was the object of an unspoken rivalry between her parents. "So what role do I play in this game? I am a pawn. Sadie is supposed to be there as my teacher and actually you, mother, are using me to keep track of your husband. This is child abuse."[206]

Louis was flighty, absent, boastful, pleasure-seeking, cocksure, while Joséphine was always patient, reasonable, perfectionistic, hard-working. "[The] men were charming. The women in the family were the strong ones."[207] They both admired and encouraged their daughter's talents from a young age, giving her painting equipment and hanging her drawings on the wall; they were very proud to have her working in the atelier. Constantly self-analyzing from adolescence, Louise quite early on felt an obsessive need to write: diaries, letters to her family and friends, often drafted before they were sent. If her writings occasionally bear a trace of the lyric sentimentality of her nature, they also reveal a profound moral conscience. In her diaries, she often described the affectionate presence of her brother, Pierre, with whom she liked to play, but rarely mentioned her older sister, Henriette, unless it's to refer to her infertility or disability: "my sister, who always inspired a great deal of compassion in me, and who desperately wanted children and never had any, and who hobbled around with a cane and a stiff knee due to water-on-the-knee."[208] When she referred to her sister's marriage in 1927 to Georges Bonnotte, it was generally in negative terms. "When [Henriette] got married, my jealousy was so intense (rage) that I became sanctimonious and religious, devoting myself to my mother's health, as a form of revenge. [. . .] I do not especially want to get married [. . .] what I want is for her not to get married."[209]

Her childhood memories of sexuality returned later on: "Hysterical symptoms can always be traced to repressed sexual memories usually having occurred (experiences). The memories may become conscious much later, at puberty—My father walking around in his nightshirt holding his genitals."[210]

One of her earliest childhood memories occurred when she was three years old, during the war: the building concierge who carried her down to the basement during the air-raid warnings openly hit on her mother: "The janitor put his hands on top of her hand and I felt that he was making a pass at her. [. . .] I was absolutely repulsed by this. [. . .] I understood that he made a pass at her. I assumed that she liked it, because if a man makes a pass at a woman it is a compliment."[211] Then as a teenager: "I had just witnessed the encounter of my sister with a neighbor's son when he was fondling her. She resisted for the simple reason that she was menstruating—so blood appeared on the scene. I thought he was killing her—the point of view of the young child. My sister was boy crazy."[212]

Sexuality was repressed and considered dangerous. For a long time, Louise held on to this feeling, inherited from her education. "When I was young, sex was talked of as a dangerous thing; sexuality was forbidden."[213]

There is no trace during this time of the difficult relations she had with her father or of his affair with Sadie. It is not until the 1950s and her turn to psychoanalysis that what was repressed in her past would return to the surface; and in her first major retrospective in 1982, she would finally translate this revisited childhood into words and images, so that we might understand its mystery and its drama.

Becoming an Artist, 1932–1938

I didn't have the security of any kind of religion, so in the end, that is
how I became an artist—to find a mode of survival.

At her father's urging, Louise took a cruise on the Baltic Sea in July 1932. Her
chaperone was Madame Luer, a friend of Louis's whom he had met in Nice.[1]
Traveling with them was a group of doctors: Jacques Dubarry, who practiced
at the Hôpital de Bordeaux, Maurice Baccharach, whom Louise later saw
regularly in 1934 (if the number of appointments she noted in her agenda
that year are anything to go by), an obstetrician named Daniel Ferré and his
wife, and a few others.

The ship made several stops. In Denmark, Louise visited Kronborg Castle, built near the city of Helsingør (Elsinore), where Shakespeare set his
tragedy *Hamlet,* and Copenhagen, where she visited the statue of Hans
Christian Andersen's Little Mermaid. She saw the Kjenndal glacier in Norway, stopped at Visby on the Swedish island of Gotland, and traveled
through Gdańsk (Poland), Vyborg (then in Finland), and Leningrad (USSR).
Her father had given her a camera, which allowed Louise to document the
trip. In some photos she is very elegant, wearing a pleated skirt and a beret
tilted to one side, standing on the gangway of the ship with Madame Luer
and her travel companions, or in front of Kronborg Castle, or posing beside
The Little Mermaid. It was a pleasure cruise, meant to be relaxing and lei-
surely for Louise, who had just passed her philosophy *baccalauréat* with
flying colors.

Joséphine wrote her daily letters, as she often did when Louise was away.
"I had two injections, one in the leg that still hurts and one in the arm which

is fine. [. . .] I went on my own so you can see that I'm quite well and you should not be the least bit worried about me. You should be happy and enjoy the trip. Think often of 'madame empty pockets' [*la poche percée*]."[2] "Above all, be happy."[3] She could not restrain herself from giving an update on her health. "The news here is excellent. [Dr.] Baudraut told me that his treatments would make a new woman of me. [. . .] Then I will be able to travel and the house will be joyful. [. . .] Every evening you must think: I have a father, a mother, a home waiting for me. They love me, and that will make the sun shine on my homecoming."[4]

She was delighted that her daughter had gone off traveling, that she might benefit from the sea and from the change of scene, but especially so that she might escape the dreariness of caretaking. "Your letter was adorable, and the photos were such a pleasure to see, you are so pretty, you know. [. . .] You will love the sea after having spent time there. The thought of you in Russia today makes me happy."[5] Louise also received a letter from her brother, Pierre: "Ricot [Henriette's nickname] changed her dressings and the wound is almost entirely healed. [. . .] I hope that the good news of your exam[6] didn't mar your holiday, and that the relief has made you more patient and sociable. [. . .] Come back to the house like a good little girl who's never been in Soviet lands."[7] Only these letters and a number of photographs that she brought back account for this first major trip abroad.

She would return to the USSR in 1934 as one of a group of Paul Colin's students.[8] This second visit, from mid-April to mid-June, was very important to Louise. Discovering communism and Russian art was a turning point in the awakening of her political and artistic consciousness. In a letter of April 30 to her father, composed on notepaper from the Metropol Hotel in Moscow, she described being awed by the preparations for the May 1 celebrations: "Everything is covered in red; eight story buildings disappear behind monumental stars presenting photos of Lenin and Stalin. Yesterday immense flags with the hammer and sickle floated above all the constructions, illuminated by large projectors. Everywhere parades, military marches headed by marching bands. Thousands of Russians in rags contemplate in all the store windows the realization of the five-year plan and the projects of the second one— For this celebration near-white bread and vodka are being distributed everywhere."[9] She returned to France by ship via Antwerp and was home in Paris by June 7. This exposure to a Soviet society brought her into contact with a group of young students and with the anti-communist weekly *Gringoire*[10] who commissioned her to write an article describing her impressions of what she'd seen. Her reflections on this stay in the USSR were invaluable, for André Gide's severe indexing of the misdeeds of communism wouldn't be written until 1936. In her diary, the young woman gave her opinions on the advantages and disadvantages of the Soviet model.

Right from the start, Louise admitted to having encountered various problems writing the article, which Georges Champeaux, the journal's film critic, asked her to do for them. It was meant to comprise three parts: "Soviet students; May 1st celebrations," and "a humorous account of the boat trip." But "none of the three is finished."[11] "To be a journalist, you have to address a large audience, a very large audience. [. . .] A journalist is by necessity superficial. [. . .] [He] shows what he himself has seen. The 'I' shouldn't be continually hateful [. . .] it must be simple, it is a colloquial style. [. . .] A reportage is a film, [a] series of striking images, quick, cut-up. Journalist doesn't equal writer or polemicist. First and foremost you have to look for current events, picturesque, to be presented simply [. . .] even an insignificant character is interesting. [. . .] He's a photographer."[12] Despite the very precise and accurate advice she gave herself, Louise had a hard time writing the piece. In the draft which she saved, she emphasizes the trouble she had in finding a point of view:

> It is very difficult for tourists who visit Moscow to be impartial [. . .] if they have prepared before visiting: they will be influenced by what they have read, and everything they see will be through the lens of this documentation, or one's preconceived ideas [. . .] one arrives in a world in which everything is so contrary to our way of seeing things [. . .] in which everything is such a challenge to our institutions & mores that it is difficult to envisage the ~~depth~~ longevity of such a regime. The facts shock us, without our being able to [. . .] explain them. [. . .] Finally we must, in order to judge properly, abandon our own personalities, our prejudices [and] our political convictions. [. . .] The Bolshevik problem concerns all nations, because, in each one, injustice abounds, [people] who suffer in their heart of their spirit, from justice or the need for truth.[13]

Louise was clearly skeptical of propaganda, although sensitive to the beneficial aspects of communism.

On September 25, 1934, she said that she had to edit the grammatical mistakes and rework the article[14] in a different direction, in order to "Say what is good about the USSR: their role as educators: expenditure for the education of the masses."[15] She also noted the important role given to young people, their faith in the new religion, the power of patriotic feeling: "Thought is detrimental to action on one hand and faith makes it tremendous therefore the Russians are <u>dangerous</u>.[16] [. . .] Communism has a great ability to propagate itself and seduces all the workers and quite a few intellectuals."[17] These reflections on communism allowed her to interrogate bourgeois morality, the degradation of capitalism, savings, and inheritance, as well as the division of labor: "it is even necessary that many think without producing," "a man who works with his hands cannot be an intellectual." Ought we to see here a reference to her own family, and her own difficulty choosing between theory and practice? "If it is indispensable to elevate the level of the masses it is dangerous to increase the number of the half-educated."[18]

At this time she was reading Romain Rolland, Lacretelle,[19] Péguy, Barrès, Renan, Gide, Fournier, Valéry, Giraudoux, Fromentin, Rivière, Aymé, Giono, and Huxley, at least judging from the list she kept in her diary.

Her commitment and her intellectual curiosity were sincere, but her lack of political discernment prevented her, no doubt, from perceiving *Gringoire*'s rightward drift. Its unofficial political director was the journalist and writer Henri Béraud,[20] whose political orientation moved from left to the extreme right, to the point of becoming an anti-Semite (as was the case with many intellectuals in the 1930s). Champeaux therefore expected that Louise's testimony would fit in with this general outlook. This would be especially surprising of one of Paul Colin's students, given the art teacher's well-known left-wing political engagements. Louise no doubt felt pulled by both sides, and tried to chart her own path, to find her own truth. Given the contradictions she perceived between the dangers and benefits of the Soviet regime, her difficulty writing this article for *Gringoire* is understandable, and it remained unfinished.

Louise's interest in politics can also be seen in an entry[21] dedicated to an event that took place at the Bal Bullier on January 18, 1935, the first open meeting of the left.[22]

Police presence in the street [. . .] Socialist and Communist Youth [. . .] Cachin arrives and then Blum [. . .] they are down on Mussolini [and defend] a people who fight for their independence and haven't even the slightest notion of freedom. [. . .] Léon Blum refers to his Italian friends who have died, a profound and sweet joy, joy to finally have the same program of action and to be reunited with Cachin (buttering up), this coming-together made possible because people wanted it and because it is the expression of the will of the people. Applause. Coordination, fusion of the whole proletariat. What separates communists from socialists is a question of organization, of perspective within the country. Memory of Jaurès. Then he talks about the USSR, he believes it wants peace and he unreservedly encourages its politics and its economy. [. . .] He is down on Italy, crude caricature of Ancient Rome. [. . .] Marcel Cachin—the foreign element, as Jaurès put it, doesn't exit [. . .] We must chase away the fascist danger [. . .] [antifascist organization, meeting of February 12].[23]

The meeting was very important, because it was there that the CGT (the labor union that was close to the socialists) and the CGTU (close to the communists) agreed to a day of general strikes, in response to the bloody events of February 6, which saw the rise of the far right;[24] the SFIO (the French Section of the Workers' International) and the Communist Party called for a demonstration to be held in Paris where the two processions could come together. This day was the first timid step of rapprochement between the socialists and communists, who had been enemies since 1920, and planted the seed of the antifascist union which led in 1936 to the Front populaire government, a coalition of radicals and socialists that had the communists' support.

This interest in social movements indicates that Louise was attuned to the tense and worrying atmosphere in the 1930s, a period during which intellectuals were split between fascism and communism. This was the era of the Action française's demonstrations, of the rise of the far right and the troubles that would lead to the Front populaire in 1936. Louise did not live at a distance from the world; the militant student circle in which she moved was also, for her, a form of rebellion against her father: "It was because he 'didn't like' the workers that at the time of the revolt (18 years old) that I turned towards them, and towards religion; it was because he was a free-thinking bourgeois that I became both (USSR and little red church)."[25]

Introspection

"This is my diary.[26] I do not start it with the intention of ever letting anyone read it, not even to reread it myself. No literary or educational pretentions. I am currently living an eventful life, rich with the most varied impressions—I very often <u>need</u> to confide—I didn't suffer from it when maman was with us—since her departure this need of expansiveness is harmful to me."[27]

The 1930s were a particularly rich and eventful period. In response to her grief and the terrible absence of her mother, Louise threw herself into a number of activities. She undertook studies at the Sorbonne as well as artistic apprenticeships in several schools and academies. She demonstrated a clear desire for independence from her father; living on her own for the first time, she tried to earn what she could to sustain herself, leading guided tours at the Louvre, serving as *massière* at the Grande Chaumière art school and as an interpreter at Fernand Léger's studio.[28] Since her trip to Russia, and under the influence of Paul Colin, she felt even more engaged in the political and ideological history of her time. The diary she kept during the 1930s is therefore an invaluable document—not only does it keep track of what was happening in her life, but it inventories the moral and existential questions she was asking herself at the time, concerning love, politics, religion, and her vocation as an artist.

Love and Turbulence

A number of suitors came to court and flatter this beautiful, cultured, sensitive young woman. Among those most faithfully besotted by her was Raoul Kanoui, the brother of her friend Raymonde from the lycée; he sent her several letters and postcards and tried to see her before he left Paris for Switzerland on January 4, 1933.[29] "He was a writer," she said, "a highly important peripheral person." "He used to talk to me about René Crevel. [. . .] He knew he was going to die, that's why his last letters were so cherished by me. I still have them."[30] Raoul Kanoui died of tuberculosis in Leysin, Switzerland, on March 28, 1933.

Jean-Paul Meunier was another of her dear friends.[31] Was he nearly her fiancé? "Papa arranges my marriage to Jean-Paul Meunier. At the end he defeats his own purpose."[32] She also had a brief relationship with a certain Roger Conrad, an architect:[33] "When I considered that my friendship with Conrad had been a fiasco and when we stopped seeing each other I lost courage (or dignity maybe) and I went back to Antony. Reason given: I could not afford an extra rent."[34] And finally, there was Jean Pelletier, whom she met, no doubt, through the artistic types who gravitated to the Académie de la Grande Chaumière, where she also studied. He became a fighter pilot during the war, but he never stopped thinking of Louise, recalling the good times they had together in Montparnasse and Saint-Germain-des-Prés. He wrote to her in New York several times: "Hardly a day goes by that I don't think about Vavin, la Grande Chaumière, 18 rue Mazarin,[35] the bibliothèque Sainte Geneviève, Boul'Mich, and so many other good memories. [. . .] How is your painting going? Do you still have the same faith?"[36] They kept up their friendship and went on writing to each other despite the distance: he received a postcard from Switzerland where Louise must have gone in 1938 and wrote to thank her and ask for her address in New York, as he was meant to travel there. He was still writing to her in March 1940: "I very much regretted not having seen you during your trip to France [in summer 1939]. For me you remain a living symbol. Neither time nor distance have succeeded in erasing from my heart the respectful memory that I have of you. [. . .] I am at the front now, in a night fighting squadron. [. . .] I entertain the hope of maintaining a regular correspondence with you."[37]

Then there were the more serious contenders, those whom she really did almost marry: first Henri Smadja,[38] whom her father imposed on her in 1933, then Georges Landeman in the fall of 1934,[39] and finally Roger Besnier in 1936. The Smadja episode almost ended in tragedy. During a health cure in Luchon in August 1933, she again attempted suicide by swallowing Gardenal, in protest at the forced marriage: "I produce a husband for you (Smadja). I need my peace. I have paid enough for you. Now you take care of yourself. I was not up to the task. Second attempt at suicide. This must have touch[ed] my mother's family. They began to prepare a trousseau for me."[40] What happened in Luchon[41] would frequently appear in her writings as a nightmare. She threw herself from Smadja's car, consumed a bottle of barbiturates in front of her sister, Henriette,[42] then asked Dr. Richiez for help. "I can't remember anything at Luchon: I threw myself from Smadja's car and swallowed a bottle of Gardenal. Henriette is there, why."[43]

In September 1934,[44] Louis Bourgeois again took it into his head to try to marry off his daughter. This time he turned to Georges Landeman,[45] the son of one of his friends, who was close to some other family friends, the Van Brabants. The engagement was announced officially only at the end of 1934; Pierre mentioned the ceremony in a letter to their father.[46] Previously, he had asked them to delay the party: "As I asked Lison, I would be happy if she could delay her engagement so I could attend. [. . .] What do you think of your future son-in-law? What does he do? I know from Louise that he is tall, blond, and twenty-five years old."[47] "Dear Papa [. . .] I want to ask you something, while giving you a chance to catch your breath after the final preparations for Lison's engagement party. I have to put in for my next leave within the next two weeks and I would like to include the wedding request with my request. [. . .] Of course if they haven't been printed yet there's nothing I can do."[48] In her diary from August 1934, Louise described going to the notary's office for the prenuptial contract, often mentioned Georges Landeman's name, and referred to a summer holiday in Quiberon.[49] The betrothal ceremony took place January 15, 1935,[50] but at the last minute she called off the engagement.

Finally, in 1936, Louise's hand was once again sought, this time by a man called Roger Besnier. This young engineer was the son of a certain N. Besnier, a land surveyor and friend of the family who lived and worked in Marseille and then Algiers. She seems to have met Roger as early as 1934, because his name appears frequently in her date book from that year. Roger Besnier moved to Algeria and officially asked her to marry him on November 23, 1936, in a letter sent from Rouïba, in the suburbs of Algiers: "Without indulging in useless preambles, would you accept to become, in the more or less immediate future, my wife[?] Companion of good days and bad. I've changed, Louison, I'm no longer the same carefree young man of twenty. [. . .] You have made me someone capable of thinking, Africa has made a man of me."[51] Louise hesitated and did not reply immediately, which made the young man fret with worry: "It is no longer the combative soul of three weeks ago who writes to you but a saddened heart. I have just reread for the hundredth time perhaps the only two letters I have received from you in fourteen months. [. . .] you hold all my happiness and my father's joy. [. . .] Louison, think for a moment if you are likely to find a more promising partner than myself [. . .] if I must continue loving you in silence, please tell me; having to wait is very painful."[52] Roger's father even went so far as to intercede with Louise on his son's behalf.[53] "My dear Roger [. . .] I should have replied more promptly to your father['s letter]. Please present him with my apologies, I was very surprised and profoundly touched by it. You, my dear Roger, have asked me a question so serious that I ask just for a bit of time to think it over, I cannot just this moment give a definite answer one way or the other. Would you like for us to correspond for a while as friends?"[54] In spite of this polite refusal, Louise and Roger maintained a friendly relationship, as demonstrated by the letters and postcards they sent each other.

While still in Algeria, Roger Besnier happened to catch a newsreel which included a documentary on Paul Colin and his school called *Les mains de Paris*; he wrote to Louise to tell her he thought he saw her in it, and to his great pleasure recognized her among the students.[55] He invited her to visit Algiers—"you who so love to travel"—building up the exoticism and the picturesque charm of the city.[56] He certainly had no ties to the art world: "I didn't know you were at the Beaux-Arts? What is your role there? And your exhibition '37 project?"[57] They continued exchanging letters after the young woman went to New York: "I haven't forgotten what a good friend you were to me, [and everything] I owe you." "I am waiting for you, come and see me, the 'plums' have not yet fallen here."[58] Later, Louise spoke of Roger Besnier as one of those she had helped, whose confidence she had helped restore.[59]

In 1938, she was courted by the son of another friend of her father's, Jacques Bauml, who also worked in the antiques business. She described his visits to the Louvre, particularly on the occasion of the *Exhibition of English Painting*,[60] and his trips to Chantilly or Rambouillet:

Sunday, went to Rambouillet with the Baumls to visit their friends Daniel & Co. There was Daniel's father-in-law (the mayor of Rambouillet) etc. . . . bourgeois milieu, rich, well behaved, who will raise children like Cécile Chasse,[61] Claire . . . Van Brabant, etc. [. . .] I had a brutal revelation, and that's why I've been sick for two days. [...] I no longer belong to this milieu, though I still esteem it; I feel like a stranger there and I have seen that it never would be enough for me anymore. [...] My dream would be to return to it full of knowledge and talent, to feel admired by these people to whom I am nothing at present; as for joining their side [...] it's too late, I no longer belong among them.[62]

She broke with her father's coterie—antiquarians, collectors, politicians, public figures—at the same time as her suitor: "I wanted to explain to Bauml that we couldn't possibly marry, and that it would be pointless to continue to see one another . . . idiot. [...] A decision made in the heat of anger, of bitterness, of fatigue, is an impulse and therefore pernicious."[63]

In spite of Louise's distance, Jacques Bauml, who was very much enamored, continued to pursue her, even after her marriage to Robert Goldwater in September 1938:

My ridiculous timidity prevented me from telling you everything I wanted to [...]. I sincerely desire your happiness, and I hope your husband will give it to you. If by chance that should not be the case, I simply would like to tell you that I would always be at your disposal if ever you were to think of me. I have always been ready to sacrifice everything for you, everything except your own happiness. Unfortunately, I have always feared that neither my financial situation nor my health would ever permit me to give you the happiness you deserve [...]. I realize how out of order it is to write such things to a young bride [...]. In case you should not find lasting happiness in New York [...] I hereby promise to wait for you, for years if necessary, and not to become engaged to anyone else.[64]

Their friendship lasted until 1949, which we know because Louise invited him to the United States: "I was touched by your offer to facilitate my trip to America."[65]

Louise had other suitors about whom she was more discreet; she left a list of their names in her notebook: Maurice Billaud, who also accompanied her to the Louvre, Maurice Baccharach, one of the doctors on the Baltic cruise, whom she continued to see in 1934, and finally Dr. Richiez, whom she must have met at the Hôpital Necker, where she was seen regularly for her chronic sinus problems—he was the doctor who operated on her.[66] Hence the stay in Luchon, a thermal spa town in the Pyrénées that specialized in the treatment of respiratory issues. She had a number of appointments with him in July 1934, and he even went to see her in Antony: "I must also mention Richiez, he telephoned twice today, I forgive him the anger he caused me yesterday. No, not anger, let's be more precise. I believed he was avoiding me so as not to have to thank me for my little chair and I struck him from my life and my heart [. . .]. I felt Yvonne's kindness[67] this evening, she was happy when she saw [that] Richiez returned to me. She isn't jealous of the feelings I inspire."[68]

Her attraction to doctors was no doubt related to her mother's illness: "I imitate my mother (be sick) to interest Richiez. I take care of her to be useful to him."[69] Did she think of Robert Goldwater, whom she would marry in 1938, as a kind of doctor, as someone who would take care of her? "My mother didn't believe in doctors, but I do, I only wanted to marry a doctor, and that's what I did."[70] For her, the word "doctor" meant "he who takes care, protects."

"Rules to Live By"

In the end, Louise broke up with all her paramours and remained alone, while still pursuing friendships with some of them. She was the kind of woman who is more often loved than loving, but, as she said, it is hard to be loved and not to return the feeling: "It is easier to feign love when we don't feel it than to pretend indifference when we are in love. If you want to be loved, be lovable and inaccessible."[71]

This explains her prevarications with her various suitors. She was equally torn between her need for independence and solitude, her father's desire to see her married off, and her vocation as an artist, which was becoming more and more important to her: "Marriage: there are young women who get married just to get married. I do not speak for them; be sincere and present yourself as you are. [. . .] Content yourself at home, in your house, with yourself, that is to say alone. Seek out the company of those who have a soul, the others aren't worth anything. Study the people in the world and keep yourself removed from them."[72] "You have to know how to get people to tell you what they know and what they can teach you, without getting their hearts caught up in it," she wrote in her diary on September 10, 1934.[73] In the lists of recommendations she drew up for herself, which she called "rules to live by—advice,"[74] her worries and concerns are apparent: health, order, work, economy, the need for solitude.

The diary is full of recipes for life, lists of things to do to fight against depression: eat healthily, rise early in the morning, tidy up, beware of worldly and bourgeois people who are supposedly interested in art but who have no soul and only respect famous people. "Impose yourself," she wrote. She worked very hard and without ceasing, avoided superficial pleasures and always sought to learn, to understand, to perfect herself. "Ah, my youth is escaping [but] I cannot resolve myself to marry."[75] It would take a lightning bolt in 1938 for her to decide to take that step and leave everything behind.

"Little Red Church"

The priests and the faith that already sustained the young woman of the 1920s only grew in the years after her mother's death. Louise went to midnight mass at the Lazarists: "It was very beautiful—I am happy because I feel that faith is within me."[76] On Christmas Eve 1937, she went alone to Saint-Pierre-de-Montmartre: "Dear God, I love life so much and I love you so much [. . .]. Allow me to pay my debt and take pity on my heart."[77] The feeling of guilt, which would only grow within her, found support in the Catholic church—later she would evoke the "sins of the flesh" and the denial of the body.

In her diary she kept a list of her prayers and the things she asked of God: health, peace, work, and prosperity for her family and everyone she loved. "May Maman's good counsel continue to grow in our hearts where she sowed it: wisdom, tolerance, courage." And for Henriette: "May she have children."[78] Her faith was sincere but remained a secret. All the other members of her family were atheists—or free thinkers, as they called them at the time—and it was difficult to discuss religion with them. In the interviews she gave during the 1990s, she denied having been religious, just as she denied having been in psychoanalysis.

In 1936, eager to be baptized, she asked Henri Torre, president of the Légion d'honneur, to be her godfather, a request he could not grant. "I cannot, alas become your godfather. The judgment of the prelates on this subject is absolute. Baptism is essentially a spiritual act [. . .]. I won't love you less for it and I will be spiritually what I cannot be judicially."[79] She remained on friendly terms with Henri Torre, who gave her tickets to an exhibition of Rubens's painting and who was delighted to see her "sink back . . . into the serene naïveté of antique tapestries."[80] In the end, her teacher and friend Yves Brayer would serve as her godfather. The baptism took place at Saint-Sulpice on February 12, 1937. She also made her first communion on March 19, 1937: "I would like this day never to end. I see Yves and I am [a] massière at the studio. I love him," she wrote in her diary.[81] Louise went to mass regularly at this time—Saint-Sulpice, Saint-Séverin, Saint-Étienne-du-Mont—and she may have had a romantic relationship with her godfather during 1937: "During this vacation I have suffered too much from solitude, I am finished loving Y. B. [Yves Brayer], completely finished, but it brought on a depression whose cause I can only understand now."[82] This ambiguous relationship with her teacher returned during her analysis: "Remember *la belle et la bête* [beauty and the beast] with Brayer—charge of hypocrisy. I knew that he was crazy about me but that he would lean over backward [*sic*]. Reaction Bd St Michel when I meet Brayer the secret is from him (fear of what) not being able to handle encounter. I do not know you."[83] They were not able to see one another during Louise's trip to France in 1939, but she did hear from him when the war started in 1940.[84]

Father and Daughter

When she left the family home in Antony in 1934, which was under renovation—her brother, Pierre, subsequently lived there and wrecked the place—it seems that she first lived in student housing (at the Foyer des étudiants, 93, boulevard Saint-Michel), where she went by the name Valérie ("I am happy and proud to call myself Valérie," she wrote in her diary[85]—it was her mother's middle name). She gave math classes to a young girl called Andrée, noting the appointments and fees in her 1934 datebook, and worked as a retoucher at a photographer's studio in place de Clichy, as well as at the Bon Marché as a salesgirl.

In 1936, she rented a studio at 31, rue de Seine, in the same building as the Akademia Raymond Duncan (brother of Isadora), and later the Gradiva Gallery, founded by André Breton in May 1937. There was also a prosthetics office, Perot & Co., which no doubt inspired her later work with crutches. She would go so far as to say that she was struck more by the visions of these prosthetics than by the surrealist works she saw at the Gradiva Gallery, which had an entryway designed by Marcel Duchamp and showed work by Wolfgang Paalen and Óscar Domíngez, among others. Although she didn't hang around with the surrealists (too old for a young student like herself and too far from the aesthetic orientations of her academic training), she did mention the gallery in a note in November 1951.[86]

In October 1937, she moved to 18, rue Mazarine. "Every time I moved house, I found my hope restored."[87] Her father put her in charge of transforming Antony; a number of pages in her diary are covered with plans for the house, budgeting costs and estimates from builders. She was assisted by her uncle, Alex Fauriaux, who was an architect, but spent a great deal of time keeping up with the work, taking particular care with the accounting and drawing up plans for various apartments. These transformations were intended to create a small apartment for Pierre on the first floor while the rest of the house would be rented out, with Louise benefiting from the income this brought in. A robust series of letters exchanged in the 1940s with her tenants, Gaston and Yvonne (Vonnette) Bocé, indicates that even from afar Louise kept a close eye on expenses, as well as on the accounts her father sent her, while also remaining attentive to the family's complaints or gratitude. They made her godmother to one of their children, Claude, and the letters they exchanged during the war were a blend of family news and problems with the boiler. She sent her trusted friend Jacques Bauml to keep an eye on a lawsuit she brought against an ugly sign hung by a neighbor, for disfiguring the facade of her building.

The 1930s saw the bonds strengthen between father and daughter. Louis Bourgeois lived on the boulevard Saint-Germain and continued to travel throughout France and abroad. Louise regularly wrote tender letters to her father and took care of him. He never stopped traveling (to the south of France—Antibes, Cannes—but also to Switzerland) but came back regularly to look after the shop with Germaine, his secretary and assistant. Louise was demonstrating her independence but remained close to her father, whom she adored and who adored her in return. "You are a pair of *enfants terribles*, but I love you all the same," he wrote in 1933, referring to Louise and Pierre.[88] The correspondence Louise kept up with her father during these years reaffirmed the ties that bound them together: "You, my darling, are my only concern. Be good, and write to me often."[89] "You are no longer a child, so I won't tell you to be calm and reasonable. I will only tell you to be well in body and spirit."[90]

Louise experienced a mild depression in early 1938: "I am coming out of a long torpor. I do not want to say illness, because my health is strong and I want to keep it and to believe it strong." She discovered, she said, her fundamental optimism at the nadir of her unhappiness: "after each depression I feel this solid foundation, young and pure. By pure I mean that it has its roots only within me."[91] Her attachment to her mother was still very strong, and she took strength from it. "The only person whose name is inscribed is maman, it's the only word that remains unstained and without tears, it's the [most] beautiful, the only disinterested one, and the only one I love."[92] This is why the maternal figure returned with such intensity at the end of her life, in her sculptures as in her writings. In spite of her fragility, of which she was well aware, Louise could delve into herself to find the resources necessary to overcome these episodes: "I just cured myself on my own [. . .] because there is order around my bed I have taken down all the engravings that were on the walls—all the inscriptions have been erased, all the papers picked up and the clothes carefully put away. Order in my environment called for order within, that is to say for peace in my mind. [. . .] This pride which tenses my will like a continuous iron bar. I silenced it [. . .] I stopped fighting, I resigned myself, and suddenly the tension of being sick relaxed and my heart began to sing."[93] Later in life, when anxiety overcame her, she would write on her notebooks and prints: "Calm down, Lison"; "Be Calm."

In addition to the stay at Luchon in 1933, another in Quiberon in 1934, and a quick trip to London with her father in September 1936 (as indicated by a ticket to the British Museum), Louise went to Switzerland in early summer 1938 to stay with Madame Laager, whose son, Werner Fritz Laager, a Swiss architect and painter, she had come to know well at the Grande Chaumière.[94] In a letter to her father, she describes this short visit, swimming in Lake Zurich, stopping in Basel, the box of paints she gave him as a gift. A report undertaken by a private detective[95] describing the young man[96] and his "honorable and solvent family" was sent to Louis in 1938. Was he wary enough of this friendship to have Laager and his family put under surveillance? Was he afraid his daughter would abandon him? Whatever the reason, this detail speaks volumes about the ambiguous relationship between Louis and his daughter.

Pierre

Relations between Pierre and his father increasingly degraded during the 1930s, along with the young man's psychological state, eventually leading to his being interned in the asylum at Ville-Évrard in December 1945. Louise remained close to her "Pierrot" throughout these years; she often saw him in the early 1930s, though she worried about his instability, as much on a mental as on a material level. After attending the Lycée Lakanal in Sceaux, then the Lycée Montaigne in Paris, Pierre began his studies at a mechanics' training school. In 1931, he lived on the avenue Ledru-Rollin in Paris. He became involved three times in quick succession: once to Ninon; to Yvonne, who was a worker in the tapestry atelier as well as a cleaner;[97] then to Marcelle Prégant. He left each of them in turn in search of something better. After his military service, carried out in Strasbourg from 1932 to 1934, he asked his father if he could move back into the one-bedroom apartment upstairs at Antony. He was often short on funds and asked for help, casting around for a job as a driver or a mechanic. He acted like a child who was constantly being found guilty, judging at least from the affectionate letters he sent to Louis: "Papa, I'm asking you to write to me, it's not mean, you don't know the ideas it gives me, it seems to me you are mad or angry or I don't know [. . .]. I will leave this here and embrace you like your little Pierrot, as I once was."[98] He got into a car accident and spent three days in prison (after initially being sentenced for ten). A later psychological report described him as violent, irritable, and fickle and noted that he had been angry with his sisters since 1938. While he lived at Antony, he looked after the garden and tried to support himself by selling fruit and vegetables. But repeated violent incidents—destroying walls, accusations of theft, complaints from the neighbors—led to his internment and diagnosis with schizophrenia.

In spite of all this, he remained close with Lison and tried to join her in New York in 1945, but she asked her father to prevent him from coming, concerned that his presence would ruin her marriage.

From Studio to Studio

"I studied art in all the studios in Montparnasse [. . .] I went from studio to studio. My father's 'tough love' meant I had no money. He hung on very strongly to the money because he wanted me to get married. I was totally unable to conceive of getting married. I wanted an art education, and I didn't want to go into the government schools."[99]

Louise first enrolled at the Sorbonne in the autumn of 1932 and studied mathematics and geometry (solid geometry and differential calculus, to be precise), two subjects that were, in her eyes, reassuring, harmonious, and stable. She liked the rigor and purity of mathematics; there could be no error in arithmetic: "Studying geometry, I learned a system in which things proceed without surprises. One is, essentially, safe. [. . .] It never failed you. Never betrayed you. [. . .] It was a world of order that I wanted."[100] But by the end of February 1933, she was disappointed (she later said) to learn that there were not, in fact, as she had thought, any certainties in mathematics, since non-Euclidean geometry could see two parallel lines meet.[101] She then turned to studying art. The various schools she chose—Colarossi, Julian, Grande Chaumière, Ranson—and her singular education, bringing together scientific, theoretical, and artistic instruction, testify to the richness and complexity of her personality, which demonstrated on numerous occasions her independence and her hunger for knowledge. She refused to restrain herself to a single framework and needed to hash things out with different professors. It is also noteworthy that she wanted to study in private institutions; the style of teaching at the École nationale des beaux-arts, where she nevertheless also studied, was very academic, and they didn't admit many women. Women were also not allowed to draw the male nude, whereas at Colarossi, Ranson, and the Grande Chaumière, they could. Later on, Louise took devilish pleasure in describing these sessions and the models' inadvertent erections, which she found very touching. That, she said, was how she understood masculine fragility. The ateliers were free, open, and attended by many artists and foreign students.

Louise also had to earn a living, since her father, hostile to this idea of an artistic career, wanted to see her married off at any cost. She used her fluent English to work in Fernand Léger's studio and to look after American artists. "'If you let me sit down and work with you I will translate anything.'

[. . .] For years Fernand Léger was my best teacher."[102] She was also a massière at the Grande Chaumière and could thereby develop her gifts as a teacher. Finally, her classes at the École du Louvre as well as her regular visits to the museum allowed her to become a docent there in 1937–38. She passed her exams by a hair's breadth in June 1937: "For Mademoiselle Bourgeois, with great indulgence, we have, in the end, asked a few questions to which she replied well. We gave her a passing grade."[103] "I'd taken my degree in Art History at the École du Louvre. That is one of the reasons they took me as a *daucent*. It was very recherché as a job, but I found it very exhausting to talk really loud to crowds of people, and I had nowhere to eat."[104]

In 1934, she also took some classes at the Académie Colarossi, as well as a class with the famous poster designer Paul Colin, whose school was first held in his home in the rue Duperré at the foot of Montmartre, then on the rue des Martyrs from 1929 to 1932, then from 1932 in a faux-Gothic *hôtel particulier* at 13, rue Montchanin (today rue Jacques-Bingen, near the place du Général-Catroux, in the 17th arrondissement). "'Paul's school' was unconventional, lively, and very bound up with Colin's life, and therefore with Parisian life," remembered one of his former students, the poster designer Villemot.[105] The school had about a hundred students from all nationalities, including a large number of women, and there was an annual dance, organized by the students. "Paul Colin was very free with his students, and he knew how to maintain a very artistic and non-conformist atmosphere."[106] Classes were offered in drawing, studying forms, volumes, and values, and included two hours with a life model, as well as invited talks and studio visits. "At Colin's, posters: a poster should attract attention [. . .] through a central point, should not disperse it on the page. [. . .] If drawing the Tower of Babel, do not draw a tower, too simple and banal, but the idea of a tower, which may be in this case a construction, ex[ample] two cubes, one on top of the other."[107] Perhaps Bourgeois remembered this lesson in constructive simplicity when she created her own towers, *Mortise* (1950) and *Memling Dawn* (1951), which brought together wooden forms on a central stem. Paul Colin's students eloquently recalled their time there: "A lively, intense atmosphere, perhaps a little chaotic, but full of warmth thanks to Colin, who was always present and always attentive. Affection and respect was strong on both sides," said another former student.[108]

From 1933 until 1937, Louise was also registered at the Grande Chaumière, in the oil painting studio with Yves Brayer. The art school, founded in 1904 by Gustave Courtois and Claudio Castelucho, was free to attend, and directed by two women after 1909, Martha Stettler and Alice Dannenberg. This historically cosmopolitan site of intellectual and artistic life of the early twentieth century attracted eminent professors and a number of foreign students. Louise took classes with Yves Brayer, Robert Wlérick, and André Lhote. A well-known photograph taken by Brassaï shows her in the sculpture studio working on a classic head in the style of Bourdelle. Brassaï took several other beautiful portraits of the young artist, hair sensibly pinned up, wearing a blouse with a Claudine collar and looking in the mirror. The photographer was able to perceive and reproduce all of his model's best qualities: subtlety, elegance, fragility.

Yves Brayer (1907–1990) played an important role for Louise; he was a professor, a lover—at least, he loved Louise—and a godfather. An academic painter who specialized in Provence landscapes, whose work was far removed from her interests, he nevertheless taught her the fundamentals of composition, color, and spontaneity. "At Brayer's the 18th of May 1936," she wrote, aware of the importance of the sketch which after the first draft would have to be enlarged in a careful, obedient manner: "A work done quickly and spontaneously is generally more interesting than a long patient one."[109]

Louise often said that it was Fernand Léger who had encouraged her to work as a sculptor by helping her discover the third dimension: "He was a stormy person, very massive, and since he was a very bad talker he said: 'I don't know why you paint, Louise. Let me show you something.' So he took a shaving of wood and he hung it under his shelf and said: 'Look, the wood turns around like this. This is sculpture.' So I made some drawings of it. He said: 'Louise, you are not a painter, you are a sculptor.'"[110] Is this experience of a suspended form turning in space the source of the spiral woman, the artist's recurring self-portrait? In any case, as early as 1935–36, Louise was taking sculpture classes at the Grand Chaumière with Robert Wlérick (1882–1944). She had her first show from June 23 to 30, 1936, with artists from the Grande Chaumière: with instructors Lucien Simone, René-Xavier Prinet, and Yves Brayer, and with other students: Fontanarosa, Papandreou, Pottier.[111]

In 1936–37, advised and supported by Yves Brayer, she began at the École nationale des beaux-arts,[112] studying first with André Devambez (1867–1944), head painting instructor, and then with Georges d'Espagnat. She also took courses in perspective, architectural history, and art history and began taking additional art history classes at the École du Louvre. She visited the Exposition universelle of 1937 on September 12 and carefully noted each kind of butterfly she saw,[113] but curiously she did not mention the Spanish pavilion, which was showing Picasso's *Guernica*.

Louise took her role as massière at the Grande Chaumière very seriously. She was not only in charge of collecting everyone's dues, organizing the studio's expenses, and recruiting models—often sex workers—but also of assisting the instructor in correcting students' work and giving them advice. In this way she received several letters from a certain J. M. Granier, a painter in Aix-en-Provence, who thanked her and congratulated her on her pedagogical talents: "Thank you for the excellent correction and for the hope you gave me [. . .]. Your teaching is so clear that you helped me make real progress."[114] She also helped a young woman named Colette Boisseau who lived in Montpellier. Colette Richarme (1904–1991)—as she was known after her marriage—was a faithful friend during and after the war. But in 1937–38, Louise dispensed advice on the composition of her paintings and kept her informed of upcoming exhibitions; she gave her news of goings-on in Paris, with the students, at the school, and of their instructor Yves Brayer, who showed at the Charpentier Gallery in February 1938: "Good reviews from the right-wing press, less flattering from the left,"[115] she wrote with an ironic tone, lightly mocking the massive publicity campaign undertaken by the artist, which provoked a scandal. Louise was no fool—not easily duped, as she liked to say. She admired her teacher, but she was not blind to his faults.

She considered taking the exam to gain a teaching certificate and to that end began preparing for it with Monsieur Rey, one of her teachers at the Louvre.[116] From morning to night she worked on her techniques: perspective, architecture, modeling. Her departure for New York in the autumn of 1938 would prevent her from achieving this. She told Colette about her first attempts at sculpture with Wlérick: "It's difficult, but now I have a better grasp of form!! [. . .] You just need a few kilos of clay, and you'll see what a leap forward (or rather into depth) you'll make. It's worth a thousand drawings."[117] Next she studied with Othon Friesz (1879–1949) and André Lhote (1885–1962) at the Grande Chaumière. She learned from Lhote that "a canvas is an arrangement of lines, surfaces, and volume on a plane [...] read *Le cœur et l'esprit*," she wrote to Colette; "it will teach you far more than all the teachers in the world."[118] She also mentioned the new canvas she was working on: "It seems to be my first really personal painting and is far to the left of Brayer."[119] This is no doubt why she soon left Brayer's studio for that of Marcel Gromaire (1892–1971). Her mentor was "broad-minded" about it; he understood and encouraged her: "You will gain nothing but good from it, because your mind tends naturally that way."[120] Richarme, who was older and married with children, played a maternal role for Louise. "I need to smell grass, earth, and the wind from the sea. I feel as if I have not left the gray streets of Paris for a century, and that I haven't heard your soft, reasonable voice and your maternal tones for a century either."[121]

What kind of work did Louise produce during these years? Academic drawings: studies from a life model (nude men and women), copies of antique plaster casts, and numerous self-portraits, either in a schematic, art deco style (face slightly tilted and turned at three-quarters, hair tied back) or in a very realist style, or with the face covered in a network of dashes and lines. The paintings from the 1930s, which Louise also carefully preserved, mostly depict female nudes, moving from Lhote's late cubist influence—simplified, massive, geometrical forms—to Devambez or Friesz—with a colored background, more fauvist or like something from Matisse—and, finally, Gromaire—imposing, sculptural nudes in gray-brown tones. Louise had a sense of volume: she almost only ever painted sculptures, as Léger pointed out to her. She also painted self-portraits at the easel—affirming her identity as a painter—as well as a hospital scene, a religious scene (motivated by personal interest?), and *Mother and Child* (1936), a more intimate picture, more personal, in composition as well as in style. The simplification of figures in the paintings and drawings of 1930–40, in a deliberately childish style, can be found only in a large canvas depicting a fruit harvest.

Louise was still in search of her true calling: "I found my vocation and will no longer work in any direction but that," she wrote on Christmas 1935, the day she turned twenty-four.[122] Of course, she would do nothing of the sort. "Don't think too much, move forward, let yourself go";[123] "the most important thing is to dare," she wrote in 1937.[124] She was trying to find herself at the same time as she sought a new milieu, having broken with her father's bourgeois high society. She remained perfectly lucid, however, of the fact that the art world could be insincere as well. This inconsistency was a constant feature of her personality.

Attending these different schools helped confirm her vocation as an artist: "The primary task of the artist is concentration—to achieve a total, friendly silence. This I learned in the academies of Paris where one drew all day long from the model. [. . .] I was also there in search of ideas—and so I pursued them by going from one academy to the next, and one teacher to the next. [. . .] It was not my classmates I liked it was all the teachers. I had complete confidence in them; it was my teachers who replaced my family."[125]

In 1939, when she returned to spend the summer in France after her first eight months in New York, she worked with Roger Bissière (1886–1964), whom she particularly appreciated for the creative freedom he allowed in his classes at the Académie Ranson. His influence may be seen in her first paintings of overlapping scenes, with a simple, childlike design. From July 7 to July 20, 1939, she showed with several painters and sculptors, the Group '38–'39 from the Académie Ranson, which was located at 7, rue Joseph-Bara.[126] Her opinion had already changed a great deal: "When I think of the amount of time I wasted sketching and studying anatomy at the Grande Chaumière!!" she wrote to Colette Richarme in June 1939.[127] All the same, she still invited her friend to come and work with her at Ranson's, where Gromaire also taught.

Louise, who had chosen the path of suffering from the very beginning of her career as an artist, liked to cite Vincent van Gogh's letters to his brother Theo: "Art is a battle, you have to have some skin in it, to know how to suffer without complaining."[128] She noted that Van Gogh read a great deal (Kant, Shakespeare), that he "loved books as much as paintings."[129] She was also aware that to be an artist is to be asocial, a "monster" for other people, in search of an ideal. "Balance can be found in resigning the self to its own oblivion. Give yourself over to an ideal useful to your fellow men—could painting be that ideal? Yes—so be a painter and know peace."[130] "Only the artist will fulfill himself completely. [. . .] An artist perceives, behind all illusions, this innocence of life which is the only background capable of bringing out the truth from the pain, from the happiness of any human experience."[131]

To be exigent, to work regularly, to live a healthy, methodical life: this was the ethical and aesthetic program by which Louise abided all her life. Art was, for her, the re-creation of experience, the tool by which we come to know ourselves. It was above all a sacrifice of one's life.

Love at First Sight

The front window of the boutique Aux Vieilles Tapisseries: *Panneaux et Fauteuils en Tapisseries Anciennes* (The Old Tapestry Shop: Hangings and Armchairs of Antique Tapestries) found at 174, boulevard Saint-Germain[132] was composed of large windows with metallic corner molding; white curtains, narrow and bordered in lace, hide the upper half. On one side of the boutique, with its old-fashioned decor and large gilded lamps, her father continued to show restored tapestries and antique furniture; on the other, Louise created her own little art gallery, buying and selling modern and contemporary work.

"At the end of June, to take my mind off my teaching exam, I went to the showrooms with my father. I bought some contemporary drawings, then I exhibited them in a part of the house in the Boulevard Saint-Germain, which I have transformed into a gallery."[133] She showed drawings, prints, posters, and sometimes paintings by a range of artists, including Maurice Utrillo, Suzanne Valadon, Henri de Toulouse-Lautrec, Félicien Rops, Constantin Guys, Amadeo Modigliani, Édouard Vuillard, Pablo Picasso, Delacroix, Pierre Laprade, Charles Dufresne, Pierre Bonnard, Paul Sérusier, and André Utter, among others. Louise took this business very seriously, as it allowed her to meet critics and collectors and thereby to get to know the modern art scene.[134] But it also allowed her to earn money, even to become quite well off: "[Bauml] must be a bit jealous that I sold so much [. . .] I made 12,900 francs in two months. [. . .] If this continues you will be able to rest in the sun," she wrote to her father on August 28, 1938,[135] while she looked after what she called the "shop" on her own. Louis had gone to Switzerland (Bern, Lausanne) to go fishing and to have a rest. This new occupation took up all of her time: "Since I started buying modern drawings and paintings again and set up my little shop (I called it a gallery in a spirit of irony, it wasn't very big, but it was going well), I've had no time for work."[136]

A photograph shows Louise sitting in an armchair in the corner of the shop that she considered her art gallery; behind her she had hung on the wall or placed on shelves a disparate number of figurative works. Although her gallery was perfectly situated in the heart of Saint-Germain-des-Prés, Louise was risk averse and did not invest in contemporary art or the Parisian avant-garde. She sold mainly classic works with commercial appeal, by artists who had already achieved recognition—which no doubt explains her success. She also acquired two etchings by Picasso from Fernand Mourlot. And August 24, 1938, at three o'clock,[137] a young American man entered her shop, elegant, serious, and slender, and bought a Picasso engraving from the Saltimbanques series, *Au cirque* (*At the Circus*, 1905–6), for the sum of 2,800 francs.[138] The young man was an art historian who was spending a semester in France, having recently finished his PhD thesis on the influence of non-Western art on modern painting.[139] His name was Robert Goldwater.[140] For Louise, it was truly love at first sight. Nineteen days later, she married him. She told the story of their miraculous meeting to her father: "On Friday a friend of my first customer[141] came and stayed for quite some time, I showed him everything I had, and lent him two books. Saturday evening he returned and in five minutes, he bought the Picasso *Les Saltimbanques* [for] (2,800 francs) which I asked him to pay for in dollars. I bought [it] for 700 francs—it's the best deal I've made [...]. He also asked if I would have lunch with him today and I've just come back, we went to the Place du Tertre, then to the bank, then to see some merchants."[142] Louise had a good head for business—thanks to her mother's practical mind and her father's commercial background—and she did not lose it when she moved to New York, very conscious of what things cost and the profits that could be made in the art world. From the outset, Louise and Robert's relationship was rooted in the love of art and painting—and Louise confessed that Robert immediately helped her glimpse another world. She was more explicit with her painter friend, Colette Richarme, on the basis of their mutual attraction: "One day a friend who had bought a Picasso from me, and who came back to give me lessons on the modern movement in France and in America, suggested that we might be able to work together in New York. In between conversations about Surrealism and the latest trends, we got married, and I am just about to go see him onto the boat at Le Havre. I hope to join him in October. [...] My husband is thirty years old. He loves painting and teaches at New York University."[143]

Robert "gave her lessons," she said. The young artist realized very quickly that her training had been too classical and had not sufficiently opened her eyes to the art of her own time. Although she did see surrealist films and visited André Breton's Gradiva Gallery and the International Exhibition of Modern Decorative and Industrial Arts, which was held in Paris in 1925,[144] she hadn't yet found her own path, confining herself to academic work in her various studios and experimenting with a very few techniques. Robert appeared, therefore, as an ideal companion: "He has beautiful brown hair, a sporty hat, beautiful hands and light blue neckties."[145] He loved painting, was aware of contemporary trends, and, especially, he was very much in love. Louise was, too, as attested by the rapidity of their marriage and their first love letters. Louise Bourgeois and Robert Goldwater married in the strictest intimacy at the town hall of the 6th arrondissement in the place Saint-Sulpice, with two American witnesses, friends of Robert's living in Paris at that time: Georges Blumenthal and Laurence Vail,[146] whose wife, Kay Boyle, was also present. In a wedding photograph taken in the courtyard of the town hall, Robert wears business attire, while Louise is wearing a long suit with a straight skirt, made of a fabric with a geometric pattern, a fur stole around her shoulders (the fox her father gave her?), a toque hat perched on her head.

Because Robert needed to travel to New York on September 21, to begin teaching the autumn term, the wedding was held quickly. So quickly that there was no time to inform either of their extended families or Louis Bourgeois's friends and clients, who complained. "Everyone coming back is scandalized [. . .]. When I told them I was leaving, they are angry that I didn't tell them."[147] Louise nevertheless received congratulations from her friend Lydie Adolphe: "you haven't said if [. . .] the young man who visited multiple times ended up taking his green Picasso. [. . . Have you . . .] taken your exam at the École du Louvre?"[148] All the same, Louise was very proud of this love story; she told her friends about it when they met at the Bibliothèque Sainte-Geneviève on September 22, the day after Robert's return to New York: she was "greeted with whoops of joy by [the whole group]," showed them pictures, and wrote her new, married name: Mrs. Goldwater. "You have been unanimously declared very nice," she wrote to Robert.[149] But she was worried about her imminent departure and felt a certain nostalgia at leaving the world that was so familiar to her, and this part of Paris that she loved so much: "In the Place du Panthéon, coming down the steps, books under my arm, I looked at the clear blue sky [. . .] I saw the trees in the Luxembourg rise up at the bottom of the rue Soufflot [. . .] instead of going to the Luxembourg station, I thought of you and I asked myself 'will I be able to continue loving the same things now that I love him' and I heard you say 'yes.'"[150]

The little art gallery she had built up with so much care, which had given her the chance, thanks to the Picasso engraving, to meet Robert, was very important to Louise: "I met my life's companion through it, just as I had dreamed I would—or rather not dared to dream."[151]

Robert and Louis got on well, apparently, in spite of their differences. According to Louise, Louis considered Robert a "real man," which was not always the case with his other son-in-law, Henriette's husband, Georges Bonnotte.[152] Louis was no doubt also proud of his daughter's union with an intellectual who came from a good (and wealthy) Jewish family in New York. When he wrote to the Goldwaters in 1938, he said that he held their son in high esteem, particularly for his sense of humor: "I was very taken by your son Robert who made himself so endearing during his too short visit to Paris."[153] No doubt this was rote politesse, as Louise later recalled that the relationship between her father and her husband was not as good as all that. "Robert had a very dry sense of humor. Very few people understood it precisely because you couldn't quite make out what he was saying or implying. Whereas, my father was Rabelasian you know, enormous humor. He had a lot of it but it was gross. I saw my father's face fall with dismay by the remarks Robert made. That for me was the test."[154]

Although both Louis and Louise thought immediately of expanding their tapestry business across the Atlantic, and the sales contacts that could be made there, her departure was heart-wrenching. "He is pained to see us go but doesn't dare do anything to keep me here."[155] Louise thought for a moment of delaying the trip but knew that her husband wouldn't understand. Robert apologized to his father-in-law for asking Louise to leave in haste, pointing out the threat of war and the alarming news the papers carried, while reassuring him that Louise would be happy and loved.[156]

On board the *Aurania,* the Cunard White Star ship that carried her to America on September 30, Louise thought again of her meeting with Robert. The wedding had taken place very quickly—Robert left nine days later—and Louise had to prepare her own departure with little notice. Between the difficulty of obtaining a visa at the embassy, buying her ticket for the crossing, planning to be away from the gallery "for a year," dealing with Antony, and the transport of her furniture, Louise was quite busy. The young couple spent their wedding night at the Auberge des Navigateurs at 49, quai des Grands-Augustins, according to a letter on the hotel's stationery. As soon as he left, she wrote to him every day. In her early letters, Robert's intellectual influence is apparent, but so is her distress: "Last night I read Jules Romains, as well as the beginning of [James] Joyce, which I easily understood but which frightened me a bit, because the first night I spent as a woman married but alone was heavy, dark, full of nightmares."[157] Louise was a cultured young woman: capricious, artistic, passionate, demanding, and serious; but she also possessed all the characteristics of a good wife for her era: she had calling cards made in her new name as well as in Robert's and bought her trousseau at the Bon Marché, good-quality sheets, light brown toile des Vosges sheets that she had monogrammed with their initials. She understood that her husband liked having nice things: "If friends come to stay, it is important to have beautiful linens."[158]

She thought as much about her new house as of the new family she was going to meet in New York—which made her slightly apprehensive. On his end, Robert was worried about her date of departure. Would her visa be granted in time? Would there still be room on the ship? His father knew people who might help her.[159] Robert wanted to send her money so she could buy a first-class ticket, but especially so she could join him as soon as possible. He mentions their wedding night, which they had intended to spend in Grasse but which they finally spent in the hotel in Paris, with a view over the Seine and Notre-Dame, concluding that it was the most beautiful place for two newlyweds. Robert was a candid and besotted young lover. "I feel in my heart great peace and contentment. It seems so natural that you are my wife [. . .] it feels as if I have always known you and loved you."[160]

Louise's analysis later on was more discerning. "He was running away from his mother and establishing himself. Not his father (like me), but his mother (who was German). So he was delighted when he realized he could bring home the very opposite of his mother with her German background and I was supposedly easy going. At least I talked that way in French. So you see it was a victory for him. And as far as I'm concerned, it was a victory for me, because he was the opposite of my father really."[161]

All the boats were full, but with a little help from the embassy Louise managed to find a place on a boat to Montreal. Her father and sister took her to the port of Le Havre, but security measures prevented anyone from boarding with her. They left, alone and sad.[162] Despite the excitement of travel and the love that carried her across the ocean, this departure was traumatic for Louise. On the very first day at sea she wrote a letter to her father describing her feelings at length over five pages: "When I left you Friday evening I suddenly felt very sad, I went up to the deck to see you and Henriette as you were receding into the night, and then I couldn't see you any longer and I felt the ship was like a prison. [. . .] I didn't want to see France's coastline recede on the horizon, which was for me such a harrowing symbol."[163] Then she gave a detailed daily accounting of the crossing, admitting to feeling apprehensive about meeting Robert's parents.

Louise also wrote to her husband. "Here I am on board, I just left Papa and Henriette who came to see me off. I thought I would be able to show them my cabin and stay a few minutes with them before departure but allegedly because of the political events they were denied access even to the deck so Henriette cried screaming that she would not see me again and Papa suddenly looked twenty years older than he was bending down to give me a kiss. Then from the boat I saw their two shadows walking into the night [. . .] [they] left so sad holding each other's arms."[164]

A heady new love and a speedy wedding, a leap into the unknown and nostalgia for what she left behind—add to this the tense political backdrop, with the threat of war becoming more and more real in Europe: it was the autumn of 1938. Louise was well aware of the growing tensions after the German invasion of Czechoslovakia, and she noted the number of Austrian immigrants: "We went to dinner at Pékin in the rue Cujas. She [Lydie Adolphe] had a meeting with some Austrian refugees, a man and a woman who complained all the time and were bitching about France because she hadn't gone to battle for them—so I became pacifist to the extreme and as gay and happy about my fate as they were sad and discouraged."[165] Nevertheless she was optimistic and took refuge in her happiness,[166] while remaining lucid: "Louise, you are going to burn your wings," she wrote to Colette.[167]

What was Louise running away from? What did she expect from this great departure, or from Robert? In spite of her enthusiasm, we can already detect the anxiety of the exile, the feeling of having abandoned her people, and the fear of not being understood—which she summarizes to Robert in a rather charming dream: "My dear husband [. . .] I dreamt about you, we were running one after the other in a street full of skyscrapers. And I was laughing hard and you were kissing me telling me that it was forbidden to laugh so hard in New York, that it was shocking, and I laughed even more loudly on purpose."[168]

"It would seem that many threads of memories have woven themselves around my heart to keep it here."[169] Between the power of memory, the abrupt separation, and the guilt of the exile in wartime, the future history of the "runaway girl" began to take form.

———

The Runaway Girl, 1938–1945

I married an American . . . I left France because I freed myself or escaped from the house. I was a "runaway girl" . . .
I escaped from a very troubling family.

The crossing from Le Havre to Montreal aboard the *Aurania* lasted thirteen days. Louise was nervous about how long it would take but used the time to write long letters to her father and to Robert, who sent her daily telegrams, to such an extent that the *sans-filiste* (telegraph operator)[1] smiled whenever he saw her, "probably thinking 'this kid seems quite happy' and he's right."[2] With great amusement she described the ferocious hatred between French and English Canadians; the waves, high as houses; the terrible seasickness; the books she found in the library—Giono, Céline, Marcel Aymé, "all kinds of books, each as shocking as the next";[3] onboard entertainment; her walks on the bridge; the ship's extremely English decor, "ridiculous but touching and well-intended."[4] She also planned to continue working while on board: "I am traveling first class and I will paint all the time."[5]

Louise said she was impatient to explore Canada, with its resinous wooden houses named for villages in France, its fox and bear furs. Delayed by a conference in Chicago, Robert could not come to meet her in Montreal; they were reunited in New York. He asked his friend Andrew Ritchie's wife, Jane,[6] to go and welcome her. "How did you do it[?] She is perfectly wonderful," Jane immediately wired Robert.[7]

This was a bit of flattery, of course, but it also partly explains the way the newlyweds had instantly been besotted with one another. At twenty-six, Louise had an undefinable charm, the physique of a well-behaved young woman, elegant, and romantic, but with an impish, intense blue-eyed gaze, a hint of both audacity and inhibition, power and delicacy. She was cultured, intelligent, and spoke English with an impossible French accent; above all, she was eager to discover new horizons: sentimental, familial, and artistic.

A work called *The Runaway Girl* (c. 1938), painted soon after she arrived in New York, alludes to her journey.[8] A young woman with very long hair appears in profile, holding a small suitcase and floating above a band of blue representing the ocean or the sky. Below her are the craggy peaks of mountains; above, a long, low house along a river in which bobs a small figure.[9] Is it a reference to Choisy and the Seine, or Antony and the Bièvre? Are its peaks those of the Creuse she saw in childhood? Here, Louise expresses the passage from one continent to another, the long Atlantic crossing and the situation of a young woman finally freed of her cumbersome family ties. Another canvas painted a few years later, the counterpoint of her departure for America, is called *Reparation* (1945): in it, Louise brings a bouquet of flowers to lay on her mother's and paternal grandparents' tomb in the Clamart cemetery.[10] In the background we see the sculpted hedges of Montchauvet, looking like people or toys, ghostly silhouettes which greatly marked her in childhood and return as a decorative leitmotif in a number of her drawings and prints.[11] In one painting, there is flight; in the other, guilt and memory. Exile was very painful for Louise; she was constantly torn between France and America, between two languages, and two worlds.

She carefully recorded her arrival in New York and her first impressions of the city in the frequent correspondence she kept up with her father. Transatlantic mail was gathered at a fixed time at the Gare Saint-Lazare to be sent on to Le Havre and then taken away by boat.[12] The same was true for mail going the other way: Louise had to run to the port of New York to send her letters. In spite of the distance, the exchanges between them were abundant. At that time, people wrote each other often and carefully preserved the letters they received. Robert and Louise (who signed herself "Louise Goldwater") lived at 63 Park Avenue, not far from his parents. An untitled painting showing the elevated train in New York, a yellow taxi, and a shop selling wine and liquor evokes her new urban surroundings.

Louise sent photographs to her father and early on spoke a good deal about her in-laws. She immediately liked her father-in-law, Sigismund Schultz Goldwater (1873–1942), who was the city health commissioner:[13]

"I do have a great friend here, my father-in-law [...] , he's an important man, his name is in the papers everyday." Robert and his father loved each other but were too much alike; they didn't speak very often and were "both kind of withdrawn," though "Robert much less since we got married [...]. Father is also [...] a top professional in his field."[14] The Goldwater family's prominence was confirmed by a *New York Times* article on October 9, 1938, announcing the marriage of Robert Goldwater to Miss Louise Bourgeois.[15]

Her mother-in-law, Clara Aub (1874–1958), was fairly grand and expertly presided over her house, but "[she] knows everything which means she knows nothing."[16] (Louise did not mention that she also wrote poetry.) Mrs. Goldwater was "very ambitious for her son." She wanted Louise and Robert to entertain more.[17] She was slightly shocked by Louise, finding her distracted and not quite ladylike, a gentle reproach that her father echoed in turn: "I understand her reasons for not finding you sufficiently coquettish."[18] Clara Goldwater was very present in Louise's life, but Louise made her well aware that Robert was hers: "when she goes on about all the things she owns, I make sure she understands that he is 'mine.'"[19] "[M]y mother-in-law resents this, for she believes the home-language is sacred and precious and she thinks that her son is becoming too French for her taste."[20] "I don't speak English well enough she is quite right about this but it is the only French thing that I have, this possibility to speak French with Robert."[21] Although she spoke English fairly well, thanks to multiple trips to Great Britain, as well as with Sadie, it was difficult for Louise not to be able to communicate better. She had trouble expressing herself at dinner parties; the English language felt like an insurmountable obstacle, a barrier between people. She was frustrated at having to struggle with people who "seem to say that I was an idiot because I didn't get the nuances and their thoughts right away."[22]

Luckily, Robert supported her: "you have no idea how kind he is [...]. [I] am a bit worried about the future but when he smiles at me I feel I'm the happiest woman on earth."[23] "[H]e is seen as a serious and hard-working and smart man which is the absolute truth."[24]

Louise was very proud of Robert, of his intelligence and his connections. She spoke often of his book on (what was at that time called) primitivism, boasting about his good qualities, as well as the advantages of her new life, to Colette Richarme: "in New York I shall be joining artistic circles. Othon

Friesz is there at the moment, so is Fernand Léger. [De] Chirico and Salvador Dalí are Robert's friends and will be in our house regularly. Picasso[25] and André Breton are also coming [to New York]. These names may not mean much to you, because they are all much more 'avant-garde' than Brayer. Breton, for example, wrote the Surrealist Manifesto, and I know that this will make you laugh, for the present at any rate."[26]

She listed her husband's precious gifts: "Robert is far more intelligent than I and much more methodical, so he manages my enthusiasms and helps me channel my energy in one direction. It's very sweet to have someone you love beside you. Since I lost Maman, I doubted whether it would be possible, and sometimes I'm so happy it makes me cry."[27] "I am becoming more reasonable sometimes I feel I resemble Maman more and more."[28] She later said that Robert reminded her of her mother: "I married my mother when I married Robert. I loved in Robert the quality that my mother had. I have never seen my mother angry, ever. My mother never lost her cool."[29]

As for Robert, he was proud of his wife's paintings and explained them to his entourage, while she talked up his book. "I can see people thinking: 'those two are strong because they work for one another.'"[30] This complicity, and these intellectual affinities, played an important role in the development of Louise's art.

Of course, for Louise, New York meant museums to discover, especially those showing modern art. She also went to see a Broadway show: "Afterwards we walked up the avenue that was bustling and scintillating and loud. It is a magnificent and troubling scene and one is wondering whether it is an evocation of Heaven or hell."[31] Louise vacillated between attraction and repulsion: though she very quickly understood what drove New York's dynamism—the dense crowd, the agitation, the intensity of life—she remained well aware of the inequalities found there: "there is a terrible fight for survival it is visible on the tense faces and swift gaits [. . .] everybody is running and suspicious of one's neighbor."[32] However, she was immediately enamored of the architecture, the skyscrapers, and especially the pure blue skies which she described in 1947: "But the New York sky is blue, utterly blue. The light is white, a glorious white and the air is strong and it is healthy too. There is no foolishness about that sky. It is a beautiful thing. It is pure."[33] "The city is a wonder that no one can imagine back home and everything is done at a baffling scale and speed."[34]

Yet the enthusiasm of discovery was followed by loneliness and sorrow. "What a strange life I'm leading here. I've been wanting to write and ask you to come and get me several times—New York is just so harsh [. . .]. I'm not usually so emotional but I would have given anything to have a grandmother or a sister for a day."[35]

On November 11, 1938, she heard drums in the street and remembered the Armistice of 1918 in Paris and the processions in the street. "[A]ll the lights were up and we sang La Madelon [. . .]. Away from the mother country, one becomes quite sentimental."[36]

"The weather is wonderful," she noted that autumn. "[But] mentally, I'm a bit disoriented and worried because life is completely different here; the state of mind above all is a bit frightening."[37] But, she wrote reassuringly, "I don't regret having left except I miss you and from time to time I miss Henriette too."[38]

Louise and Robert began looking for a new apartment; the place on Park Avenue was much too small. The kitchen was in a closet, and Louise painted "between the bed and the window."[39] Louise was determined that when they found it, she would bring over some of her old French furniture, in order to "own something that [. . .] comes from my country in this totally new world."[40] She was particularly eager to perfect the image she gave of being an impeccable housekeeper. She describes buying elegant dresses, the solid silverware engraved with her initials that Robert gave her as a gift—though it wasn't from Christofle, she noted, for she had kept her luxurious habits. She spoke often of money, what she received from France (the rent from Antony), her joint account with Robert, the sales of tapestries, problems with customs and importing works of art.[41]

Robert, who taught at New York University near Washington Square, had set his sights on becoming a professor at Queens College. His book *Primitivism in Modern Painting* was published in late November 1938.[42]

Louise began to paint as soon as she arrived, despite the difficult conditions. Whatever time they did not spend "socializing," she wrote, "I am spending [with] a brush in hand [. . .]. [T]he house is full of oils and colors but Robert is sweet and helps me as much as he can. He poses for me, stretches canvases for me."[43] At the same time, she made contact with several dealers, including Durand-Ruel, to meet with Othon Friesz and especially Louis Carré,[44] who knew everyone in the art world and with whom she was relieved to be able to speak French, although she did not "consider [him] an eagle," convinced that she knew more art world people than he did—not to mention Robert, whom she called "an expert in African art."[45] She also spent time with Robert's circle of friends, who came in for one of her implacably sharp but accurate judgments: "all social climbers if you ask me. They fight each other like wolves. Women are the same, maybe worse, they never think about having children, they only want to get away from their husband[s] and make it on their own."[46] Very quickly, Louise understood everything about America, as much about social relations as the economic situation and the differences between Europe and the United States: "[T]hey don't care about saving, they spend, consume and produce a lot and it makes for a heated environment that wears down Europeans and makes them anxious."[47]

The lithograph she made as a Christmas card[48] in 1938 depicts "the arrival from Paris to New York of a native of St Germain."[49] She had left her heart behind, said her husband.[50] She still dreamed of opening a shop selling antiques or tapestries ("a gallery like the Perls have here small but in a good location where they are from morning to night"),[51] but for the moment, she lacked the funds to launch such a business. She asked her father to send her some tapestries and went to the auction houses to find out how much she could get for them. "Before and after our wedding, Robert told me he didn't want to hear about business, saying there could be conflicts of interest, since he could be suspected in the press to have a vested interest in the things he'd be talking about."[52] Like any other museum type, Robert tried to keep art history apart from the market. However, he suggested to his father that Louise work as an artistic adviser for the murals commissioned by public hospitals. When his father agreed, Bourgeois exclaimed: "I was so happy it's the greatest joy I've had since I've arrived here."[53] She had already suggested he consider "splendid" Mexican frescoes as well as Gothic tapestries, as a way of demonstrating that it is possible to be "modern and still remain in that tradition."[54]

The two were frequently invited to the Goldwaters' country home in Huntington, a beautiful seaside property on Long Island. Louise described painting his aunt Thérèse's portrait there one afternoon. She warmed to her sisters-in-law, Janet and Mary.[55] Louise and Robert left to spend a few days in Boston between Christmas and New Year's, and stayed at Harvard, where

Robert had done his degree. The landscape around Boston and the room where they stayed reminded her, she wrote to her father, of the trip they had taken to England almost three years earlier.[56]

Unsure how much to believe what she read in the papers, Louise was extremely concerned about the political situation in France and in Europe. In October 1938, Robert had written to Louis to apologize for their hasty departure after their marriage, citing the imminent risk of war.[57] She shared the reactions she encountered in America with her father: "[Édouard] Daladier behaves like a horrible dictator [. . .]. Italy and Germany are detested by all and so is Chamberlain but the France of the Front Populaire garners all sympathies. Among the people I meet several are anti-Nazi Germans but the nicest are the French [. . .]. All the Americans I meet greet and listen to me as if I came from a blessed country."[58]

A subject of a more personal nature also preoccupied her, as she confided in her father: she wanted to have a child and to bring it to France with her the following summer.

> I was worried because I was thinking that perhaps I wouldn't be able to do that but I saw a doctor who told me I was in perfect health [. . .]. Robert [. . .] declared he didn't want a child for one or two years [yet] [. . .] because we are not rich, because they would bear a Jewish name and that Jews are made to suffer and that he doesn't want to raise kids to be sent to war [. . .]. I would love for you, my dear Papa, to tell me what you think about the issue of children for me it is the most important one in life and I can only talk about this with you.[59]

This declaration underscores the importance of maternity in Louise's life and art, as evidenced in her numerous works on the theme of the pregnant woman and, at the end of her life, in the gouaches depicting childbirth and newborns feeding at their mothers' breasts. In her 1939 diary, she carefully noted the dates of her period, her appointments with her gynecologist, Dr. Rodgers, the days she ovulated, and the months that remained before the birth of a child.[60] Louise, like a good hysteric, worried she was sterile—which is one of the things that led her to adopt a French orphan in 1939.[61]

These questions concerning maternity and Jewishness, which she mentioned here to Louis for the first time, are significant both in terms of the close relationship she maintained with her father as well as her own relationship to Judaism. In June 1935, she copied out a page from Jacques de Lacretelle's novel *Silbermann,* which tells the story of a young Jewish man, the son of an antiques dealer, who goes to America to flee persecution and to try to launch a career as a writer.[62] In 1939, she wrote to her father again: "I'm also quite worried about anti-Semitism here which is increasing because of the refugees."[63] In 1954, she gave her sons her surname, not only to keep her father's name alive after his recent death, but to protect them from McCarthyism and anti-Semitism.[64]

Even after her marriage, Louise still needed her father. After her mother's death, he was the only person in her family she felt she could rely on, though Henriette kept up regular contact. Louis felt abandoned and alone; he sometimes complained about her departure for the United States, envying the Goldwaters yet writing to them to thank them for their hospitality toward his daughter. To combat his loneliness and boredom he went fishing, traveled, took a cruise on the Mediterranean. With the threat of war growing ever stronger, his business was suffering.

However, he did understand Louise's decision; he was proud of her husband and only wanted her to be happy in her new life. "Nurture your happiness and treasure it," he wrote to her, reassured to know that she was safe and well away from the war.[65] The tenderness and shared solicitude conveyed in their letters is not in keeping with the negative feelings Louise later expressed about her father. For a long time she was torn between hatred and love.

In the letters Louise exchanged with Colette Richarme, she spoke willingly and precisely about art and painting. And they demonstrate the importance of her marriage to Robert and her departure for America, how determinative they were for the course of her artistic career. Living in New York not only gave her access to a great deal of modern art but also enabled her to benefit from the advice and unfailing support of her husband: "I have much more confidence [*foi*] now, [I am] far calmer and more assured than last year; Robert has contributed to it so much, by making me carry an idea or a piece of work, once started, through to the end."[66]

Louise was well aware that she and her friend were on very different paths. One more "traditional" ("you also value the opinion of people who paint the way people used to paint two hundred years ago")[67] and academic, the other more contemporary: "in matters of painting the young are always right."[68] She dispensed some advice: read the *Cahiers d'art* rather than *Beaux-arts,* look at Picasso, the great master, and show at the Salon d'automne or the Tuileries rather than the Salon des artistes français.

1939, a Year Full of Menace

The year 1939 was particularly hectic for Louise, in a personal as well as a public sense. In October, she and Robert moved into a two-bedroom apartment with a beautiful view, in a building at 333 East Forty-First Street, where he could have an office to work in. They bought a car—a Plymouth 1936—which looked exactly like Louis Bourgeois's Chrysler and made, Louise said, the same racket. At the beginning of the year, Robert was hospitalized for a serious pulmonary illness. Louise, an experienced nurse, looked after him tenderly and fed him the healthiest meals. Her husband's sickness brought her closer to her in-laws.

Robert worked very hard, but since he had taken the teaching job at Queens College, his colleagues at NYU thought he would never lecture or write another book or article ever again. Louise was aware of this difficulty and did all she could to help him build on the prestige his book had brought him.[69]

Much to the Goldwaters' dismay, Louise and Robert wanted to return to France. Not only did Louise want to see her father, as he hadn't been able to come as planned in April, but she wanted to visit the rest of her family and pick up some of her things from Paris and Antony. She asked her father to send her drawings and a couple of paintings: "as much stuff as you can manage," frames, boxes, iron rods with hooks.[70]

Little by little, she seemed to be adapting to her new life: "You know that we are very happy my dear Papa and if you are sad you can come share our happiness—with heartfelt kisses your Louison who loves you."[71] Her bond with her father was still very strong, but her offer for him to come and share in her happiness was, to say the least, ambiguous. Their complicity was total ("I believe that if you come to meet me on the other side of the world if we are together we will form a little world of our own and we will say boo to the people who do not understand us"),[72] but it was not so much love for her father that she expressed here as much as the need to re-create the world she had left behind, of which Louis was a symbol.

To her father, too, she noted that under her husband's influence she became serious and reflective. She said: "Robert has taught me to be more organized and methodical."[73]

Of course, Louise made reference to the increasingly worrying political situation: "Every day the newspapers here give us terrible news [. . .] I read the speech of [Édouard] Daladier and I was devastated; he is very much liked here. There is a large anti-German campaign in the United States—and Chamberlain is not very highly esteemed."[74] "[A]nd people organize protests to 'stop Hitler,' all of this is really sad."[75] "[E]very body is very anxious for nobody doubts the American intervention in case things become worse in France and England. [. . .] I have a hard time understanding the point to which economically and sentimentally America depends on Europe."[76]

Back at home, Louis described the distribution of gas masks, reservists being called up, and daily Parisian life, with shops closing and people leaving.

Louise and Robert's trip, which was planned for June 1939, was considered very dangerous, given the threat of war. "My in-laws are trying to push back or cancel this trip but I am adamant about it and our tickets are already bought for June 29 on the *Champlain*."[77] "Whenever I think about this trip to France my heart starts beating out of sheer happiness."[78]

The Goldwaters did all they could to dissuade them from going. "My in-laws are pretty upset about our upcoming trip. [. . .] His mother thought 'my son is lost.'"[79] Despite their warnings, Louise and Robert boarded the *Île-de-France* on June 21 and arrived at Le Havre six days later. "I think the real reason for my present happiness is the thought of seeing my own country again," she wrote to Colette Richarme.[80]

During the summer of 1939, which they spent in Paris, and despite the heavy atmosphere there, Louise planned to work on frescoes at Ranson with Bissière and to take classes with Léger at Gromaire. She brought along four of her canvases which were to be shown at the Académie Ranson, as well as the works of some young American painters.[81] Paris seemed sad and changed to her; all anyone talked about was war. Colette Richarme invited the Goldwaters to visit her in the south, but they instead went to Geneva to see the exhibition of works from the Prado in Madrid: "The most beautiful masterpieces by Velásquez, Greco, Goya. Never has an exhibition moved me so much."[82] Robert worked at the Bibliothèque Doucet, while Louise prepared for the Salon d'automne. She attended the baptism of her godchild Claude Bocé, the daughter of her tenants in Antony, and saw her friends Jacques Bauml and Jean Pelletier.

At this time she was fascinated by Picasso and his links to the poets Guillaume Apollinaire and Max Jacob; she was deeply interested in the relationship between words and images, in cubism and surrealism, in the visual and the literary arts. "As a creator of images, the poet is close to us, which is why I read Joyce, Jarry, James, and Gertrude Stein."[83] She was breaking definitively with traditional figuration and drew a great deal: "I do unshaded drawings, as thoughtful and delicate as they used to be emphatic, and I go on working at a form for days and days."[84] She took advantage of the trip to see her entire family and to send some furniture from Antony to New York: "Last year I suffered terribly from not having anything from my former setting [*mon ancien cadre*] around me."[85]

Robert and Louise were still in France on September 3, the day of the general mobilization and the declaration of war with Germany. Their return to America obviously became more complicated. But Robert, thanks to his contacts as well as his father's, managed to find room on a boat leaving from Bordeaux on September 30, the *Manhattan*.[86] Louis Bourgeois, who had spent the month of August in Évian, urged his daughter to leave as quickly as possible, because the news was alarming: "Are you not the most precious thing in the world to me [?]"[87]

This new separation, under ominous, worrying circumstances, was painful for Louise: "I am very sad," she wrote to Colette. "With my home [*ménage*] on one side and my country on the other. [. . .] I feel like a motherless child. I haven't felt that way in two years. Not since the days in the rue Mazarine."[88]

A French Child

Before they left, Louise and Robert visited an orphanage in Bordeaux[89] to see a three-year-old boy named Michel Olivier whom Louise hoped to adopt—not only because she feared not being able to have children but also because she hoped in the face of war to take with her some "precious" part of France. The adoption process was long and complicated; in the end the Goldwaters had to leave without the child, who would not arrive in the United States until May 1940. Only Colette Richarme knew about the plan to adopt—"I didn't tell my in-laws or my father"[90]—and helped Louise with the administrative side of things. "Have you written to Bordeaux about the child? [. . .] I curse the 'nitpickings' of the public assistance authorities there."[91]

The adoption says a lot about Louise's complex relationship to maternity and her attachment to France. She decided to adopt a child because she thought she wouldn't be able to have one of her own, and this was traumatic for her. But she became pregnant soon after they returned home—a frequent phenomenon, apparently. Louise was very grateful to Robert for understanding her desire for a child and for supporting her attempt to adopt. "I ask so much of Robert, and I can't help thinking that there are very few husbands who would do as much [were they] in his place."[92]

The orphanage informed her that she had to go through the government offices in Paris and that she shouldn't expect a response before three months' time. Louise, emotional, began to accept that the adoption might not work out. In January 1940, she finally received permission, but social services wouldn't allow such a young child to travel by sea alone. Louise thought for a moment of having him sent over on a plane.[93]

Finally, after eight months of correspondence, it was arranged that little Michel would be accompanied by a nurse[94] on the last American ship, the *President Adams,* which was making a stop in the Mediterranean.[95] His arrival in New York on May 21 was a real event, not only for the Goldwater family, but for the press, since the boat also carried British refugees. Three newspapers including the *New York Times* and the *New York Post* covered its arrival, which was delayed by twenty-four hours due to fog, especially to see the French orphan. "French war orphan here to join foster parents" and "French orphan yells loud *'non.'*"[96] Refusing to disembark from the ship, Michel had to be taken off by force.

Louise was waiting for him on the quay, very moved: "I am at the ship at 8:30, terrible wait [. . .]. finally arrived. The child looks to be in good health although he has a cold. The nurse cries when she leaves him, he was a little king on the ship. The wait on the dock was difficult. The Michelette is

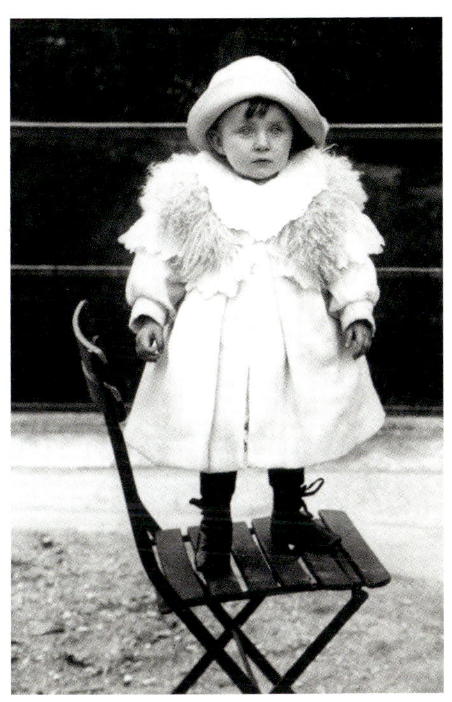

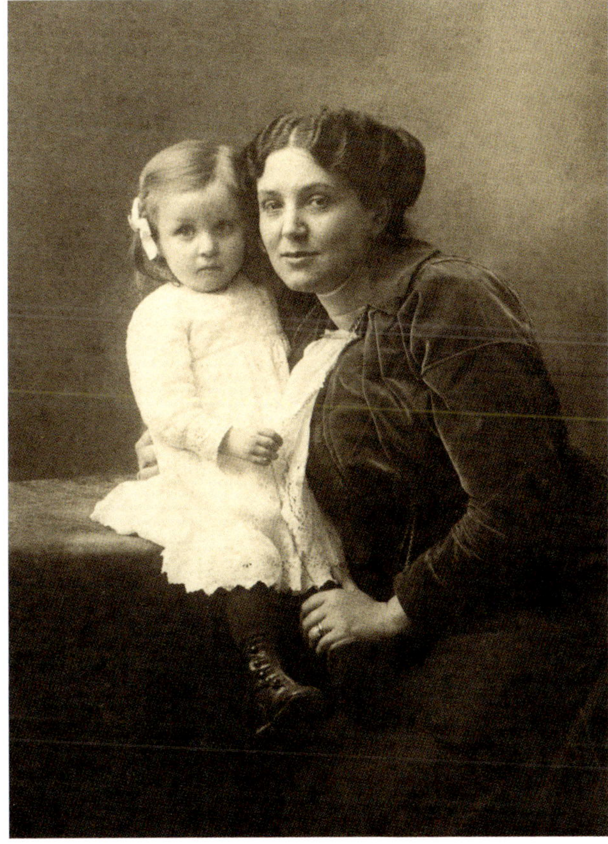

Louise Bourgeois, 1913

Louise Bourgeois with her mother, Joséphine, 1914

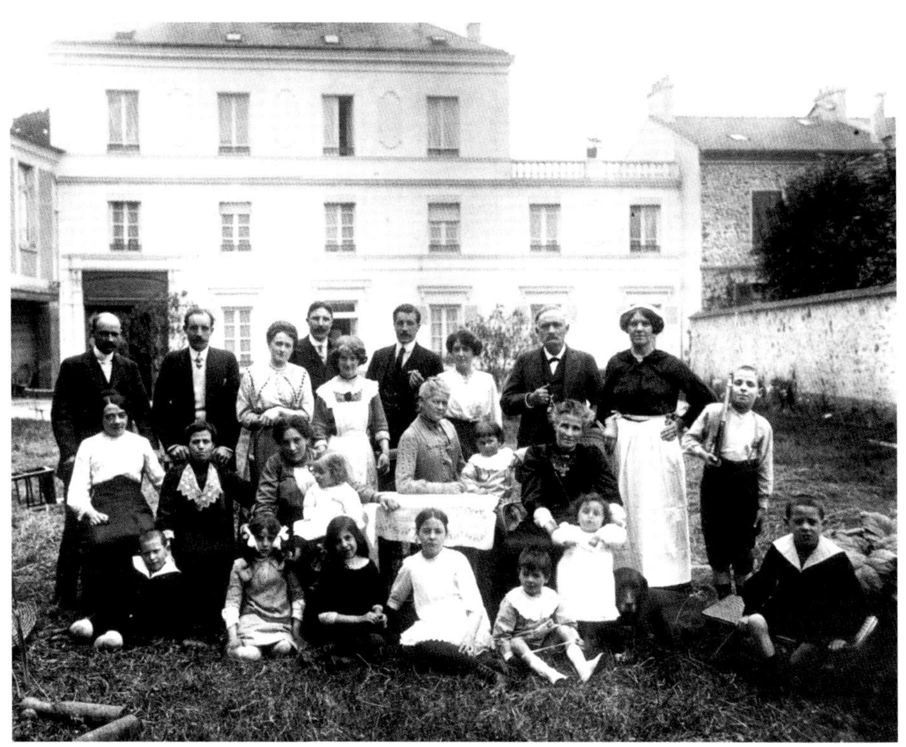

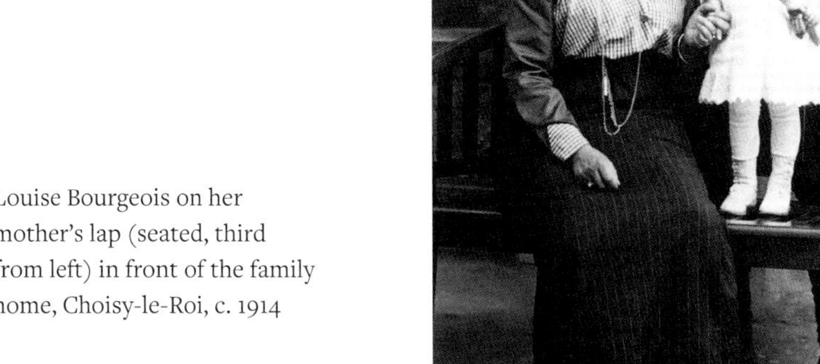

Louise Bourgeois on her
mother's lap (seated, third
from left) in front of the family
home, Choisy-le-Roi, c. 1914

Louise Bourgeois with her
parents, Joséphine and Louis,
1915

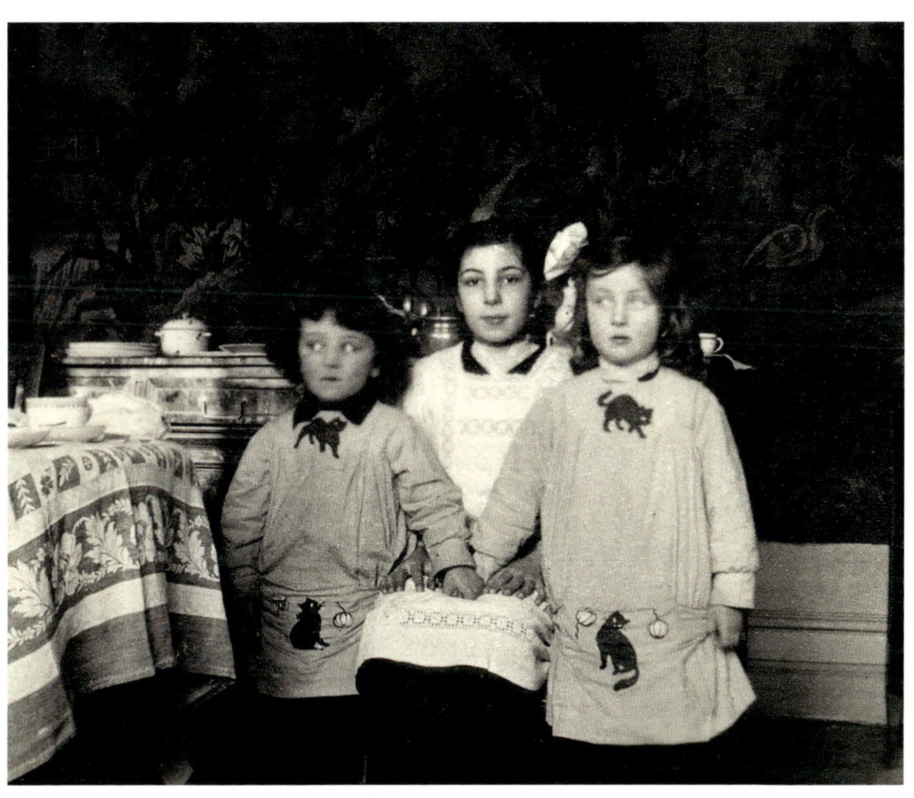

Louise Bourgeois (right) with her brother,
Pierre, and sister, Henriette, c. 1917

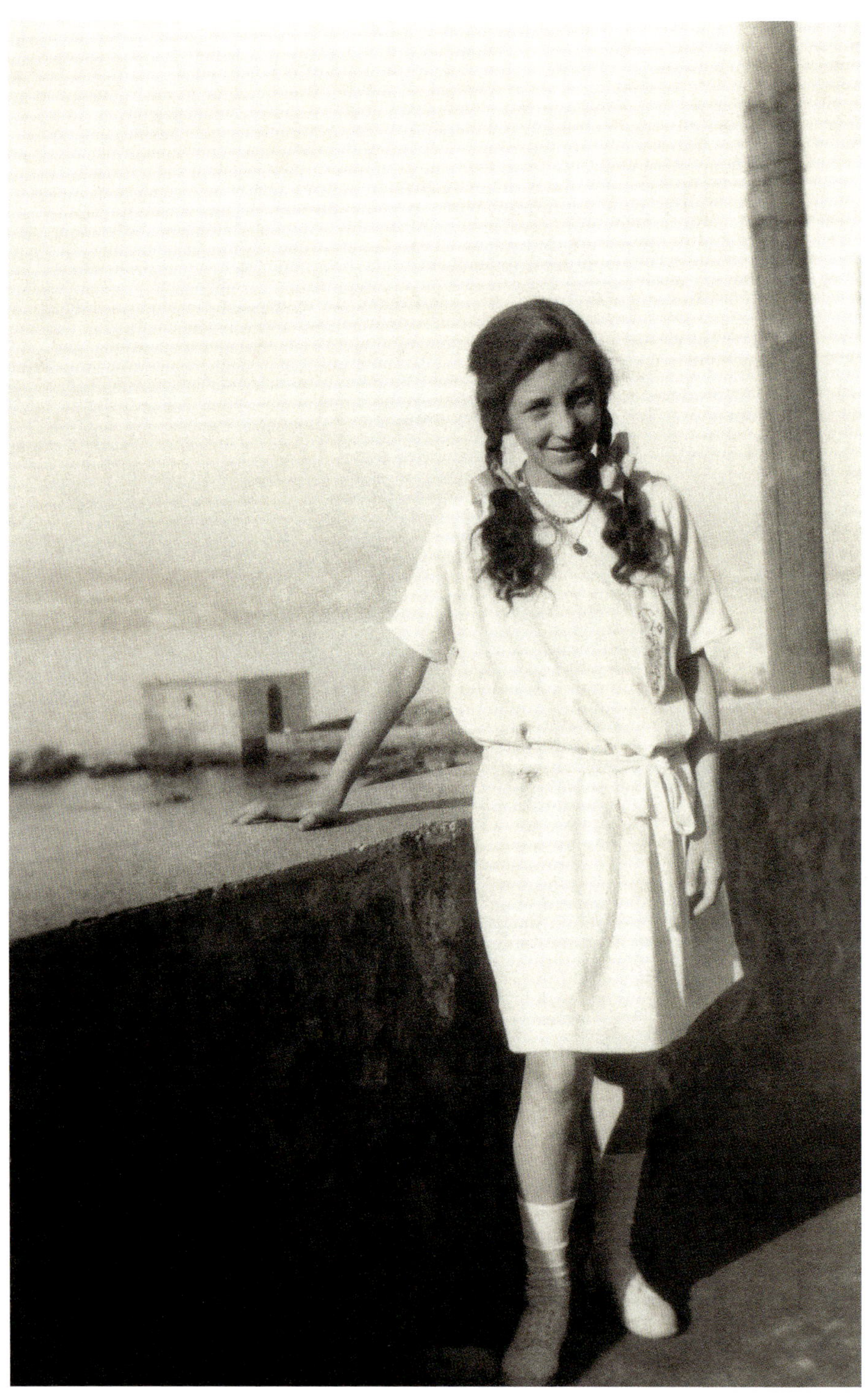

Louise Bourgeois wearing Coco Chanel, Cannes, 1925

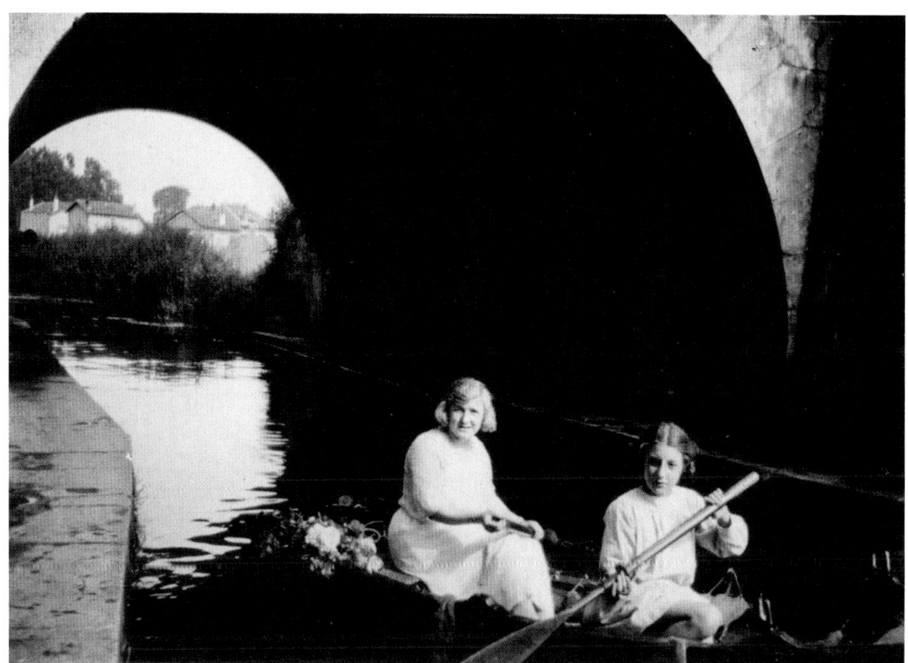

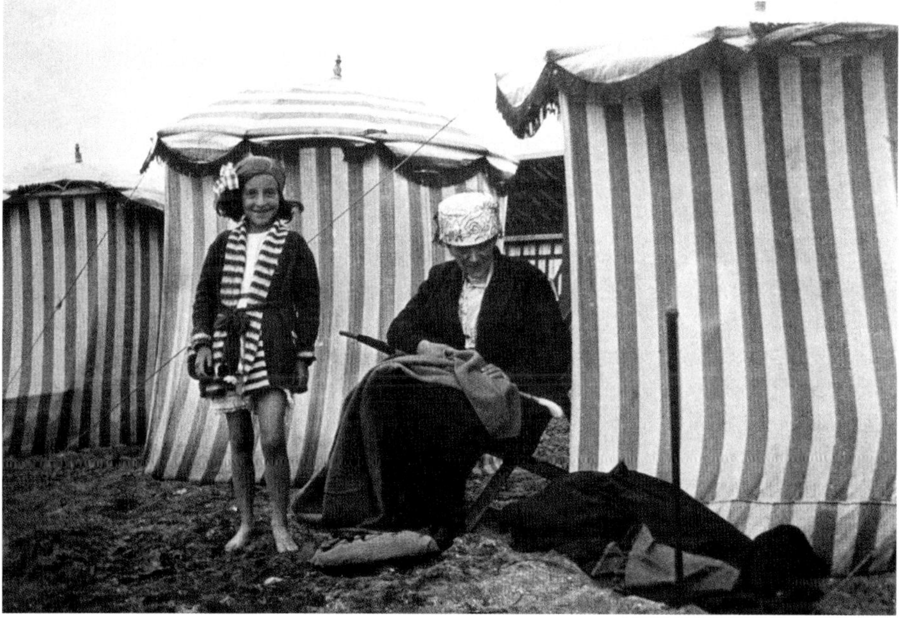

Louise Bourgeois with Sadie Gordon
Richmond on the Bièvre river, Antony, 1923

Louise Bourgeois with her mother,
Joséphine, Deauville, Normandy, 1922

MEMENTO

Le mois de Novembre a été
pour moi un assez bon
mois j'ai été 11ème j'ai
j'ai été toujours bien
avec maman
j'ai toujours été bien avec
Papa
je ne me suis pas arrive-
ment disputée avec René
et Henriette
je n'ai pas menti
j'ai bien appris mes
leçons

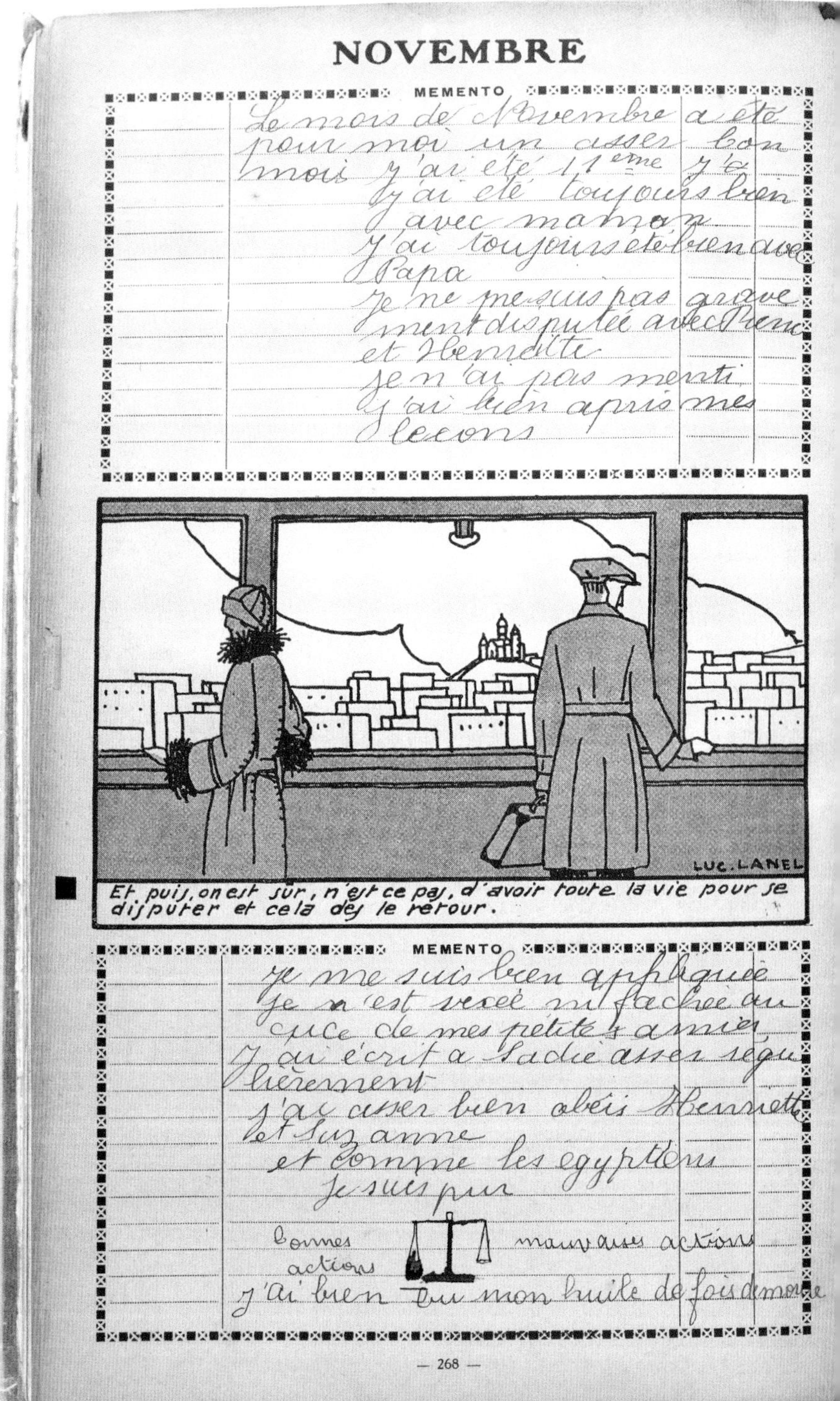

MEMENTO

je me suis bien appliquée
je n'est vexée ni fachée au
cuce de mes petites amies
j'ai écrit à Sadie assez régu-
lièrement
j'ai assez bien obéi Henriette
et Suzanne
et comme les egyptiens
je suis pur

bonnes
actions   mauvaises actions
j'ai bien bu mon huile de foie de morue

Pages from Louise Bourgeois's 1923 diary

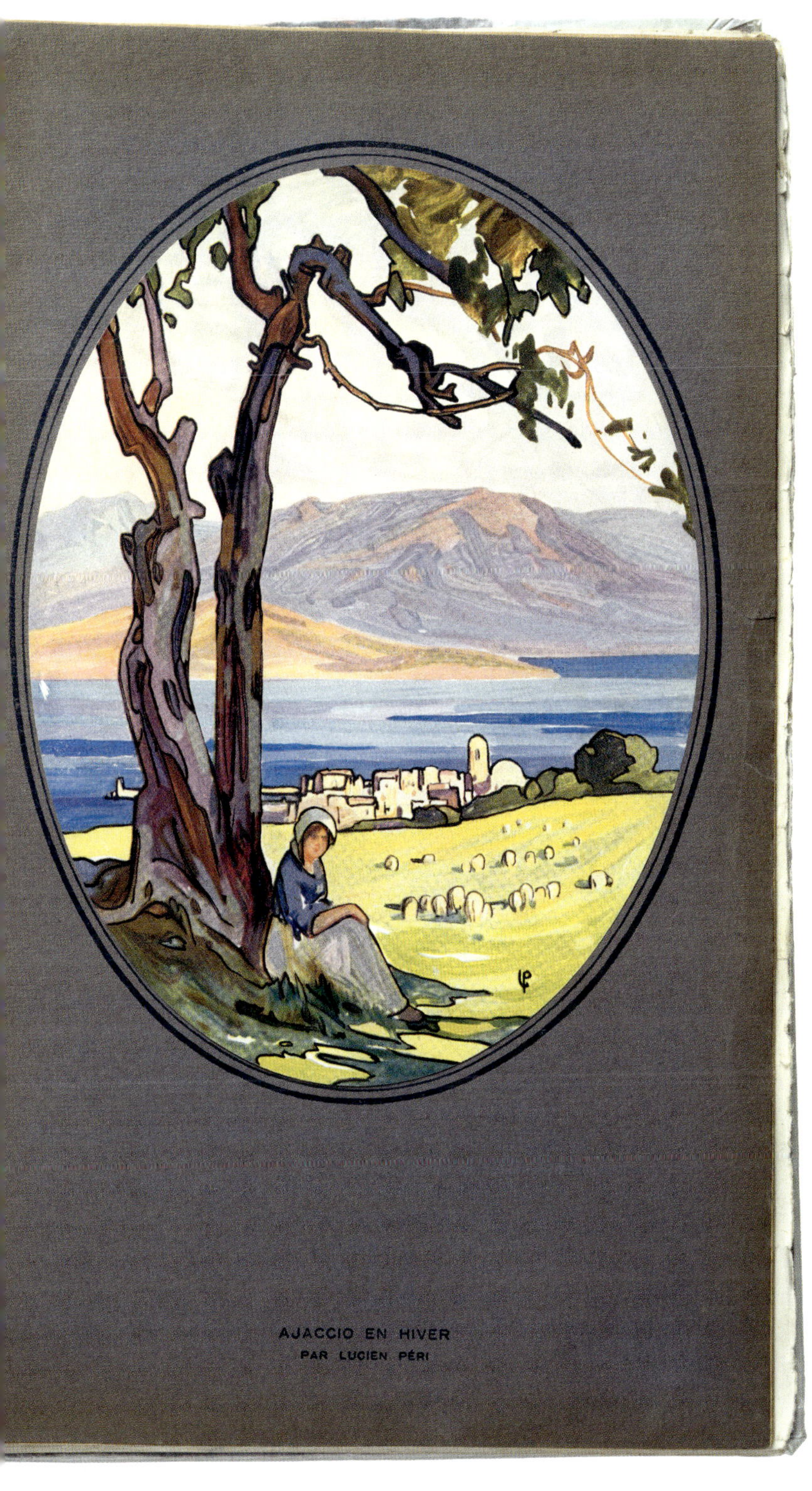

AJACCIO EN HIVER
PAR LUCIEN PÉRI

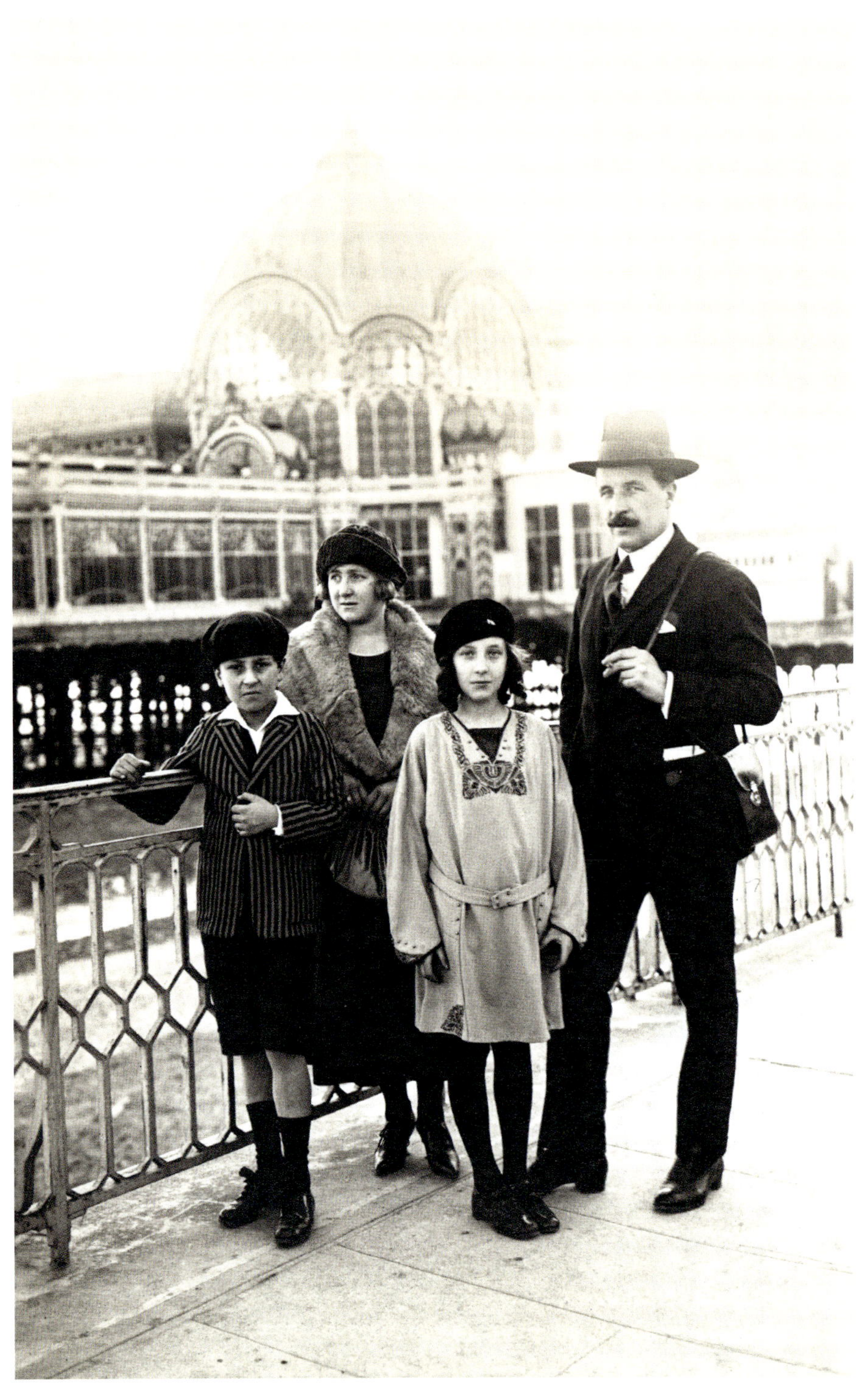

Louise Bourgeois with her brother, father,
and Sadie Gordon Richmond, Nice, c. 1923

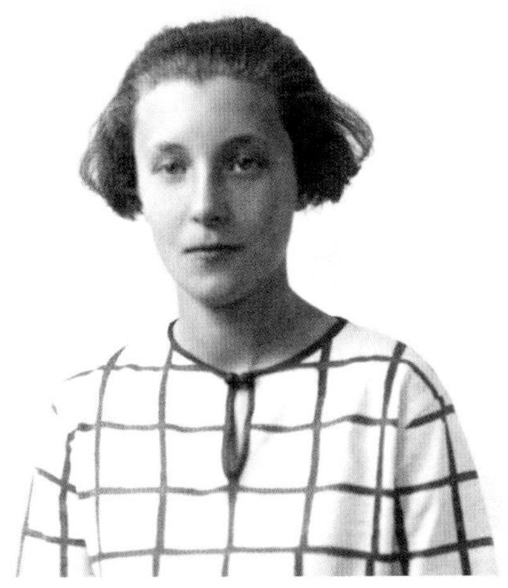

Louise Bourgeois wearing Paul Poiret, 1926

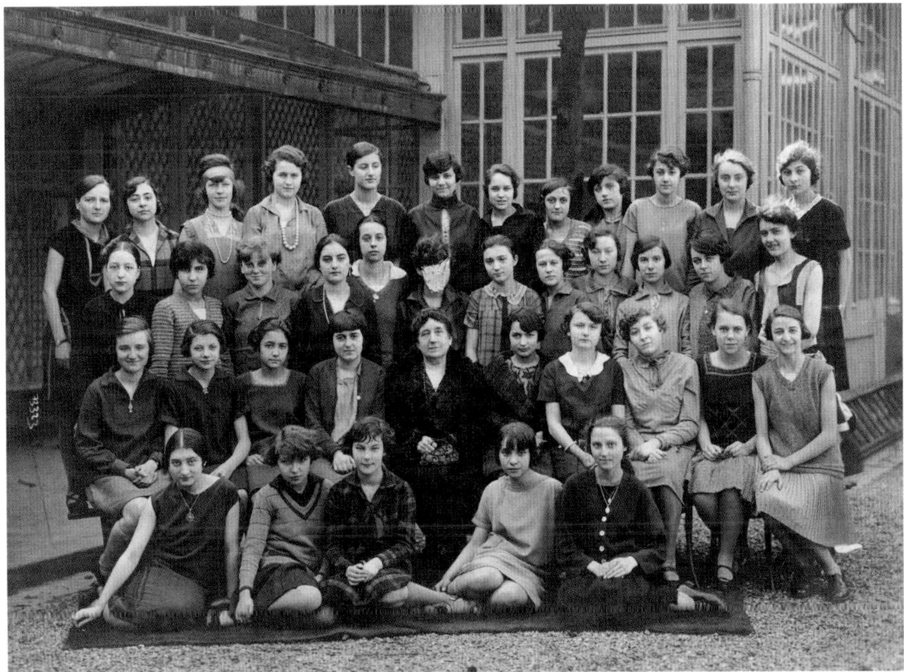

BELOW
Louise Bourgeois (center, face erased) with her classmates, Lycée Fénelon, Paris, 1927.

Louise scratched out her face in the picture because she hated her new haircut.

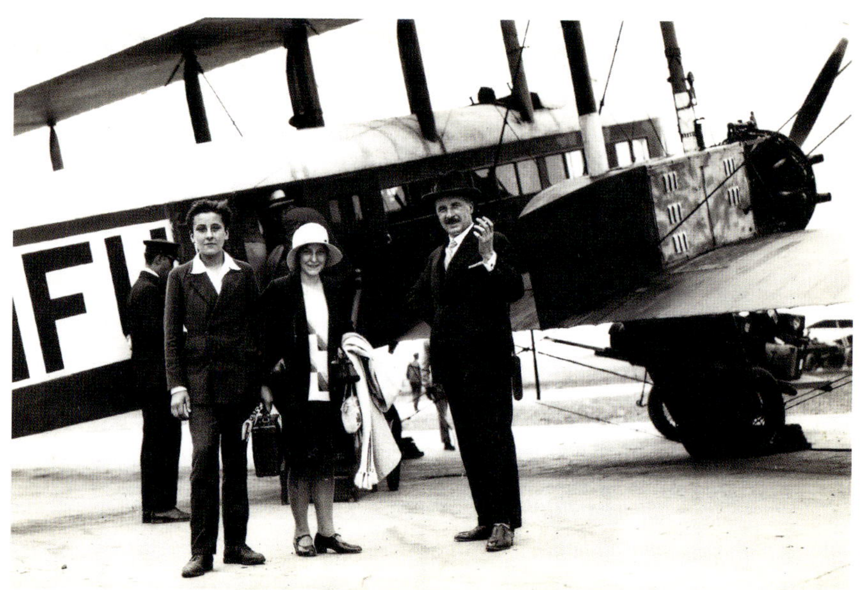

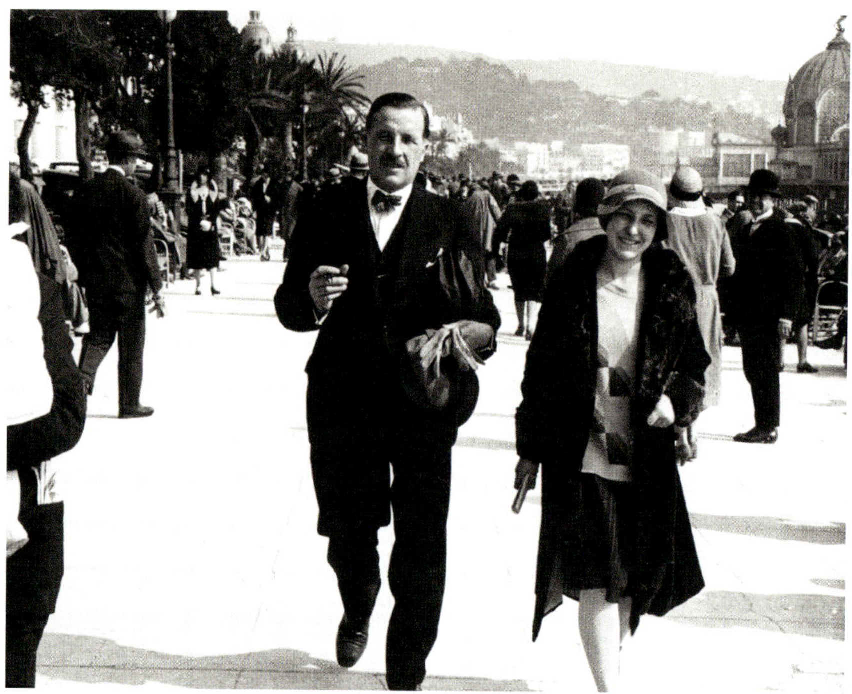

Louise Bourgeois with her brother and father
about to fly from Nice to London, 1929

Louise Bourgeois wearing clothes by Sonia
Delaunay with her father, Nice, 1929

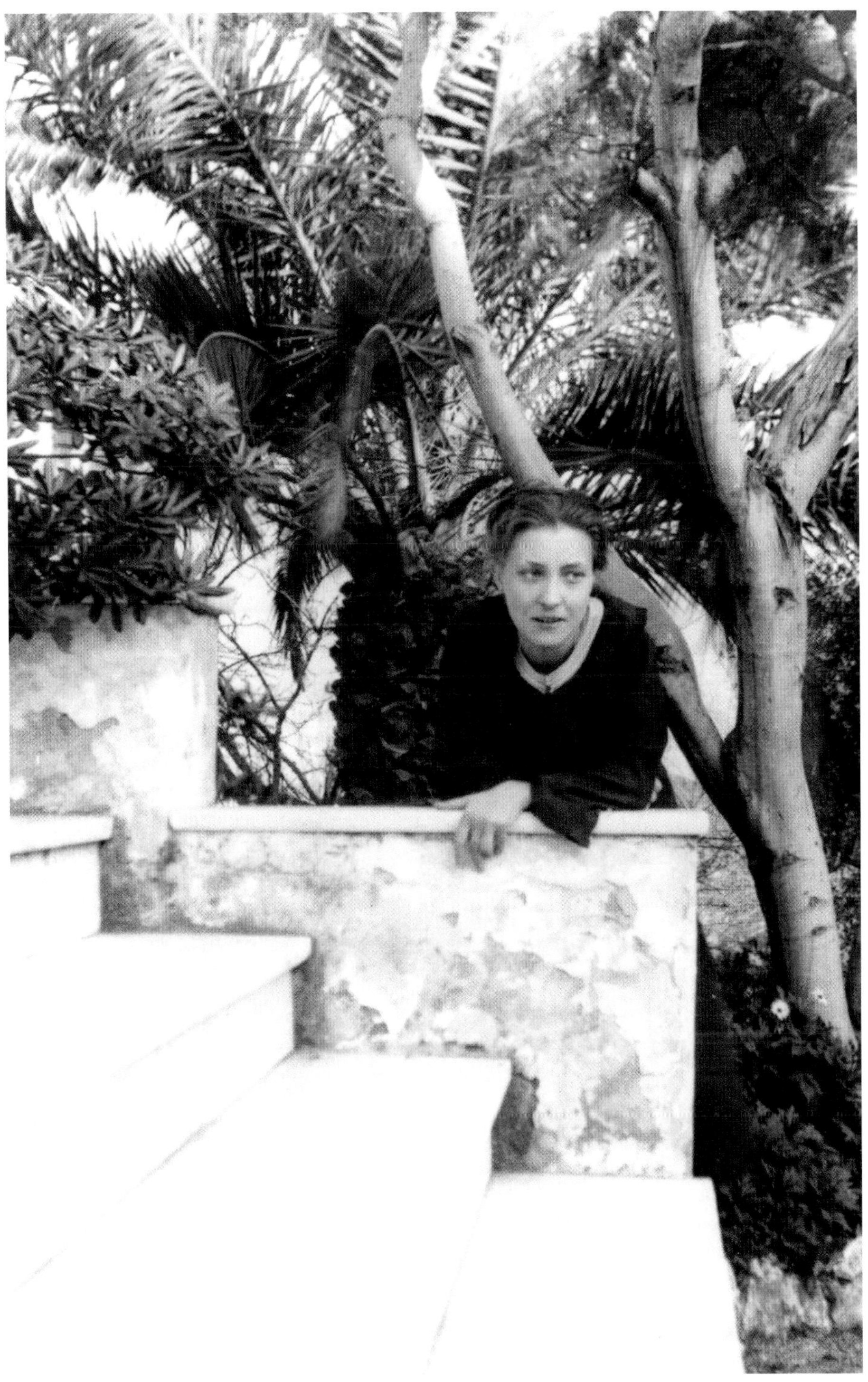

Louise Bourgeois at the Villa Pompeiana,
Cimiez, Nice, 1931

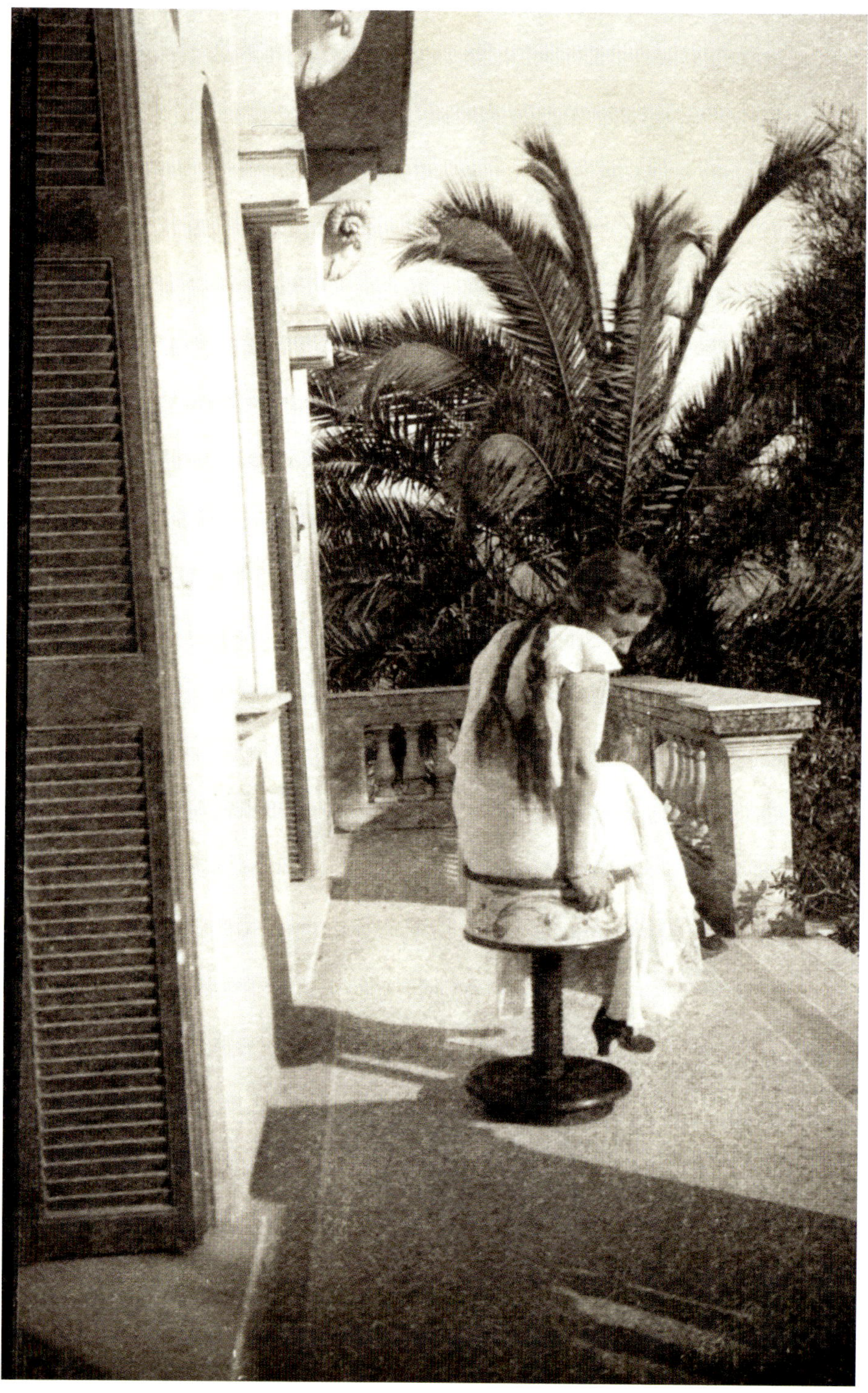

Louise Bourgeois in the south of France, 1932

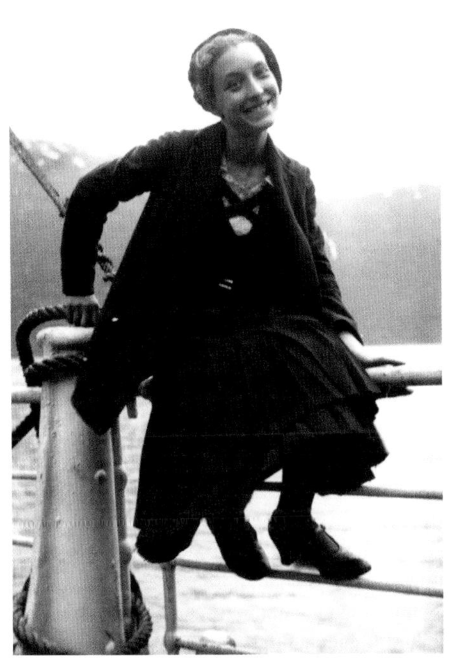

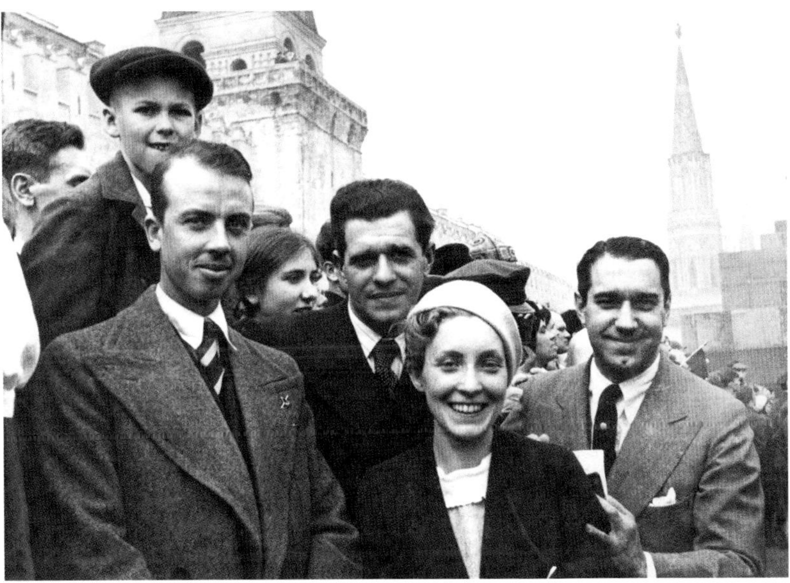

Louise Bourgeois on her first trip to the Soviet Union, 1932

Louise Bourgeois with fellow art students of Paul Colin
during her second trip to the Soviet Union, Moscow, 1934

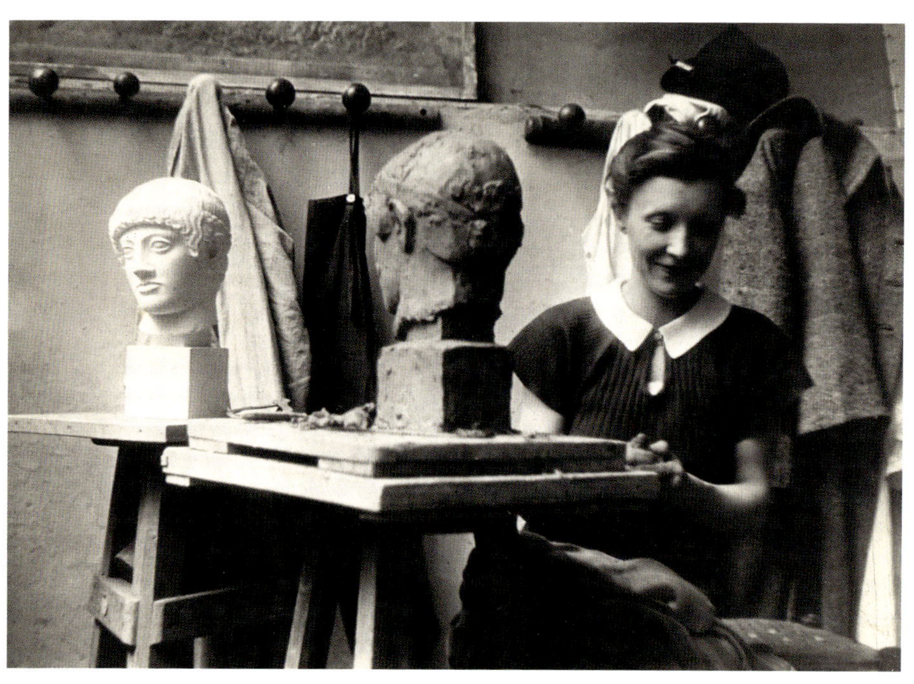

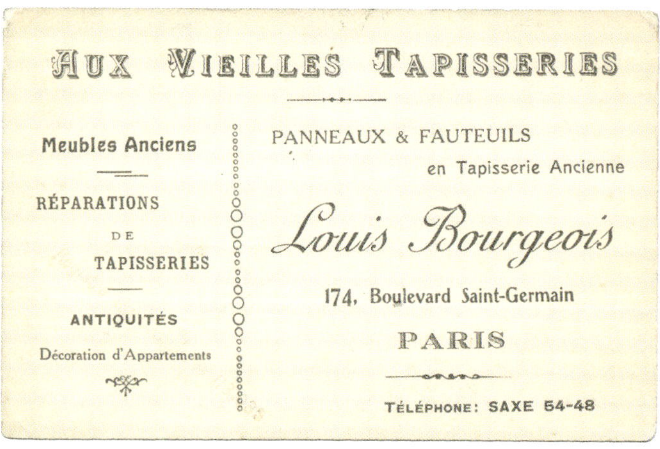

Aux Vieilles Tapisseries

Meubles Anciens

RÉPARATIONS

DE

TAPISSERIES

ANTIQUITÉS

Décoration d'Appartements

PANNEAUX & FAUTEUILS

en Tapisserie Ancienne

Louis Bourgeois

174, Boulevard Saint-Germain

PARIS

TÉLÉPHONE: SAXE 54-48

Louise Bourgeois at the Académie de la Grande
Chaumière, Paris, 1937. Photograph by Brassaï

Louis Bourgeois's business card, c. 1930s–40s

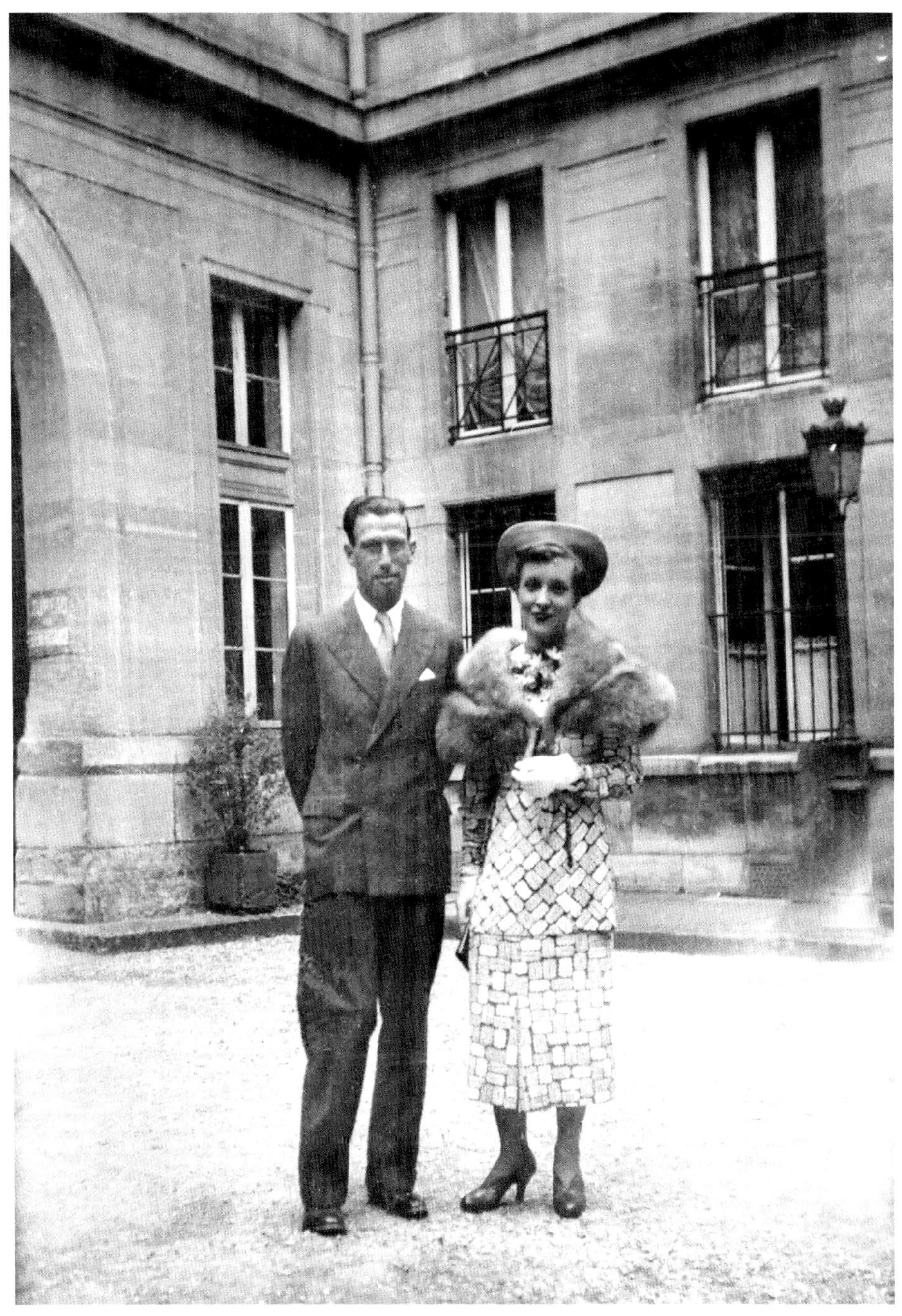

Louise Bourgeois and Robert Goldwater after
their civil ceremony at city hall in Place
Saint-Sulpice, Paris, September 12, 1938

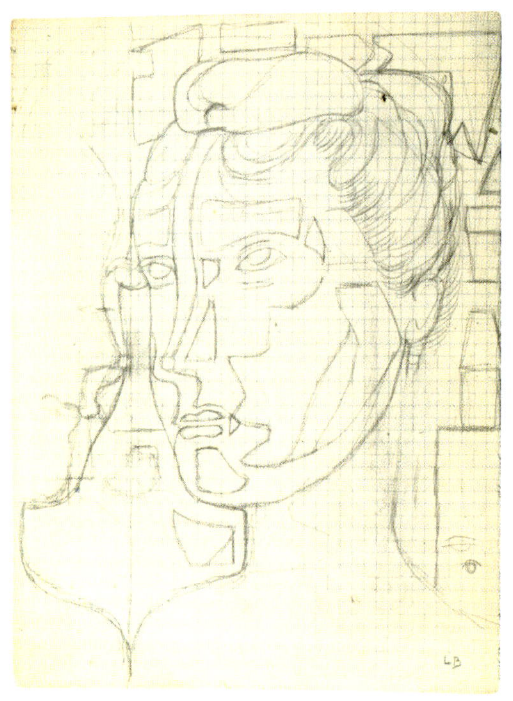

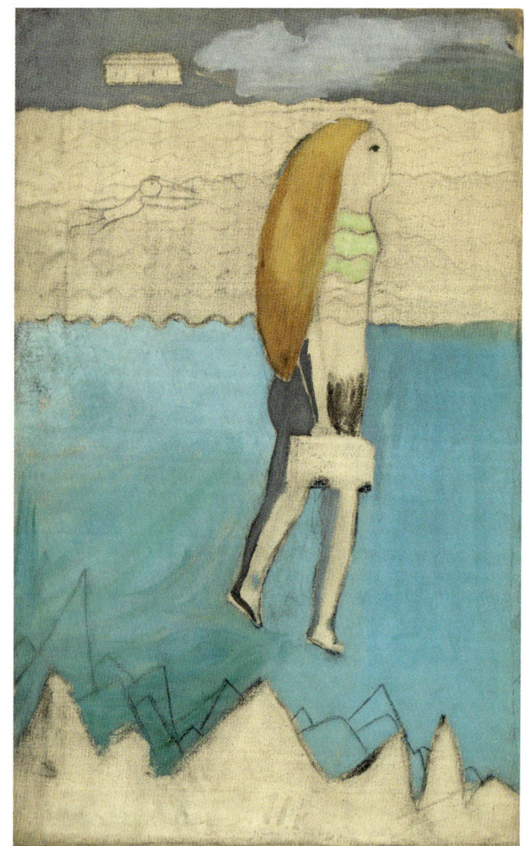

Self-Portrait, 1938. Pencil on
graph paper, 11 × 8½ in.
(27.9 × 21.6 cm)

The Runaway Girl, c. 1938. Oil,
charcoal, and pencil on canvas,
24 × 15 in. (61 × 38.1 cm)

tired."[97] She had no shortage of praise for the little boy: "He has proved to be very robust. He is, as well, intelligent and highly sociable," she wrote to Colette Richarme.[98] She decided to apply for Michel to take her father's name: "Will we regret giving Papa's name to Michel[?]"[99] Louise hoped for Michel to attend a French nursery school, which was at that time run by nuns, but Robert seemed to "detest" the idea. His hesitation reminded her of Henriette's "narrow-mindedness when she was getting treated by [the nuns] in Clamart and was bad-mouthing them."[100] In the end, the child went to school from 9:00 a.m. to 5:00 p.m. every day. Robert often looked after him, teaching him his letters and numbers. Around this time Louise became very interested in children and jotted down her thoughts about their upbringing and psychology.[101] She loved to bestow nicknames on people, so she called her son "My Michelette": "Difficult day for my Michelette," she wrote in her diary a few days after he arrived in New York.[102] But was the feminization of her son's name—which she repeated with her third child[103]—only an affectionate gesture or, more profoundly, the desire for a daughter or for a *Fillette* (1968) who would bring together the masculine and the feminine? She admitted that "the child is too spoiled. The coming days are going to be difficult."[104] Suddenly arriving in a new country, after a long ocean voyage with strangers, was a shock to the child, especially given that his adoptive mother was pregnant. Michel, who was then four years old, had strong memories of his birthplace, Souillac, saw "duckies [*coinscoins*]" everywhere he looked,[105] and talked about the people who had looked after him at the orphanage. He didn't find it easy to adapt; he cried at night, yelled, was afraid of dogs, cried for the door to be left open,[106] made a terrible scene on the first day of school, but in the end he got used to his new family. He was "very large, unaware, randomly kind or cruel. He's no dummy and charms everyone, without exception. [. . .] It's not likely we'll have to worry much about his future."[107] Alas, the future would very much prove otherwise.

Jean-Louis was born July 4, 1940, six weeks after Michel arrived. The previous February, Louise wrote that her obstetrician, Dr. Rodgers, had "taken out my ring saying the child will not fall out. we shall see."[108] It was terrifying.

The birth of her son was the most beautiful moment of her life, she later said,[109] and in a rare occurrence, indicating how important writing was to her, she precisely detailed the different phases of childbirth in her diary—that very same day: "[Contractions] every 5 minutes, [. . .] [get Michel dressed] Mother calls a driver from the village [. . .] Rodgers is coming from the country as well. At 10 a.m. we arrive at the hospital [. . .] the pain continues, even stronger, Rodgers breaks my waters [. . .], I am taken down to the labor room in a bed with bars all around. I am in unbearable pain so I am put under. My arms and also my legs are tied down. There are 5 people around me, icy, looking at me. Jean-Louis Thomas makes his entry 8 pounds 7 ounces [. . .]. Very beautiful evening and very beautiful night [. . .] Robert is happy, perhaps, I don't know."[110]

Motherhood, so longed for, was twinned with her love of country: "I would like for Jean-Louis to resemble Papa— All day I think about France. The little one is beautiful— In the evening Michel comes to visit with Robert and Mary, he is unaware and self-centered. I wish I could work and forget everything."[111] Louise was torn relentlessly between her maternal instinct, her vocation as an artist, and her desire to flee. And at the same time, she intensely experienced the joy of being a young mother: "He is becoming more beautiful every day and when he is lying by my side and I am looking at his blond hair in the light it is as if a peaceful wave were overcoming my mind and the future."[112]

"As for my Jean-Louis," she wrote to Colette Richarme, "he's a beautiful little thing. I was happy to name him Jean-Louis. Of course my in-laws wanted to give him an English name, but I'm very possessive over him and Robert has promised me that we can have him naturalized during our next trip to France."[113]

Louise was ferociously French. The question of naturalization was a genuine obsession of hers, a testament to her visceral attachment to her homeland. A few months before Jean-Louis was born, she was already asking her father to look into the conditions under which "our darling Baby girl or Baby boy"[114] might receive French nationality. On learning that the child would be French if it was born in a French colony, she considered for a time going to give birth in "Saint-Pierre,"[115] but her father strongly dissuaded her: "you will be better cared for by Robert and his family."[116]

Getting along with her in-laws was not always easy. "Father comes, he is calm sensitive and kind [. . .] Mother [. . .] Discussion, argument—not a tender word not even a little crumb of warmth not even a crumb of respect. [. . .] I am disgusted and my disgust encompasses all the old people who judge and bicker while the young are struggling to accomplish something."[117]

The birth of Alain, so soon after Jean-Louis (barely fifteen months), somewhat worried her father, as well as her father-in-law. In fact, as early as March 26, 1941, Louise writes that she was either sick or pregnant. "Robert is depressed about the family (growing) and the price and work of Easton."[118] "Father is sick. We tell him about Nicolette."[119] The young mother was overwhelmed, though she had a lot of help from her in-laws as well as a nurse. She was tired and complained often, particularly at Robert's parents' house in Huntington: "tired from going up and down the stairs—I can't carry Jean-Louis and the groceries from the ice room to our room to feed Jean-Louis [. . .] tired and angry I want to go. It is difficult for me to cope with the couple for I can't go in the kitchen."[120]

In her diary, she described her second experience of giving birth in great detail, on November 11: "I don't feel well, the baby is heavy and unsettled." The following day: "Alain Matthew Clément is born. [. . .] The child arrives at 2:30PM." Amid the anesthesia, crying, and general fatigue, the baby, who was born late—*The Reticent Child* (2003)[121]—"seems to be well, he is redder and darker than Jean-Louis."[122]

Art Making and Life

"You must have heard," she wrote to Colette Richarme, "that there was an exhibition of 400 paintings by Picasso here (forty years' work). It was so beautiful, and it revealed such genius and such a collection of treasures that I did not pick up a paintbrush for a month."[123] Louise's admiration for Picasso, clear since she purchased some of his engravings from Mourlot in 1938, was confirmed during this period. In March 1939, she read the article "Picasso, Works from 1930–1935," that had appeared in *Cahiers d'art*[124] and made some notes of her own: "Picasso paints what is true; true movements, true feelings. [. . .] Picasso is an enthusiast. He says so, and that is why his works are young. Skepticism is the beginning of decadence. [. . .] All movements painted by Picasso have been <u>seen</u> and <u>felt</u>; he is never theatrical. The Surrealists are theatrical. New York painting, the painting that wants to be or is fashionable, is theatrical. Theater is the image of life and Picasso sees life or rather <u>reality</u>! Keep your integrity. You will only count, for yourself and in your art, to the extent that you keep your integrity."[125]

With such an aesthetic declaration Louise signaled her profound divergence from the surrealists in exile, but also the distance she put between herself and American painting. Desire for authenticity and truth is a constant in her artistic practice. She also wrote about Van Gogh, whose catalogue raisonné she had just seen: "What can one add that is new when there is such genius around? If art is for personal satisfaction only, it is too much of a selfish pleasure."[126]

Robert was very close to his professor and colleague Walter Friedlander, whom Louise invited to meet her father in his shop in Paris: "I told them that your house is like a museum." She was always very proud of her father and of his knowledge of tapestries: "If they see that you are rich, proud, and free (and this guy will tell everybody here), they will be impressed and I will feel less small—I've always needed you but I do now more than ever."[127] This feeling of pride also revealed the slight inferiority complex she felt in the wealthy, urbane art world to which she now belonged. She was always trying to foreground her culture, her training, and her French origins.

Hoping to earn her own living in order to be "useful" and not entirely dependent on Robert, Louise decided to sell antique prints and engravings. At the New York Public Library, she looked at books on popular imagery and went looking for images of Épinal among the dealers. In a notebook dated February 20, 1940,[128] she copied out with extreme care the cultural and folkloric characteristics of each French city, noting the museums specializing in engravings and the names of collectors. This deep dive into old French customs was, doubtless, a way for her to maintain contact with her country and its traditions.

At the library, she became interested in a work on Odilon Redon, published in 1944, then wrote a review of John Rewald's book on Georges Seurat,[129] as well as an article about James Whistler, which appeared in *Pour la victoire*[130] in 1942—all of which foretold her future art critical writings on Gaston Lachaise, Joan Miró, and Francis Bacon.

She had read Jules Renard's *Journal* in the maternity ward after giving birth to Jean-Louis, finding it terribly depressing, "given how much [. . .] bitterness there is [. . .] under a comical or smiling face. There is lots of Molière, minus the genius of his large and concentrated suffering."[131] Louise was a voracious reader with eclectic tastes: "All of Hemingway," Louis Aragon's *Les cloches de Bâle*, the poetry of Charles d'Orléans, Paul Verlaine, Paul Claudel, Maurice and Eugénie de Guérin, and Charles Péguy, Victor Hugo's *Choses vues*, and André Malraux's *Les conquérants* kept her company throughout the 1940s.

Engravings and Drawings

Louise enrolled in classes at the Art Students League in November 1939, soon after her arrival in New York, taking a life drawing class with the constructivist Vaclav Vytlacil,[132] whom she found to be a good instructor.[133] There she made her first prints—lithographs, woodcuts, drypoints. She went on to study with Harry Sternberg and with the painter Will Barnet (1911–2012). These works consist of realistic scenes, interiors, still lifes, the country house in Easton, Connecticut, that she and her husband bought in 1941. A number depict states of waiting and solitude. Some show a perfect wife and housekeeper in her home, with her husband as he reads and works; another, a sleeping young woman, a grimacing "monster,"[134] and a child collecting its tears in a vase.[135] This duality also turned up in her letters to her father. She depicted herself as a happy mother and an organized, practical housewife, but her fear, her loneliness, and the difficulty of living this double life can be detected in this work. "Divided inside,"[136] as she said herself, Louise disclosed the different sides of her personality, which we can see distinctly in her *Self-Portrait* (ink on paper), of 1942: an adult face, serious, staid, partially darkened by a kind of beard made of lines, on the small bust of a woman-child.

The drawings from the 1940s evoke pregnancy and motherhood. Here, too, Louise provides images full of ambiguity. Pregnancy—so longed for, the source of so much happiness—is also portrayed as a state of fragility; the pregnant woman is always afraid of falling or losing the child she carries (*Girl Falling*, 1947). She depicts childbirth in two drawings from 1941. One of these shows an adult-sized baby attempting to emerge from its mother's body, forming a two-headed torso—*Untitled (Woman Giving Birth)*, 1941—as if the woman were giving birth to herself.

And, when the "wild beasts"—as she called her children—were hanging on her skirts and keeping her from working, she would devour them like an ogre (*Untitled,* 1943). Elsewhere, in a kind of glass bubble vase, an androgynous child appears between its parents' profiles as if to form a link between the couple. She also drew Michel, the children in the bathtub, newborns suspended from her tears. A charcoal drawing of 1945 shows a man holding a young girl in his arms, a possible reference to Bourgeois's suicide attempt.[137] As early as 1947, she was drawing spiders with geometric feet, as well as an abstract female Saint Sebastian, pierced with arrows, two themes that reappeared in the 1990s.

On October 21, 1942, Robert's father, Sigismund, died. "We lost Father. he did not suffer."[138] No other information is given.

Louise revisited her childhood through her sons. She now had three children, making a family of five much like the one in which she had grown up. This similarity did not escape her father, who, upon learning that Louise was pregnant with Alain, wrote, not without a gentle reproach: "You go on saying that you've had second thoughts about the birth of a third child, it's obviously nearing and had you considered these thoughts perhaps you would [have] been more reluctant in Bordeaux." But, he added, "there were three of you as well [. . .] and but for your mother's ill health [. . .] you will then be the five of you as we were ourselves and I wish you to be happy as we were."[139] "All five" was the theme of a number of later works: a woman, sculpted or drawn, always surrounded by five "packages," and her late flower drawings have five petals.

The Second World War

From 1940 to 1945, Louise spent her time looking after her house, caring for her three children, making art, and sending packages and letters to her loved ones: Colette, Paulette, Henriette, Germaine, Yvonne, and especially her father.

On June 10, 1940, she noted in her diary: "Italy has entered the war against us," that is, against France and England; on November 2, "Roosevelt's speech, all races all colors coming from all over the world . . . we are American a little light in the dark future,"[140] experiencing these events as simultaneously French and American. Exile was harder to bear during wartime; while her heart and thoughts were turned toward France and her family, she remained a foreigner in her adopted country.

In August 1941, Louise, Robert, and the two children moved to 142 East Eighteenth Street, a building called Stuyvesant's Folly, which has since been destroyed.[141] Finally Louise had a studio of her own. She found she could also work outdoors on the roof of the building, which allowed her to experiment with sculpture as well.

Louise and her father continued to write to each other almost every week. She talked about the Americans' attitude toward the war, the way they hesitated between getting involved and staying out of it, as well as her own hopes for a Free France; he described how difficult it was to get supplies, France's division into two zones, and the censorship of the mail. Louis left Paris in June 1940, settling in Saint-Michel-Loubéjou, in the Lot department of southwest France. He was taken in by friends not far from his nephew Maurice Bourgeois, who ran a hardware shop. In the countryside he didn't suffer as much from the restrictions on food; he lived off the land, fishing and hunting. Pierre found himself a prisoner, so to speak, when the Germans took up residence for a while in Antony, but Louis refused to see them in Paris. He warned Louise to be careful what she wrote in her letters, which were required to contain only family news and no opinions about politics. When he returned to Paris in June 1941, he found the Parisians resigned to their fate, the city plunged into complete darkness, food and coal difficult to procure. Pierre, who always managed to get by, was at that time recovering in the Val-de-Grâce hospital. News about Pierre was contradictory: Louis spoke of the scandal he had caused in Antony, using words like "terror," but also attempted to reassure his daughter, telling her that everything was fine.

Like anyone living far from home in time of war, Louise worried about her loved ones, and she sent them everything they couldn't find in France. She managed to get shoes to her father, as well as fabric for a suit, powdered milk, sardines, butter, cod liver oil, and vitamins; to Germaine she sent clothes; to Colette and Yvonne, toys for the children. All she could think about was their state of health and their deprivation, as well as the soldiers' well-being: "Tell me what I can send to the soldiers. Knitwear? Books?"[142]

In her letters to Louise, Colette Richarme appealed to her sense of patriotism: "You who remain so French, talk to people around you—tell them about the heroism of our France, the miseries that it's experiencing. I am [. . .] horrified by America's recent egotistical mentality. [. . .] Dear friend, be a messenger on your country's behalf, talk [to people], lead [them], convince [them] so that help for a wounded France might arrive in abundance . . . and not before it's too late."[143]

Paris to New York

Life in New York was rich and complex. Hundreds of refugees were arriving, having passed through the Antilles and been turned away by Cuba. Between 1940 and 1945, New York became the intellectual capital of the world, a varied assemblage of Jews fleeing Nazism: artists, writers, journalists, editors, professors, and anthropologists. Several groups formed, including one around André Breton—bringing together André Masson, Max Ernst, Jimmy Ernst, Yves Tanguy, Roberto Matta, and Kurt Seligman. But there was an older guard as well: Ossip Zadkine, Jacques Lipchitz, Marc Chagall, Amédée Ozenfant, Fernand Léger, and Marcel Duchamp. An affinity grew between Breton and Claude Lévi-Strauss, who was teaching at the New School of Social Research. The boundaries between disciplines weakened, which allowed for fruitful new encounters.

Many of the surrealists had left from Marseille via Varian Fry's network, and in some cases, with financial help from Peggy Guggenheim.[144] They were welcomed into Louise's home, where French was spoken, though their young hostess couldn't abide what she called "pontificating father figures." Louise was more interested in intellectual issues than artistic ones and actively supported the political and literary initiatives taken by the Resistance. She wrote an article for the journal *Pour la victoire*,[145] went with Zadkine to the Pontigny meetings being held in the United States,[146] encouraged Robert Goldwater to meet with Pierre Lazareff (a meeting arranged by Varian Fry), who was at that time working for La Voix de l'Amérique,[147] a radio service sponsored by the Office of War Information, contacted Jacques Mauritain's secretary on November 23, 1942, and curated an exhibition on clandestine cultural activities during the Occupation in 1945. Of all the artists who had landed in New York, she got on only with Marcel Duchamp and Joan Miró, who first came to New York in 1947, after the war—though she could sometimes be malicious about them in private. Louise was deeply frustrated during this time, as a young artist and, moreover, the mother of three children, which is to say that in the decidedly macho environment of

New York, she didn't exist. She revolted against the paternalist figures she left behind in France and who, during the war, arrived in New York en masse: "André Breton, Marcel Duchamp, and the Elders were there. It was a very small circle and everyone met everyone. I had mixed feelings toward them, however, since they were not interested in women, period. They were interested in rich women, of course, but that is a special breed of women. Secondly they were not interested particularly in young women and I was a student when they came. Thirdly, they were not interested in other artists. They were interested in themselves."[148]

They each had different experiences of exile. André Breton, for example, did not take a positive view of America: "I don't like exile, and I mistrust those who are in exile," he declared later.[149] He obstinately managed to speak not a word of English during the five years he spent there, so as not to "pollute" his French. But the painter Yves Tanguy experienced his lack of English as an impediment: "Not managing to speak English made me more and more anxious and nervous. They seem to completely loathe European artists here, all they talk about is American art."[150] Breton supported himself by speaking on La Voix de l'Amérique. However, with Duchamp's help, he organized the exhibition *First Papers of Surrealism* at Peggy Guggenheim's gallery in 1942.

Louise often bad-mouthed the artists she knew: she mocked Masson[151] for not speaking English and not knowing any American painters; she criticized Miró and his wife, Pilar, for being narrow-minded and even fascist. She railed against Chagall's faux-naïveté,[152] attacked the Matisse family, Pierre Matisse,[153] as well as Georges Duthuit and his son Claude, with reference to discord within their families, said of Henriette Nizan that she "was quickly consoled after Nizan's death,"[154] or that "Tina Jolas is an insolent woman she was kicked out of high school."[155] Her criticisms could be scathing, but they were amusing and often hit their mark. Her sarcasm can partly be explained by the indifference these exiled French people had toward her, which fed her inferiority complex, but also by the difficulties she was having finding a gallery and being recognized as an artist in her own right, rather than seen only as Robert Goldwater's wife.

Similarly, her relationships with museum curators were bound to be complicated and ambivalent. She judged the taste of their friends Russell and Eleanor Cowles[156] "conservative" and believed Russell hadn't done enough to help her: "He doesn't want to talk about my concerns about finding a gallery [. . .]. He wants to see me energetic happy and disinterested. For that to be possible, I'd have to have a personal and professional life completely separate from him, and with him always be beautiful and charming. Not to spend time being sentimental or to ask anything of him."[157] She thought the same thing about Meyer Shapiro: "Do not mention to Meyer any money question, I did and he did not like it, when he does not like what you say, he does not discuss he shuts like a clam."[158]

She did jot down details that brought together things that interested her: one of Masson's sisters, Sylvia, married Georges Bataille, "civil servant at the biblio nat [Bibliothèque nationale] and publisher of Documents (money from Wildenstein)";[159] the publication of the *Anthologie de l'humour noir* (1942) and the names of writers mentioned by André Breton: "André Breton's [anthology of] black humor," Jonathan Swift, Sade, Lichtenberg, Thomas de Quincey,[160] as well as Roger Caillois, Klossowski, and the review *Acéphale*.[161] She read Pablo Picasso's *Desire Caught by the Tail*, Henri Bergson, Marmontel's memoirs, Albert Camus, Henry James, Henry David Thoreau, André Gide, and subscribed to *Les temps modernes*.

She built relationships with important dealers, such as Pierre Loeb, Julien Levy, Curt Valentin, and Peggy Guggenheim, to whom she proposed, in May 1946, an exhibition which emphasized the connections between European and American artists: "Pollock, Rothko, Paalen, Bourgeois, Ben Shaw, De Kooning, Jimmy Ernst," and others.[162] But finally "Peggy's show" was called off.[163]

In fact, Louise felt much closer to the abstract expressionists, Americans such as David Smith, Mark Rothko, Adolph Gottleib, Willem de Kooning, Franz Kline, Louise Nevelson,[164] David Hare, or Stuart Davis, who was "concerned with Russia, politics, the war; he dislikes the communists."[165]

Jean-Paul Sartre arrived in New York on January 12, 1945, as a journalist for the Resistance, sent by *Le Figaro* and *Combat* to give an account of the American war effort. His trip was paid for by the Office of War Information. On May 15, 1945, he stayed at the Hotel Victoria, then did a tour of the country as a star speaker. His talk at Yale was badly received—it was seen as a sign of French cultural imperialism. "Even Jean Paul Sartre, last year [1945] managed to speak for two hours without any mention either of his work or of the political situation in France, or of Franco-American relations, or of young French writers and artists' ambitions and plans. It was quite admirable. I happen to know that he was looking for someone to publish his books and it is my view this was his real aim."[166]

In addition to New York, the Europeans were drawn to peripheral spaces: Mexico, where Benjamin Péret and Remedios Varo settled, and Martinique, birthplace of Aimé Césaire. Louise became interested in these new lands, as well as in their artists and writers and the indigenous arts that were made there. That is how she came to meet Wifredo Lam and his wife, Helena, and became interested in Mexican art (Frida Kahlo, Rufino Tamayo, José Guadalupe Posada), as well as in votive offerings and Spanish religious art. On April 3, 1948, she met the Chilean poet Vicente Huidobro. She also knew the painter Roberto Matta, no doubt through her Chilean friend Nemesio Antúnez. Breton's forced stopover in Martinique allowed her to discover the West Indian poet Aimé Césaire. On April 30, 1944, she wrote: "André Breton. [. . .] David Hare says that Aimé Césaire is in Haiti. I look for *Tropiques*."[167] Louise became fascinated by Césaire and wanted to meet him: "Since Aimé Césaire was in the Antilles, I had no way of communicating with him and so I repeatedly asked Breton to put me in contact with him. He was very jealous and simply never gave me Césaire's address, never forwarded my letter to him."[168] Clearly, Louise remained critical of Breton: "last time that Mr. Breton calls to say that he is busy and cannot show / *Tropiques*."[169] He was also having difficulty selling his book on Martinique.[170]

She also made mention of the works of anthropology she was reading: Margaret Mead's *Male and Female*[171] and Claude Lévi-Strauss's *Structures des institutions populaires*.[172]

She and Robert became friendly with Le Corbusier, who sometimes came to dinner.[173] Le Corbusier drew a portrait of Louise with her braided chignon, as well as a drawing of a long-haired woman seen from behind in the form of a crow.[174] The Goldwaters also spent time with the architects José Luis Sert[175] and Frederick Kiesler.

Her intellectual curiosity led Louise to go and see three surrealist films by Maya Deren, which she seems to have found greatly disappointing; the next day she wrote: "Worn-out Symbolism [. . .] clichés, nothing new, the audience is quite over this."[176] She attended concerts by John Cage and ballets by Merce Cunningham,[177] as well as performances of classical and contemporary music (Haydn, Bach, Darius Milhaud) and opera (*Don Juan*). This sprawling topography of Louise's interests, ranging from the American avant-garde to European modern art, confirms that she quickly acquired a thorough knowledge of the art world in New York. Of course, she was much younger than the famous French artists who were there at that time, but she went to openings whenever she could[178] and kept up to date on everything that was happening in the art world, including the polemics and debates that divided it. However, she disliked socializing: "we do not see anyone. I am sick of seeing people."[179]

In spite of the great number of activities she undertook during the war, she was often depressed. Louise regularly confessed her distress, her anger, her inability to work even in good conditions: "bottomless sadness of days without work."[180] She had some dark days and was often very hard on herself, going so far as to write that the painting she showed at the Whitney was horrible.[181]

But she always remained lucid: "Louise is too preoccupied by herself," she wrote in her diary.[182]

Against Surrealism

Her position on surrealism had already solidified. In a letter of 1942 to Alfred H. Barr,[183] then director of the Museum of Modern Art in New York, Louise asked herself if one could place the surrealists' research into dreams, the unconscious, and automatic writing in the same category as psychiatrists, biologists, and biochemists. Wary of psychoanalysis and the uses the surrealist painters made of the unconscious, she always gave precedence to the objectivity of science. She declared later that she was not a surrealist but an existentialist, that she preferred Charcot, because he was a scientist, to Lacan, whom she called a "con man."[184] In the end, "the unconscious is my friend," she would say, since she had direct access to it, without having to resort to the interpretation of dreams or automatic writing.

Her husband shared her distrust of surrealist painting. In *Primitivism in Modern Art,* he writes that "by deliberately composing their subjects out of Freudian iconographic symbols, and so lifting them into consciousness, [the surrealists] both alter their meaning and restrict their understanding." In his view, they had lost their "irrational, subterranean communicative power" and moved "from the direct emotional plane to the allusive and the literary."[185] He also critiqued their academic, realist style.

Louise and Robert loved Picasso and African masks and defended a certain "authentic" primitivism. They were interested in Dubuffet's work with children's drawings, graffiti, and art by people with mental health problems. They denounced, however, false naïveté: "There is a type of artist who wants to appear naive—Alfonso Ossorio, for example, or Jean Dubuffet, or even Philip Guston. Whereas the genuine naive, though truly talented, is helpless, the *faux* naive is the crafty one [. . .] Dubuffet is not Adolf Wölfli—one is a put-on and one is genuine."[186] This declaration illuminates Louise's singular position toward primitive art: she is a completely "authentic" artist, while also a very educated and cultured one.

Marcel Duchamp

It has become commonplace to draw connections between Louise Bourgeois and Marcel Duchamp, given that they were both born in France but naturalized American[187] and shared many preoccupations: the importance of sexuality and the erotic, an ambivalence toward gender, and a decidedly French sense of humor. They even bore a physical resemblance to each other, as clearly attested to in Douglas Gordon and Anna Gaskell's photocollage of 2001–4.

But Louise's relationship with Duchamp was an ambiguous one; her feelings for him were mixed. Although she did not completely see him as a surrealist, she forcefully rejected the paternalism he represented: "Breton and Duchamp made me violent. They were too close to me and I objected to them violently—their pontification."[188] She recognized, however, that "he was not macho at all."[189] She told a story from childhood related to her adolescent fear of sexuality, which says a great deal about her capacity for feeling, as well as her relationship with Duchamp:

Duchamp, he didn't say very much, but he was a good listener. [. . .] once in the garden—I was fifteen or sixteen, no older than that, and nature meant a lot to me—I was digging, and I found two snails completely joined together. I looked at them and there was revulsion. It was too much to take. I detached them and threw them down, and I ground them under my foot.

Duchamp said: "Please do not exaggerate, Louise." I said: "Marcel, I do not exaggerate." [. . .] He did not want to talk about his sex, and the secret of Marcel Duchamp, as everybody knows today, is that he was married to a peasant girl from Normandy[190] and he started to talk to her and be clever, and she would not take it. "Look here," she said, "we are here to fuck, don't tell me stories, just shut up," and then he was reduced to impotence and she left him. He was absolutely crushed. What happened after that? He lived with Mary Reynolds[191] when we knew him.[192]

This singular vision of Duchamp returns in another interview: "Yes[, we were friends]. He was a great intellectual but he suffered very much. He suffered from the fact that he was unable to make love with his wife [. . .]. All his life he felt that he could not have made a woman sexually happy."[193] Louise recognized that Duchamp had helped her but projected a form of sexual impotence onto him that seems completely fabricated, given what we know of his numerous liaisons, although some of those close to him did refer to physiological difficulties. When Francesco Bonami said to Louise that sex played an essential role in both of their lives, she retorted by saying that he was twisting her words: "I just said that it destroyed Marcel Duchamp. I didn't talk about you or me!"[194]

Louise well understood, however, the older artist's need to be in control: "Duchamp did not trust his emotions. He worked very hard at looking cool. I don't think that he felt cool. He wanted to put up a good front."[195] "If you had asked Duchamp [about his sexuality] he would have said: 'Well, why talk about sex? Is that important?' He would not have admitted that it was terribly important. But he was very witty, and people would have accepted this answer. Bacon, if you had asked the same question, would have said: 'My God! I'm dying of it! [. . .]' Pierre Bonnard would have responded: 'Do you want to make me cry?' And Miro would have said: 'Oh, it's amusing.' If you would ask Louise Bourgeois: 'Sex? What do you mean, it does not exist.'"[196]

The subject of sexuality was a complex one for Louise. She never stopped talking about it while at the same time minimizing its importance; she rejected such readings of her work, in order to foreground her knack for sublimation.

As for whether Marcel Duchamp was sexy, she responded that she had always found him quite *un*sexy. "Duchamp was a charmer. He was very sociable. He got along very well with Robert, they shared a sense of irony and a sense of humor. Duchamp liked to tease people."[197] "He was coy in the sense that he pretended to do nothing. But in fact he was a workaholic. He was working and nobody knew it. He pretended to be indifferent—'la belle indifférence'—but he was very engaged. He looked very fine and debonair, but he suffered like a dog. He was not cynical; he was a romantic who could not admit it."[198]

Homeland

At this time, Louise was putting all her energy into supporting Free France. "The Free France movement is sizable in New York and I am a member of the welcoming committee. That is to say that when a Free France boat arrives some of the sailors come here to spend the evening and they tell us how they left France. They only stop in New York on their way to England or rather by way of Montreal—Canada. From London [. . .], they go to Africa."[199]

With the help of Marcel Duchamp, she organized an exhibition in June 1945 on the role of the underground media within the Resistance entitled *Documents France, 1940–1944: Art—Literature—Press of the French Underground*. The cultural service of the French embassy as well as the library at Columbia University helped her gather books, posters, and journals that gave a sense of intellectual life in France during the war and of Resistance activities. Duchamp recommended she ask for help from Katherine Dreier,[200] who replied: "Mr. Duchamp telephoned me and I told him about your collection of Underground Papers of France which you desire to exhibit somewhere. [. . .] Later [. . .] he mentioned [. . .] that he was going to see Mr. J. J. Sweeney,[201] Director of the Museum of Modern Art, regarding them."[202]

From Eugene Scheffer, a professor at Columbia, Louise borrowed documents of the French avant-garde, some of which had already been on display at the Maison française,[203] for an exhibition at the Norlyst Gallery. She listed what had to be included: newspapers (*L'humanité, Le populaire, La revue libre, Résistance*), art (Bonnard, Picasso), posters, books (about Dubuffet, Vercors, Éluard, Aragon, Jean Cassou, Sartre, Gide) as well as photographs of Paris during the Occupation.[204]

She wanted the exhibition to tour several universities, since it would only last two weeks at the Norlyst Gallery. They printed a flyer for their show: "Anti-Nazi press, art, poetry, prose."[205]

This initiative was important in the political context of Franco-American relations at that time. The Americans tended to minimize the role of the Resistance in France, since the only French people they saw were émigrés. Providing information on clandestine cultural life in France was thus a symbolic militant act.

Louise was also preoccupied by the tragic fate of her Jewish friend Rahissa Frenkel, who had been her tutor in Nice. She invited her to come to New York as early as 1940, but Frenkel, unaware of the danger, didn't want to leave France.[206] Later, Louise received a letter from Frenkel's sister, Berthe,[207] asking her to ask American agencies to help find Rahissa. On October 25, 1945, Louise looked for her in vain among the lists of prisoners of war, deportees, and refugees.[208]

First Exhibition, 1945

"I have all sorts of ideas and plans in my head and I'm all set to write, or to draw—anything—but physically I'm very tired and calm and feverish. I'm irritable with the children, highly sensitive, as if on the verge of tears. But this condition seems favorable to intellectual work," she wrote in her diary.[209] For Louise, a state of nervous fatigue and elusive concentration went hand in hand with intense intellectual activity.

On the same day, June 4, 1945,[210] Louise opened her Resistance show, *Documents France, 1940–1944*, as well as her own first solo show at the Bertha Schaefer Gallery in New York, *Paintings by Louise Bourgeois*, in which she showed work including *Interior*,[211] *Natural History, Mr. Follett: Nursery-Man, The Potter's House, Pilgrims, Design in Purple and Blue, Connecticutiana*, and *Runaway Child* (on loan from J. B. Neumann). The invitation reproduced the painting *Mr. Follett*. Follett was a gardener in Easton; she depicted him with tulips. But there was more still for her to cope with; during these two artistic events, her son Jean-Louis was sick in the hospital.[212]

Focusing her attention on her work, she offered unsparing commentary on her own paintings, judging *Natural History* not big enough, with too much going on within it and lacking any abstract qualities.[213] Her notes from that time describe the technical problems of the "pictorial kitchen": glazes, wax, glue, the use of petroleum instead of turpentine to avoid colors running, and contrasting pure colors, burnt sienna and Prussian blue.

Louise was still in an experimental phase, moving from realist subjects (self-portraits, Robert reading, Michel, couples, her childhood house) to more nature-based ones (trees, leaves, plants, hedges) while also working on more abstract compositions, with schematic figures. In all of this we can already see a throughline leading straight to the work to come and her obsessive thematics, which will find expression as sculptures or prints and emerge later in other forms: the child inscribed in the bodies of its parents or between their profiles,[214] or the painting *Red Room* (1947), which prefigures two Cell works, *Red Room* (*Child*) and *Red Room* (*Parents*) of 1994, and finally the interlaced couples fused into one that will appear in fabric and aluminum in the 2000s.

Her interest in the vegetal—trees with their roots; herbariums—was quite pronounced at this time, as demonstrated by a series of paintings titled *Natural History*, which are different compositions of trees, roots, foliage, and fruit. Louise commented on this work: "The slow life of a plant given unified and consistent expression in terms of abstract forms. [. . .] The life of a plant in three parts: First the whole picture of the plant itself, with root, stem, and leaves; second the flowers of the plant; and third the fruit. These three stages of evolution in the plant are at once consecutive and interdependent; they are, at different times, both part and whole. Hence a NATURAL HISTORY."[215] In order to gain a better understanding of her subject, she went to the New York Public Library and consulted agricultural encyclopedias and works of botany—she made some very detailed drawings of greenhouse plants—and studied the paintings of Georgia O'Keeffe.[216]

Louise wanted to make "a painting that consists of several areas [compartments] completely closed-off. (Idea board) is a challenge to the idea of unity and of composition—Extreme caution is necessary,"[217] she wrote in her painting notes from this period; she was also attempting to "treat the painting like a tapestry with a large painted frame."[218]

In this composition and style, we can detect the influence of her instructor Roger Bissière, or of Joaquín Torres García, with whom she had collaborated in 1943,[219] creating a tapestry based on one of his works for the exhibition *The Arts in Therapy*. Hence the long horizontal panel *Connecticut-iana* (1944–45), in tones of red and black, which presents motifs of birds, flowers, and fish, in different sections. The title was a reference to the family's country home in Easton.

The reception for this first exhibition was on the whole very positive.[220] One critic detected a Mexican influence, while another thought Louise was the wife of the writer Stephen Bourgeois, but both emphasized the originality of composition and iconography in *Natural History* and *Connecticutiana*. Nevertheless, Louise was disappointed: "I didn't sell anything before or after the exhibit—only one painting to a friend who would have bought it anyhow."[221]

Family

Life in Easton—with her three children, her husband, naps beneath the trees, games, box hedges, nature all around, the garden—was essential to her well-being and brought back memories of Antony. The house she grew up in and the one in Easton were ongoing sources of inspiration during this period.

Louise was very active and handy around the house; she painted the walls of the kitchen red, trimmed the vines, dug a hole for drainage, did leveling work to make the house inhabitable, oiled the tools and kept them organized, built shelving, and all the while took care of her children: Jean-Louis, whose health was fragile and necessitated several stays in hospital; and Michel, who was in therapy—he set a fire beneath the kitchen table and wanted to kill Alain. "[H]e needs a boarding school for boys [. . .] so instead of being nervous we can be tender. He also needs a lot of tenderness," Louise wrote.[222]

She described her daily life to her friend Paulette Place[223] and gave her news of some French artists:

Michel is nine years old. [. . .] [He] is in boarding school near Philadelphia. I go to see him every month and he spends the holidays with us.[224] [. . .] Jean-Louis looks like me. He is blond and pink and has terrible temper tantrums. He is very good in class—Alain is sweet, shy, like his father. He is smart and balanced. The three get along. During the summer we go to the country in Connecticut [. . .]. We have a small house which looks like a Provencal *mas*.[225] Last summer Masson was our neighbor with his wife and his two sons. They just went back to France very disappointed because America did not appreciate them enough which is completely unfair. Zadkine went back too, also Léger and Lipchitz are getting ready to go back. Breton has a mission for Haiti—. Many French people come with missions from France [. . .] and if they give lectures it is always on boring generalities and to a very small audience. [. . .] Two young ones from pre-war Wifredo Lam and Matta have had success here. Both from Picasso's group.[226]

In return, she asked Paulette's husband, Georges Place, to tell her what was happening in art in Paris.[227]

He Disappeared into Complete Silence

Louise continued with her engravings and used Stanley William Hayter's[228] studio, Atelier 17, to create her first illustrated book, *He Disappeared into Complete Silence* (1947). Her relationship with Hayter was, as was often the case, ambivalent. She was furious with him when his book[229] came out and her name wasn't in it: "fulmination + anxiety over Hayter's book."[230] "[G]reat nervousness over the fact that I have not been put in Hayter's book for reproduction."[231] But she indulged his caprices: "poor genius Hayter with his haunted face, his pressing talk, his sudden hates. [. . .] Like a poor jewel in a sea of shit—Hayter is sicker than me [. . .] I understand him and I love him for his suffering. But damn it all it was not love Hayter was afraid of. I think he was sleeping with everybody."[232]

Her book is composed of nine plates facing short, enigmatic texts in prose—ironic and cruel, and referencing events in her personal history. There followed a story of unrequited love, a childhood memory when her mother buried a lump of sugar in the earth, the destruction of a building, a decapitated head, the force of a mother's love not strong enough to keep her child, and a marital dispute that devolves into an act of cannibalism: "Once a man was angry at his wife, he cut her in small pieces, made a stew of her."[233] The fear of abandonment, the "shrinking self-confidence," motherly love—a panoply of complex feelings that took the form of geometric houses, explicitly referencing the skyscrapers of New York: "My skyscrapers are not really about New York. Skyscrapers reflect a human condition. They do not touch."[234] These stylized figures stand in for loneliness, marriage, the family, sadness (suggested by a veil of rain, obscuring the image), incomprehension, violence, and cruelty, feelings which feed all of Louise's work and later found purified form in her sculpted figures. This foundational work, which brought together text and image, also shows how crucial words, and writing, were to her artistic process.

"It's the story of a very young person who is hoping to find a soul mate," Louise noted. "The works of the 1940s reflect this state of waiting and despairing."[235] It was also, she said, "a descent into depression," but "You can stand anything if you write it down. You must do it to get hold of yourself. When space is limited, or when you have to stay with a child, you always have recourse to writing. All you need is pen and paper."[236]

Another parable, also dating from 1947, she consigned to an agenda book, though it was later published as a screenprint on fabric in 1992 as *She Lost It*: "A man and a woman lived together. On one evening he did not come back from work and she waited. She kept on waiting and she grew littler and littler. Later a neighbor stopped by out of friendship and there he found her in the armchair the size of a pea."[237] Louise identified with the pea. This metaphor later returned in her writing.

The critic Marius Bewley[238] wrote a short text that served as an introduction to the book: "They are all tiny tragedies of human frustration: at the outset someone is happy in the anticipation of an event or in the possession of something pleasing. In the end, his own happiness is destroyed either when he seeks to communicate it, or, perversely, seeks to deny the necessity for communication. The protagonists are miserable because they can neither escape the isolation which has become a condition of their own identities, nor yet accept it as wholly natural." Isolation and difficulty communicating were at the very heart of Louise's work as a sculptor, and they can also be detected in the *Femme maison* series of paintings.

"All this architecture is affectionately dedicated to L. C. [Le Corbusier],"[239] she wrote in her diary. Louise met Le Corbusier at Hayter's. The architect seemed attracted to the young woman and showed curiosity in her paintings, but his romantic interest was unreciprocated. "I respect L. (and admire him up to a certain point) but cannot love him because he has an intelligence of the mind and not intelligence of the heart. I love him like I love my tools my electric saw or my electric drill."[240]

The Puritans

A third text, also dating from 1947, recounts the difficult unrequited love affair she had with Alfred H. Barr Jr., the director of the Museum of Modern Art. It was published only in 1990, in a book of engravings called *The Puritan.* In it Louise describes the architecture of the museum, a place where people worked efficiently, where everyone was immaculately turned out and refined. "In this structure there was a man, there always is, [. . .] he was very fine. [. . .] Everyone there was very fond of him and looked up to him. He accepted this because apart from being civilized he was kind. There was a definite well-organized, successful and ambitiously satisfied feeling about the place. The trouble came when one of the doors was left open and apparently someone came in. [. . .] She saw him, she saw he was good and of course she loved him." Something happens between them; they see each other occasionally. "But there it was. There [. . .] was silence. First an expecting silence, and then the silence of the completely dead."[241] This summary of the text, in which Louise describes her relationship with Barr—her husband's professional associate—tells us much about the young French artist's place in the context of New York, about her personality as well as Barr's, a man who, refusing her love, she would later call a "puritan." It points to the essential, persistent difference between French culture as Louise embodied it—free, chaotic, impertinent, direct—and American reserve—proper and structured. The feelings of love she experienced at this time were inextricable from those of friendship, of the admiration she felt for this man and his power in the American art world. It was Barr who first bought her sculpture *Sleeping Figure* (1950), for the museum, in 1951. If we are to believe Peggy Guggenheim, Barr "looked like Abraham Lincoln. [. . .] He was shy but very charming, and I liked him at once."[242] Louise was interested in every last thing about him, in his tastes—"Alfred enjoys [. . .] different breakfast food with cream + sugar. In the evening he does not read, he listens to music or [his wife] Marga reads to him. Since 1927 he has *The Funeral of Phocion* in his bedroom. Now he has another Poussin."[243]

She avoided going places where she knew he would be, in order to spare herself the pain of seeing him. "I have not slept for the last 3 nights thinking about the opening at the museum, on Tuesday I decide not to go in order not to see Alfred Barr."[244] Even though she felt rejected—"he probably doesn't think of me"[245]—she didn't want to completely give him up. But she was well aware of what she was endangering: "self destruction under the form of destruction of my marriage."[246] By the end of the year, she wrote: "the breakdown has come [. . .]. [I] am not going to make a fool of myself with A. [. . .] He is museum director and I need him—I got to play the game again as if nothing had happened—I got to go to 57th on Saturdays and keep a straight + smiling face."[247]

Putting on a good show, hiding her feelings to protect an important professional relationship, but also to spare her husband and Barr's wife—it was a difficult balance to strike, and Louise felt the stress of it. She was tired of society life: "The cocktail parties are useful because one meets many people, a select group, of which we are all more or less a part. But as time passes hearts sour where there was never true affection at any moment there isn't ever any after. I only like the people who like my work,"[248] she admitted. Her anger flared up at everyone: "You got angry at Eileen, Catherine, Nemesio, Albert Erskine, St. Gillette, Alfred Barr. Why? You want to eat them and to them, what happens? Socially, I want nothing—nor emotionally—sexually I want something."[249] Her rages provided an outlet for her to vent her frustration: "In a deep sense temper tantrums are healthy they are an expression of defeat and a form of orgasm—with Alfred."[250] There was nothing more to say.

In 1990, when *The Puritan* was published, Louise added a postscript: "I wrote *The Puritan* in 1947. It's the story of someone so frightened by his love that he withdraws."[251] Afraid of desire, afraid of love. Louise later said that Alfred Barr was not in fact indifferent to sex, as his biographer, Alice Goldfarb Marquis, insisted: "(that is an insult), only repressed."[252]

Reflecting on the first time she met Robert Goldwater, she confessed to Alain Kirili: "when I met this American student who was a puritan, I thought it was wonderful. And I married that guy."[253] This attraction to puritanical men was doubtless a means of escaping from the overwhelming sexual promiscuity she encountered in her own family. But Louise would also say that she loved puritans because she found them sexy, and because it was a challenge to seduce them.

The Femme Maison, 1945–1950

Even though I am French, I cannot think of one of these pictures being painted in France. Every one of these paintings is American, from New York. I love this city, its clean-cut look, its sky, its buildings, its scientific, cruel, romantic quality.

Louise's second solo show took place in the autumn of 1947 at the Norlyst Gallery.[1] "These are paintings of a city dweller . . . brown stone houses and jails . . . the bee sleeps in the dark and her domain is the sky. In her reduced geometrical space a cruel and blind life goes on."[2]

This text, which compares Louise to a reclusive bumblebee, was written by her friend Nemesio Antúnez, the Chilean painter.[3] On the back of one of the invitations, Louise jotted down these poemlike lines, possibly addressed to Nemesio: "I know you will understand my statue, because it does not make any noise, it does not bother you. [. . .] You do not need to elect me, but do not abandon me. [. . .] I will continue working for you."[4] The text echoes a photograph in which we see Nemesio in the garden at Easton, steadying the life-sized sculpture *Observer* (1947–49) with his hands.

Robert Storr, who met Nemesio at the National Museum of Fine Arts in Santiago, Chile, in 1993, has written[5] that Nemesio confessed to having had an affair with Louise in 1947. It was a complete secret, and Louise made no reference to it; she only described Nemesio's charming smile in her diary.[6] Unless something she wrote later in her life is a veiled reference: "I accept responsibility for the Antúnez failure and in accepting this error of youth, I am able to forget him (or to forgive him, forgiveness falls like a hair into a soup) it is not a question of forgiveness but of understanding, what happened is the scientific reality of the attraction of the student to the professor."[7]

It was in fact Antúnez who was in love with Louise, as an invitation he sent her in 1986 attests: "I have loved you for over forty years,"[8] and, elsewhere, "I haven't betrayed you!"[9] Their physical relationship was apparently somewhat complicated: "To come back to recent years, with Neme[sio], I used to say no to everything, became a rock, night and day, and even made him [think] that he was unintelligent, all this because I was afraid of being myself. I would rather break than be a woman."[10] For a woman who declared herself "without secrets," this was, perhaps, the only one she kept. And it is possible she was angry with Nemesio, and indirectly with Robert Storr, for having revealed it.

Although their affair ended around 1950, their friendship continued into the 1980s. Antúnez stayed at her place when he came to New York and helped her with difficult tasks; on August 8, 1990, his telephone number at the National Museum of Fine Arts in Santiago is written in her diary, and one day she discovered some clothes he'd left behind: "I find Antúnez outfit: hat, bag, jacket: the rest has been thrown out: cape, bedspread."[11]

Exhibited in her second solo show, the four *Femme maison* paintings are emblematic of Louise's work. Their blend of the organic and the geometric, of rigidity and malleability, of architecture and viscerality, is a metaphor for the structure of her psyche. Bringing together these two disparate dimensions, the female body and the house, Bourgeois manages to go beyond the mind-body split, the dichotomy between reason and feeling, of cerebralism and sensuality. Louise, in her ambivalence, embodied the coexistence between these antagonistic elements. The house also represents her despair, the feeling of being oppressed, the need to escape.

The work of the philosopher Gaston Bachelard has often been cited in reference to the iconography of the body-house.[12] "The house is body and soul, the human being's first world, a symbol of maternal refuge, of the protective warmth of childhood and memory."[13] We imagine the house, he writes, as a vertical being: it rises up, its verticality assured by the twin poles of the basement and the attic.

Some critics have also compared this image of a nude woman who is half house with a work by André Masson, *Le bâillon vert à la bouche de pensée* (1938),[14] which shows a mannequin whose head is locked in a cage.[15] This formal similarity seems somewhat simplistic. Not only is there no way of establishing that Louise saw this particular work,[16] but the significance of these two pieces is completely different. Louise's paintings owe very little to surrealism; for that matter, she saw few members of that group at this time. Her paintings are more interested in a kind of primitivism and magical thinking, more in line with her husband's tastes.

Louise sought above all to explore the concepts of imprisonment and claustrophobia—which Antúnez understood well—but also to find imagery to express the duality of her personality: a nude woman who hides and exposes herself at the same time. We might also detect an attempt at flight, to flee from above, as one of the paintings suggests, her arms reaching for help, or, in another, her hair taking off into the sky. One woman is given a bust in the form of a brownstone, from which her two legs emerge, spread; a central stairway leads to a vertical slit which serves as both a doorway, or her sex. "It's a tragic house, because the lights aren't on, we don't know what's happening, the door is very dark [. . .] it's clearly someone very erotic, who doesn't know that she is erotic."[17] The house also refers to the body of the mother, from which stems the antagonism between maternity and sexuality.

The four houses she depicts, each in a different style, could be those of Choisy, New York, Easton, and a courthouse with a neoclassical portico—a tribunal, that is to say, a place where people go to have disputes. These houses—while evoking particular memories for Louise—are the organic and architectural incarnations of her emotions.

Louise rejected the feminist readings that saw in *Femme maison* "an example of art made by a woman,"[18] one caught in her familial environment—which was indeed Louise's situation, no matter what she said, with three children to raise and a husband who worked all the time. Her identity is "absorbed or obscured by the domestic realm, which she in turn nourishes and supports."[19] In English, *"femme maison"* can be translated literally as "housewife." In 1944, she referred to one of the paintings as "the House Picture."[20]

These paintings offer, then, multiple readings. What is certain is that the femme maison is an essential image in Louise's work, all throughout her life, conjugated in different forms and materials—in marble, in fabric, and, in one instance, with a plastic Barbie doll. It marked the beginning of her move into sculpture: the body, by means of architecture, becomes volume in space. "[T]he effect I want to achieve can't be done with paint. what I want is a substance."[21]

Another theme appears in her paintings of 1946–47: the woman on the roof. At this point, Louise had started working on the roof of her apartment building. In a canvas from 1946–47, she painted a woman's head near the roofline of a building, her hair blowing wildly in the wind. Behind her, three little heads (those of her children?) emerge from the building's chimney. In another painting, *Red Night* (1946–48), she painted—against a bright red background—a bed, on which a woman lies with three little round heads nestled against her body. Her family was omnipresent. A small painting from this period contains a message to her sons: "little boys no more food after 4:00 / keep your appetite for Callie's dinner."[22] Finally, a large canvas that contains a fictive view of the Cour Carrée at the Louvre is entitled *Regrettable Incident in the Louvre Palace* (1947); does it refer to the days when she was a docent at the museum in 1937–38 and the way the war wounded haunted her?[23] Or is it an allusion to a date she had there with Jacques Bauml when they went to see an exhibition?

A few newspapers ran pieces on Louise's exhibitions: "Once a pupil of Léger, she has gone on to evolve a personal style in one of the most vital traditions of art today—the humanization of abstraction and surrealism into a pictorial, symbolic idioms [*sic*]. Her technique is impeccable, and [. . .] she shows a thoroughly French love for rich textures and subtle nuances of color."[24] Although the *Art News* critic emphasized the feminine aspect of the domestic world symbolized by the house, the writer also noted that through her concise style, Louise avoided too literal or anecdotal a reading.

These two important first solo exhibitions show that after the war, Louise was not entirely isolated or unknown. She was also included in the second, 1945 iteration of *The Women*,[25] curated by Peggy Guggenheim in her Art of This Century gallery, one of the centers of avant-garde art.[26] Also in 1945, Louise took part in the annual show at the Whitney Museum, thus embarking on a regular collaboration with that institution which would last several years.

In 1947, Joan Miró came to the United States to paint a large mural in the restaurant of the Terrace Hilton Hotel in Cincinnati. He also visited New

York, and it was at this time that Louise met him through Hayter at Atelier 17. Several photographs document an evening that Miró, Louise, and Miró's wife and daughter spent together, during which he draped himself in a large fabric banner covered in arcane symbols, likely created for the International Surrealist Exhibition of 1947 in Paris. In one of these, he is sitting on a chair as if it were a throne, his feet resting on books about Picasso, with Louise kneeling at his knees in an imploring pose. They are acting out a scene together, Ingrès's *Jupiter and Thetis*. This theatrical game attests to the friendship between the two artists but also to the indirect links Louise maintained to the surrealists. It also prefigures the performance she would undertake much later in which she wrapped two bodies in a printed banner made of fabric.[27]

In the late 1940s, Louise began making her first sculptures, in carved balsa wood, on the roof of her building or in Easton: "in the wooden constructions, instead of nails there should be wooden 'pegs.'"[28] At this time, she also saw much of the painter Attilio Salemme, whose abstract and geometric figures bear some resemblance to what she created in wood.[29]

In April 1949, Louise took part in a group show at the Peridot Gallery, alongside artists Willem de Kooning, Bradley Walker Tomlin, Hans Hofmann, and others. Another sign of the reputation that Louise was then building: she posed for the renowned photographer Berenice Abbott that same year.

And when Robert was invited to San Francisco for a round table with Marcel Duchamp on the situation of artists after the war, Louise went with him.[30] Other participants included Gregory Bateson (an anthropologist), Andrew Ritchie (a curator at the Museum of Modern Art), Frank Lloyd Wright (an architect), George Boas (a philosophy professor), Kenneth Burke (a philosopher), Darius Milhaud (a composer), Mark Tobey (an artist), and Alfred Frankenstein (the editor-in-chief of the arts and music section of the *San Francisco Chronicle*). This interdisciplinary discussion underscored how invested American intellectuals were in art at the time.

Tangled Drawings

Drawing—repetitive, obsessive—was an activity that Louise constantly engaged in. At this time she was accumulating quasi-"automatic" drawings, so many that they became her calling card, with their thick overlapping lines like manes of hair.

Louise had, at that time, very long hair, which reached down to her waist. It can be seen in a photograph that shows her from behind, sitting at her easel; or in another, in which Jean-Louis is combing it. Onto the canvas she is painting, as if looking in a mirror, long, tangling locks that also remind the viewer of thread, waves, and mountains. Her drawings in charcoal or ink also depict tangled material. The page is invaded by long, undulating lines, which cross and tighten to form hanging oblong balls of yarn. Louise hung these chevelures everywhere, on the walls of her study and in the house at Easton, "hair in water, hair in flames, hair that dries before the fire, smoked skeins of wool."[31]

Two years later, she wrote: "my drawings are an arsenal of forms that I love [. . .] forms hanging from the ceiling. [I] prepare some boards to hang on the wall on which I can present my drawings."[32]

News from France

Louise was always up to date on events in France and responded to the Allied landing in Normandy in June 1944 by printing a holiday card called *Normandy Landing*, on which she depicted the French coast and copied out a poem by Aragon: "Do you remember those nights when upon us lies / Night which comes from the heart and no morning hath."[33] And she added: "The sixth of June. / A great morning / The darkness lifted up and we saw the light / coming from the West."[34] On August 25, 1944, she wrote in her diary, "Paris is free," and on August 26: "battle in Paris again."[35]

She heard from her father, but also from her family and friends: her maternal grandmother, Mémère Bathelot, had died in 1942;[36] Sadie went to visit Louis before following her husband to India. Louis returned to Paris in October 1944 and confessed that he was "grateful to America for having cast out the barbarians."[37] He was very moved to return to his shop, in which Louise had left so many memories. Paris is all decked out, he wrote in May 1945, to celebrate the Allied victory. American cars and trucks were applauded as they went through the city; young people threw themselves onto them. But "everyone is hungry, thirsty for something else besides fruit juice with saccharine, men want to smoke, women want to wear stockings."

They lacked enthusiasm for the dance halls: "a few dancing attempts [but] there wasn't enough energy, people are too tired to dance before the buffet."[38] He also told Louise that he had seen footage of President Roosevelt's funeral in a newsreel and had been very upset by it: "I was very touched and the entire audience was sad [. . .] everyone believes that it was his love for France that made him drag America into the war."[39] The house in Antony, which was located on the road to the Leclerc division, had suffered greatly. Louis hoped to be reimbursed for war damages, in order to undertake the major renovation work necessary to restore it. But, regardless, he said he was happy "to have been delivered from the Krauts."[40]

Pierre

During the Occupation, Louise's brother, Pierre, ravaged the house at Antony. He cut down all the trees[41] and sold them off, reducing the garden to a construction site. In late 1945,[42] he decided on a whim to go and see his sister in New York. Louise worried about what she called his "loony plans" and asked her father to intercede.[43] "I barely managed to keep him from leaving, his suitcases were already in Le Havre [. . .] and he was getting ready to embark in Antwerp."[44] Luckily, Louis was able to stop him from leaving and bring him back to Paris, "astonished and furious as a lion in a cage."[45]

In early 1946, Louis tried again to reassure his daughter; on May 15, 1946, he wrote: "You can rest easy about Pierre for a while. I can't say more but that's what matters."[46]

Louise always kept mum as to her younger brother's mental illness and internment. She saw him only one more time, in 1957, when she visited him in the hospital with Alain, who remembered it well. The worsening of Pierre's mental health was a permanent worry and source of suffering. Did her interest in psychiatric illnesses originate with her brother? Was she angry with her father for shutting him up in a hospital? Or was she worried about hereditary destiny?

Pierre was taken from Antony on December 19, 1945, and committed, first at the psychiatric Hôpital Sainte-Anne in Paris, then at Ville-Évrard, and finally at Villejuif. Louise was informed of the situation only later. Doubtless her father—aware of the affection between his children and worried that Louise wouldn't understand his decision—was trying to protect her. He later tried to justify the decision: "It wasn't my choice to commit Pierre Bourgeois [. . .] I had three children and I housed them [. . .] until 1945. [He] is 33 years old."[47] He went regularly to see Pierre in the hospital, then, finding he couldn't—or wouldn't—go on paying for it, asked for him to be transferred to an institution in the provinces (in the Vaucluse) where he would be able to work, in particular by looking after the garden, which would also lower the internment fees.[48]

The story of Pierre, torn between uncontrollable violence and a desperate desire to stabilize himself, is a tragic one. On one hand, the psychiatrists' reports—"assaults on his neighbors [. . .] mental disturbance [. . .] prone to anger, a liar"[49]—or information given by his neighbors to the police in La Croix-de-Berny—"[hangs out with] shady characters [. . .] mores [. . .] against nature [. . .] has leanings toward men as well as women and even children of both sexes [. . .] black market"[50]—are damning, but no doubt unreliable, given the frequent denunciations and false testimonies of the time. On the other hand, before his internment he wrote to his father to share his plans for Antony, eager to plant flowers and become a horticulturist.[51] He tried to reassure him by saying he hadn't destroyed anything and was taking good care of the house.[52] In this sense, we can understand that being forced to leave Antony was devastating and destabilizing.

Louis Bourgeois regularly went to see American films at the cinema to get a better idea of what his daughter's life was like. When he received the invitations to her exhibitions, he was astonished to discover that she had continued to paint—"you didn't tell me you were still working, it doesn't surprise me as [. . .] you have always been courageous"[53]—and asked how she managed to reconcile art making with her responsibilities as a mother. He was particularly proud of her work on the *Documents France, 1940–1944* exhibition: "I want to congratulate you and can recognize your energy that has remained the same."[54]

Like many French people after the Liberation, Louis had a positive view of Americans. To those who complained and begged, he pointed out that the Americans had lost twice as many men as France and that they entered the war to save the French. "I can assure you," he wrote to Louise, "that it isn't wise to criticize America in my presence."[55]

He was, however, surprised by the artistic path his daughter had chosen, sensing how far she had come from him and his tastes: "you [are] still interested in modern painting: tell me then, are the Americans still interested in antique tapestries?"[56] He recognized that he wasn't keeping up with the new generation's ideas, aware that he was no longer the audacious young man he had once been but a bourgeois grandfather; the radical socialist and anti-religious firebrand was now reasonable and restrained in his old age. "You will think that Papa rambles a bit, it's true, but please try to see the great tenderness I bear toward you: the modern spirit, the turbulent youth, and communism scare me a bit, and I think a little moderation would go a long way."[57] However, he mocked his own sentimentality, which he found slightly ridiculous.

In Louise's letters, she sent her father news of the children: Alain, still as sweet and easy-going, had a bad eye and had to wear a black patch over one of the lenses of his glasses (Louise painted it sky blue with a white clover on it so the children at school wouldn't make fun of him);[58] Michel, who was at a "very good" boarding school in New England, "a kind of extravagance [*un genre de folie*] on our part";[59] and Jean-Louis, who looked like his grandfather and knew how to read. She also talked about their vacations and the gardening at Easton and the numerous packages she sent to France. She thanked her father for sending her an Hermès scarf and a tapestry bag which reminded her of her mother and the atelier at Antony.[60] Finally, on learning that her sister, Henriette, wished to adopt a child, she allowed herself to give her some advice, having some experience in the matter: adopt a child as young as possible (though she also allowed for a child who was old enough to know they were being adopted), be well informed as to the intelligence and character of the birth parents, and "be very sure no one will come to claim them later on."[61]

She also worried about Antony; she was fond of the place, and she hoped to stay there on an upcoming trip to France with Robert and the children. She imagined building a new house in the garden or adding a floor to the existing house. She described the new renters' financial difficulties and had some fairly harsh things to say about them: "if tenants become masters against the 'capitalists,' what is the point of building anything?"[62]

She also resumed corresponding with her friend in Montpellier. As soon as the day of victory had arrived, on June 9, Colette Richarme described her husband's return from imprisonment, thinner and aged. She asked Louise to send her cod liver oil and vitamins for the children.[63] She also congratulated her on the Bertha Schaefer exhibition in June 1945, saying she very much liked the painting that appeared on the invitation and praising the simplicity she had achieved.[64]

Reunion, 1948

In May 1948, almost ten years after his daughter's departure for America, Louis came to spend two months in New York (May 22–July 23) to finally meet his three grandchildren and the Goldwaters in Huntington. After several weeks in New York, they left on a road trip[65] by car around Canada (Montreal, Quebec, with a trip to Saint Laurent and Niagara Falls), returning via Maine and Massachusetts, and finally arriving in Easton, where they had dinner with their neighbors, the Prendergasts,[66] in their home.

Canada—which Louise was properly visiting for the first time after a decade in North America—made a mixed impression on her. "Everything is English. Not a smile, puritan, honest, dry and clean. Food is possibly less expensive than USA [. . .]. We don't see a single interesting building. A very new country, without a past, where the people work hard, colonial mindset, but they seem happy and well nourished. No beer or wine; almost all the products are American—Coca-Cola and Esso are everywhere. Not a trace of the French."[67] After Montreal, which she found "very lively" and "pretty English,"[68] they visited Quebec City: "cathedral: bourgeois people who go to mass, clean, dignified and self-contained. Pretty houses 18th C. with a porch. [. . .] The homes remind me of Tours and the province."[69] Finally they saw Percé, a beautiful village in the province of Quebec, located on the tip of the Gaspé Peninsula, which featured a rock with a hole in it (pierced, or *percé*) and a natural park full of birds and numerous craftspeople: "People look like Tamayo, make baskets [. . .] bad road."[70] On July 14, they crossed the border to drive down the coast of Maine, and slept in Cambridge: "Cambridge Harvard, Beacon Hill."[71]

But the thing Louise would remember[72] about her father's trip was an episode that tarnished the image she had of him. She would tell the story later: they spent night of June 8 in a nightclub,[73] Leon and Eddie's on Fifty-Second Street:

I was there with my father, and it was four in the morning and the prostitutes were unemployed. My father, in his macho attitude, said "Well, let's see the girls." The row of prostitutes were given the signal to appear. They appeared, posturing one after the other trying to be attractive to my father. I witnessed the scene. With a flick of his wrist, he dismissed #1, #2, #3, looked a little longer at #4, and got a glint in his eye at #5. I became interested in the failure. I identified with those that failed. It's about defining my low self-esteem. You realize how terribly difficult it is to make it. The desire to please is the motivation and there are no rules. It's Russian roulette. My identification was with the fallen ones, so I thought the judge a fool.[74]

This identification with the girls not chosen says much about her understanding of femininity, and her ambivalent relationship to her father, given that Louise projected herself into the role of the potential mistress.

There is a photograph of this evening showing Louise beside her father. They sit at a table in the nightclub after their meal: he is very elegant in a tuxedo with a bowtie, a small mustache, hair slicked back, smoking while glancing sideways; she wears a patterned dress, her hair prettily styled, a discreet smile on her lips as she eyes the photographer. The anecdote about her father's behavior is typical of the ambiguous relationship Louise had with him. Later, she described other, similar scenes, in which she was denigrated because of her gender, flattered and spoiled, more like a lover than a child—this attitude would always unleash feelings of inferiority and indignation. "My father said on 18th Street: 'Do you remember how beautiful our past was?' I said: 'I do not know what you mean.'"[75]

Once Louis had returned to France, he and Louise resumed their correspondence. Louise and her children listened to the League of Nations meetings, which were broadcast on the radio, and rejoiced at the rights of women that were to be included in the new constitution. She informed her father that the boys' French was improving bit by bit, reminded him of the places they'd gone together, including the *toile de Jouy* exhibition at the French embassy, and reported on the conversations she'd had with Paul Prouté concerning engravings. She also proudly described her sculpture exhibition at the Peridot Gallery: "All the important artists in New York came and the two directors of the Modern Art Museum did too."[76]

In 1949, the apartment had grown too small for the family—Alain had to sleep with the maid and Jean-Louis was banished to the dining room when Michel came home from school—and the Bourgeois-Goldwater family once again turned their thoughts toward a new residence and dreamed of finding a three-story brick house from the late nineteenth century: "these little houses attached one to the other with a small backyard have a Proustian charm."[77]

Her correspondence with her father breaks off at this point,[78] because in September 1950 Louise arrived in Paris with Robert and their two youngest children; they stayed for nearly a year. Louise kept all the letters they exchanged from 1938 to 1950 carefully tied with a red-brown ribbon.[79]

"My letters to Papa," she went on to write, "are, no matter how long ago they were written, UNCOMFORTABLE. Deep embarrassment. Awkward desire to avoid 'the real subject' (embarrassment of a child who has committed a crime, lying, petty theft, disobedience), embarrassment when one mentions these forbidden subjects, blushing. Embarrassment at showing oneself naked. Shame."[80] This confession reveals the much more complex feelings about her father that she would later share.

Robert Goldwater

Louise's early years in America, marked by her entrance into the New York art world, the company of exiled European artists as well as American artists, were tightly bound up with and conditioned by her husband's professional and aesthetic commitments.

Robert Goldwater, who was born in 1907, was a brilliant art historian, who after finishing his undergraduate studies at Columbia University (he obtained his BA in 1929, the year MoMA was founded), went on to do a master's at Harvard in 1931, and then his PhD (published as *Primitivism in Modern Painting*) at New York University. "When Goldwater wrote his thesis," writes the art historian William Rubin, "modern art was not considered a serious subject of discussion."[81]

Goldwater was a professor at Queens College[82] from 1939 to 1956 and also taught at the Institute of Fine Arts until his death in 1973. In tribute to the place that was so important to her husband, Louise would create a silver sculpture of the building, *The Institute* (2002), as she had previously done in marble for her house in Choisy-le-Roi. Goldwater was also the editor of the *Magazine of Art* (1947–53), as well as the first director of the Museum of Primitive Art, which was later absorbed into the Metropolitan Museum of Art. *Primitivism in Modern Art*[83] is recognized as a foundational study and a pioneering work in its field. His list of publications indicates the rich interdisciplinarity of his interests, from Senufo statues to modern sculpture, from Gauguin's sculptures to Mexican art. For a long time, Louise refused to comment on the artistic and intellectual affinities with her husband, going so far as to censure all mentions of "totems" or "fetishes" in texts on her work. However, these affinities no doubt provided an important basis for their mutual understanding and their relationship. Robert recognized Louise as a singular artist, for whom art was a form of exorcism, while Louise saw in her husband's writing a validation of the path she had chosen.

In 1950, Robert was one of the first scholars to be awarded a yearlong Fulbright scholarship in Paris. As Barr's biographer relates: "Robert Goldwater . . . and his wife were writing Barr long letters about the miserable working conditions there. Not only had Goldwater and another Fulbright fellow, Millard Meiss, been unable to find an apartment, [but] they were disheartened by antiquated research facilities and uncooperative archivists. 'The fact is that art history here is still carried on in the tradition of the bourgeois scholar inheriting and building his own library and working "privately,"' Goldwater despondently wrote."[84]

This trip to France, which should have been a joyous occasion for Louise, was not without its complications. What to do with the children? Where should they live? At Antony? Boulevard Saint-Germain? She had to find a studio and a Parisian gallery to show with. It was in this spirit that she drew up a list of galleries to approach as well as a portfolio to show Daniel-Henry Kahnweiler.

Her return to Paris, more than ten years after she had first left, would prove completely overwhelming.

Homesickness, 1950–1960

In spite of [my] youth and happiness there was something dead, and I had to resuscitate it. And what I had to resuscitate was the right to be unhappy, the right to be in mourning for France. It's very simple but it's very violent. It's phenomenally persistent, but it's something I have conquered.

How did Louise move to sculpture from the painted, drawn, or engraved image? To some extent she was formally inspired by the vertical towers of New York, which she discovered from the rooftop studio of her apartment building. "Suddenly I had this huge sky space to myself and I began doing these standing figures."[1] She turned her outdoor space into a privileged place to work, which served as an escape from the claustrophobia of domestic life. The skyscraper, the height of which impressed all the French people who visited New York, allowed her at least momentarily to make a fresh start and escape the heavy weight of her past.

But the transition was also the result of a "revelation" that emerged from her everyday life. To fight her homesickness and ward off the loneliness and anxiety that beset her whenever she was home alone, she cut up milk cartons, folding them and piling them up into towers that she painted black and moved around as she liked: "After the men would leave, I would experience total chaos, meaning solitude, a wrenching solitude. Then I realized I could have control over another form of expression, over another world. I could create these forms, paint them black, which expressed sadness. I could group them together, throw them to the ground and destroy them. This feeling of empowerment helped me control my homesickness. Sculpture was revealed to me as a means of expression thanks to a carton of milk, thanks to its simple triangular form, something useful, indispensable."[2] "No doubt it's a kind of fetish," she explained, "but all the triangles from this period, I would never have been able to part with them."[3]

Sculpture was from the start, then, a form of exorcism. Through it, Louise managed to displace her feelings of pain and powerlessness onto a physical thing, to give form to her torment in order to master it, to let it pass from her body to another "body."

Some of her sculptures were carved from cedar wood, the same material used to make the water towers that sit on the rooftops of New York—Louise would later convert a water tower into a large work entitled *Precious Liquids* (1992). But at this time, Louise was only using tall, thin planks or found pieces, which she could then easily cut down with a razor blade and assemble into the desired shapes. To give them form, she had to size, cut, recut, and dig into them—actions which allowed her to release her aggression and violence.

She first showed these sculptures at the Peridot Gallery, from October 3 through 29, 1949. In April of that year, she had taken part in a group show with Willem de Kooning, Bradley Walker Tomlin, and Hans Hofmann. For this solo show, she was invited by Louis Pollock, the director of the gallery, on the recommendation of Arthur Drexler, the poet, architect, and curator in the department of architecture at MoMA.

In 1949, Louise had a lot to prove. She wanted to show that she spoke English well,[4] so she gave English titles to her works: *Woman in the Shape of a Shuttle, Friendly Evidence, New York City Doorway with Pillars, Captains' Walk on Irving Place Building,*[5] *Persistent Antagonism, The Tomb of a Young Person, Woman Carrying Packages* (now called *Woman with Packages*), and a more horizontal work: *Blind Vigils* (now called *The Blind Leading the Blind*).[6] Some titles are explicit, referring to tapestry, architecture, domesticity, maternity, the child who can wound with a knife. Others refer to people Louise knew: *Portrait of C. Y.* refers to Catherine Yarrow,[7] a surrealist artist with whom Louise found herself in conflict: "But this one I exorcised, I got rid of [her] by making a statue, putting a name on this statue"[8]—and by, for instance, hammering nails where her chest might be, as done in some African fetish statues. Others had more ambiguous, multiple meanings. Such was the case for *Persistent Antagonism*—a title that well suited Louise herself—which she at first connected with her feeling of loneliness ("because I was isolated from my entire family, suffered from it")[9] but which she later framed as a work that "refers to sex, men showing off their penises. It is irritating. The macho bit is irritating. I have nothing against the penis. It is the wearer of the penis."[10] The first is a sentimental, psychological interpretation; the second sexual, anatomic. They are not mutually exclusive, given that on a formal level the sculpture does show a sharp phallus, like a knife. The knife is a frequent prop in her work: *Dagger Child* (1947–49) or *Femme couteau* (1969–70) capture the suffering caused by separation or castration. "Exile or alienation is a necessary (not sufficient tho' [*sic*]) condition of work."[11]

All these characters have a story: the *Woman with Packages* (1949) refers to Louise weighted down by chores and housework, with her three children hanging from her skirts. A similar configuration can be found in *Quarantania* (1947–53), which brings five figures together on a base—Louise, Robert, and their three children: "I had children around my waist. This is the origin of the *Quarantania*. I was carrying my packages."[12] These "five totemic poles assert the phallic dominance in a family of four males."[13]

The Blind Leading the Blind (1947–49) is the largest construction, composed of three horizontal bars clustered together and supported by seven pairs of legs.[14] It is without a doubt the most abstract work of this period, given that in the other totemlike works, we can generally make out bodies, heads, arms. This sculpture exists in several colors: black and red, black, pink, and some with additional pairs of legs. Its title refers to a painting by Pieter Bruegel the Elder, *The Blind Leading the Blind* (1568),[15] but Louise sometimes gave a different, more positive account of the biblical story: "Brueghel's painting is a pessimistic vision, because they're falling: instead of trusting their own consciousness, they're trusting someone else. Obviously it's fatal. Because they can't see, they cling to one another."[16] The composition recalls the family photograph taken in Mont-Dore in 1920, in which we see young Louise guiding her father, who is playing at being a blind man with a cane.[17] It also brings to mind the statue of Antigone and Oedipus at the Lycée Fénelon. Blindness is linked to sexuality: "Blindness comes from the shame that I felt beside the people who surrounded me. Since my father was a ladies' man, I had to turn a blind eye to his mistress who lived with us. I had to close my eyes to the fact that I was a bit of a sadist with my brother. I had to close my eyes to the fact that my sister was sleeping with the man from across the street. I was disgusted by everyone. Especially for erotic reasons, sexual reasons."[18] Three versions of the sculpture were painted pink in the late 1970s, and one of these was retitled *C.O.Y.O.T.E.*, after the name of a sex workers' rights organization (Call Off Your Old Tired Ethics), in yet another reference to sexuality.

But—as was often the case—Louise told different stories about the piece, depending on the context. In another version, it represents the adults' legs gathered around the table when as a child she would hide beneath it, with her brother or her cousins. Legs, which are a persistent motif in her drawings, would appear again in the 1980s.

The *Personages* are for the most part painted white, with a few touches here and there of blue or black. They often culminate in a point, which emphasizes their fragility and suggests they might be driven directly into the ground. She preferred this installation, without pedestals, and displayed them each in relation to one another. They could also be leaned against a wall. Louise also worked on them in Easton, arranged them in the garden, assembled them, photographed them—they went everywhere with her. She could move them around as she liked. This is what she did, for example, with *Portrait of Jean-Louis* (1947–49), an abstract image of her son, which took the form of a long wooden knife with a split handle, whose phallic upper portion is pierced with little windows evoking a skyscraper.[19] It was a fetish object that Louise could carry with her, a sculpture being somewhat easier to carry around than a child.

The second showing of the *Personages* took place in the same gallery a year later, from October 2 through 28, 1950. This time, the titles were in French, and constituted a genuine manifesto: *Figure qui apporte du pain (Figure Bringing Bread)*, *Figure regardant une maison (Figure Watching a House)*, *Figures qui supportent un linteau (Figures Supporting a Lintel)*, *Figure qui s'appuie contre une porte (Figure Leaning Against a Door)*, *Figure qui entre dans une pièce (Figure Entering a Room)*, *Statue pour une maison vide (Statue for an Empty House)*, *Deux figures qui portent un objet (Two Figures Holding an Object)*, *Une femme gravit les marches d'un jardin (A Woman Mounting the Steps of a Garden)*, *Figures qui attendent (Waiting Figures)*, *Figures qui se parlent sans se voir (Figures Talking Without Seeing Each Other)*, *Figure endormie (Sleeping Figure)*, *Figure pour une niche (Figure for a Niche)*, *Figure quittant sa maison*

(*Figure Leaving Its House*), *Figure de plein vent* (*Figure in the Wind*), *Figure emportant sa maison* (*Figure Carrying Its House*). The poetic repetition of these actions suggests lived history.

The insistence on architectural elements and constant references to the house are a striking aspect of Louise's work. They are memories of childhood, which appear suddenly like photographic snapshots. "[T]he titles indicate exactly what I mean. There's no mystery at all! [. . .] But there is a great intensity and a very great personal emotion. This is apparent in the constant repetition of the word 'figure,' which expresses the fact that I had left my entire family in Europe [. . .] the homesickness was doubled by a sense of abandonment. I felt I had abandoned them."[20]

For Louise, these sculptures truly had presence; they were substitutes for human beings, idols with supernatural powers. "Now even though the shapes are abstract, they represent people. They are delicate as relationships are delicate. They look at each other and they lean on each other."[21] Sculpture was a material way for her to re-create the past, in order to control and manipulate it. By disseminating her sculptures throughout the gallery and arranging them in clusters as if at a party, Louise presented one of her first immersive environments.

These two first exhibitions were a mitigated success. Her friend Marcel Duchamp came to see the 1949 show with the art dealer Pierre Matisse. Some critics[22] were sensitive to Louise's expressions of loneliness and to her representation of the spatial relations between people, as well as to the elementary, sometimes biomorphic forms, which they described as totems because of the way they echoed African fetishes. *Art News* reported on the "disturbed spirit at work,"[23] emphasizing the feelings of estrangement that emit from the works, their uncanny impact. But in the *New York Times,* Stuart Preston was severe in his judgment: "I, for one, find them neither convincing as symbols nor pleasing as forms," he wrote.[24] Louise was crushed: "devastating review in the *Times,* Stuart Preston."[25]

Her friend Arthur Drexler, who helped stage the exhibition, saw the poetic magic in the work and detected a "surrealism" that was closer to Lewis Carroll than André Breton: "I stepped into her studio [. . .] and it was like finding yourself in a strange French movie by Jean Cocteau. There stood this very small, intense woman—extremely svelte, handsome—wielding a huge cleaver with which she worked on balsa wood. Time and conventional notions of reality were annihilated. She was alarming as she attacked the wood with a kind of innocent magic that was obsessive, yet also poetic. [...] I remember thinking that when I entered her studio it was like passing through a mirror into another world."[26]

After the formal simplicity of these early stacks of monolithically sculpted wood, Louise undertook more complex sculptures, assemblages of found elements, threaded onto a central rod. *Memling Dawn* (1951) is composed of a stack of black wood blocks forming a square column, and *Mortise* (1950) is a stack of red and black wood blocks notched and embedded in one another. *Femme volage* (1951) and *Spiral Woman* (1951–52) are also formed of fragments strung together; these kinetic, unstable works give the impression of being propelled from the inside out; as the curator Katherine Brinson writes, "The layers fling themselves outwards from the central axis in a tornado of centrifugal energy."[27]

In 1951, Alfred H. Barr bought *Sleeping Figure* (1950) for MoMA. Louise wrote him a letter explaining that the two long parallel arms that hold the figure in place could be moved around; she added holes for this purpose and two sets of shoulders, one happy and one sad. "However I am not quite sure about the plasticity of the gay one, so I will send you only the serious one." She noted that it could function in different environments—inside, outside, in a dark space or a light one, alone or with other works, standing up or laid down. But although it could be manipulated, it was fragile and should not be placed in an unstable position.[28]

Reading this letter with an awareness of Louise's feelings for Barr, this advice—valuable, subjective ("it is the role of the owner to take care of it") but also deeply ironic ("If there is in the process, damage or breakage the artist could be called upon to repair it, paid a reasonable fee, he should be happy to handle old works of his")—is particularly touching. Was Barr able to read between the lines and perceive the more personal meaning hidden there?

Louise's recommendations for how to present the work are confirmed by a number of photographs taken at Easton, in which we can see the figures installed in a number of contexts—outdoors, on a wall, in a group—and posed in different ways, like marionettes, or puppets.

Impossible Love

Her flirtation with Barr wasn't completely over yet. Between 1950 and 1953, Louise continued to be haunted by him: "my desperately falling in love with impossible A. B. coincides with a deep depression—1) does a bad physical states [*sic*] produces sadness or is it the sadness that puts me in bed?"[29] Part of her work, she said, was inspired by her relationship with Barr, for example, "the series of drawings I made during the winter + which I consider very fine work in spite of or because of my relation to A. B."[30] Occasionally she rebelled against this emotional dependence: "on Friday at the end of the day when I realized that I thought AB did not care for me I had a horrible fit declaring that I wanted to leave for France."[31] Their professional relationship made such breaks that much more difficult to bear: "if you are an artist it is good that the painters know that you have powerful friends but if you show up at a lecture with Mr. Barr you cease to be an artist and become Mr. Barr's girlfriend."[32] Nevertheless, she tried to disengage by numerous means: "the only way to detach oneself from a man is to despise him. A. B. is the timid type he doesn't dare look at the painters and talk to them."[33] No matter how lucid her perspective or how much she criticized him, she reserved her harshest judgments for herself: "I wake up at 5 [a.m.] furious against A. B. because I had the weakness to write to him and I am a sucker people laugh at, I am going to write to him, Mr. Narcisse, that he loves himself but nobody else does."[34]

Her emotional state had a negative impact on her health and exacerbated her already extreme sensitivity to the judgment of others. Louise was incapable of reading anything about herself or any of her contemporaries, so devoured was she by jealousy. Her frequent disagreements with Robert made her extremely anxious and fearful, which manifested on a physical level: "awful state disagreement with Robert (personal), great tension + fear that things are not going to go right [. . .] desire to escape daily."[35]

But in this entry it is clear that this was also a period of great creativity for her: "terrific tension beforehand partly sexual [. . .] wake up [. . .] in great excitement ideas rush on at great speed and intensity—intense physical well being sinusitis completely gone and breathing deep and easy well being of an after climax."[36]

She continued to participate just as energetically in the New York art world. In April 1950, she took part in a three-day, closed-door symposium at Studio 35 with other artists (William Baziotes, David Hare, Robert Motherwell, Mark Rothko, and others), organized by Robert Goodnough and directed by Richard Lippold. Each of the speakers was asked to present their work and give their perspective on contemporary American painting and sculpture. A few months after the symposium, Adolph Gottlieb initiated a protest in the form of an open letter to the Metropolitan Museum of Art,[37] questioning the conservative policies adopted by the museum toward modern American art. Seventeen painters and ten sculptors joined him. Louise was one of a handful of women[38] to sign the letter, but she did not appear in the iconic photograph[39] of the group that appeared in *Life* magazine and heralded the emergence of the New York School.[40] Several signatories of the letter formed a group calling themselves the Irascibles. The letter unleashed a polemic between the old and the new guards and solidified the nascent abstract expressionist movement. Hedda Sterne,[41] the only woman in the photograph, later emphasized the abstract expressionist painters' misogyny: "they all were very furious that I was in it because they were all sufficiently macho to think that the presence of a woman took away from the seriousness of it all."[42] The misogynistic climate that Louise so often denounced during this time was clearly felt by other female artists as well.

In November 1950, Erick Hawkins[43] (the dancer and choreographer, who was also married to Martha Graham) asked Louise to design the set and costumes for a ballet. Hawkins had already collaborated with the Japanese American artist Isamu Noguchi on two ballets, *John Brown* (1945) and *Stephen Acrobat* (1947).

Hawkins was an ardent admirer of Louise's work and wrote her numerous long letters, sending her poetry by e. e. cummings on January 24, 1951, and comparing her to Calder and Brancusi.[44] Nevertheless, the pay was quite bad, which upset her: "I work for Hawkins at the rate of $25 for 3 figures. He calls me a housewife. I could twist the neck of the world. I am leaving my gallery, my husband and when the figures are done I will tell him what I think of him. What can cure you from frustration and hate. Is it to sleep with a man is it to work."[45]

Robert often served as an intermediary between Hawkins and Louise to arrange the conditions for their collaboration. Louise took her time responding to the choreographer and mainly discussed her *Sleeping Figure*, the sculpture Barr acquired for MoMA in January 1951, and the museum's recent exhibition of abstract sculpture. "I am very touched by your offer of protesting against my not being there," she wrote to him.[46] But "go and see the *Figure Endormie*. I hear it is being shown now in the new acquisitions show."[47]

Louise received Hawkins's commission while she was abroad in Paris. The distance complicated her collaboration with him, and in the end, nothing came of it. It was an ambitious project set to music by Henry Cowell, involving marionettes, a clown, and an angel for whom Hawkins had asked Louise to design a pair of wings. Back in New York, she wrote, "I do not work any more. Hawkins job is over. No prospect of being able to isolate myself for the necessary concentration."[48]

Finally she contributed to a different, more modest show, *The Bridegroom of the Moon*, proposing an assemblage of personages made of wood and papier-mâché, standing on little bases or supported by kickstands on the back. Set to music by Wallingford Riegger, the performance took place on January 19, 1952, at Hunter Playhouse. Louise convinced her friend and rival Louise Nevelson to help put together the black and white painted sculptures—this was the beginning of Nevelson's own practice of creating sculptures out of painted black wood, according to Robert Storr,[49] some of which bore a striking resemblance to Louise's *Personages*.

In the early 1950s, a new school of American sculpture was taking form, which was the subject of many exhibitions, articles, and books; its principal representatives were Herbert Ferber, Isamu Noguchi, Richard Lippold, David Hare, Seymour Lipton, Theodore Roszak, and David Smith. Louise occupied a marginal place in this movement. Not only did she not work with metal, like most of the New York School, but she also didn't consider her figures to only be sculptures; she called them, rather, her "statues," an outdated term, one reserved mainly for ancient or "primitive" works. For Louise, abstract forms were always full of emotional meaning.

Return to France

On October 26, 1950, the family finally returned to France for Robert's sabbatical year;[50] they stayed until September 1951. Louise, who hoped to visit several of her friends from childhood—Jean Pelletier, Cécile Chasse, Annie

Segalen—carefully planned the trip. Later on she said that their departure for France had other motivations, of a secret and political nature: "[Duchamp, Ozenfant, and I] were investigated by McCarthy in 1951. We had different fates. Duchamp had powerful friends, so he was safe. Ozenfant was a very awkward person, original and independent. When he was attacked he would attack back like a child. So he was kicked out of the country. But I defended myself. I was interrogated several times after I made an application to become a citizen. My defense was that I had no connection with or knowledge of what the men I was involved with were doing politically."[51] This version of the story was also confirmed by her son Alain, who explained that Louise feared the anti-Semitic climate in America and thought her children would be safer in France.[52]

On the boat journey over, her anxiety and low-level depression continued, exacerbated, as usual, by her return to France. In her diary she wrote: "I do not know why I do not jump in the ocean."[53]

Once in France, they went to Antony first to stay with Louise's sister, Henriette Bonnotte at 36, avenue Gabriel-Péri. Then, through the artist Day Schnabel, Louise found a little house with a studio that belonged to a sculptor named Müller in the 14th arrondissement at 77, rue Daguerre,[54] which she rented until 1955 before periodically subletting it to the young American painter Shirley Jaffe.[55] When they moved in, the house was not at all comfortable. The children had to sleep in the kitchen with the gas stove; the rooms overlooking the street were noisy, and there was much work to be done. But these inconveniences did not prevent Louise from having a piano sent.[56]

Jean-Louis and Alain were registered at the Lycée Hoche in Versailles; Michel was left behind in America, in the care of his grandmother and aunt Mary. Louise returned to the Latin Quarter, the Gibert bookshop, the Café Capoulade. She took classes in aesthetics with Étienne Souriau at the Sorbonne and worked at the Grande Chaumière. She visited the Louvre regularly (especially the Cabinet des Estampes with Robert).[57] She also returned to rooting around in the family archive, rediscovering her mother's account books, or the list of opera records she listened to in her youth.[58] Her time was also taken up with joint ownership problems at Antony, the taxes on cleaning the Bièvre, ongoing litigation with the tenants. In November she went to Monthléry with Henriette, then to Meudon, and saw the Arp show at the Galerie Maeght.

In the early spring of 1951,[59] the family began a road trip around France. They set off for Saint-Benoît-sur-Loire but also went to visit the home of Louise's Fauriaux grandparents in Aubusson, where she had lived for a short time during the First World War: "Aubusson [. . .] houses hewn from granite."[60] She observed that the "Creuse is a strong, fast river," noted that there were fishermen there, and rediscovered the terraced garden behind the house.[61] Next they went to La Chaise-Dieu, Le Puy (to see the Black Madonna), then stopped over in Aubenas (palm trees, olive trees), Avignon ("cypress hedges to protect from the Mistral—*mas* [farmhouse] bordered with sycamore trees"),[62] and Aix, where it was still cold. "Robert is exhausted."[63] The mimosa was not yet in bloom. They drove back up through the deserted Ardèche, stopped at the Hôtel Mariquita in Magagnosc, went to Montpellier (to see Bruyas, Courbet, and Delacroix), Saint-Gilles, and the Pont du Gard. The children sang in the car. They slept at Montélimar, then passed through Lyon, Cluny, Autun ("lovely"),[64] Saulieu, Vézelay. Finally, April 8, their massive trip was over; they returned home, after stopping off on April 7 to see Louise's childhood friend Annie Segalen and to get something to eat in Versailles.

Louis's Death, 1951

The next day, April 9, 1951, she wrote in small, tight handwriting in her diary: "Papa passes away." Below was written "(Leleu[65] manager of the Nationale)." Did she have a meeting planned with him? Then on April 12, "Papa's burial service in St. Germain des Prés. Music is beautiful. Bowers takes care of the boys.[66] Jacques B. comes with Edouard Germaine + Nadia + Luer[67] keep to themselves."

It was a terse statement and a sudden death. Louis Bourgeois, aged sixty-six, died at the clinic run by the brothers of Saint-Jean-de-Dieu, in the rue Oudinot. Had the lifelong atheist found God at the end of his life? He received the final Catholic rites and was buried in the cemetery at Clamart, after a religious ceremony in the church of Saint-Germain-des-Prés. On the death announcement,[68] Pierre's name was included, although it would seem that he had not even been told of his father's death.

If we are to believe the letter Louise wrote to Annie Segalen, Louis died suddenly, with no warning.[69] If Louise had known her father was ill, how to account for this long trip to the south of France and, especially, the infrequent mentions of him in her diary since her arrival in France?[70] Had the family reunion—with all its repressed memories—not been as idyllic as she had expected? Did she love her father only from afar? She had apparently begun to feel ill at ease with Louis during the trip to Canada in 1948. Louise remembered that her father always wanted to ride in the backseat to admire her beautiful hair. "Rage on Canadian trip. 'Sit in front, I will be able [t]o look at your beautiful hair. Servant master attitude comes out with Robert." She remembered watching Robert struggle with the suitcases in the pouring rain.[71] She also remembered her father's need for "constant proofs of love and admiration. In Huntington work on the car seat for compliments and reassurance and flattery."[72]

Maybe Louis had let himself die of sadness: "When he realized that Robert had wiggled me out he let himself die."[73]

Louise's grief was devastating: "Losing my Father—it is as if I was castrated I lose everything even my equilibrium—Post-mortem scene April 1950 rue Daguerre—I was not able to walk in the room without holding on what a collapse—of the digestive system and dizziness."[74]

Louise received a number of condolence letters[75] from her father's business contacts, but also an affectionate and sensitive note from her mother-in-law, Mrs. Goldwater. Everyone knew how attached she was to her father. "Dear, my dear Louise, What a shock your father's sudden taking off must have been to you! [. . .] I know how you loved your father [. . .] it must be a deep regret to you that you were not with him at the last, it must be an equally deep satisfaction that [. . .] you gave him and yourself the joy of seeing each other." For Mrs. Goldwater, Louis had been "charming" and filled with great energy.[76] Janet, Louise's sister-in-law, confirmed this: "He was so vigorous and youthful and full of vitality."[77]

Losing her father triggered deep feelings of abandonment, just as her mother's death had done. The experience of mourning a parent, this time so unexpectedly, was very painful and dramatic for Louise. "Then, on April 9, 1951 came the news of the sudden death of my father. I fainted when I heard this news. My whole world fell apart, including my desire for a show."[78]

The month of May was taken up by problems concerning her father's estate,[79] putting together a *conseil de famille* to serve as executors, emptying the apartment, and determining its future. An inventory had to be made of the shop, as they could not buy it, and they had to go to Drouot to sell the merchandise.[80] Louise and Robert went to the family tomb in Clamart and noticed that the gate had disappeared.[81]

Meanwhile Robert, who couldn't get much time off from his research, was busy visiting museums and taking professional meetings.

By June, the Goldwaters were back on the road. "Anvers, exhib. Ensor. [. . .] Holland is very beautiful. [. . .] Everybody is blond and neat. Modern houses freshly painted [. . .] windmills, roads looking out on the countryside, meadows, cows, and the smell of wet hay [. . .] full of canals, double windows and double doors [. . .] Holland is abstract in the very construction of its country [. . .] art doesn't represent it, it renders it visible."[82]

No detail escaped Louise's sharp eye, and her critiques were as forceful as ever. In July they went to England, where David Sylvester introduced them to Francis Bacon,[83] an artist she greatly admired and on whom she would later write.[84] "I like Bacon's work unconditionally. It hits me and makes me tick. To look at his paintings makes me feel alive."[85] That August they also met with Ben Nicholson, Douglas Cooper, and John Richardson.

Depression

Very quickly, Louise began to exhibit signs of the depression that had been dormant since the 1940s: dizziness, fainting spells, fatigue, pain. Dr. Jean Mercier prescribed atropine.[86]

In early September, the Goldwater family boarded the boat to New York: "exploration of the boat in first class—the lateral bridges are quite beautiful [. . .] the dogs have the best spot on the boat,"[87] she noted in her diary. But also: "Jung / *Modern Man in Search of a Soul*—he is much less dogmatic than Freud and less troubling.[88] "I am happy to be arriving. It is difficult to isolate oneself on the boat."[89] This allusion to Carl Gustav Jung is not surprising coming from a young woman who lived in the United States, where the Swiss psychiatrist's ideas were favorably received.

Soon after her return to New York, a long, severe depression set in: "very low energy [. . .] all day in a chair [. . .] depressed day—do not go out—no interest in anything, no music, no radio, no work, no reading, no thinking, no project, no eating at all."[90] "In Paris I was in bed practically the whole time Fulbright year 1951."[91] This was confirmed by her sons, who reported that at that time their mother was almost constantly in bed.

Louise first consulted doctors complaining of hormonal problems, then of an "infection of the nervous system," but she quickly made the connection between these physical symptoms and psychological problems—what she illustrated with a triangle, writing "sexual life / sinus / work" at each angle.[92] She felt immature and neurotic.[93]

On October 24, 1951, she began an analysis with Dr. Leonard Cammer.[94] By the following January, she began seeing Dr. Henry Lowenfeld,[95] whom she would see regularly between 1952 and 1966, then on a more occasional basis until his death in 1985.

Louise made the decision to change analysts in December 1951. It was not an easy choice to make: "In front of the analyst problem (making a decision on who to see) I am very afraid 'not to make it': tantrum against Robert. Am also afraid to go into drastic and extreme steps. The Reich[96] is an extreme (ask McD).[97] A four years four times a week man is an extreme. (Catherine Y.)[98] A psycho-therapist is an extreme."[99]

In fact, she had already been in contact with Dr. Lowenfeld in late December 1951. She had been concerned about the therapist's Reichian side and the frequency with which he expected to meet. She wrote a devastating, deeply violent text on December 31, which concludes with the words: "This letter is addressed to Dr. Henry Lowenfeld."[100]

The 1950s would be punctuated by numerous sessions with Dr. Lowenfeld (three to four per week), dream narratives, and hundreds of psychoanalytic writings—the earliest of which were awkwardly typed on the typewriter—which Louise kept all her life.

It was also a period during which they made numerous trips to France. Robert and Louise spent the summer there with their children, from June to September, every other year from 1953 until 1961. In 1952, Louise decided not to go, "because of the excessive emotional strain."[101] Then she regretted it, talked it over with Dr. Lowenfeld, and felt ready to reconsider the trip. But Robert refused to reopen the discussion, and they abandoned the idea.[102]

Between Paris and New York, 1953–1960

A third solo show took place at the Peridot Gallery from March 30 to April 25, 1953: *Louise Bourgeois, Drawings for Sculpture and Sculpture*. It was well received by the critics, who were particularly interested in the drawings.

This was the first time Louise showed them alongside her *Personage* sculptures. The critic for *Art and Architecture*[103] said he was impressed by the drawings, which reminded him of masses of hair, waves, and oblong, striated forms that looked like muscles. They were "strange, disturbing, and rather obsessive work" whose "enigmatic reality" recalled dolmen or the moai statues of Easter Island.[104] "[S]tudy of knots—symbolism of knots, braids, tangles, knotwork, letters, ornaments, pebbled [*rocaille*], lacing, lace, hooks / continuity solution," she noted in her diary to explain her approach.[105] Meanwhile in *Art News,* Fairfield Porter underscored the fragility produced by the quiet, familiar presence of the sculptures.[106]

Forêt (*Night Garden*) (1953) signals a new direction in Louise's work. In that sculpture she abandoned the rigidity of isolated, geometrical figures in order to bring different abstract elements together into one compact mass: bulbs, cattails, hollowed-out pieces of wood. She painted them black—hence the title—and added a few touches of white and dark red. The title of the work refers to her childhood, when as a little girl she would cross the garden at Antony in the dark, encouraged by her father so she would be less afraid. The same compositional principle—oblong figures combined on a base—can be found in *One and Others* of 1955. Louise attributed this new interest in the group, in the relationship of the self to others, to the comfort brought by the presence of her husband and children. Her work shifted, little by little, from the mise-en-scène of the solitary individual to a group consciousness. "At first I made single figures without any freedom at all . . . now I see my work as groups of objects relating to each other. . . . But there is still the feeling with which I began—the drama of one among many."[107] This unusual sculpture drew the attention of the *Art Digest* critic, for whom this nocturnal garden was a "private poem of restraint and seclusion."[108]

Despite the success of the show, her depression was debilitating. Earlier in the year she wrote that she was "paralyzed in bed (by fear)"[109] and found that she was unable to accompany Robert to Cleveland, where he was meant to travel for work. And she was wracked with guilt: "indecision makes me mean conflict for days—after eight negative decisions I am relieved—the day after I am ashamed and sad not to have gone."[110] She was summoned to court to make Michel's adoption legal. Then on March 27, 1953, with Robert's consent, she filed to give her surname to her other sons, Jean-Louis and Alain. From then on all three of the couple's sons would be called Bourgeois, given the name of the mother and not of the father. That is—the name of the mother's own father.

On June 17, 1953, the family boarded the *Queen Elizabeth* for France. Louise looked into the Société analytique de Paris before leaving, and drew up a list of names including Marie Bonaparte, Françoise Dolto, Jacques Lacan, Daniel Lagache, and Serge Lebovici.[111]

It is unlikely that Louise met Lacan that summer, though she later called him long-winded: "I am suspicious of words. [. . .] I distrust the Lacans and the Bossuets because they revel in their own words."[112] She did, however, find his work very interesting: "I was seduced by Lacan['s] process of thinking [. . .] Lacan is anti-everybody."[113] Much later, she watched video recordings of his seminars and read Élisabeth Roudinesco's book about him.

It was at this time that she began to think about drawing in red China ink, as she would later, sketching concentric spirals or bulbs like mountain ranges. It was more powerful than oil painting, she thought. She often went to the Louvre, to the Musée des arts décoratifs, and worked at the Grande Chaumière, where she had a locker.[114]

Robert maintained a cordial professional relationship with the art critic Michel Seuphor.[115] As early as 1951, Seuphor asked Robert for photos of Louise's work to include in his next article.[116] At that time, Galerie M.A.I. (Meuble, Architecture, Installation) had offered her a show, with a catalog prefaced by Seuphor.[117] But Louise backed out of the project when her father's death left her overwhelmed and unable to prepare it. Robert then wrote to Seuphor, saying, "Louise is at the moment at one of those points often reached by artists who work not as a métier but more directly with their own emotions where all practical decisions seem almost impossible to make . . . Everything seems terribly difficult because it carries her away from the kind of intense concentration she needs just now [. . .] tell Mr. Gervais how much we both appreciate his immediate understanding of Louise's work and his practical expression of his understanding."[118] This explanation well summarizes Robert's profound knowledge and understanding of Louise's singularity as an artist, as well as her fragility.

In the summer of 1953, Louise was on the brink of finally achieving her dream: to have a solo show in Paris,[119] at the Paul Facchetti gallery, accompanied by a catalog featuring a text by Michel Seuphor: "I would willingly call this walking forest, like something out of Shakespeare, a symbol of humanity," he wrote with regard to the *Personages*.[120] This impressive, poetic essay highlights the magical aspect of Louise's work. The allusion to Shakespeare's *Macbeth* emphasizes her work's personal, human dimension, as well as its emotional impact: "Louise Bourgeois immobilizes us, salt statues, fixed forest. She strips us down to the bone, leaving us the only eloquence of the bone: the fact of being." Seuphor also touched on the poverty of her materials, the austerity of her figures, and what he calls a "return to divine humility."[121]

But her depression and anxiety drove her to cancel, once again, the show that had been planned for July. "[V]ery hard day—I do not want the show. Robert goes to Facchetti [. . .] I refused: the texts for the book are not ready except Seuphor's preface."[122] This story about the catalog was surely an excuse. For that matter, Louise was worried about the contents of Seuphor's next book about sculpture[123] and of the status he granted other artists: "Lardera + did Seuphor include Stahly in his book?"[124]

But Robert did all he could to create the best possible conditions in which she might work and to convince her to take part in this show. To give her some quiet time on her own, he took the children to Brittany and then to Bordeaux, where he wrote her a very moving letter, a testament to the strength of his love:

> My love [. . .] As I have been thinking of you all the time that I drive, and constantly when there are fields and houses and kinds of people you would enjoy. If only you will live in the present, and do what it gives you so much pleasure to do, and not worry about the past. (I will get anything you want from Antony.) You can do your one piece for Facchetti—and that is all there is to do for the show. It will be a <u>step</u>, marked by the catalogue + book— which, as you have always said, will stay + will be seen and sent to all those who did not come to the show. I know how great an effort it is, + how difficult it is to get started, but it will be worth it to you. I put it to you as a challenge—and I will give all the help I can, which isn't much I know, but give it with all my heart and love— If only I could tell you how much you are a <u>presence</u> for me, when we are together, and when we are apart, which after all has not been often in 15 years. How you have extended my eyes and my emotions. How much grace and laughter there is in what you do. It is why your sadness is so terrible, because you can be so happy [. . .] I have not told

you often enough how much I love you. [. . .] I have no existence except as we exist together. You are for me a presence, it is the only way I can say it.

This declaration of love, tenderness, and emotional support demonstrates Robert's awareness of Louise's unstable state but also indicates what she had done for the timid, reserved young man that he had been when they met: "Whatever I write now (I mean really whatever art I see) is a combination of academic method, which is pretty poor in itself, + a large part of your esthetic vision."[125] As with any other couple, they influenced each other reciprocally.

When he was in Bordeaux, Robert took the children to Margaux to see Michel's former nanny, Madame Cursol, who was delighted to see the little boy who had left thirteen years earlier. The trip must have been an emotional shock for Michel, who complained less than usual and seemed to appreciate the trip.[126] In a different letter from the summer of 1953, Robert seems confident again, persuaded that Louise has been able to make some progress and work well in their absence, which pleased him greatly: "Everything seems to be getting together to make the show a success."[127]

But Louise was not able to get over her anxiety. The next month the family left for Italy, visiting Florence on August 17, Vicenza (and the Palladian villas of the Veneto) on August 24, and Turin on August 25, as well as Verona, Siena, and Venice. A photograph shows the five of them together, parents and children, smiling in a gondola. The trip was good for Louise's morale: "A far away person is not real anymore for L. unless there is obsession. In Italy, I lost the very memory of American friends."[128]

On their return from Italy they stopped in Grasse, then on September 1 they went to see her friend Cécile Chasse, who had recently been married, in Montceau les Mincs. She seemed especially happy to have freed herself from the obsession with the "house of [her] dreams." In this process of liberation, she suddenly felt disgust at the thought of what she had previously loved. The house in Montchauvet might come to her, but she didn't want to know anything about it: "Is the resolution to an obsession not to hate what one has loved and to love what one hates?"[129]

On September 4, 1953, Louise noted: "I am going to commit suicide or be paralyzed, or explode, or be seized with dysentery because this injustice has been committed: as it so happens, Day Schnabel[130] is in *Art of the 20th.*"[131] Her jealousy of other artists was as violent as ever.

On September 10, 1953, Robert and Louise were crossing the ocean again on the *United States.* Stretched out in the sunshine on a pair of deck chairs, they tenderly held hands.

Depression prevented Louise from making very much work between 1953 and 1960. She did take part in several group shows: at the Allan Frumkin Gallery in Chicago (1953), the Stable Gallery in New York (1954), the Walker Art Center in Minneapolis, where she showed *Forêt* (*Night Garden*) from May 23 to July 2, 1954. In 1954, she was also invited by Mr. and Mrs. Frank Didisheim to show in their private garden in New York, alongside Louise Nevelson and Nemesio Antúnez; she showed *Spring* (1948–49), with its fertile budding curves, and three other sculptures including *Memling Dawn* (1951).

Robert and Louise spent a long weekend in August 1954 on Long Island in the "Red House" with Elaine and Willem de Kooning and Franz Kline.[132] Louise was, then, still part of American artistic life. She made a few more wooden *Personages*, radical and minimalist, as well as one last grouping of oblong forms on a base: *One and Others* (1955). This work was shown at the Whitney's annual exhibition in 1956 and was acquired by the museum the same year.

In 1954, she was photographed with a young Robert Rauschenberg at the opening of the Eighteenth Annual Exhibition of the American Abstract Artists group, which was held every year at the Riverside Museum.

In June of the following year, the Goldwaters returned to France. In Paris, Louise attended a sale of engravings at Drouot, accompanied by Paulette and Georges Place. She went to a few science bookshops and wrote a list of rare books (Walter Scott, *Robinson Crusoe* by Daniel Defoe, and *Gulliver's Travels* by Jonathan Swift) and engravings (Constantin Guys, Géricault) with an eye to opening her own bookshop.[133]

In July 1955, the Goldwaters left for Brittany: Belle-Île, Hôtel du Phare at L'Apothicairerie, Douarnenez, and Roscoff.[134] Louise and the three children returned by boat from Cherbourg on September 11, while Robert returned by plane.

Of this period we are only aware of one sculpture, photographs of which were taken in the studio on the rue Daguerre: a female figure with long floating hair forming a kind of phallic protuberance. It is no longer extant.

Louise sublet her studio[135] to Shirley Jaffe and her husband, a former GI who wanted to live in France.[136] This transaction was arranged by Joan Mitchell and Day Schnabel. Shirley remembered Robert's kindness; he would stop in to see her from time to time and was interested in her work, whereas her relationship with Louise was more complicated. Louise did not like her paintings, and seemingly ignored them, which did not prevent her from asking a number of personal favors from Shirley, such as babysitting her son Jean-Louis or going to see her brother, Pierre, in the asylum at Villejuif.

At decade's end, despite her fears of not being included, Louise would indeed be featured in Seuphor's *Dictionnaire de la sculpture modern* in 1959.[137] In her book published in 1955, Carola Giedion-Welcker[138] compares her to François Stahly and describes the combination of simple forms arranged in a harmonious group.

Erasmus

Finding herself unable to create new work, Louise turned to the idea of starting a business. In January 1956, she opened a shop called Erasmus Books and Prints, initially located in Greenwich Village,[139] selling books and engravings. In so doing she was building a place that reminded her of the shop on the boulevard Saint-Germain, that allowed her to satisfy her hunger for business and her love of books: "The return to the father. His tastes, garden / his books Diderot his profession antiquarian. Conflict about a book shop (substitute for the shop),"[140] she noted. She had letterhead stationery printed, featuring an image of Erasmus, as well as advertising leaflets.

"Having a picture gallery isn't a profession or even a métier, but a feminine occupation,"[141] Mr. Mieier told her.[142] Robert did not seem to be in favor of this initiative, which led to a certain amount of discord between them. In 1958, Louise moved her store to the first floor of 922 Madison Avenue but had to close her doors in December 1959. During a stay in Amsterdam in July 1959, Louise wrote: "stay in Amsterdam is coming to an end—and not a word has been uttered about Erasmus. I do not quite understand what I came here to do. [. . .] What is the point of being unemployed."[143] The shop was a commercial failure and lasted only four years, an experience that left Louise distraught. "[T]he terrible crisis that occurred when I opened Erasmus II—the fear and the terrible depression of the early days at 922 [Madison Avenue]. It was the refusal to leave Erasmus I which represented a world of guilt [. . .] but this omnipotent world of guilt [. . .] is also that of the all powerful father [. . .] the world of childhood of dependency."[144] She brought her whole stock of books home. This bookshop, where she would spend entire days without selling anything, was a sort of refuge for her. She quickly realized that starting it was a means of psychically regressing: "It was a way of going back to my past—to my own childhood. The fear of depression was very real—and of abandonment. I was disappointed in myself. It was a business, but it was out of this world. It allowed me to stay outside the house—to not become a hermit."[145]

French Critics

Although her work did not find much support in America, she was nevertheless favorably mentioned in the French art press, in publications such as *Cimaise* and *L'œil*. And though Robert didn't support her commercial project, he was still a faithful admirer of her work, underscoring, in one article, the "poetic halo" surrounding it and the "remarkably personal conception of forms and the shifting way they relate to one another [. . .]. She employs forms of unusual simplicity, stripped of all that is not essential. She frees herself from fanciful ideas about material and surface, to such a point that she only paints her statues in a few elementary colors, white, black, terracotta, symbolizing light. Her earliest work dealt with isolated figures, the chasms that separate them; her more recent work brings them together in a way that is just as moving, but more tender."[146]

In 1957, Louise took American citizenship, while Robert became the first director of the Museum of Primitive Art, continuing all the while to teach at the Institute of Fine Arts at NYU.

Come summer, they left again for Europe. Louise saw her uncle Alex Fauriaux in Paris, who was an architect in Montchauvet, to talk about doing some work at Antony. She drew up a list of booksellers and bookshops and gathered information from the Syndicat de la librairie ancienne et moderne for Erasmus.

In June 1957, the Goldwaters went to London. Louise went to some auctions at Sotheby's: "I feel very much at home as at the hôtel Drouot or Parke Bernet."[147] It was a world of objects, therefore real, but unsatisfactory, she added. She visited the British Museum and saw the Parthenon marbles on June 27, 1957. Then she visited different bookshops (British Publisher, Antiquaria Bookseller), still on behalf of Erasmus. At this time, she knew she was losing money with the shop and that she couldn't go on paying a certain Mrs. Bertheim (if that was her name) to help her. In her notebook she admitted to the loneliness that she experienced in a tea salon on New Oxford Street, in front of Wren's church, in a student neighborhood full of booksellers and Chinese and Indian people: "I feel lonely, I always tumble [. . .] into this wall of silence. [. . .] this may be a sexual solitude [. . .]. Maybe I should re-read Sartre and Kierkegaard. This subject of solitude is really what interests me most now."[148] Not its cause, she specifies, but a remedy.

She also went to Clamart to visit her parents' graves and to see her paternal grandparents' home. She describes this return to the sites of her childhood in a small notebook: "I went to Clamart saw 64 rue de Paris the cemetery [. . .] I buy a red geranium for Papa and a white work of art for Maman." The neighborhood where she had spent her childhood was in very bad condition:

What was once the cité Lesniers is now a ruin. [. . .] The grandparents' house is not any worse than 4 years ago. It's a total come down but all the tenants are there even Madame Brun. She sees me and comes to the window [. . .] I get scared and I run away—I regret it, she is so old. On my way back I think of having a glass of lemonade but the thought makes me nauseous, and here I was thinking this visit would not bring any recall—I start getting a stomachache and the loathing and reflux follow. [. . .] Hot flashes on the forehead, I would like for someone to talk to me kindly and to tell me that I'm kind. [. . .] I detested everybody in the family really everybody except my 2 parents of course.[149]

These encounters with the past were physically painful. Seeing these places so greatly changed was wrenching. "[A]t 172 [boulevard Saint-Germain],[150] the recall does not come—What's the use of coming back to Europe—the present relieves nothing from the past."[151]

On July 6, Louise and Robert went to Amsterdam; they then visited Leyde and finally Austria (Kitzbühel and Innsbruck).

In 1958, Louise took part in the *Nature in Abstraction* exhibition at the Whitney.[152] The building where the family had lived since August 1941 (Stuyvesant's Folly) was going to be knocked down. So they moved to Chelsea, to an apartment at 435 West Twenty-Second Street, a narrow brownstone that looked very much like the one she would occupy from 1962 until her death, at 347 West Twentieth Street.

Robert and Louise spent the whole summer of 1959 in Europe: Brussels, Amsterdam, Aix-en-Provence, and Saint-Martin-du-Canigou in the Pyrénées.[153] On their return to Paris, they seem to have seen Michel Leiris, Jacqueline Delange, André Masson, and Georges Henri Rivière,[154] a testament to their shared interest in ethnography. On her return, in October, Louise arranged by correspondence for the Rota & Gay foundry in Paris to cast *Sleeping Figure* in bronze. The Museum of Modern Art allowed her to send the original, which was in their collection, to France—how times have changed!

Michel Seuphor was still a supporter of Louise's work and mentioned her in an article on contemporary sculpture for *L'œil*: "For quite some time in New York, Louise Bourgeois has been building totemic figures which are very rudimentary but strangely endowed with spirit, which she calls *astonished figure [forme étonnée]*, or *sleeping figure [figure endormie]*, or simply *understanding [entente]*."[155] "Her unusual work clearly influences a number of young American sculptors."[156] He also referenced her in his study of twentieth-century sculpture,[157] alongside quite a few women:[158] "I will only refer to Louise Bourgeois's totems, which convey an acute sense of human solitude, wreathed with secret drama."[159] The bibliography at the back describes a "very pared back work, imprinted with a secret poetry, full of subtle reservations, [which] has exerted no small amount of influence in America."[160]

Another influential critic, Michel Ragon, mentioned Louise's work in an article on American contemporary art in *Cimaise* magazine in 1959.[161] He noted the appearance of a new school of sculpture whose leader was David Smith, influenced by Julio González, Jacques Lipchitz, and Alexander Calder, and refers to the most significant practitioners as David Hare, Theodore Roszak, Seymour Lipton, and Herbert Ferber, a homogeneous group working mostly in metal and soldered iron, while two lone artists, Louise Bourgeois and Louise Nevelson, worked in wood.

Pierre's Death

On February 5, 1952, Robert wrote on Louise's behalf to Dr. Bergeron, Pierre's doctor, to find out how he was. "Amongst other things I would like to know what diagnosis was issued concerning his case." He particularly wanted to know if Pierre was aware of Louis's death[162] and to let him know they would visit at the end of June that year, "given the great affection that linked my wife and her brother."[163] Dr. Bergeron replied to Louise on February 9: "Madame, your brother has been the object of a request to be institutionalized at the end of December 1945. [. . .] He displays symptoms of schizophrenia and is quite affected in his thinking, his affectivity, his behavior. For two years, I had hoped that he would get better but [he is] opposed to treatments, in spite of several attempts. [. . .] We had to assign him to the pavilion for agitated patients, for he was getting impulsive and violent."[164]

Louise went to see her brother in Villejuif only a couple of times during her trips to France; on August 25, 1957,[165] she took Alain, who retained a vivid memory of the visit: "I found him charming. As far as I know, Louise only went to see him once, and she didn't talk about him."[166]

Louise always felt guilty about Pierre, aware that she had, in some way, abandoned him, and because their father didn't love him: "Since I got the love and attention I felt guilty vis-à-vis Pierre."[167]

But she didn't hold Louis responsible: "Yesterday [I] saw that Papa really did not give up Pierre to the Antony agents but actually protected him from a worse fate by preventing an official intervention later. In fact if the psychological results were disastrous Papa acted for the best according to his ideas and his means."[168]

This mythical uncle sometimes sent his nephews—particularly Alain, who was his favorite[169]—rambling letters accompanied by childish drawings. Pierre also wrote to his beloved sister, whether for her birthday or when

Paris was liberated: "My dear Louison, [. . .] Jaffe brought me a pomegranate which I ripened beside your photograph. Thinking of you keeps me young, and sometimes I dream about when we went swimming in Cabourg. [. . .] Did you get my little drawing? [. . .] Pierre who adores you so much."[170] He urgently requested his release from the hospital: "You have to make your request for them to let me out in writing."[171] He also asked for permission to travel to America; Shirley Jaffe could organize it.[172]

Afraid of seeing her brother, Louise sent her rue Daguerre subletter in her stead. Jaffe very generously looked after Pierre and went to see him several times at Villejuif. She told Louise that Pierre remembered a school he attended as a child as being a hospital; he mentioned Henriette and their father, whom he described as "a terrifying man." He was sweet and kind and would write to Louise to ask her help to get out.[173]

"He was very tall," Jaffe said. "In the beginning it was difficult, then he got used to me, to my being there. When Louise understood my attachment to Pierre, she ordered me to stop visiting him."[174]

Pierre died in May 1960, at Villejuif. "He [. . .] didn't complain about anything, and in the morning we found he had passed away. He was lying in a normal sleeping position, and neither the nurses on duty in the dormitory nor those sleeping next to his bed heard anything. [. . .] A sum of 6,800 francs was found in his clothes and given to the bursar's office. [. . .] Next of kin have one year to collect it," wrote the nurse.[175]

Henriette told Louise[176] that she had had to bring a sheet and some clothing for their brother's burial; he was very changed, had grown thin, and resembled their father. It was a sad ending, lonely and impoverished, for this younger brother, of whom she had been so jealous and whom she had loved so much. Louise never spoke of her brother or of his internment, but for the rest of her life she kept the legal and medical documents concerning him, as well as his letters and drawings, which, when she saw them later, devastated her.[177] Her ambivalent relationship with psychoanalysis, as with mental illness, no doubt stems from this family trauma.

"The Unconscious Is My Friend"

The analysis is a jip [*sic*] / is a trap / is a job / is a privilege / is a luxury / is a duty / is a duty towards myself / my husband, my parents / my children / is a shame / is a farce.

Louise had a rich and complicated relationship with psychoanalysis, to put it mildly; she denied its role in her life but was so fascinated by it that it completely consumed her for over thirty years.[1] "Have you been through analysis yourself?" she was asked in 1993. "No, but I have spent a lifetime in self-improvement—in self-analysis, which is the same thing."[2]

Suspicious by nature, she resisted becoming dependent on anything. As an artist she also feared losing her inspiration: "The problem was whether or not analysis would interfere with my work by dissolving the necessity of image creation."[3] She later expressed this reticence in an article on Freud: "The truth is that Freud did nothing for artists, or for the artist's problem, the artist's torment—to be an artist involves some suffering. That's why artists repeat themselves—because they have no access to a cure."[4] This negative comment acknowledges both the syndrome of repetition and the inability of psychoanalysis to cure certain problems. "Am sick and tired of Freud and Co," she wrote. "It does not apply to any trouble I know. I do not want to understand. I want to be 'cradled.'"[5] Louise wanted nothing more than to please and to be loved, but she was afraid of transference. Falling in love with her psychoanalyst would only land her with another authority figure to admire and reject, like her father.

From the beginning of her analysis, she was aware of these two problems: where is the boundary between creativity and depression? "Freud says:

art is a form of neurosis. vs. neurosis is a form";[6] how to go about containing these ambiguous feelings for one's analyst? "You are coming to save me, you are a hero. L[owenfeld] on the white horse. [. . .] The confidence and trust and devotion is complete. You have the key to all my problems and now I can be a starfish and sleep in the peace on the sunny sand."[7]

Louise was aware very quickly of the possible attraction she felt toward Lowenfeld: "Another 'falling in love' or showing off for sympathy begins."[8] Her first reaction was rejection, shame, and guilt: "I feel sorry and hate myself at the same time," and, further on: "Forget about L. and try never to see him again. Unpleasant and frustrated memory (Jacques and Richiez)."[9] But then her sense of humor took over and she found a way around it: "L. is not a handsome man anymore. He is no man at all. I have suppressed him as a man (since he did not want me) but he becomes a brain."[10] No longer the hero on horseback, he became just a doctor who might be able to help restore order to Louise's life, who could "clean" and "put in order" her problems. "He is still a hero (without a body)."[11]

Louise would pass through all the contradictory steps of analysis: discouragement, hatred, resentment, hostility. In early February 1952, she wanted to throw in the towel: "I want to stop the analysis, think that it is boring and takes too much of my time. The hours are wrong and I do not want to make an issue of it."[12]

In the beginning, she did not think Lowenfeld was a good psychoanalyst. He was self-important,[13] "he breaks my morale and keeps me from getting well."[14] She was worn out: "you do not want to say anything Dr. L. It is ok. But I am tired of talking."[15] "L. is not a capable doctor. He does not help me or understand or get any good from me. I feel abandoned or rather uncounseled."[16] She dreamed that Lowenfeld had many female patients, and in the dream she thought he showed "a mild and vaguely disguised favoritism [. . .] he stays extra time with me telling me stories because I am sick."[17]

She had frequent morbid fantasies: "Contraption to kill L. several time[s]";[18] "With an absolute decision and coolness I shoot and the bullet goes straight thro[ugh] his heart. The 'cavalier' is L."[19] He appeared in her dreams at the same time as her husband: "On Central Park West I accidentally come upon L. who is having an epileptic seizure. He jumps and twists around like a soul in damnation. I get closer and devour him with my eyes. [. . .] Robert insists on going to see Ferren.[20] He starts to undress in their room. I am ashamed and want to leave when they go to bed."[21] She described a fantasy that involved forcing her way into his home: "I kick out L. and his wife threatening to ruin them if they don't let me stay in the apartment. [. . .] I then begin to examine each room. [. . .] I want to know everything, see everything, control everything."[22] Louise thereby revealed her desire for omnipotence, which also manifested itself through manipulation: "I manipulate them, they do not manipulate me."[23]

She was however also very attached to him. She couldn't bear it when he was away or traveling and desperately resented his abandoning her: "If I was not afraid of the police," she boasted, "I would break your neck."[24]

Final piece of evidence: "The analyst is costing me too much" (*L'analyste me couche* [*sic*] *trop chère*, literally, "The analyst is putting me to bed too expensive/too dear").[25] Quite the Freudian slip, which speaks volumes about her conception of sexuality as well as her relationship to money and, of course, to psychoanalysis!

Lowenfeld

But who was the illustrious Lowenfeld? A fairly unorthodox Freudian, born in Berlin in 1900, analyzed by Otto Fenichel and Sandor Rado. His wife, Yela,[26] was also a psychoanalyst; they met in Munich. He was close to Annie Reich,[27] who was married to Wilhelm Reich and considered to be a Marxist practitioner. He fled Nazi Germany, first to Switzerland, then to Prague, and finally sailed for New York on May 16, 1938, aboard the *Normandie*, the same year as Louise. She could not have found a more attentive listener, given Lowenfeld's particular interest in the relation between art and psychoanalysis (in 1941, he published a paper called "Psychic Trauma and Productive Experience in the Artist")[28] as well as in bisexuality and creativity. However, when he arrived in New York, he returned to mainstream Freudianism and, once the Cold War set in, became disenchanted by communism.[29] Above all, he was a German Jew, like Louise's mother-in-law, rootless like she was, and a humanist who was very sensitive to art and literature.

Louise herself had a good working knowledge of psychoanalytic theory because it was influential not only for the surrealists but for American painters in the 1950s, such as Mark Rothko and Jackson Pollock. She read a number of authors: Otto Rank, Sigmund Freud, Wilhelm Reich, and especially women: Anna Freud, Melanie Klein, Karen Horney, Helene Deutsch, Marie Bonaparte, Maria Montessori, since "Freud has written nothing on women."[30] She kept many books on psychoanalysis in her library[31] but displayed a certain defiance toward them: "Pluses and minuses of readings. Why am I scared of dirtying myself by reading books about psychoanalysis. Fear and mistrust of transference. Jealousy."[32]

What was at stake for her was to learn not only about herself but also about education in general; for a long time she had been interested in child psychology. In the early 1960s, she even applied to New York University with the intention of studying it: "In the last two years I have done considerable reading in the psychology of the arts. I would now like to add a formal training in psychology to the insight into the interpretation of visual forms given me by my personal experience of the last fifteen years. My purpose in undertaking these courses is therefore a double one: 1) To enrich and deepen my own future artistic production. 2) To acquire the necessary theoretical and experimental foundations so that I will be able to find a useful position in the field of diagnostic testing and remedial care of children."[33]

On one book—the appropriately titled *The Divided Self* by R. D. Laing[34]—she noted, prudently: "I do not see any purpose in reading this book." The work of the antipsychiatrist was nevertheless very close to her own preoccupations, if we are at least to judge by their titles. It is striking to see the degree to which the perplexing and unclassifiable *Knots*[35] (1970), a "collection of logical-psychological poems" (according to Félix Guattari), resembles the form and content of her own poetic-psychological writings. She was also reading books about sex,[36] which point to the troubles she was having with Robert, to which she sometimes alluded: "It is the sexual energy my father had and Pierre still has. Robert has very little, Alfred has very little, my mother had very little. Hawkins has a lot (he does things,) but it is displaced. [. . .] Artists in general have a lot. but the flow of it does not seem quite satisfactory. In many cases I know it is quite the opposite of course it is 'the' reason why they have become artists."[37] Later, in the 1970s and 1980s, she read Bruno Bettelheim and Françoise Dolto.

She was an avid reader of literature. "After that awful time I want to read (Proust is a little too detailed and need[s] an attention too concentrated) Virginia Woolf,"[38] with whom she sometimes identified; it was also crucial for Louise to have a "room of her own." She mentions Jean-Paul Sartre as well: "Before falling asleep I read Sartre 10PM *Le Mur* and *La Chambre*."[39] During this period she also read Colette's *Sido* and *La retraite sentimentale* (*Retreat from Love*),[40] as well as Françoise Sagan's *Bonjour tristesse*. All books in which she recognized some part of herself, since they were about childhood or allowed her to project herself into the characters of women in love with their fathers.

In 2004 and 2010, several boxes containing Louise's writings from 1952 to 1966 (loose sheets of paper, but also agenda books) were discovered. These writings, now known as the "psychoanalytic writings," allow us to listen in on her thoughts, feelings, and dreams during this long period of depression and analysis.

She evoked memories, impressions from childhood, analyzing her father's character, and her mother's, reflecting on the nature of their relationship[41] and her contradictory feelings about her parents, her brother, her sister. Her own family is prevalent as well, Robert, the three children, her role as mother, good and bad. Her father appears as immature, tyrannical, miserly,[42] mocking, and charming. He was always away, leching on women, trying to please, talking too much, being hypocritical and authoritarian, and yet everyone adored him. Her mother put up with him in silence. They did not argue; Louise saw her cry only once.[43] She worked hard, was gentle and patient, and accepted her husband's bad behavior. "I inherited," Louise would say, "my mother's rationality but my father's foolish heart."[44] These texts also give a precise outline of her depressive state and her physical pain: the cramps and feeling of vertigo in the center of her stomach, followed by diarrhea,[45] pain in the solar plexus, in the arch of her ribcage, under her sternum.[46] And then there was the insomnia, which would be with her all her life.

She suffered greatly from her dependence on her husband, the burden her children represented, and her difficulty working. How to be a woman, a good wife and mother, and an artist, all at the same time? Several obsessive themes run right through her work: jealousy, anger, guilt, frustration, abandonment, sex. "I am enraged I am the rage the resentment and the hatred I wrote yesterday in my diary—Why?"[47] Her violence often expressed itself as a desire to kill or to kill herself, "in real life I identifie [*sic*] with the victim, in my art I am the murderer."[48]

But the most curious thing is that she constantly performs this self-analysis on paper, which functions as a pendant to her sessions with

Lowenfeld; in these thousands of compulsive, repetitive texts, she writes down each of her thoughts, feelings, dreams, and nightmares, without restraining herself, wanting to say it all, understand it all, analyze it all, control it all. Writing was for Louise a form of exorcism, and had been since her daily practice of keeping a diary in childhood; it was a way of knowing herself, healing from what tormented her by giving it a name. "[T]his danger was coming from within and only this incessant flow of words could keep it at bay if not master it."[49]

During her psychoanalysis, this practice was even more important to her. Words were "transitional objects," said Donald Kuspit.[50] They allowed her to relive her fears, to reactivate the past, to free associate fragments of sensations and violent emotions. "If a word strikes you it is because it relates to a past experience."[51]

Some of the early texts were typed on a typewriter, often at night or when she was alone. These were often addressed to Lowenfeld; she used carbon paper so that she could keep a copy for herself, sometimes sending him the original. The vast majority are handwritten, in a variety of inks, formats, paper types, and so on.[52] Written in a mix of French and English, they indicate the difficulty she felt in finding the right language. This writing practice, which drew on automatism and free association, was fulfilling for Louise in the sense that it allowed her to develop her taste for wordplay, children's songs, and antiquated proverbs, which lent a particular tone to her writings. "[T]he mandrake devours / devours whom. Devours me Melanie Klein / can cope with her—the merry-go-round of Melanie Klein / dictionary page 591 for mandible with a D. / take it apart with a t— / a little game with the dictionary or game / of helter skelter— / note the words that come to mind."[53] Their sessions could also be seen as part of a game, like a play in which Louise and Lowenfeld were acting, a drama in several acts moving from love to rejection to indifference.[54]

Some texts took the form of poetry: lists of fears, incantations, rhyming repetitions. Others were denser and more chaotic, unclear in their associations, but all shedding dramatic light on the way she was torn to pieces by the antagonism of her own psyche, her fight against the disintegration of the self, the symptoms of a paralyzing anxiety, and the violent feelings of aggression and rage, which made her feel guilty. She was caught in a vicious circle, moving ceaselessly from anxiety to aggression and then on to culpability.

These are the confessions of a woman confronted with problems having to do with her identity, the multiple facets of her personality—a particularly sensitive woman, the mother of three, the wife of a prominent art historian, an artist of singular vision, a woman in exile weighed down by her family history. As the years went on, we can see the slow progress of the psychoanalytic work, bringing past trauma to light, reactivating it through memory and relived experience.

God the Father

In the 1950s, with the help of this analytic work, the unconditional and excessive affection Louise felt for her father as a child gave way to a rejection of him. But this belated hostility was also a way of hiding her love for him—a forbidden love, for which she felt guilty. When she was little, she did all she could to be his favorite: "need to be approved of by the Father. My father loves me, I work so that he loves me."[55] She was always on his side: "[I am] the only one who can rightfully stand next to Louis Bourgeois in a picture gallery—Pierre who is off his rocker [*taré*] + my sister belong[s] on my mother's side (proved by their brown hair)."[56]

However, in her psychoanalytic texts and her subsequent declarations, she was extremely lucid, "dissect the psychological anatomy of the father"[57] by listing all of his faults. Louis had no limits or rules, believed he could do as he liked,[58] and did not feel guilty about his absences or about being financially dependent on his wife, whom, according to Louise's uncle Alex, he had married for her money.[59] He was proud of himself for doing his duty in the war, for paying his taxes, for his travels and then his education: "'how good he has been to his children' 'how good he has been he has been to his parents.' how good he has been to his country."[60] Easily flattered, he always fished for compliments and spent money in order to be respected and admired. Although he was proud of the worldly company he kept at the auction houses, he was a "lone wolf,"[61] his only true friends those he had fought alongside. "My father never belonged to the house. [. . .] My father stood as a figure of success in the family."[62]

He had a great deal of respect for self-made men and those who were successful in business and was proud to employ two dozen people: "'At the age of twelve just out of middle school, I was earning a living and was giving everything to my mother.' Later he hated anyone educated. 'They're all high-falutin' good-for-nothings.'"[63]

Louise quickly realized that his love had something unhealthy and incestuous about it. He dressed her as if she were his little mistress; he told her she didn't look after herself enough, she wasn't feminine enough, so he bought her furs, and dresses from famous couturiers, like those he bought for Sadie. "I used to hate everything he bought me. I thought it always was show off and not of my type. It was always for a tramp."[64] Louise, on the other hand, preferred to dress like a studious, independent young woman, with the air of an artist or a saint.[65] A number of ambiguous childhood memories connected with her father nagged at her. The ceremony of slippers and bathrobe and his smell of amber eau de cologne, scratching his back, kissing him on the lips, the jokes he would make with an orange peel,[66] the way he terrorized her during mealtimes: "In the little dining room at Antony, the smallest criticism bothers me. I can't even lift up my head or talk anymore. I can't finish eating my food. Louise is picking at her food, Louise is sulking. We have to give her a tougher personality."[67]

Above all, Louis had certain disturbing habits: "My mother did not see any danger in letting [. . .] my father take me to bed [. . .] at the age [of] 16. She did not object to my father kissing his two daughters on the mouth. In fact she never criticized him for anything."[68]

But though she tried to "kill" her father, she knew she had a need for that sort of guardian figure: "I literally cannot live or function without the protection of a father."[69] "The return to the real father is blocked need of approval from 2nd father."[70] She said she needed to find someone who could help her forget the bad father, the cause of all her pain: "[I] cannot forgive the bad father how am I supposed to grow up well with such a father [. . .] to own a good father enables you to forgive the bad one."[71] But this was only a fantasy: "this new father must be abandoned or renounced because it is the eternal lost cause—the ambivalence about the father uses 2 fathers, the bad old one and the wonderful new [one]."[72]

Her difficult relations with men—which included impossible, unrequited love, sexual frustration, and seduction—stem from this Oedipal source: "your fear of men comes out of your relation to your father."[73] She was afraid that her father would "eat at" her marriage:[74] "when I am well with my father I want to kill my husband; the allegiance or fixation to the father."[75] It also prevented her from fulfilling herself as an artist: "Since he closed for me the door of man-woman relationship[s], and since business means less to me than friendships it is kind of bad. If the windows of creative work are closed too, then it is really bad."[76]

Louise, however, often compared herself to Louis. They had the same weaknesses: the impulse to flee, a lack of confidence, the constant need to be loved and admired, a lack of identity, integrity, dignity. The constant feeling of rejection. But her father was a social success because he was a good businessman and lover, as well as a good communicator. This was not the case for Louise.

The feeling of being rejected made them both like "starfish," an image she used in her writing. "Drama of a completely exposed starfish," a vulnerable, powerless mollusk. "Image of a Starfish. I am a starfish spread out, I cannot be anything but that and anyone can or will step on me. The starfish cannot change itself into a bird can it."[77]

Louise's protective feelings toward her mother counterbalanced this forbidden love. She was jealous of her mother as she had been jealous of Sadie. "It's never my turn— My father and her in Chartres [. . .] My father and Sadie."[78] "Keep me from going in my father's bedroom in 174."[79] She listed her anxieties: "I am afraid of suicide / I am afraid of a divorce / I am afraid of insanity / I am afraid of incest"[80] and described the "incestuous trauma [. . .] I will get myself dressed for a father figure."[81]

We will recall that when her mother died, she literally tried to replace her: "One day my father put me in such despair that I took my mother'[s] place in her bed that no one had ever touch[ed] of course since she had gone. To this day I remember the deep relief and peace it gave me."[82] This usurpation, far from upsetting her, gave her pleasure. Louise's mother deprived her of her father; therefore, in some way, her death left the field wide open. "When my mother did wiggled [*sic*] herself out by dying. I became not only a feared and forbidden sexual object but a victim to be sacrificed for his 'crimes.' Reread *Iphigénie*. To what should a father sacrifice his daughter."[83]

Maman

Joséphine Fauriaux had married an immature young man, an emotional one to boot, because she loved imaginative, adventurous people and admired their courage. But she did not see the risks posed by this excessive feeling and refused to understand the melodramatic situations he provoked, finding them utterly foreign lands—in this respect she was just like Robert.[84] Joséphine regretted not having an education and carried the Académie française's grammar book around the studio with her, reading the pages she had marked with a ribbon.[85] She ruled over the atelier with an iron fist, saying that whores made the best workers because they had expert fingers.[86] She was an impeccable housekeeper, a lover of spotless rugs and shiny parquet. Louise inherited this mania for cleanliness: she had a phobia of dirt and during her depressive spells would spend her time cleaning the house, tidying it up, and putting things away.

Her mother, she said, didn't love Pierre—too lazy—or Henriette, who always lied and never said she was sorry. "She suppressed also her religion that was mild but existent, she also suppressed her social views, she was a follower of Louise Michel. She believed in work and independence for Women, that she taught me."[87] Louise admired her mother's determination, calm, and dignity: "My mother had (or acted as if she had) compassion."[88] She spoke little, Louise recalls, and never complained.

> [. . .] My mother never had a chance to [have] a personal friend, man or woman. He would not have tolerated it. The closest it came to it is Mr. Langard that he threw out like a dog. My mother had no enemy and I never heard her express real resentment though she employed many people. [. . .] She worked for him like a slave, even when she was very sick in Cimiez. She may have been counting to hold him on his inability to form a lasting relationship even with a woman. She said once many come and go but the "wife" remains. At the end once I saw her cry.[89]

Her mother was always a refuge for Louise. "My mother loved me and also she put me at peace."[90] "I used to hold my mother's hand, and I felt then that mine were strong because they had a soothing power."[91] But she would turn against her, finding her castrating: "It's my mother who dispossessed me from my big Father + P."[92] "My mother is the castrating one it is the first time that she appears in this role (Marie Bonaparte and everyone has said it) it is the mother who is castrating the daughter—and it is she who endures rage and revenge as I become a woman I turn against Robert."[93] Whence the numerous dreams in which she appeared like a threat, in which she hated her and killed her. "[T]he horrible J. mother is there looking at me instead of him—I [h]owled in terror though she only looks at me through a little triangle (god's eye)."[94] This allusion to the divine eye and the omnipotent mother shows that the Christian morality of her youth was still very much with Louise, and the triangle is a symbolic trinity that runs throughout her writing.

This was not the only image she attributed to her mother: "then the mother['s] rear end reveal[s] itself moving it is a piece of an enormous monstrous snake."[95] She had to be decapitated: "Decapitation again [of] Maman who after having been cheated on for ten years [. . .]."[96] She would accomplish this symbolically in her sculpture *The She-Fox* (1985).

But Louise was always ridden with ambivalent, contradictory feelings. She was angry with her mother for having tacitly accepted her father's affairs and for having manipulated her: "This is what my mother did. She used me to keep him."[97] Despite this violence—"I think that it is directed against my mother in the past"[98]—she remained attached, emotionally dependent, and complicit. "[B]ut silly you I am not going to love him I simply want to steal him, to dispossess him, and I will come back to you. Both of us we are going to steal him, we are going to eat him. Let's not detach from each other it is a women's pact— My father has betrayed me with other women but my mother has never betrayed me."[99] This cannibalistic desire presaged *The Destruction of the Father* (1974) and fidelity to the mother, the late tribute to "Maman," to whom she called out for help in moments of anguish[100] and whom she will need more and more at the end of her life. "You need a mother. I understand, but I <u>refuse</u> to be your mother because I <u>need</u> a mother myself."[101]

Louise was constantly torn between these two loves and felt deeply culpable as a result: "to eat to kill to devour to come to kill the mother to incorporate the father to take his strength and to be killed as a punishment."[102] Because the mother also represented death: "You know this woman that you call your mother—she really is 'Death' her body is like a wicker basket underneath her dress—I am atrociously flabbergasted to have lived so long without knowing and Thank God without being in conflict with her."[103]

The Mistress

Another source of Louise's jealousy was Sadie, her au pair. She first alluded to her second role in December 1951: "Very young and gay servants; Marthe and Marcelle. Then Sadie who was his mistress as proven to me by Suzanne Lamoine. Is it possible that my mother did not know the obvious, Did she resented [*sic*] it, did she encourage it. Hotel des anges (Le Cannet)."[104]

At this time, Louise appeared to accept the relationship as just one among many, as a fact. She even seemed to feel some compassion. The feelings of betrayal and hatred would come later. "Kill. The killing— The stabbing to death. [. . .] Is it Sadie back of it all[?]"[105] Sadie came to her in an "atrocious dream," dressed in a fox fur: "a tan fox around her neck sends me into a rage and I reproach my father for having made me unfit for married or professional Life. [. . .] I am being jipped [*sic*]. Dream where Sadie + my father do jip [*sic*] me, it is a fact."[106] She became aware of this unhealthy, hypocritical relationship only during the 1950s through her analysis. It was then that feelings of hostility toward Sadie and her father emerged.

On November 15, 1957, she wrote: "Suddenly, I perceived my jealousy and hate of Sadie which was never conscious. I would have to watch this earea [*sic*] of Sadie very carefully because I have never been aware of disliking her. This jealousy was utterly repressed. [. . .] The word Sadie reminds me of nothing except the fact that I was always in good terms [*sic*] with her. I was jealous of her shoes though and my father used to buy her clothes; leather suede jacket; my mother used to like her and be nice to her—that is a fact. Henriette and Suzanne were jealous of her and she Sadie was jealous of me."[107]

An Uncertain, Divided, Multiple Self

Louise was well aware of her mental fragility. She confessed that she was afraid of being mentally unstable, like her brother: "Fear or worry no 1. I have Pierre's trouble and will fall apart slowly and surely. So the sooner the better, and let us be thru with it. No solution."[108]

"Immature, neurotic, psychotic, do not grow, do not love, do not. acceptance of his mate is necessary for change. Idealization of romantic love does not love—mature love is security."[109] She especially suffered from an unhealthy lack of narcissism, which came "in a state of great physical fatigue I become so impressionable that I identify with everything. Incapable of non identification, the self is very weak."[110] Later, she spoke at more length about this fear of depersonalization: "I do not want to forget Louise anymore she is all I have."[111]

She described this fear as being somehow related to a fear of the void: "I do not have to live in an empty world, world of vacuum (Marie Bonaparte). I can create my own artist world of omnipotence + fantasy. I have to control space because I cannot stand emptiness."[112] This fear was also associated with falling: "My early work is the fear of falling."[113] *Mademoiselle Rien,*[114] "empty house"—these themes appear in her writing until the end of her life. "The void anxiety is the only one," she wrote in her diary on March 19, 1986.[115]

She was able to exorcise her fear through graphomania, this daily obsession with filling up pages, darkening the paper, or even, when she was able to move past these crises, through her work as a sculptor: hollowing out, shaping, giving form to the void. Her psychic structure had a fault line that she ceaselessly attempted to fill in. And everything passed through her body: emotions, moods, nerves, anxieties, impulses, desires.

She had no self-love. She was ashamed of her body, hiding and neglecting it. She scraped her hair back into severe chignons, dressed in dark colors, with blouses buttoned to the neck or the pinafores of a good little girl, just as she had done in her youth, when she told herself "I was too fat and ugly and I found peace and relief in the catholic religion that tells you that anything connected with body and flesh is sinful."[116] The feeling of being at fault, being guilty, and having to make sacrifices also comes from the religion that she turned to after her mother's death.

She sometimes called herself a "bluestocking,"[117] as did Robert, for example, in a letter of 1938 telling her he had announced their marriage to his family. It was in response to his sister's concerns,[118] given that a young woman of twenty-six—an intellectual, an artist, and unmarried—was, at that time, already a "spinster."

She was afraid of incest and madness but also of suicide. She often returned to the foundational moment when, provoked by her father's mockery, deep in grief[119] after her mother's death, she threw herself in the Bièvre. "SCENE AT THE RIVER, [...] When the scene at the river is remembered the tenseness (throwing up is such that 2 little papers in the sign of a cross release a refuge and running for help feeling."[120] Louise still sometimes turned to religion when she felt she was at the edge of the abyss.

She felt rejected and unloved and filled with self-doubt, especially during the period when she could not manage to work. "I want to be successful, bought, shown, loved," she wrote at the end of a list of rules to protect her state of mind, her work, her appearance, and her exchanges with other people. "Unsuccessful with gallery colleagues. (Moral indignation and jealousy) complete insomnia."[121]

"Fear no 7. Inability to establish working conditions. Studio, gallery, colleagues."[122]

Making work, however, was the only thing that seemed to save her from her anxiety. "When you do not work you reduce to the size of an insect. Your energy turns into hate. When you work you could run in joy carrying the house on your shoulders."[123] "Anguish, anguish woke me up. I go to the workroom. On the tables there is no room to place anything. the anguish is choking me. I need to tidy up, I need to put things away, my work is not done."[124]

"Eternal Theme of Phallism"

Louise was one of those rare artists who have been able to verbalize their obsession clearly and concretely:[125] "The shame of being dirty has been for me almost as important as the problem of Penis envy."[126] "'If I had a penis' says the little girl 'I could defend myself' laments the little girl. [. . .] If a woman is afraid to be attacked by the penis weapon the little girl wants a penis to defend herself against what—in both cases it is a weapon, offensive or defensive."[127] But thanks to her reading in feminist psychoanalysis—Karen Horney in particular[128]—she quickly understood that the penis is only a symbol and that the desire she felt was for a man's power. In her cannibalistic moments, she hungered for "the fruits of the father" in order to absorb his power.[129] The desire for a phallus went hand in hand with the fear of castration.[130] Louise wanted to be the owner of the phallus and be all-powerful, and feared separation and abandonment. She had all the physical symptoms of hysteria: cramps, heaviness in the stomach, contractions in the diaphragm, diarrhea, insomnia.

Her parents had expected her to be a boy, and as a child, she played at being a tomboy, ill at ease with femininity. But she was still her parents' little girl, manipulated and torn between the two emotional poles of father and mother, adored one moment, detested the next. She had no self-confidence, was self-destructive, and destroyed everything she loved. "My mother is what I am, my father is what I want."[131] Her rejection of femininity persisted in the following years. "Refusal to accept being a woman. [. . .] To be a woman is dangerous."[132]

Jealousy was, for her, an intensely violent passion—"my strongest emotion"[133]—which set in as early as childhood. "I was ferocious about wanting the whole undivided attention of my parents. Was as jealous as a tiger."[134] The rivalry she felt toward her siblings should perhaps be understood in the context of the death of her parents' earlier child. Louise did not speak of it often, and when she did, it was in contradictory terms,[135] but it surely impacted her mother's mental health as well as Louise's relationship with her mother: Joséphine's unconscious guilt, depression, and fragility had an enormous emotional effect on Louise. In 1959, she considered this: "I wished and feared death [. . .] I was always afraid to die—identification with a dead sister."[136] But she was able to turn this repressed trauma into a source of creativity. "[T]he other fellow is getting the thing I want, it makes you see red, ready for anything. Gushing of hate, and destructive impulse. The creative energy seems to be related to that gushing of emotional force slightly diverted by a soothing hand. [. . .] That reassurance which transforms the hate into work, may come from a certain amount of past success, or a 'certitude' of attaining some may be a form of being wanted."[137]

Her feelings of abandonment began at birth and were firmly entrenched after her father went off to war. But later, it was she who abandoned her family: "The abandonment of Papa by Louise, of Pierre by Louise, of Henriette by Louise who doesn't even write to her. The abandonment of the shop which was so important to Papa. During all of last week I felt 'deserted.'"[138] "I have felt guilty about my having abandoned my father."[139] Her proclivity for self-destruction, which had set in during adolescence, only strengthened: "Destruction of the loved object = visible of sadism vs. masochism. Destruction of what you loved most is a way to appease of guilt feeling [*sic*]."[140] When the child cannot blame its parents, it takes the blame for itself and thinks it needs to pay the price.

Years later, Louise would recognize a criminal impulse within herself, as well as her predilection for cruelty: "It's in the blood [*l'appel du sang*], it's the uncontrollable need to totally destroy [things.] [. . .] The sadist in me comes out in my unhealthy attraction to velvet-eyed men [*yeux de velours*]."[141] She claimed to be at the same time victim and executioner: "Don't forget the masochist loves a sadist and the sadist loves the masochist."[142]

Good Mother, Bad Mother

Her feelings toward her sons were equally possessive and ambiguous. Of Jean-Louis, she said: "when I saw that he was escaping me (Jean-Louis) I wanted to possess his friend—I have deprived him of his friend and I appropriated him."[143] She also noted earlier that she was incapable of "establish[ing] reasonable and peaceful" relations with him.[144]

She knew Michel had problems, that he had a difficult time adapting: "Michel is a second Pierre as shown in his drawings, behavior, appearance. Michel took Pierre's place. when I 'abandoned' the older. No solution."[145] When Michel came home from boarding school on the weekends, it created tension in the household, from which she sometimes preferred to take refuge in bed rather than fleeing and never coming back.[146] She even imagined Robert and the boys enjoyed her crises because they put her in a position of dependency, though they were also terrified by them. But the last thing she wanted was to hurt them, and she tried to make herself useful.

As for calm, placid Alain, he was too much like Robert and therefore like her mother, and that annoyed Louise more than anything.[147]

She loved them ferociously, though: "The children have long ago realized that I love them as much or more tha[n] they could ever [have] dreamed of being loved and they are not afraid and enjoy to see [*sic*] how far they push me. Robert too."[148] Louise—a depressed and anxious mother—feared the insistent demands her children made on her and preferred to stay in bed once she had fulfilled her maternal obligations—which she did all the same.[149]

A mother's love could extend as far as murder, she wrote, casting herself in the role of a twentieth-century Medea. On December 31, 1951, as her "crisis" was beginning, Louise wrote a strange narrative and addressed it to Lowenfeld, whom she had not yet begun seeing regularly.[150] In it she described being shut up in the house and ridding herself of her children, Jean-Louis and Alain, either by killing them or by sending them away. In this project she was in perfect harmony with Michel, who understood her despite the "gravity of the situation." She tells him she loves him most of all: "everyone always loved you," which calms him: "His twitched little face relaxed." But then he refused to take care of his brothers the way Louise had asked him to. "No it is your job," he replied. This story, which she called "the drama," is suggestive of a murder: "I tried to kill them is [*sic*] self-protection." She reveals a great psychic fragility: "These pages are a call for help."[151] The allusion to Medea, who in some versions of Greek mythology devoured her children, often returns in her dreams and her writings: "Medea / worse revenge than suicide / end of analysis."[152] However her husband, she wrote, was a dependable person, responsible, perfectly sane, intelligent, and well-intentioned: "he has the extraordinary and unique privilege of making me sink straight down into the kind of despair that makes me a dangerous person. I say that he is unique because left alone in my living cell that includes my three children I am able to function [. . .] I wish someone will make him understand that for the good of his family he is temporarily asked to leave."[153]

In the face of this inescapable reality, stuck with her children and her husband, unable to find the time and space in which to work, she thought often of fleeing, identifying once again with her father, who neglected the family home.

The Husband

Louise often talked about divorce and separation during this period. She needed to be alone to be able to work, a "room of her own" in which to do so. But she was well aware of the financial problems that that would pose, as much for herself as for her children. She looked askance at her marriage: "R[ober]t has married me because I was not a Jew. Never looked at my work, explained nothing of his position in America, went into marriage blind folded—woke up later. Neme[sio Antúnez] likes me because I was French. [. . .] We live in a state of passive resistance which holds no less hostility for being silent."[154] She notes, as well, their different backgrounds and educations: "I was brought up as considering money as an end in itself. Robert was brought up as considering money as a mean[s]."[155] And she expresses a desire to be free: "against Robert, [I] want a job."[156]

"Conflict over the gallery—a stronger ego would give me courage [. . .]. Inferiority complex. The independence necessary is seen as a drive away from R[ober]t."[157]

Robert was very supportive of her analysis, which we know not only because he sometimes accompanied her to Lowenfeld's office but especially because he paid for it. This brought back feelings of dependence from childhood: "This refusal to grow up was expressed by my wanting Robert to pay for my analysis."[158] Lowenfeld would call Robert in to see him, whether to make a communal decision about a proposed trip to Europe in 1952 or to discuss their marital problems: "Robert goes to L. [. . .] there [do] not seem [to be] any physical obstacles to our sleeping together. Robert calls L. about a name."[159]

Robert was taciturn, impersonal, unreachable, and would say nothing after evenings with friends, offering no commentary at all: "What enrages [me] is R.['s] inability to talk, to tell [a] story to interest me."[160] She also reproached him for having no authority over the children, since he was always busy with work.

He also appeared in Louise's dreams, identified with her mother. "[T]he deep disturbance is against Robert (mother figure)."[161] "To blame R[ober]t for leaving me in the dark—it is to blame Maman for not telling me what I wanted to know: not instructing me, not telling me what was going on."[162]

He was a calm and reassuring presence. But could he be mother, father, and husband all at once? Louise described their sexual problems several times: "Fear no. 5. Inability to reach intimacy with Robert, sexual problem. Also am ashamed of R[ober]t being my scapegoat."[163]

Louise also thought he was turned on by the fear of her violent outbursts;[164] this fed her ambivalent feelings about him, which moved from rejection to the need for reassurance.

But despite this discord (which was above all a reflection of the discord with her father), Robert was a rock-steady source of support for Louise, especially during this long depression. He answered professional correspondence on her behalf, played go-between with Erick Hawkins, galleries, and museums, even took care of shipping her work. He believed in her and did all he could to restore her self-confidence.

"Psychoanalysis Is My Religion"

The 1950s were thus a critical turning point for Louise.[165] As she turned forty years old, she lost her beloved father but found in Lowenfeld both a stand-in and a means of reorienting herself, which helped her overcome this serious depression and especially to begin working again in the early 1960s. After a period of some years during which she felt completely impotent, she began to develop a new kind of sculpture, leaving behind the rigidity of wood and turning to more supple and liquid material such as plaster and latex, creating more plastic forms with emphatic sexual connotations.

Louise became aware that she was beginning to locate the place where her work and her analysis came together. "What belongs to the sculptor and what belongs to her psychoanalyst?"[166] Early in her analysis, she noted: "I have a strong impulse to 'make a figure usual size 5 ½ feet' on the workbench in a material soft like a woven material the word mattress came to mind FROM material no doubt. And to wrap up said figure in string. The roasted filets of my youth were wrapped in string. This figure I feel myself drawn to make is going to dissolve or appease my anxiety."[167]

Drawing, too, had a restorative power: "Untangle hair, clarify, put in order. Rake. Make braids. Weave. Make skeins. Tidy-up. Make peace and order and rest. The lines are flexible and do not cross. Sensibility. Neither force nor conflict."[168] It was calming and soothing; it helped tend her wounds, put aside obstacles, find protection.

During this decade she and Robert traveled to Paris every other summer, beginning in 1953. Louise had difficulty coping with the dichotomy between these two artistic milieux, which were more and more divergent and competitive. She grieved what was lost: the houses that were no longer there, France, childhood, the past. Analysis became a means of working through grief, rooting around in the past in order to cut herself off from it.

Writing and analysis occupied all of her energies; she was completely committed to it, on an intellectual and emotional level as well as a therapeutic one. When she declared that she was no longer undergoing an analysis but was performing a self-analysis, we must understand that none of her symptoms had disappeared, that she was suffering as much as before. The talking cure had not completely worked, given that she would not shed her aggressive power or the emotion brought back by the past; rather, they would feed her creativity. "I need my memories. They are my documents. I keep watch over them. They are my privacy and I am intensely jealous of them."[169] The first part of this phrase later reappeared in another format, embroidered on a French mail sack placed on the bed in one of her first *Cell* installations (*Cell I*, 1991).

As Juliet Mitchell rightly notes,[170] she did not "have" an analysis, she "used" it, she made use of it. Or as Mignon Nixon writes, she treated psychoanalytic theory as an object to be manipulated, like her sculpture, just as she saw other people as potentially useful objects. Lowenfeld was an object.[171]

"Why did I need so long with L.—ask him if it is customary to have to write down dreams + recall like these pages. it is very time consuming but it gives me the 'joy of creation' that I used to have after working. Beside[s] I build up strength. The result is not 'art' useless except as a catharsis."[172]

Louise saw art and therapy as linked, because for her psychoanalysis did not breed dependence, or the destruction of her creative capacities, but allowed for self-knowledge and the achievement of total freedom. She was able to turn her troubles into "psychic material."[173]

What made her artistic practice so unique was that it was fed by the primitive impulses of her unconscious. Very few artists have gone so far in the precise study of their psychic functions or the construction of their identity, and the path that led her from profound depression and suicidal ideation to the Oedipal complex would in the 1960s produce decisive work, which in part resulted from the analytic process.

However, we must be careful not to read her work solely through the lens of psychoanalysis. Not only does her work signify far beyond any interpretive approach, as the multiple readings she herself performed of it suggest, but because she crafted the narrative of her life in such a way that it perfectly fit the textbook definition of the Oedipal complex, we must be on our guard. Perhaps we need an anti-Oedipal approach? What might a pre-Oedipal stage look like? The detailed study of her neuroses and fantasies has much more to do with the history of psychoanalysis than the history of art. What is useful to us here is the possible relationship between cure and creativity. During the 1950s and into the 1960s, her unconscious served as an echo chamber for the Freudian model; instead of being able to work, she overinvested in fantasies, dreams, and sensations and devised her own narratives. Her relationship to the father she adored and abhorred, the love and hatred for the mother, desire for the phallus and for castration—these were as much imaginary models as lived situations, repetitive patterns that became the raw material for writing and sculpture. Her excess of feeling and her extreme artist's sensitivity lend a passionate intensity to her psychoanalytic writings. It was a question of her unmastered interior chaos, of her "volcanic unconscious."[174] When she again became capable of giving it form, after 1960, her art freed her from impotence, though not from the invasive symptoms which were, after all, so necessary to her.

Louise described herself as fierce, fragile, a killer, constantly torn between antagonistic polarities, and her personal drama tapped into universal, archaic myths. "A chthonic art," as the Lacanian psychoanalyst Paul Verhaeghe called it,[175] which travels from the edges of time carrying with it all its violence and ambivalence; she was closer to the Magna Mater, the phallic woman, and Baubo's laugh[176] than conventional Freudian mythology because she never lost her sense of humor. Part of her work always escapes interpretation, although she admitted that a psychoanalytic interpretation didn't bother her because it was a scientific approach.[177] Her art was a desperate attempt to represent or give form to something unrepresentable; she brought material to life in a symbolic and not a narrative fashion. "For me, sculpture is the body. My body is my sculpture,"[178] she later said, disappearing behind her work: "I don't have an ego. I am my work."[179]

Louise was "sly [*maline*]";[180] she had a profound sense of humor: "life is so funny. Life is so ridiculous."[181] She deconstructed all patterns and archetypes; whereas her art is completely controlled, it finds its source not only in her unconscious and her feelings but also in her deep knowledge of art history.

The Organic Refuge, 1960–1970

A lair is a refuge, but sometimes, a refuge can be a trap if there are not two exits. This is not one of my fears. I do not expect to be trapped.

The change in Louise's art and life in the early 1960s was radical. She was evolving a new plastic vocabulary that was the opposite of the wooden figures of the previous decade, although certain themes, such as those of the house or the body, remained consistent. "There also has been a similar gradual change from rigidity to pliability," she noted, "and a change from upright verticality to spiral forms and structures that open up within an enveloping skin to reveal internal rhythms."[1]

After attempting to rid herself of homesickness by "standing up" people from the past, Louise needed to create a new home, to take refuge inside of a nest, to build herself a protective shelter. This search for interiority, profound and subterranean, was no doubt one of the results of her analysis. From now on, Louise began to explore the realm of the maternal, a theme to which she would fully devote herself in later decades. "[R]eturn to the mother. yesterday in my sculpting I made drawings of breasts pressed against each other; there was a double attitude to be like a mother and liked by a mother."[2] She would also use these "part objects" to explore ambivalence about gender, which is one of the essential components of her identity.

This evolution from outside to inside space necessarily called for a change of material and technique. She gave up using wood, which had to be stripped or hollowed out and which she found too rigid and short-lived, and turned to plaster or latex: liquid, supple, malleable materials, which were better suited to the organic subject matter she was exploring. "[A]ll the shapes have in common the fact that originally they were poured, and could be obtained only through that process."[3] "I am not interested in materials," she said, "they are simply a tool: which does not mean that I don't respect materials; plaster, for example, is a substance which has much to give to whoever works with it. If you pour your plaster, the plaster will take form [*le plâtre va travailler*], it will settle [*il va s'installer*] from liquid to solid, it has a life of its own, independent of the sculptor. Plaster and cement move, and offer no resistance; they enable a dialogue."[4] She no longer worked by subtraction but by addition, moving from a central core out to the periphery. This turn to flexible, organic forms is the counterpoint to the rigid, monolithic geometry of the vertical constructions. Louise's art always oscillated between two opposing poles, whose emblematic figure was the femme maison, a hybrid of architecture and flesh.

This central motif took a variety of shapes—a nest or a den, animal dwellings which confirm the original, savage aspect of this work. The nest is, according to Bachelard, "the image of a simple house [...] the natural habitat of the function of inhabiting."[5] The inside of the nest imposes its form; it is a house built by the body for the body. Bachelard quotes Jules Michelet: "'The instrument that prescribes a circular form for the nest is nothing else but the body of the bird. It is by constantly turning round and round and pressing back the walls on every side, that it succeeds in forming this circle.'" "What an incredible inversion of images!" Bachelard comments. "Here we have the breast created by the embryo."[6] The dens—what Louise called *Lairs*—are the result of internal pushing, of modeling from the inside.

The experimental nature of the early plaster works—*Spiral/Summer* (1960), *Maison* (1961), *Labyrinthine Tower* (1962), *Lair* (1962)—signal the direction her sculpture would take. Here, the spiral—a constant theme in Louise's work—is made of a metal thread rolled back on itself and covered with plaster. "The spiral is an attempt at controlling the chaos," she said. "It has two directions. Where do you place yourself, at the periphery or at the vortex? Beginning at the outside is the fear of losing control; the winding in is a tightening, a retreating, a compacting to the point of disappearance. Beginning at the center is affirmation, the move outward is a representation of giving, and giving up control; of trust, positive energy, of life itself."[7] Louise presents the spiral as a dialectic between activity and passivity, a metaphor for her personality. "Torn by opposites of violence and tenderness— The sculpture twisted is violence [. . .] in one piece the inside is violent the surface is peaceful and enveloping."[8] Spirals also feature in a number of drawings from these years. "The drawings express the feminine tender aspect."[9]

The layered sausagelike forms suggest entrails: they appear in a latex sculpture, made by rolled-up intestinelike forms with a strongly scatological connotation. In her 1965 diary she wrote, "Sea of faces versus sea of faeces,"[10] as if referring to pieces like *Lair* (1963).

The standing, but somewhat leaning, *Labyrinthine Tower* (1962) is a forerunner of the phalli to come, as well as the implicitly sexual aspect of the sculptures she made in the late 1960s; but here, the phallus is fragile; it leans and looks as if it might fall over. Its form and ambiguity recall Brancusi's famous *Princesse X*.

Louise was moving in two opposite directions: one animalistic, made of twists and contortions, of visceral spillages, resulting in work in which the hand of the artist is very much present, as in the overlapping finger grip of *Clutching* (1962); and another more rational and geometric, like the simplified house which is a counterpoint to the organic work. "I think these methods preserve the fusion of geometric and organic forms which interests me."[11] The small-format sculpture *Maison* (1961) confirms Louise's interest not only in architecture and mathematical precision but also in the home, the dwelling, which was one of her obsessions.

In 1962, Louise and Robert moved once again, to a tall, narrow brownstone at 347 West Twentieth Street. At this time Chelsea was a working-class neighborhood, in pretty shabby condition, inhabited mainly by Puerto Rican immigrants. The meat market was close by; Louise liked to stroll there and talk to people. Her studio was on the garden level, below it the basement foundation was set with large, round stones, and there was a small garden backing catty-corner onto a schoolyard, which enabled her to plant trees and prune them and to listen to the children shouting; across the street stood the brick tower of Saint Peter's Church. She would stay there for the rest of her life.

"The Diseases of the Femininity"

This return to making art was accompanied by certain developments in her analysis.[12] Louise still suffered from attacks of anxiety, rage, and aggression, but she had begun to accept and understand the ambivalence of her relationships. Her depression was "connected with my father on the analytical situation—the rage is connected with my mother."[13] "Robert is suddenly cast in a new role— Instead of being a taboo brother figure—he becomes a mother figure."[14] But in discovering this, she also believed it was unfair to assign him the role of mother. Louise realized she had trouble growing up, leaving childhood behind and accepting her femininity: "Now that I am no longer physically suicidal, I direct my attack against Robert and am in despair over it— The question is what do I hate is it to be a woman / to have been jipped [sic] by being a woman / to be jipped [sic] / to have lost at the game, the big game."[15] She acknowledged a feeling of inferiority—"you are nothing since you are only a woman"[16]—which she explained as a form of castration: "when a man is present, I'm different and I feel castrated, I feel something is missing and it makes me uncomfortable."[17]

Her relationship to her father wavered between love and hate: "I was never conscious of the hate I had for my father until today," she wrote on February 26, 1960.[18] Her feeling of guilt was in fact linked to sexuality: "there is no more guilt because there is no more sex [. . .] I want to go back to darkness and warmth—to bed," she wrote, in a state very close to depression.[19] Later, about her return to Paris in 1964, she noted: "during this trip [. . .] I was no longer as afraid to love my father and that consequently the guilt or remorse is lighter."[20] And much later, she realized: "I am not my father."[21]

She was still susceptible to outbursts of violence and inclined to "destroy what is most dear to me—my husband—and my work."[22] The threat of self-destruction forever hovered nearby: "It is failure—I spoil a plaster piece wide metal electric shade is poured in—cheese cloth, burlap, impossible to separate from the mold. I persist, nothing works, rage (of the helpless) finally I break the tools, the mold, plaster is everywhere from the floor to my hair and my throat—I have to give up, renounce, pay for the damage."[23] It is clear that the return to work, although a sign of health, was not always peaceful. It never would be. Doubt, a lack of self-belief, the fear of showing her work, and the fear of success would persist for years, even during rich periods of creation.

After regretfully closing her little bookshop due to financial difficulties, she looked for new occupations in teaching and studying.[24] In 1960, she taught for a year in a public school in Great Neck, on Long Island, then in 1961, she took classes at New York University (School of Arts and Sciences), including "Evolution of French Theater from the Renaissance to Symbolism" and "Currents of Fifteenth-Century French Painting," two subjects about which she was passionate and in which she excelled.[25] She would teach for many years; it was a way of getting out of her head and building relationships with other people. It also permitted her to make some money, thus becoming less dependent on Robert. In 1963, she taught at Brooklyn College, and then again in 1968.

In the draft of her application to NYU, Louise composed a biographical note in which she emphasized her training in psychology: "In recent years, thinking about my own problems as an artist, and discussing them with other artists, I have become more and more interested in understanding the psychology of art, and it is in this direction that I now wish to resume my formal academic training."[26]

In the summer of 1961, Louise returned to Europe with Robert, first to London and then to Paris, where she met the poet Henri Michaux on June 12 at his home at 16, rue Séguier.[27] Louise was still eager to learn, to develop her intellectual capabilities, alongside her creative work. The name Michaux features regularly in her writing.[28] He interested her because of his own experience of violence and suffering but also because he was both a painter and a poet. In particular, Louise asked him if he started painting because he couldn't write or because the effects of the drugs prevented him from concentrating.

Something "Repellent"

In 1964, eleven years after her last solo show at the Peridot Gallery, Louise finally had her own exhibition at the Stable Gallery:[29] *Louise Bourgeois: Recent Sculpture*. She showed, among other works, *Labyrinthine Tower* (1962), *Double Negative* (1963), *Lair* (1963), *Lair* (1962–63), *Rondeau for L.* (1963) and *Fée couturière* (1963). At the same time, she showed drawings at the Rose Fried Gallery. The shock was palpable: the sculptures were found to be strange and troubling, surprising those who saw them:

When the January, 1964 exhibition at the Stable Gallery opened, brilliantly installed by Arthur Drexler, it was as disturbing to those who recalled the artist's earlier work as it was to those unacquainted with her past. Radically transformed, the techniques and forms appeared to reverse outward manifestations. It was as if an old acquaintance once darkly lean, elegant and aloof, had come back from a long journey transformed: fleshy, chalky, round and organic. These new sculptures seemed to have the capacity to quiver and ooze. No longer would one immediately associate them with figures; no longer did their scale appear analogous to our own. [. . .] The effect of this exhibition was not ingratiating for the work was powerful but rather repellent. It exerted much the same fascination as an aching injury, demanding an effort from us, drawing our concentration.[30]

This "aching injury" had an obvious sexual connotation, especially when applied to a mouth- or vaginalike fleshy brown latex sculpture (*Le regard*, 1963). The big drops or suspended sacs in the *Lair* sculptures had openings which allowed one to glimpse their internal structure, the hidden tunnels and subterranean passages which transformed the viewer into a voyeur. These nests expressed at once the violence of retreat and the imprisonment and tenderness of protection.

Fée couturière[31] was named after a kind of bird, which echoes the dominant theme of the nest. "The *Fée couturière* is a little bird. The title was in French from the start. It's a room where there are holes, several floors, and it's like a labyrinth. You can put your hand inside and we don't know where the entrance is, or the exit. It's a bird's nest suspended from a tree. At the top there is a hook and the piece can spin. It was shown at the Musée Rodin (by the way the garden of the Musée Rodin is very welcoming and it's very agreeable to show there)."[32] The title also, more obliquely, referred to Louise's mother, who was associated with the work of a seamstress and whom we will again encounter as a spider and repairer.

Another piece, *The Quartered One* (1964–65), was a reference to carcasses suspended in a butcher shop. It resembled a piece of meat waiting to be chopped up. There are square or rectangular openings in the front which suggest windows and doors, and it has two "pockets" on either side. These motherly forms sometimes resemble parts of the human body, a way of evoking the fragmented self. In *Inner Ear* (1962), Louise explores the cavelike space with its complicated system of thin membranes. Hearing was for her one of the most crucial senses, as she would later show in the enormous marble ear paired with a gong, in *Cell IV* (1991).

This journey to the inside of the body would yield almost anatomical sculptures, which speak to her longtime interest in medicine: "But my body becomes material—and I express what I feel through it."[33] In *Torso, Self-Portrait* (1963–64), Louise presents a ribbed spinal column like a stem and its leaves, flanked on top and at the bottom by breasts and buttocks. The plaster is white, like bones. A similar anatomical structure appears in a drawing of 1968. Most of the sculptures explore the relationship between external and internal space, between the skin and the skeleton. Louise was attempting to give form to the formless, at once inside and on the surface; she was interested in the reversibility of forms: "is there such a thing as a one piece mold (yes a glove or a rabbit skin) turn[ed] inside out[?]"[34]

These new works appeared ten years after the beginning of her analysis. Louise referred to Lowenfeld in *Rondeau for L.* (1963), which may have also been called *Rondeau du soir;* it was a small plaster sculpture, cast in bronze, and constructed by coiling circular forms that looked like a wave or long, curved fingers around an empty center. The title was taken from a traditional Gascon dance of the fifteenth century, which was danced in circles or in an open chain and which had a repetitive rhythm.[35] The endless movement of the interminable analysis: this baroque excrescence echoes Rodin in its crude treatment of surface. It is also a robust tribute to the man who was helping her navigate and survive the chaos of the unconscious. Working with this material, clay or plaster, allowed her to concentrate, to grab hold of the outside world by building connections between herself and others: "Sculpture is the others or rather clay is the others and the sculptor is the ego. These are concrete and precise situations."[36]

The fleshy brown latex *Portrait* (1963), which belonged to her friend Arthur Drexler (now in the MoMA collection), is a segment of entrails nailed to the wall, viscera revealed, a flayed figure, the skin of Marsyas, which can also be found in the later bronze *Rabbit* (1970). These two sculptures can be seen as self-portraits and describe her suffering and soul searching better than she could. She still wrote in her diaries about the way she did not feel loved, but she made some progress in terms of "the Relearning of Dignity [...] I would like to be able to love myself somewhat. It seems to me that it is around this that tolerance of the other starts. Like a dumbo I think I am going to cry."[37] She explained her mental fragility in terms of her repressed sexuality and castration complex: "my garments and especially my undergarments always have been a source of intolerable suffering because they hide an intolerable wound."[38]

Critics of the time were aware of how radical and original her practice was. Only Michael Fried seems not to have admired it. He claimed that the work was "bereft of both formal intelligence and expressive content," with the exception of *Rondeau for L.*, which was, for him, the most successful piece.[39] Daniel Robbins wrote the first real analysis of Louise's art.[40] He was impressed by the singularity of her work, which was very much not in line with most of the art of the time. Louise was, for him, an "puzzling artistic phenomenon."[41] She created a world all her own, based on her emotions, her intimate natural knowledge (nests, earth, landscapes), of the body and its anatomy. Whether it was a question of drawings with vegetal connotations, as in *Eccentric Growth* (1960) or *Concentric Growth* (1965), or a variety of udders, hills, and breasts—all these lumps and bumps that compulsively fill up the pages of her drawings—Louise explored motifs of germination and birth, the world of fertility. This tendency could be seen in the work of some surrealists and would be developed by sculptors such as Ferber, Lipton, and Roszak, but Louise's work was different[42] because it was exploring the potential of these organic forms in a very personal way.

William Rubin also noted this specificity, asking Louise about Robbins's declaration that she was "not connected to the New York world" and if she felt any affinity with contemporary American sculptors or other artists exploring similar themes.[43] She replied: "I do not feel any affinity with the sculptors you name," and said that "the theme of eclosion appears in a piece called *Spring* that was shown in the Peridot Gallery in 1950." The only artist who might have unconsciously influenced her, she said, was Arp, whom she admired and found very likable. She met him in 1960, in New Canaan, Connecticut.

Unlike the critics, Louise perceived a strong link between her recent sculptures and those from the late 1940s and 1950s: "They have the same simplicity. Instead of being 'phallic' as in the past, the recent sculptures are in the shape of spirals; so instead of having a linear direction they have a circular or spiral direction. [...] Whether these works are of the figure type (upright), or of the cocoon type, they obey this law of immediacy, a desire to stand for something, to be positive; or perhaps the contrary, to retreat into something."[44]

Return to Paris, 1965

In May 1964, Robert and Louise traveled to Athens, Lisbon, and Paris. Before her solo show at the Stable Gallery, Louise had taken part in an exhibition of American sculpture at the Claude Bernard Gallery in Paris (from September 30 to October 31, 1960) with Louise Nevelson, Isamu Noguchi, David Smith, and others, then in 1962 in a show of female artists at Mount Holyoke College in Massachusetts. But the most important show for her was at the Musée Rodin in 1965: *États-unis: Sculpture du XXe siècle,* curated by René d'Harnoncourt, the director of MoMA in New York. Held in the chapel and the garden of the museum, the exhibition was conceived to show the evolution and specificity of American sculpture ranging from the days of Gaston Lachaise, William Zorach, and Elie Nadelman up to the most recent trends. Louise also took part in the *Salon de la Jeune Sculpture* (Young Sculptors' Salon), curated by Denys Chevalier, which was also held at the Musée Rodin. She showed the bronze versions of *Spring* (1948–49) and *Sleeping Figure* (1950), and the plaster *Fée couturière* (1963), with the last hanging from a tree. For this trip in 1965 she decided to stay in Paris for a month on her own (from April 22 to May 21). She turned down Henriette's invitation to stay in Antony—she found her sister a bit invasive—and stayed instead at the Hôtel de l'Avenir, at 65, rue Madame. In her small, peaceful room under the zinc rooftop, lit by a camp lamp, Louise lived and drew like a young student, eating saucisson, chocolate mousse, oranges, and milky tea,[45] and sometimes a good choucroute. At those times she felt "like a queen."[46] It was cold and rainy in Paris; she never left the house without being "bundled up like an onion."[47]

It was the first time she had gone to France without Robert,[48] and this trip, made for professional reasons—the installation of her work at the Musée Rodin, visits to foundries to cast her little plaster models in bronze, contacting galleries, and visiting museums—was a lonely ordeal, a constant battle against anxiety and depression. She kept track of her difficulties and her often negative impressions in a notebook[49]; but she wrote Robert regularly, long, rational letters in which she describes Parisian life in detail, asking after the children and the cats, Champfleurette and Tyger, as well as the house. These parallel writings—the diary and the letters—are so different in their form and content that we can see how divided Louise was between duty, the desire to please Robert by showing him how capable she was of getting on by herself, and the anxiety that overcame her when she remembered something from childhood and was plunged back into her obsession with the past. However, this time it seemed as if "the past ha[d] disappeared." She could visit the places she had loved—the Luxembourg Gardens, the Lycée Fénelon, Saint-André-des-Arts, her student housing, Antony, Clamart, the shop—and she no longer felt the "constant impossibility to be moved." No doubt because "the desire to recall the past was too strong and invaded the conscience." She described her sensations: "At the Café de Flore, I feel nothing, I am bored, I wait for it to end." And: "I am bored, everything is a drag, it is not my fault. I would like to talk to people, be able to look at them and to listen to them. I think 'so what' a subject of the past and yet I know that the past will take its revenge and that I will think in the future, how lucky you have been to go back to Paris and you haven't done anything with it."[50]

This trip was not like the others. "Paris is the city of my father, he is there at every step: the statue of Diderot that he liked, his neighborhood, his trees, his public bench, his Petit Saint-Benoît, his Champs-Elysées which I missed this time—also his distaste for misery and poor people."[51]

All the familiar places let her down, except those linked to Robert: the rue de Médicis, the Pons patisserie.[52] And it was also for the love of Robert that she tried to return to a normal social life, to see people, to work: "Will I be able to do what Rob[er]t expects from me. It makes me sick today."[53] She was aware how lucky she was and wanted to take advantage of this time, whatever it took. She saw her friend Paulette Place, her sister, Henriette, Jacqueline Delange,[54] Denys Chevalier, Hélène Kamer,[55] and especially Shirley Jaffe, her former tenant in the rue Daguerre. She asked if Shirley was angry with them about the lawsuit they'd had to file about the sublet and conflicts over the cost being too high. In spite of this dispute, they remained close and saw one another often. "I was very pleasant and she will come to *La Jeune Sculpture*."[56] Shirley's studio, in the rue Daguerre, had been completely renovated—it was painted white and was lovely. As for Louise, she was trying to buy an atelier-apartment. She visited a number of places, including the studio of a sculptor called Hilquily, but none of them were what she was looking for. She was also trying to find an inexpensive foundry for a bronze of her *Fée couturière*. Someone mentioned Batalia in Milan, but she didn't have time to visit during this short trip.

This Parisian stay yielded a dalliance which she called "the Boulton affair."[57] She met Patrick Boulton on the boat, and "in my solitude," she wrote, "I stayed close to Boulton."[58] She didn't dare to act on the flirtation and couldn't admit it was happening, but it still bothered her; she didn't write to him, so as not to appear clingy, but she desperately waited for him to call.[59]

Louise, who could not stand an unfaithful husband, set herself a rule that she could not go near a married man. But Patrick Boulton was "neither a poof nor married";[60] she was willing to do anything to attract his attention—such as writing him charming letters or inviting him to coffee. But in the end, she let it go, out of pride, though it did sting: "After 'The Renunciation' of P. B. I am so tired that I cannot walk on the boulevard Raspail. What I did to satisfy my vanity (libido) I would not be able to do today for one million [dollars]."[61] She had also realized that Boulton wasn't worth it: "P. B. has revealed himself in turn to be a worthless person and the only trouble in this whole affair is that I did not realize the danger."[62]

She continued to experience attacks of depression and anxiety in Paris: "I am going to pass from the Strength Zone to the No Strength Zone. The passage is a sudden worry extremely fortuitous with perspiration on the forehead—suddenly I do <u>not want</u> anything any longer."[63] She went on filling up her diaries and her letters to Robert with an abundance of complicated feelings: jealousy, shame, and betrayal regarding her father, guilt at having abandoned her family, her envy of her cousin Jacques who had bought a house at Montchauvet, Henriette's complaints, and frustration with Germaine, who inherited a sum of money after finding her father's "jewels" in the basement of the shop (Bourgeois planned to give a gold and diamond signet ring to Michel).[64] But although she was reexperiencing these attacks of violence and terror which made her shake like a leaf, they "only last an hour instead of drowning me."[65]

She read Wilhelm Reich, William James, and, on board the boat, Benjamin Péret, *La légende de l'Amérique du Nord*, Borges, *L'officiel du mode*, and

Françoise Gilot's book on Picasso, which she found "interesting but very poorly written unfortunately."[66]

Her letters to Robert were as tender as ever—"My dear little one, I embrace you and love you," as were Robert's to her: "My darling, your husband who loves you." They attest to the closeness of their relationship and their love and understanding during this period.

The installation of her sculptures in the garden of the Musée Rodin went well, although Louise wrote that the plaster sat outside for three days in the rain[67] and that it required an enormous machine to suspend it from the branch of a flowering cherry tree, protected by a tire. She was happy with the opening, the dinner, the conversations she had with the other artists. "[Denys] Chevalier was there with 5 sculptors they were all really quite nice and all of a sudden I was at ease with everybody and we were all chirping like birds." "I would very much like for them to love me enough to love my sculpture or vice versa."[68] Nevertheless, she still had a couple of complaints: "Lee Bontecou was qualified of [*sic*] needle work, minor art";[69] and in the catalog for the *Salon de la Jeune Sculpture*, her piece was reproduced upside down.[70]

Louise saw her young friend Henri Zerner,[71] whom she found "wonderful," and attended several openings with him: she saw "a woman sculptor from Malakoff"[72] at Caroline Lee's foundry, and "an English pop [artist] at Iris Clert's."[73] It seems that she was especially taken with Andy Warhol's opening at the Sonnabend Gallery. "[There] was an incredible mass of orange poppies offered by Andy himself to all the young men, Zerner giggled in total happiness."[74]

The previous week she had seen Yves Klein at Alexander Iolas Gallery, and Niki de Saint Phalle in Soisy-sur-École, having been invited by the artist herself.[75]

Seeing art, she said, allowed her to get back on her feet, though she was critical of what she saw in Paris: "They copy here what has been bought by the museum of modern art (that tells you everything). [. . .] Chamberlain[76] has made dozens of followers."[77] These observations indicate that Louise was completely up to date with the artistic developments of her time and that she could be interested at the same time in the avant-garde as well as in tapestries by Calder, Gilioli, or Prassinos. She saw the Salon de Mai—"not bad—a bit jumbled but interesting"—and an exhibition at the American Cultural Center: "the artists are fighting for the attention of the Americans."[78]

Her interests also extended to "primitive" art, and she went to the Musée de l'homme for the opening of the *Masterpieces of the Musée de l'homme* exhibition, curated by Michel Leiris and Jacqueline Delange. The mise-en-scène was a little overdramatic—"black ceiling, light for each object in the d'Harnoncourt style"—and she didn't recognize all the pieces. But at least it was not the "dusty desolation of the rest of the museum."[79] At a dinner hosted by the Delanges,[80] they described the compromises some curators and collectors had had to make with the sometimes dubious African commercial art market. Louise therefore discouraged Robert from writing a preface for the Tishman collection,[81] which was to be on show at the Musée de l'homme, because although it was a good one, it obeyed a mercantile logic. Robert took her advice. Louise kept up with Robert's friends and professional contacts. She saw the Leirises and Daniel-Henry Kahnweiler, who "sends you his best."[82] However, she noted: "I didn't go to the Michel Leiris communist show at the Odeon.[83] If he is willing to recognize me I will perhaps go tomorrow. (I met Jean Laude at Iolas's)."[84] The political context was always present. She described Ahmed Ben Bella's appearance at the Palais de la Mutualité and André Malraux's speeches on television: "many people are dissatisfied with him. He follows de Gaulle like his shadow."[85] Further on she specified that the Delanges were ardently political, they were "anti-Vietnam" and read *L'observateur*.[86] Finally at La Hune she ran into Max Ernst, who stared at her "out of his limpid blue windows [. . .] but the day before [. . .] those eyes were glacial [. . .] I didn't recognize him."[87]

After several weeks, she missed her family. "Your letters are the only ray of sunlight on the capital."[88] "I don't see what is important and the why of my stay,"[89] she confided a few days later. She was worried about Jean-Louis, who was going to be seeing a new therapist. "I see that things are not going very well with J. L. [Jean-Louis], luckily you are a saint."[90] Jean-Louis wrote what seemed to her a sarcastic letter, which was not entirely a bad thing, since he had a tendency to hold back.[91] Alain worked hard, and Michel, according to Robert, had trouble finding stable employment.

Robert sent her typewritten letters in English, in which he talked about his schedule, their children, housework, and professional obligations and tried to reply to her questions. The house seemed empty, but everyone was proud that she had been able to travel on her own. Michel was happy to see her off on the boat; Jean-Louis went to hear Panofsky and left Dr. Lieberman for another psychiatrist, Dr. Myerson. Michel found work thanks to "Temporary Office Help" and was looking for a job at the Port Authority for June; he took several boxes of books. Robert saw a Niki de Saint Phalle show in New York, which he called "curious and clever,"[92] and passed on her contact information in Soisy-sur-École: "She will have returned by the time you get this [. . .] Jean [Tinguely] will be away."[93] He took care of showing two of her works at the Chelsea Art Festival. Dore Ashton asked after her, he said; she said she was "disheartened" by the commercialism of Clement (Greenberg?) and Harold (Rosenberg?). Robert described a dinner he attended at the home of Vaclav Vytlacil with Annette Michelson, who wanted to see his work; she was with Susan Sontag. He mentioned that he was taking part in a symposium on African art that Douglas Fraser had organized at Columbia. Bruce Barton invited her to "a party"[94] at Rosenquist's and was surprised to learn that she had gone to France. Shirley Jaffe shouldn't complain anymore now that she has a handsome studio. He told her not to worry about Henriette and sent all his love.[95]

Her personal problems were compounded by Jean-Louis's psychological issues; he had been in therapy since adolescence.[96] Louise still felt she was forever incapable of helping her children, though she thought of them all the time: "I am unable to help Jean-Louis, Michel, and Alain, so I feel guilty and violent and self-destroying."[97]

"We have (after Lowenfeld advice) forced Jean-Louis to go back to Lieberman—Mrs. Jennings at the hospital explains that you can do only what you are ready to do—Jean-Louis is set against the doctor which has upset us very much—I find a measure of pity in Jennings['s] interpretation."[98]

Jean-Louis began seeing a new psychoanalyst, Arthur Myerson, whom Louise also saw, and the relationship between mother and son (and especially mother and analyst) was very complicated: "Contract. I accept Myerson['s] secrecy agreement if he will accept my secrecy about him. What I feel about him is none of his business. We both know it and we both know that the other knows it but we will not talk about it."[99]

1966, an Eccentric Year

"I want to be pretty, nice, popular, have friends for dinner, be successful as a sculptor, push myself like everyone else, but above everything else, be liked."[100] Louise wrote this in her 1966 diary, a year that would be punctuated by an exotic trip and a pioneering exhibition.

In April, she and Robert went to the first World Festival of Negro Arts in Dakar, Senegal (from April 1 to 24, 1966). Curated by Alioune Diop, editor of the journal *Présence africaine,* with the help of Michel Leiris, the festival aimed to demonstrate the vitality and quality of African culture. The event—which was attended by the Senegalese president Léopold Sédar Senghor—presented both classical and contemporary culture, mixing traditional and folk dance with Duke Ellington. It was also a chance to put on the first global festival of Black arts: *L'art nègre: Sources, évolution, expansion,* which took place at the Musée dynamique de Dakar and traveled to the Grand Palais in Paris. Much of the work was borrowed from the Musée de l'homme in Paris and the Museum of Primitive Art (MPA) in New York. Funded by Nelson Rockefeller and directed by Goldwater, the MPA was initially reticent concerning the borrowing conditions in Dakar, though it actively supported the initiative and the way it highlighted African countries' contribution to human civilization. According to Louise, Robert's letter to the curators at the Musée de l'homme made a strong impression: "Your letter to the musée de l'Homme about necessary guaranties for the exhibition of Dakar [*sic*] was very appreciated for its force and its pertinence."[101] A conference was held from March 31 to April 8, composed of art historians, anthropologists, writers, and artists, including Jean Laude and Roger Bastide. Robert was on the research committee and gave a talk, while Michel Leiris spoke about aesthetic sentiment and Black Africans, a text that was then reproduced in his book *Afrique noire: La création plastique,* cowritten with Jacqueline Delange.

This trip to Africa must have been quite striking for Louise, but she said little about it. In an interview with Colette Roberts in 1968,[102] she described meeting Malraux on her visit to the Musée dynamique de Dakar and was sorry that several African American artists refused to participate in the exhibition so that their work would not be labeled "*art nègre.*" And she was particularly concise in her description of the trip: "Dakar looks like Montpellier. Dakar is the French figure of the South."[103] She later told Xavier Girard: "My decision, early on, was to leave ['primitivism'] behind. I am a rational, empirical person who refuses authority, whatever form it may take."[104]

Her letters show that she was keeping up with her husband's work, that she still praised his book on "primitive" art, met with his professional contacts (Jean Laude, Jacqueline Delange, Michel Leiris), but although she usually described the places she visited—the people, landscapes, art, and culture—with caustic wit, she remained silent about this event. Though she did take several photographs while she was there, in her diary, she wrote only "Dakar Africa" on March 30 and "Nigeria book to Alfred Barr" on June 6.

After Dakar, they visited Côte d'Ivoire and Nigeria, as far as Kano, alongside Robert Farris Thompson and Roy Sieber, returning via Lisbon. She brought a small vial of perfume for her friend Henri Zerner.

Leiris thanked Robert warmly for sending him his book: "Dear Robert Goldwater, I received your book. You know how keen I was to own it! [. . .] This book is truly a pioneering work and one of the 'great classics' in the field of research that interests us both."[105]

Robert and Louise spent the month of May 1966 in Portugal and Spain, then returned to New York in early June. This seems to have been a good period for her, and she managed to take some pleasure in life: "All I want in this world is to sit in the sun on my terrace—to take care of my hair with my newspaper and my cats."[106]

Eccentric Abstraction

Louise's evolution toward soft, organic sculptures and her turn to new materials marked a turning point in the history of American art, which Lucy Lippard acknowledged in the exhibition she curated in autumn 1966 at the Fischbach Gallery: *Eccentric Abstraction*. Bourgeois stood out as the oldest artist among a new generation: Bruce Nauman, Eva Hesse, Keith Sonnier, Alice Adams, Gary Kuehn, Don Potts, and Frank Lincoln Viner. Most of these artists came to sculpture from painting, and their work had nothing to do with the style of the 1950s or with pop art: "The makers of what I am calling, for semantic convenience, eccentric abstraction, refuse to eschew imagination and the extension of sensuous experience while they also refuse to sacrifice the solid formal basis demanded of the best in current non-objective art. [. . .] Abstraction is a far more potent vehicle of the unfamiliar than figuration, and erotic sensation thrives on the unfamiliar."[107]

Lippard was arguing for a different kind of abstraction than the minimalists had been practicing, one that made room for emotionality, intimacy, and sensuality. The art of the three women presented—Eva Hesse, Louise Bourgeois, and Alice Adams—allowed her to sketch out new visual and theoretical categories. It was Arthur Drexler who first introduced the young Lippard to Louise's work; Lippard had been a student at the Institute of Fine Arts, where Robert taught. She was struck, she said, by this artist from an older generation who managed to produce such original and audacious work compared to younger artists.[108] Her work was less aggressively detached and more poetically realized than that of some of the younger artists, even though, like them, she was aware of the disquieting, almost repulsive powers of art.[109]

The invitation to the opening was made of pinkish rubber, consecrating the triumph of floppiness in the world of sculpture and the arrival of new material (fabric, plastic, latex) to express the organic, the biomorphic, to emerge from the formalist and puritanical rigor of the dominant minimalism. Lippard's points of reference were Meret Oppenheim, Salvador Dalí, Yves Tanguy, Yayoi Kusama, and Claes Oldenburg. But she insisted that the movement was different from surrealism. "Eccentric abstraction" was not a simple development of that movement but a response to the relative failure of it in painting. The relationships between the internal and the external, between the earthly and the visceral in Louise's flexible latex casts define the site of metamorphosis rather than the act, she wrote, in her essay on the topic published in *Art International*.[110] She also insisted on the visceral power of these works, which she called "body ego"—the voyeurism and physical sensations they provoked, as well as their erotic and scatological dimensions.

Though it was not shown in *Eccentric Abstraction, Le regard* (1963) is a prime example of her concerns. The sculpture is an egglike mass of brown latex with a slit on top which allows a glimpse of an ocular globe inside of it. With its labial folds the gap references female genitalia but also the eye, its soft, wet, concavity constituting a feminine version of Giacometti's *Pointe à l'œil*, an allegory for women's lack of a scopic gaze. A vagina-eye that calls to mind certain surrealist drawings, as well as Georges Bataille's *Histoire de l'œil*. This metaphorical fusion of forms and ideas, typical of Louise's work, made *Le regard* "the vaginal equivalent of *Fillette* (1968)."[111]

Landscapes

From 1963 to 1967, Louise created a series of works on the theme of landscape, which she called *Soft Landscape*. Domes, hills, clumps of mushrooms—these sculptures were created using latex and wax, and then resin, aluminum, and alabaster, moving from soft materials to harder ones. She eradicated the opposition between these materials, "to disrupt the binary logic of 'softness' and 'hardness,' qualities they often manage to hold in tension."[112]

In *Double Negative* (1963), she juxtaposes fullness and emptiness, positive and negative space, under and above ground. This desire to show the underside of things, the reverse form, is characteristic of her dualistic vision of the world and her own psychic split. Every element is placed beside its opposite. In her formal experimentation during this period, she plays with the contrast between convex and concave.[113] The *Soft Landscapes* are like an extroversion of the *Lairs*: "In a refusal to come to grips with the problem you project yourself at the horizon. The landscapes explode in a desire to escape, to get some distance from yourself and eliminate anxiety. Terror is turned outwards towards the understanding of the universe. The introjection of the landscape is the lair."[114]

She let the material spill and spread, forming strange craters and folds not unlike the human body. These soft landscapes show that she was interested in an anthropomorphic view of nature in which bumps and hollows have a strongly sexual connotation but also allude, according to the artist, to topography—of the Parisian basin, which Louise discovered as a child during her walks from Choisy to Clamart, or the toposcopes such as the one she remembered visiting at the Tour Biret.[115] These reliefs reproduced the hills of the Creuse of her childhood or the Lascaux caves, which she visited in 1953: "[H]ollow forms appeared first in my work as details, and then grew in importance until their consciousness was crystallized by a visit to the Lascaux caves with their visible manifestation of an enveloping negative form, produced by the torrent of water that has left its waves upon the ceiling."[116]

These "landscapes" of the 1960s are like the volcanic eruption of a prenatal state, a chthonic world, entirely feminine, Mother Earth herself.

To attain the results she desired, she experimented with different materials. Latex was, for her, a medium halfway between sculpture and painting; it was a liquid that solidified while remaining fluid, a material close to something like skin. It was her material of choice at this time.

First Trip to Italy, 1967

Louise's sessions with Lowenfeld were becoming less and less frequent, because she found herself more capable of going out alone, visiting new places, and meeting other artists. After a short visit to Paris in early July 1967, where she stayed at the Cité des arts and showed her work,[117] she went to Italy with Robert[118] and stayed on alone to cast her recent plaster sculptures in bronze, make casts from wax models, and experiment with marble. This long trip on her own (from August 27 to November 11, 1967) was a turning point in her life and professional career. Like her diary, which became more elliptical, her letters attest to a profound change. She and Robert wrote to each other almost every day: the technical details involved in casting, financial difficulties (Louise was always worried about production costs; Robert told her to keep going and to not worry about expenses), little local anecdotes, wariness of the other artists who were there. But her first stay in Pietrasanta was characterized by energy and intense production. She was staying at the Auberge Ballerini, making friends with a local named Mario and his wife, as well as the workers. She split time between the Tesconi and Tommasi ateliers, for bronze, and Erminio Cidonio's for the marble; he was the director of the Henraux marble quarries in Querceta. She compared their prices and capabilities: "There are things for marbles: full shapes and things specifically for bronze: slender shapes."[119]

Pietrasanta, whose name literally translates as "sacred stone" (also called "Little Athens"), is a charming medieval city in northern Tuscany, near Pisa, Lucca, and Viareggio. It has a majestic rectangular piazza with a church, some old Renaissance houses, and a theater, but above all it is the city of marble workers, given its proximity to Carrara, at the foot of the Apuan Alps. It is a spectacular landscape of marble fields, with stone peaks so white it looks like they're covered in snow. Dirt paths meander between quarries and caves, littered with enormous blocks of different colored marble. The trucks go up and down the quarries of the different ateliers, of which Henraux is the best known.

There Louise made a few versions of *Sleep* (1967 and 1968)[120] in bronze, plaster, and white marble. The white marble piece, which she referred to in her letters as *"Le grand sommeil,"*[121] was the largest. A smaller bronze version, titled *Untitled (Sleep)*, was dedicated to Alfred Barr.[122] Can we read this leaning phallus as a symbol of masculine power? Or, as she later said: "a little animal recoiled in upon itself in order to gather its forces for waking up the next morning."[123] It was a kind of disguised self-portrait, a sleeping woman who is emerging slowly from her stone. The theme of animality and organic development were still dominating her work. Louise was making sculptures that were both pure forms—*Attentive Figure* (1967), *Germinal* (1967), *Point of Contact* (1967–68), *Tits* (1967), and *Black Torso* (1968–69)—as well as figurative work: "one gives me a rest from the other and are worked upon more or less at the same time—overlapping within the week."[124] She tried casting a heart, a lung, a liver, and the splayed corpse of a rabbit.[125] "I have been thinking about those plaster[s] of animals for the past week [. . .] I made drawings of them, a lung, a trachea, a liver, a heart."[126] The workers brought her these organs, which they kept in a refrigerator, so she could make a mold and then cast them in bronze. This kind of work—very original for its time—contrasted with the academic nature of the abstract sculptures being made at the same moment by artists like François Stahly, Antoine Poncet, Jacques Lipchitz, Isamu Noguchi, Lorenzo Guerrini,[127] and Alicia Penalba: "Penalba is very much like Nevelson, but we got along relatively well."[128] All these artists worked between Carrara and Pietrasanta, where they had studios and made their work in the greatest secrecy. "The suspiciousness of the other artists toward me makes me sad—everyone works in private."[129] Louise was always afraid that her work would not be shown, but she was also afraid to show it: "All of a sudden I am a little nervous, I can't push myself like that—I might not ever succeed in getting any respect."[130] However, some Italian friends helped her propose some sculptures to a gallery in Milan; the Italian representative for the Marlborough Gallery, Carla Panicali, came to visit the ateliers, and a young Japanese admirer sent by the Barrs was also very curious about her work.[131]

She felt naive beside these professional artists who were successful, with their galleries and commissions. She was somewhat critical of the commission that Stahly had received via Darthea Speyer for Nelson Rockefeller's private estate in Tarrytown, New York. She envied them while fearing finding herself such a situation. "When things are going well I am afraid of success."[132] Although she remained primarily solitary and independent, she did spend some time with artists, made day trips to Viareggio, Arni, and Pisa, where she saw Pisano's deformed statues, "rough and very touching."[133] She also went to Rome,[134] before leaving for New York, and on Robert's advice saw the Berninis at the Villa Borghese and the Barberini Palace as well as Borromini's chapel. She had earlier made a piece called *Homage to Bernini* (1967), "[the bust] from Versailles," she specified.[135]

Louise's social skills improved greatly, and she found the energy to work in spite of the moments of impotence in which she felt completely lost.[136] "I hope that you are not despairing of me," she wrote to Robert, because she was beginning to get back to herself: "the phoenix, poor periodical phoenix, was reborn once again from his ashes."[137] Robert was very enthusiastic: "I am very proud of you and know that the work you are doing will be very fine [. . .] you have been making a tremendous effort."[138]

Robert replied regularly to her letters, encouraging her, pushing her to make more and in better conditions, taking care of her application for a Guggenheim grant, sending photographs of her work to be written about in periodicals, and so on. He was a devoted husband who understood and protected her.[139]

She worried often about the boys: about Jean-Louis and his therapists, his difficulty settling down. He was suffering, she thought, from a complex concerning Robert, since they had the same intellectual and aesthetic interests (he later wrote a book—*Spectacular Vernacular*—about traditional adobe architecture in West Africa, West Asia, and the American Southwest). Michel seemed to have found a girlfriend: "do you believe they sleep together[?]" Louise asked.[140] And she worried that Alain was unhappy: "he would want you to admire him."[141]

Louise's turns of phrase and use of expression was jarring; she often said things like "it's literally raining cats and dogs [*comme vache qui pisse*],"[142] "what you are saying about Swenson is hilarious [*roulant*],"[143] "my heart skipped a beat [*mon sang n'a fait qu'un tour*]!!,"[144] her little pensione was "generous instead of being skimpy [*généreuse au lieu d'être étriquée*]."[145] Whether in her diary or her letters, Louise frequently adopted an informal tone: "Too funny [*il y a de quoi rouler à rire*] [. . .] my interpreter is a gnome, very intelligent, he reads Marcuse,"[146] "makes me want to tear my hair out [*de quoi s'arracher les cheveux*]" and "the big cheeses [*les grosses légumes*] of the 2 museums and of NYU."[147] Robert did not necessarily understand some of her old-timey French expressions, but their familiarity made him laugh. Louise particularly appreciated a good sense of humor.[148] She mocked other people, yes, but also herself: "When I start making fun of myself (quoting [using] prefabricated language [*expressions consacrées* . . .]) I am on the verge of anger. [. . .] 'Is it where it belongs, if it is not I cannot do anything' is the *expression consacrée*. Quoted as a joke by Rob[er]t. I feel snapping come up and anxiety start."[149]

Always attuned to the political climate of the time, Louise read such African American writers as Richard Wright, James Baldwin, and Ralph Ellison.[150] This interest for Black writers and civil rights demonstrations was made concrete in a series of small sculptures of the 1970s. She remained wary of hippie pacifism: "Rotten foundations—Tel Aviv calls to everybody at the UN against the Aqaba strangulation—nobody budges—'commitment' mean[s] nothing, pulling itself by its boot strap it does fight, what do the hippies think of that[?] how can you honestly be a pacifist when the arbitration boards do not enforce their judgements[?]"[151]

In September 1967, Robert told her that their mutual friend Varian Fry had died at their home in Easton.[152] They asked Lipchitz to speak at the funeral, which Louise did not understand ("why not you or Alfred"), because Lipchitz was "complaining about himself, condescending to the nth degree"; a "monster" who acted like Varian was "a lost soul," a failure, that he had never gotten over "the excitement of the exodus."[153] But although she was harsh toward successful artists such as Stahly, who, in her opinion, was a little much, she supported other artists and regretted that the old sculptor she'd met through Darthea Speyer, Jacques Zwobada,[154] was so little known.[155]

Part Objects

Fillette (1968) is no doubt the piece that is most emblematic of Louise's work, thanks to the famous photograph by Robert Mapplethorpe; it has become a secondary attribute, a sign by which she is known. This latex sculpture suspended from a hook embodies a great deal of ambivalence: between masculine and feminine, hard and soft, strength and weakness.

Her pronounced sense for irony, tenderness, and cruelty can be heard in the title: by calling a penis a "littlc girl," she freed herself from traditional modes of thinking about and representing the phallus. The title lends the work a childish, girly element. The male sex organ is presented as a fragile, tender thing like a newborn—it has the same color, size, and soft skin. Louise treated the phallus like a child to be cradled and protected, as evidenced by the pose she struck for Mapplethorpe. "When I hold a little phallus like that in my arms, well, I find it is a very sweet object, certainly not one I would ever harm, that much is clear. My kindness is directed towards men."[156]

Both a fetish object and a substitute, *Fillette* could also be considered a self-portrait. "Portrait of the artist as *Fillette*,"[157] as Rosalind Krauss put it, rightly analyzing the phalli, breasts, vaginas, and bodies in Bourgeois's works as so many part objects, that is: "an object towards which a partial drive is directed, without the whole of the person necessarily being perceived as a love object"[158]—for example, the breast for the mother, the penis for the father, and so on, "all the person becomes a breast that thrusts itself to give— This was an identification of all day with a part of the body," Louise wrote.[159] With Melanie Klein, the term "object" acquired the meaning it has been given in psychoanalysis: although incomplete, this part of the body is bestowed with personlike characteristics. *Fillette* looks a bit like a face, with two eyes at the top and a kind of pinched mouth at the bottom. She described the "collar" as that of a French schoolgirl's uniform.

For Donald Winnicott, there are good and bad part objects: the breast can turn against the newborn and eat it right back, with feeding becoming another way of devouring.

But above all, Louise managed to blend masculine and feminine, erasing the differences between the maternal and paternal figures. The spheres at the bottom are both testicles and breasts; the vaginal opening, at the base and the top, scrambles these distinctions and "forces male and female to merge."[160]

In antiquity, the phallus was a symbol of power, fecundity, and virility; it was an object of veneration that played a central role in initiation ceremonies, and its size recalled the Greek myth of Priapus. The fragility Bourgeois wanted to evoke at the same time refers back to a memory of childhood: "I remember the model in life drawing class at the Beaux-Arts getting an erection. He was embarrassed and I was amazed at how vulnerable he really was. [. . .] The sexual impulse of women is not so visible and can be denied. [. . .] A man's cannot, he cannot lie and that is why men are so nice."[161] "The phallus is the subject of my tenderness. It's about vulnerability and protection. After all, I lived with four men, with my husband and three sons. [. . .] Though I feel protective of the phallus, it does not mean I am not afraid of it."[162] Between menace and protection, the whole complex relationship between eroticism and sexuality is contained there. She would ceaselessly move between claiming it and denying it: "I have been told that there is quite a bit of eroticism in my work. Well of course there is, since I am constantly interested in the human body. But I don't feel the eroticism myself."[163]

When it came to certain subjects, Louise felt a strong ambivalence, and her work gave form to this binarism; however, she did note the distinction between eroticism, sexuality, and pornography: "One must differentiate between sex, which is a function, and eroticism, which encompasses so much more. First, eroticism can be real or imagined, reciprocated or not. There is the desire, the flirtation, the fear of failure, vulnerability, jealousy, and violence. I'm interested in all these elements."[164] She would experience this whole range of emotions in her relationships with men.

"The life of the artist," she also said, "is basically a denial of sex."[165] Her work was partly motivated by the desire to ward off her anxiety: "The fear of sex and of death is the same." And: "Art comes from the inability to seduce. I am unable to make myself be loved. The equation is really sex and murder, sex and death."[166]

Janus

That same year, 1968, Louise made other hanging works: the *Janus* series (*Janus, Janus fleuri, Janus in Leather Jacket, Hanging Janus,* and *Hanging Janus with Jacket*). They resemble rotating, stuck-together penises. "In the fruits of the father there is a hanging object / downward direction [. . .] the fruits of father are rather fingers and fiddling use or downright upsurging and aggressive."[167]

The juncture where these two outgrowths meet recall the slit of the female sex. Once again, Louise brought together masculine and feminine in this strange two-headed organ which could also be seen as breasts. The duality signified by the title *Janus*, which summons the two-headed divinity, one turned toward the past and the other toward the future, can be found in almost all the work from this period. "*Janus* . . . is a reference to the kind of polarity we represent. . . . The polarity I experience is a drive toward extreme violence and revolt . . . and a retiring. I wouldn't say passivity . . . but a need for peace, a complete peace with the self, with others, and with the environment."[168]

In short, interpretation is the viewer's privilege, and we can discern there "a double facial mask, two breasts, two knees. [. . .] It is perhaps a self-portrait—one of many."[169]

Back to Italy, 1968

Louise's second trip to Italy, from May to October, was marked by her stay in the small city of Querceta. Louise was looking for a studio where she could both work and live. After several unsuccessful attempts, including a hasty forced departure from an old house she had found on the Via XX Settembre, she chose to stay with the marquis Aïmone Negretto di Cambiano (of the august Colonna family), who rented her the ground floor of his house at Via Cugina 17, in the village of Querceta. The house was not very comfortable and required a number of changes and renovations which Louise, being a practical-minded person, oversaw. She had a few pieces of furniture brought from Paris (from the flat in the rue Daguerre) and after several weeks moved in with the marquis, who was himself an artist. She had a bicycle for getting from one atelier to another, because she was still working with Tommasi and Tesconi, but also very much with Henraux, who had a new artistic director (Chitti) for the marble work. Before finding a convenient studio, she made a mosaic portrait of Easton,[170] and the mosaic work of the artisans reminded her of Aubusson.[171]

She created models in plaster or plastic, which the workers then enlarged. Important work emerged during this period: *Cumul I* (1969, first titled *Village drapé*),[172] *Chapiteau* (1968), *Colonnata* (1968), which was the name of a small town in the mountains, and several bronzes, including a bronze cast of the wood *Personage* sculpture *Listening One* (1947), which was initially called *Attentive Figure*. Her works in black and white marble involve a number of oblong forms gathered together and emerging from a rough-hewn block. Louise explored many forms—phalli, artillery shells, pipes, houses. The fingers that pressed and molded the material to give it form can be seen in *Germinal* (1967); they protrude from a hemispherical base, like plants.

What led Louise to work with marble and to make these long trips to Piestrasanta? At that time it was a place where many sculptors and designers gathered, people who, on the initiative of Erminio Cidonio, and with the help of evolving technologies, wanted to develop new modes of sculpting with marble and open it to other styles. Cidonio, then, invited Italian artists (such as Lorenzo Guerrini, or Gio and Arnaldo Pomodoro) and international ones to come and experiment with making a wider, freer range of forms. Dealers and gallery owners came to visit the ateliers; there were exhibitions, as well as a biennale. But according to Louise, "They are provincial as opposed to the international."[173]

Pietrasanta was an important creative and cultural site for overhauling stone and marble sculpture. When she applied for funding to return to Italy, Louise insisted on her desire to experiment with the traditional technique, because she found the material to offer both resistance and softness.[174] She would not begin working with marble for another decade, but as early as 1957 she was thinking about its potential, writing (and playing on the pun between the material and the toy) that "a marble that does not find or is not found by the palm of a hand may easily become a bullet—of course the warm palm which is a mother can be a bad one."[175]

Although Louise noted a number of technical and financial details of the work she was doing, she said nothing about her subjects, her intentions, the forms she was making, as if all these new sculptures came to her instinctively and almost unconsciously. "[M]y idea (talk about gestation with a high dose of evanescence) took shape yesterday, when I attached my 4 pours (Tesconi) together. Months of unconscious drives including the time in Paris and to my shame no small amount of revolt and despair; [it] suddenly jelled."[176]

However, she paid close attention to the work the other artists at the quarries were doing. She was very critical as well, and aware of her own uniqueness. With regard to the upcoming Carrara biennial (which would be canceled in the end but in which she was meant to participate), she specifically told Robert that she didn't want to be lumped in with the official Paris school (Stahly, Poncet) but preferred to be considered alongside the young artists from the Fischbach Gallery with their "soft objects." For Lucy Lippard's upcoming show on soft sculpture,[177] she agreed to lend the latex *Portrait* (1963), *Warm Mountain* (1963),[178] and *Torsade* (1962).

She made *Fillette* before she left and decided it would be indecent to lend it to William Rubin: "I do not know if it is possible to give 'la fillette' to Bill it is very indecent; I didn't see it as such before seeing the photo."[179] Robert agreed: "I have looked at it again and carefully and it seems to me that unless it is seen as a penis it doesn't really work as a form."[180] At the time, it was a difficult work to put in circulation, and Louise had to eventually admit its erotic component.

She got on well with the sculptor Jean-Robert Ipoustéguy because, in her words, "we have the same problems," and "Ypousteguy [*sic*][181] has something of Bill de Kooning in his air of approachability and his shrewd eyes [...] and his sense of humor which emerges when he has had 2 or 3 drinks."[182] But Robert, who was writing a book on sculpture, didn't see the connection with her work.[183] Louise agreed: "I see that your description of Ypoustéguy is correct [. . .] my work is close to his only in the sense that we are not from the official Paris school (Stalhy Poncet) nothing else," she replied simply.[184]

Louise was resolutely modern and anticonformist. She who at one time had fervently believed in God was now horrified by the religious processions and celebrations in the village: "These medieval attitudes make me desire the modern, in everything—Particularly that religion repulses me [. . .]. Between De Gaulle and Negrotto it's enough to make you want to tear your hair out!"[185]

The news from New York was all about Alain's upcoming wedding to Jessica. He discussed the list of invitations with his parents, and Louise tried to behave—as always, in all circumstances—like the perfect mistress of the house. But she did not care for society events: "I like weddings with 4 witnesses."[186] Nevertheless, she ordered a silk dress in Italy and was "happy that Alain is getting married [. . .] I hope that he will be as good a husband and father as his Father."[187]

Michel bought a bus, for taking children to school, he said, but he then disappeared and never picked up the phone; he was still friendly with Mary,

Robert's sister: "Only affection and patience can get the better of his wild streak."[188]

Jean-Louis was taking classes at Columbia and seemed interested in art history, although it was very fraught for him, given his brilliant father. "Jean-Louis who is so afraid not to equal you or even to please you."[189] The art historian Dore Ashton, however, found him charming: "[She] said that Jean-Louis was a wonderful young man, and had made a real impression on her."[190]

Some have called Louise a bad mother, but when you see the important role her children take in her letters, the constant attention given to their worries, their professional activities, their love lives, it becomes clear that Louise and Robert were like all parents, worrying about or congratulating their offspring, accepting each child's individuality and wishing only their happiness and independence. However, her sons apparently did not at all feel this parental attention, neither as children nor as adolescents, judging their parents too preoccupied by themselves, their relationship, and their work, never showing them tenderness or love. In a conversation with his father, Jean-Louis reproached him for never being able to express his feelings. He even believed that the different members of his family were not close to one another and were incapable of communicating.[191]

In July 1968, Paulette and Georges Place's son Jean-Michel[192] came to do an internship at Kraus, a publisher in Mamaroneck; he went out to have a drink with Robert in New York,[193] but he had a serious car accident which required he be hospitalized and sent back to France. Robert and Alain took care of the paperwork. Louise was still very close to her friend from childhood as well as to her husband, whom she consulted on a variety of practical matters. She remembered that she had given her father's stock to Paulette for nothing![194] Paulette was meant to join her in Italy, but in spite of their friendship, Louise preferred to go on working undisturbed.

While Louise was away for those few months, all the domestic and familial tasks fell on Robert, who was at that time very much occupied with work: a book on Rothko and another called *What Is Modern Sculpture?* (Louise was of course included, with a reproduction of a *Personage* sculpture, *Quarantania*, from 1947–53). Above all, he was busy with a major upcoming exhibition at the Met, to open the following spring, from the Museum of Primitive Art. He was to be in charge of the catalog and had to postpone a teaching job at Princeton. In spite of his numerous commitments, seminars, and articles,

Robert was still an excellent husband. He took care of his wife's family (writing to Henriette, who wanted to sell her house), of the children, of the house, of the shipping of works and furniture. He advised Louise as to which pieces to reproduce in William Rubin and Wayne Anderson's articles, booked her travel, bought beautiful blocks of marble (Belgian black, for instance) required to produce her work, and above all, wrote to Louise nearly every day.

At this time they seem to have fallen in love with each other all over again, as their daily letters and intimate confessions attest. Louise asked her husband: "What do you do these days when you feel romantic?"[195] "When you are away it is a sort of vague permanent st[ate]. When it gets acute, then I go to bed too late and even then I sleep very badly, and don't work very well besides. I hope that you won't get too close to the Count," he responded with a hint of jealousy, but happy that Louise felt renewed love for him.[196]

Molotov Cocktail

Louise mentioned the protests of May 1968 in Paris, which she discovered by reading the headlines—she read *L'Express*, Arthur Koestler, and Marshall McLuhan. That year she made a sculpture with an evocative title, *Molotov Cocktail* (1968), a bronze oblong form (a bomb, an egg, a head?) that she gave to William Rubin. "Just now there are many protests . . . from all the intellectuals in France. . . . Across the whole world, I think. This is praise. At the time I was teaching. I was teaching and all my students were protesting . . . there were debates because they [the students] absolutely refused to go to Vietnam [to fight]," she said.[197] Shocked by the repressive force employed by the police against the Black community during the big civil rights protests in the United States, she made little torsos from black Belgian marble, which were both homages to Black Power as well as sexual forms (*Black Torso*, 1968–69).[198] She also noted the death of Malcolm X: "Malcolm X has been shot,"[199] and made references in interviews to her commitment to the civil rights movement.

On September 16, 1968, she attended the anarchists' convention in Carrara, which was the occasion to create the first International of Anarchist Federations and where she heard Daniel Cohn-Bendit, who would continue his political career after May 1968: "We laughed a lot at lunch. At the International Anarchist Congress which has always been based in Carrara, the discussions were held in French and Cohn Bendit was there, with others. The Carrara police (everlasting tradition) does not intervene in these battles, of which there has been quite an assortment."[200]

When Louise learned that Robert Kennedy had been assassinated in June 1968, she was like all Americans deeply shocked and wondered about a possible conspiracy. But oddly, when her husband told her Marcel Duchamp had died, to whom she had been close,[201] she made no written response.

She continued to keep a regular diary, noting her thoughts and constantly self-analyzing. Some aspects of her personality are as present as ever, such as her fear of having her models stolen—"what is going to keep the marble worker from selling my models[?] How to keep from giving him the idea"[202]—the fear that someone would take advantage of her, wariness mixed with curiosity toward other artists, the fear of being bold. But she began to take her career in hand with more and more authority; she took pleasure in working and learned "the school of giving up,"[203] because she had finally found a way to fight against periods of depression and to find a balance between private and professional life: "1) there is one thing you have to insist on, absolute solitude when you work [. . .] 2) work and life go together 3) the premises must accommodate your husband his work the house and my work."[204]

This stay was particularly beneficial for her, though she continued to be torn by a kind of doubling that manifested itself between her life writing, in which she meticulously detailed her moods, and her more reasonable correspondence with Robert. "I felt terribly happy in Italy. I was in the sun all day and doing what I wanted. I was a picture of health and happiness, and at the same time I was doing the 'hysteric' woman, actually. So, there is a great, great distance between what you are and what bothers you."[205]

In March 1968, she agreed to a long interview with Colette Roberts for the Archives of American Art.[206] The interview, which was never published, was the first in a long series and reveals a very liberated Louise Bourgeois, who spoke of other artists, even if often in very critical terms, people she had known in France, those who had influenced her, and the state of contemporary art in New York and in France. She didn't speak very much of her work or of herself. In the second part of the interview, she struck out a number of sentences, a practice she frequently engaged in thereafter. The interview began with an acerbic critique of the exhibition that was held at the Willard Gallery of a sculptor whom she declined to name (it was Richard Lippold) but whose work she believed was vastly overestimated. "And this is ridiculous." This was not bitterness, she said, given her body of work piling up at home, infrequently shown, but a problem of justice and injustice. "This is said without bitterness because I go on working as well and maybe better if the work is not disposed of and used." Louise was wary of success; it could kill an artist.

She described visiting Bonnard when she was in Le Cannet, being taught by Léger on the rue Blomet, and by Bissière,[207] whom she liked very much, at the Académie Ranson. Then on her arrival in America, a departure that was a blessing for her, spending time at Hayter's studio, where she met Miró, Antúnez, and his brother Zanartu. When she was asked about Marcel Duchamp, she replied that he was more her husband's friend than her own, because they had a similar attitude. In her opinion, Duchamp was completely authentic, she respected and recognized his influence on contemporary art. The same went for Man Ray. She drew the line, however, at minimalism and pop art: one was more architecture than art, and the other was the best American propaganda in Europe. "There is a freshness there that everybody loves." However, she was not easy on the critics, whether it came to Clement Greenberg, who told painters what they should paint—"And he actually paints his own painters"—or Harold Rosenberg, who seemed more interested in ideas about art than in art itself. She preferred Wayne Anderson, an art historian who had written a book about sculpture that mentions her work.

She also agreed to discuss "primitive" art, how she had discovered voodoo rituals at the Brooklyn Museum, and recognized that the nails stuck in *Portrait of C. Y.* (1947–49) were no doubt a product of this influence. She also said that she was always sensitive to the emotional aspect of art, to its magical power.

Her last comment is a premonition of her long career: "My credo is that I hope I will live long enough to say most of the things I want to say. That's it."

The Great Mother

All of the lumps, protrusions, spherical and egglike outgrowths from this period resemble mammary glands as much as phalli. She called them *Cumuls,* after the round, cumulous cloud. "They are clouds, cloud formations, I don't see anything sexual in them,"[208] she said later. In fact, they were originally landscapes, "terrains," thus suggesting her intimate relationship to the earth, and to nature.

She linked the maternal figure to this element: "The mother is the Earth, the mounds of Bourgogne and or Provence or of Easton where one falls asleep on the warm grass. [. . .] The fruits of the mother are attached to the body on the whole surface of the diameter of the sphere—they could not be more attached and they also have a button voilà they are spheres and demi spheres."[209]

After having "killed off" the mother in analysis, Louise regularly returned to this beloved figure who, as early as the 1960s, was a reference point for femininity, fecundity, sweetness: "as long as I am under the influence of the good mother—as long as I am in good terms with her whatever the cost may be [. . .] it is all manageable. [. . .] I kept the vision of the oasis. Maternal figure who encircles in her arms her possessions to protect them—it is more than tenderness, it is not tenderness at all, it is protective and happy, it is maternal love. This piece made me think back to my mother and I felt how much she had protected and loved me."[210]

We see again here the emotion she felt and expressed when Jean-Louis was born, Louise the good mother. "I'm on all these landscapes, unconscious landscapes, soft, the end of softness—even the *Cumuls* all belong to the same group. [. . .] The last landscape I made was a landscape of udders. Well, just picture a female dog, or a cow; you put her on her back and you have a very interesting, moving, live, and flexible landscape. Everything comes back to that. If you hold a naked child against your naked breast, it is not the end of softness, it is the beginning of softness, it is life itself."[211]

Louise continued to obsess over the anthropomorphic landscapes that appeared with the *Cumuls* at the end of the 1960s. After the hard smoothness of marble, which echoed the softness of breasts, the generous udders of woman or earth—"they are anthropomorphic and they are landscape also, since our body could be considered from a topographical point of view, as a land with mounds and valleys and caves and holes"[212]—she made two even more disconcerting works out of latex and plaster: *Avenza* and *Avenza Revisited* (both 1968–69). Avenza is the name of a small village near Carrara. The ocher tones of the latex, as well as the texture of the material, evoke skin and flesh; their connotation is clearly more organic. In *Avenza Revisited II* (1968–69), Louise reused the mold for *Avenza* but added material to the sides, which allow for it to be lifted off the ground, as if it had legs, and arranged tubelike loops to hang inside of it, which looked like entrails. *Amoeba* (1963–65) was in her mind a kind of formless ectoplasm, beneath which we can make out a gestating fetus.

Robert's book *What Is Modern Sculpture?* was published by MoMA in 1969. It dedicated a section to Louise and included a commentary on *Quarantania I*, a work made between 1947 and 1953. Was it by way of thanks that she made *Portrait of Robert* (1969): a small head emerging from a cluster of what might be fingers—those of the sculptor—or phallic forms? One more wink at masculine equipment. And finally she signed a contract with the Knoedler Gallery, which would include her work in two group shows in 1970 and 1971.

William Rubin, the head of the painting and sculpture department at MoMA, wrote a wonderful piece about her work in *Art International*.[213] This support of Louise's work was fairly surprising from an art historian whose tastes tended to run to surrealism and abstract expressionist painting. He also invited Louise to participate in the exhibition he curated at MoMA in 1969.[214] To write his article, he drew on the interview he'd done with her via letter,[215] in which he asked her very specific questions. "Louise Bourgeois is a vigorous, tenacious artist," he wrote. From the outset he marvels at her uniqueness in the American art world, citing her status as an immigrant and her relationship with the surrealists. But he believed that her work made better use of the hidden possibilities of surrealism. Her singularity was also a function of her honesty and the immediacy of her feelings, whether in relation to figurative or abstract sculptures. He likened the latent sexuality of *Sleep II* (1967) to the work of Arp and Brancusi. And above all, he understood the poetry of her art and her strong personality: "Her ideas have a poetic and plastic resonance seldom found in sculpture these days, not to speak of a distinct, forceful and illuminating personality. It all adds up to beauty of a very personal kind."[216]

Third Trip to Italy, 1969

Louise returned to Italy from April to May 1969, and then again in the autumn, from September 15 to December 16, 1969.

The Ballerini pensione had closed, so she stayed at the Hôtel Italia, reading Borges, Orwell, Gide, and Kurt Vonnegut.[217] But she told Robert that *Le Monde* and *Encounter* interested her more than contemporary fiction, although "Philip Roth was very amusing."[218] She was working on a bronze version of *The Quartered One* that was to be shown at MoMA (in its show entitled *The New American Painting and Sculpture: The First Generation*, from June 18 to October 5, 1969), offering two potential positions for the work: hanging from the ceiling or placed on a pedestal.[219] She wanted to know if Rubin was including her great rival Louise Nevelson in the show.[220] Robert reassured her that her work would not be in it. "I would very much like for [William] Agee's text on my work to be interesting,"[221] she said.

She gathered together bits of scrap metal and struts and assembled them on a pedestal. She had a column made of Arni marble which, when placed in the room, had "an incredible face, but people would have said that it was a penis."[222]

She also made two very different works, a series[223] of smooth, vertical forms in black Belgian marble, and another series of bronze sculptures with sharp angles, *Blades* (1969). In her letters, she also references a work made of found objects and scrap metal (and uses "the rusted rolls of an object that one sees in New York by the A&P a conveyer belt on which the cans are put"); she found it "very simple and rather elegant."[224]

"I sculpted marble for the first time, all afternoon."[225] To make a piece with twelve small columns on a base: "They are people huddled against each other, around a larger central shape. [. . .] The surfaces of the tops are lightly slanted like faces that are drawing near or oscillate."[226]

She reunited with the regulars: Pomodoro, Gonzalo Fonseca, whom she saw often, Noguchi, and Henry Moore, with whom she had dinner one night.[227] "I was very apprehensive—I was seated next to the master who asked me what I was working on, I explained to him the forms of the 20th century (derived from the industry and from containers) he was interested and surprised and came off his godlike act; enough for us to have a good time."[228] She used his private atelier at Henraux for a time, but on the master's return she was taken out, since she hadn't produced enough models ("I can't go any faster"), and then she no longer had a place to work. "I said that if I was taking too much space, I could put myself in the loos. This remark saddened everyone—so I responded that it would perhaps bring me luck. They laughed."[229]

She also met a lot of new people: the young French sculptor Jeanette Cardoux, Deborah A. Stott, who was studying with Rudolf Wittkower and was Jacques Lipchitz's biographer, and the Polish artist Alina Szapocznikow,[230] with whom she struck up a friendship. "[T]he renowned Polish woman artist arrived yesterday; she has a face like a crumpled rag."[231] Alina invited her to the Meridiana, where she was living, and showed her some photographs and catalogs: "It is body parts immersed in moss Gallo style[232] + Marisol[233] but better. Talking freely she told me (she is 35 years old: 17 year old son) that she had spent 5 years between 13 and 18 at the Auschwitz camp—I was so surprised that I wasn't able to shake the impression. Her father and her brother died there her mother who was a medical doctor survived—I asked very stupid questions regarding the graffitis [*sic*] and I have asked what they were thinking. She told me: we were sitting stark naked, piled up and we were fighting for a potato—I thought that I would never again stop being grateful."[234] But in spite of her feelings of friendship and admiration for Alina, she observed that "her energy and ambition are unsurpassed to the point of being obsessive."[235] She did not share her rolled constructions with her, "because she could make a more interesting use of them!?!?"[236] Here, too, Louise demonstrates her strength and her weakness; she has the intelligence and the ability to recognize Alina's talent, to admire her strong personality and the originality of her creative practice, but at the same time she mistrusted her, afraid she would steal her ideas.[237] "The situation of being confronted with another woman always depresses me," she wrote.[238]

Her relationships with the other artists improved; she became friendlier, looked for a house to buy with La Papa,[239] the wife of Gualtieri di San Lazzaro, who was the editor of the journal *XXe siècle*. Visiting farmhouses on the mountain excited her and reminded her of her uncle Alex's "stone madness [*maladie de la pierre*]."[240] Louise loved the idea of acquiring property, but in Italy she quickly gave up on her fantasy. Her walks through the sunny autumn countryside reminded her of childhood visits to the south of France.[241]

In October, she took a train up to Paris to deal with some issues with the estate and stayed with Henriette. She went to see the Viera da Silva show at the Musée d'art moderne de la Ville de Paris and visited Brancusi's studio. She mentions the Paris Biennale[242] and had dinner with Denys Chevalier at the Rotonde, but "it would be better to see Restany or Otto Hahn,"[243] who were in her view more up to date on the contemporary situation. She had dinner at the home of Alina and her husband (Roman Cieslewicz),[244] their son, and some of their friends, "very modern very young and very ambitious they all were communists and had but one idea: make it to the United States. The only one who made it of their group is Polanski (Roman) the cineaste who was a classmate of theirs."[245] This return to Paris went well: "Paris is after all the cradle of my life and the cradle of my marriage!!! That's it I am going to cry."[246] "I am happier today than I ever was in my younger years—I understood this deeply during my last trip to France—when I was able to see things soberly, without emotion and without regrets and that allowed me to appreciate and enjoy (reasonably) the present—but above all to appreciate it."[247]

"My dear sweet little husband and 'cultural advisor,'"[248] "Tell me what you're doing and what you think about my whole life revolves around it."[249] Robert is not only her most devoted and precious counselor but also the "tutor" on whom she can rely to overcome her anxiety attacks. During these trips to Italy, Louise showed how loving she could be toward her husband: "I would like to get back home because I want to make love— There is nothing to add today—because I cannot think about anything else—I wonder what you think about this."[250] Robert's response to her desire was reasonable and measured: "I also think that about that a lot, but I hope that for you it has passed somewhat—only for the moment,"[251] arguing that there was time for everything. Their letters also show the degree to which she confided in her husband, sharing her weaknesses and fears: "I tried but this letter is no good. It is only my love for you that gives me the courage to send it."[252]

"I am at the same time very sentimental and very inhibited."[253] "I wonder what in the world I am doing here. Luckily I never wonder why I work. The day when I will be able to cry everything will go fine. But I am not there yet."[254] Violence was a constant theme in her private writings and psychoanalytic confessions. Louise regularly experienced destructive and sadistic impulses, and she was unafraid to discuss them:

Violence is what pleases me most—I feel at ease in it—I adore frightening people (for want of a better show) but after I have atrocious fears. I do not understand the mechanism very well but have witnessed it thousands of times. But if I do not succeed in expressing myself in violence (in a civilized manner if possible) depression and self-destruction appears. All of this on a rhythm of 28 days has appeared here [just the same] as anywhere [else]. [...] I have doubts vis-à-vis my work and produce extremely slowly because of violence turned against oneself in the form of unconscious resistance.[255]

In her diary, she referenced political events: civil war in Nigeria and Israeli defense minister Moshe Dayan's politics, which she called "arrogant."[256]

She continued to draw, regularly. "[A]ll the drawings on the diagonal are 'on the attack' for years; throw yourself in the water, you're not afraid, go ahead," she wrote to encourage herself on January 15, 1969. For these fears were still with her: she feared that she had not done enough to save her Jewish friend Rahissa; she was still "suspicious of my colleagues [...] suspicious because of defenselessness."[257] "I want [Henry] Moore to respect me but I don't want to show him my work—suspicious. I'm starting to fear the visit."[258]

Louise was often overcome by feelings of powerless and insignificance, frustration and discouragement, which she had to ceaselessly fight off. She understood, however, "the difficulty of being a professional sculptor for example I did not know what was done in Paris (the Biennial) I get stuck in the daily grind of saving 4 cents."[259]

This third, very long stay in Italy thus allowed her to finish the different versions of the *Cumuls,* to cast several plasters in bronze, to invent other forms, but also to conceive of new little works in marble: defenseless women without arms, *Harmless Woman* (1969), *Fragile Goddess* (1970), and above all *Femme couteau* (1969–70), which signaled a new stage in her artistic practice—her feminist commitment—as well as anticipating a turning point in her private life: *The Destruction of the Father* (1974).

CHAPTER 8

————

The Destruction of the Father, 1970–1980

It is a very murderous piece, an impulse that comes when one is under too much stress and one turns against those one loves the most.

The 1970s were, for Louise, a time of political and feminist commitment, as well as a crucial turning point in her professional and personal life: she suddenly lost her husband in 1973. This third major tragedy coincided with a confrontation with her past, which she gave form to in two essential works—*The Destruction of the Father* (1974) and *Confrontation* (1978). Both of these immersive works give a new, monumental dimension to her sculpture. These funerary rituals were also true scenes of initiation, which celebrated her liberation from domestic constraints and her ambivalence toward masculinity and femininity while also allowing her to explore the riches of her unconscious. From then on Louise lived alone, without husband or children, face to face with herself. The end of this decade corresponded with long-overdue public recognition, as if the path she had chosen—solitary, autobiographical—was more aligned with the needs of a new generation of antiformalists. The art world also saw, during this time, the return of a more subjective sensibility.

Knife-Woman

The works of the early 1970s attest to an ever-present volcanic capacity for violence and of a vision of femininity that recalls, in its archaic idols with missing heads, the fecundity of prehistoric sculptures—for instance, *Fragile Goddess* (1970)—as well as the ambivalent fetishism of *Femme couteau* (1969–

70). The body of the woman became a sharp phallic object, as if every eroti-
cized female body were the equivalent of the penis. *Femme couteau* symbolizes
both vulnerability and defensiveness, even aggression; it embodies the duality of the artist and the sculptor's work. The knife was turned, not against
men, Bourgeois specified, but against those who would attack her. It could
also be used for cutting off arms and heads, to keep only the roundness of
the belly, thighs, and breasts. "My knives are like a tongue—I love you, I hate
you. If you don't love me, I am ready to attack. They're very double-edged."[1]
The first version, made in 1969–70, is in pink marble, depicting a fluid drap-
ery that sheathes a pair of breasts: "This marble sculpture—my *Femme
couteau*—embodies the polarity of woman, the destructive and the seductive.
[. . .] In the *Femme couteau,* the woman turns into a blade, she is defensive.
She identifies with the penis to defend herself. [. . .] We are all vulnerable in
some way, and we are all male-female."[2] The body of a woman transformed
into a bladed weapon is, after *Fillette,* one of the most significant tropes in
the art and personality of Louise Bourgeois, who, as a sculptor, was herself a
"knife-woman." The apparent softness of the material, its pink color, its
erotic female forms, breasts and vulva, but also masculine, give it its air of
being "double-edged": for and against penetration. The armless women, such
as *Harmless Woman* (1969), and *Fragile Goddess* (1970), generously propor-
tioned and resembling the Venus of Willendorf, also exist in several versions
and materials. Their smallish size allows them to be held in the hands, to feel
both the sensuality of their curves and the menace of the pointed object. In
the same spirit, but more explicit, the *Femme pieu* (1970) is a sort of brown
wooden shell, balanced but unstable, whose belly is pierced with multiple
sewing needles. Pleasure and pain are united.

Louise continued to explore different techniques and materials, filling a
glove with wax[3] or sticking colored straight pins into a small wax sculpture
depicting a mother and child.[4] This interest in found objects and their
fetishistic power led her to create a bronze cast of an animal heart (*Heart,*
1970): a soft muscle, full of arteries, the headquarters of emotions, a hunk
of flesh that could be torn out both literally and figuratively; later we will
see hearts suspended behind the stairway in *No Exit* (1989)[5] and a flayed
rabbit (*Rabbit,* 1970) that she first cast in Pietrasanta in 1967. The flayed
rabbit hanging upside down with its entrails on show is a self-portrait of the
artist, who always felt she suffered like a beast: "A person who has been

rejected is like a dead animal, so dead, poor animal, and if you look closely, it's a rabbit that's ready to be cooked. All its entrails are hanging out, it's someone who's suffering. It's a story about isolation."[6] It was also a reference to the street singing she remembered hearing when she was a little girl at Antony: *"peaux de lapins"* (rabbit skins) whenever the traveling salesmen passed by, hawking their furs.[7]

Family tension was ever present: she worried about Jean-Louis, who was severely depressed in late 1970s. Louise went to see his psychoanalyst, Dr. Myerson: "During the whole month of November we dealt with the terrible shock of J. L.'s withdrawal from all work, all friends, and from us."[8] "Is J. L. unable to talk (as before Nov. 1963)[?] Is J. L. refusing to talk, to show controlling power over the analyst[?] Is going from one to another a way to prove that he is not curable[?] He is right or the doctor is wrong. [. . .] J. L. is looking for someone who agrees with him."[9] Alain, in an attempt to escape this too-heavy atmosphere, abruptly got up from the family meal one evening and walked out the door.[10] He told his father that he (Robert) and Louise "seem to strike terror into every member of the family."[11] Was it to try to resolve these problems with Jean-Louis that Louise went to the Institute of Family Therapy on January 2, 1973, to see Dr. Blaustein, a friend of Henry Lowenfeld's? Faced with the dilemma of being a woman and an artist, a good and a bad mother, Louise responded in her own way: "My work having made me a better person, I was a better mother. But taking a great deal of my time, it has kept me away from them."[12]

There had also been a good deal of political uncertainty, given ongoing hostilities between Israel and its neighbors, culminating in the Yom Kippur War, which broke out in September 1973. Louise wrote in 1970, at the time of the first Rogers plan for containment in the region, that "[US Secretary of State William] Rogers says: Israel does not need planes— Who says? And who knows? [. . .] Rogers or Israel—how nice," she noted, sarcastically. "The French feel defensive and guilty about the deal with Jordan but the Americans pass judgment instead of saying, 'We feel bad about this.'"[13] Her friend Alina Szapocznikow wanted to come and see her in New York, and Louise wasn't enthusiastic about the idea, which in turn made her feel guilty: "Alina is coming. I do not say Alina does not need my help, or does not need to come to America (since she has such a nice studio in Malakoff) but I say I cannot help. It is too much for me. I feel bad about it and cannot sleep."[14]

Finally, she threw away material for which she no longer had any use. "I let [it] go. I break them detach myself the symbol no longer symbolizes anything—it's out of date, useless, to me and to anyone else the milk cartons [remaining from her earlier sculptures], have burned [. . .] why cover my work? To hide?"[15]

"I Am Tired of France and the French"

Louise had a particular affection for young French art historians, educated, well brought up, and charming.[16] She noted the names of André Chastel,[17] Jean Leymarie,[18] André Fermigier,[19] and also that of Dominique Bozo,[20] who had come to see her in New York on February 8, 1970. She had already struck up a friendship in 1958 with Henri Zerner, whom she met in the print study center at the Metropolitan Museum of Art, where she was looking for a portrait of Erasmus to use for the stationery for the shop she named after him. The young man was bewitched by this petite, bizarrely dressed woman with the strong French accent, and went several times to visit her at Erasmus and bought two Géricault lithographs from her.[21] He also became a close friend of the Goldwater family, particularly Jean-Louis, regularly visiting them at home. Louise sometimes confided in him about her immense sadness at her difficulties with Michel, who seemed to be drifting farther and farther away from his family.[22]

Then, in the 1970s, she frequently saw Dominique Bozo, Françoise Cachin, Patrice Marandel, and later Xavier Girard. Bourgeois met Marandel[23] in 1969 at a dinner hosted by Zerner; he was charmed by Louise, "this little slip of a woman dressed like the ace of spades,"[24] and was an early defender of her work, encouraging museums to show and acquire it. In December 1971, he wrote an article on her for *Art International,* and in 1981, he curated a solo show for her at the Renaissance Society in Chicago.[25]

Bozo had an affectionate relationship with Louise, almost a flirtation. They met through Marandel when Bozo arrived in New York in 1969 on a Focillon fellowship. "I was certainly aware that he relied on charm. I liked that, but I am no pushover. [. . .] I don't suffer Don Juans lightly. I've been told that he was a loyal friend, and that he believed only in amorous friendship."[26]

They saw one another regularly, whether in Paris or New York, and wrote each other long letters. Dominique Bozo was the first French curator to buy an important work from her; in 1973, he acquired *Cumul I*,[27] which would be shown at the Musée d'art moderne in 1974 before being absorbed into the collection of the Centre Pompidou. He sent several French colleagues and friends to meet her, including Françoise Cachin,[28] who one day tried on, in the basement of Louise's house in Chelsea, a multibreasted latex costume Louise created around the time of her famous performance of 1978, *A Banquet / A Fashion Show of Body Parts*. She later wrote to Louise, telling her that she was unhappy in the new museum at Beaubourg, and talked to her about her partner and daughter, Georges and Charlotte. He also introduced her to Isabelle Monod-Fontaine,[29] whose husband sometimes slept at Louise's house. But curiously, Dominique Bozo never wrote about Louise's work and did not organize a big exhibition in Paris, as she ardently hoped he would.[30] However, she did like talking with him:[31] "When I think of D[ominique] B[ozo], I can't help being sarcastic. [. . .] I had learned not to expect anything of him; and yet I liked him."[32] To please him, she went to see François Rouan's show at the Pierre Matisse Gallery in June 1976; she found it beautiful, sober, subtle: "I understand why you like him," she wrote, "but I prefer his texts to his paintings."[33] Later, on the accompanying catalog, she noted: "Robert Storr identifies with Bozo, Dominique was an anti hero. [. . .] Alfred Barr never got a PhD."[34] Sexuality, flirtation, power—she lumped them all together with what she referred to as powerful men, art critics or curators, whose friendship she cultivated for many reasons, but also because they could buy her work. Dominique was meant to serve as witness to Louise's fake marriage[35] to her student Pietro Cicognani, but when he couldn't make it, he sent Xavier Fourcade in his place.[36] Louise sometimes felt clumsy and maladroit in their game of seduction: "I can't forgive myself for the outburst I had in front of you";[37] "I'm ashamed of my violence, I like you so much, as you know."[38] Dominique replied: "[Your] violence doesn't bother me, it suits me."[39]

And yet their aesthetic tastes diverged at this period: Bozo was a great supporter of Simon Hantaï, whom he helped to discover, François Rouan, and the artists from the Jean Fournier Gallery, Joan Mitchell, James Bishop—artists of an abstract, formalist tendency, far removed from Louise's sensual and rather figurative subjectivity. He told her all of the twists and turns his career had taken, the Henry Moore show he was overseeing, the future Picasso Museum he had been tapped to run, and his resignation from his post as director of the Musée national d'art moderne at the Centre Pompidou in 1986.[40] She wrote him about thirty or so letters between 1972 and 1991.[41] She was meant to come to Paris with other American artists for the inauguration of the Centre Pompidou in 1977: "The whole of the American school is turning up at Beaubourg for the opening. Can you let me know if Pontus[42] included me among the Americans or the French or not at all? It's very important for me."[43] Alas, not at all, which indicates just how eccentric and misunderstood her work was at this time.

Louise agreed to write a short text in the tribute book that was made in his honor after his tragic death in 1993, *D. B.: The Good Public Servant.* With her corrosive sense of humor and her eye for detail, she noted that he was a man who blushed: "D. B. was the only man I ever saw blush," and that, despite his handsome figure, his legs were too short.[44]

On May 9, 1970, Louise created a plaster cast of her friend Henri Zerner's face, which she would later do again with Xavier Girard.[45] In Zerner's case, it was to try out casting a bust in preparation for one she was commissioned to do of Peter von Blanckenhagen, a scholar of Roman art and a colleague of Robert's, for the Institute of Fine Arts.[46] Because she was not accustomed to this kind of work, and given his physical disability, she wanted to do some test casts on someone else. Since the first cast of Zerner didn't take very well, she drew Zerner's portrait, as she would also do in 1972 for von Blanckenhagen.

During the summer of 1970, Louise and Robert went to Saint-Paul-de-Vence to attend the opening of a show at the Fondation Maeght, *L'art vivant aux États-Unis* (Living art in the United States), curated by Dore Ashton. Louise showed *Clamart* (1968), a large piece in white marble, and Peter Agostini[47] contributed a sculpture whose round, erotic forms were distinctly reminiscent of Louise's work from the 1960s. Her reactions were, as usual, paranoid, but also caustic and clear-sighted: "No one invites us for so much as a drink—all the American artists complain. All the French artists ignore us."[48] "The whole exhibition is just a frame for Yunkers[49] / South American dealer from Caracas, who is going to show Yunkers, I am incapable of speaking to him, because I would like a show for myself."[50] This presentation of American art in France took place in a very particular political context, the anti-imperialism that most of the American artists shared; artists signed a petition that was circulated at the same time as the exhibition, against the recuperation of art and culture by a racist government supporting fascist regimes.[51]

Pietrasanta—Paris—New York, 1970–1972

On July 20, 1970, Louise and Robert left for Pietrasanta; Robert stayed with her there for a month, and then their correspondence resumes.[52] Louise stayed on until October 19, 1970, and in that time she made some new pieces, including geometric towers carved from travertine stone and titled *Serpentine* (1968–70). She was also working with round bits of found marble and little cylinders whose edges she shaved off diagonally, in order to show their tilted faces. She placed them directly on the ground in a tight group, representing a crowd, like a demonstration of students or workers. Similarly her *Number Seventy-Two* (*The No March*) (1972) refers to the protest march against the Museum of Modern Art, a conflict she referenced in her collages, engravings, and numerous editions filled with the inscription *No.* "I want to say 'no,' but I am a pushover. Obedience is the big word . . . sometimes I obey, but I am never convinced. I go through the motions because I have been taught to be obedient . . . but behind this, I never give in."[53]

Her works in marble, such as *Baroque* (1970), were sometimes difficult for the artisans to make: "it is a very complicated baroque piece in the mood of *Clutching*"[54] in yellow Siena marble, but made five times bigger. She also worked on a percussion instrument that she hoped to dedicate to Jean-Louis: seven thin columns affixed to a crosspiece. In order to create the aural component of this xylophone, she asked Robert to get some information from his colleague Denise Paulme or her husband, André Schaeffner,[55] who was friends with Pierre Boulez. Could he "write a few lines for this new instrument"?[56] Louise also worked on Peter von Blanckenhagen's portrait, as he was in Italy at this time. She had made a first attempt at his face in March 1967, which she was trying to rework, since Robert remarked that it looked more like an imprint than a sculpted portrait:[57] "I will listen to you for the portrait although I <u>respect</u> what a mask from the live original procures—it is simply something else than an interpretation."[58]

Jacques Lipchitz came to visit: "The old master was there this morning with his mane in the wind like an old tree, I didn't talk to him but smiled from afar."[59] A dinner was organized in his honor at the pensione with thirty-four sculptors. Louise was very proud to be seated beside Lipchitz and to act as hostess: "To be important for two hours was <u>very</u> pleasant."[60]

She also often saw her friends the Poncets, to whom she made a present of a little house made of black Belgian marble, Henry Moore, Alina Szapocznikow, and La Papa. But this year, "the sociabilities do not interest me—only the models occupy me and the resistances to vanquish in this smaller scale work consume all my energy."[61] "I even thought (a bit late in the game) that marble is my vocation—I have the impression that I could work on the same piece for months without getting tired of it."[62] This material, which brought strong resistance together with an extreme softness, particularly suited her.

She was attempting to bring to New York a dog called Cosimo, who had been lost and wounded. He had followed her around the previous year, and she had him vaccinated and tried to get someone to look after him. This dog was very important to her because *he* had adopted *her;* he later appears in the short films she made on West Twentieth Street with Pietro Cicognani.[63]

Always curious and up for an adventure, Louise wanted to try returning to New York by boat via Genoa, Algiers (in order to see the Casbah), and Morocco, but the cruise was expensive and complicated. She wasn't stingy, she wrote, but she was always afraid of spending too much money: "I don't dare tell you what the pictures cost, the hotel is paid I hope that there will still be a spot on the boat in tourist class. I am not very proud of myself and feel the size of a pea."[64] She wrote from Genoa, where the boat was stuck for a few days because of a strike. It was a communist city, beautiful but dirty, she said; she visited the old town, the Roman churches, the port, and the narrow streets.[65] On October 28, the boat finally left, and Louise was "very happy to see the coast of France."[66] The beginning of the trip shows her working hard, socializing, still very much in love—from afar—with her husband: "Speaking of slender bodies I would like to touch yours—I feel very lonely in bed."[67] But the final letters, before her departure, betray the return of her feelings of guilt (being far from her family for birthdays and Thanksgiving), anxiety, and depression: "I feel very isolated and don't give a damn about anything."[68] "The magic word[s] I love you, I believe that if I was never to hear it I would want to die [. . .] I am so depressed that I can't shake off the dark ideas. If I don't work soon I will go to France or throw myself in front of a truck."[69]

The following year, 1971, she made *Le Trani Episode* in marble, terracotta, plaster, and plaster and latex. It followed the logic of the 1960s work in terms of its ambivalence toward gender. Trani is a small Italian village near Carrara. The oblong forms are simplified here and represent elongated breasts which could also be a pair of phalli. The association of breast milk with sperm is a tribute to life. The novelty here is that the two overlap: "Because these forms are empty it becomes a container, the inside is hollow. If you lift up the top, you will find a box of secrets."[70] Louise also managed to reference the refuge of the maternal breast, the warmth of bodies pressed together, the desire and the buried treasure of childhood, for the way the piece rocks evokes that of a cradle. She later cast the piece in bronze and also remade it in luminous alabaster, as part of *Precious Liquids* (1992).

Back in New York, her social life picked up again and she mingled with a younger generation of artists; on April 4, 1971, she noted the names Tony Smith, Andy Warhol, and Robert Morris in her diary.

Out of friendship for the artist Jean Revol,[71] she wrote a short text for his exhibition: "The paintings endlessly repeat the same terror. Jean Revol is presently preparing a book, *The Invention of the Image;* its title comes from Goethe's words: 'When terror grips me I create an image.'"[72] The same could be said of her own practice.

In July, her cat died: "Champfleurette leaves us [. . .] without a sound, purring and listening. 10 PM."[73] She also cited a book by Samuel J. Warner in her diary: "read Warner selfdefeatism [*sic*] 'double polarity,'"[74] because she always defeated herself as an artist: "You are an artist if you say you are—why did you say that. (I am an artist if my life is a work of art.) Can you prove it. You are an artist if you had had [*sic*] shows."[75]

On June 6, 1972, Robert and Louise went to Paris again and stayed at the Hôtel du Danube.[76] She went to the Café de Flore. On June 15, she returned to Pietrasanta (where she would stay until July 20) to finish *Number Seventy-Two* (*The No March*) and to see her friends Hugh Honour and John Fleming in Viareggio.

"State of Shock," 1973

As early as 1967, Louise wrote in her diary that Robert's arm was bothering him and mentioned a hemorrhage.[77] In March 1973, Robert was very tired:

"Robert is very tired + irritated also when I come back at 6:30."[78] On March 26, he died suddenly in his sleep.[79] Dr. Bry Benjamin signed the death certificate, and the funeral was March 29.[80] This death was another shock for Louise: "when my father died I lost my equilibrium. when Rob[er]t died I fell in a state of shock for a year."[81] On May 7, she wrote: "It is in Janet + Alain that I am going to find echoes of Rob[er]t."[82] His sister and son looked so much like him and reminded her as well of her own mother, reasonable and calm.

Robert's heart attack has often been ascribed to the different sources of the stress he was under: disputes about Mark Rothko's estate[83] and the huge responsibility as head of the Museum of Primitive Art. Little by little, Louise realized the extent to which Robert played an important role in her life and saw only his virtues: "Robert has never made any demands on me except when it concerned <u>my</u> work [. . .] career,[84] his demands on me in both cases were functions of the demands of his conscience," but in that case, "the indirect moral imperative[s] were too much for me."[85] "Robert was the darling of the ladies."[86] She tried to overcome this painful loss by attempting to preserve a trace of him, arranging the living room exactly as it had been when he was there: "intimate waxed, shiny—he loved it, it was his favorite room. I loved the bedroom best with its cochineal red heart, bed spread, mysterious and warm."[87] In the autumn, an exhibition was curated in his honor at the Museum of Primitive Art (from October 1973 to February 1974); his colleague Jacqueline Delange, the Africanist at the Musée de l'homme, was commissioned to write one of the texts for the accompanying catalog.[88] Robert Goldwater was an important figure in the American art world, esteemed by his colleagues and students,[89] even though some found him slightly cold and intimidating. Louise continued to welcome the students that Robert sometimes invited over for dinner and looked after the books in his library, which were carefully preserved so that his professional archives might be donated to the Archives of American Art.[90] "[T]he challenge of Rob[er]t being immortal / Bateson, obsession, all his books, students, friends, he is not gone," she wrote in her diary on June 6, 1974.[91]

She fought to withstand her loneliness and struggled to go on making work: "I am an artist with the whole house as a studio, I am not week [*sic*] nor crushed. I do not need a family, Rob[er]t would be proud of me and that is enough."[92] Her husband's death reminded her of her father's: "when my father passed away I built in NY a memorial to him recollecting the beautiful

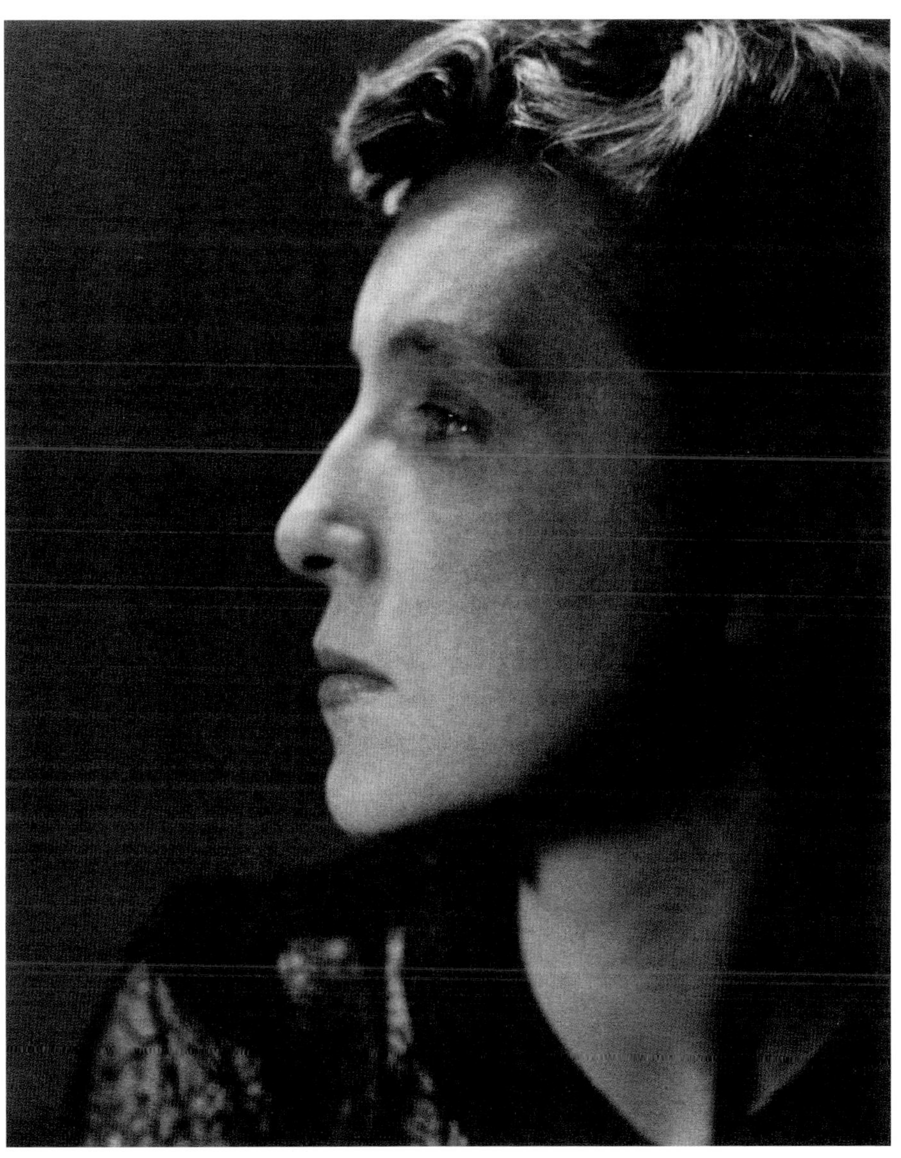

Louise Bourgeois, 1949.
Photograph by Berenice Abbott

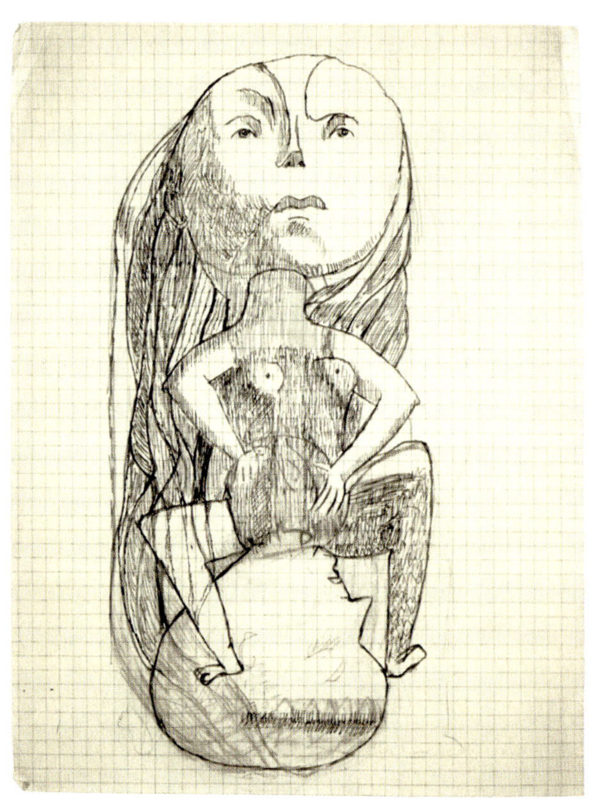

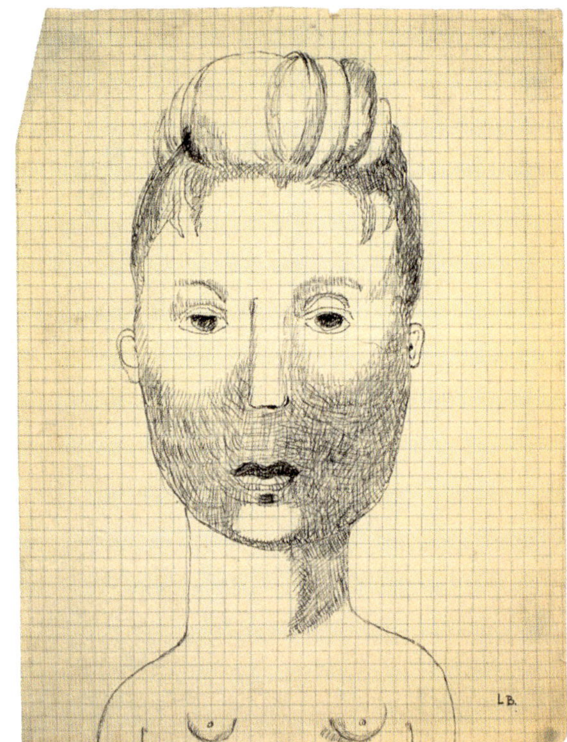

Untitled (*Woman Giving Birth*),
1941. Ink and pencil on graph
paper, 11 × 8½ in. (27.9 × 21.6 cm)

Self-Portrait, 1942. Ink on graph
paper, 11 × 8½ in. (27.9 × 21.6 cm)

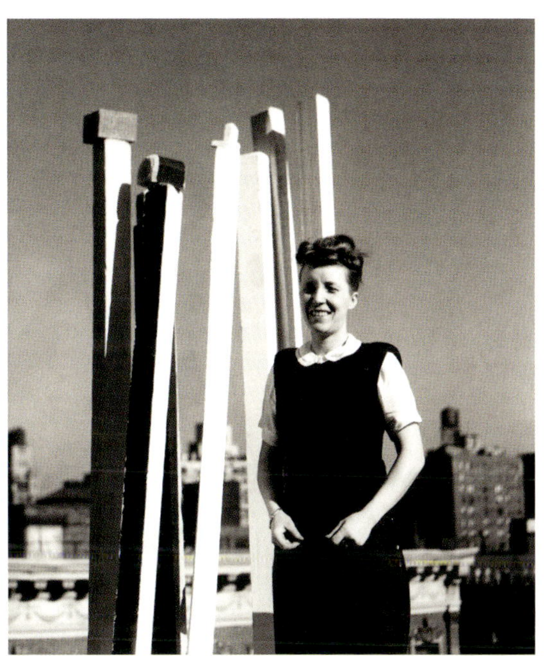

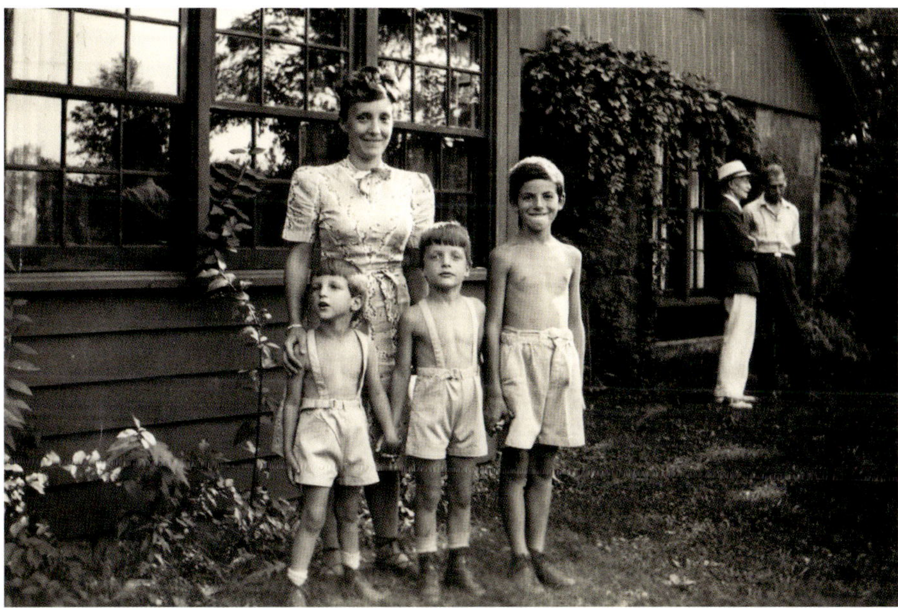

Louise Bourgeois with *The Visitors Arrive at the Door*
(no longer extant) on the roof of her apartment building,
Stuyvesant's Folly, 142 East 18th Street, New York, c. 1946

Louise Bourgeois with sons Alain, Jean-Louis, and Michel,
Easton, Connecticut, 1945

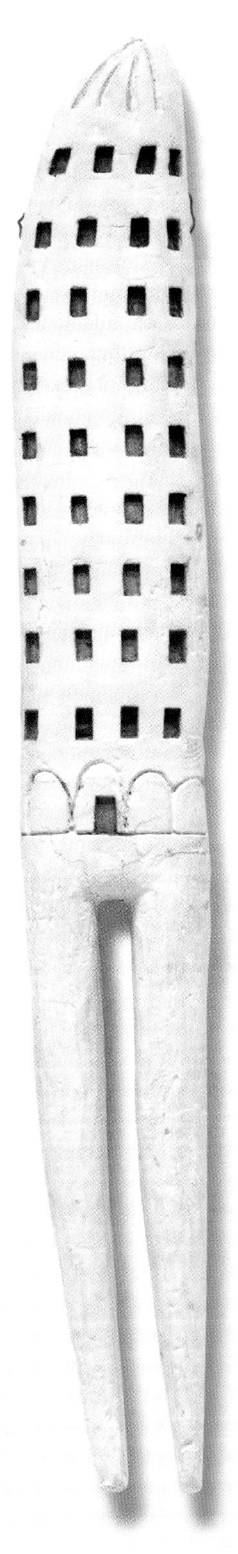

Portrait of Jean-Louis, 1947–49.
Painted wood, 35 × 4 × 1¼ in.
(88.9 × 10.2 × 3.2 cm)

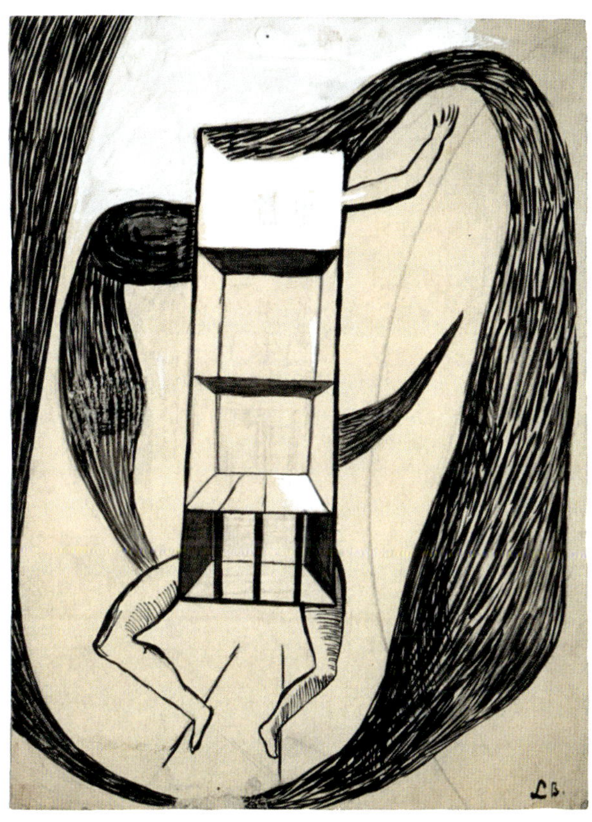

Femme maison, 1947. Ink, gouache, and pencil on paper, 12¼ × 9¼ in. (31.1 × 23.5 cm)

RIGHT

Exhibition announcement for *Documents France, 1940–1944: Art—Literature—Press of the French Underground* curated by Louise Bourgeois, Norlyst Gallery, New York, June 4–19, 1945

documents france 1940-1944
art - literature - press of the french underground

UNDERGROUND ANTI-NAZI PRESS

its purpose was the organization of an effective resistance. its newspapers, tracts, and pamphlets were addressed to the general public, to trade unions, and to professional groups:
defense de la france
resistance
combat
le franc tireur
la revue libre
l'insurge
liberer et federer
le populaire
m.o.f.
l'humanite
le peuple syndicaliste
jeune garde
cahiers politiques
les cahiers du temoignage chretien
le palais (de justice) libre
l'universite libre
etudiants de la classe 44
l'ecole de bara
le medecin francais
appel a l'intelligence francaise
debats de l'assemblee consultative provisoire
la convention de la haye
le patriote
le patriote lyonnais
l'instituteur francais

ART

posters, le marche noir,
participez au recensement,
il compte sur vous,
liberation posters
photographs
100 photos of german occupation
paintings
pierre bonnard
pablo picasso
jean dubuffet by louis parrot
jean dubuffet by pierre seghers
letter from jean paulhan to jean dubuffet
articles by rene huyghe, jean cassou
art magazines

POETRY

louis aragon (francois la colere): Broceliande (manuscrit); le musee grevin (editions de Minuit); les yeux d'elsa; le creve-coeur.
jean cassou: 33 sonnets composes en secret (editions de minuit).
jacques decour (decourdemanche): pages choisies (editions de minuit).
pierre emanuel: combats avec tes defenseurs.
loys masson: delivrez nous du mal.
pierre seghers: le domaine public; chien de pique.
poetes prisonniers (editions de minuit).
poesie 42: pour les quatre saisons (*pierre emanuel, loys masson, andre de richaud, pierre seghers*).
poesie 44: (*paul eluard, max jacob*).

PROSE

louis aragon: le crime contre l'esprit (editions de minuit); la facon de vivre et de mourir de gabriel peri; saint pol roux ou l'espoir, temoignages.
debu-bridel: angleterre (editions de minuit).
(*mortagne*): le marque de l'homme (editions de minuit).
jean bruller (vercors): le silence de la mer (editions de minuit).
elsa triolet (jean le guern): l'arrestation.
jean-paul sartre: la nausee; l'homme et les choses (poesie 44).
problemes du roman (confluence).
les cahiers de la liberation (editions de minuit).
andre gide: la justice avant la charite (combat).
gertrude stein: problemes du roman.

ACKNOWLEDGMENTS

this exhibition would not have been possible without the generous cooperation of the following:
office of war information; columbia university library; french press and information service.
messrs. louis clair, marcel duchamp, peter c. rhodes, eugene sheffer.
i wish to express my sincere thanks to all of them for their kind assistance.

norlyst gallery
59 west 56
new york city 19

JUNE 4 to JUNE 19, 1945
EXHIBITION ARRANGED BY LOUISE BOURGEOIS

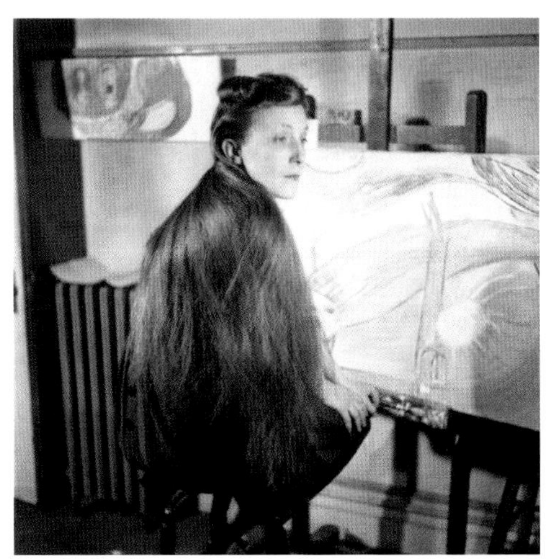

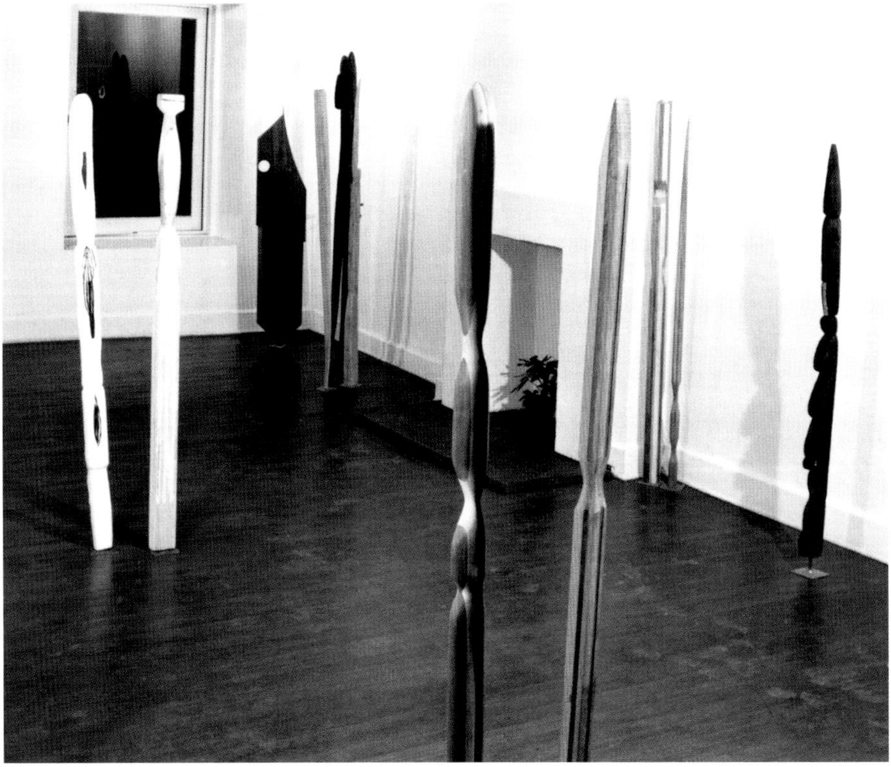

Louise Bourgeois in her studio, New York, c. 1946

Installation view of *Louise Bourgeois: Sculptures*,
Peridot Gallery, New York, October 2–28, 1950.
Photograph by Aaron Siskind

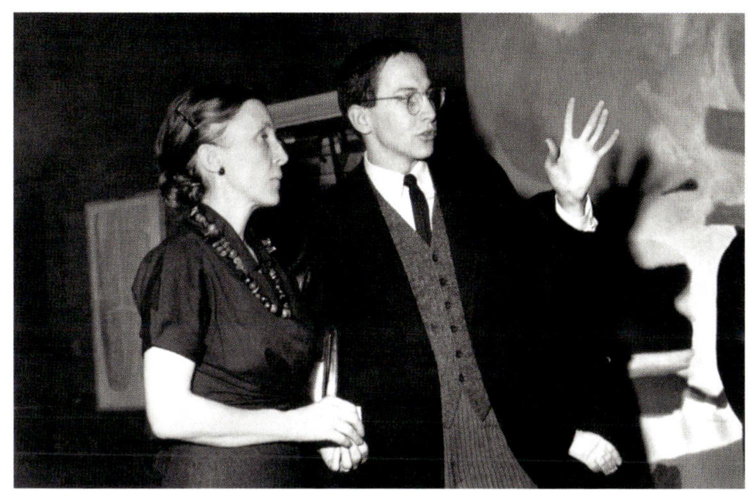

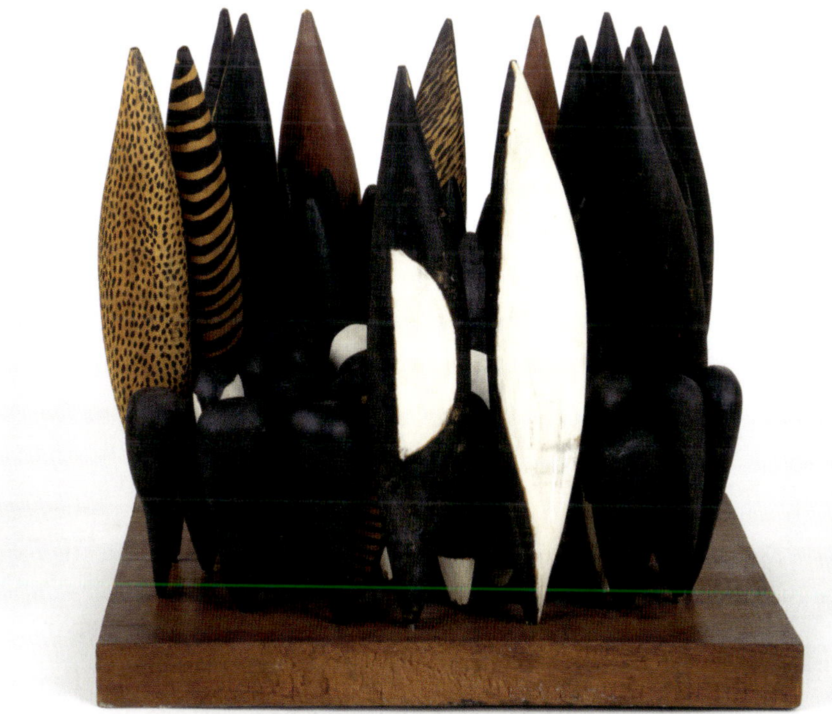

Louise Bourgeois and Robert Rauschenberg
at the *Annual Exhibition of American Abstract
Artists,* Riverside Museum, New York, 1954

One and Others, 1955. Painted and stained wood,
18⅝ × 20 × 16⅞ in. (47. 3 × 50.8 × 42.9 cm)

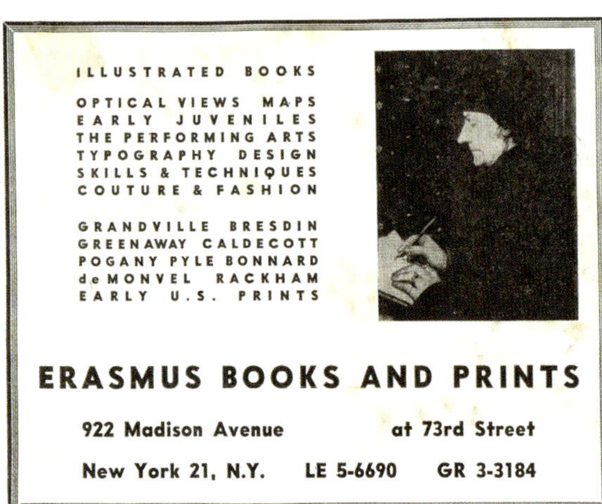

ILLUSTRATED BOOKS
OPTICAL VIEWS MAPS
EARLY JUVENILES
THE PERFORMING ARTS
TYPOGRAPHY DESIGN
SKILLS & TECHNIQUES
COUTURE & FASHION
GRANDVILLE BRESDIN
GREENAWAY CALDECOTT
POGANY PYLE BONNARD
de MONVEL RACKHAM
EARLY U.S. PRINTS
ERASMUS BOOKS AND PRINTS
922 Madison Avenue   at 73rd Street
New York 21, N.Y.   LE 5-6690   GR 3-3184

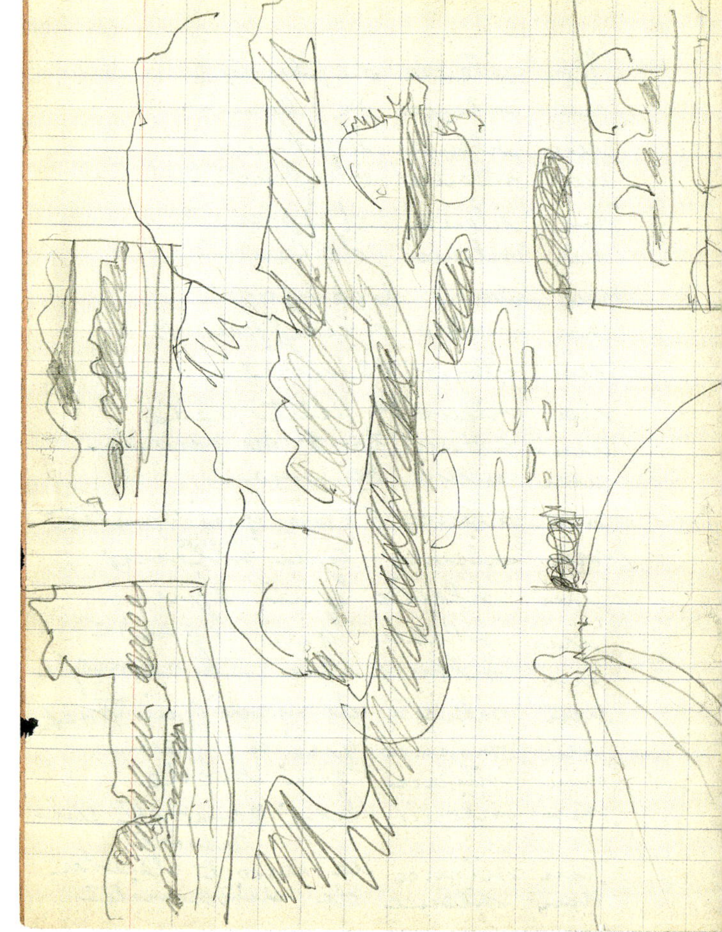

Following the summer trend il y a eu hier un tangible, positif
Return à la mère. hier dans ma sculpture j'ai fait des dessins de
seins pressés les uns contre les autres; il y avait une double attitude to be like a mother and liked by mother.
the emphasis was on the hilltop - Pursing of the lips
et tout le corps tendu pour donner un
pursing the lips Kiss like
sucking toute la personne
devient un sui qui se
tend pour donner - leur
était une identification de toute
la journée avec une partie
du corps

aussi dans la sculpture souci de direction
Dans les fruits du père il y a objet pendu
direction vers le bas.
Dans les fruits de mer il y a thrust forward. larger size warmth between the nos
demi de sommeil. c'est bien pour mettre sa tête
dessus. c'est le même ordre de grandeur que la tête ou qu'
les fesses. les fruits de père sont plutôt fingers and fiddling
un ox down right upsurging and agressif - la mère et la
Terre, les mamelons de Bourgogne et de provence une d'autre
où l'on s'endort sur l'herbe chaude. aussi les fruits du Père
sont semi détaché du corps comme des fruits sur un arbre
les fruits de la mère sont attaché au corps pres la pleine
surface du diamètre de la sphère - il ne pourrait
pas l'être davantage et en même temps ils ont un bouton

un sommeil de mort
un sommeil ami.
un sommeil tordu
un sommeil de pierre
un sommeil de marais
un sommeil rose
un sommeil rose et propre
un sommeil rose thé
un sommeil rose sale et
pourquoi pas.
un sommeil d'adoration
un sommeil de mal au cou
un sommeil de lumière trop
cru
un sommeil tout doucement
un sommeil de repos
un sommeil de fuite
un sommeil de refus
et un un sommeil de refus
total
un sommeil de comme il faut
et un sommeil de je m'en fous
un silence n'est pas forcément un
sommeil
Le sommeil dit dans le sens où il

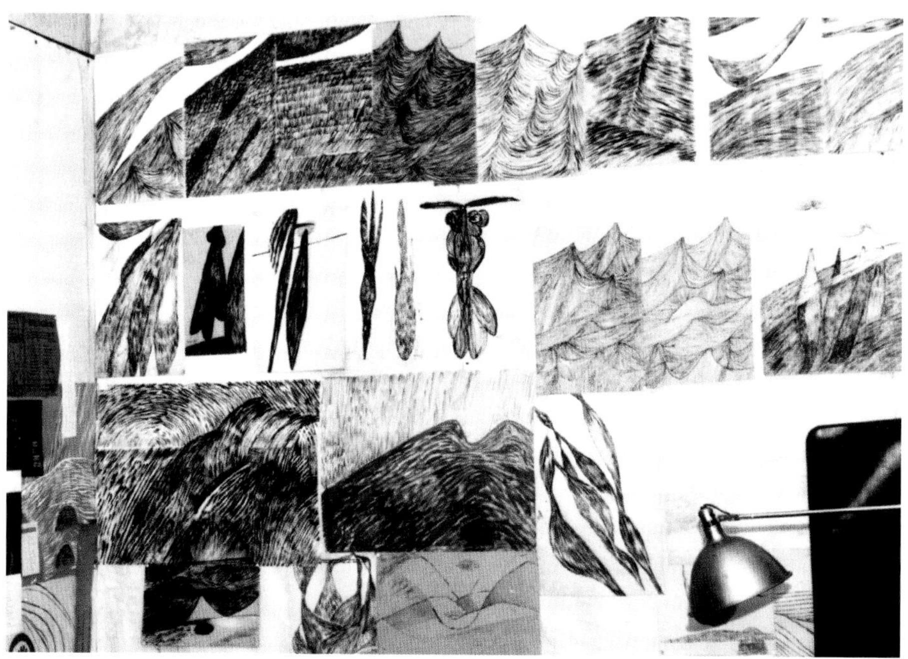

Louise Bourgeois's drawings pinned to the wall,
New York, 1962

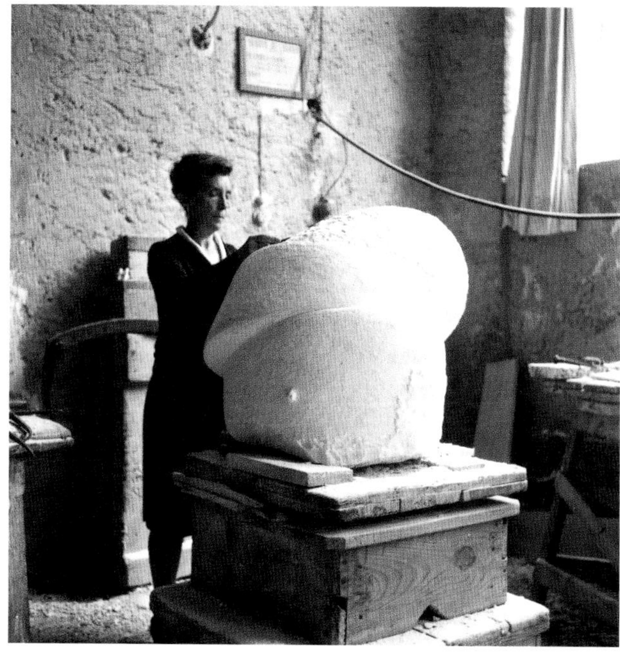

Louise Bourgeois with *Sleep II*, Pietrasanta, Italy, 1967

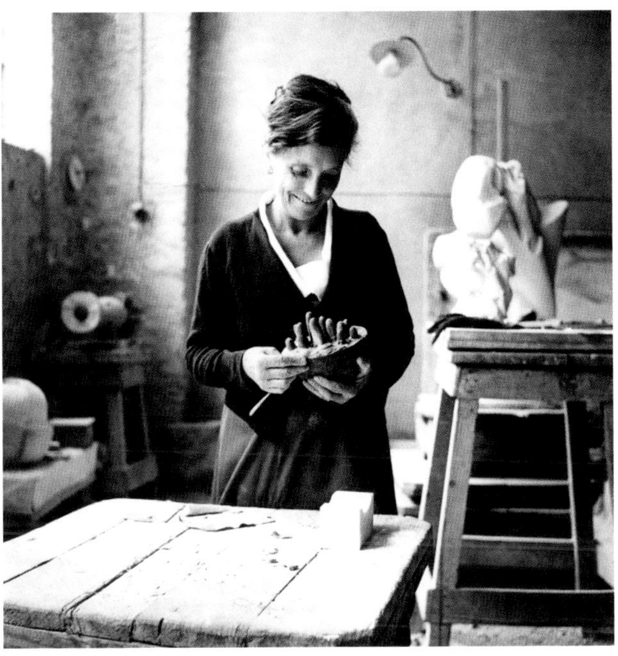

Louise Bourgeois with *Germinal*, Pietrasanta, Italy, 1967

Letter from Louise Bourgeois to Robert Goldwater
(recto/verso), April 29, 1969. Ink on paper

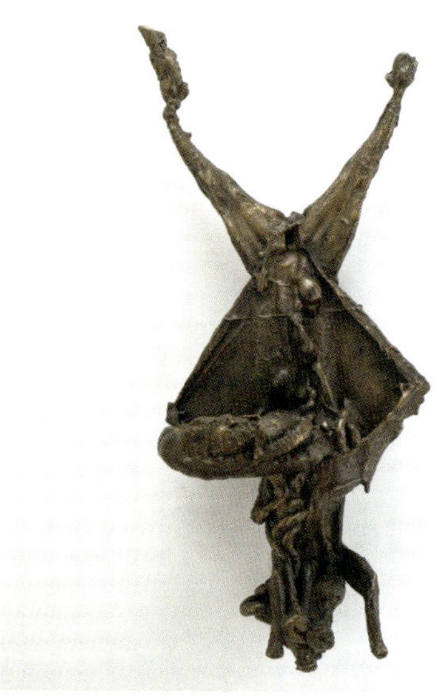

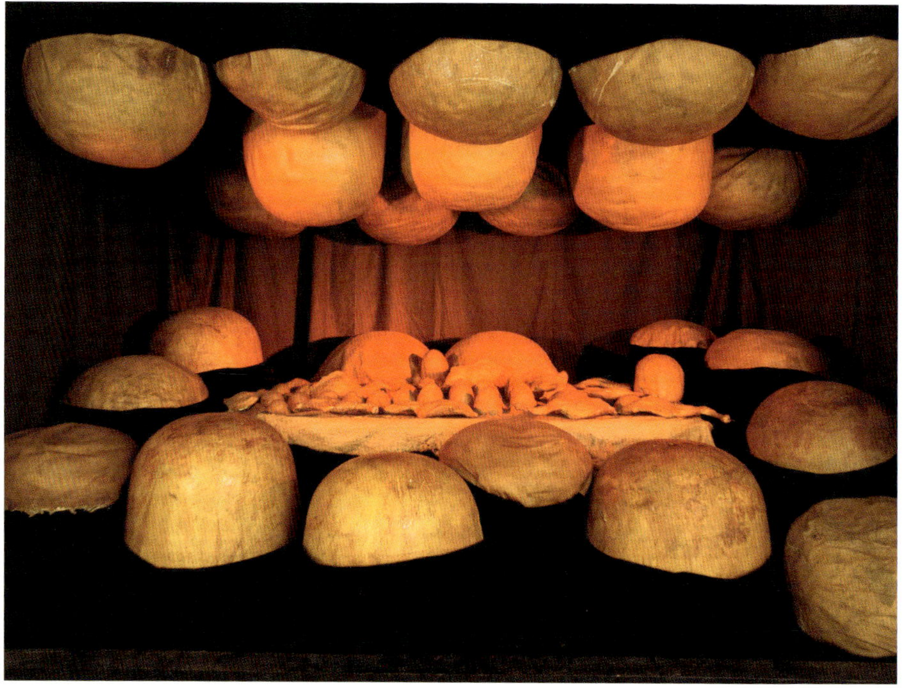

Rabbit, 1970. Bronze, 23 × 11⅜ × 5⅞ in.
(58.4 × 28.9 × 14.9 cm)

The Destruction of the Father, 1974. Latex, plaster,
wood, fabric, and red light, 9⅝ × 142⅝ × 97⅞ in.
(237.8 × 362.3 × 248.6 cm)

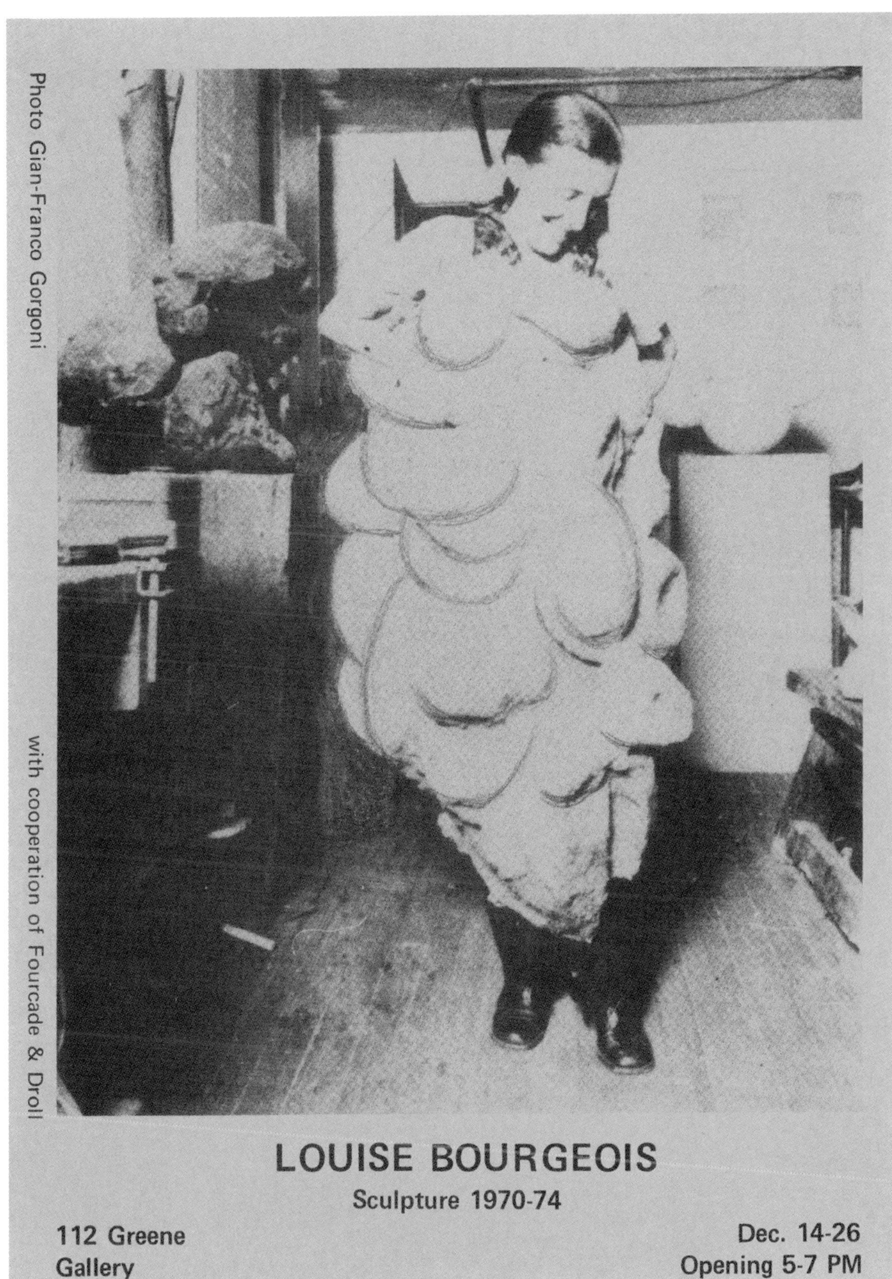

Exhibition announcement for *Louise Bourgeois:
Sculpture 1970–74*, 112 Greene Street, New York,
December 14–26, 1974

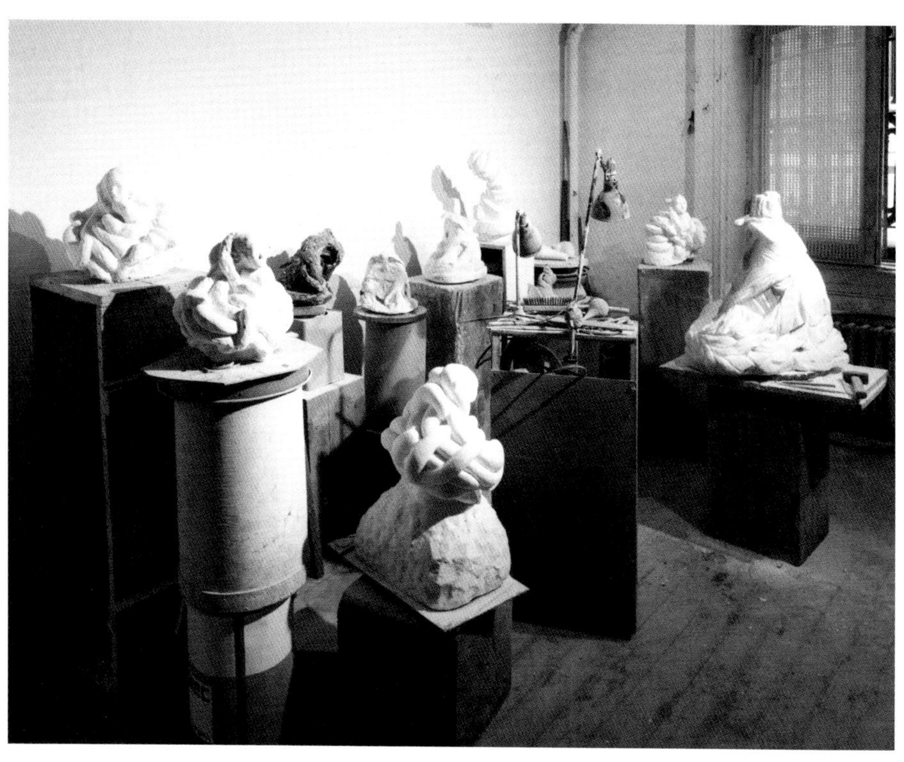

Louise Bourgeois's work in her home studio,
New York, 1982

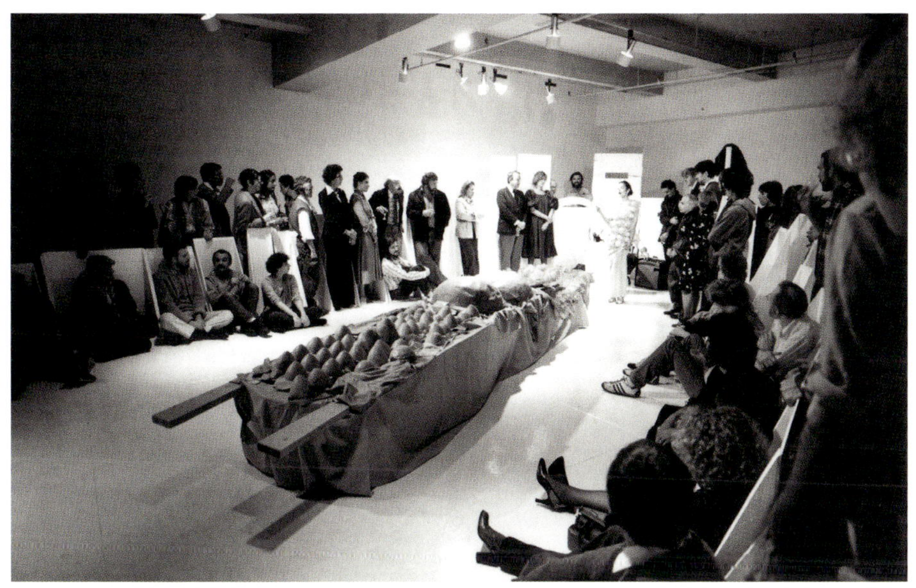

Louise Bourgeois's performance, *A Banquet / A Fashion Show of Body Parts*, staged around her sculpture *Confrontation*, Hamilton Gallery of Contemporary Art, New York, October 21, 1978. Photograph by Peter Moore

Invitation to the feminist dinner party in honor of Louise Bourgeois hosted by Mary Beth Edelson and Ana Mendieta, New York, March 14, 1979

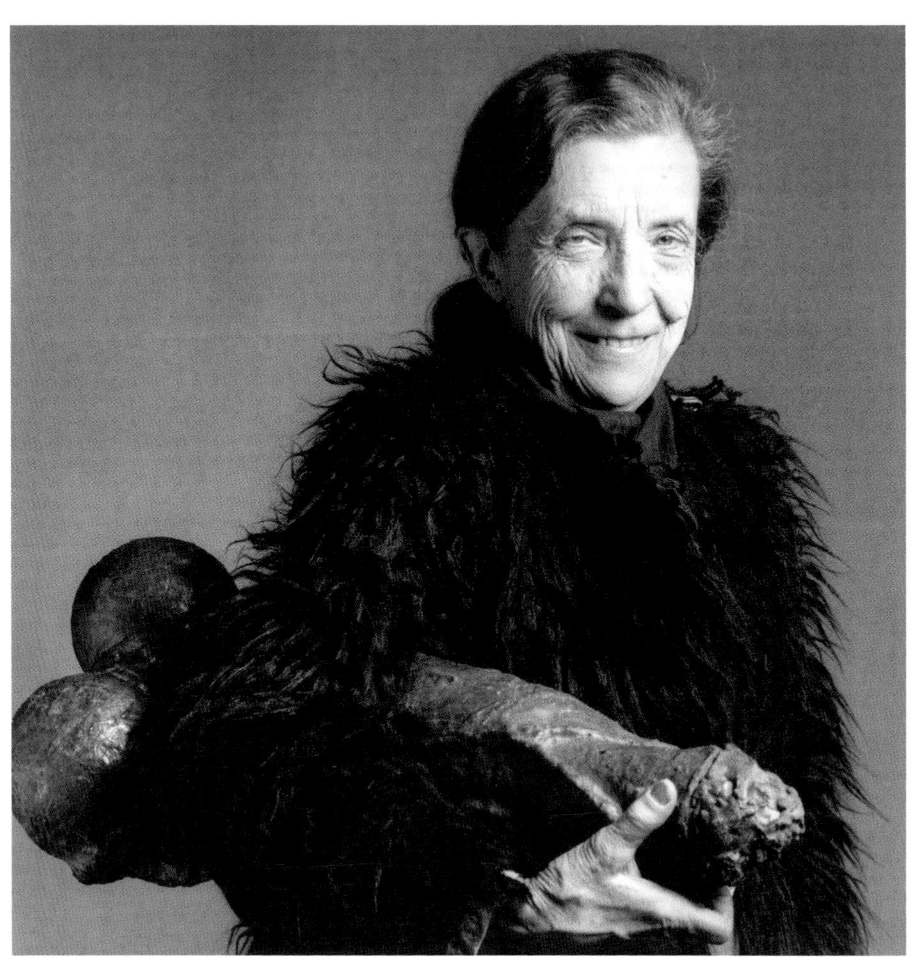

Louise Bourgeois, 1982.
Photograph by Robert Mapplethorpe

past and refusing to let go / when Rob[er]t passed away I turn the house into a museum refusing to let anyone in."[93]

But as early as April 1973, Louise was inviting over younger artist friends, such as Joyce Kozloff, Nancy Spero, and Vivien Corso; above all, she was becoming more and more involved in the young feminists' liberation movement and appreciated their company. She wanted to give a party for Joyce, but "[Nancy] Spero has usurper [*sic*] my party for Joyce."[94] Kozloff remembers another detail from an opening night party held at her place, to which Louise absolutely insisted on bringing a meat dish, although only a cold buffet had been planned. Louise rang the door early that morning saying, "The butcher's here!" and attempted to cook an enormous leg of lamb in the artist's tiny oven.[95] This anecdote says much about her complex relationship to food, especially to meat, which, as a good housekeeper, she insisted on but also abhorred.

Empty House

After Robert's death, Louise felt deeply lonely in their house. This physical experience of emptiness plunged her back into psychic anguish: "The perception of the inner void gives me vertigo; an anxiety uncontrollable [. . .] the vertigo hangs at the edge of the abyss, at the edge of the well [and] enters one's consciousness."[96] "[T]he empty house means that I am identified with the void, it isn't out there any longer / I am the void, quite tiring but I become active instead of passive— Then it's a matter of filling it up, collecting. Collecting is stupid."[97] Empty and full, active and passive, this infernal, dialectic spiral dominated her life. "[F]ear of emptiness, Marie Bonaparte [. . .] intuition of the damage caused by the thought—I have nothing. Terror of emptiness, of the void. [. . .] I have no one to go out with me, I have nothing, no cloth[es], no charm [. . .] no job, no interest, no right to show myself, nothing to do."[98]

She set about filling the void—Robert's absence, her feelings of abandonment—through the accumulation of things and memories, endlessly re-creating the past. "Robert loved to be trusted, entrusted with—he did not leave a 'single' personal paper apart from his family—no diary. I left a mountain of it. Ego for me. No collection—he would live for the present moment. I live in the past or in the future, the horror of the present."[99] Once she had processed the shock and devastation of his sudden death, she was able to develop her career as an artist on her own, without the support or the gaze of her art historian husband. For a long time Louise refused to speak of Robert, to include him in films about her, to refer to their shared aesthetic affinities, especially non-Western art.[100] Robert had become a taboo subject. Then, at the end of her life, when she was beginning to create her sculptures of couples, returning to the theme of the family, she became more willing to discuss him, with much tenderness. A small selection of their early letters was published in 2015, after her death.[101] But we will have to wait for the forthcoming edition of their many letters to further understand their emotional connection, their role as parents, and the strength of their bond, in spite of the tensions and differences of opinion that marked the beginning of their marriage and their apparently unsatisfying physical relationship.[102]

Louise happily began teaching at the School of Visual Arts (SVA) in January 1974 and was quite well suited to the maternal role of professor and mentor, which she would play there until 1976 and at other art schools until 1983. She loved her young students. Then she returned to Paris from July 2 to 23, 1974, staying at the Hôtel du Danube near Saint-Germain-des-Prés. She saw the artist Dorothea Tanning, went to Düsseldorf to see a dealer called Galloway, who didn't even look at her photos, stopped off in Cologne to see the cathedral. During her stay in Paris she visited Dominique Bozo and Paulette and Georges Place. She mentions Georges Place again on July 18, as well as the name Nadine Pouillon, who worked at the Musée national d'art moderne and was in charge of acquiring *Cumul* for the museum. She also went to see her sister, Henriette, and her cousin Jacques.

Back in New York, she saw her psychoanalyst.[103] She read R. D. Laing's book *Knots* (1970),[104] which was very close to her own poetic writings, as much in their form—lists of words, linear outlines—as in their contents, which had to do with the need for love and recognition. Laing was very fashionable during this time among New York intellectuals. In her copy of *Knots,* Louise marked the following passage: "He is devoured by her being devoured by him not devouring her."[105] An interweaving of knots, desire, and cannibalism which Louise would herself make material in *The Destruction of the Father* (1974). She returned to Laing in the 1980s: "See in Laing: invasion of privacy, territory, silence, noise within my space."[106]

However, a young friend of hers from this time, the writer and filmmaker Chris Kraus[107] (who was with Sylvère Lotringer at the time) tended to be critical of the star of antipsychiatry: "R. D. Laing never figured out that 'the divided self' is female subjectivity."[108] Louise was well aware of women's multiple identities: "Why not be yourself," Robert said, "but there are so many selves."[109]

Feminism, Politics, Eroticism

I have no comment. I'm a woman, so I don't need to be a feminist.

Without claiming to really be a feminist, Louise participated in a number of feminist events and exhibitions in the 1970s.[110] In December 1970, there was a protest during the opening party of the Whitney's annual show, dedicated to sculpture, against the small percentage of women included. She protested despite being one of the few women in the show, her *Noir veine* (1968) having been included. The art critic Grace Glueck wrote a piece for the *New York Times* about this first militant feminist demonstration in a museum, describing the eggs and tampons scattered through the rooms and even on the artworks in the show.

Another demonstration was held two years later, to call for more attention to be paid to female artists—"MoMA Prefers Papa," went the slogan on everyone's pins. She joined Chryssa and Lee Krasner in fighting the museum's discrimination.[111]

In March 1972, she took part in the *Thirteen Women Artists* show organized by the Women's Ad Hoc Committee, housed at 117–119 Prince Street in New York—one of the three main feminist organizations, along with Women Artists in Revolution (WAR) and Women Students and Artists for Black Art Liberation. Later that year, she took part in *American Women: Twentieth Century* at the Lakeview Center for the Arts and Sciences in Peoria, Illinois, and *American Woman Artist Show* curated by GEDOK at the Kunsthaus Hamburg.[112] Then in 1974, she contributed to *Women's Work: American Art, 1974* at the Museum of the Philadelphia Civic Center during FOCUS, a series of citywide events celebrating the achievements of women in the visual arts, as well as several others.

In 1977, four young female art historians curated an exhibition called

From Women's Eyes at the Rose Art Museum at Brandeis University in Massachusetts. Louise was chosen by Deborah Wye, who was just starting out; thus began a long working friendship. In 1978, Louise appeared in a photo-collage[113] by Mary Beth Edelson, surrounded by Nancy Spero, Pat Lasch, and Michelle Stuart, and then in a photograph of the feminist dinner party Edelson and Ana Mendieta gave in her honor on March 14, 1979.

Louise's position on feminism—as usual—was ambivalent, and later she gave contradictory answers when asked about the label "feminist." As Elisabeth Lebovici writes: "Is she? Or isn't she?"[114] It's hard to say absolutely yes or no. We can't forget that Louise was of a different generation, for whom the term did not have the same meaning; for her, there was no specifically feminine art, and she defended the artist's work more than her gender. "A woman has no place as an artist until she proves over and over that she won't be eliminated."[115] "For better or worse, I am a woman, I can become a better artist, so it occupies more importance in my consciousness."[116] She also disapproved of some feminists' tendency to see themselves as victims. However, she also declared: "The women got together not because they had things in common but because they lacked things."[117]

And yet it was no accident that the women's liberation movement claimed her as one of its own. She was among the first to reconfigure "an aesthetic in which 'the personal is political'" and to place the body and sexuality at the heart of the "'sexual wars' between two contending feminist priorities: the right to be free of sexual violence and the right to sexual pleasure. Bourgeois was divided between these two options," between pleasure and violence.[118]

Not only was her work included in a number of feminist exhibitions, but she also actively took part in the many debates, conferences, and interviews which were held at this time. For the roundtable discussion "Does Art Have a Gender?" which took place at the YMCA on February 16, 1972,[119] Louise contributed a short text that was more about the success and the role of the artist, the need to show one's work, and the system of galleries and dealers, than about gender and sexuality, although she recognized "the frustration of the woman artist." Rather, she insisted on the interior necessity, on the inability to develop, and on the fact that "the solitary artist is going to be a thing of the past with his soul, his omnipotence, his pride, his patience and his destiny."[120]

The question of feminism is bound up with questions about the representation of sexuality and the erotic, considered characteristic of her work. "There has always been sexual suggestiveness in my work," she admitted in 1974,[121] insisting again on her ambivalence about gender, and on the importance of sexual education as natural and not dangerous.

In 1974, she was included in a group show at the Erotic Art Gallery. She took part in a meeting on the theme of the erotic in art, moderated by Anita Steckel.[122] The discussion was filmed,[123] and we can see Louise in a black apron dress and a white shirt with a round collar, that mischievous smile on her lips as she talks about her work with long-haired women in trousers and flowered shirts, who are talking about discrimination against female artists when the work is explicitly sexual. When it's her turn to speak, Louise says that she has more often suffered from being called a "woman artist" than an erotic one. Because her work is allusive, she says, suggestive, not literal or figurative; they are landscapes and not only sexual organs. But at the same time she says that the work she has recently showed at the Whitney, an accumulation of columns pressed up against one another, had been seen as a cemetery, or a bombed-out city, but that in fact it showed a number of penises, "because one hundred is better than one."[124] The young participants laugh at this. Her work was as ambivalent as ever, like *Janus* (1968). Louise held onto her contradictory perspective, sometimes rejecting a sexual interpretation, seen as too reductive, sometimes standing up for it.

Elsewhere in the political realm: in January 1972, she published a letter in *Art in America*[125] defending the Judson Three, artists accused of burning the flag, and called for a lottery of artworks to raise money for their legal defense; then in 1973, she supported the staff strike at MoMA.

A Feast for Cannibals

Louise would again build up a collection of maternal and phallic forms in *The Destruction of the Father* (1974). She covered a table with a tablecloth made of globular lumps of latex. In the center, she placed two enormous hemispheres and a form resembling a growth, indicating that we are in the domain of the erectile and the phallic. From the ceiling she suspended equally enormous spherical forms that could be interpreted as breasts, buttocks, or clouds. The whole thing emerged directly from the above/ below landscapes of the 1960s and the *Cumuls,* but here the setting evokes a cave, a cavernous space full of nooks and folds, or the inside of an enormous mouth.[126] The dark, closed space gives the viewer a sensation of entrapment, of violence and claustrophobia. Another title for the piece was *The Evening Meal,* which brings to mind a ritualized cannibalistic feast; its soft yellowish forms are cast in a red light and resemble bloody entrails and severed limbs. The reference, she said, was to family meals and the ambiguous love/hate relationship that she experienced with her father. It was the materialization of a scene lived sixty years earlier, when she imagined that the whole family was devouring him for revenge: "The room is dominated by a table, the horrible, terrifying table presided over by the father, who sits at its head and pontificates. And the others, the wife and children, what can they do? They sit, silent. The mother, obviously, tries to satisfy this tyrant, her husband. The children are nervous. . . . My father was overcome with annoyance, when he looked at us, and he always explained to us what a great man he was. So much so that, out of patience, we grabbed hold of him, threw him onto the table, tore him limb from limb and devoured him."[127]

This cannibalistic aspect of the work is confirmed by the fact that Louise cast pieces of animal bone and meat bought at the meat markets close to her house. The destruction of the father also symbolizes that of the husband, not the individual person, but as a public figure. The murderous rage that had dwelled within her for years was finally expressed in this spectacular piece, which was shown in December 1974 at 112 Greene Street Gallery, with works from the 1960s. It was Louise's first solo show in ten years. Despite its monumentality, it was created in the basement of her house in Chelsea. This no doubt contributed to the claustrophobic, subterranean aspect of the piece. "The sculpture represents both a table and a bed. [. . .] These two things count in one's erotic life: dinner table and bed. The table where your parents made you suffer. And the bed where you lie with your husband, where your children were born and you will die."[128]

But destroying the father did not resolve the complicated relationship with the mother: "I want no rivalry with a mother figure. It turns me into a guilty killer."[129]

The piece had a major impact. It made the cover of *Artforum,* and Lucy

Lippard wrote an important essay: "Louise Bourgeois: From the Inside Out."[130]

One of Louise's first filmed interviews dates from September 1975. It was made by Lynn Blumenthal and Kate Horsfield, who were filming interviews with artists for the Video Data Bank at the Art Institute of Chicago. For the first time, Louise spoke on the record about her childhood, her training in the Parisian academies, her interest in teaching. Some of the footage shows her class at SVA with students she introduced. She chose this setting because she wanted the "video [to] act as sculpture."[131] She very quickly realized the artistic potential of this new medium, and she took an active role in this and the later films that were made about her.

The rest of the footage, which comprises the final version of the film, was filmed in her house in Chelsea, a vertical space which was like a sculpture to her, that had to be constructed, repaired, and inhabited from the basement to the attic. This first official interview shows a politically committed Louise Bourgeois, engaged in the civil rights struggle and very concerned about the artistic situation of her time: "I consider myself a minority. I consider myself part of minority." When she is asked about her influences, she begins by looking back at her difficult relationship to the surrealists during the war years, recognizing that if she fought violently against them, it was because she felt too close to them. They were, for her, a "counter-influence." The other reason for her wariness was the secondary role they accorded women in the movement and the fact that they only liked, as she put it, wealthy women and collectors. She added that she much preferred political artists of that period, such as Gertrude and Balcomb Greene, who were close to Russian constructivism and nonobjective art.

She spoke a bit about her childhood and about the war, but she particularly emphasized the relationship between her body and her sculpture, her desire to please, the compulsive obsession to repeat. This interview allowed her to specifically locate her feminism, which was not directed against men. We cannot fight with them, she said, only ignore them, as they have ignored us. These statements were measured and extremely generous. We have to let go of desires that only bring disappointment—"ashes," she said—in favor of acceptance and giving. "The aim in life is to give without mentioning it, you see, without any feeling of the need for return." This generosity also appears in her diary, associated with the concept of renunciation—"Read about the Catholic Renunciation"[132]—which she associated with the rupture with Sadie and with her father.[133]

Fake Marriage

In 1974, Louise took a liking to one of her students at SVA named Pietro Cicognani,[134] a handsome and worldly young man, Italian on his father's side and Russian on his mother's,[135] who spoke French very well. He took her class on copper engraving and remembered that she was a very good teacher who pushed him to go further "towards the interior of his soul"[136] and to improve his technique.

"My best student is an Italian. He's a little crazy, but the creativity and the energy there is fantastic," she said in her Video Data Bank interview.[137] She added that she could not put into words what she felt for him.

Very quickly she developed a friendly and protective relationship with him. Then he left for Paris for a year, to take architecture classes at the École des beaux-arts; she sent him to the Musée national d'art moderne to see if her sculpture *Cumul* was well presented. In the letter he sent to her, Cicognani insists on the erotic aspect of the work, talks about orgasms, of "making love to a statue,"[138] and describes his life as a student. When he returned in 1976, he lived with Louise for over a month, and she did the cooking—something she hadn't done since Robert's death. Pietro remembered meeting her sons, Jean-Louis and Alain, who, in his opinion, "was the one she loved the most, he was her favorite, she respected him."[139] They talked about poetry and enjoyed a true friendship and intellectual understanding. At the time, Cicognani was fascinated by death and designed all kinds of tombs in homage to Baudelaire.[140] Louise filmed him with her camera while they talked. But she was jealous of his social life and his girlfriends, who she sometimes phoned at three in the morning to find out where he was. When he slept elsewhere one night, she waited for him at the top of the stairs and threw logs of firewood on him, which narrowly missed hitting him. Pietro admired her work and wanted to help her. He introduced her to his posh Italian friends, Carlo "Carletto" Perrone, the grandson of Marie-Laure de Noailles, and a collector friend, Gian Giacomo Attolico Trivulzio, who bought her portrait of Marcel Duchamp.

At the opening for the exhibition *Sculptors' Drawings* (May 29–June 8,

1976), he "proposed marriage"[141] to her, which he saw as a conceptual art piece. Cicognani compiled a dossier consisting of copies of their passports with their photographs, the marriage license from City Hall in New York (June 1976), and a statement from a witness, Xavier Fourcade, who was standing in for Dominique Bozo.[142] These documents from October 1976 were mounted under plexiglass and released in an edition of nineteen as Cicognani's final art project. The fake marriage was to be followed by a divorce in Hawaii in the following days. Pietro confirms that he had imagined the ceremony as a denunciation of the institution of marriage and a reflection of its futility. Louise was delighted to take part, to have this relationship with a charming young man, whom she looked after like an adopted son. But at the last moment, following the advice of his mother, Elena (who was also in correspondence with Louise), Pietro gave up the project, which was judged to be too risky (he was worried she wouldn't divorce him), and left for Italy. Louise, who took him to the airport, was very hurt. Their relationship was never the same. Pietro always felt a bit guilty, as he hadn't considered the ways the project could be misunderstood. Louise continued, however, to play a maternal role and to worry about him; she insisted he "immediately" see a therapist.[143] "To sublimate your feelings of extreme violence, it might be useful to visit Dr. Henry Lowenfeld a couple of times," she wrote to him on July 27, 1977, while reassuring him: "I never thought said or wrote that you were crazy, you are reasonable, even—and always intelligent."[144] She wanted, then, to bring him to see her own psychoanalyst, Henry Lowenfeld. He categorically refused, thinking that sublimation was linked to artistic creation and that suffering was also part of it.[145]

"What a difference between Pietro's 'departure' and Cosimo's. Never again, *vive la solitude* [long live solitude]!!!!!!"[146] she wrote in her diary on January 15, 1976, comparing the young man to the stray dog she'd brought back from Italy. Louise was torn between her maternal and amorous feelings for the young man. She was reading Roland Barthes's *Lover's Discourse* at this time,[147] as well as his essay on Pierre Loti, in which he described the debauched gay parties in New York at this period and the erotic drive that led to death.

Louise, who spent time with young artists and went to many gallery events, had her doubts about what they were calling performance art, which was becoming quite fashionable: "a happening is not a work of art, it is merely an experience. An experience is merely a solitary transformation of the self. Happenings have been concessions done to the viewers who become participants, but it is not [a] call upon the creativity."[148]

Similarly, she was critical of what she called accumulations: "burying things inside things does not make a sculpture, no more than accumulating. Process of elimination is more subtle because it represents a choice, a decision."[149]

Finally, Louise was skeptical about whether these exhibitions were at all useful. "Why do you want to show your work[?] What does it do for you? Is it any use? Do you fear criticism, take it personally, fear sarcasm[?] Warning: you are exposing yourself."[150]

She still felt herself to be in a rivalry with Louise Nevelson: "Nevelson never made any progress (see last show) because she had success too easily. No one ever criticized her."[151] Initially their relationship had been a friendly one, and they ran into each other regularly; in 1948, Nevelson had even asked to meet Louise's father, to ask him to give his opinion of an antique tapestry. She was so insistent that Louis took a strong dislike to her, asking who in the world this broad was.[152] Nevelson also came to see Louise when she did the set design for Erick Hawkins's ballet and was no doubt inspired by her black wooden sculptures.

But the friendship quickly transformed into competition and jealousy, as Nevelson found real success in the 1950s and 1960s while Bourgeois was in the height of her depression.

Confrontation, 1978

Four years after *The Destruction of the Father*, Louise made another monumental work, called *Confrontation*, which was part of her show at the Hamilton Gallery of Contemporary Art in New York (September 16–October 21, 1978). On the final day, she staged a performance called *A Banquet / A Fashion Show of Body Parts*, in which several participants donned latex costumes she made herself. This show, which Louise pitched to the young art dealer Patricia Hamilton, was a true adventure and an event that proved to be a turning point in her career. The show garnered quite a lot of press.

Confrontation consists of a long table surrounded by an oval composed of wooden boxes resembling coffins, painted white, and in which one might sit; the table is like a stretcher, designed to transport the wounded and the dead. It is covered with a blue plastic tablecloth on which Louise placed different organic elements made of latex: lumps, breasts, a penis. Was it the remains of a meal, a massacre, a sacrifice?

Some of the organlike forms are old and wrinkled, others young; it's a comment on the inversion of the sexes and the love of the old for the young, or the young for the old: "*Confrontation* has to do with sexuality between generations—the attraction of one generation toward the other, of an older person for younger. It goes both ways. Because it is not possible, it ends in death."[153] Was she alluding to what happened with Pietro or to her gay friends who often went out with younger men?

"Each of these boxes represents one of us. We have to stop running and take our places in the circle and face ourselves in front of each other. That is to say, to face how limited and uninteresting we are. Every one of us has to do this in front of everybody else. At that point, we have grown up. Nothing can let us escape this confrontation."[154]

Louise decided at the last moment to organize the performance. But how would they go about finding performers on such short notice? asked Patricia. It seemed impossible. Then she had the idea to invite art historians, critics, and strippers.[155] All replied in the affirmative.

The performance Louise created around this piece was an extraordinary spectacle. Dressed in a tunic and dark trousers, hair in two braids, she circulated among the participants, and then squeezed herself into one of her little boxes, delighted with the situation, and highly amused by the parade of art world luminaries, which incarnated "the element of entrapment, humor, and teasing that is present in all my work."[156] Some of the performers wore latex dresses adorned with multiple sets of breasts; some were half-naked and swaddled in gauze like newborns. An emcee, standing before a lectern, read a text written by Laura Tennen and Harold Koda. Participants included the art historian Gert Schiff and Louise's student Robbie Tillotson, who paraded up and down, as in a real fashion show. Other art historians and curators, including Susi Bloch, Peter von Blanckenhagen, Marcia Tucker, William Lieberman, Patrice Marandel, and Lowery Stokes Sims—as well as artists such as Jackie Winsor, Ron Gorchov, Nancy Graves,

Isaac Witkin, and John Willenbecher—were in the audience, often seated in their own boxes.

An aggressive soundtrack blared from the speakers. The performance artist Suzan Cooper, who was one of Louise's closest friends at this time, provided the vocals, a throbbing song called "She Abandoned Me," accompanied by a violin. Dressed in a transparent latex sheath, with her electric haircut and her terrifying monologue, she was the epitome of punk, which pleased Louise: "Punks are rude, loud, outrageous, and anti-taste. They have contempt for authority. They are nice. They are also totally ignorant, which is sometimes refreshing."[157] The photographs and film from the event attest to the wild and joyful atmosphere that evening. For many, it was a revelation; for Louise, it was the beginning of a new approach. From this moment on, she was a guiding light for the next generation.

The installation underscored, once again, the dominant themes of her work: the blending of the body and architecture, organic and geometric, isolation and gathering, food, sex, and death. It also heralded the *Cells* series she would create in the 1990s.

These coffinlike boxes reappeared, in black and red, in a series of abstract sculptures, stacked on tall metallic bases. Called *Structures*, they all referred to houses: *Structure IV: Boat House, Structure III: Three Floors, Structure II* and *V*, both entitled *Goodnight House* (all 1978). To create these wooden sculptures she turned to a student in her printmaking class at SVA, Mark Setteducati. She called him one day in the mid-1970s and asked his help restoring and installing one of her *Personages,* and then he began to visit her regularly. Mark was the perfect assistant, a faithful friend and great admirer until the end of Louise's life: he later did card tricks and magic tricks to distract her. He was impressed, he said, by her class and her elegance, and said that Louise was the kindest and most benevolent person he'd ever known—which contrasts starkly with other people's impressions of her but is revealing of the contradictory sentiments Louise could inspire.[158]

Louise was under contract with the Xavier Fourcade Gallery, but after the success of *Confrontation* at Hamilton Gallery, she promised Pat a show of recent work. Under pressure from Fourcade, she had to let it go. This turnaround bothered the young dealer, but it did not diminish her friendship or her faithful support.[159]

Louise also created her first public commission: *Facets to the Sun* (1978), an assemblage of small bias-cut columns placed on the ground in front of the Norris Cotton Federal Building in Manchester, New Hampshire.

Partial Recall

The final works of the 1970s tend toward the abstract and geometric, as if she felt the need to react against the bodily and emotional excess she experienced. She made another minimalist take on the theme of architecture with *Maisons fragiles* (1978), which is composed of two fragile steel constructions in a precarious equilibrium that nevertheless holds; they recall the imagery of stilts and houses in her first illustrated book of engravings, *He Disappeared into Complete Silence* (1947). She also made a series of "nests": *Nest of Seven, Nest of Five, Nest of Four* (all 1978), composed of steel tubes inserted inside of each other and cut into sections on the diagonal. The resulting cross-section looks like an oval spiral, a form she would obsessively return to in her drawings of 1993–94. The beveled forms echo the columns in *Number Seventy-Two (The No March)*. These "havens" were impenetrable or already occupied; the repetition of the circular motif creates a labyrinthine surface. Louise had rediscovered geometry. The final significant sculpture in the evolution of her work this decade is *Partial Recall* (1979), an assemblage of whitewashed planks of wood on top of which she posed semicircles, arranged from smallest to biggest. They recall the burgeoning forms of *Cumuls,* but here they are flattened. After having restaged her past so dramatically, she found a certain degree of rest in the "partial memory": "*Partial Recall* has to do with forgiveness and with integration, as aggression has to do with explosion and disintegration. It is difficult to recall forgiveness, one needs to be blessed at the moment. Aggression is very easy to recall."[160]

Like the nourishing earth or a cloudy sky, this celestial, terrestrial configuration, reassuringly geometric, paternal and maternal at the same time, can be seen in several drawings of this period. It seems to be the antithesis of *The Destruction of the Father.* But the rounded form also resembles the tombstone that marks the Bourgeois family plot in the cemetery in Clamart. *Partial Recall* was shown at Xavier Fourcade's gallery in 1979. The day of the opening, nothing was ready, tools and paint pots littered the floor, the wooden planks had been badly installed and had fallen over. Louise was in tears and didn't know what to do. But she reacted quickly, calling her children and friends (Alain, Mark Setteducati), who got to work finishing the painting and fixing the wooden panels.[161]

On October 28, 1979, she went to Paris with Suzan Cooper;[162] they met Rosette Lamont, a theater critic who specialized in Ionesco and Beckett, as well as Roger Blin, because Louise wanted to nudge along Suzan's career in the theater. During their extended stay,[163] she saw her friend Dominique Bozo, who had just opened a major Picasso show at the Grand Palais,[164] met up with her friend Colette Richarme from Montpellier, Paulette Place and her son Jean-Michel, and Henriette, who had just had an operation. She dined with the artist André Cădere, made a trip to Clamart, and visited the Musée Bourdelle and the Musée Rodin. Her mental health was not good; she suffered from insomnia, and she was overwhelmed with rage while dining at a restaurant which she used to go to with her father, called Le Petit Saint Benoît. "Summary of my 'emotions' seeing Paris again: Pierre Friloux the schemer, Arlet Bon [a dancer and choreographer], Nadine Pouillon, Rose Marie Horchild [*sic*], Suzan Cooper, Michael Orlowitz."[165] And "The mother pig who gives out her truffles, that's Louise to Friloux, Cooper, Pouillon and Bozo."[166] Suzan wrote directly in Louise's diary: "Louise gives me at the airport, $200 = 800 francs," and "I love you. Thank you, XOX Suzan."[167]

Returning to New York, Louise described a meal at Beaubourg: "Lack of recognition—injustice. The fury of the Beaubourg 'free lunch.' There is no trace of sex anywhere. Challenge, the first to understand, the first to invent, it is a sport where the best is first—competitive + inventive."[168]

As the decade came to a close, Louise had amassed a larger following in the media. It was the beginning of her long interviews, which sometimes gave rise to books. Deborah Wye showed her work again at the Berkeley Art Museum at the University of California in a show called *Louise Bourgeois: Matrix / Berkeley 17*.[169] She also met the critic Paul Gardner,[170] with whom she struck up a friendship. The turmoil of the years following Robert's death made room for occasional moments of something resembling equilibrium, as she wrote in a diary entry in February 1979: "I go upstairs in Rob[er]t room + in the boys room. I perceive the floor as being at <u>peace</u> again after painting the ceiling (all the latex pieces are there!!!), this feeling of a turmoil being put to rest invades me. The chaos has been conquered. Suddenly I do not need the affection of Paul Gardner anymore. This is a very rare occurrence."[171] She had found some peace of mind, as evidenced by the infrequency of her sessions with Lowenfeld: "Lowenfeld, I do not go, enough [*la barbe*]."[172] During the summer of 1979, her Chilean friend Nemesio Antúnez was in the United States and worked out of her basement. Meanwhile she worked doggedly on a difficult piece and reflected on the ways her process had developed to cope with moments of difficulty:

> *La petite épine dorsal* (genesis) I am obsessed all day long with it
> when I have mastered
> the how, reduced to 3 formula
> I relax, when
> I am free again, terror
> has set in and I cannot use
> the saw.
> when I own it
> I do not have to
> use it. I transcend it + abandon it
> when it is "possible" I am satisfied
> and can dispense with it
> it is not a permission that I
> need, it is a certitude, a
> *garantie*, a test.[173]

An article about Louise by Eleanor Munro appeared in *Ms.* magazine,[174] as well as a profile in *Vogue.*[175] However, it would still take a few more years, and pressure from several critics and artists, for the Museum of Modern Art to decide to give her a large retrospective of her forty years of work, which would finally open the door to more widespread success and recognition.

The Body in Pieces, 1980–1989

Everyday you have to abandon your past or accept it and then if you cannot accept it you become a sculptor.

Early in 1980, Jerry Gorovoy, a young artist who worked at the Max Hutchinson Gallery in SoHo, wanted to include a piece by Louise in a show he was putting together: *Ten Abstract Sculptures: American and European, 1940–1980*.[1] Louise met with him and agreed to let him include *C.O.Y.O.T.E.* (1947–49; retitled and painted in 1979), a pink version of *The Blind Leading the Blind*.[2] But when she saw the sculpture installed in the gallery, she immediately wanted to take it out of the show. Jerry took her to a café to discuss it with her and, in short, convinced her to leave the piece in.

Yet in spite of the artist's initial mistrust, Jerry was soon invited to visit her home, where he discovered decades of work and hidden marvels. He described it as being a genuine treasure trove, a jumble of sculptures in wood, marble, plaster, and latex, some of which had never been shown, as well as hundreds of drawings. Quickly won over (like the young curator Deborah Wye)[3] by the significance of the work, so original and yet so little known, he decided to organize a show later that year devoted to her iconography as a way of exploring her childhood memories and her dreamworld.[4] For the first time since her show at the Norlyst Gallery in 1947, Louise showed her early paintings, including the *Femme maison* series, as well as a few engravings and drawings. These particularly interested Jerry, who had interned at the Drawing Center in New York. Their meeting was a decisive one, with a profound effect on Louise's life and work. Gorovoy sincerely loved what she made, the abstract and more biographical work alike, and wanted to share it with a larger audience. Then, little by little, over the course of the 1980s, their relationship developed from one of respect to include tenderness, and affection, eventually becoming a loving and deep friendship lasting thirty years, until Louise's death.[5] Jerry, said Alain Bourgeois, was the ideal son, the one she'd liked to have had.[6] Young, free, with both the sensitivity of an artist and the instincts of a dealer, he quickly became indispensable, serving as assistant, secretary, model, and muse, taking care of all requests, preparing exhibitions, and looking after her on a daily basis, in her life as well as in her creative process. Louise was able to work in these favorable conditions, while Jerry took care of building her reputation and showing her work, which she didn't like to do. Not only did he prevent her from destroying her work, but he nudged her to participate in major international exhibitions, making her, in spite of her age, into a contemporary artist.

For quite some time, Louise had had a penchant for younger men, as indicated by her infatuations with Pietro Cicognani, Henri Zerner, Dominique Bozo, and Xavier Girard. But her relationship with Jerry was more profound and necessary because it involved every aspect of her life and work—which he would defend to the end. It was not always an easy one, especially at the beginning; it took time to adjust to one another, to win each other over. Jerry was calm, reserved; he withstood Louise's bouts of anger and obsessive jealousy; he anticipated her anxiety attacks before they occurred and took the time to reassure her and rebuild her confidence, in order to allow her to continue with her work and develop it further. He took care of her like a "shrink," a friend, a mother.

By the end of 1980, Jerry visited more and more often. In January 1981, he came for dinner,[7] and in February she said of him: "Jerry is a polite little girl."[8] They grew closer, and a few years later Louise noted in her diary how delighted she was to listen to him speak for an especially long time over dinner.[9] Jerry introduced her to John Cheim, at that time working at the Robert Miller Gallery, in March. And eventually he left a job at the Sidney Janis Gallery to make himself more available to her.[10]

Around the time that she met Jerry, a major turning point in her solitary life, she also acquired a large studio in Brooklyn, at 475 Dean Street. It was a former denim factory, which included the previous owners' old sewing machines. These immediately reminded Louise of her mother's atelier. The particular atmosphere of the place, a blend of junk shop and industrial building, located in a rough, if not outright dangerous part of Brooklyn, would be an important inspiration for her. She could gather her thoughts in solitude, take advantage of the light from the enormous windows, hear the familiar sound of pipes, attend to the noisy, vibrant spectacle of the neighborhood. This new space not only allowed her to create large-scale works and to take in the entirety of her work at once but also gave her an excuse to escape her claustrophobic house. Every morning, Jerry picked her up and drove her to Brooklyn in his Chrysler. Now she had a house and a studio, like any other professional artist of a certain stature.

But the biggest change in her life at this time was the major retrospective that MoMA organized in late 1982,[11] which inspired a number of solo exhibitions, first in the United States and then in Europe.[12] Louise left Xavier Fourcade's gallery for personal reasons (she no longer got along with its director),[13] but also because the gallery was too associated, in her eyes, with the great names in modern art. From then on she showed with Robert Miller Gallery, which was more open to younger artists and to women as well.[14] In fact, she was always "terrified" of Xavier Fourcade,[15] though she recognized that he was, like her father, an excellent salesman.[16]

This new life, this new beginning at the age of seventy, still included moments of fear, rage, and violence, in spite of the long-awaited recognition and the steady friendship of Jerry Gorovoy, Deborah Wye, and the art historian Robert Storr, who were her closest friends during this decade.

After refusing to discuss her private life, Louise finally revealed her family history, which she had explored and dissected for years during her analysis. Her sessions with Henry Lowenfeld were few and far between—two in 1980, three in 1981—and he died in 1985. Digging around in the past was no longer therapeutic but had become, instead, a source of inspiration. To re-create it was to control it; she reexperienced her emotions in order to transfer them onto her sculpture. It was a story she would tell and retell— she called it Scheherazade's complex, the compulsive need to speak, to tell stories, to put words to memories and feelings, in order to survive: "Shéhérazade talks to ward off castration, assassination. She talks as a last defense. It is a pretty miserable motive, useless + dangerous, silence is wonderful!"[17] Or: "I talk to avoid killing or being killed," she said.[18]

Henriette

Louise's older sister, Henriette Bonnotte, died on July 9, 1980. She made a note in her diary: "police inquiry into my sister's death. Phone call: [. . .] I assume the expenses for Henriette's burial; local Coroner's office. Invoice of the funeral home." Louise did not attend the funeral, although Henriette was her last link to her French family (her relationship with her cousin Jacques and Maurice had fallen by the wayside, though she had remained in contact with her niece Claire Bourgeois,[19] Jacques's daughter, who was a painter and lived in Montchauvet).

In tribute to her disabled older sister, Louise made two suspended sculptures of legs: one a kind of articulated prosthesis (*Henriette*, 1985); the other (*Legs*, 1986) composed of two long, thin rubber legs, one of which is slightly longer than the other, a reference to Henriette's limp. Her relationship with her sister had always been ambiguous, a blend of jealousy and compassion.[20]

She said of a sculpture representing her sister: "It is a pathetic vision."[21] Then she backtracked, saying: "I'm not sure it is pathetic, it is a very positive and friendly vision of my sister, who always inspired a great deal of compassion in me, and who desperately wanted children and never had any, and who hobbled around with a cane and a stiff knee due to water-on-the-knee. So, she had this very, very strange profile when she walked and I was very sorry for her. There is no wit at all."[22]

Louise was still preoccupied by her children, and especially by Alain, whose judgment she feared and whom she associated with Robert: "Alain, I love for his kind wisdom. Robert, I love for his allegiance. Robert remained to you [*sic*] through the whole dinner."[23] "To Rob[er]t + Alain. I hope you still love me."[24] Louise needed to be loved by her children but also by her grandchildren: "I call Alain and tell him thank you. Gratitude for giving me beautiful grandchildren, depression recedes."[25]

At the end of March 1985, the children's favorite aunt, Mary Goldwater, Robert's older sister, died in the hospital after a long struggle with Parkinson's. The three children each reacted in their own way; Alain wanted to go to the cremation, Jean-Louis said he would be proud to go, and Michel, who was particularly close to his aunt, also wanted to be there and to make himself useful. "[L]esson: love did it. My boys loved her. Obituary mentions the four nephews. My love for Mary paid off. The four jewels in her crown."[26]

The Young New York Art Scene

Louise continued to follow the goings-on in the contemporary art scene and was interested in young artists such as Robert Malaval, Jean-Michel Basquiat, Andy Warhol, and Keith Haring, whom she'd taught at SVA. In October 1979, she was invited to the Maison Française at Columbia University and met young French artists who were based in New York, including Bernar Venet, Jean Dupuy, Arman, and Patricia Caire.

She went to see them perform as well. "My behavior concerning Pierre Friloux[27] has been a total withdrawal except for going to 2 performances. The risk was that they would themselves withdraw—on the contrary like Carl Andre, [Jean] Dupuy and [Hans] Haacke, they bite the hand that feed[s] them to get publicity—I unconsciously failed to fall for it."[28] Louise could not hold back from making barbed statements aimed at these fashionable artists. She had to see the filmmaker Michael Blackwood about a film project, but she was petrified: "the sudden + total withdrawal, stone face and wooden stare worked also with Blackwood."[29]

Her friendship with Suzan Cooper, the talented young performer with whom she had traveled to Paris in October 1979, continued during the 1980s, but Louise worried about her drug habit. She had no patience for drug use: "Suzan [Cooper] takes hashish!! If I can think of Pietro [Cicognani] or Paul [Paulsen] has [*sic*] a forbidden drug it gives me a grip on the problem."[30]

She went to New Orleans in January 1980, where she was given a prize for Outstanding Achievement in the Visual Arts at the National Women's Caucus for Art conference. She was accompanied by her friend Patricia Hamilton, the art dealer, who recalls that at the moment her name was called to receive the prize, Louise disappeared, having fled, and was discovered sitting in on a session on pornographic lesbian theater.[31]

Her rivalry with Louise Nevelson was still very much alive: "I experience Nevelson as a parasite sitting on me."[32] She frequently turns to the image of the parasite in her writing, applying it to useless people, flatterers, sycophants, but also to parents, children, cousins, her father's mistress, elderly people, everyone who makes use of people for their own ends: "The parasite was the robber."[33]

Louise still saw Françoise Cachin and Patrice Marandel, who was annoyed, she said, not to have been involved in the show at MoMA. "Jerry spends the day here. Patrice [Marandel] calls, he is very hurt by being put out of the modern show."[34] Toward the end of the 1970s, she had met Paul Gardner,[35] with whom she quickly struck up a friendship and who was often her date for social occasions.[36]

On January 20, Louise went to the Feminist Institute.[37] In her diary, she describes her ambivalence toward militant feminists, after learning that women were joining the army: "Registration of women in the army—a Tormenting hatred of the Woman (monthly one) has expressed yesterday in a compulsive running away."[38] But her engagement with and support for the feminist movement continued during this period. She noted in particular the name Guerrilla Girls[39] in October 1985, and also Janet Fish.[40]

On June 3, 1980, she attended the opening of an exhibition at MoMA curated by William Rubin, *Picasso: A Retrospective*,[41] as much to see Dominique Bozo—the show included a number of never-before-seen loans from the future Picasso Museum in Paris—as out of interest in the artist.

Face to Face

In late July 1980, Louise met the young art critic Xavier Girard, through Marie-Claude Beaud.[42] Louise was quite taken with him, and he came back to see her the next day. "Louise greeted me with a somewhat brisk politeness, as if she were trying to make herself likable by getting to the point. We were in the corridor which leads to the back room with the large windows lit up by the garden, when she turned towards me with a smile and asked: 'What are you afraid of?'"[43]

Their relationship was one of fast, stimulating friendship. Together they went to a show for the blind at the Grey Art Gallery at NYU,[44] and Louise took him to a Mexican restaurant to eat very spicy food. He told her all about going out to clubs in New York, his friendship with Lynda Benglis, and eventually wrote a short text for Louise's show at Max Hutchinson's gallery.[45] He came to see her often, talked with her about Nice, which he knew well, about

Bonnard, and one day, out of the blue, she told him, looking him straight in the eye, "Tomorrow, if you like, I will do a cast of your face."

Everything was ready in the studio, and a friend came to help: "You need two people, but you have to move quickly and precisely, you have to keep moving."[46] The first words Louise said when he turned up at her house—"what are you afraid of"—came back to him.

Xavier Girard's memory of this experience is somewhat mixed; he recounted it years later in a book, analyzing it with meticulousness and a touch of good humor.[47] A blend of fear and fascination, not only because the hot plaster and the feeling of being smothered was quite disagreeable but also because he felt somewhat as if he'd fallen prey to a cannibalistic ritual, to the rapid seizure of his face, to a symbolic transaction. The art of sculpture with all its instruments and liquids is situated somewhere between cooking and healing; the mask directly translates the real person into the material, which is the essential equation underpinning all of Louise's art. She loved this academic process, which she no doubt learned during her sculpture classes at the Grande Chaumière. She had already made several sculpted portraits, as well as plaster casts of the faces of her close friends Henri Zerner and Peter von Blanckenhagen. But for Louise, a cast was not a portrait. She also kept, all her life, her mother's death mask.

Return to Italy, 1981

Louise decided to return to Italy, from August 25 to October 3, 1981. Jerry went with her to Carrara to see the ateliers and the people with whom she had worked (Pasquini, Nicoli). She picked up the old plaster models she had left with the artist Gonzalo Fonseca and tried to begin some new work. They stayed at the Hotel Michelangelo. During this season, it was empty: "deserted Carrara. Not even a restaurant."[48] They went to the beach at Avenza (which inspired the name of works from 1968–69), but Louise had trouble getting started and finding new ideas. She did make a number of small works in marble and new versions of the *Femme couteau*. Since Louise hadn't prepared any models to give to the marble workers, she let herself be inspired by her early paintings and drawings. The marble sculptures of the *Femme maison* were directly inspired by her paintings of houses, reproduced in the catalog *The Iconography of Louise Bourgeois*, from 1980, that Jerry brought with him.

She also wanted to make a sculpture of a woman suspended by the hair but soon realized, while experimenting with a Barbie doll she'd found, that it would be too difficult to make in marble. She then positioned the doll horizontally in a backward arch, after the hysteric's pose, but it was too stiff. She finally decided to imprison the doll in an earthen building, a clay tower, thus creating a new version of the *Femme maison.*

Although in the end the trip was productive on an artistic level, it was dramatic on a personal one. On September 18, Jerry was joined by a friend, Mark Snyder; they went together to visit Lake Como, Florence, and Milan. Louise obviously took it very badly: "Arrival of Mark Snyder, they rent a car at the airport [. . .] sudden <u>violence</u> to force me to go to Pasquini [. . .] heartbeats [. . .] I'm afraid of having a heart attack."[49] "The presence of Mark makes him totally uptight ι violent against me."[50] Louise responded sarcastically to this feeling of abandonment: "Snyder is like your shadow (he never leaves you)."[51] Louise and Jerry were at that point obliged to share their intimate lives as well. Jerry pushed her to work, to create new forms. "I learned in Carrara how to be totally concentrated," she wrote in her diary on September 19, 1981. From this stay dates the new *Femme maison* in marble, in particular one made from a plaster cast of Jerry's shirt, which made a draped pedestal on which Louise positioned a houselike shape. "Small T[-] shirt piece is finished [. . .] pregnant woman with wooden leg."[52]

She also made several sculptures of *Fallen Woman:* a small woman's head posed at the end of a rounded stick like the handle of a hammer. It is unstable because the rounded body rocks to one side then the other, and the head might break. The theme of the fall continued in her work: "My early work is the fear of falling. Later on it became the art of falling. How to fall without hurting yourself. Later on it is the art of hanging in there."[53] This physical fear, inherited from a childhood memory of vertigo from her first steps on the balcony, took on a symbolic dimension: the woman in decline, who has failed, and fallen.[54]

Houses

The theme of the house, which takes shape both in very complicated and baroque works as well as extremely simplified ones—like the small, curved rectangular house made of white marble—took physical form when she bought her son Michel a house on Staten Island. Michel never lived in it. Although they remained close, he never wanted to depend on his adoptive family. "Do not throw Staten Island at me [says] Michel. You better keep it Louise. Effect of Staten Island purchase on Michel."[55] He also later refused the gift of the house at Easton. Louise was very hurt by this refusal because Michel loved going there, and she wanted to leave him something. In 1984, she thought of offering it to Jean-Louis to celebrate his marriage to Carollee Pelos. "I give you Easton, in full ownership. The title had been left by Rob[er]t to the attorney who took care of the transaction when we bought in 1941."[56] But in the end the house went to Alain and his family.

The empty house on Staten Island reminded Louise of her desire to flee. "My passion for buildings (that are always abandoned) stands for an attempt to leave home and find another lair."[57] It also reactivated her anxiety: "Journey into nothingness, emptiness / not the void not the chaos / nothingness is better."[58] One of the forms her anxiety took was to feel like an empty house because she closely associated her body with architecture.

In 1981, eight years after Robert's death, Louise felt very lonely: "I need someone to live in the house with and separate from me upstairs [. . .] Michel comes to talk about [*sic*]."[59] Michel was very present during this period, despite his feelings of rejection, and took an active role in Louise's life. She was already thinking of her will, of what would happen to her work, to the inheritance she wanted to leave, at this time, to Jerry and Jean-Louis: "To be added to my will Jerry Gorovoy is to be my executor in charge. [. . .] Selling my work with Jean-Louis he is to be artistic executor too. Louise Bourgeois."[60] Although Louise never talked about dying, she was very concerned about what would become of her work.

The MoMA Retrospective

The beginning of the decade took shape around the preparations being made for the huge retrospective at MoMA, which opened in late 1982. A group of artists and critics had been calling for this show since 1973,[61] according to a letter addressed to William Rubin.

The task of curating it finally fell to Deborah Wye, a curator of prints at MoMA, who had already shown Louise's work[62] and who knew her well during this time. She was assisted by Alicia Legg. Wye remembered Louise showing her all her work on slides and that she showed her the work in her basement by quickly turning on, then turning off, the light. She was afraid to show everything, to reveal herself. For Wye, this encounter "changed her life," as she put it.

The critical response was very positive, and everyone agreed: this was long-overdue recognition for a great artist. "Louise Bourgeois is finally where she belongs: among the top American sculptors, and at the apex of feminist art." She is "in a category all by herself," wrote Kay Larson in *New York* magazine.[63] She would remain in this category all her own, on the margin, swimming against the current of whatever was in fashion. And that is no doubt the source of her power. If she remained little known for so long, it is because of her discretion and her reluctance to impose herself and her work. Subjective experience was the material from which she started, but although the forms she created were often simple, their meaning was complex. This retrospective was just one more step in her trajectory, and with or without the success it brought, she continued on her path. Louise often confessed that it was her very indifference to the market and to museums that permitted her the freedom to carry on making work, unconstrained.[64] And, she said, in 1971, "recognition will come in time, and this is enough for me."[65]

Kay Larson and others insisted on the specifically feminine aspect of her work.[66] For them, Louise was the first artist to have seriously explored physical interiority, the ambiguity of maternity and sexuality, as well as the difficulty of being a woman, all leavened with a good dose of humor. She could be seen laughing in the pages of *Time* magazine, in her striped dress, with one leg resting on the enormous penis in *Sleep II* (1967).

Another young man appeared in 1981: Robert Storr, who became a close and devoted friend. He first came to see her to ask for artwork images for the *Harvard Advocate*, then returned regularly to see her during the 1980s.[67] He was immediately won over as much by her personality as by the singularity of her work. In 1985, he started making plans to write a book about her.[68] Louise mentioned a contract[69] between them and worried when the book wasn't appearing: "total block about Rob[er]t Storr book."[70] Robert Storr was, for Louise, a paragon of all the virtues. He spoke French, was a writer, had an artist's sensitivity. He wrote several articles and numerous books about her, included her in exhibitions; he was a confidant during this decade.

Deborah Wye visited her regularly throughout 1982 to plan for the MoMA show, but Louise, who was finally being recognized and sought after by all these young people, couldn't resist manipulating them, playing them off one another—Debby, Jerry, and Robert. "Horror Transfix about Jerry + Debby / strategy game. I little Louisette maneuver them on the chess board to a corner / when they are trapped; Sledge hammer does the Rest."[71] A slightly cruel "game of billiards," and one she would repeat numerous times, replaying the way her parents and Sadie had manipulated her in childhood.

Louise had to revisit the past to prepare the catalog, consulting her archives and photographs; this inspired her to use all this material to tell her story in a slideshow she called *Partial Recall*,[72] which was included in the exhibition. But she refused to include Robert Goldwater in it: "very serious refusal to include my husband in the film: it is a cop out on my part: to be judged on my merit not as a wife, not as a woman but as an artist devoid of all her excuses and assets or embellishment. I am accused of being ungrateful by the women (unmarried ones)—I am accused of being ungrateful by the men / my objection is a feminist one."[73]

This first work of memory transformed into images was a turning point in her life, which became clear to her only later: "Homesick. Memories flash as if on a screen—the script for the film (MoMA) (exorcism). Relive these 24 years in prose and in image. [. . .] Acting out again + again. Remember, psychoanalyze, exorcism. It's no use, none at all—theater—the void anxiety is the only one."[74]

She also published a version of the voiceover in *Artforum* (December 1982) under the title "Child Abuse." The title could easily seem misleading, but the abuse in question was not incestuous; rather, the betrayal and manipulation that made her childhood so deeply traumatizing. Louise chose the photographs and oversaw the layout. The text is preceded by two photographs side by side of her as a child, walking with her mother in one and her father in the other on the mountain at Mont-Dore. In both photos the parent has a hand on her shoulder, especially her father, who is pretending to be blind; all three of them have canes. In the next spread, a sculpture of two marble eyes[75] is followed by a photograph of Sadie and Louise in a boat on the Bièvre. Then there is an image of a high fence punctuated with two columns—the caryatids of the Château Vaux-le-Vicomte—facing a marble

Fallen Woman (1981) sculpture.[76] Finally, there is an image of the bottom stairwell in her house, with the sculpture *Maisons fragiles* (1978) on one side, and *Fillette* (1968), suspended, on the other. Antigone and Oedipus, the gaze and the mistress, the faraway past, the fallen woman, the fragile house, and of course the phallus: it is a photographic summary of Louise's universe. The spreads, commissioned by Ingrid Sischy,[77] spoke of Louise's difficulty letting go of the past; it focused on her parents' and Sadie's betrayal: "So what role do I play in this game? I am a pawn. Sadie is supposed to be there as my teacher and actually you, mother, are using me to keep track of your husband. This is child abuse."[78] Sadie belonged to Louise because she had been hired to teach her English. "I thought she was going to like me. Instead of which she betrayed me. I was betrayed not only by my father, damn it, but by her too. It was a double betrayal."[79] Every time Louise told this story, it brought her to the edge of tears. "I am sorry to get so excited but I still react to it."[80] She also could not understand how her mother could have tolerated the situation and imposed it on her children. Even if, as she said, having a mistress was par for the course in France.

Why did Louise feel compelled to tell the story of this particular childhood trauma, at the very moment when her work was being recognized for its innovative character and its formal invention? In interviews from the 1970s,[81] Louise refused to talk about her private life, so that the interviewer could focus on her work. Only in her psychoanalytic texts and her personal writings did she mention Sadie, her parents, and this fracture in the psyche which was a major cause of her mental fragility.

There may have been several reasons. The process of aging prompted her to turn more and more toward her memories, and the upcoming retrospective required her to look through her archives. But these were not the only reasons; Louise used this old family story to create an autonomous work, be it *Partial Recall* or "Child Abuse." She found a visual form that suited her need to tell a story, to construct an autobiographical narrative, bringing together text and image, her life and work, which were now one and the same. Perhaps—since she was so often ahead of her time—she sensed the importance that subjectivity, sensitivity, and figuration would assume in the art world of the 1980s. This familial drama would become— reductively—a major trope in the interpretation of her work. But it also fascinated those who like Louise had Oedipal relationships with a seductive, untrustworthy father. They recognized themselves in Louise's story and could project themselves into her emotions, her hysteria, and her contradictory feelings.

Portrait of Louise with *Fillette*

A good portrait of Louise was needed for the MoMA catalog. Off she went in April 1982 to be photographed by Robert Mapplethorpe, a renowned artist by that time. The shoot worried her. Eccentric and coquettish at the same time, she thought hard about what to wear: "[I] prepare [for] MAPPLETHORPE. Monkey coat, black satin slacks, Ferucci pink sweater."[82] Pink and black, fur and satin: it was to be a classic seduction.

"So on the day of this appointment at Robert's studio, I thought 'What can we bring? What prop can we bring?' [. . .] So I got *Fillette* (1968), which is a sculpture of mine, which was hanging among others. I knew that I would get comfort from holding and rocking the piece. Actually my work is more me than my physical presence. [. . .] You see the triple image of the man you have to take care of, of the child you have to take care of, and of the photographer you have to take care of."[83] It was Louise herself who had chosen to be photographed holding *Fillette*. Intimidated by the session with Robert Mapplethorpe, who was famous for his overtly sexual work, she went armed with a defensive weapon: a phallus. She knew that Mapplethorpe would be delighted by the size of the organ and would recognize it as an ironic wink at his photographs of nude men, which Louise knew well: "Mapplethorpe's phalli are not there only for the beauty of the image or to create a scandal. They are not only exhibiting their virility. When we see them that way, like flowers or exotic fruit on the studio table, we tell ourselves they are in danger. Their vulnerability is real. We want to protect them."[84]

On the contact sheet with its many shots, it becomes clear that Louise knew how to be photographed, presenting many different facets of her personality; she held the phallus in her arms like a newborn, or under her arm like a baguette, with a heavy dose of irony.

In 1983, she traveled to Italy again with Jerry, feeling much better this time around: "I am much stronger than 2 years ago, familiar with the place and am able to like people, look at them and talk to them. The hotel is a living museum of antique furniture every piece is authentic mostly Italian

XVIII [century]. Crazy armoire, piano benches, consoles, mirrors, commodes, nightstands, aquatints, frames, cabinetmakers (orgy of). I read Jean-Jacques Rousseau (sorry for himself). *Reveries of the Solitary Walker* [. . .]."[85]

Next they went to Morocco, to Tangiers, as part of an exchange with the School of Visual Arts. During this trip, Louise met Paul Bowles.

On December 5, 1983, the French minister of culture Jack Lang conferred on Louise the medal of Officer of Arts and Letters, one of the many prizes that she received during this period.[86] Louise agreed to write speeches for the receptions but didn't like attending the ceremonies and often sent someone else in her place: Robert Storr for the MacDowell medal in 1990, later Jean-Louis for the National Medal of the Arts, awarded by Bill Clinton at the White House in 1997.

In September 1984, one of her sculptures (*Pregnant Woman I*, 1947–49) was shown in the controversial exhibition *"Primitivism" in 20th Century Art: Affinity of the Tribal and Modern,* curated by William Rubin and Kirk Varnedoe at MoMA. She attended the very starry opening night party with Jerry Gorovoy and saw some of Robert's old friends there, including Hélène Kamer-Leloup.

Tutelary Figures

After daring to stand up to and even destroy the authoritarian image of the father in *The Destruction of the Father,* Louise continued on the warpath, creating tender and cruel portraits of tutelary figures, paternal and maternal, embodied by two mythical animals with heavily symbolic functions: the Sphinx and the fox. For Louise, her parents were monuments. These headless divinities majestically inaugurate the sculptures of the 1980s while also picking up on and reworking some of the foundational themes in her work, the *Femme maison* and the *Lair.* At the same time, they start down a new road: the body in pieces, the castrating dismemberment that began with *Fillette* (1968). This decade would be marked by cutting and fragmentation: the human body is a unit composed of different parts, and each "part object" refers to a specific person: "Well, the body is always dismembered, of course, what a child does to a toy."[87] Louise sculpted "from nature":[88] eyes, legs, feet, hands, mostly in marble, one of her preferred materials during these years, a consequence of the time spent in Italy. She blended abstract forms and figurative elements. In exploring her childhood memories, she relieved her past and translated this psychic experience through her own body, the site of emotions: "Suddenly I move my leg, or suddenly I move my arm, suddenly I move my thumbs, so we are in the physical, we are in the body's languages now. The stone becomes the body. [. . .] What happens to my body is repeated in the stone, except that then it has to add a formal meaning."[89]

Nature Study (1984) depicts a monstrous creature, somewhere between human and animal, masculine and feminine. This Sphinx (male or female?) with clawed paws, decapitated, with three pairs of breasts and a phallus between its legs, comes from the plaster cast of a hunting dog that Louise found in a dumpster near her foundry. "[W]e work on wax of dog," she wrote in her diary on January 2, 1985. This dog already had its head cut off, its tail between its legs.

The sculpture was placed high atop a pedestal so as to dominate the spectator, whose eyes would be level with its genitals; this position allowed the viewer to see that the creature was very strangely sexed: its long tail between its legs looks like a second penis. Louise herself said that it was an image of her father: "Because my father demolished me, why would I not demolish him? I take a really masculine animal and I give him breasts to mock myself, and then after I give him breasts I give him another pair, why not? And then I cut off his head. It's a kind of teasing. Because my father teased me, I will tease him."[90] Louise's piquant sense of humor helped her avoid the association of the multiple breasts with Artemis of Ephesus, and the missing head with castration, displacing these formal inventions onto the level of the game or the joke. This was something she had already pulled off in *Confrontation*, or in *The Destruction of the Father*. Serious works dominated by black humor: "[B]eyond the tragic, there is Black Humor. There is Dada."[91] The blend of male and female genitals, the inversion of roles referring yet again to the presexual state of the perverse, polymorphic child, for whom sexual difference has not yet been defined.

This brilliant bronze figure, polished to reflect like a mirror,[92] was followed by the unsettling darkness of the black marble *The She-Fox* (1985), a portrait of the mother as a fox, with *Fallen Woman* (1981) at her feet. It was a protective, if somewhat frightening vision of maternity. The crafty animal seems to have been an apt image for the artist's mother, whom she would later re-create as a spider: "The appellation 'fox' means I considered my mother to be a very intelligent, patient, and enduring if not calculating person."[93]

The rough-hewn marble base, the dark color of the material, the underdefined forms, align the mother with the savage, the animal, the "dark continent," which contrasts with the enlightened, learned male. The missing heads clearly have a sexual connotation; all headless bodies are associated with castration. But this mutilation was also a form of exorcism and testify to the child's sadomasochistic feelings toward her parents. The power of the mother is terrifying and drives her to violence: "So, I would try and hurt her, and this time I did. I cut her head off. I slit her throat. Still, I expect her to like me. The tragedy is: Is a person who I have treated like this going to like me?"[94]

"I have been inhabited by a ferocious mother-love. In that way [*The*] *She-Fox* is also a self-portrait."[95] She is the good and the bad mother, who devours her children and is devoured by them. A cannibalistic impulse drives both children and lovers: "The fulfillment of desire is the devouring of one's partner."[96] It appeared during the 1950s: "everything is my fault. I wanted to burn, bury, kill and + eat up my mother."[97]

"[*The*] *She-Fox* is the portrait of a relation. It is an expression of the faith a child can have in a parent and of the violence between the strong and the weak. This is the meaning of the piece."[98]

The third sculpture in this series is *Blind Man's Buff* (1984), which gives us yet another version of a phallus endowed with breasts. Somewhere between *Labyrinthine Tower* (1962), whose leaning erection she used again here, and the *Cumuls*, this disturbing sculpture was intended to be touched rather than seen. The bulbous proliferation emerging from the marble calls out to be caressed by the blind.

During this period, Louise also made a series of large pairs of eyes: *Nature Study (White Eyes)* (1986), *Nature Study (Pink Eyes)* (1984), and *Nature Study (Velvet Eyes)* (1984). The last referred, for Louise, to the soft gaze of the person we love: "my velvet eyes softness comes from my real gratitude. I want to thank, to pay, to kiss, to love + say thank you. Not before in anticipation [but] after the fact in gratitude."[99] In a block of gray marble she carved out two deep holes, where two ocular globes float. She opted for a realist approach, including dark pupils and the whites of the eyes. For her second public commission, she proposed a sculpture of two spheres resting on a block of marble: *Eyes* (1982).[100]

The eyes are the window to the soul; a conduit to our feelings and our truths, they are the best way of communicating with the world and with the other. "Because the eyes never lie. If a woman doesn't look you in the eye, it's an admission that you are having an effect on her. Her eyes would betray her. That's how demure women behave. They are the interesting women."[101]

This insistence on the eye, the organ of sight, already the subject of numerous drawings[102] and a latex piece from 1963 (*Le regard*) can be understood not only through the erotic metaphor of the eye (the pupil is a black hole that awaits penetration) but also because the cut-out eye alludes to blindness and castration. Louise was obsessed with the myth of Oedipus, and a number of her works refer either directly or indirectly to this foundational question. Perhaps she recalled the statue of Oedipus and Antigone she saw at the entrance to the Lycée Fénelon and which she wrote about in her diary: "Fénelon + Œdipe / Rivière [Georges Henri], Leiris what you can do on charm."[103]

Paris 1985, Galerie Maeght-Lelong

In early 1985, Louise's first solo show in Paris took place: *Louise Bourgeois: Rétrospective, 1947–1984*. It was held at the Galerie Maeght-Lelong, thanks to its director, Jean Frémon, who met Louise in the early 1980s and quickly became an intimate friend, remaining so until her death. Louise made it clear she wanted to break through in France, and she found in Frémon an influential ally. "The thing about [Louise] and me is this: when I met her, she knew she was a great artist, but she lacked recognition, whereas I directed an important gallery—which she knew. After that, the power dynamic shifted, but we remained close."[104]

Louise arrived in Paris on February 2 and stayed at the Hôtel Royal Monceau. She ate oysters at the brasserie La Lorraine at place des Ternes with Jean-Michel Place and his wife, visited the flea market at Saint-Ouen and the Marché Biron to see some tapestries (Verdure et Teniers, sixteenth century).[105] On February 5, she had lunch at the Café de Flore and was filmed at the gallery as well as, several days later, some places around Paris and her childhood home.[106]

It was a difficult trip; Jerry remembers that she called him for help when she was shopping at Printemps. She noted it in her diary: "attempt Printemps, I cannot stand it / Jerry rescues me."[107]

On February 6, she went to check in at the gallery, where the work was being installed. "[F]or the first time I go to gallery: [*The*] *Blind Leading the Blind* at the back of the room, everything away from the walls."[108] *The Quartered One* was suspended in the middle of the exhibition.[109]

Worried about the opening triggering her anxiety, she asked Jean-Michel Place to be her date.[110] She wore black trousers, an oversized light blue silk blouse, and on her head, as was often the case, a little cap. She smiled at everyone, seemed happy, was given flowers, saw her friends. "Blue silk coat. Opening in Paris 6–8. Charivari."[111]

While signing prints at the gallery, she ran into her friend the painter Jean Revol and mentioned having seen Hubert and Teri Damisch.[112] She had lunch with her dear friend Paulette Place, who always welcomed her warmly and faithfully into her house whenever she came to Paris. "Paulette is a proof that goodness exists," she wrote in her diary.[113]

Georges and Paulette Place's children remember her visiting their house in the 1950s and 1960s. They went to Montchauvet several times to visit her sister, Henriette, with her dogs and her orthopedic shoes. They met Louise's children, who at the time spoke only English. Above all they were struck by the friendship between these two very different women: "the white angel and the black angel."[114] Louise wasn't yet a well-known artist, and it's not clear whether her audacious, sensual work, which they only discovered later, were quite to Georges and Paulette's tastes. But their children remember a strong friendship between the two women. Paulette inherited some of Louis's furniture—his desk is still in the Place family home.

The show did not receive much press.[115] The little there was underscored the autobiographical aspect of the work: "Louise Bourgeois: *Sculpteur pour tuer le père* [sculpting to kill the father]," ran *Le matin de Paris*'s headline, going on to call it "one of the most impressive autobiographical theatricals ever fed by love and hate."[116] For Geneviève Bréerette, who would become friends with Louise, "her life is the source of her art,"[117] and she emphasized the rawness of the works' sexual energy. However, in *Le quotidien de Paris*, Philippe Dagen was skeptical of the "heavily Oedipal symbolism" and criticized the work as "too literary" and "lacking in variation"[118]—quite a severe judgment, which he would later recant.

In the middle of the 1980s, French museums were still uninterested in this French-born American artist. The exhibition went to Zurich, while a separate one went to the Serpentine Gallery in London, curated by Stuart Morgan, who would later do a long interview with Louise.[119]

What were these years of visibility like for Louise, when she was more and more sought after for interviews, films, and photographs? Her writings were still full of mentions of fear and low self-esteem. Entire pages were covered in litanies: "I do not deserve it, I do not deserve it, a show, a fan [. . .] a photographer [. . .] I test my strength and ability to cope, to cope, with temptation, with seduction."[120] "Success or good news is terrifying and provokes attack, anxiety attacks or aggressive + murderous attack, it is the fear of the alter ego. I do not want to be rewarded or exalted I detest it, it makes me bite, it is not ingratitude, it is not fear, it is terror."[121] "Fear, Four / fear is intolerable and shameful. [. . .] The raison d'être of my work is to prove I'm not afraid."[122]

Cut

Louise wrote on several of her drawings phrases such as, "I love you, do you love me? I love you, even if you don't love me." In *Je t'aime* (1977), she wrote "*je t'aime, je t'aime, je t'aime . . .* " (I love you, I love you, I love you) over and over, line after line, like a schoolchild being punished: "Desire: write me one hundred lines, no, two hundred lines." This persistent question testifies to an insatiable need for love and comfort, as well as a desire to please. Louise often said that her work was driven by the need to be loved by other people.

In the 1980s, she made a decisive return to drawing. Abstract or figurative, embroidered drawings, text-based drawings, on a multitude of materials, colored paper, burned paper, sewn paper, as well as latex. She also drew her tools: pins, scissors, flowing red blood. Red was her color, the color of passion and love. In a drawing (*Untitled*, 1986), a small pair of red scissors hangs between the legs of a larger blue pair, like a child emerging from its mother's body—"*Ma mère et moi*" (Me and my mother) is written below. In others, instruments which are used to cut or slice are carefully described.

Cutting and separating were one of Louise's obsessions, emerging from the trauma of abandonment and of birth itself: "The umbilical cord cutter. They cut me, separated me, I am going to cut everything around me, absolutely everything—I want the monopoly of cutting, the trees, at 345, all the cutters. I am the cutter who cuts everything. I cut the books, the stones, the wood of the trees. I cut them off, I cut them short."[123]

Threats of suicide, love, anatomy, repeated abstract forms, connected, or not, to the sculptures—these were the dominant themes of the drawings, which were shown several times, first at the Robert Miller Gallery and then abroad.[124]

Louise continued to reference her complicated relationship with her mother and father, and her delicate position between the two, because she was aware that she identified with them both.[125] Writing allowed her to process her oldest memories and to fight against anxiety. "ART IS AN ESCAPE: From Hell life (terror)."[126]

Luckily, she was learning to anticipate and master these periods of anxiety, thanks to her work, and in between bouts she had moments of happiness and calm, when she was alone in her studio in Brooklyn or when she waited on the steps of her house in Chelsea for Jerry to pick her up.[127] "I am free, I'm waiting, I'm living, I'm not afraid, I don't want anything, I don't need anything, I owe nothing to anyone, that's happiness standing still in the sunlight."[128] Among her reassuring memories, she recalled holding her mother's hand when they traveled alone, her protective mother who must be protected. "She sees me as a bodyguard—I see her as a refuge."[129]

When she returned to New York on February 10, 1985, she got to work on a large piece of marble through which she wanted to see the light appear.[130] But this desire for "transparence" was possible only several years later, when Louise received a big block of marble from Carrara, which she would pierce in several places. This monumental sculpture, entitled *The Sail* (1988), hollowed out here and there by holes and tunnels, presented two contrasting sides: one smooth, with a slit in it like an eye, and another, riven with agitated lines like the sails of a ship.

She described technical difficulties, the tools she needed, and referred to some works as the "Bachelard pieces,"[131] confirming her interest in the philosopher and the impact his writing had on her work.

Punk Lady

Louise hung out with young people, especially artists, whether her students (Keith Haring), pop stars such as Andy Warhol, whom she ran into at their simultaneous solo shows at the Robert Miller Gallery,[132] or Bernar Vernet and Robert Malaval: "I love all artists and I understand them (flock of dea[f] mutes in subway). They are my family and their existence keeps me from being lonely."[133]

Around this time she also became friends with Livio Saganic,[134] a young Croatian sculptor whom she mentions several times in her diary from 1985 and with whom she had a close but ambiguous relationship—as with Pietro Cicognani—rooted in artistic understanding. Louise cooked for him (leeks and lamb chops), took interest in his love life—in particular his relationship with the sexologist Shere Hite, author of *The Hite Report: A Nationwide Study of Female Sexuality* (1976)—offered to let him stay in the house on Staten Island and to help him at SVA. But their relationship was not without an element of seduction and revealed her need to be loved. Another link connected them: they were both "outsiders," exiles. Livio particularly remembered the way the mirrors were installed in the bathroom: "The mirrors were rigged in such a way—placed in the corners around the toilet and tilted down—that a man could watch himself or be watched while he pissed."[135] Louise did have an affinity for voyeurism, as the many *Cells* containing mirrors will attest, as well as the films in which she plays with mirrors to look at or trap the Other.

Her inclination toward younger people can be understood as in some degree pedagogical: "Love between teacher + student has to be present for the learning process to take place."[136] But that was also her opinion of life itself: "Students educate their teachers, children educate their parents (Jerry, Michel, Neri)."[137] She got on very well with people younger than herself: "I live with people of a certain age, less than thirty-five or forty. I understand them, I can push them once in a while but I don't do it on purpose. [...] But my love is with them. I relate to them and there is an exchange."[138]

She also befriended a younger generation of women, as evidenced by her friendships with Suzan Cooper[139] and Chris Kraus, who was in a relationship with Sylvère Lotringer at the time.[140] Louise went to a talk Lotringer gave at Columbia about Antonin Artaud, a poet she particularly admired. Kraus says that Louise gave her a gift of a pumpkin-colored wool bouclé shift dress that she had worn to accompany Robert Rauschenberg to his first opening on Tenth Street.[141] She told Kraus: "The only hope for you is marrying a critic or an academic. Otherwise you'll starve."[142] Louise introduced her to

Marshall Blonsky,[143] whom she must have met through Xavier Fourcade. On December 15, 1985, Louise noted: "the cherry on the cake. Chris is pregnant. Sylvère is the father. Louise is the founder of the Fund for Chris' Baby. Suzan is godmother."[144] In the mid-1980s, Louise was a charismatic presence, sought after and adored by the avant-garde, intellectual, and marginal feminists—the New York City underground scene which centered on drugs, performance art, psychoanalysis, and structuralism. She regularly went out at night, especially to the Mudd Club with Andrée Putman, Livio Saganic, and Paul Gardner, whom she would call at all hours of the night.

She had long been interested in performance art, as is clear from *A Banquet / A Fashion Show of Body Parts* (performed around *Confrontation*, 1978). The *Cells,* which she began in the 1990s, are like sets from arte povera theater. She noted in her diary names such as Grotowski and Kantor[145] and took part in a reading of Picasso's *Desire Caught by the Tail,* produced by Françoise Kourilsky's Ubu Repertory Theater at the Guggenheim on October 25 and 26, 1984.[146]

Louise also describes how she met Roland Barthes and his then-disciple Renaud Camus and brought up the subject of love affairs between an older person and a younger one,[147] a theme which had preoccupied her since *Confrontation* and which she sometimes experienced through her students or the young men she encountered. "Barthes is important to me—I met him not long before he died—but like Gaston Bachelard, I read him when I was in my 60s.[148] So it's not that they influenced me, but that suddenly their existence was revealed to me. Barthes had a passion, and you know, any passion has a double effect. [. . .] He told me right to my face, 'You know it was a tragedy because I fell in love with my students, one after the other.' And I thought to myself 'What a fool.' But I didn't say anything."[149]

She also wrote in her diary, "Lacan and the problem of Grace. Psychoanalysis + structuralism. Can you reduce an experience to words, to intellect, yes or no[?]"[150] She mistrusted theory as much as ever, often claiming to be an existentialist, someone who believed in experience, and not a surrealist, much less a structuralist. But she was interested in intellectual trends, especially those which involved psychoanalysis; she discussed these subjects with different visitors and friends and noted it all in her diary.[151]

In the summer of 1986, there was a major exhibition dedicated to twentieth-century sculpture at the Centre Pompidou, called *Qu'est-ce que la sculpture moderne?* (What Is Modern Sculpture?), curated by Margit Rowell.[152] Many American critics rightly commented on the fact that Louise's work was not included: "it is surprising that Rowell could not find room for a sculptor as distinctive as Louise Bourgeois. French patriots will be irked by her certainty that the contribution of native Gauls to modern sculpture compared with achievements in painting as slight."[153] In spite of her friendship with the Pompidou's then director, Dominique Bozo, and the substantial retrospective at the Galerie Maeght-Lelong, Louise's work did not always manage to penetrate French institutions. She was considered eccentric, her work too far removed from the canons of formalism.

In 1987, Louise met with the critic Donald Kuspit[154] a number of times for an interview and was troubled by the personal nature of his questions: "Kuspit, resistance against 'psychoanalysis.' I am jealous of my <u>sacred</u> subject."[155] "Donald Kuspit visit is very heavy. I could <u>kill myself</u> for having said this. Off with your head."[156]

In a long interview with the artist Alain Kirili[157]—which she considered important because for the first time she was able to discuss the autobiographical and French origins of her *Personages*—she touched on her problems with France. They were both Franco-American sculptors, they both felt they belonged in two different cultures, and they both had the same reactions when confronted with American puritanism.

No Exit

Louise made a second series of *Nature Study* works in 1986 in which roughly cut blocks of marble serve as bases for spiral cords, complicated knots tied around large fingers or in thick braids, resembling, as well, masses of intestines. In one, a child's hand emerges from the tangle. In another, a hand emerges from the mass holding a female figure. The obsessive repetition of the same motif was one of the key elements of Louise's practice. It is unsurprising, then, to rediscover, emerging from the marble, the spiral—that image of torsion and opposition, the plaster versions of which she had experimented in the 1960s. But here the umbilical cord and the vigorous tension of forms gave the work a visceral violence, as if a piece of flesh had been torn from the stone. The harder and more resistant the material, the more important and painful the struggle, because resistance was directly linked to the subject being expressed. The marble had to be cut as if cutting into the self, she commented, with reference to Bachelard. "It is a fight to the finish at every moment."[158]

By contrast, the small *Spiral Woman* in polished bronze from 1984, suspended over the void—sometimes installed above a black slate circle on the ground—is caught in a winding coil from which emerge only her legs and arms, an expression of fragility, solitude, and powerlessness. Louise identified with this small, hesitant figure, who spins in the air: "Spirals—which way to turn—represent the fragility in an open space. Fear makes the world go round."[159] The image of the twist comes also from memories of the tapestries that had to be washed and wrung out to dry and from Louise's desire to wring Sadie's neck. In the film *Art City* by Chris Maybach and Paul Gardner, we see her violently wringing a rag.[160] This gesture may also be a reference to torture.[161] The same goes for the large wooden wheels in the sculptures she called *Shredder* (1983).

After building nests, dens, and little houses, Louise felt the need to create spaces in which she or the viewer could physically enter. *Articulated Lair* (1986), her second environment after *Confrontation* (1978), is a refuge composed of forty-eight metal panels folded accordion-style and arranged in a circle. At the center stands a small stool, on which one might sit to be alone or meditate. At one end, there is an escape door. Oblong forms made of black rubber and resembling vegetal pods or the tapestry weaver's shuttle hang in front of some of the panels. Painted black, white, and blue, the panels are reclaimed shelves from her Brooklyn studio, which used to be an old garment factory. These colors had personal meaning for Louise: "Nothing can satisfy the need to cover everything in blue / the opposite side is black— The black from suicide, the black dot, the deep black of a well of solemnity."[162] Blue had a calming function; she needed sky blue after a spasm of jealousy, she wrote; blue is a defense, just as sugar and coffee are stimulants.[163] The stairs in her house in Chelsea were painted blue and black.

For the second time, Louise gave her sculpture a theatrical, performative component, in that the viewer or the artist is offered a seat and can then withdraw in its protective structure. The work—flexible and pivotal in more ways than one—was shown from May to June 1986 at the Robert Miller Gallery before being acquired by MoMA. Mark Francis exhibited it in Paris in 1989 at the *Magiciens de la terre* (Magicians of the Earth) exhibition,[164] a means of signaling what a unique artist Louise was.

After this work on enclosure, a subject she'd already addressed in *He Disappeared into Complete Silence* (1947) and in the *Femme maison* series, Louise made two installations at the end of the 1980s, which she called *No Exit* (1989) and *No Escape* (1989). Each includes a wooden stairway to nowhere, surrounded by a sort of screen in the shape of a half-circle. In *No Exit*, Louise placed two large wooden balls at the foot of the stairs, transforming the staircase into a phallus rising from the center of a feminine circle. Behind the stairs, in a nook like a child's hiding place, hang two light blue rubber hearts, visible only through a peephole. They are little signs of affection that bring a note of comfort to this seemingly pessimistic vision of life, experienced as a Sisyphean punishment: rolling the same rock up and down the same hill. "Our salvation is in two hearts. The issue is how much do you care for somebody else. It is how much you have been able to trust. The trust is a thing I've never been able to reach. It's pretty sad. It's sad, but you get used to it."[165] Ladders that knock into the ceiling in the *He Disappeared* engravings from 1947 (number 8), stairways to nowhere—direct allusions to Jean-Paul Sartre's play *Huis clos* (*No Exit*): "Jean-Paul Sartre said in *No Exit*, '*L'enfer c'est les autres*' (Hell is others). I say that Hell is the absence of others—that's hell."[166]

In March and April 1989, these two works, which foreshadow the *Cells*,[167] were shown at the Galerie Lelong, while two large marble sculptures, *The Sail* (1988) and *Pass* (1988–89), were at the Robert Miller Gallery. Louise was working in two different lanes at the same time, going opposite ways, in very different materials. She continued exploring marble, which she enjoyed working with, as in *The Sail* (a work she was particularly fond of), as well as creating assemblages of found objects.

"I Love You, Do You Love Me?"

Starting in 1988–89, she returned to printmaking, working in lithography with Judith Solodkin at SOLO Impression and in intaglio with Harlan & Weaver. There she met Felix Harlan, with whom she would collaborate until the end of her life, rediscovering the passion she had when she was just starting out. She also worked with Benjamin Shiff of the Osiris imprint, and

Peter Blum; together Bourgeois and Blum would produce a number of books and engravings. The first example is *Anatomy,* a portfolio of ten drypoints and one etching, published in 1989–90,[168] which was also the first time she worked with Felix Harlan.

In October 1988, Louise and Jerry returned to Europe, where her first drawings show took place in Amsterdam at the Overholland Museum.[169] Louise attended the opening, though she was reluctant: "The trip is very difficult. I do not deserve such luxury. I feel <u>embarrassed</u> uncomfortable and it makes [*sic*] self defeating. [. . .] <u>fear of success.</u>"[170]

They then went to Carrara where she continued working in pink marble, for a second series, *Untitled (with Foot), Untitled (with Hand), Untitled (with Growth), Untitled (with Hands)* (all 1989), which moved between abstraction and figuration. On bases of pink marble, she placed smooth spheres from which emerge here a leg, there a hand, or three hands. These primordial forms which blend both mother and embryo are allusions to birth and to procreation. Each bit of material contains a human element within it. Louise conferred life on flesh-colored marble and engraved on the bases these phrases: "I love you," "Do you love me?," "We love you." An obsessive affective credo, expressing the inexpressibility of love.

Another exhibition of her drawings was held in Paris at the Galerie Lelong.[171] Dominique Bozo acquired a series of tangle drawings from the 1940s and 1950s in black ink for the Fonds national de l'art contemporain.[172]

In early 1989, Louise went to see the Andy Warhol show at MoMA and, in September, the Picasso/Braque show to meet up with Dominique Bozo. She was given the College Art Association's Lifetime Achievement Award but didn't think she deserved it: "I do not deserve this invitation. [. . .] I am afraid to accept this honor because I do not think that I deserve it."[173] Since she couldn't be there for the ceremony, she wrote a text explaining the reasons for her absence. "I dread questions. [. . .] This situation terrifies me. It makes me feel like St. Sebastian about to be punctured with arrows. [. . .] Being put on the spot gives me a shot of adrenaline which I sense as a physical challenge, and whatever form my behavior takes, it makes me ashamed. In Charcot's time, in La Salpêtrière, doctors theorized that under extreme stress, a person's body automatically arches into a rigid, bow-like figure. I try to avoid this."[174]

Louise felt unworthy of her success—she even said she wanted to hide it—and was always haunted by guilt. By Pierre's ghost, who needed her, or her mother's ghost, who needed her, too. Sometimes overwhelmed with the desire to kill, she equated sex and violence: "Equation of sex = violence" as well as between sex and death: "Violence is a need [. . .] like fear or the libido. Raw violence appears in tantrums + suicide threats."[175]

For Louise, her work referred neither to history nor to philosophy, religion, or myth, "except for those that appeared in my early life [. . .] they are all personal references, experiences, private vocabulary of the 20th century."[176] Personal experience with universal resonance. In spite of the agonizing tension and profound internal division of which she was aware—she felt torn in two—she went on inventing and creating, and as the years went by, she became prolific. "Art is my religion. Art always allows us to reach the truth. Art keeps us sane, *équilibré* [balanced]."[177] And so she wrote in her diary, on January 14, 1989: "Dear God give me the strength to go on."

CHAPTER 10

———

Becoming a "Star," 1990–1999

The Cells represent different types of pain: the physical, the emotional
and psychological, and the mental and intellectual. [. . .] Each Cell
deals with fear. Fear is pain. [. . .] Each Cell deals with the pleasure of
the voyeur, the thrill of looking and being looked at.

The richly abundant work produced in the early 1990s confirms the motif
of the house as the central, preeminent theme of Louise Bourgeois's oeuvre.
In the *Femme maison* imagery, the *Lairs*, and the *Cells*, as elsewhere in her
work, the house is a metaphor for the body, a dialogue between inside and
out, formed of passages and openings such as windows and doors, or those
that allow us to see, hear, and smell. The device of the accordionlike doors
forming an enclosure, as in *Articulated Lair* (1986) or *No Exit* (1989), paved
the way for the monumental sculptural environments she would call the
Cells. The term "cell" evokes not only the biological organism but also a
place of solitary retreat, whether clerical or carceral. These semienclosed
spaces, into which the eye or the viewer may enter, are "sites of memory,"
magic rooms in which a secret ceremony is carried out or in which an
ancient fear or suffering is reenacted in order to exorcize it.

The older Louise got, the farther back she traveled in time, venturing
closer to her earliest childhood memories. As she aged, her ambitions grew,
and she believed it was important to reconstruct past emotions, theatrically
yet on the scale of lived experience. "My emotions are inappropriate to my
size. My emotions are my demons. [. . .] It is not the emotions themselves,
it is the intensity."[1] These *Cells*, with their "walls" of old glass-paneled doors,
or grilles, allowed her to bring together a jumble of symbolic objects, to

| 257 |

stand in for the eternal protagonists of the family drama, or our complex affective relations with others. This decade was punctuated by invitations to major international exhibitions; for each one, she prepared new work. *Cell I* to VI (*Carnegie International,* Carnegie Museum of Art, Pittsburgh, 1991–92); *Twosome* (*Dislocations,* MoMA, 1991); *Precious Liquids* (*Documenta IX,* Kassel, 1992); *Cell* (*Arch of Hysteria*) and three more *Cells* on the theme of childhood, loneliness, and voyeurism for the 1993 Venice Biennale. Before she created these large pieces, Louise was making singular works such as *Ventouse* (1990), which echoes the placement of suction cups on her sick mother's back; *Le défi* (1991), a blue wooden shelf filled with glass containers; and *Mamelles* (1991), a long frieze of pink rubber breasts. They were an important step toward the *Cells.* Despite her age—over eighty years old—Louise did not stop creating, renewing her visual language, or exploring new sculptural techniques and materials in a dynamic, organic, endless process, each discovery opening out onto new terrain. She made large, curved needles, larger than human-sized—as in 1992's *Needle* (*Fuseau*), which refers to the tapestry business and the family workshop. Next came the suspended clothing, soft sculptures in fabric, and, following this thread, the figure of the spider, a final homage to her mother. She was extremely prolific during the 1990s, developing her writing as well as her sculpture—not only in her diary and the inscriptions on her insomnia drawings, but as art criticism or as poetic writing in her illustrated books. Louise had incontrovertibly become a star of the contemporary art world, showing at all the biennials (Venice, Lyon, São Paulo, Gwangju); she was an icon, highly sought after for films, photographs, and interviews. Finally, that long-desired recognition came from the French, with several public commissions (the Manufacture nationale de Sèvres, les Gobelins, the town of Choisy-le-Roi, the Bibliothèque nationale) and major exhibitions (Centre Pompidou, Musée d'art moderne de la Ville de Paris, Musée d'art contemporain, Bordeaux).

In the late 1990s, Louise organized a weekly salon, to make up for Jerry's absence on Sunday afternoons, receiving visitors and young artists who sought her advice. She was ever more haunted by the past, by the memories she had accumulated, noting everything down in her agendas, recording interviews on cassette tapes because she was always afraid of confiding in others. She wanted to control her own image and sometimes went so far as to censor things that bothered her. However, she agreed to participate in several documentary films and proved herself a born actress, excitable and very funny. It was the apotheosis of her artistic career, a position that allowed her complete freedom to create and to take on important challenges, including the monumental commission from the Tate Modern's Turbine Hall in 2000.

The Death of Michel

However, this decade began with a painful loss: the death of her adopted son, Michel, in April 1990. Though he had somewhat distanced himself from his family, he continued to visit Louise regularly; they had always had a strong, relaxed relationship. He lived alone as the superintendent of a building on Mulberry Street, in Little Italy, where he made a few friends, went by Mike, and occasionally saw his brother Alain.[2] Michel appears in a photograph from 1977 taken by Mark Setteducati, at a ceremony at Yale University: small and stocky with a black mane of hair, a pronounced nose, and a thick mustache.[3] He was rough-hewn in build but had a sweet disposition, at least according to those he was close to. Louise had a particular bond with this French child who had such a difficult time adjusting to life with his intellectual adoptive family in New York. According to Alain, Michel had trouble fitting in from the very beginning: he was dyslexic, emotional, fickle, a bad student, more interested in nature than in his studies.[4] Setteducati said that he was never at a loss for words, that he was both direct and distant, and very kind. Jerry, who often ran into him at Louise's house, also found him charming. On April 20, 1990, Alain notified Louise that Michel was very sick and drove her with Jean-Louis to Saint Vincent's Hospital so she could see him one last time. He died on April 27: "5PM Michel passes away at St. Vincent." Not much is known of the nature of his illness. Louise gathered with Michel's brothers and all his friends to hold a memorial in a local bar.

She was thinking more and more about her foundation and planning who would serve on the board and in what capacity:[5] "Advisory Board: no dealer according to Jerry / Richard Marshall, Debby Wye, Rob[er]t Storr, Jane Timkin, Rob[er]t Pincus-Witten, Dominique Bozo, Ingrid Sischy, Brenson, [. . .] Glueck Grace [*sic*], Rainwater (Bobby) Adato Perry, Geldzahler."[6] Her children would be honorary members, as would her grandchildren, Claire and Alex; she also considered her lawyer, Ira Lowe.[7]

Louise wanted her foundation to be headquartered at her studio in Brooklyn, at 475 Dean Street.[8] She also imagined that she would divide up her archives between the foundation and the Archives of American Art.[9] These preparations demonstrate her keen organizational sense and her concern for the future of her work and legacy.

Although her grandchildren saw her as distant, indifferent, even cold, Louise kept up with their studies and professional successes: "Bravo! Claire is admitted at Oberlin."[10] She wanted to give Claire two Louis XVI corner cabinets from her father (though she would not, in the end, make this gift, and used them in the *Cell* titled *Red Room* [*Parents*] two years later)[11] and had her come by once or twice a week to organize her archives. However, they both found it difficult to communicate with each other. Claire Bourgeois clammed up, just as Mâkhi Xenakis[12] would later: "Claire 11 A.M. (mute as a *nutte* [newt]) *le mutisme de Claire* [Claire's refusal to speak] gets to me."[13] With Alex,[14] things were no easier,[15] because they were tied up in her relationship with Alain, his father: "How do we break that vicious circle[?] I am not a Saint, I am not your mother, and I am not your father. I am something quite special either your grandmother or your friend."[16] Despite her apparent coldness (in fact due to a surplus of feelings), she thought of them all the time: "Claire, Alex, Alain are on my mind."[17]

Her old fears were still hanging around. "Don't confuse the thrill of fear with erotic thrill and the thrill of your attack, related to fear, aggressivity and sexuality, what come [*sic*] first."[18] With time, however, she felt that her wounds were healing: "intestinal hysteria calmed."[19] And, "To help concentration: you have to admit failures (pink + blue) as a mother, as a planner, as a friend, as a doer, as a woman, as a 'fashion plate,' as a speaker, as a film worker."[20]

European Tour

In 1990, Louise was finally given a retrospective exhibition that toured the European museums: Frankfurt,[21] Munich, Lyon, Barcelona, Bern, and Otterlo. Still not Paris, though, which disappointed her greatly and which is difficult to understand. A proposal was made to the Centre Pompidou, but it didn't go anywhere. It was, in the end, the Musée d'art contemporain in Lyon[22] and its director, Thierry Raspail, who were lucky enough to receive the show. An important catalog was created, which would be the first French monograph on Louise. Thierry Raspail reflected on her lack of visibility in the country of her birth: "To say that Louise Bourgeois's work is little known in France is a euphemism. What strange attitudes we have, so ignoring what we see before our eyes, cutting ourselves off from it out of conformity, and unequivocal blindness."[23] He fondly remembered his joyful, festive trips to see Louise in New York, where she made him drink vermouth down to the dregs.

On July 5, 1990, Louise attended the opening in Lyon. She stayed at the Hôtel Terminus, and had dinner with Dominique Bozo and Michel Troche as well as her new dealer, Robert Miller. Trips to France were as anxiety-inducing as ever: "I'm afraid and I have a terrible fear of going to Lyon. I have a terrible fear of being revealed, lacking, inadequate."[24]

The response in the media was mixed: the specialist journals were enthusiastic, but the daily newspapers barely noticed it. A critic for *Art Press* who attended the opening night referred to the artist's "radiant energy," her mocking, acerbic tone, her vitality, and the striking contrast between her confidence and extreme fragility.[25] Robert Storr published a long interview with Louise in *Galeries Magazine*[26] on the subject of this tribute in her native land: "And yet here you are, and it seems as if you will beat the odds? — That's true, that's true," Louise replied. The Americans ridiculed this lack of recognition: "The site of her triumphal traveling retrospective is not Paris—the Pompidou Center turned it down—but Lyons's Musee d'Art Contemporain."[27]

After Lyon, she and Jerry went down to Le Cannet, visited the Musée Bonnard, and verified that the Villa Astrid was not the Villa Marcel she remembered from childhood. "We leave Le Cannet[28] hotel Grande Bretagne for Carrara. Lunch La Spezia."[29] "The sterility of reality and the magic of memory [. . .] Seen again, found again, Le Cannet is nothing."[30] On the road with Jerry, traveling by car, they stopped at a flea market where she bought the famous glass suction cups she would use in *Ventouse* (1990), in reference to those applied to her mother's back to treat her illness. This would be her last trip around France. After a short stay on the Côte d'Azur, she returned to Carrara, Italy, where she reunited with Nicoli.

Louise returned to Europe for the opening of the Fondation Tapiès. On November 5, she arrived in Barcelona, checking in at the Hotel Colón. "At

6:30 am, so nauseous I could kill myself."[31] Old memories returned; she describes her fear of germs, Legionnaires' disease in the bathroom: "[The] period of trauma anorexia, afraid of drinking, eating, touching, even of washing myself, contamination, afraid of moving, especially, cold."[32] Because she was so afraid of germs, she required the newspaper be ironed before she would touch it, refused to see people if they had a cold, and took various other hygienic precautions. Louise was always obsessed with cleanliness. "I detest filth, dirty dish rags in the storage room, blood on the dish rags, dirty laundry, the hamper, the handkerchiefs."[33] She associated bad smells and dirt with memories of childhood and with the servants ("Maids were everywhere / enveloping our lives as children like a dirty towel")[34] but also with the smells of the sewers, which brought back Paris, Antony, and the Bièvre.

After the opening at the Fondation Tapiès on November 6, she went to Carrara, stopping off in Rome and Pisa; this would be her final trip to Italy. Louise still complained about the Italian people's manners: "I want to assert myself and they won't give me the chance. That's why the Italians yell or bark, instead of talking. [. . .] It's absolutely antisocial, sometimes I am the path to the social: cut off the people who are yelling. Sometimes I'm the one who's yelling."[35]

Cells of Meaning

The first *Cells,* numbered *I* to *VI,* were shown at the *Carnegie International,* in Pittsburgh.[36] *Cell I* is a small square room closed off by a set of blue wooden doors, with an iron-frame bed covered in rough canvas bags from the French post office onto which she embroidered phrases: "I need my memories, they are my documents," "Art is the Guarantee of Sanity," and "Pain is the ransom of formalism." These phrases summarize Louise's entire approach to art and are present in her texts and in many of her works, testimony to the artist's inescapable pain and the cathartic function of her creative practice. Beside the bed she placed a low table, on which stand a variety of glass objects—tubes, bottles, and beakers. An atmosphere of stifling solitude, desperation, and melancholy resides in this space which is so like a prison cell or a hospital room (with its medicinal vials and a book on tuberculosis)[37] or like the set for a play by Kantor or Grotowski.[38]

She frequently turned to glass during this time; it can be found in almost all of the *Cells,* in varying forms: found objects, gas lamps or laboratory equipment, flasks, vases, blown glass, jars. "The glass suggests the infinite fragility of the human person. [. . .] If I talk to you, I may break everything. But, that's not my fault; I can be very, very sorry afterwards. But a break in a piece of glass can never be hidden."[39]

In one *Cell,* there is a collection of Shalimar bottles, her favorite perfume; in another, a pink marble leg; in yet another, a large marble ear and a gong. Then there is one featuring two balls of wood, and, finally, in *Cell VI,* a small blue stool in a claustrophobic room created by four blue doors. Some *Cells* refer to the senses: smell, hearing, touch. The perfume symbolizes the ephemerality of pleasure, the effluvia of the past; it is the essence of a person or a place. When asked her favorite scent, Louise responded: "Smell of the garden after the rain."[40] Smell, an immediate physical sensation, often opens the door of memory, through which some element of the past can enter the present. Its evocative power is so strong that Louise reported once having fainted in a hotel room upon catching a whiff of a typically Parisian sewer smell. The intensity and the physical effects of scent are a frequent refrain in her writings: eucalyptus reminds her of Le Cannet ("the smell of my childhood is eucalyptus, eucalyptol essential oil used in medicine"),[41] the leather smell of shoes, the creosote of the Paris metro, or . . . the smell of feet: "The smell of the feet is not the odor of defeat, it's the opposite, it's an adored smell, euphoric and intoxicating, nostalgic and exciting and erotic."[42]

Wooden chairs, stools, mirrors, globes, fragments of the body rendered in marble, glass objects, sharp objects—like the paper cutter in *Cell III* and the band saw in *Cell (Arch of Hysteria)*—are recurrent motifs in this series. Most of the first *Cells* were closed off with wooden doors or French doors, reclaimed from her studio, and offering a solid feeling of refuge like a house.

Louise was always interested in literature, curious and on the alert. Paging through Inge Morath's photograph collection *Portraits*—which included Louise—Peter Blum[43] had the idea to commission Louise and Morath's husband, the playwright Arthur Miller, to create an illustrated book together, which would eventually become *Homely Girl: A Life* (1992). Miller accordingly went to the studio in Brooklyn to see the "senses" of the *Cells* and drafted a text, the story of a young woman who falls in love with a blind man. Louise's accompanying series of ten drypoint prints depict flowers growing on stems and from broken branches and clouds over a mountain range. In a second volume, she made color photolithographs with medical images of various eye diseases. The motif of the eye and its corollary, blindness, reappear in this new form.

Twosome

On being asked to curate an exhibition called *Dislocations* at MoMA in 1991,[44] Robert Storr invited Louise—by this time a leading light of the contemporary art world—to contribute, along with Bruce Nauman,[45] Chris Burden, Sophie Calle, David Hammons, Ilya Kabakov, and Adrian Piper.

For this show, she made a kinetic work, unusual for Louise. In contrast to the verticality of the houses or the *Cells*, she worked with horizontality in the form of two enormous cylinders on a track, so that the smaller one enters and is ejected out of the larger. Louise found the old gas tanks on Staten Island. The layout of the door and three windows pierced in one of the tanks resembles the family's country house in Easton, Connecticut. The tanks are lit from within by a flashing red police light. The sexual connotation is clear, the mechanical element that moves like a piston emphasized the degree to be which it could be seen as a "fucking machine."[46] But this primary relationship between two elements also symbolized, for Louise, the child which emerges from its mother's body and keeps returning there because it cannot manage to sever the umbilical cord. *Twosome*, she said, represents "the efforts of the child who seeks his independence at all costs, who escapes parental tyranny and doesn't know what to do with his independence, so he returns."[47] As usual, Louise supplied other interpretations: it was also a dialogue between a man and a woman: "It's a psychological relationship. Everyone wants to see a sexual one in it. It's presexual. It's the attraction of the masculine and feminine elements before fornication."[48] This alternation between attraction and repulsion tells us much about her conception of the erotic, which envelops physical desire, maternity, seduction, and all dualistic relationships, from resistance to acceptance. "It relates to birth, sex, excretion—taking in and pushing out. In and out covers all our functions. In and out is the key to the piece. [. . .] Two people make an environment. One person alone is an object."[49] The mechanism was constructed with the help of a computer and was included in the exhibition no doubt because it integrated new techniques. It was one of her favorite works, suggesting a multiplicity of unconscious meanings: "There are several layers of interpretation in it. The deepest, most secret level is about pleasure. And pleasure is erotic."[50] Whatever their precise meaning, the red lights inside these black forms have a tragic connotation. The red and the black, so dominant here, will be echoed in two *Cell* pieces in 1994, titled *Red Room (Parents)* and *Red Room (Child)*.

Louise was quite well known by this point, and the feminist movement recognized her as a leader. Somewhat in spite of herself, Louise played an important role in the changing of the title of the Guggenheim SoHo's inaugural exhibition in their new downtown space.[51] Originally entitled *From Brancusi to Beuys: Aspects of the Guggenheim Collection,*[52] the show contained almost exclusively works by men, except for Louise. This caused feminist organizations like the Guerrilla Girls and the Women's Action Coalition to launch a campaign to get the organizers to change the title, and it became: *From Brancusi to Bourgeois.* Her friend Andrée Putman, whom she had known since the 1980s, when they went clubbing together, was there for the opening on June 25, 1992, as well as Michel Guy. Louise—a small, charismatic woman—was welcomed in triumph. She commented on the use of glass in her work *Le défi* (1991): "Showing the glasses (it looks like a shop), ambivalence. What's hidden, and gender confusion. The glass as nightmare."[53]

Precious Liquids

Michel's absence was an ongoing source of sadness and guilt. Louise dreamed of a shop for him on Atlantic Avenue in Brooklyn:[54] "Yesterday was the day to celebrate, but I couldn't do it because I am always guilty of abandoning my dead. $25,000 is due to St. Vincent's [for Michel's hospitalization]. The sculpture of Michel has to be built."[55]

New anxieties arrived in 1991 when Alain fell seriously ill. Jessica, his wife, called Louise on November 6 to tell her that he had a collapsed lung and was in the Methodist hospital in Brooklyn. Louise celebrated his birthday on November 12 in his hospital room and brought him presents. On December 20, she wrote[56] that the fact that Alain was still in the hospital destroyed her: "going to visit Alain in Methodist Brooklyn Hosp[ital] liquidates me, stunned, destroyed, [. . .] reduced to tears—reduce[d] to silence!!!"[57] He still hadn't recovered in January 1992 and was moved to a different hospital, which terrified Louise: "Alain changing hospital wrenches me out of shape [. . .] I pace like a sick pig, but I don't attack anyone. Anger suits me."[58] There was more cause for concern in May 1994: "Alain is in [the hospital] Lenox Hill [. . .] I cannot cope because of Alain['s] hospitalization."[59] These worries were compounded when Jean-Louis's wife, Carollee Pelos,[60] also fell ill and had to have surgery.[61] She was hospitalized again on October 11, 1993.

Perhaps it was because of these clinical environments, as well as the specter of AIDS,[62] which was decimating the artistic community in New York, taking with it several of her close friends (Gert Schiff, Nigel Finch) that led Louise to create her piece entitled *Precious Liquids,* as well as several writings about illness during this time: "The Precious Liquids—Rain, the sink, hot + cold, the washing, the drinking taken in intravenous feeding [. . .] blood, semen—emptiness again[?]"[63] Words such as "sperm," "urine," "tears," "milk," "sweat," and "blood" recur regularly in her notes during these years. "Some diseases are considered shameful because sinful," she wrote in 1991 about one of her *Cells*: "in bed, crouching in fear, the person in this *Cell* is hiding. [. . .] He is physically sick and afraid of death."[64] Later, concerning one of her spiders and the fear around mosquitoes, she said: "The subject is in reality much more the fear of mosquitoes, of AIDS or infection, than that of the spider. It's a defense against something evil. It's the eternal battle between good and evil, we can see it's everywhere. And truly the evil is AIDS."[65]

On the subject of blood, Louise recalled her period appearing in the infirmary at the Lycée Fénelon: "A period is a 'blessing,' eternally grateful to my mother. Blood means kill him. I kill or I am killed."[66] Louise willingly became a mother but saw herself as both the executioner and the victim: "In real life I identify with the victim, in my art I am the murderer."[67] Elsewhere, she played with the anagrams crime/*merci*.[68]

Louise also referenced birth, sex, food, and excrement. "[I] have a morbid attraction to the shit, covering up for the revulsion. Revulsion at everything including the self."[69] The sex drive, however, was stronger: "Fear, fear [. . .] the only way to stop fear is to give in to the erotic, the attraction."[70] That's why sublimation was so useful: it was a form of resistance: "Sexuality is sublimated in the intensity of effort necessary to learn, to understand, to connect, to associate in creation."[71]

Created for *Documenta IX* in Kassel, in 1992, *Precious Liquids* is a masterpiece, a pivot point between the two *Cell* typologies. Unlike the windowed spaces of the other pieces, this one is closed off and dark. Container and contained are coupled in a cause-and-effect relationship, because the interior of this enormous tank is intended for the storage of large quantities of liquid: it is a water tower of the kind found on New York City rooftops. The eponymous precious liquids are, for Louise, all those produced by the human body, those humors which spill forth under the shock of an emotional blow: love, fear, pleasure, suffering. "Since the fears of the past were connected with the functions of the body, they reappear through it. The glass becomes a metaphor for the muscles of the body. It represents the subtlety of the emotions, the mechanism and the instability. When the muscles of the body relax and the tension goes down, a liquid is released. Intense emotions physically become liquid, a precious substance."[72] Inside, there is an iron bed frame fitted with a sheet of metal that has the appearance of an old trough. It is slightly concave, and a drain with a small pool of water is at the foot. It is surrounded by four steel-pipe structures with tiered branches holding multiple glass receptacles, as if in reference to IV poles beside a hospital bed. Across from it, two rubber globes flank an immense man's coat, under which hangs a white dress embroidered with the words "*Merci/* Mercy." On the other side are two wooden balls and an illuminated version of an older work (*Le Trani Episode*, 1971). The large coat stands in for the father, authority: "The little dress taking refuge in the big coat represents the child who has undergone strong emotions and has been able in the process of growing up to feel compassion for the big fool, the flasher."[73] The play on words, "*Merci*/Mercy," thanks and pity, express the double feelings of gratitude and compassion that Louise sometimes felt for her father. The privileged place that the child is given within this coat seems to indicate that the liberation has finally taken place. "The piece, *Precious Liquids*, is about a girl growing up and finding passion instead of terror. She stops being afraid and she knows passion. The little dress taking refuge in the big coat represents the child who has undergone strong and frightened emotions. The big coat is a metaphor for the unconscious."[74]

The moral of the piece is inscribed in a piece of iron encircling the tank: "Art is a Guaranty of Sanity." Louise thus reaffirmed the credo she had already announced on the bed in *Cell I* and repeated many times. Understanding and managing our fears allows us to move forward every day.

In her diary, Louise described the different steps involved in making the piece, the technical difficulties she encountered taking the tank apart and bringing it down from the roof of her Brooklyn studio building: "George Lapcik has to take the water tower down."[75] Using this relic of the New York City skyline reminded her of making her earliest sculptures in wood on the rooftop of Stuyvesant's Folly on Eighteenth Street.

The Centre Pompidou wanted the work for its collection,[76] which at this time included only *Cumul I* (1969). Dominique Bozo and Germain Viatte[77] went to New York to negotiate the acquisition. In honor of her long friendship with Bozo, she agreed to lower her price but requested that the work be shown immediately upon arrival in Paris. "I will sell *Precious Liquids* on the condition that it will be erected on arrival."[78]

Louise Bourgeois, Art Critic

Louise didn't like the term "art critic." She was often very hard on critics,[79] wary of them as of art historians; she saw the role of the artist as being separate from knowledge and theory, in spite of her husband's profession and her own studies at the École du Louvre: "I am not interested in art history. My husband taught it, so I had my fill at home!"[80] Another of her contradictions. Now famous in the art world, Louise was often sought after to write articles for *Artforum* on subjects that were important to her. The first was on Sigmund Freud's collection of antique objects, which she called "Freud's Toys."[81] "When I look at this catalog of Freud's collection, I think of Madame Tussaud's Wax Museum."[82] After analyzing his reasons for having such a collection—pleasure, social standing, something to look at during long silent sessions with patients—Louise, drawing on her knowledge of Freud's writings and her own time as an analysand, goes on to give a sarcastic description of psychoanalysis: "I see his office with the half-dead hysterics there as a pitiful place. I don't want to exaggerate, but I call them maggots."[83] Freud, she writes, wanted to save these poor people's lives because he truly believed that analysis could lead to rebirth. His collection of objects from all civilizations inspired him to believe, as well, in the power of culture. For Sigmund Freud, collecting after the death of his father allowed him to locate his place in history. In the same way, Louise kept her father's pebble collection after his death: "My father had one collection and I found it. I still have it. It was a box and inside there were pebbles. There were hundreds of pebbles, and he had it on his desk. He said, 'Every time I have a beautiful moment, it proves to me that life is worth living, and in gratitude I put a pebble in the box.' So he was collecting beautiful moments."[84]

In her essay, Louise argues for a distinction between art and artifact. For her, Freud's objects have little aesthetic value; the little Tanagra statuette from the Hellenistic period is just a manufactured product to be placed in tombs, replicated thousands of times. "A toy is fine, but it is only a toy. It's not a reality. [. . .] The artifact is a manufactured object; a work of art is a language. The artifact has only an educational or sentimental value. The work of art has an *absolute* value. How could Freud have had an eye for esthetic quality when the esthetic of some of these objects is so low?"[85] She concludes with a reflection on the uselessness of analysis for artists. "People sublimate and turn to art," she writes, "because, first of all, they would like to be sexual but they are afraid, and second, they feel guilty." For Louise, "you [. . .] do not have to be religious to be afraid of sex," and "the need of artists remains unsatisfied, as does their torment."[86]

"Gaston Lachaise, Père Lachaise"

Louise has been compared to Gaston Lachaise, another American artist born in France who made deeply erotic sculptures, whose audacious distortions were evocative of sex organs.[87] It seems natural, therefore, that she would be invited to write about him.[88] Louise knew his life and work well and emphasized his affair with the artist (and his muse) Isabel Dutaud Nagle. "Why the obsession with breasts and cunts?" she asks.[89] What did he have to prove? For Louise, Lachaise was no Don Juan, and unlike what some feminists, shocked by his representations of the female body, had to say about him, Lachaise did not exploit women: he loved them. A famous work like *Abstract Figure* (1930–32), also known as *Breasts with Female Organ Between*, reflects an original vision of his relationship with woman "as mother, as lover, as ideal, as god."[90] "It is a compliment to grant the sex object such power that it can trigger such passion."[91] Louise always went against the grain of the politically correct.

She also wrote an article on Joan Miró, to coincide with the MoMA retrospective of his work in 1994.[92] After noting that she knew Miró in the 1930s in Paris, when he showed at the Galerie Pierre and had "shake[n] off the hold of Breton," and again in New York in 1947 in Hayter's studio Atelier 17, she confronts the question of the naive artist. For Louise, Joan Miró was authentically naive: childlike, innocent, sincere, his work an expression of deep feeling. But in spite of her admiration and feelings of friendship toward him, Louise could not restrain herself from several (justifiably) pointed observations about his dependence on his wife, Pilar, and especially his sculpture, which she found uninteresting: "There is more to sculpture than a blob of clay with a fork in it."[93] Miró was too successful and, in her view, yielded to the pressures of the marketplace. She concluded by congratulating MoMA on three excellent historical retrospectives—Picasso, Matisse, Miró—but, she argued, they were "stuck in the past" because they did not explore the artist's "inward vista." They demonstrated no interest in the "behavioral sciences"; they ought, she wrote, to aim "to equip us better to understand *why* we do what we do."[94] This observation echoes Picasso's comment that a science of man was needed to understand the work of an artist. And above all, it allows us to understand why it took so long for Louise's work to be recognized: she was more interested in the subjective and unconscious interior processes by which artists create than in the form and history of art.

The Venice Biennale, 1993

In June 1993, Louise represented the United States at the Venice Biennale. It included both recent pieces in marble, older works, and, most importantly, four new *Cells*,[95] three of which had cages made of grilles or windows, one of which was a manifesto: *Cell (Arch of Hysteria)* (1992–93). It was the most violent work of this period. On a bed embroidered over and over with the words *"je t'aime"* (I love you), a man stretches out in the posture of the hysterical arch. His arms and head have been cut off, perhaps by the circular saw beside him. Louise was interested in Charcot and hysteria, as her reading attests:[96] "Except that in my *Arch of Hysteria* it's not a hysterical woman— that's a nineteenth-century misconception—but a hysterical man. That's why Jerry lent me his anatomy."[97] The use of Jerry Gorovoy as model had nothing to do with Charcot's theatrical demonstrations of hysteria. Jerry was not being "directed"; he was part of a two-person drama, but not one being performed onstage. It was, rather, a psychodrama[98] that was being

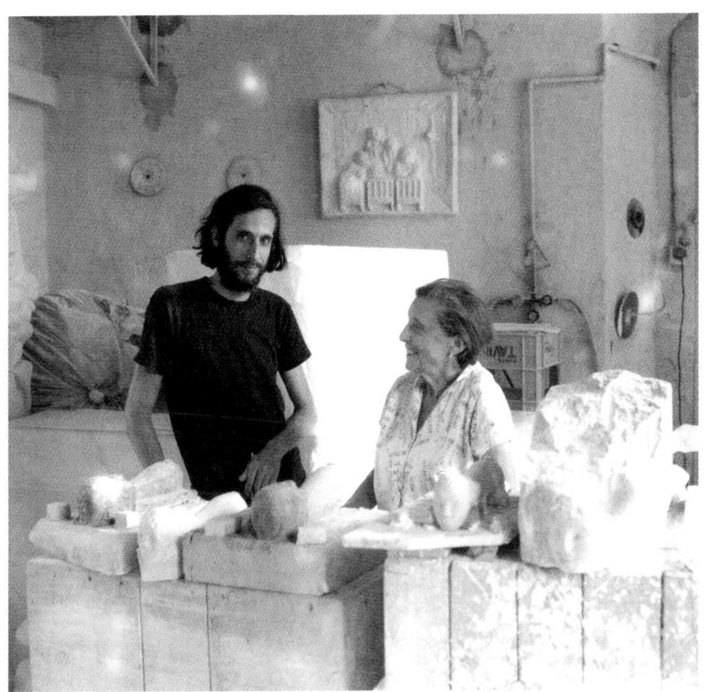

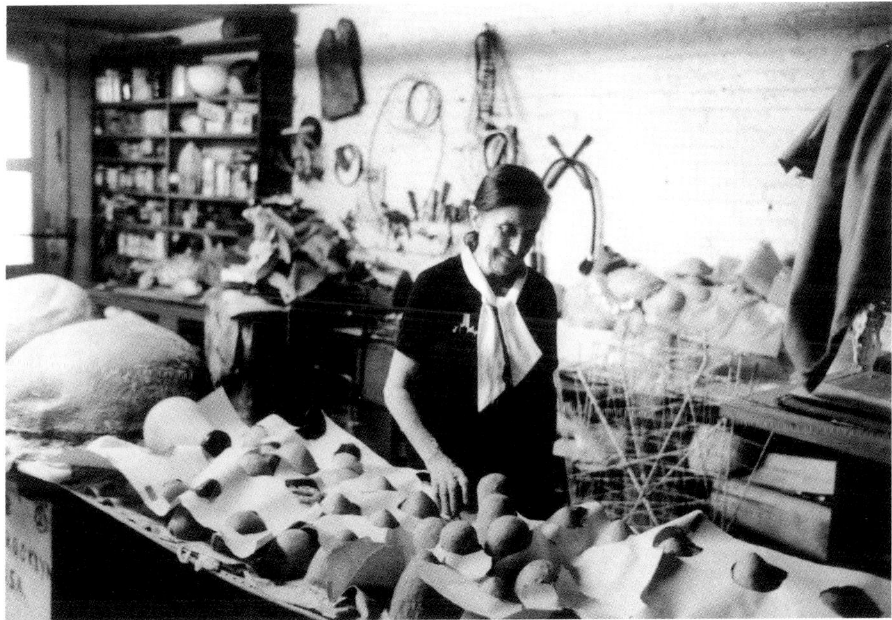

Louise Bourgeois with her assistant Jerry Gorovoy,
Carrara, Italy, 1981

Louise Bourgeois in her home studio, New York, 1982

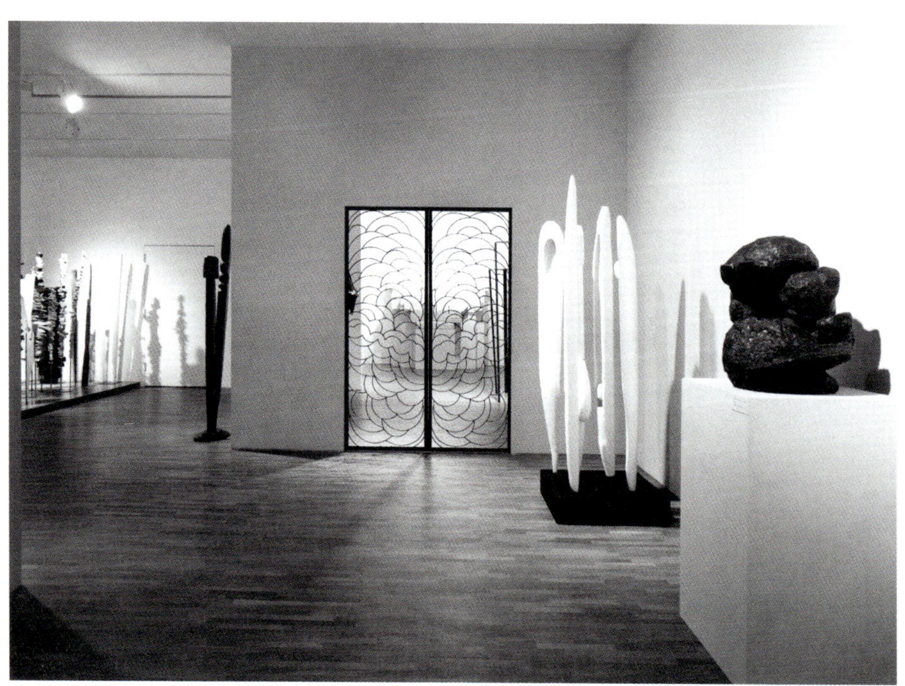

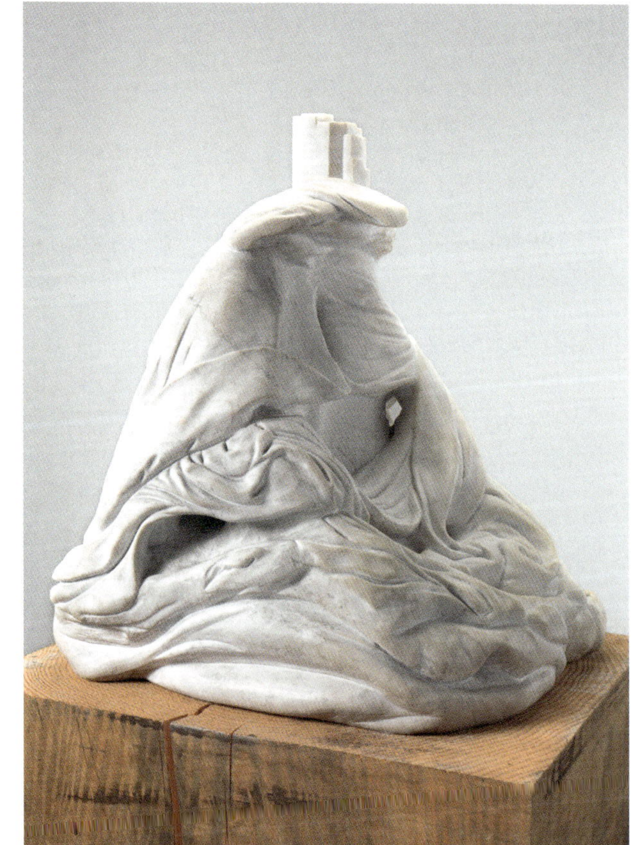

Installation view of
*Louise Bourgeois:
Retrospective*, Museum
of Modern Art, New
York, November 3,
1982–February 8, 1983

Femme maison, 1982.
Marble, 25 × 19½ × 23 in.
(63.5 × 49.5 × 58.4 cm)

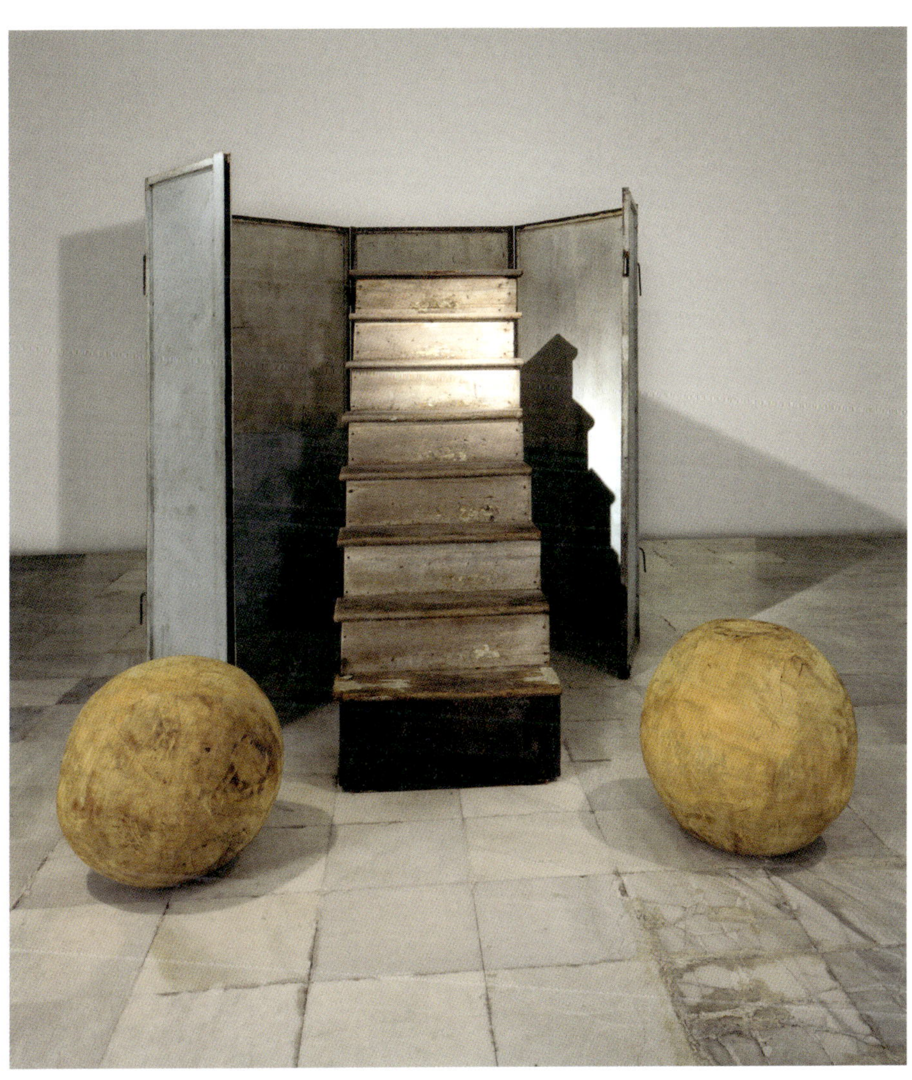

No Exit, 1989. Wood, painted metal, and rubber,
82½ × 84 × 96 in. (209.6 × 213.4 × 243.8 cm)

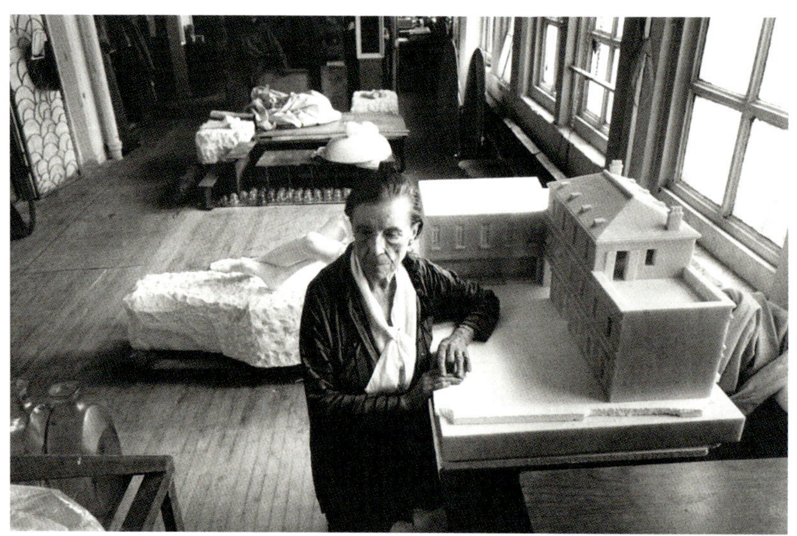

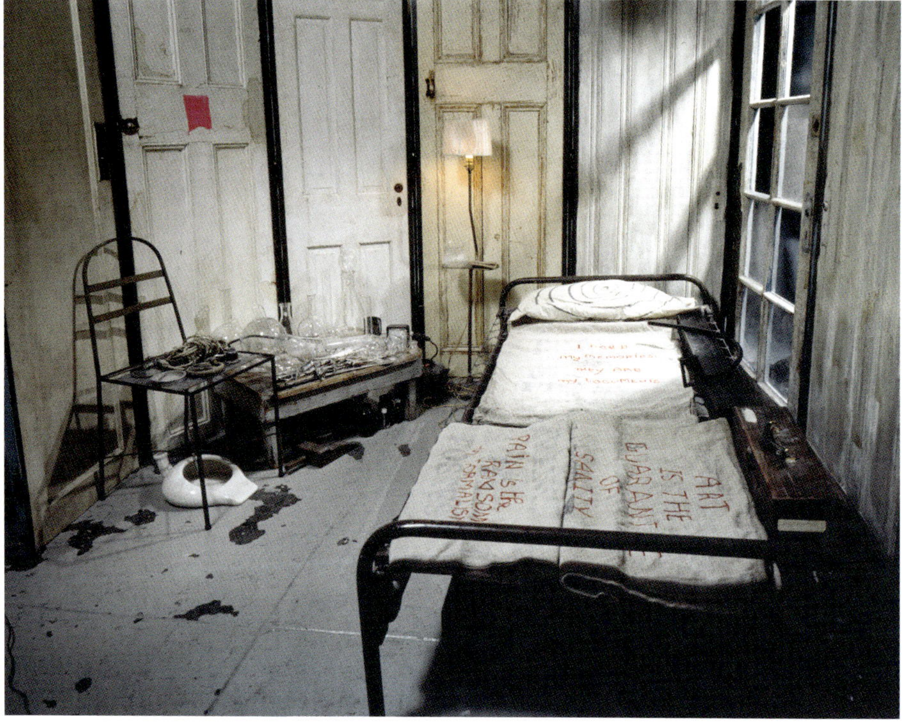

Louise Bourgeois in her studio, Brooklyn,
New York, 1991

Cell I (detail), 1991. Painted wood, fabric, metal, and
glass, 83 × 96 × 108 in. (210.8 × 243.8 × 274.3 cm)

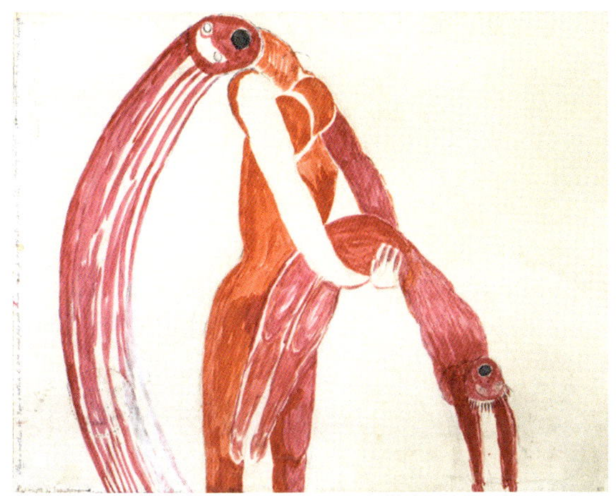

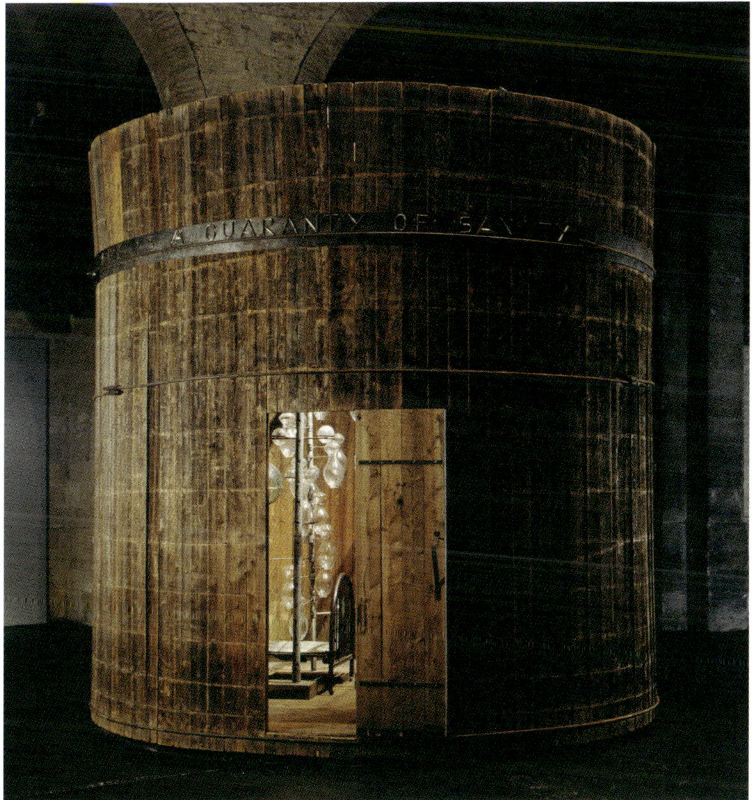

Altered States, 1992. Gouache, ink, and pencil on paper, 19 × 23¾ in. (48.3 × 60.3 cm)

Precious Liquids, 1992. Wood, metal, glass, alabaster, rubber, fabric, embroidered fabric, water, and electric light, 167½ × 175¼ × 175¼ in. (425.5 × 445.1 × 445.1 cm)

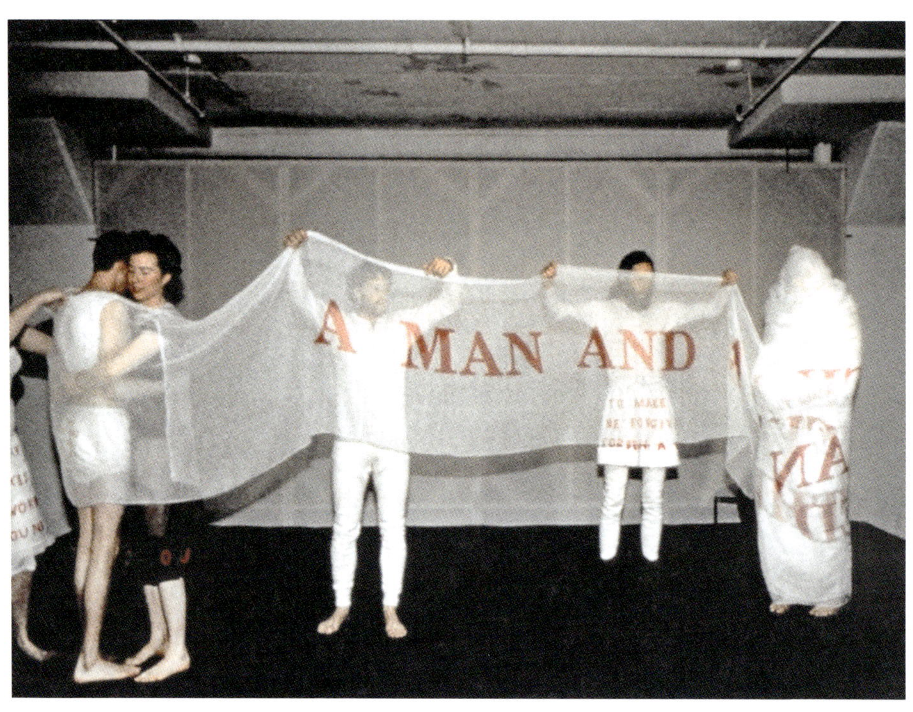

Louise Bourgeois's performance, *She Lost It*, at the
Fabric Workshop, Philadelphia, December 5, 1992

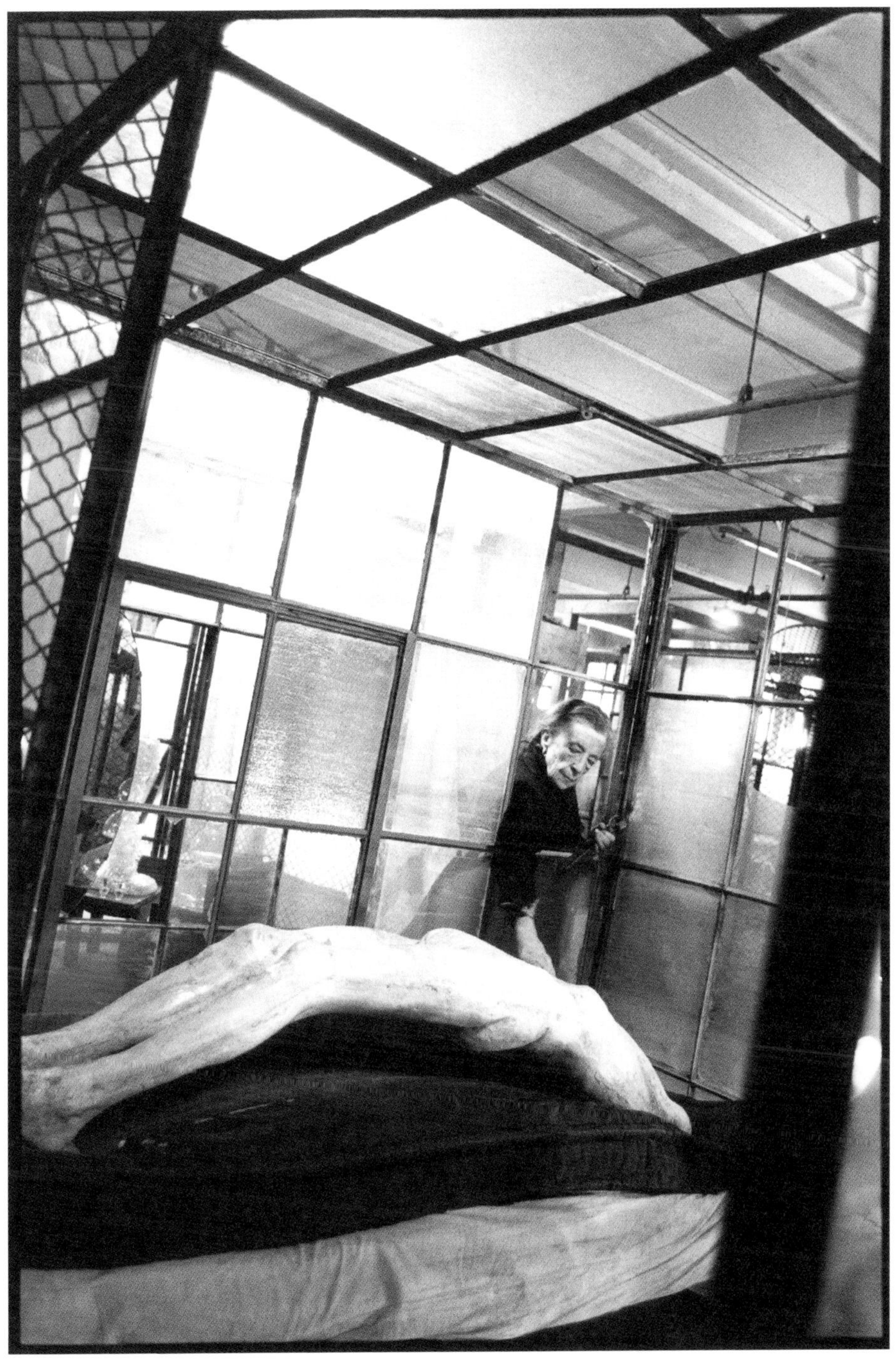

Louise Bourgeois with *In and Out* (in progress),
from the *Cell* series, in her studio, Brooklyn,
New York, 1993

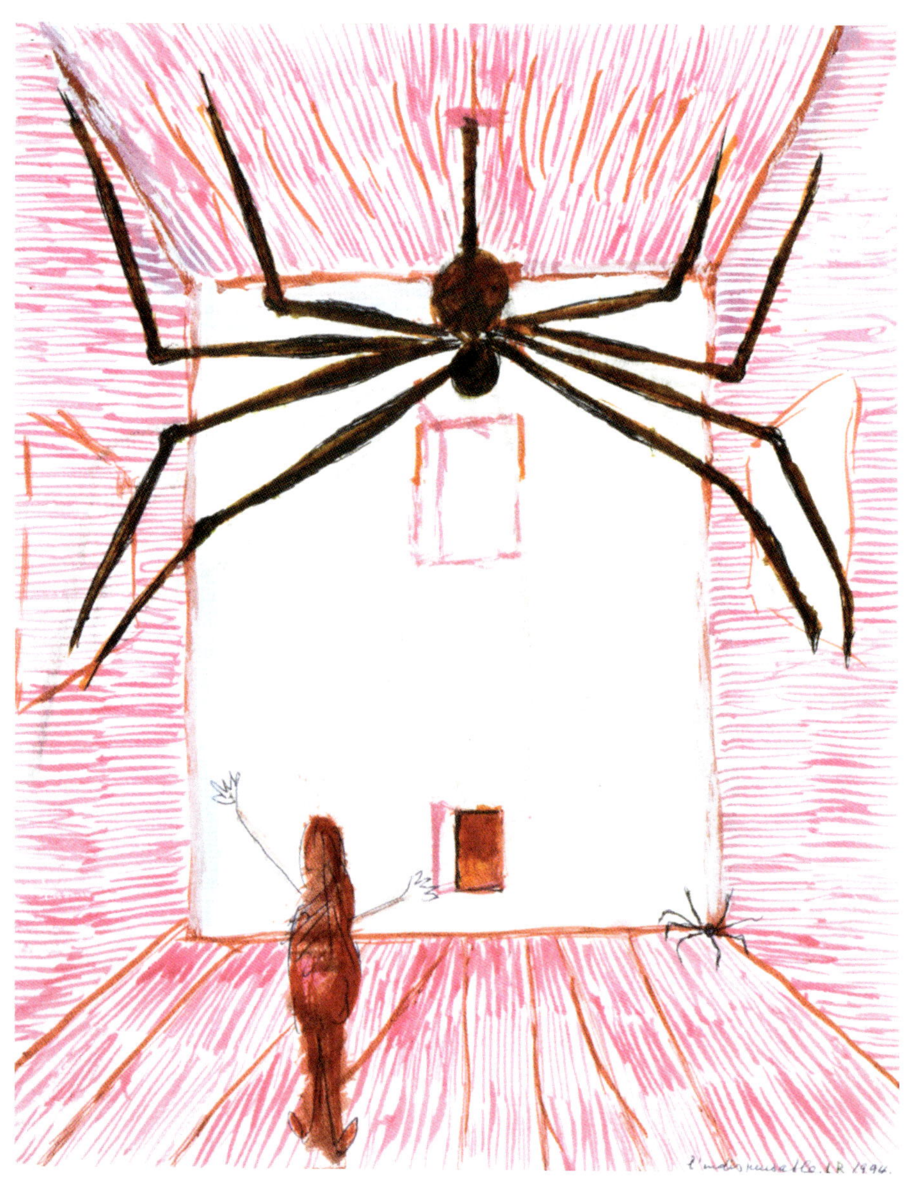

Spider (*l'Indispensable*), 1994. Ink, watercolor,
and gouache on paper, 10 × 8 in. (25.4 × 20.3 cm)

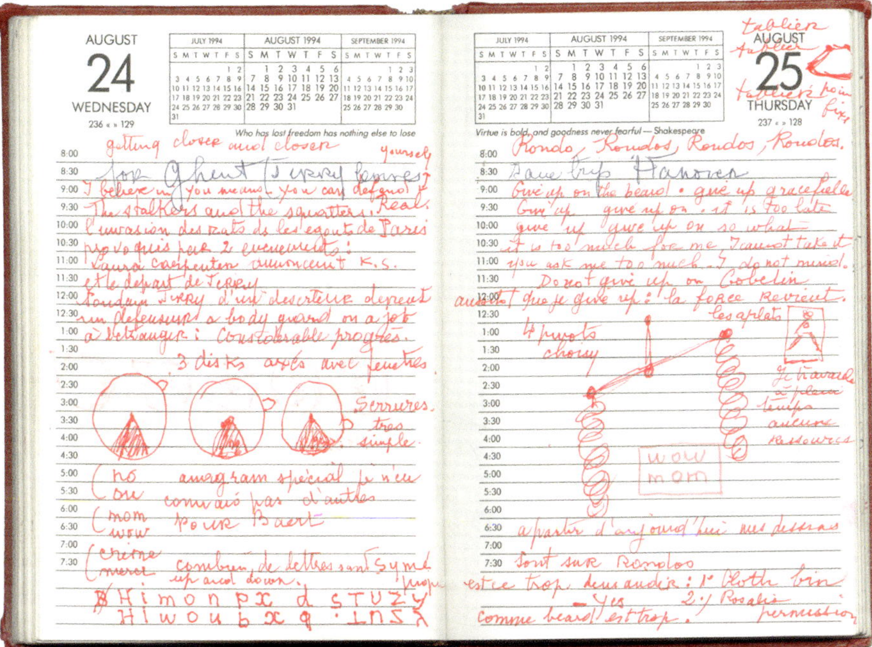

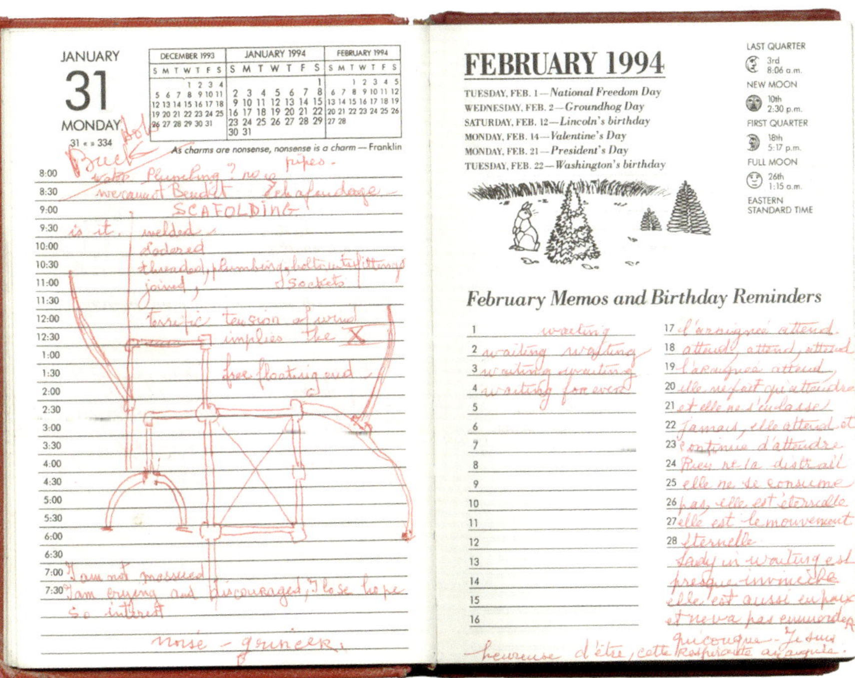

Pages from Louise Bourgeois's 1994 diary

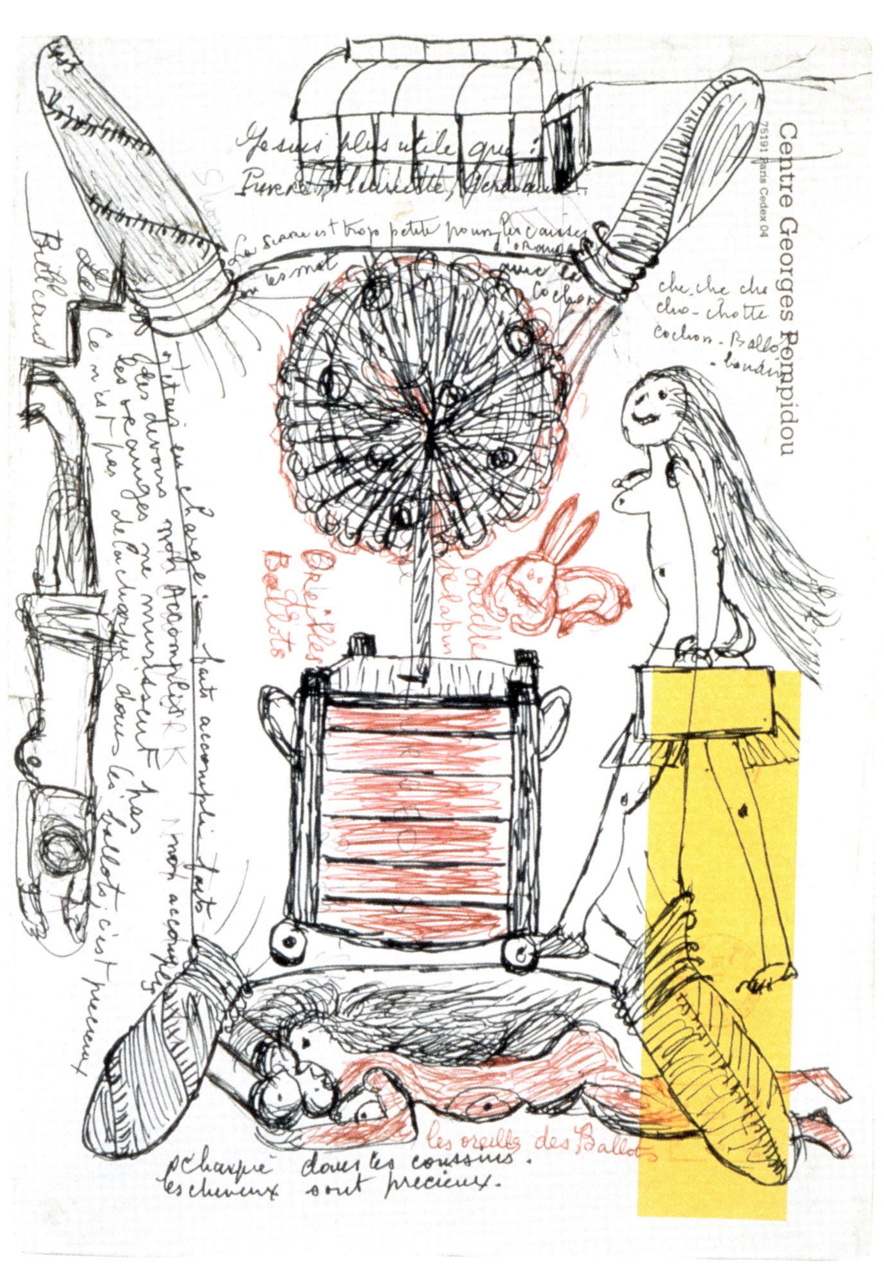

The Insomnia Drawings (detail), 1994–95. Series of
220 mixed media works on paper. Detail: ink, pencil,
and correction fluid on paper envelope, 12 × 9 in.
(30.5 × 22.9 cm)

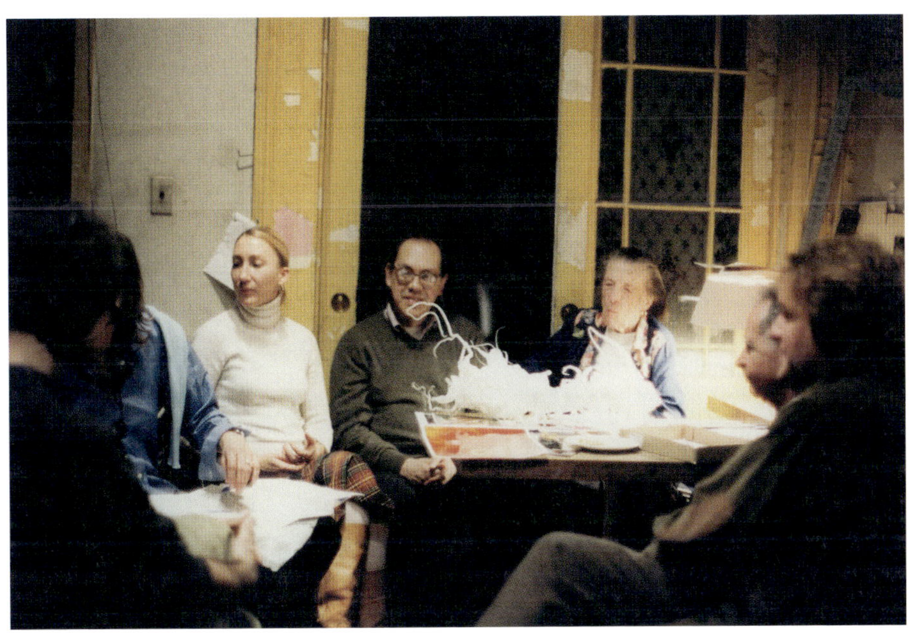

Louise Bourgeois with Paulo Herkenhoff (center)
and guests at a Sunday Salon hosted in her home,
New York, 2001

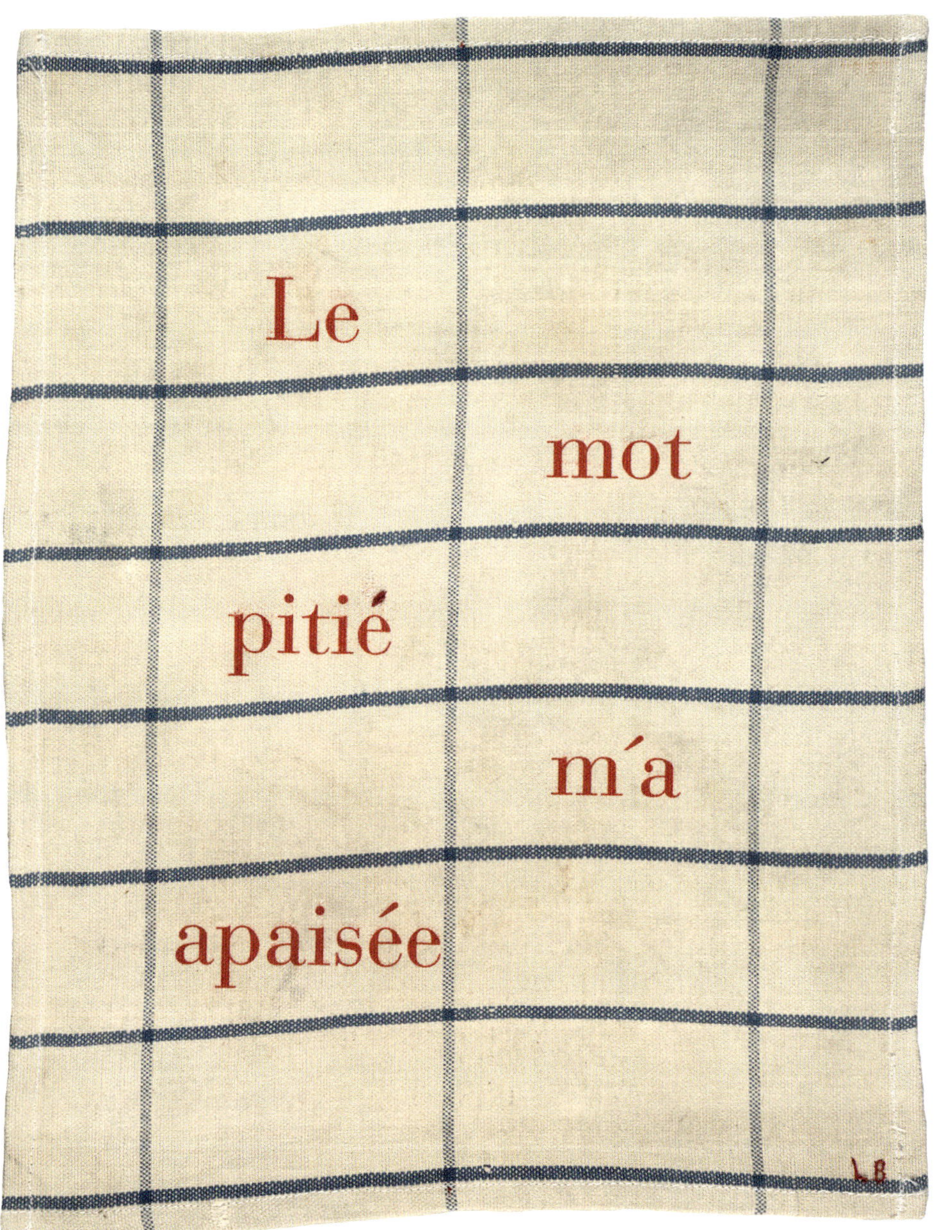

Le mot pitié m'a apaisée, 2002.
Lithograph on fabric,
13¼ × 10½ in. (33.7 × 26.7 cm)

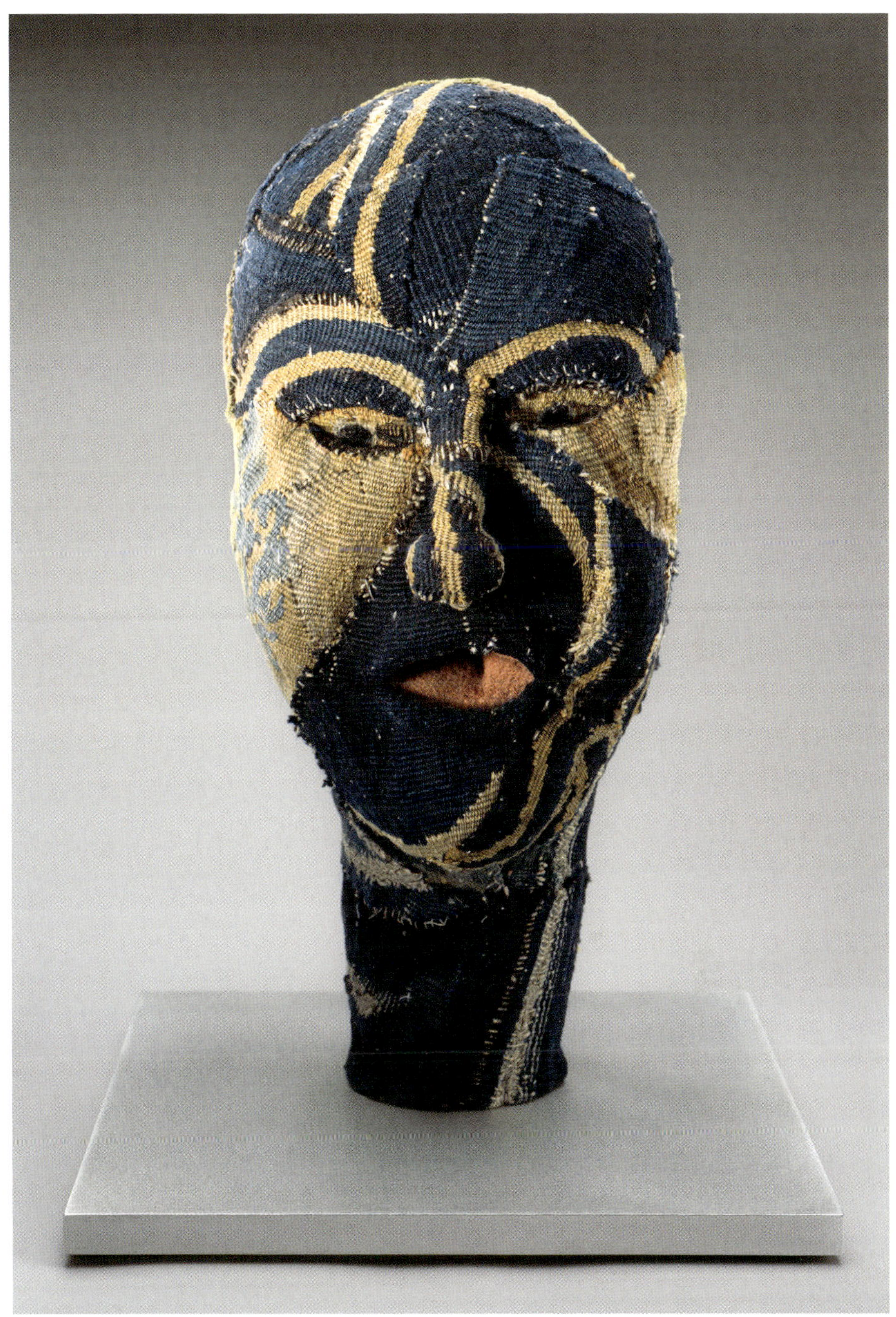

Untitled, 2002. Tapestry and aluminum,
18 × 12 × 12 in. (45.7 × 30.5 × 30.5 cm)

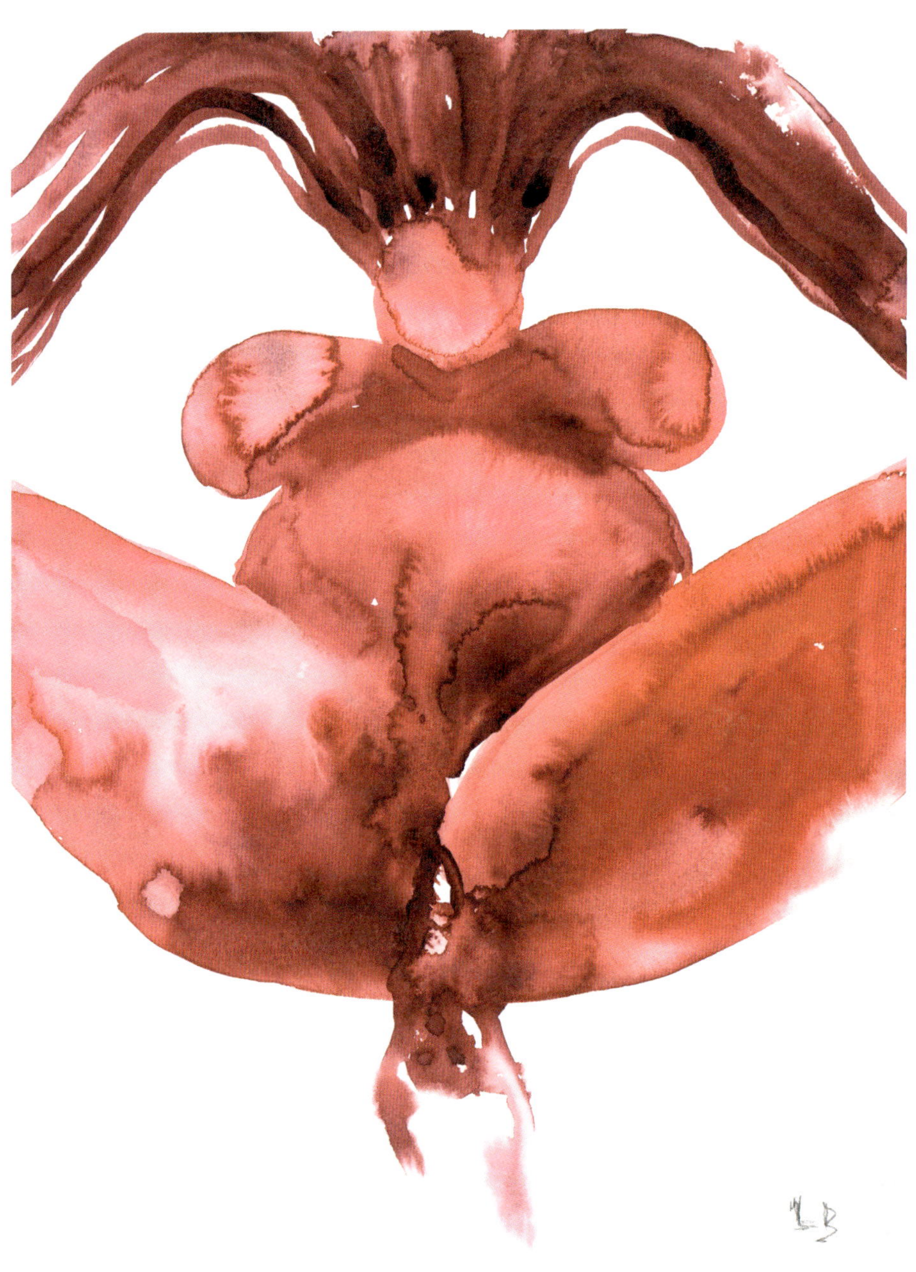

The Birth, 2008. Gouache on paper,
14⅜ × 11 in. (37.1 × 27.9 cm)

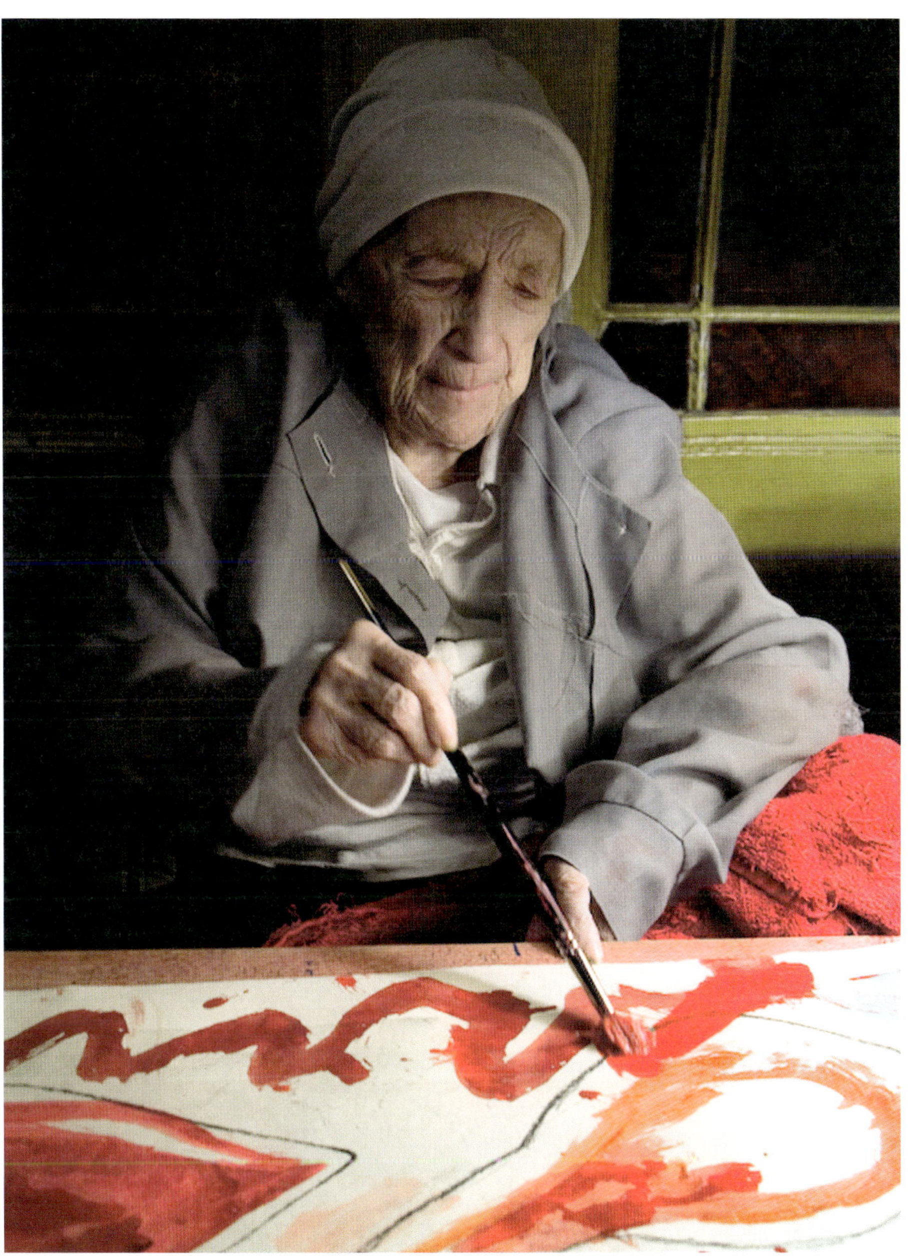

Louise Bourgeois with *La famille*
(in progress), New York, 2008

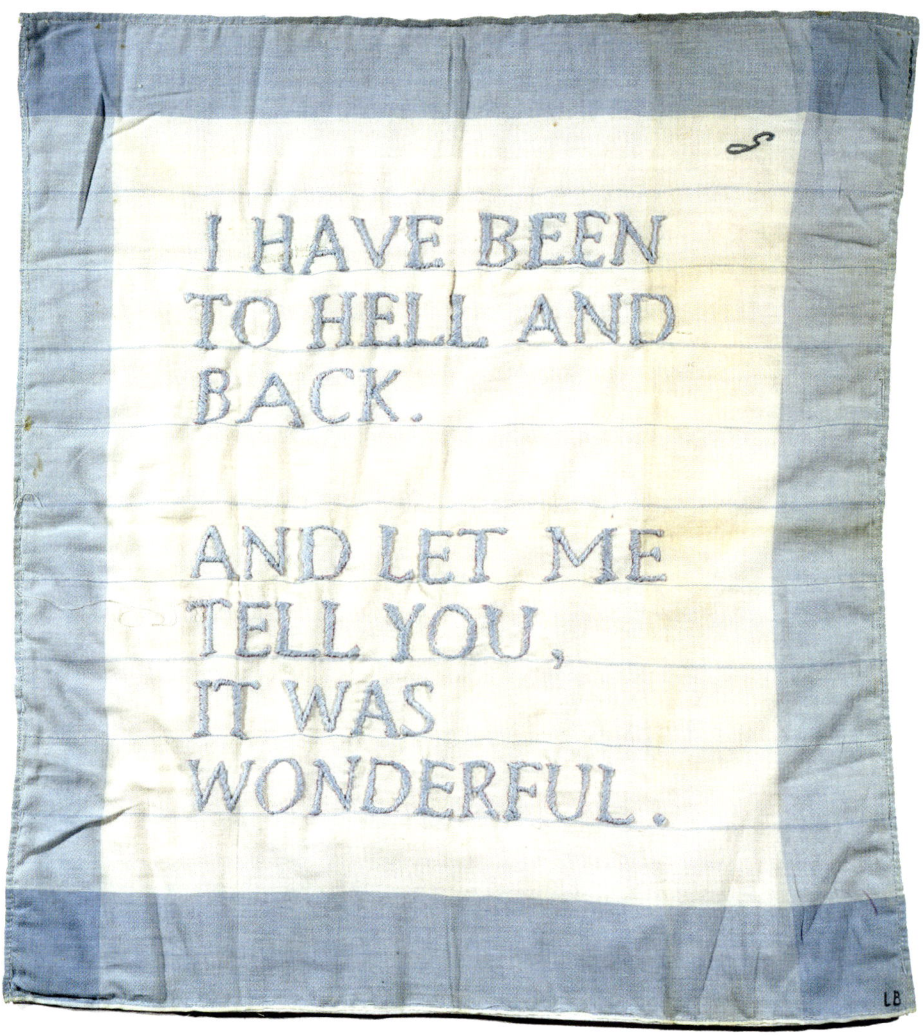

Untitled (*I Have Been to Hell and Back*), 1996.
Embroidered handkerchief, 19½ × 18 in.
(49.5 × 45.7 cm)

played out between the declaration of love on the bedspread, the threat of the blade, which has the air of a punishment hanging in the air—being cut into pieces, castrated—and a blend of joy and suffering suggested by the position of the body. In taking a man as her model, Louise was inverting the traditional roles of sculptor and muse. Louise often declared, when denying that she had been in analysis, that she was more interested in illnesses of the nervous system than in those of the mind: "It's neither mental nor physical, it's nervous!"[99] The nervous system and its reactions were, for her, the link between the physical and the emotional; it was the core emotional and affective network of the human body. She had already illustrated hysterical symptoms with a man's lower leg and foot midspasm (*Cell III*, 1991), and she spoke often in her diary about cramps, intestinal hysteria (diarrhea), of sweat, palpitations, insomnia. She also made drawings and engravings representing a child pulling backward into a hysterical arch between the legs of its mother. And later a small figure in pink fabric appeared, reversed and suspended.

"The *Cell* with the figure or arch of hysteria deals with emotional and psychological pain. Here is the arch of hysteria, pleasure and pain are merged in a state of happiness. Her arch—the mounting of tension and the release of tension—is sexual. It is a substitute for orgasm, with no access to sex. She creates her own world and is very happy. Nowhere is it written that a person in these states is suffering."[100]

Cell (Choisy) (1990–93) is the most symbolic work of the series presented in Venice. Its walls are now grilles, or glass casement windows that create different perspectives; they frame the sign from her father's shop, Aux Vieilles Tapisseries. Inside she has positioned a marble model of her childhood home in Choisy-le-Roi, pink as flesh, on a nineteenth-century workbench with, poised above it, the blade of the guillotine. This was a double reference to France and to its history; it was there "to show that people guillotine each other inside a family. The past is also guillotined by the present."[101] The house in Choisy was destroyed in the early 1970s to make way for the Théâtre Paul Éluard.[102] "You just have to abandon every day your past. And accept it. And if you can't accept it, then you have to do sculpture!"[103] Louise was only too aware of the weight of the past. She needed her memories, which she explored in order to exorcise them, to get rid of them. Otherwise, she said, we cannot live; we dwell in melancholy and nostalgia.

Other *Cells*—*Cell (Eyes and Mirrors)* (1989–93) and *Cell (Glass Spheres and Hands)* (1990–93)—allude to the gaze, to the necessity of looking in the mirror to know oneself, to the value of education, to the relationship between teachers and students.

In another *Cell* from the same period, *Cell (You Better Grow Up)* (1993), Louise references the passage from childhood to adolescence to maturity. "The artist, like the child, is passive. The artist remains a child who is no longer innocent yet cannot liberate himself from the unconscious. The acting out of his terror is self-involved and pleasurable. Some artists act all their lives instead of thinking. Self-expression excludes learning. [. . .] The tiny figure inside the stacked glass shapes is cut off from the world. That's me. The little hands are mine. They are self-portraits. I identify with the dependent one. [. . .] So the moral of this *Cell* is, you better grow up."[104]

Cell (Three White Marble Spheres) (1993)[105] is a square cage, its door partly open, with two large white marble spheres and one small one resting inside. Are they breasts? Or parents with a child, the triangular family, the essential trio at the heart of all Louise Bourgeois's work? This group from the series concludes with this mother cell, primeval, at the origin of the world, by returning to the geometrical simplification of spheres in a square.

This international exhibition in Venice (in which she showed the following *Cells: Arch of Hysteria, Choisy, Eyes and Mirrors,* and *Glass Spheres and Hands*) had a major impact and contributed greatly to the recognition of her work. One would have thought she'd have won the Golden Lion, but alas not.[106] She received only special mention and was greatly offended, as she confessed in her diaries as well as to Robert Storr,[107] who was the one who broke the news. "Rob Storr to announce: a mention in Venice. Reaction: 1) fuck yourself. 2) attack of Clorox cleaning."[108] This was how strongly she reacted. She had to wait until 1999 to receive, together with Bruce Nauman, a Golden Lion for lifetime achievement. When she was asked if this show in Venice had been important to her, she replied no, "Personally, no exhibition is important. The progression in the work is important."[109]

A Born Actress

Starting in the early 1990s, everyone wanted to film Louise. In her studio in Brooklyn, in her house in Chelsea, with Jerry, without Jerry, with her children, without her children—they wanted to know everything about her life, her memories, her art training, her family history, her early work, and since she was such a marvelous storyteller and a charismatic individual, she was highly sought after by French, English, and American filmmakers. Every time, she found the filming inconvenient, but every time, she took a wicked pleasure in it. She liked to show off while hiding behind the role she was playing. Her extreme sensitivity could lead to angry outbursts or to a rupture with the interviewer, whom she often wanted to toss out; then, feeling guilty, she would make them come back to give them a present and thus be forgiven. She was both terrorized and fascinated by this mise-en-scène of herself. Two films were made to coincide with the Venice Biennale. The first was a French film made by Camille Guichard,[110] filmed in 1993. Louise chose the interviewer herself—the critic Bernard Marcadé,[111] who didn't know her work very well but whom she doubtless wanted to seduce.[112] In the film (and in two others) Louise recounts, with accompanied gestures, the famous episode involving an orange peel that her father carefully cut up: "It's a little trick that my father learned in the trenches which he often showed us at the table at the end of a meal with a peeled orange. You take a knife and cut a woman out of the orange peel, the head, the shoulders, the breasts, the belly. You put the pith of the core at the place where the genitals would be so that when you peel it, you have a figure with lovely hair and something between its legs. My father would say: look children, it's amazing, look what she has. She's the perfect image of my daughter, not Henriette, but Louise, but Louise has nothing there!"[113] She used one of the peels in a collage drawing called *Orange Episode* (1990). This figure of the phallic woman alluded to the artist's masculine side and, consequently, the difficulty she had accepting her femininity in the face of her father, who was crude, mocking, and contemptuous toward women. She retained a traumatic memory of this "teasing" and, with this foundational episode to which she returned so many times, we can begin to understand the penis envy she discusses in her psychoanalytic writings of the 1950s and 1960s and her fear of castration. In this dialogue with Marcadé, Louise revealed her way with words and her keen sense of humor. When he emphasizes the symbolic power of cutting off her male model's head and legs, she is impatient and replies that this is part of her freedom as an artist:

"My poetic license is to remove the arms, to remove the head and then, if I want, to fetch them back, get the arms and put them on again—and to consider them, to consider all these things. [. . .] We can put it there, look! [. . .] Consider the version 'without' and consider the version 'with' [. . .] it makes him part of History, part of Eternity."

"But headless, all the same!" Marcadé says.

"Well, he can't have everything."[114]

Around the same time, she was also taking part in a film by Nigel Finch called *Louise Bourgeois: No Trespassing*.[115] There was a great deal of tension and some misunderstandings between filmmaker and subject, but this only makes the resulting film more affecting. From the very beginning Louise balks at what is asked of her and is impatient when Nigel doesn't understand something or asks her overly personal questions, concerning, for instance, her bitterness toward *"hommes à femmes"* (ladies' men). Louise says he's trying to make a fool of her and reproaches him for making her repeat herself. Nigel did not always understand Louise's reticence: "What I'm trying to understand is what it is you're so worried about, what is it you're resisting?" he asks her gently. Without answering, she holds up then hides behind a No Trespassing sign. Later, she adjusts the rhythm of a metronome—fast then slow, then fast again—to illustrate her mood, to the rhythm of its beat. Later still, she breaks a ceramic plate and stomps on the shards: "The broken plates protected me from an 'argument,' I overcame a terrible feeling of frustration, frustrated at not seeing Nigel."[116] "I use anger. [. . .] It is my way of defending myself. Sometimes it frightens people."[117] Her violence was a way of expressing her anger when she was asked a question about Sadie and her father's betrayal, which she still could not get over. It is an eternal resentment, she admits.

In a film by Chris Maybach and Paul Gardner, Louise again displayed her innate talent as an actress, her comic timing, her sense of humor.[118] She begins by energetically cleaning her sink with a dishrag, which she violently wrings, evoking the workers twisting the tapestries to dry them. She rolls her head around in a circle to limber up and declares that finally she is ready. Later we see her in *Red Room (Parents)* (1994) with a marble sculpture, the front of which is a draped form reminiscent of the robes in Greek and Roman statuary and the back of which is a bare buttock, which she rotates to display and lightly spank.

These films were also an occasion to see how Louise dressed herself. She transitioned from refined elegance—silk blouses, earrings, lipstick—to a boyish, sporty little outfit with a large smock hiding her ample bosom, a baseball cap, and a pink faux-fur jacket with a pink sequined hat. All her clothing signaled her particular, original, and extravagant sense of style: a blend of school uniform, priest's vestments with tightly buttoned white blouses, and brightly colored punk elements.

Finally, two American filmmakers, Amei Wallach and Marion Cajori, recorded her between 1992 and 2008 for a documentary called *The Spider, the Mistress, and the Tangerine,* a very thorough film that showed in commercial theaters and allowed the audience to follow the development of Louise's work right through to her final pieces.[119] This film—no doubt the most important and poignant on Louise Bourgeois—was in the making for many years and was a "cinematic journey inside the life and imagination of an icon of modern art," according to the filmmakers.

The Little Glossary Maker

In 1947, Louise wrote a short text that she returned to in 1992 for *She Lost It,* a performance on December 5 at the Fabric Workshop and Museum in Philadelphia.[120] The story, which is reminiscent of the parables in *He Disappeared into Complete Silence* (and was probably drafted for that publication), was screen printed on a long scroll of cotton gauze. During the performance, the scroll, which was rolled around Robert Storr, was slowly unfurled to reveal the printed text, and then rewrapped around an embracing couple.[121] The text tells the story of an abandoned woman whose neighbor finds her sitting in her armchair, reduced to "the size of a pea." The performance was accompanied by magic tricks performed by her faithful friend Mark Setteducati. Jerry Gorovoy and a few others also took part, wearing black and white garments (underwear, aprons, skirts, long johns) on which several phrases had been embroidered in red and blue thread: "I had to make myself be forgiven for being a girl" or "The cold of anxiety is very real." The female counterpart of the embracing couple wore a black skirt embroidered with: "Fear makes the world go round."

Around this time, she published another text from 1947 as *The Puritan,*[122] an illustrated book of engravings. This was the text that revealed her love for Alfred H. Barr. Writing became an increasingly important part of her creative practice, in spite of her still active wariness toward words (she continued to write in her diaries as well). Louise had genuine literary talent, and her turn to writing was more than merely therapeutic. She loved making lists, playing with words, looking things up in the dictionary, blending English and French, while remaining aware of the way meanings changed according to the context: "English vocabulary is devoid of verbal clichés (for obvious reasons). Is it out of context or very much in context. My English has <u>never</u> been criticized ever by my family, my friends, my students, my neighbors. I feel very much at ease in English. Almost more comfortable than in French (full of clichés and Parisian accent)."[123]

Her diary, which contained lists of names and appointments as well as reflections on her moods and those of others, served as a kind of prop to lean on when necessary: "What my <u>diary</u> gives me and costs me, the diary must be seen as a distinct, living entity."[124] It was an attempt at authenticity, at self-analysis, at controlling her emotions, at apprenticeship and self-knowledge. "I believe, rock solid, in the form of a journal, diary, now I can reread it."[125]

Often writing of herself in the third person, she calls herself a *petite glossarienne* (little glossary maker).[126] Was this a reference to Michel Leiris's book *Glossaire j'y serre mes gloses?* She had several of his books and knew him through her husband. Or did she make it up herself?

Her writings, diaries, and notebooks are filled with wordplay, real or invented proverbs, and clichés, as if articulating French phrases was a kind of fetish, a transitional object, which reassured her by connecting her to France. *"Le fer debout et le faire couché"* (do it standing up or do it lying down);[127] *"La chasse au Mari en Endalousie [sic] (et au Japon) marier bien, ou mal mariée, hystérie"* (husband hunting in Andalusia [and in Japan] marry well or badly married, hysteria);[128] *"Le cor de chasse* [talk in clichés], *Le cor au pied* [talk in proverbs], *se gargariser* [to revel in]";[129] a French expression (*"faire pipi dans un violon, parler à un mur"*) that she rendered in English: "pissing in a violin, talking to a wall," meaning wasting time on pointless activities;[130] *poudre d'escampette* (hit the road), *sainte nitouche* (goody two-shoes), *l'avoir à l'oseille* (to be frustrated), *la mouche du coche* (self-important), and *la zizanie* (trouble) are expressions typical of her generation that constantly recur in her writings.[131]

Reading Louise's writing better allows us to understand the way her mind worked: "I never talk literally; you have to use analogy and interpretation and leaps of all kinds."[132] However, strangely, she claimed to have no confidence in language: "I am suspicious of words. They do not interest me, they do not satisfy me. I suffer from the ways in which words wear themselves out. I distrust the Lacans and the Bossuets because they revel in their own words. I am a very concrete woman. The forms are everything. . . . With words you can say anything. You can lie as long as the day, but you cannot lie with the re-creation of experience."[133]

Several allusions to Lacan indicate, however, their shared interest in wordplay: "History, his story, *histérie*, mystory [*sic*]."[134] "Seamstress, Mistress, Distress, Stress."[135] Louise was quite severe toward Lacan, though she did read Élisabeth Roudinesco's biography of him[136] and watched videos of his seminars. She believed that although he did play with words and interrogate language, it was also necessary to "demystify" him.[137] Because his publications were only "transcriptions" of talks he gave, they were not made to be read.[138] Her view of Lacan was, as usual, mixed: she admired him and was interested in the way he thought ("I was seduced by Lacan['s] process of thinking [. . .] Lacan is anti-everybody")[139] but reproached him for having "stolen" Bataille's wife, Sylvia, and also for having "stolen from" Jewish psychoanalysts only to bestow his love and compassion on Jewish women.[140] While we're at it, we can also see here her profound links with Judaism: "I was saved by the Jews," she confided to Jerry, referring as much to Dr. Lowenfeld as to Robert.[141]

Despite her issues with Lacan, her interest in psychoanalysis remained as strong as ever: "The return of the repressed started after the children['s] birth. Post birth pregnancy depression instead of working with Lacan and Dolto."[142]

Insomnia Drawings

Louise had long suffered from insomnia—it was her constant companion—but it grew worse as she aged. There were many reasons for it: nighttime cramps, angry outbursts, anxiety. She tried all possible treatments, and in her final years she took a number of medications[143] that helped her sink into a deep sleep. But the intermediate zone between being awake and asleep, when the senses are in a heightened state of alert, also allows one to uncover recent or long-buried memories and to explore the unconscious. In a particularly intense period of insomnia between November 1994 and June 1995, she drew, wrote, and scribbled on all kinds of paper in order to calm her anxiety. Long lines of red and blue, forming a long skein of childhood memories, like the rivers that crisscross the map of France like its central nervous system, overflowing and flooding its houses, the troubled waters that rock so many Ophelias[144] to sleep in their arms. Water runs everywhere, inundating the images and texts, as if it were the source from which flowed the artist's imagination. For Louise, water was the symbol of unconscious energy and the mistress of language. Together, these 220 drawings reveal the close relationship between drawing and writing for the artist. They share some of her childhood fears and memories and tell us much about the way her unconscious worked: variations, repetitions, poetic and musical phrases, lists of names, wordplay, a constant back-and-forth between the peaceful sublimation of aesthetic pleasure and the ceaseless reactivation of the past, the source of emotions and the driver of creative energy. Louise moves through abstract and geometric forms and figurative, realist drawings. "The abstract drawings come from a deep need to achieve peace, rest, and sleep. They relate to unconscious memories." The realist works are the "conquest of negative memory, the need to erase it and to get rid of it. These drawings are pinned down in time and location. They rely on the accuracy of memory. Far from inducing sleep, the realistic drawings are problems to be solved."[145] The work weaves together three principal themes: nature, sewing, and geometry. The movement of water becomes a flooding or abstract motif; flowers and petals form rosettes. The knitted stitches loosen into interlinked loops or strands of unidentifiable words.[146] The rivers and mountains are also masses of hair, skeins of wool, needle eyes with threads hanging down. The figurative drawings are often linked to a text: Louise's houses, her rivers (the Creuse, the Bièvre, the Hudson), the map of France, the locks on the Bièvre, the orange trees in the Luxembourg Gardens, Ophelia, caryatids.

We find here her favorite expressions: *zizanie* (trouble), *Pâmoison* (pass out), *soupe au lait* (touchy). The concepts of silence and expectation dominate, "lady in waiting, nothing else." The idea of the void, of nothingness, returns as well: "I am *Mademoiselle Rien* [Little Miss Nothing]."[147] The passing time, in the form of a clock, is also omnipresent; Louise counted the hours of the night. The drawings also contain numerous references to music—she wrote on music scores and listed the tangos, operas, popular songs of her youth. She would hum: "*Je cherche après Titine, oh ma Titine . . .* [I'm looking for Titine, oh my Titine]."[148] Then there were her plays on words, her games of alliteration: *nier, nie, nid* (to deny, deny, nest), *charpie* (torn cloth), *chipote* (rummage), *chiot* (puppy), *chiotte* (loo), and so on.[149]

"The Year of the French"

Curators, critics, artists, writers, politicians[150]—they all flocked to see Louise, whether motivated by business or friendship or a combination of the two.[151]

During a long stay in New York[152] toward the end of the 1980s, the young artist Mâkhi Xenakis shared her work with Louise, hoping to receive encouragement during a time of extreme fragility and self-doubt. Louise immediately understood Mâkhi and helped her find herself, and the two kept up a special relationship. Louise sent the young artist on a kind of photojournalistic mission to take pictures of the sites of her childhood in France. Mâkhi sent Louise photographs of the Lycée Fénelon, notably of the sculpture of Oedipus and Antigone located at the bottom of the staircase. The two artists shared certain themes and problems: Medusa, Medea, the spider, the eye, the Oedipal complex, fear, lack of confidence, and trouble managing the challenges of having a family and an artistic practice. Louise wrote a text for Mâkhi's show at La Box at the École nationale supérieure d'art de Bourges, France. Mâkhi made a book about their encounter: *The Blind Leading the Blind*.[153] But Louise was not always kind to those she loved and wanted to help; her attitude was a blend of severity, frankness, perversion, manipulation, and profound benevolence. "The Fragile Goddess is sitting and lurking, [. . .] Makhi like her subject is mute, totally mute [. . .] like a well, she gives off such anxiety that I try to start a reaction as if I were throwing a little pebble into the well, listening, listening for the stone to hit the water so to speak. What is there in the well this silent presence, is it alive[?] These drawings prove that there is an active underground life and that without looking for verbal communication, we find it visually. In this way we trust Mâkhi. I trust her and after this beautiful exhibition I expect further proof of her talent."[154] She also kept up with a young art critic, Marie de Brugerolles, who briefly helped organize her archives.

In May 1992, I went to see Louise to propose an exhibition of her drawings in the graphic art department of the Centre Pompidou. She took careful notes about each of my visits, writing down the names of the members of my family, of my hotel in New York, and so on. She wrote about the hiccup in our plans[155] when the show had to be pushed back because of the retrospective at the Musée d'art moderne de la Ville de Paris in 1995. I saw Louise regularly between 1993 and 2000, because after the drawings exhibition, I wrote the first monograph about her work in French.[156] When Bernard Marcadé organized the *Féminin-masculin: Le sexe et l'art* show at the Pompidou,[157] we had a number of conversations about ambivalence, the role of the erotic and sexuality in her work. Louise's work was at the very heart of that exhibition, situated at the intersection of Marcel Duchamp and Picasso; moreover, she was an important point of reference for a number of contemporary artists. The question of gender, of the feminine and masculine parts of her personality, recurs often in her diaries: "If I am pushed into a 'masculine' position, I go wild + I am going to hit you. To scream, yell, and carry on is not feminine."[158]

Quite a few of Louise's works were included in the show—about a dozen, including the spectacular *Twosome* right at the entrance. We asked her (as well as some of the other artists such as Robert Gober, Jean-Michel Othoniel, and Jean-Michel Alberola) to contribute something to the catalog, so she supplied a list of French words that ended in *-otte: Bonnotte, bonne note, chipote, crotte, parigotte,* and so on, that gives way to a text on the way those letters are often used to create pejorative feminine endings: "*Il parle, elle parlotte* [. . .] *il cuisine mais elle popote* [. . .] *La femme de l'amigo est une amigotte.* [. . .] *La chamotte est la femme du chameau.*"[159] Bernard Marcadé selected some of these "otte" words, and different excerpts were put to music by Satch Hoyt and Ramuntcho Matta, based on an idea by Brigitte Cornand.[160] This song quickly became Louise's theme song, not only because of its humor and wordplay, but because of her particular delivery, her inimitable voice and intonation, and especially the syncopated *c'est ça, c'est ça,* which repeats throughout. This "rap" single has been included in many exhibitions and was played on several radio stations.

In the 1990s, Louise regularly saw Jacques Soulillou, a writer and art critic who since 1991 worked in the French cultural service in New York. He wrote a book on art and crime called *L'impunité de l'art*[161] and often discussed the subject with Louise; when it was published, it was dedicated to her. He and Bernard Marcadé often had intellectual and theoretical conversations with Louise, which kept her curiosity alive but sometimes irritated her: "Jacques Soulillou and Bernard Marcadé's verbal acrobatics are harmless, but they're still annoying."[162]

Jacques Soulillou, who knew African art quite well, asked Louise (along with André Magnin) to write something on the Senegalese sculptor Seni Awa Camara for a book on African contemporary art.[163] Louise knew her work only from photographs and it is surprising that she agreed to do it, given what we know of her resistance to the idea of her work being influenced by the art of Africa. But she got on well with Soulillou and she respected and admired the artist, a potter who made fertility figures and terra-cotta sculptures of her strange visions. That she sold her sculptures at the Marché Bignona between the tomatoes and the fruit, smoking her pipe in the sun, obviously only contributed to her appeal for Louise.[164]

La Maison Française at New York University paid tribute to Louise on November 15, 1993; Soulillou organized the event, and Rosalind Krauss gave a talk at the Institute of Fine Arts.[165]

This same decade, Louise was finally asked to do a major retrospective at the Musée d'art moderne de la Ville de Paris.[166] Suzanne Pagé and Béatrice Parent were the curators.

She also received several public commissions during this time: a tapestry for Les Gobelins (directed by Yves Sabourin), made from a drawing of a feminized Saint Sebastian, but which did not particularly satisfy Louise, and porcelain sculptures for the Manufacture nationale de Sèvres. The directors there—Georges Touzenis and Geneviève Gallo—came several times to oversee the project, which resulted in editioned porcelain versions—some with polished gold—of *Nature Study* (1984–86) and *Fallen Woman* (1996). She then received a commission for a new building being constructed by Dominique Perreault for the Bibliothèque nationale de France. She had long conversations with the architect and with Alfred Pacquement, who was in charge of the project; after proposing a spider, which was turned down, she decided to make an abstract sculpture, an enormous scalloplike form of curved and polished aluminum that fans out and offers multiple reflections. This wall sculpture, *Toi et moi* (1997), is reminiscent of a wood construction from 1978.

Meanwhile, the town of Choisy-le-Roi had invited the artist to create a sculpture to be placed in front of the town hall, to commemorate her family's history there. This would become *Les bienvenus* (1995), two large aluminum spiral cocoons that were hung from trees.

As part of a contemporary sculpture installation in the Tuileries Garden in Paris, the curator Aude Bodet commissioned a work from Louise; she proposed *The Welcoming Hands* (1996), a series of six hand poses in bronze that was originally created for and presented to Battery Park in New York, across from Ellis Island, but in the end was installed near the Jeu de Paume in 2000.[167] Aude Bodet and her husband, Didier Semin, became close friends with Louise and named their first child after her.

Rainer Mason also commissioned an engraving from her to benefit the print collection of the Louvre.[168]

In 1995, on the suggestion of Jean Frémon, Louise received a commission from the Théâtre du Vieux-Colombier to pay tribute to Marguerite Duras.[169] She made a series of eleven wooden panels inlaid and collaged with metal circles, oven plates, game tokens, and horseshoes.[170] She had an ambiguous relationship to Marguerite Duras, though she did weld their names, *Louise* and *Duras,* on two steel blocks in a second work dedicated to the writer.[171] Many critics and people who knew them tried to associate them with one another. They were a pair of "angry old ladies," nonconformists, liberated and fascinating, whose works were both rooted in their childhoods and their relationships with their mothers. When she received the commission, Louise wrote in her diary: "Vieux-Colombier, [. . .] Neauphle-le-Château, childhood, Choisy, Yann Andrea, Duras."[172] But she couldn't resist a dig at Duras's literary style. In one of the books she owned,[173] *La pluie d'été* (1990), she had some biting, acerbic things to say: "Jean Frémon could write a parody of Duras's literary style. Anti-american, a Communist. *Ça biche, ça bigle, ça va mal, alors on s'embête* [What's up, it sucks, not great, and we get bored]. I underlined the word 'ça' twenty times. It's her Achilles heel, that 'ça'—anti-bourgeois, affected vulgarity, counter to good manners. She saved herself some trouble, remaining silent. She's mocking."[174] It is particularly ironic that she picked up on the overuse of "ça," given that Louise abused it herself when she spoke, as evidenced by the song "Otte." In *Le square* she noted: "Andrea only appears in 1981." And elsewhere: "Yann Andrea appears page 7."[175]

At around this time she was also reading Nathalie Sarraute, including *Enfance,* and Sartre's *Les mots,*[176] but she continued to assert that "To read books serves me of <u>nothing, nothing, nothing</u>. Words serve me of nothing, nothing, nothing. Only experience allows me to understand."[177]

It was at this time that another Frenchwoman who would play a key role in her final years entered Louise's life. Brigitte Cornand, a journalist and filmmaker specializing in films about art, went to see her in January 1995 to make her first film, *Chère Louise,* which again featured Bernard Marcadé in a sequence in which Louise discusses the text with the *-otte* endings. Mark Setteducati does a card trick, which amuses Louise; she again discusses the trauma around Sadie and shares that her habit of breaking dishes was her mother's technique for calming her father's angry outbursts. Louise recognized that she had made work that was both feminist and antifeminist and explained to Brigitte the meaning of the Ophelia drawings in which she clings to her young lover. After the film Brigitte returned to see Louise regularly, to help produce the rap single "Otte" and to record an episode for Radio Nova with Elisabeth Lebovici and Bernard Marcadé. Bit by bit, Brigitte became an indispensable confidant who was there throughout the 2000s and who made more cinematic portraits of her dear friend, including *La rivière gentille* (2007), as well as an album of childhood songs, *C'est le murmure de l'eau qui chante: Songs* (2002). Louise actively took part in setting up the shots for the films, by turns playing around or making trouble and singing now and then; she was cheerful or pensive, meditative or quiet. In these films she demonstrates the many sides of herself, from the little girl to the old woman, always funny, always ironic.

Reparation, Restoration

Louise's mother is endlessly associated with tapestry, with restoration, with everything related to sewing: needles, thread, distaffs, bobbins, weaving. In the deepest metaphorical sense, she is like a spider with her web. In 1992, Louise began a new series of works.

Titled *Poids* (1992 and 1993) or *Needle (Fuseau)* (1992), these spindly sculptures feature elements—flax or glass orbs filled with blue liquid—suspended at the far ends of long, curved steel rods. Their equilibrium is maintained through the use of counterweights, which have an extreme precision to them and remind us of the artist's keen eye for detail. One features two blue spheres which look like eyeballs; another has a crystal pendant; still another shows an eye pierced with needles, beneath a bell jar. Separately, Louise also formed vertical towers of found pipes paired with strange objects. In *Tower* (1992), she suspended a red heart and glass droplets. In *Sutures* (1993), she further developed the reference to the family sewing atelier by attaching a number of bobbins of silver, blue, and gray thread on metal fixtures that stem from a central vertical pole like tree branches. *In Respite* (1992) features a pink rubber pendant that recalls the teardrop forms of *Articulated Lair*. Here, it serves as a pincushion for a number of needles threaded to connect to the surrounding spools. She said that when she was growing up, "all the women in my house were using needles. I've always had a fascination with the needle, the magic power of the needle. The needle is used to repair the damage. It's a claim to forgiveness. It's never aggressive, it's not a pin."[178]

The Parisian gallery Karsten Greve showed Louise's work at this point, including a few of her new sculptures—*Spindle* (1992), *Poids* (1992, two versions), and *Eye* (1992)—in a show which received a good deal of press coverage. The art critic Stuart Morgan wrote a long piece in *Beaux-arts* magazine,[179] in which he expressed surprise at the press's reaction to her work—merely polite and almost annoyed—and Louise's absence from the French art world, which he attributed to the "disturbing" aspect of her work.[180]

Spider Woman

The spider jumps from one pinnacle to the next, holding on,
weaving her thread like a silkworm.

The accumulation of pincushions and threads (which also recalls the Three Fates) is a metaphor for destiny, the thread of life, the passing time.[181] These threads led Louise to create the figure of the spider. On the back of one drawing, she wrote: "Spider, *la mère coupe le fil de l'araignée*" (Spider, the mother cuts the spider's thread),[182] and for an illustrated book: "The friend (the spider—why the spider?) because my best friend was my mother and she was deliberate, clever, patient, soothing, reasonable, dainty, subtle, indispensable, neat, and useful as a spider. She also knew how to defend herself, and me." This text is accompanied by nine drypoint prints on the theme of the spider in the book titled *Ode à ma mère* (1995).[183]

For Louise spiders were useful creatures because they ate mosquitoes, whereas for many other people they represent death and femininity; they have bad reputations and are often perceived as hairy beasts that lure their victims into their webs in order to devour them. In contrast, Louise identified with them. *Maman*—the largest of Louise's spider sculptures—is her mother, she said, but also herself. She made sculptures of spiders in different sizes: a medium-sized spider with smooth, pointed feet whose glass belly is filled with blue water; a giant, terrifying spider with twisted feet; a family of five spiders, each one larger than the next. The spider is her *Maman*: "I shall never tire of representing her," she wrote in *Ode à ma mère*. And that is why the spiders proliferated and became her trademark: they are a sign of gratitude. The monumental *Maman* can be found around the world—in London, Tokyo, Bilbao, Ottawa—attracting beneath its legs an audience of terrified adults and children who nevertheless delight in huddling beneath the enormous arachnid, which becomes no longer scary but protective. Her maternal side is underscored by the twenty marble eggs in her abdomen. In a *Cell* piece titled *Spider* (1997), we find only three eggs: the three Bourgeois children, and Louise's three sons. In fact, the spider motif had haunted her since the 1940s: the first spider drawings date from 1947.

The ambiguity of this figure is a good fit for the double entity of the mother: good and bad, protective and threatening, which was so important to Louise. She herself often assumed the role of Medea: "if you leave me, if you abandon me (To Robert): if you separate me from you I will kill, I kill your children (Medea)."[184] Sometimes in her drawings, she paired the spider's long, hairy legs with the Medusa's serpentine locks. For a long time, Louise was conscious of this ambiguity: "All daughters hate their mothers. In Freudian terms the daughter blames the mother for the loss of the penis. [. . .] I am deeply grateful not to have gone through this ordeal."[185] As a mother, Louise was aware of her own shortcomings, the lack of time she had for her children. Though she knew she "wasn't perfect," she believed she was "good enough, all the same."[186]

The word *"Maman"* had another meaning. Every month since the late 1930s, she had used this word to indicate the dates of her period in her diary, writing *"maman garanti."* It was a sign of fertility, which she accepted, because for her procreation was creation. *Ode à ma mère* concludes with these words: "Forgive me, Maman, who lies, who lies, I lie, I thought I knew, I was out of it Maman. Wait for me, don't run. I'm coming. I need you."[187]

Louise never got over her mother's death or the feelings of abandonment it caused.

Having finally reconciled the double images of the father and the mother, and reconstituted the discordant couple, she was able to confront the "primal scene" and represent her parents' bedroom, the forbidden lair of the marriage bed.

Red Rooms

Two new *Cells, Red Room (Parents)* and *Red Room (Child)*, debuted in 1994 at the Blumarts gallery, to coincide with the publication of *Album*, which brought together a number of photographs from her past, captioned by the artist.[188] The title *Red Room* comes from a painting from 1947. For Louise, red signified passion and pain and, when paired with black, tragedy. The symphony in red and black that she orchestrated was formed in two distinct *Cells,* one representing the parents and the other the child, created from dark wooden doors taken from a courtroom. The parents' room is signified by a large red bed on which a child's toy train and a xylophone still in its box have been placed. Atop a pair of triangular cabinets on either side of the bed sit two of Louise's marble sculptures depicting veiled torsos on one side and exposed buttocks on the other. Across from the bed, there is a large, pivoting oval mirror. The space is sparse, neat, symmetrical. It suggests a happy couple—there is a cushion on which the words *"je t'aime"* are embroidered, as well as the reference to children via the toys. Only two details trouble this impression and threaten the peaceful household: a resin object, of an organic but unidentifiable shape, which hangs above the rubber-covered bed; and a rubber finger stuck with a pin that emerges from the bed itself. Sex, with its demonic energies, can threaten the family home.

The children's room is diametrically opposed to this one. It is a treasure trove, a joyous mess, full of all kinds of different pieces, made of glass, fabric, rubber. In the middle, we see a stand with red spools of thread and three optimistic blue ones (Louise and her two siblings, or her three children). Enormous hourglasses made of what look like coiled red sausages attest to the inexorable passage of time and the precariousness of life, which hangs by a thread. The relationship that emerges between the two rooms, between the adult and the child and vice versa, the aura of the forbidden that hangs over the marital bed where the erotic ceremony and the mystery of conception take place, came directly from Louise's unconscious—and the collective unconscious as well. In reexperiencing her childhood traumas, she gives form to the foundational myths of the unconscious (the Oedipal complex in particular) and the cycle of reproduction, life, and death. The bed, which appears frequently in her work, was for her the site of birth, of pleasure, and of death. In one text, she lists the different beds she has known, the bed tidily made, the linen sheets of her newlywed days, with their initials embroidered ten centimeters high, then the *lit bateau* (literally: boat bed, in English sleigh bed), whose shape made her think of the Egyptian funerary boats that she saw in the Louvre and those that cross the River Styx.[189]

This primal scene hearkens back to her earliest works on maternity, the unifying thread of her work. Maternity, understood in the larger sense of the matrix—the capacity to give birth, to germinate, to grow, to reproduce, to give refuge: the house, the womb that is also a tomb. Aging allowed her to fish freely in the very depths of her unconscious; liberating all that was previously repressed unleashed her immense creative powers.

"The Fashion System"

After exorcising these obsessive images of childhood and the mother, Louise suddenly felt the need to rummage further through her house, from the basement to the attic, opening cabinets and closets and taking out, one by one, her old clothing and linens.[190] She drew and printed on handkerchiefs, sometimes stitching on little bones, doll arms, or buttons; on one she added a cat perched on red high-heeled shoes.[191] On another, she embroidered a phrase that is an aesthetic manifesto unto itself: "I have been to hell and back. And let me tell you it was wonderful."[192] This sadomasochistic credo was echoed by the artist Dominique Gonzales-Foerster, who wrote it on a large banner suspended in the Tate Modern for her Turbine Hall commission in 2008, above a reproduction of *Maman*, one of several reproductions of art by well-known artists such as Alexander Calder, Claes Oldenburg, and Coosje van Bruggen.

Louise also started manipulating her own clothing. It is unsurprising that fabric would be her final material; clothes are like a second skin, they mold not only to the body but to the mind, wrapping in their folds the scent of a precise moment in time, memories of a way of living and a time of life. They are relics of the people who wore them; they remain when the person who wore them cannot.

Clothing is a form of protection, a dwelling, a "woman-house," with its own architecture and form. From a very young age, Louise's parents dressed her in clothes by the great designers—Chanel, Paul Poiret, Sonia Delaunay. She made an inventory of her trousseau: linens, undergarments, dresses, coats, and slips, which she suspended from metal "poles," or cut up, pieced back together, and stuffed to make soft sculptures. Sometimes she hung them from ox bones used as hangers, bringing actual skeletons into the work, not for their morbid or animalistic connotations, but to echo the structure of our bodies. The clothes float, like ghostly markers of absent presence. In one of these works, a red dress is elongated by an animal tail, a hybrid figure which recalls the engravings from this time that blend felines and femininity. The sequined black cocktail dress and pink flowered summer dress allow us to imagine Louise at specific moments of her life. "Clothing is also an exercise of memory. It makes me explore the past [. . .]. They are like signposts in the search for the past."[193] Louise never threw anything away; it was wasteful, and in any case, "Throwing out and abandoning one's possessions is a bit like dying unless you can share them with someone else."[194]

In 1996, she created *Cell (Clothes)*, a largely black and white space featuring clothing and stuffed dummies: long hanging shirts, legs sheathed in black stockings or pantyhose, draped on stools, a lamp covered with a blue blouse serving as a lampshade. In this ceremonial, carnivalesque atmosphere, the air is heavily scented; it is bodily, sensual, evocative of old laundry rooms or dressing rooms at the theater.

After stripping bare her wardrobe, Louise continued to sew, cut, stuff, and swaddle, using terry cloth, berets, woolens, stockings, and pantyhose—not to mention bed linens, towels, tablecloths, and napkins. Life-size figures are sometimes shown in elegant glass cases, as if the artist wanted to create some distance from the disagreeable effect of their textures and to transform them into mummies, or newborns in incubators (see *Torso*, 1996). Most figures are headless, though *Single II* (1996) has two heads, breasts, and pronounced genitalia. In three black-fabric sculptures of headless couples in tight embrace, such as *Couple III* (1996), the female figure is endowed with a prosthesis.

Louise continued to develop her eternal themes—castration, sexual embrace—with this new material, fabric. The first fabric sculptures—two embracing couples (one with a prosthesis) and two single, headless figures— were made for an installation in the bell tower of Saint Pancras Church in London, in 1996. The theme of the couple took on even more importance in her final years, as the little blue and pink couples from 2001 attest (shown at the Cheim & Read Gallery).[195] Louise was fascinated by the phenomenon of coupling: "The couple copulating is seen through the eyes of a young girl. Are they fighting? Are they enjoying themselves? Is one killing the other? It refers to the age when I could not understand what they were doing, what they saw in each other, and what they were pursuing in each other. It is the question of an arrested traumatic experience," she wrote in the commentary she provided for the catalog accompanying the exhibition at the Fondazione Prada in 1997.[196] The first couples were dressed in old clothing or con- structed of black fabric, the color of mourning; later ones were mostly pink and blue and often suspended, tightly bound to each other. The anguished view of sexuality—"I am exasperated by the vision of the copulating couple, and it makes me so furious, it upsets me so much, that I chop their heads"— calmed in time, became more tender: "I would never separate a couple."[197]

One of the last cells of this decade, *Spider* (1997), allowed her to explic- itly link the figure of the mother with her métier, in the form of scraps of tapestries attached to the grilles of the cell, which forms a circular room beneath a large spider and includes an armchair to take refuge in, as one would in the mother's lap.

Cannibalism

In the early 1990s, Louise met Paulo Herkenhoff, a young Brazilian curator and art historian. He became a friend and confidant and created links for the artist with South America. "The road to friendship runs through Chile. [. . .] The road to Chile, dedicated to Nemesio Antúnez, Osvaldo Tortora, John Garcia, Clara CDS."[198] Paulo first invited her to participate in the São Paulo Biennial in 1996, where she showed her recent "pole" pieces with the bones and suspended clothing;[199] then he asked her to show her drawings and sculptures in Rio de Janeiro.[200] He invited her back to the Biennial in 1998, when he was the curator, organized around the theme of cannibalism and titled *Antropofagia*. Louise showed *The Destruction of the Father* (1974), *Couple III* (1998), and *Untitled (Two Chairs)* (1998). The theme of cannibalism was an apt one, given its presence throughout her work. She referenced it in her illustrated book *He Disappeared into Complete Silence* (1947):

> Once a man was angry at his wife, he cut her in small pieces, made a stew
> of her.
> Then he telephoned to his friends and asked them for a cocktail-and-stew
> party.
> Then all came and had a good time.[201]

In 1943, she drew two figures, one with defined breasts, both devouring a child.[202] And then there was *The Destruction of the Father*, the cannibal's feast complete with leftover bones, which explicitly references other famous banquets. Contemplating the Biennial, Louise lists in her diary: "7 banquets for Paulo: Gargantua, Don Juan, Socrates, Buñuel, Cannibal."[203] A number of writings, throughout her life, make reference to flesh-eating, cannibalism, ingesting the father in order to internalize his strength and power: "to eat to kill to devour to come / to kill the mother to incorporate the father to take his strength and to be killed as a punishment."[204]

Louise's creative process, like that of many writers and artists she admired, was driven by the cycle of digestion and excretion, whether in the form of allusions to predatory spiders who consume their prey or works that devour their various components—"I mean that the sculptures were eaten up by later sculptures. So, they reappeared part in other places"[205]—or the vows that are transmitted from generation to generation ("it is absorbed by your children + continue[s] to eat its way through generation[s]").[206] She also saw a connection between cannibalism and melancholy—"Fear of death appears after the devouring to eat is to make everything equal to devour is the same as to copulate"[207]—and between eroticism and death: "the height of desire is to devour one's partner."[208]

With Paulo Herkenhoff, she took on another theme that was close to her heart and structures her work—topology: "Project of Paulo includes: atlas, cartology, hydrography, topology, geography, topiary."[209] She remembered the hilly landscapes she saw as a child, the toposcopes of the Tour Biret, the topological maps at the Musée de l'armée: "Lacan: I begin where he flees. Topology, on the 3rd floor of the military museum."[210] These hills returned as the rounded forms of the 1960s and helped her see the relationship between negative and positive space, "topology or the reverse & the place."[211]

Passage Dangereux

The invitations were piling up for shows at galleries and museums. *The Personages*, at Saint Louis Art Museum (1994), a drawing show at University of California Berkeley Art Museum & Pacific Film Archive (1996), organized by Lawrence Rinder; *Blue Days and Pink Days* at the Fondazione Prada in Milan (1997), an invitation to show in Vienna with Helmut Lang and Jenny Holzer (1998–99). Then retrospectives set to take place the world over—in Mexico, in Seville, and in Yokohama.

She showed again at the Guggenheim SoHo, as part of the French exhibition *Premises* (1998), curated by Bernard Blistène, Alison Gingeras, and Alain Guiheux.[212] She submitted a large *Cell* called *Passage dangereux*, a long grilled corridor that features—among many other elements—furniture suspended in the air as if from the attic in Antony, an electric chair, and a miniature iron-frame bed on which legs suggest a couple midcopulation.

Urged by Jerry Gorovoy and Cheim & Read Gallery, she agreed to be shown alongside the German sculptor Franz Xaver Messerschmidt and Francis Bacon,[213] the latter of whom she had met through David Sylvester in London in 1951. She had written a piece on his work; he was an artist she admired and understood, and she felt close to him.[214] She was sensitive to the artist's quite particular physique—"Bacon's face was fat, squashed and contorted as if someone had sat on an overripe melon"—and his violent emotions: "He was dying of too much passion. His suffering communicates. I sympathize." She noted that he had a sadomasochistic side; sex, alcohol, and gambling were the primary drivers of his creativity: "He twisted his figures, which were mostly male, like a pretzel into a Möbius strip of attraction and repulsion."[215] In her view, all Bacon's portraits were self-portraits.

In 1999, she was invited by the curator Harald Szeemann to take part in the Forty-Eighth Venice Biennale, and she astonished everyone by showing three new fabric works, one of which was particularly dramatic: *Three Horizontals* (1998), which featured three pink terrycloth figures, laid out on a metal wheeled cart. Mother, daughter, child: the three ages of life are stacked one above the other like Russian dolls lying as if on the surgeon's table or in a torture chamber. There is violence in the embryonic, acephalic form representing the child or the newborn. It was on this occasion that she finally received the Golden Lion for Lifetime Achievement.[216]

In Madrid, Jerry Gorovoy and Danielle Tilkin curated a show around the theme of architecture.[217] That subject brought back memories, which she noted in her diary: her friendship with Le Corbusier and Frederick Kiesler, her childhood crush on her cousin Jacques Bourgeois, who became an architect, Auguste Perret, the strange buildings she saw as a young woman passing through Bourg-la-Rein such as the tower of the Maison Hennebique made of reinforced concrete, but also the adobe houses of Mali on which her son Jean-Louis was an expert.

The public commissions poured in. In Chicago, she was invited to create an outdoor sculpture for a park commemorating the activist Jane Addams, who created Hull House, a settlement house for immigrant women and children. She made six granite blocks on top of which she placed bronze hands clasping one another, which she called *Helping Hands* (1993). In Pittsburgh, for the Agnes R. Katz Plaza, she made a huge bronze fountain of stacked triangular forms, decreasing in size as they go up, and which changes color at night. Surrounding the fountain are three pairs of granite benches in the shape of eyes: *Fountain and Benches* (1999).

Nicholas Serota and Frances Morris[218] went to see her in July 1999 to ask if she would agree to undertake a large installation in the Turbine Hall for the opening of the Tate Modern in 2000.

Deconstruction of the Father / Reconstruction of the Father

The 1990s also saw the publication of several books of interviews. Multiple art critics interviewed her at length, and she proved very candid. She told her stories, not out of narcissism, but because she interested people, even if she was wary of them, and these exchanges—about her childhood memories, her ideas about art, her philosophy of life—were a chance for her to consider at length the questions that haunted her, to fill the void on certain days, and to develop strong bonds with these various interviewers. With Christiane Meyer-Thoss,[219] Louise spoke more freely about sexuality and maternity; with Donald Kuspit,[220] about psychoanalysis. With Henry Geldzahler[221] and Douglas Maxwell,[222] she talked about her childhood and her training. She also agreed to long radio interviews with French journalists: Jacqueline Caux and Monette Berthomier, for Radio France.

Finally, given the accumulation of interviews and poetic writing published over the years, Hans Ulrich Obrist[223] and I suggested publishing the entirety of these interviews. Louise actively participated in this project, which she took very seriously. She accepted, with Jerry's assistance, to publish some excerpts from her diaries. She is the one who came up with the title: *Deconstruction of the Father / Reconstruction of the Father*. It was as if a negative phase was ending, and she hoped, through bringing together these texts, to reconstruct her past. She still regularly saw her biographer and friend Robert Storr but was sorry that the monograph he had been working on for more than a decade still hadn't been published. He could not finish it, because Louise was still quite active and endlessly creating new work. It seems they had some kind of disagreement, because she noted: "The descent into hell / annihilated / after a discussion of his text with Rob[er]t Storr and Rosamond [Bernier]."[224]

This hyperactivity, at more than eighty-five years of age, was sometimes unpleasant. "I have made many promises: Baccarat, Karsten portraits, interviews, articles that I could not possibly keep. Promises are easy, the payments difficult. I am the victim of my own unconscious pacts [. . .]. The sources of inspiration can be found deep in the desire to please."[225] It brought with it too much pressure and fatigue. "It is impossible to satisfy you. You're asking too much of me. I cry Kaput, Kaput [. . .] I don't want to see you anymore, with your demands, reproaches, warnings [. . .]. It is my claim to glory to be able to tell you *merde* [shit]."[226] "I worked so much that I deserve to be let off, please please leave me [a]lone."[227]

The "chapter of fear" was reopened, "fear or rather terror shatters me, confuses me, and makes me spinning around [*sic*], completely deprived [. . .]

I am totally destroyed by fear, I am avidly assaulted [. . .] I am on the other side of despair, and this happens to me 4 times a day. I am fed up, I want to let go and see no one, run away, lock up, good evening."[228] This confession comes after a long complaint on the subject of reparation, restoration, and the possibility of salvation. "Evangelism is my salvation,"[229] she wrote, while claiming not to be religious. But the theme of the sacrifice of Christ had been a constant in her writings: "I would suffer in my body because of the bloodstained rags," she wrote in 1964. "Like Christ suffered for man and would sacrifice himself for him, for his redemption—it is the meaning of martyrdom, and of women saints."[230]

Louise described the technical difficulties she encountered in making an important and complex work, pointing the finger at many collaborators next to whom she felt powerless.

But her ferocious will to live remained intact: "Why get up. Why do. Why live? Because I'm interested? Because I want [to]."[231]

The Sunday Salons

"I love my Sundays. They are for others, I listen to them. Silence, warmth, and kindness reign there; free for the asking," she said.[232] Then again, "The children are bored on Sundays [. . .] you are depressed on Sundays [. . .] I don't draw on Sundays, I only do second-rate writing."[233]

She was totally lost when Jerry wasn't there—"When Jerry left this morning, hammer blow I can't escape, it's like getting my heart torn out, no more no less. They used to rip the hearts out of animals who were still alive"[234]—and needed to find a way to fill her Sunday afternoons. So she opened her living room to young artists, musicians, writers, and poets in need of advice and people passing through. The rules were clear: everyone had to bring an example of their work and reply to a certain number of awkward questions about their artistic motivations and their financial situation. Louise was very clear: she wasn't "an employment agency" or a "publishing firm"; "To call yourself an artist is not an excuse," and "unsolicited material ends [up] in the garbage pail outside,"[235] statements that point to her dark sense of humor and high expectations when it came to art.

Each "salon" had its own ritual, depending on the participants. It could veer from group therapy to fits of weeping, because Louise could be very cruel on these Sunday afternoons. She noted in her diary the day she made some young woman cry, and did try to control herself: "[Sunday:] I'm not going to upset anyone."[236]

To help Louise receive all these visitors, Robert Storr, Jean-Louis, Paulo Herkenhoff, or Brigitte Cornand would be present; Louise served little cookies and sometimes alcohol. It was a chance for her to do herself up—to put on make-up, dress a certain way (always unique); then she would emerge from the tiny kitchen and appear at her worktable with a wicked smile on her face. Everyone sat in a circle and awaited the high priestess, who was liable to slip off or clam up, content just to look around her, amused by all the people who loved and needed her.

Pouran Esrafily[237] filmed all the salons. She also made a film, *Abandon* (1998), about Louise's childhood and the trauma of Sadie. Robert Storr's daughter played Louise as a child, and actors were hired to play her parents and the mistress, trapped in the cage of *Passage dangereux* (1997).

In spite of her success, her entourage, the Sunday salons, the Christmas birthdays that brought together family and close friends, Louise felt more and more like a child, "The Runaway Girl who didn't grow up,"[238] as she put it; "the passage from childhood to adolescence never happened. I left the premises without leaving them."[239] In spite of her advanced age, she seemed not to have grown old, and she saw herself as a young girl: "If I were not looking at myself in the mirror, I would believe I was 18 years old. Life has not changed me—I am happier today than I was at 18."[240]

Louise continued to take interest in everything; in her diary she mentions the artists who came to see her and what her close friends have been up to: Brigitte had dinner with David Hammons, Sylvère Lotringer gave a talk on Simone Weil, Marie-Laure saw the Antonin Artaud show at MoMA. Her friend Paulo, who had a "traumatic relationship with the telephone,"[241] left for Argentina. She wrote down, "Helmut Lang from Vienna curates a show. . . ."[242]

Curiously, in these final years, religion returns as a leitmotif; Louise said her prayers and often discussed the religious education she hadn't received with Brigitte Cornand. After psychoanalysis, after art, she had a habit of taking refuge in religion: "I enter my studio like a church," she wrote in 1990.[243] On July 24, 1999, when Frances Morris came to visit to discuss the Tate Modern commission, she wrote the *Hail Mary* prayer in her diary. And on September 24, she wrote the title of another: *The Lord's Prayer.*

Looking through her archives, Louise discovered the letters her father had sent her—about seventy-five documents: "It's mortifying to realize what Robert endured," she wrote in her diary.[244] Always careful to respect her husband's memory: "I disrespect Robert's memory by forgetting: Professor, writer, father, and husband."[245] "All that remains to us are our children, when I think of Rob[er]t I am speechless I can only cry the first time [in] exactly 20 years."[246] For Louise, it was imperative to keep her memories intact. She sometimes worried that her memory was failing, that it was ridden with moth holes.[247]

As frequently occurs in old age, the songs and lullabies of childhood returned to her easily, and she clung to them, the territory of her language-country. "Fire, [call] the firemen, the house is burning / I don't want papa, and don't want maman / I want my little husband to smile at me."[248]

In spite of these indirect appeals to her father, her mother, her dear husband, Louise still saw herself as "Madame Rien," or a "Lady in Waiting,"[249] the title of a 2003 work which depicts a little woven spider perched on a tapestry armchair.[250]

However, in the 1990s, she did experience intense moments of happiness: "I am so happy that my heart is going to burst,"[251] she declared in a text where she referenced the Carte du Tendre[252] and listed the names of all the old and new friends that surrounded her.

Petite Maman, 2000–2010

Petite maman / don't leave me / don't abandon me / I need you / I can't do anything without you.

The long, slow weaving work that Louise performed on her childhood memories and her emotions took spectacular form with the monumental installation she created in 2000 for the Turbine Hall, on the occasion of the Tate Modern's opening. Three immense steel towers were distributed throughout the space: two featured spiral staircases leading up to platforms surrounded by large oval mirrors; the third was a rectilinear tower with a spiral staircase on one side. Visitors were encouraged to climb the steps and sit in the wooden chairs provided at the top. Louise worked on a double scale, monumental and miniature; inside the towers she placed a number of smaller works, including small bronze or fabric figures under bell jars, which referred back to the theme of the good or bad mother. These sculptures were preceded by others—*Topiary IV* (1999), a small steel tree with blue bead fruits, wearing a dress; one of her legs is amputated at the knee, but she has a crutch to prop herself up. *Le père* (1998) features a chair (symbol of authority) dominating three tiny chairs beneath it, representing the three children.

These constructions were unusual for Louise but borrowed from certain recurring formal and thematic elements: they reference the skyscrapers of her engravings from 1947, the opposition between the organic and the geometric, the hard and the soft, the large oval mirrors that featured in *Cell (Twelve Oval Mirrors)* (1998), and the spiral staircase had already appeared, in smaller scale, in *Cell VII* (1998) and was reminiscent of the one that descended to the basement in her house in Chelsea; finally, the motif of the vertical tower symbolizing both ascent and fall, imprisonment and freedom, refuge and trap calls to mind her earliest *Femme maison* paintings.

By inviting the viewer to take part, Louise was trying to provoke unexpected meetings between people, inspiring them to look at themselves in the mirror and to see the surrounding space from different perspectives. The curator, Frances Morris,[1] described how the show came to be. After sending Louise the plans and videos of the Turbine Hall space, Morris received, by certified mail, an image of a tower with a spiral staircase, which she found magnificent. The next day, she received another image, and the third day still another. Louise had identified the challenges of the space and proposed this massive installation, both in keeping with her work and perfectly adapted to this immense industrial space.[2] In the midst of it all was a giant spider,[3] *Maman*, conceived specially for that space and shown there for the first time.

The titles she gave the towers were loaded with meaning: *I Do, I Undo,* and *I Redo.* These three actions apply to weaving, a sequence of positive and then negative and then reparative actions. "*I Do,*" she writes,

> is an active state. It's a positive affirmation. [. . .] Things are fine and peaceful. I am the good mother. I am generous and caring—the giver, the Provider. [. . .] *I Undo* is the unraveling. [. . .] There can be terrific violence that descends into depression. [. . .] It is the view from the bottom of the well. [. . .] It is the return of the repressed. I take things away. I smash things, relations are broken. I am the bad mother. [. . .] The guilt leads to a deep despair and passivity. [. . .] *I Redo* means that a solution is found to the problem. [. . .] You get clearer in your thinking. You are active again. [. . .] In terms of relationships to others, the reparation and reconciliation has been achieved. [. . .] There is hope and love again.[4]

This declaration was a psychological and creative manifesto. The dialectic process was a way of going beyond the opposition between construction and deconstruction, passive and active, which allowed her to fend off depression, fear, the anguish of never being loved.

Oedipus

Louise returned to the theme of the family[5] in these final years, repetitively, obsessively—the relationship between the mother and child, the father and child, the couple, childbirth, or the quasi-incestuous proximity among the various members of a family. "I have three frames of reference. [. . .] My father and mother [. . .] my own experience [. . .] the frame of reference of my children. And the three are stuck together."[6]

Three drawings of seven figures huddled together from 1996, the fabric sculpture *Seven in Bed* (2001), and the lithograph *Eight in Bed* (2000), are significant in this regard. In the sculpture, seven little figures made of stuffed pink fabric are laying down on a mattress, tightly wedged together as if in a box of sardines, pressing up against one another. Some have two heads which face either way, kissing greedily. These are not children but sexualized beings, all the same size; the number seven refers to Louise's extended family: the parents, the three children, and her two orphaned cousins. "From the moment I was born, I was involved in constant rivalry with others. My brother, my sister, my cousins, my neighbors—I considered them all rivals. I wanted to seem like someone who was just as good as the others, I was very ambitious. It was exhausting and, I think, pretty negative."[7] To explain the situation, she points out that every Sunday the children all went into the parents' bed.

The two most important works in this new series of smaller sculptures are *Oedipus* (2003) and *The Reticent Child* (2003), which was first shown in 2003 at the Sigmund Freud Museum in Vienna.[8] For the latter, Louise arranged six characters on a stainless steel table, as if onstage: two pregnant women, a woman giving birth, a baby hidden under a layer of pink gauze, a man standing with his head in his hands, and a child curled up in bed. A large concave mirror, hammered in some places and nailed to the edge of the table, reflected a distorted view of the scene from behind. The doubling of the figures and their extension based on the viewer's position made the tableau that much more unsettling. Their small size, and the materials chosen for the figures (five are made of pink fabric and one of pale, flesh-colored marble), made them fragile and vulnerable. These little fabric creatures, puppets, or dolls straight from the hands of the artist replay the primal scene in the life of the mother, giving birth to a "reticent" child: "There is a child who simply refused to be born. His birth was quite late. Was there something that he perceived that prevented him from wanting to leave the womb and go out into the world? How much of who he will be, his feelings and actions, will be predetermined by this refusal to appear? How will this child face the future? Will he be shy, reduced to silence, awkward or even hostile? He is the reticent child. He was reticent. But I found him out."[9] This reserved child, born late, whom Louise claimed to have "revealed," was Alain Bourgeois, her youngest son, who mostly kept his distance in order to protect himself from the family drama, opting for a more rational way of life—he became a lawyer, then a judge, as well as a photographer.

A triptych of drawings and prints from 2004, also called *The Reticent Child*, show a little baby cozy in its mother's womb, then in her breast, and then finally its birth. This primal scene appears often in her late work.

The other tableau, called *Oedipus*, also arranges a variety of figures, this time on a wood table encased in glass, ten little fabric sculptures that touch on an essential theme in her work—the myth of Oedipus, which first appeared as a reference in her sculpture *The Blind Leading the Blind*, from 1947. We recognize the Oracle (a two-headed Janus), Jocaste feeding Oedipus at her breast, the infant Oedipus with the pinned ankles, King Laius falling victim to Oedipus, Oedipus contemplating his fate, the Sphinx, Oedipus having sex with his mother, Oedipus realizing what he's done, the Blind Man (a head with pins stuck in its eyes), and an aged Oedipus being led by his daughter, Antigone. All the protagonists of the Greek tragedy are present, as well as the three ages of man from the Sphinx's riddle, as if Louise, at this stage of her life, finally felt the need to exorcise her "incestual" relationship with her father.[10] On August 5, 2000, Louise wrote about this play in her diary, noting: "Antigone, Œdipe Rex, Jocasta. Charity. In Louis Malle:[11] The mother says 'I put you out of your misery because I am charitable.' [. . .] She was raped at Charité-sur-Loire. Charity begins at home. Forgive yourself. Incest disguised as Charity. Sadie was your protector." An enigmatic declaration that, beneath the wordplay (Charity and the town of Charité-sur-Loire) and the allusion to the Louis Malle film, confirms her fear of incest and the protective role Sadie played between Louise and her father.

In the early 2000s, Louise drew more and more, even adopting new techniques. Since she rarely left the house, whatever work she could do at her table with a sheet of paper, pencils, or a brush became a regular, necessary activity. Her final drawings are typical of her late style, and as was often the case in her work, they vacillated between abstraction and figuration. They featured, for instance, repetitive drawings of concentric circles or grids, but also couples, pregnant women, childbirth. The former were a kind of purification ritual; they are detailed and incisive and were each given a title.

Tous les cinque (2004), a series of forty-seven drawings, was shown at Cheim & Read alongside *The Reticent Child*.[12] Each composition consists of five vertical lines formed of stacked red circles, like glass pearls, which appear between fine vertical lines. The title is explained on the first drawing, where five names appear: Robert, Louise, Alain, Jean-Louis, and Michel, in that order. On the back of one of the last drawings, the artist wrote, "the father, the mother, and the three children." Was she referring to the family she was born into, which she associated with her own family? She repeated these drawings obsessively, as in others that present intersecting blue and red lines like the framework for a tapestry, *Untitled (C.I.A.)* (2004).[13]

In 1998, Louise made several drawings in red ink, composed of stacked ovals, like the stacks of fabric, with names and words written inside of them. This series was an homage to Robert as a father. In one of the drawings, she notes how much Alain resembles him: "When I look for Robert, I find Alain. The Father is Robert, his son is there." She also wrote: "Life began when I met Robert in June 1938, nothing before."[14] In 2002, she made another tribute to Robert in the form of an architectural model, made of silver, of the Institute of Fine Arts building at New York University, where he taught for many years: "The Institute played an important part in my life. For many years my husband Robert Goldwater taught there. The four o'clock Friday lectures and tea were events I enjoyed. The best parts were the questions from the students."[15] This incredibly detailed model echoed the one she made of her childhood house for *Cell (Choisy)*, replicated in pink marble. But *The Institute* (2002), which resembles a reliquary, doesn't allude to family, or France, but to her husband's masculine, erudite spirit and that of American art history; Louise made a gift of the edition to the institute to finance its research programs.

Couples, Maternity

Beginning in 2007, she also made other drawings on wet paper with a large brush dipped in red gouache. This turn to the fluidity of gouache (which, diluted in water, spreads across the surface of the page), allowed the bodies she drew to fuse, to submerge the infant in its mother's belly, to inflate the breasts and penises. The forms spilled freely onto the paper, with a minimal amount of control.

The fabric couples that appeared in the middle of the 1990s returned in the early 2000s, but this time around, there were fewer decapitated bodies, monstrous couplings with fetishized prosthetics, or life-sized figures made of old clothes attached to a hook. Now they were usually entire figures, rendered on a small scale, in pink or blue terry cloth or knit, tightly embracing, often suspended by a thread, which suggested their fragility. This obsession with the couple at the end of Louise's life is a sign of the ambivalent erotic drive which wavered between attraction and repulsion. If the entire basis of her practice was above all a question of the relationship between the self and others, romantic love was also a central concern. The need for affection, and tenderness, and recognition above all, in spite of everything, of the benefits of living with someone, which comes through in the rehabilitation of the role played by Robert in their family life, as attested to by her writings and drawings. But above all, the couple was inextricably linked, for Louise, to having children, to maternity.

Pregnancy, like childbirth, was for her an ambiguous state, at once painful and erotic. That is why the subject takes so many different forms in the 2000s: little pink fabric sculptures, large red gouaches and prints. Louise didn't leave out a single step: conception, pregnancy, childbirth, breastfeeding, postpartum depression. It is hard not to recall here that the first famous Louise Bourgeois was a midwife to Queen Marie de Médicis, nicknamed La Boursier,[16] born in Paris in 1563 on the boulevard Saint-Germain. Louise the artist paid tribute to her namesake by illustrating a facsimile of the first Louise Bourgeois's book from 1636, *Recueil de secrets* (Collection of secrets).[17]

Few artists have represented childbirth so often or so explicitly: the child emerging from the mother's body or attached to the umbilical cord; but in her writings Louise also mentions her fear of not being able to have children, the heavy responsibility they represent, the ambivalence of maternal feelings that can pass from hatred to love, the pressure she felt to fulfill her role as mother. The bad mother (as depicted in the drawing *The Bad Mother*, from 1997) lets the milk flow from her naked breast while her child clings to her leg, and the good mother (another drawing, *The Good Mother,* from 2003) is like an icon of the Mother and Child as she rocks her newborn.

The childbirth scene appeared as early as 1941, when Louise sketched her own labor, which she described in her diary in great detail.[18] If this first image related directly to her own experience, the later ones were a metaphor for rebirth, creative power, and the cyclical way extreme old age returns one to the state of being a newborn. Maternity is the source of life and death. This is what her large red gouaches show magnificently at the end of her life.[19] Overflowing and dripping breasts, couples embracing, inflated bellies with burrowing babies, multiple mammary glands surrounding babies, children emerging from their mother's sex, legs spread wide: these images are deeply touching, because they are shakily done, but also radical in their affirmation of a certain vision of fertility; they are allegories of Life and Death. The maternal *womb* from which we emerge at birth is also the earthen *tomb* that we return to when we die. A small pink fabric sculpture representing a child emerging from between the thighs of the mother, attached by its cord—itself connected to the mother's navel—is called *Do Not Abandon Me* (1999). Who is abandoning whom? Birth can be understood in two different ways: it is the first abandonment, the infant must leave the mother's body, it is expelled, but the mother also feels abandoned by this part of herself that is leaving her. The cord which connects them is a bond of codependence that haunts familial relationships. Louise was still exploring this ambiguity. It was no accident that maternity returned in such a precise, regular way at the end of her life. It was for her a vital event, essential, profoundly connected to the creative act. But above all, at the end of her life, Louise saw herself as the baby.

Heads, Pillars

While she was making these multifigure compositions, Louise was creating heads made of scraps of different pieces of fabric—bits of tapestry, striped canvas, towels, fleece.[20] These patchwork faces, sometimes bandaged like mummies, were, in a way, vanitas which incarnated the various steps of the human condition, from birth to old age to death. Some cry out but their mouths are sewn shut, their gaze is fixed, immobile, frozen for all eternity. Others look like burn victims, with quickly sewn-up bandages. Louise took particular care with the details, fitting the tapestries closely to the forms of the faces. After cutting off many, many heads, she began to focus on the theme of the uncompromising self-portrait of the artist facing physical decay. After these imposing single heads, she went on to make others, as well as groups of two or three in different fabrics for a number of *Portrait Cells* (2000) encased in glass vitrines. Columns or pillars of stuffed fabric blocks, stacked on a rod, date from this period as well. Despite the change from hard to soft materials, these vertical forms echo her *Personages* from the late 1940s to 1950s.

Louise often returned to older works, remaking them in fabric; and so she returned to her pregnant women, her women-houses, her knife-women, the arches of hysteria, all reworked in tapestry. The return to the past, and to repetition, is characteristic of her late style, and she could not operate otherwise.

I Remember . . .

The years 2000–2010 were the last decade of the artist's life. By now in her nineties, she worked over and over with fabric, old linens, and clothing,[21] not only to make sculptures but also for a series of fabric collage books. Her turn to this material can be explained in several ways. For an elderly woman, fragile, who got around with great difficulty, it was a light, flexible material that she could work on at home, either alone or with the help of a seamstress, Mercedes Katz, for the detailing. In cutting, sewing, repairing, restoring, Louise returned to her childhood in her mother's studio, with the seamstresses and their needles and thread. "I was born in the rag business and not in the Food business. Let us not confuse things."[22] She chose and prepared the bits of fabric, cut them roughly to what she desired, and asked Mercedes to assemble them with more subtlety and discretion. She wanted the stitches to be less prevalent, to disappear; her own stitching was often not very fine.

The needle had many meanings for Louise: it referred to the women's work in her mother's tapestry restoration studio and it was also the tool of repair, of bringing together scattered materials. She wrote: "Saved by the needle: No pins. No stapler. No tape. No glue."[23] And later, in her diary: "I've spent my life making holes everywhere, whether with a needle or a chisel."[24]

The first book she made from bits of cut up and collaged fabric is *Ode à l'oubli* (2002), a way of fighting against the loss of memory by transforming old clothes, handkerchiefs, and linens, kept since the 1930s, into collages and patchwork compositions. The cover of the book was made from a scrap of her trousseau embroidered with her monogram: LBG. Through this patient work of cutting, sewing, and collaging, Louise remembered moments lived with these clothes, and at the same time, by cutting them up, she erased or transformed them. She was conscious that reactivating the past could also invent false memories, because she wrote on one page, "I had a flashback of something that never existed." Or rather was it a case of something she had denied and repressed? "The return of the repressed," she wrote on another page.

The second fabric book was a tribute to the river of her childhood, the Bièvre, which ran through the bottom of the garden in Antony and in which the workers washed the tapestries, but also on which she took boat rides with Sadie and Pierre. The text of *Ode à la Bièvre* (2002) evokes memories of the scent of the garden in Antony and of the muddy, fertile earth in which they grew geraniums, peonies, asparagus, pink and white hawthorn, purple tamarisk, and cherry trees. When she returned to Antony in 1951 with her children, she noted that "the river was gone. Only the trees that my father had planted along its edge remained as a witness."[25]

A third book, this time on handmade paper with music staves, called again on her memories of her French childhood: *Paris toujours Paris* (2006). It opens on two pairs of red and blue maps of France thumbing their noses at each other. On the following pages, Louise noted in her trembling handwriting all the places that were so important to her: 77, rue Daguerre, the École du Louvre, rue Saint-Benoît,[26] the town hall in the place Saint-Sulpice.[27] It concludes with lines of famous French chansons: Jean Sablon's "C'est si bon,"[28] and Maurice Chevalier's "Paris sera toujours Paris."[29] Music, like perfume or clothes, is another vector to reactivate memories and emotions of the past.

In 2002, Louise recorded a compact disc of children's songs, traditional songs, and made-up songs, accompanied by Frédéric Sanchez.[30] Music was ever more present at the end of her life, in various forms—drawings on music scores with music notes and G clefs;[31] lists of composers and singers of popular songs; but also, and above all, she loved to sing. She wrote the words to several songs in her diary: "Maman les petits bateaux," "Tout va très bien

Madame la marquise," "Il était une bergère," "Nous n'irons plus au bois, les lauriers sont coupés." Brigitte Cornand, who knew well how much Louise enjoyed these little songs, often asked her to sing them. "C'est le murmure de l'eau qui chante" is a song Louise made up herself: *"C'est le murmure de l'eau qui bout, c'est le murmure de l'eau qui chante, c'est le murmure de ta voix qui me remplit de joie"* (It's the sound of the rushing water, it's the sound of the singing water, it's the sound of your voice that fills me with joy).[32] This sweet song was played at several exhibitions, including one at the Palais de Tokyo in Paris in 2002. Louise's work was being shown at this gallery of contemporary art, alongside work by young artists. A photograph taken by Annie Leibovitz shows her in profile looking like an old, wise woman, her face striking and craggy; it was blown up and shown in all the metro stations, consecrating her as a star. This image of a stern, conquering woman contrasted sharply with the fragile pieces on show (a newborn in a haze of pink gauze) or with the trembling voice of the artist heard in the recording.

Louise was receiving more and more invitations, of all sorts: from the Sigmund Freud Museum in Vienna;[33] from White Cube in London,[34] where she showed a new series of fabric women (mostly headless) combined with cooking utensils, including several "knife-woman" sculptures that recalled *Femme couteau* from 1969–70 but this time included a real blade, threatening to cut the woman in two.

In 2007–8, first in London[35] and then in New York at Cheim & Read Gallery,[36] she showed a new sculpture series called *Echo,* made with clothing dipped in plaster and then pulled by one end so that the weight of the plaster stretched the garment into a tall, slim pillar. When cast in bronze and treated with a white patina, they resembled her early *Personages*. These "formless" pieces, as if suspended in the void, also recall both the real clothing she hung from her "pole" pieces in the 1990s and the marble *Femme maison* sculpture she made in Italy in 1982 using one of Jerry's crumpled T-shirts. Everything she touched was immediately transformed, recycled, metamorphosed—either cut to pieces, then restitched and patched up, or turned to stone.

Passing Time

Time and its inexorable passing, its minutes, hours, and days, form the horizon of her final years. So Louise drew clocks with the arms pointing at the changing hours, the cyclical wheel of time, and she showed a large clock composed of twenty-four drypoint etchings in 2009 at the gallery Pièce Unique in Paris.[37] But one hour was particularly dear to her: ten o'clock in the morning. On a series of forty sheets of music paper, she indicated the sacred, blessed moment when Jerry arrived in the morning: "10 am is when you come to me."[38] This declaration is written across one sheet along with a clock indicating the time. The rest of the series shows pairs of arms and hands belonging to Jerry and herself. Their hands reach toward each other, touch, part ways, call for help, barely touch again. She also made variations on these arm poses in bronze.

In 2005, Louise was forced out of her large studio in Brooklyn, when plans came through to knock down that part of the neighborhood; in its place the city put up the Barclays Center, a sports and music arena.

Most of her work between 2005 and 2010 took place in her house in Chelsea. This included sewing, drawing, and printmaking, each sustaining the other. Her friend Felix, from the Harlan & Weaver printshop, regularly came to bring her copper plates, and then proofs, on which she often drew again. He had previously repaired the old press she kept in the basement and sometimes used it, so that she could see the printed image more quickly. Then he bought and installed another, even better, small press. With Benjamin Shiff at Osiris, she explored techniques that allowed her to combine printmaking, drawing, and writing on large-format paper. As her vision declined, it became difficult to work on Felix Harlan's smaller-scale plates.[39] The collaboration with Benjamin Shiff in a bigger format allowed her more freedom to work without the limitations of the frame and with larger, freer movements, which suited her. She needed encouragement and technical advice from those she worked with, who were also her friends, and kept her company during these last years.

Louise often returned to the foundational themes of her work, which she reinterpreted from different perspectives: tools, knives, hands, child-birth, couples, spiders, cats (male and female), and organic forms (*À Baudelaire*, 2008) that worked themselves into knots and hills. Some phrases from her writings were reproduced and printed on fabric or paper and sometimes used as titles: *Le mot pitié m'a apaisée* (2002); *Toi et moi* (1989–2003); *Yes, Yes, Yes*, which gained an "E" and became *Eyes* (2004); *Obsession or Confusion* (2004); *Ne t'occupe pas de toi-même, occupe-toi des autres* (2001).

The illustrated book *The Laws of Nature* (2003), which she did with Felix Harlan, shows a nude woman balancing and twisting a nude man between her legs over five images, making him do—according to Louise—somersaults. (She told Harlan that the figures in this series are playing an adult version of a French children's game, known as *faire des galipettes*, meaning to do somersaults. In fact, the expression *"faire des galipettes"* is also slang for having sex, a punning reference that Louise must have enjoyed.) *Saturday Morning* (2003–9) shows people lining up in front of the Saint Peter's soup kitchen across the street from Louise's house. "*Les plus malheureux que toi*" (those less fortunate than you), she wrote on the back of one of the proofs.

Several wonderful series also emerged from her collaboration with Benjamin Shiff. A series called *Extreme Tension* (2007)[40] is composed of eleven large-scale mixed-media panels that brought together soft ground etchings and sheets of paper on which she wrote words and phrases in English. The text was excerpted from a piece of writing in French dating to around 1959[41] that described all the parts of the body from top to bottom, with anatomic precision, naming bones as well as internal organs, including the famous nighttime cramps that had tortured Louise for years, perspiration, and palpitations. The text concludes with "the smell of the hunted animal." Fear is always, always there, crouched deep within its hiding place. Another large-scale series was called *À l'infini* (2008), a series of knots, curls, and interweavings from which escape a couple here, some fetuses in utero there—which look a bit like blood vessels, or entrails, or all the important moments of herself gathered together in a long braid. The series derives its power from the loose additions, watercolor stains, scribbled words—all hallmarks of her late style.

Does the title derive from a metaphysical meditation on the afterlife? In 1990, Louise was already asking questions about eternity, the world above and below: "Closed world of which I see the boundaries and which I can control—I am at ease in it. Is life passing me by? That is what fear does—establish the distance between the immediate + the eternal. The evanescent + the eternal."[42]

Among the final mixed-media print suites made with Benjamin Shiff were *My Inner Life* (2008), *La maladie de l'amour* (2008), and, finally, in 2010, *I Give Everything Away*, a six-paneled piece that combines soft ground etching with hand additions and texts and that may have been a way of saying goodbye. "I give everything away. I distance myself from myself. From what I love most. I leave my home. I leave the nest. I am packing my bags."[43] Louise also worked with Raylene Marasco (Dyenamix), who printed *Self-Pity* (2009, a text on fabric), *Lullaby* (2006), and *The Fragile* (2007).

Louise was ever more admired, loved, and venerated by a younger generation of artists and writers. She contributed to Roni Horn's[44] book *Wonderwater: Alice Offshore* (2004),[45] in which she noted all the names of the psychoanalysts and writers who had been important to her.[46] She and Tracey Emin worked together on the digital print series *Do Not Abandon Me* (2010), which was also published as a trade edition book.[47] In this work with Emin, which addressed Louise's primary theme of abandonment, the younger artist added drawings and words to Louise's large red gouaches of erections, bellies, and breasts. Louise also collaborated on an illustrated fabric book with writer Gary Indiana[48] titled *To Whom It May Concern* (2010). It is a meditation on the physical confrontation of the man with his erection and the woman with swollen breasts and belly. Always couples. And eroticism.

These two last books were published in 2010, the year of Louise's death. She worked until the very end. Daily activity sustained her, in spite of the insomnia, the fatigue, the memory loss, the physical weakness.

She was still accepting public commissions, including one called *Hold Me Close* (2005), a memorial for the victims of a tsunami in 2004, installed in Krabi, Thailand.[49] Louise always responded to requests for philanthropy, whether through the sale of work, special editions, or public monuments. "Do something for someone else and you will feel better. Beneficence," she wrote in her diary.[50]

Art Is My Religion

In 1998,[51] Louise agreed to decorate a desacralized chapel[52] in Bonnieux in the south of France. Her relationship to religion was always a complex one. Raised by parents who were vehement atheists and freethinkers, she had herself baptized in 1935, and it seemed as if at the end of her life religion had returned to haunt her in the form of prayers and giving thanks. For art had always been, for her, a form of religion, and the artist, in spite of her suffering, is a privileged individual. "Lord, there is no limit to my gratitude," she wrote sometime around 1990 in a magnificent prayer-poem, "Look at my drawing. Nobody could count the hills in this landscape, like heartbeats they move infinitely. Like the waves of the sea they pulsate infinitely, forever, inviolable unchanged like my gratitude toward you [. . .]. I try to make you understand how I am grateful. It is my gratefulness, my thanks, my appreciation for your kindness that will touch you and will make you know that you can not abandon me."[53] Her faith expressed itself through different channels: gratitude, meditation ("I would like to gather my thoughts and meditate"),[54] love ("Beauty is associated with love, isn't it? Maybe it's a religious thing. Christ died because of his love. Perhaps it is a religious tragedy"),[55] and finally sacrifice: "I cannot resist saving, saving from oblivion, rescuing from death, destruction, or perdition (moral). Sacrifice oneself to the saving of someone else—vows of sacrifice, of chastity, denial, teaching of the church, against sin."[56] It was more a question of adhering to Christian values and a need for absolution than allegiance to religion, since, for Louise, "whenever there is power (church) and respectability there is a danger for the artist."[57] In 1993, she confessed that she had "incorporated awareness of the Church."[58]

With or without faith, the works she created for the little chapel in Bonnieux attest to a sensuous concept of spirituality and are an incontestable success which places that site in the noble lineage of Matisse's chapel in Vence or Picasso's in Vallauris. It includes a pink marble basin for holy water filled with lactating breasts, a confessional with cushions made of tapestry and marble hands joined in prayer, a large bronze cross formed of two arms, with one hand closed and the other open (*Cross*, 2002). It contains her entire formal and iconographic vocabulary, perfectly adapted to function and place. There's even a small spider on the wall, behind the pink fabric *Mother and Child* (2001) under a bell jar.

Paris Pays Tribute

In 2008, Louise finally had the major French retrospective she had been waiting for. Thanks to the Tate Modern, which organized this traveling exhibition,[59] the Centre Pompidou finally showed Louise Bourgeois. It was a revelation for a wider public who discovered the legendary artist's work.

Unknown for far too long in her country of origin, she now took her place in the art history of the second half of the twentieth century and became a reference point for a number of contemporary artists. Seeing her work inspired very strong, very intense reactions of dizziness and physical rejection—or unconditional love. She acquired a number of new devotees, including the writer Nadine Satiat,[60] who was so moved by what she saw that she wrote a beautiful essay about it.

Then, in another final act of recognition, Jean Frémon suggested that the Maison de Balzac organize, after her death, an exhibition of eight pieces,[61] one of which is a sixteen-part fabric work collaged with beads, buttons, fasteners, and artificial flowers on the theme of Eugénie Grandet, a character with whom she identified. "I don't need to read *Eugénie Grandet*. I lived [it]. If you [don't] want to repeat Balzac. Be informed."[62] This identification with a character who was never allowed to grow up—"Eugénie Grandet didn't grow up"[63]—was a frequent one. However, Louise's life was nothing like the narrow, reclusive one of Balzac's heroine. But both were victims of manipulation, of their authoritarian fathers' arrogance, in love with their cousins, and bereft of their mothers at a young age. On a large mixed-media etching, *My Inner Life (#5)* (2008)—which shows a pregnant woman whose very long hair intertwines with an umbilical cord attached at her belly button, as if anticipating the baby who is still in her womb—she embroidered several phrases inspired by Balzac's novel on the subject of the codependent relationship between mother and daughter and the fate of girls to suffer: "My mother was right. Suffer and die. Ah! Maman, I am suffocating. I never suffered so."

Identifying with the figure who sews, cooks, mends, cleans, and keeps house was also a way for her to pay tribute to the patience of young women who nevertheless rise up against their state of dependence: "Eugénie Grandet never grew up. [. . .] I am sitting by the window. I spent my life making curtains to hide the dirty window panes. [. . .] I spent my life washing dishes, I spent my life washing vegetables [. . .] I spent my life being afraid of the cold, I spent my life darning, letting out the waists and shortening the dresses. I spent my life listening to the chirping of the birds, the water falling from the ceiling and the traffic on 20th."[64]

This work testifies to her interest in Balzac, who, like her, was dedicated to describing the contradictory feelings at the heart of the family, closed up in their domestic universe, and, more broadly, to those of the "human comedy."

Accepting Old Age

"Actually, I like old people, because they are modest and often sad. They struggle because they often feel ugly. In fact they are not ugly they are interesting like trees that have survived storms. They are not depressing."[65]

Is this declaration—one she made in the 1960s—an indication of the way Louise faced her own old age, with lucidity and courage? As she wrote in 1995, she did not feel her age; inside, she remained eighteen years old. She was happier, even, she noted, than she had been at eighteen: "I would loathe going back."[66] However, she observed in the 1980s that "Old age is an insult to beauty—no."[67]

The very end of her life seems to have been serene. As she wrote in her prints: *"Le mot pitié m'a apaisée."*[68] She did not speak of her approaching death, except on a loose sheet of paper, written when she was in her seventies: "It is not guilt. It is the consciousness of death. Seen as price [of] deliverance, Bourdaloue, Bossuet, Fénelon [. . .] Corneille, Racine. Logical conclusion of the 17th Century literature deserve not death but paradise + salvation. Sex is never mentioned, only love! The opposite of love is death."[69]

Louise knew how to make the most of her old age and the assumptions that people made on the basis of it. When, in 2007, Nicolas Sarkozy (accompanied by his wife, Carla Bruni) came to award her the medal of Commander of the Legion of Honor, Louise seemed distracted; her wicked smile indicated that she was happy to be honored in this way, but either she didn't know or was pretending not to know who had won the election that year, and so she asked Sarkozy who was the president of France. She received another "honorific" award in 2009, when she was inducted by Fernando Arrabel into the order of the Grande Gidouille of the Collège de 'Pataphysique and given the title of Exquisite Commanderess and Arranger of the World.

The familiar presence of her friend Brigitte Cornand helped her through this period of physical decline; she distracted and stimulated Louise by making her recite the fables of La Fontaine or by collaborating on a new language composed of onomatopoeias or nonsense words like "Grabigouji."[70] Louise's insomnia had worsened, and she often slept during the day to catch up on her rest.

Cornand continued to film Louise:[71] what amounted to a daily filmic journal consisted of blurry, unstaged images of Louise alone, sleeping, drawing, talking, or reciting; it is a moving testament to their relationship, their closeness, but also forms an essential visual and aural archive documenting the end of the life of a great artist. All her close friends took turns being with her. Jerry was always there, of course, but Paulo Herkenhoff (whom she drew as a big baby with chubby cheeks) visited often, as did Deborah Wye, her children, and her grandchildren. Alas, her relationship with Robert Storr had become strained.

Once she was no longer able to climb the staircase that led to her bedroom, a bed was installed for her on the parlor floor, behind the kitchen, overlooking West Twentieth Street. That way she could sit and look out the window, as she had always done, at the people who walked by and those who lined up in front of the Saint Peter's food bank. She liked "the soft February light [which came] through the window."[72] The Sunday salons continued but sometimes had to be canceled due to her worsening insomnia, which made her tired and less and less present. All these visits were useful distractions, but what really helped her hold on was her dear Jerry, who remained attentive to her every wish and mood, protecting her from disruptions. "Jerry is here, everything is here."[73] Or she would sing, "What a beautiful morning, what a beautiful day, everything is going my way."[74]

Photos and films from this time show Louise often dressed in a sky blue blouse that brought out the color of her eyes, or a large T-shirt, her head protected by a white cotton cap like those worn by newborns. Her face was wrinkled, chiseled like an old engraving plate, but her gaze was still clear and piercing. In spite of her fatigue, she perked up as soon as she got down to work. It was a way for her to fight against death, to repel the inevitable failure of the body, which she would never discuss. Because Louise had dug her nails into life. She accepted the hazards of old age—physical decline, incontinence, loss of memory—and even let herself be photographed or filmed in this state of disrepair. Alex Van Gelder's[75] photographs show her clowning around, provocative, deformed by age, while the images taken by Cornand are more moving and tender. Louise surrenders to sleep, watches the birds in her garden, or sings. In those of Van Gelder, she wears all black like a witch, she is armed with a knife, masked like Zorro, or she allows him to photograph her gnarled, stiff hands, which had always been her most reliable tool.

Reborn

Can we speak of Louise Bourgeois's late style, like that of Titian, Rembrandt, or Picasso? Old age can, indeed, exalt artists in spite of their trembling hands and failing vision, and this unsteadiness can transform into power. For Edward Said,[76] late style was either the harmonious, calming influence of maturity and wisdom, or the savage return of childhood untamed. The artist could thumb his nose at conventions and mastery. Late style is often anachronistic and therefore trailblazing, as was the case, for instance, of the "final" Picasso. It is difficult to resist finding intersections between Picasso and Louise Bourgeois, both of whom turned intensely to printmaking at the end of their lives, which allowed them to develop narratives and to return to their earliest works. Both concentrated on erotic themes—kissing, coupling—and faces like skulls. Both claimed that old age returned cyclically to childhood. But if Picasso painted like a *Young Painter*,[77] Louise identified with newborns—because Louise was haunted by the desire for the mother's breast, the return to the mother. At the end of her life, she became a baby again—perhaps she never ceased being one. Whenever she was shown her images of breasts, pregnant mothers, or babies (in the womb or out) and asked which one she was, mother or child, she systematically replied that she was the child. "I am not a mother; I am a baby!" she said in 1992.[78] And in 1965, she feared reacting like "a crybaby with a compulsion."[79]

In May 2010, Louise caught pneumonia and was hospitalized; she recovered fairly quickly and asked Jerry to bring her paper and pencils so that she could draw. Finally she was sent home, very happy to be out of the hospital, and, according to those who were close to her, she felt much better and was very alert. Unfortunately, she wouldn't stay long; the first night she was home she suffered a heart attack and was taken back to the hospital in an ambulance, where she remained in a coma for several days, before dying on May 31. Louise Bourgeois was buried beside Robert and Michel in a cemetery on Long Island (Cutchogue Cemetery), in a small, private ceremony.[80] Strangely, there is no gravestone, no names, no dates. All three are beneath the earth with no mention of their "presence" in the world. No trace of the artist who sculpted her emotions all her life and gave her body to sculpture— Louise felt her work was more *her* than her physical presence. At one time, she intended to place one of her own works on Robert's tomb, but the overtly sensual forms of the sculpture were apparently against the rules of the cemetery, which otherwise consists only of geometric stones.[81]

After a long and rich life, the end was quick, relatively easy, without physical suffering. But she was never delivered from her mental anguish: "Never let me be free from this burden that will never let me be free," wrote Louise,[82] who had "been to Hell" and returned to tell us: "it was wonderful."[83]

NOTES

Unless otherwise identified, all writings, correspondences, notes, and other papers by Louise Bourgeois are in the collection of the Louise Bourgeois Archive / The Easton Foundation, New York.

Introduction

1. Elisabeth Couturier, *Paris-Match,* June 10–16, 2010.

2. Valérie Duponchelle, *Le Figaro,* June 1, 2010.

3. Vincent Noce, *Libération,* June 2, 2010.

4. Harry Bellet, Emmanuelle Lequeux, *Le Monde,* June 2, 2010.

5. Richard Serra, speech at memorial ceremony in honor of Louise Bourgeois, Museum of Modern Art, New York, September 28, 2010. Transcript courtesy the Louise Bourgeois Archive/The Easton Foundation, New York.

6. Jenny Holzer, speech at memorial ceremony in honor of Louise Bourgeois, Museum of Modern Art, New York, September 28, 2010. Transcript courtesy the Louise Bourgeois Archive, The Easton Foundation, New York.

7. *Louise Bourgeois: Pensées-plumes,* Centre Georges Pompidou, Paris, 1995; *Louise Bourgeois,* CAPC–Musée d'art contemporain, Bordeaux, 1998; *Louise Bourgeois, rétrospective,* Centre Pompidou, Paris, 2008.

8. Louise Bourgeois, *Destruction of the Father / Reconstruction of the Father: Writings and Interviews, 1923–1997,* ed. Marie-Laure Bernadac and Hans Ulrich Obrist (Cambridge, MA: MIT Press, and London: Violette, 1998) [hereafter cited as *Destruction*]; Louise Bourgeois, *The Insomnia Drawings* (Zurich: Daros Collection, 2000).

9. Whose archives I organized for many years at the Musée Picasso.

10. Brassaï, *Conversations avec Picasso* (Paris: Gallimard, 1964), 123.

11. Louise Bourgeois, "Native Talent," *Artforum* 32, no. 5 (1994): 73–74, reprinted in *Destruction,* 271–74, quotation at 274. [Emphasis in the original.—Trans.]

12. December 18, 1994; see Bourgeois, *Insomnia Drawings,* 27v.

13. "Welcome, To my neighbors: the walls are paper thin at 347 between 347 and 349. Please be timid, be careful: about <u>banging</u>," she wrote on January 24, 1995, on one of her *Insomnia*

Drawings (1994–95); see Bourgeois, *Insomnia Drawings*, 103v. [Originally in English. The word "banging" is triple-underlined in the original.—Trans.]

14. This iconic phrase appears in her diary first on August 25, 1991, and again on November 14, 1991, and April 16, 1992. She subsequently included it in the works *Cell I* (1991) and *Precious Liquids* (1992).

15. "The only access we have to our volcanic unconscious and to the profound motives of our actions and reactions is through the shocks of our encounters with specific people." Diary, September 11, 1980. [Originally in English except for *"inconscient"* (unconscious) and *"chocs"* (shocks).—Trans.]

Chapter 1. The "Mystery" of Childhood

Epigraph: Louise Bourgeois, *Album* (New York, Peter Blum, 1994), n.p. [hereafter cited as *Album*], reprinted in Louise Bourgeois, *Destruction of the Father / Reconstruction of the Father: Writings and Interviews, 1923–1997*, ed. Marie-Laure Bernadac and Hans Ulrich Obrist (Cambridge, MA: MIT Press, and London: Violette, 1998) [hereafter cited as *Destruction*], 277–85. A number of images and texts from *Partial Recall* (1983), shown for the first time at the MoMA retrospective in 1983, were published in *Album* in 1994. [Originally in English.—Trans.]

1. Loose sheet, c. 1990 (LB-0009). [Originally in English except for *"l'abandon"* (the abandonment).—Trans.]

2. "Interview with Douglas Maxwell," *Modern Painters* 6, no. 2 (1993), reprinted in *Destruction*, 246.

3. "[T]hey had a child. My father, he was quite macho, and unfortunately the child was a girl. I am sure my mother was embarrassed, even though she was a strong feminist. The embarrassment did not last too long, since the child died." *Album*, reprinted in *Destruction*, 279. Is she referring to the first child or to a daughter born between Henriette and Louise, which seems more likely, given that they were six years apart? Louise would then be the adored little daughter, her birth following the death of another little girl.

4. "Interview with Maxwell," reprinted in *Destruction*, 246.

5. "Interview with Jerry Gorovoy," October 8, 1990, in Frances Morris, ed., *Louise Bourgeois*, exh. cat. (London: Tate, 2007), 163.

6. "Do you know that that child is your spitting image?," in *Album*, reprinted in *Destruction*, 279.

7. Eleanor Munro, *Originals: American Women Artists* (New York: Simon and Schuster, 1979), reprinted in *Destruction*, 112.

8. *Album*, reprinted in *Destruction*, 280.

9. In fact, Louise only spent the first four years of the First World War in Aubusson.

10. "The Fabric of Construction," *Craft Horizons* 29, no. 2 (1969): 34, reprinted in *Destruction*, 89.

11. "A Memoir: Louise Bourgeois and Patricia Beckert," late 1970s, in *Destruction*, 117.

12. *Album*, reprinted in *Destruction*, 278.

13. *Album*, reprinted in *Destruction*, 279.

14. "Memoir: Bourgeois and Beckert," 117.

15. "This infant, above, is not the son of François Jean. Forbidden from bearing the

surname Jean in the future," noted the magistrate's court of the Seine on June 17, 1908. I thank Nathalie Berghege for this information.

16. Diary, June 11, 1966. [Originally in English.—Trans.]

17. "Memoir: Bourgeois and Beckert," 118.

18. In 1968, she titled a marble and wood sculpture after Clamart.

19. *Album*, reprinted in *Destruction*, 278, 277. Although Louise claimed that this is an image of the gates in front of the Château de Sceaux, The Easton Foundation has since discovered that the property is not Sceaux after all but instead the Château Vaux-le-Vicomte, located in Maincy (near Melun). Sceaux may have similar statuary. However, in the photo, it's clear that the building's squarish side wings and cupola match those of Château Vaux-le-Vicomte, whereas the similar Sceaux building has a more triangular roofline. Regardless of the possible memory lapse regarding its location, the château certainly held a lot of meaning for her as a signpost of the past.

20. Louis Bourgeois to Louise Bourgeois [hereafter LB], October 20, 1939 (LIB-0026).

21. Jacques Jean to LB, February 18, 1946 (LL-0046).

22. *Album*, reprinted in *Destruction*, 281.

23. Small town in the Yvelines, on the Mantois plateau, twenty-eight miles northwest of Versailles.

24. "They treated me with more respect than my brother or sister because of my abilities and potential." "Sixty-One Questions," 1971, in *Destruction*, 92. This was a questionnaire sent by Alexis Rafael Krasilovsky, a student in Dr. Lenore Weitzman's course "Sociology of the Woman Artist" at Yale University.

25. Her sister's disability would inspire several of Louise's works, including *Henriette* (1985), a suspended bronze leg, and *Legs* (1986). See also chapter 9 in this volume.

26. Diary, September 23, 1986. [Originally in English.—Trans.]

27. Diary, December 1, 1987. On jealousy, see Juliet Mitchell, "The Sublime Jealousy of Louise Bourgeois," in *Louise Bourgeois: The Return of the Repressed*, ed. Philip Larratt-Smith, 2 vols. (London: Violette, 2012), 1:47–67.

28. "Beginning in 1904, my father was responsible, almost single-handed[ly], for the rediscovery of Aubusson and Gobelins tapestry, which he showed in his gallery in Paris." "Sixty-One Questions," 92.

29. There are photographs of Joséphine in front of the tapestry gallery in Paris (c. 1911). The sign for Aux Vieilles Tapisseries was used in Bourgeois's *Cell* (*Choisy*) (1990–93). Today the site is occupied by the bookshop L'Écume des Pages; it has the same glass facade. This is where Louise ran an art gallery in 1938 and where she met her husband, Robert Goldwater; see also chapter 2 in this volume.

30. "Self-Expression Is Sacred and Final: Statements," in Christiane Meyer-Thoss, *Louise Bourgeois: Konstruktionen für den freien Fall / Designing for Free Fall* (Zurich: Ammann, 1992), 185.

31. *Album*, reprinted in *Destruction*, 284.

32. Joséphine Bourgeois to Louis Bourgeois, July 20, 1929 (JVB-0005).

33. "Two Conversations with Deborah Wye," 1979 and 1981, in *Destruction*, 128.

34. Louis Bourgeois to LB, January 28, 1947 (LIB-0070). He was in the bookshop on the rue des Saints-Pères.

35. "A Conversation with Bernard Marcadé," 1993, in *Destruction*, 248.

36. The two epigraphs that open this section are from Louise Bourgeois, *The Trauma of Abandonment*, 2001, a fabric illustrated book with digital print and embroidery, quoted in Morris, *Bourgeois*, 293; and loose sheet, c. 1961 (LB-0374). [Both originally in English.—Trans.]

37. *Album*, reprinted in *Destruction*, 281.

38. Loose sheet, c. 1958 (LB-0858), in "Select Diary Notes, 1960–1979," in *Destruction*, 70. [Originally in English except for "Papa et Maman."—Trans.]

39. Cited in Paulo Herkenhoff, "War," in Morris, *Bourgeois*, 293.

40. "Keep me in the dark, in the closet at Chartres—prevent me from seeing," loose sheet, autumn 1959 (LB-0228), in Larratt-Smith, *Louise Bourgeois*, 2:111. [Originally in English except for *"m'empêcher de voir"* (prevent me from seeing).—Trans.]

41. Loose sheet, c. 1958 (LB-0858), in *Destruction*, 70. [Originally in English except for *"les Dames de la Croix rouge"* (the Ladies of the Red Cross).—Trans.]

42. "Letters to Colette Richarme, 1937–1940," in *Destruction*, 37.

43. "The Amputees or the crippled of the Louvre, Civil servants The Cafeteria in the Louvre's basement." Loose sheet of music paper, January 25, 1998 (LB-0798). [Originally in French except for "Civil servants" in English.—Trans.]

44. "Interview with Maxwell," reprinted in *Destruction*, 244.

45. Louis Bourgeois to Joséphine Bourgeois, January 15, 1917 (LIB-0031).

46. Louis Bourgeois to Joséphine Bourgeois, January 16, 1917 (LIB-0035).

47. Louis Bourgeois to Joséphine Bourgeois, January 15, 1917 (LIB-0033).

48. "Here I am in a good little room at the nice hotel in town." Louis Bourgeois to Joséphine Bourgeois, January 15, 1917 (LIB-0034).

49. Louis Bourgeois to Joséphine Bourgeois, January 18, 1917 (LIB-0037).

50. Joséphine Bourgeois to Louis Bourgeois, December 10, 1918 (JVB-0017).

51. Joséphine Bourgeois to Louis Bourgeois, December 10, 1918 (JVB-0017).

52. Loose sheet, April 27, 1957 (LB-0141), in Larratt-Smith, *Louise Bourgeois*, 2:53.

53. Louis Bourgeois to LB, September 20, 1945 (LIB-0060).

54. Donald Kuspit, *Louise Bourgeois* (New York: Random House, 1988), 66.

55. "There were all kinds of animals. There was a donkey, there was a pig. It was full of guinea hens that always flew—you couldn't get them back—ducks, and families of rabbits." *Album*, reprinted in *Destruction*, 282.

56. "Rédaction," loose sheet, February 5, 1927 (LB-2118).

57. The young English governess who came to teach the children English from 1922 to the end of the 1920s and became their father's mistress; see chapter 2 in this volume.

58. "Memoir: Bourgeois and Beckert," 122.

59. Munro, *Originals*, 112–13. Her father also collected pebbles. See "Freud's Toys," *Artforum* 28, no. 5 (1990), reprinted in *Destruction*, 186–90.

60. See Mâkhi Xenakis, *Louise Bourgeois: The Blind Leading the Blind* (Arles, France: Actes Sud and London: Galerie Lelong, 2008), 22.

61. Loose sheet, c. 1960 (LB-0222).

62. "Memoir: Bourgeois and Beckert," 122.

63. "Fabric of Construction," reprinted in *Destruction*, 89.

64. "Memoir: Bourgeois and Beckert," 118.

65. "Memoir: Bourgeois and Beckert," 119–20.

66. "Memoir: Bourgeois and Beckert," 120.

67. This can be seen in photographs of tapestries carefully piled in alcoves of the apartment on the boulevard Saint-Germain.

68. "Memoir: Bourgeois and Beckert," 121–22.

69. Kuspit, *Bourgeois,* 20.

70. *Louise Bourgeois,* directed by Camille Guichard (Paris: Terra Luna Films, 1993).

71. [An *Agenda PLM*—Paris-Lyon-Méditerranée—was a promotional publication produced by the railroad company that connected Paris, Lyon, and the coast, a forerunner of today's SNCF. The agendas were launched in 1913 and contained colorful advertising, illustrations, and texts.—Trans.]

72. Diary, December 31, 1923. The first entry of the diary dates from May and describes the events of January.

73. When Sadie has to leave for the holidays, Louise writes: "I made her a little drawing of the Croisette at Cannes. I wrote these words at the bottom of the page: 'I am leaving my dear Sadie with a heavy heart.' I promised her I would write every week." Diary, July 9, 1923.

74. [*Bécassine* was a popular comic about a dim-witted but lovable Breton maid; *La Semaine de Suzette* was a weekly magazine for young women in which *Bécassine* originally appeared; it ran from 1905 to 1960.—Trans.]

75. Diary, January 1, 1923. These two colors would return in later texts: *Blue Days and Pink Days* would be the title of an exhibition at the Fondazione Prada, Milan, in 1997, as well as one of her "Pole" sculptures the same year.

76. Diary, February 1923.

77. Louise's expression, which Brigitte Cornand borrowed for the title of her film *La Rivière gentille: Portrait de Louise Bourgeois* (Paris: Les Films du Siamois and Centre Georges Pompidou, 2007).

78. The child, she later said, is entirely alone, it cannot count on ridiculous adults, it can only draw on its own "physical self and reasonable self." "It was a kind of ferocious desire towards independence, and this is present in all the work." "Two Conversations," 128.

79. Diary, December 14, 1923.

80. Diary, September 17, 1923.

81. A blue notebook, seventy pages long, mistakenly dated July 27, 1926; it should say "June," as the school year is still in session. The following citations, unless otherwise indicated, come from this diary.

82. Diary, July 1926, undated, 4–5.

83. Diary, July 1926, undated, 6, 9.

84. Diary, July 4, 1926.

85. Diary, July 1926, undated, 14.

86. Diary, July 3, 1926.

87. Diary, July 2, 1926.

88. Diary, July 8, 1926.

89. Diary, July 2, 1926.

90. Diary, July 8, 1926.

91. Diary, July 3, 1926.

92. Diary, April 20, 1974, in "Select Diary Notes, 1960–1979," in *Destruction,* 72. [Originally in English, except for the French expression *"manger du curé,"* which refers to priest-bashing, or knocking the clergy.—Trans.]

93. Diary, July 11, 1926.

94. "Rédaction," loose sheet, c. 1922–23 (LB-2101).

95. LB to Louis Bourgeois, April 24, 1946 (LB-1024).

96. Notebook, 1927 (LB-2032).

97. Notebook, 1927 (LB-2032). [Louise was probably referring to the Puy de Sancy, a famous inactive volcano near Mont-Dore. "*Puy*" means hole, or *trou*.—Trans.]

98. Bourgeois's personal photographs were seen at the Louise Bourgeois Archive/The Easton Foundation, New York.

99. In the slide show *Partial Recall* (1983) and the article "Child Abuse," *Artforum* 20, no. 4 (1982), reprinted in *Destruction*, 133.

100. See Xenakis, *Blind*, 60.

101. "Interview with Maxwell," reprinted in *Destruction*, 244–45.

102. "Memoir: Bourgeois and Beckert," 117–18.

103. *Album*, reprinted in *Destruction*, 283–84.

104. Loose sheet, October 28, 1958 (LB-0266). [Originally in English.—Trans.]

105. [The original French: *Votre lettre avec votre nouvelle* [sic] *projet m'a complètement renversée. Ce n'est pas une chose qu'on puisse décidé* [sic] *en place.* [. . .] *Vous m'aviez dit dans votre lettre que vous partiez en voyage ces jours-ci et que ce serait bien si je pouvez venir avec Madame pendant votre départ. Alors si cela vous aidera, je viendrai samedi prochain le 30 (pour 8 ou 15 jours) et pendant ce temps on parlera de l'avenir; Qu'en pensez vous?* [. . .] *Si c'est oui, j'arriverai samedi soir à six heures à Saint-Lazare.* [. . .] *Je suis votre toute dévouée Sadie.*] Sadie Gordon Richmond to Louis Bourgeois, January 28, 1926 (LL-0001). Contrary to Louise's claims that the young woman had lived with them for ten years (from 1922 to 1932), in the beginning Sadie came only for a few days during their stays on the Côte d'Azur, sometimes more often, but only a few months per year, and only until 1929.

106. Diary, July 1926, undated, 40.

107. Diary, c. July 18, 1926.

108. Diary, c. January 1927.

109. Diary, c. January 1927.

110. Diary, April 16, 1927.

111. Loose sheet, April 24, 1952 (LB-0128), in Larratt-Smith, *Louise Bourgeois*, 2:39. [Originally in English.—Trans.]

112. Diary, April 16, 1927.

113. Diary, April 16, 1927.

114. "Rédaction," loose sheet, c. 1926 (LB-2117): "The most beautiful day of the vacation, or of your life."

115. "Rédaction," loose sheet, February 8, 1927 (LB-2119).

116. Unless otherwise specified, all following citations are from the 1929 diary.

117. Diary, July 19, 1929.

118. Diary, July 21, 1929.

119. Diary, July 24, 1929.

120. Diary, July 27, 1929. [Originally in French except for "pictures" in English.—Trans.]

121. Diary, July 27, 1929.

122. A reference to her British friend Beryl Tattershall; Diary, July 25, 1929.

123. Diary, July 30, 1929. Or a bit earlier: "I have 2 letters from Maman what a treat I am going to read them 10 times." Diary, July 22, 1929.

124. Joséphine Bourgeois to LB, July 23, 1929 (JVB-0020).

125. Joséphine Bourgeois to LB, July 1929 (JVB-0006).

126. Joséphine Bourgeois to LB, July 1929 (JVB-0002).

127. Joséphine Bourgeois to LB, July 1929 (JVB-0006).

128. Joséphine Bourgeois to LB, July 1929 (JVB-0011).

129. Joséphine Bourgeois to LB, July 1929 (JVB-0012).

130. Joséphine Bourgeois to LB, July 1929 (JVB-0013).

131. Joséphine Bourgeois to LB, July 29, 1929 (JVB-0025).

132. Diary, July 11, 1926.

133. Biography, typewritten loose sheet, c. 1960 (LB-1759); "Autobiographical Notes," in *Destruction*, 67. [Originally in English.—Trans.]

134. "Autobiographical Notes," 68.

135. "Interview with Jeffrey Hogrefe," April 9, 1984, reprinted in Morris, *Bourgeois*, 114.

136. [Originally in English except for "*lycée*" (high school).—Trans.]

137. Diary, October 7, 1929.

138. Xenakis, *Blind*, 62.

139. "Rédaction," loose sheet, October 22, 1922 or 1923 (LB-2102).

140. "Rédaction," loose sheet, February 22, 1927 (LB-2120).

141. From April 23 to June 28, 1932; see her registration form for the Lycée Fénelon in Xenakis, *Blind*, 44.

142. Frenkel, a rabbi's daughter, who held a BA in science and was Louise's friend and tutor, encouraged her studies, helped her study for the *bac*, and wrote to her on the occasion of her wedding (LL-0036, November 18, 1938). In 1940, Louise urged her to come and live in New York, but Rahissa, who did not feel herself to be in danger, refused to leave. After she received a letter from Rahissa's sister, Louise did all she could to track down her friend, who had disappeared without a trace into a concentration camp. See also chapter 3 in this volume.

143. Joséphine Bourgeois to LB, July 19, 1932 (JVB-0003).

144. Diary, July 9, 1929. Louise misspelled Pierre Vergniaud's surname.

145. Diary, July 9, 1929.

146. Diary, July 9, 1929.

147. Diary, July 9, 1929.

148. Loose sheet, April 24, 1952 (LB-0128), in Larratt-Smith, *Louise Bourgeois*, 2:39. [Originally in English.—Trans.]

149. Loose sheet, June 21, 1994 (LB-0551).

150. "Rédaction," loose sheet with colored pencil drawing, c. 1926–27 (LB-2037).

151. Diary, March 6, 1928. [An old French song; title uncapitalized in the original French.—Trans.]

152. Diary, January 28, 1929, Villa Pompéiana, Cimiez.

153. Diary, March 4, 1929.

154. Diary, February 18, 1929.

155. Draft of LB to Cécile Chasse, January 26, 1929 (LB-2054).

156. Cécile Chasse to LB, January 29, 1929 (LL-0391).

157. Marcel Arland, *L'Ordre* (Paris: Gallimard, 1929).

158. Diary, January 6, 1929.

159. Draft of LB to Paulette, loose sheet in her 1928–29 diary.

160. Diary, June 13, 1929.

161. Diary, June 16, 1929.

162. *Rigollot:* mustard poultice created from flour made of de-oiled black mustard seeds, supplementary decongestant treatment for respiratory ailments, invented by Paul Jean Rigollot (1810–1873).

163. Dismissed, like the other doctors, as a paternalistic figure, and guilty as well; see Diary, September 3, 1994: "I have to manage to find a good father, a professor, a scholar, a genius, a doctor—d'Oelnitz, Médeville, Bardonnault, Baudraut, Richiez, Breton, [W]ahl, Cochet at 172, a school principal. Mister Chasse [. . .], the hatred of Matta, the intruder in Gradiva, the hatred of rivals + and the father's magic private hunting grounds, my mother's disease puts me in touch with doctors—."

164. Diary, June 23, 1929.

165. This diary is composed of two small notebooks. One has the three words on the cover and the initials TDV as a monogram; the other cover has the TDV monogram and is written almost exclusively in English.

166. Loose sheet, April 24, 1952 (LB-0128) in Larratt-Smith, *Louise Bourgeois,* 2:39. [Originally in English except for *"Travail devoir vertu"* (Labor Duty Virtue).—Trans.]

167. Diary, August 15, 1929.

168. Loose sheet, September 23, 1968, 4 (LB-0468), in Larratt-Smith, *Louise Bourgeois,* 2:166. [Originally in French except for the word "guilt," which is in English.—Trans.]

169. Diary, January 27, 1993.

170. Diary, Autumn 1928.

171. Diary, August 23, 1929.

172. Diary, August 13, 1929. [Originally in English.—Trans.]

173. Diary, August 30, 1929. [Originally in English.—Trans.]

174. Diary, September 19, 1929. [Originally in English.—Trans.]

175. Diary, March 8, 1929.

176. Diary, August 30, 1929. She would install her enormous spider, *Maman,* in the Tuileries Gardens in 2008. [Originally in English.—Trans.]

177. Diary, August 28, 1929. [Originally in English.—Trans.]

178. "[M]y sacrifice has not been recognized or appreciated, or rewarded or I am frustrated for lack of appreciation, you jipped [*sic*] me of a thank you, you are ungrateful. This is why my house is full of Thank you notes and I love you. I was fooled." Diary, July 20, 1980. [Originally in English.—Trans.]

179. Loose sheet, c. 1964 (LB-0378).

180. Loose sheet, October 28, 1958 (LB-0266), in Larratt-Smith, *Louise Bourgeois,* 2:85. [Originally in English.—Trans.]

181. Henriette Petit Fauriaux Bathelot to LB, January 12, 1939 (LL-0025).

182. Loose sheet, December 4, 1951 (LB-0458). [Originally in English.—Trans.]

183. Loose sheet, April 15, 1958 (LB-0649), in Larratt-Smith, *Louise Bourgeois,* 2:77.

184. Diary, August 23, 1929. [Originally in English.—Trans.]

185. Diary, September 14, 1929. [Originally in English.—Trans.]

186. Loose sheet, January 2, 1961 (LB-0043).

187. "Coffin," loose sheet, September 23, 1968 (LB-0468), in Larratt-Smith, *Louise Bourgeois*, 2:166.

188. Paul Gardner, *Louise Bourgeois* (New York: Universe, 1994), 43.

189. Loose sheet, September 17, 1959 (LB-0124), in Larratt-Smith, *Louise Bourgeois*, 2:107.

190. Diary, June 26, 1929.

191. Diary, July 2, 1929.

192. Diary, July 3, 1929.

193. Diary, July 5, 1929.

194. Diary, July 8, 1929.

195. Diary, August 14, 1929 [Originally in English.—Trans.]; "I set myself on the path that leads of the swings and draw the house in the back of the statue." Diary, August 12, 1929.

196. Diary, July 13, 1929.

197. Diary, September 25, 1929. [Originally in English.—Trans.]

198. Diary, August 30, 1929. [Originally in English. This is a direct translation of *"crispé,"* to be tense, to be on edge—she means that playing the piano calms her down when she's tense.—Trans.]

199. The epigraph that opens this section: "It was a completely luxurious life, you know." *Album*, reprinted in *Destruction*, 282.

200. Diary, April 20, 1974, in "Select Diary Notes, 1960–1979," in *Destruction*, 72. [Originally in English.—Trans.]

201. *Album*, reprinted in *Destruction*, 283.

202. Julia Kristeva, "The Runaway Girl," in Morris, *Bourgeois*, 246.

203. "Interview with Maxwell," reprinted in *Destruction*, 242.

204. Loose sheet, c. 1968 (LB-0635).

205. *Album*, reprinted in *Destruction*, 282.

206. "Child Abuse," reprinted in *Destruction*, 134.

207. *Album*, reprinted in *Destruction*, 280.

208. "Two Conversations," 129.

209. Loose sheet, c. 1961 (LB-0020), in Morris, *Bourgeois*, 157.

210. Diary, February 22, 1949, in "Select Diary Notes, 1949–1954," in *Destruction*, 56. [Originally in English.—Trans.]

211. "Interview with Maxwell," reprinted in *Destruction*, 240.

212. Diary, comment added in 1997 to entry of July 24, 1973, in "Select Diary Notes, 1969–1979," in *Destruction*, 71. [Originally in English.—Trans.]

213. "A Merging of Male and Female," *New York*, February 11, 1974, reprinted in *Destruction*, 101.

Chapter 2. Becoming an Artist

Epigraph: "Statements, 1979," in Eleanor Munro, *Originals: American Women Artists* (New York: Simon and Schuster, 1979), reprinted in Louise Bourgeois, *Destruction of the Father / Reconstruction of the Father: Writings and Interviews, 1923–1997*, ed. Marie-Laure Bernadac and Hans Ulrich Obrist (Cambridge, MA: MIT Press, and London: Violette, 1998) [hereafter cited as *Destruction*], 113.

1. She was a surgeon's widow. The name Madame Luer appears on the cover of a 1928 diary Louise kept during her stay at Cimiez at the Villa Pompéiana and appears eight times in all in this diary. "Madame Luer arrives, she is charming." Diary, February 26, 1928.

2. A slang expression meaning "spendthrift." Both mother and daughter were very careful with their money.

3. Joséphine Bourgeois to Louise Bourgeois [hereafter LB], July 16, 1932 (JVB-0014).

4. Joséphine Bourgeois to LB, July 19, 1932 (JVB-0003).

5. Joséphine Bourgeois to LB, July 18, 1932 (JVB-0004).

6. She had just passed her *bac* (on July 6, 1932), and this trip was a present from her father.

7. Pierre Bourgeois to LB, Antony, July 26, 1932 (PB-0007).

8. Paul Colin (1892–1985), painter, designer, and poster artist, became famous in 1925 thanks to his poster for Josephine Baker's *Revue nègre*.

9. LB to Louis Bourgeois (LB-1034), in Robert Storr, *Louise Bourgeois: Intimate Geometries* (New York: Monacelli, 2016), 70.

10. Right-wing political weekly newspaper founded in 1928 by Horace de Carbuccia, with the help of Georges Suarez and Joseph Kessel. Initially a pamphleteering publication whose favorite target was Marxism, it became more and more influenced by Action française until it became an apologist for fascism. Romain Gary published two short stories in *Gringoire*, but like Kessel, he left when it became anti-Semitic in 1935.

11. Diary, 1933–1938, September 3, 1934 (LB-1777).

12. Diary, 1933–1938, September 3, 1934 (LB-1777).

13. Diary, 1933–1938, September 3, 1934 (LB-1777). [Strikethrough in the original. —Trans.]

14. [Bourgeois had originally written "depth," but she crossed it out and wrote "longevity" instead.—Trans.]

15. Diary, 1933–1938 (LB-1282).

16. [The word "dangerous" is double-underlined in the original. Thank you to Sewon Kang for confirming.—Trans.]

17. Diary, 1933–1938 (LB-1282).

18. Diary, 1933–1938 (LB-1282).

19. She even copied a page of the novel *Silbermann* into her diary, on Jewish marriage rites and the hero's departure to America—a prophetic act!

20. Henri Béraud was a famous journalist, and a friend, for instance, of Joseph Kessel's. He received the Prix Goncourt in 1922 for his book *Le martyre de l'obèse* and then traveled to Russia in 1925. He subsequently wrote an article that was very critical of the communist regime.

21. Diary, 1933–1938 (LB-1284).

22. Le Bal Bullier was a large room decorated in the North African style, located at 37, avenue Georges-Bernanos (today 31, avenue de l'Observatoire), near the Luxembourg Gardens, in the 5th arrondissement of Paris.

23. Diary, 1933–1938 (LB-1284).

24. [A riot on this day led by the extreme right at the place de la Concorde in front of the Assemblée nationale resulted in the deaths of fifteen people, shot by police. The events led to the resignation of the prime minister as well as the creation of several antifascist groups.—Trans.]

25. "Little red church" refers to left-wing Catholicism; loose sheet, c. 1964 (LB-0372).

26. Diary of September 25, 1933, to April 26, 1938 (LB-1281 to LB-1297), written on loose sheets of graph paper with a table of contents: "I. Drawing—painting—posters. sketches, illustration; II. Articles—journalism—memoirs; III. Project for house; IV. Rules to live by—advice" (LB-1291). These various subjects summarize Louise's interests during the 1930s, between her drawing classes, politics, running Antony as a real estate investment, and concerns about her life, and her future as an artist.

27. Diary, 1933–1938 (LB-1281). [The word "need" is underlined in the original.—Trans.]

28. *Massier* or *massière*: in an art studio, this is a student who is put in charge of collecting everyone's contributions, watching over the communal expenses, and assisting the instructor.

29. He lived in rue du Ranelagh, in the 16th arrondissement of Paris.

30. "Interview with Hans Ulrich Obrist," January 1995, in *Destruction*, 292.

31. J. Meunier to LB, January 9, 1934 (LL-0016). Her mother wrote to Louise from Nice in January 1934.

32. Agenda, August 15–16, 1953. [Originally in English.—Trans.]

33. Roger Conrad, noted several times in the 1937 diary and cited in a list of architects.

34. Loose sheet, December 2, 1951 (LB-0451). [Originally in English.—Trans.]

35. Louise's address in 1937–38.

36. Jean Pelletier to LB, Gibraltar, March 24, 1942 (LL-0052). [The Académie de la Grande Chaumière is a famous art school in the rue de la Grande Chaumière in Montparnasse; the rue Vavin is around the corner; rue Mazarine is near the Beaux-Arts in Saint-Germain; the Sainte-Geneviève library, popular with Sorbonne students, is in the Quartier Latin, as is "Boul'Mich," an old abbreviation for the boulevard Saint-Michel.—Trans.]

37. Jean Pelletier to LB, March 13, 1940 (LL-0139).

38. Born in Oran in 1898, died in Paris in July 1974, he was a doctor and then worked in the media from 1936, serving as editor of the newspaper *Combat*. Louise, who was in Paris in 1974, wrote his name and the date of his suicide in her diary on July 16, 1974.

39. M. Landeman senior to LB, January 24, 1935 (LL-0018).

40. Loose sheet, March 5, 1952 (LB-0461). [Originally in English.—Trans.]

41. After a sinus operation, Dr. Richiez sent her to Luchon, in the Pyrénées, to recuperate. She was alone there and felt abandoned. See loose sheet, 1967 (LB-0075).

42. "I swallow the pills when she is there [. . .] her presence [Henriette] is intolerable." Loose sheet, 1967 (LB-0075).

43. Diary, September 29, 1991.

44. See diary from 1934.

45. "I happen to travel alone to Quiberon later where my father also will abandon me I will react by glomming on to Landeman." Loose sheet, 1967 (LB-0075).

46. "At Lison's engagement party"; Pierre Bourgeois to Louis Bourgeois, Strasbourg, February 6, 1935 (PB-0062). Louise later wrote on the envelope, "Engagement party? Winter 34?"

47. Pierre Bourgeois to Louis Bourgeois, December 8, 1934 (PB-0061).

48. Pierre Bourgeois to Louis Bourgeois, Strasbourg, c. January 1935 (PB-0063).

49. See also "Landeman engagement visit"; loose sheet, January 23, 1951 (LB-0465).

50. See letter from Georges Landeman's father, thanking them for the lovely party, January 24, 1935 (LL-0018).

51. Roger Besnier to LB, Hôtel de France, Rouïba, Algeria, November 23, 1936 (LL-0150).

52. Roger Besnier to LB, December 15, 1936 (LL-0151).

53. N. Besnier (Roger Besnier's father) to LB, December 1, 1936 (LL-0148), and January 10, 1937, in Marseille (LL-0149).

54. LB to Roger Besnier, December 22, 1936 (LB-1743).

55. Roger Besnier to LB, Hôtel de la Victoire, Palestro, Algiers, November 23, 1939 (LL-0157): "I've just seen [a reel called] *Jeunes filles de Paris*, it reminded me of another film, *Mains de Paris*, where you can catch a furtive glimpse of Paul Colin's pupils." Roger Besnier to LB, c. November 1939 (LL-0053): "*Les Mains de Paris*, which features in particular Paul Colin and his school, you were present that day, which made me very happy."

56. Roger Besnier to LB, c. 1937 (LL-0152): "Algiers is a town like no other."

57. Roger Besnier to LB, Affreville, Algeria, January 28, 1937 (LL-0153).

58. Roger Besnier to LB, November 19 (LL-0154) and 23, 1939 (LL-0156). [The word "plums" possibly refers to bombs.—Trans.]

59. "I give that reassurance myself to a lot of people (Roger Besnier, Farr, Brooks, Pierre, Alfred). But I do not have assurance myself. I doubt my damn self all the time." Loose sheet, February 8, 1952 (LB-0450). [Originally in English.—Trans.]

60. LB to Louis Bourgeois, March 8, 1938 (LB-1002).

61. A friend from the Lycée Fénelon.

62. Diary, 1933–1938, April 26, 1938 (LB-1295).

63. Diary, 1933–1938, April 26, 1938 (LB-1295).

64. Jacques Bauml to LB, September 30, 1938 (LL-0140).

65. Jacques Bauml to LB, August 12, 1949 (LL-0042).

66. Father figures: "Richiez (the doctor who operated on me)"; see "Interview with Jerry Gorovoy," October 8, 1990, in Frances Morris, ed., *Louise Bourgeois*, exh. cat. (London: Tate, 2007), 127.

67. Yvonne Bocé, wife of Gaston Bocé, neighbor and concierge at Antony.

68. Diary, 1933–1938, September 29, 1933 (LB-1281).

69. "I use my mother to get to Oelnitz" (another of her mother's doctors). Diary, March 18, 1985.

70. Diary, January 27, 1993.

71. Diary, 1933–1938, December 25, 1937 (LB-1294).

72. Diary, 1933–1938, c. April 1938 (LB-1295).

73. Diary, 1933–1938, September 10, 1934 (LB-1281).

74. Diary, 1933–1938, table of contents (LB-1291).

75. Diary, 1933–1938, December 25, 1937 (LB-1294).

76. Diary, 1933–1938, December 25, 1935, "For my 24th birthday" (LB-1293).

77. Diary, 1933–1938, December 25, 1937 (LB-1294).

78. Diary, 1933–1938, December 25, 1935, "For my 24th birthday" (LB-1293).

79. Henri Torre to LB, January 6, 1937 (LL-0030).

80. Henri Torre to LB, December 26, 1936 (LL-0029).

81. Diary, March 19, 1937.

82. Diary, 1933–1938, January 1, 1938 (LB-1294).

83. Diary, June 5, 1966.

84. See also Yves Brayer to LB, January 5, 1940 (LL-0223). He told her that her work was still being shown at the Galerie Dufrêne.

85. Diary, 1933–1938, September 23, 1934 (LB-1281).

86. Loose sheet, November 1951 (LB-0466).

87. Diary, January 14, 1994.

88. Louis Bourgeois to LB, c. 1933 (LIB-0001).

89. Louis Bourgeois to LB, c. 1933 (LIB-0003). Louis was in Switzerland at this time. It seems they may have gone there together—"The trip that we took seems [. . .] very nice" (LIB-0009)—and that he stayed on after she left. He was lonely, went fishing to distract himself, and asked about her stay in Zurich.

90. Louis Bourgeois to LB, January 1936 (LIB-0038).

91. Diary, 1933–1938, January 1, 1938 (LB-1294).

92. Diary, 1933–1938, January 1, 1938 (LB-1294).

93. Diary, 1933–1938, January 1, 1938 (LB-1294).

94. See "Letters to Colette Richarme, 1937–1940," Paris, March 7, 1938, in *Destruction*, 29: "The Swiss writes to me weekly to announce his return but every week, tearfully, he postpones it."

95. Report, January 3, 1938 (LL-0183), stamped "Private police, investigation and research bureau."

96. "He's a simple, well-behaved young man, currently without occupation." Report, January 3, 1938 (LL-0183).

97. See "Interview with Hans Ulrich Obrist," January 1995, in *Destruction*, 289: "There was a peripheral person around me who was an albino. [Her] name was Yvonne. [. . .] She was extremely healthy and vivacious. She seduced my brother, she was attracted to him."

98. Pierre Bourgeois to Louis Bourgeois, June 22, 1934 (PB-0053).

99. "Interview with Douglas Maxwell," *Modern Painters* 6, no. 2 (1993), reprinted in *Destruction*, 242.

100. Munro, *Originals*, reprinted in *Destruction*, 113–14.

101. "Interview with Jerry Gorovoy and Marie-Laure Bernadac," February 1996, in *Destruction*, 349.

102. "Interview with Maxwell," reprinted in *Destruction*, 243.

103. H. Julliard to the director of French museums, June 7, 1937. Her grades were: Sculpture: 6; Egypt: 12; Painting: 11; Greek and Roman Antiques: 9; objets d'art: 14; Oriental Antiques: 8. Final grade: "60 sur 100." Archives nationales. [French students are graded in each subject on a scale of 1 to 20, with 10 being a passing grade and 20 practically unattainable.—Trans.]

104. "Interview with Maxwell," reprinted in *Destruction*, 243.

105. Villemot's recollections, cited in Alain Weill and Jack Rennert, *Paul Colin* (Paris: Denoël, 1989), 136. Louise had this book in her library; on this page she had underlined the name of one of Colin's former students, Sherman (Russian).

106. Edgar Derouet's recollections, cited in Weill and Rennert, *Colin*, 138.

107. Diary, 1933–1938, September 1934 (LB-1283).

108. Jack Rennert, *100 Posters of Paul Colin* (New York: Images Graphiques, 1977), 3.

109. Diary, 1933–1938, May 18, 1936 (LB-1296).

110. "Interview with Maxwell," reprinted in *Destruction*, 243.

111. See exhibition announcement for *Exposition de l'atelier de la "Grande Chaumiere,"* Galerie de Paris, June 23–30, 1936 (LBE-0036).

112. Yves Brayer, c. 1937: "Maître, permit me to send you one of my students, Mademoiselle Bourgeois, who has studied at la Grande Chaumière; she is very gifted, works very hard, and has an observant mind which strikes me as very promising. I would be very happy, Maître, if you would accept her into your workshop, and I believe you will be glad to have done so." Brayer, letter of recommendation for Louise Bourgeois, c. 1937 (LL-0222).

113. Diary, September 1937, monthly expenses page.

114. See J. M. Granier to LB, July 20 (LL-0218) and August 17, 1937 (LL-0219). "Your way of teaching is marvelous."

115. "Letters to Richarme," Paris, March 7, 1938, in *Destruction*, 26.

116. Robert Rey (1888–1964), art historian, instructor at the École du Louvre.

117. "Letters to Richarme," Paris, January 14, 1938, in *Destruction*, 25.

118. "Letters to Richarme," Paris, January 14, 1938, in *Destruction*, 26. She is referring to a book by André Lhote, *La peinture, le cœur et l'esprit* (Paris: Denoël, 1933) (BIB-2256).

119. "Letters to Richarme," Paris, January 14, 1938, in *Destruction*, 27.

120. "Letters to Richarme," Paris, January 14, 1938, in *Destruction*, 28.

121. "Letters to Richarme" [Paris, March 12, 1938], Paris, January 14, 1939, in *Destruction*, 25.

122. Diary, 1933–1938, December 25, 1935, "For my 24th birthday" (LB-1293).

123. Diary, 1933–1938, September 14, 1937 (LB-1294).

124. Diary, 1933–1938, September 14, 1937 (LB-1294).

125. "Statements from Conversations with Robert Storr," 1980–1990, in *Destruction*, 217.

126. Exhibition announcement for *Le Groupe 1938–1939 de l'Académie Ranson*, Paris, July 7–20, 1939 (LBE-0016): the other artists included Bissière, Le Moal, Pagava, Levine, and Stahly.

127. "Letters to Richarme," New York, June 11, 1939, in *Destruction*, 34.

128. Diary, 1933–1938 (LB-1294).

129. Diary, 1933–1938 (LB-1294). "By age 27 he loves Kant, Shakespeare, he says one has to learn to read as one learns to see or to live."

130. Diary, 1933–1938, January 1, 1938 (LB-1294).

131. Diary, 1933–1938, January 1, 1938 (LB-1294).

132. Today it is the site of the bookshop L'Écume des Pages. The facade hasn't changed very much.

133. "Letters to Richarme," Paris, September 1938, in *Destruction*, 29.

134. See "Letters to Richarme," Paris, October 8, 1938, in *Destruction*, 31: "in the past few months I have seen work by painters like Picasso, Derain, Lautrec, Modigliani, La Fresnaye, Pascin, Dufresne: all the twentieth century school and the one that preceded it."

135. LB to Louis Bourgeois, August 28, 1938 (LB-2051).

136. "Letters to Richarme," Paris, October 8, 1938, in *Destruction*, 31.

137. Robert Goldwater [hereafter RG] to LB, October 2, 1938 (RG-0003): "[Jane] left Paris [. . .] August 24 at noon, therefore three hours before I got to know you." In her 1938 diary, Louise wrote on August 24: "Robert climbs up on the desk. Borrows Berthe Weill book [*Pan dans l'œil*]."

138. Louise kept the receipt from Mourlot for this Picasso (LL-0301). Robert had the print framed and hung it in their new home.

139. Robert Goldwater, *Primitivism in Modern Painting* (New York: Harper and Brothers, 1938), expanded and reissued in 1966 as *Primitivism in Modern Art*.

140. On his first visit, Robert was accompanied by Adeline Tintner, who became a noted Henry James scholar.

141. The client was Alfred Barr, curator at the Museum of Modern Art, who was in Paris during this time and visited the gallery on July 8, 1938. Alfred H. Barr, Jr. Papers, MoMA.

142. LB to Louis Bourgeois, August 28,1938 (LB-2051).

143. "Letters to Richarme," Paris, September 1938, in *Destruction*, 30.

144. "I feel close to [art deco] because I saw the exhibition of decorative arts in Paris in 1925. I was very young at the time and it had a profound effect on me." Art deco did indeed have a pejorative connotation, but for Louise, "those works were handcrafted and very beautifully made. Later I was taught by these artists." See Henry Geldzahler, *Making It New: Essays, Interviews, and Talks* (San Diego, CA: Harcourt Brace, 1996), 285.

145. Loose sheet, c. 1998 (LB-2154).

146. Poet, novelist, Franco-American painter (1891–1968). In 1922, he married the heiress and art collector Peggy Guggenheim and then, in 1932, the writer Kay Boyle. Vail was nicknamed the "king of bohemia" in 1920s Paris.

147. LB to RG, September 23, 1938 (LB-1714).

148. Lydie Adolphe to LB, October 23, 1938 (LL-0032).

149. LB to RG, September 23, 1938 (LB-1714).

150. LB to RG, September 23, 1938 (LB-1714).

151. "Letters to Richarme," Paris, October 8, 1938, in *Destruction*, 31.

152. "Since you left, he [Louis Bourgeois] has been very much on edge. [...] He is bothered to see us go and doesn't dare do anything to keep me. [...] He likes you a lot and above all treats you like a man, something that he has never done with my brother-in-law [Georges Bonnotte] who trembles in his presence although he is fifteen years older than you." LB to RG, September 24, 1938 (LB-1715).

153. Louis Bourgeois to LB, c. 1938 (LIB-0008).

154. "Interview with Robert Storr," 1990, in Morris, *Bourgeois*, 149.

155. LB to RG, September 24, 1938 (LB-1715).

156. RG to Louis Bourgeois, October 1938 (RG-0248).

157. LB to RG, September 22, 1938 (LB-1713).

158. LB to RG, September 24, 1938 (LB-1715).

159. "There is much I can do from here through my father's contacts." RG to LB, September 28, 1938 (RG-0002).

160. RG to LB, aboard the *Aurania*, September 21, 1938 (RG-0001).

161. "Interview with Kay Larson," February 1, 1982, in Morris, *Bourgeois*, 149.

162. "After leaving you on your boat Henriette and I returned to Le Havre, very sad [...] and we wandered through the city like two afflicted souls." Louis Bourgeois to LB, October 10, 1938 (LIB-0025).

163. LB to Louis Bourgeois, October 4, 1938 (LB-1019).

164. LB to RG, September 30, 1938 (LB-1718).

165. LB to RG, September 23, 1938 (LB-1714).

166. "Your telegrams worried me. You see things much too darkly. If even by taking the worst scenario Hitler were to start a war, all the French people would not die at the same time." LB to RG, September 28, 1938 (LB-1716).

167. "Letters to Richarme," Paris, October 8, 1938, in *Destruction*, 32.

168. LB to RG, September 24, 1938 (LB-1715).

169. LB to RG, September 23, 1938 (LB-1714).

Chapter 3. The Runaway Girl

Epigraph: "Interview with Xavier Tricot," November 25, 1996, reprinted in Louise Bourgeois, *Destruction du père / Reconstruction du père: Écrits et entretiens, 1923–2000*, expanded French ed., ed. Marie-Laure Bernadac and Hans Ulrich Obrist (Paris: Daniel Lelong, 2000) [hereafter cited as *Destruction* (French ed.)], 379.

1. *Sans-filiste:* operator of wireless telegraphy (TSF).

2. Louise Bourgeois [hereafter LB] to Louis Bourgeois, October 4, 1938 (LB-1019).

3. LB to Louis Bourgeois, October 4, 1938 (LB-1019). [In French she writes "*livres aussi verts les uns que les autres,*" with "*verts*" meaning "crude," "daring."—Trans.]

4. LB to Robert Goldwater [hereafter RG], September 30, 1938 (LB-1718).

5. LB to RG, September 29, 1938 (LB-1717).

6. Andrew Ritchie was Robert Goldwater's colleague.

7. Jane Ritchie to RG, telegram, October 12, 1938 (LL-0173).

8. Called *Runaway Child* at her first solo exhibition at Bertha Schaefer Gallery in 1945.

9. Is this a reference to her suicide attempt?

10. She did this after her wedding, right before her departure.

11. She went so far as to plant hedges in the garden at Easton, which grew nicely, she told her father; they were her son Alain's domain, and he watered them regularly. LB to Louis Bourgeois, August 10, 1949 (LB-1046).

12. Louise recommended her father buy a copy of the *New York Herald Tribune* at the Deux Magots: "On the next to last page you'll find [a column called] 'Shipping and mail' the list of departing boats. If you send the letter at the station up until 5 minutes before [it] leaves, that would speed it up enormously." LB to Louis Bourgeois, December 14, 1938 (LB-2052).

13. He was also the director of Mount Sinai Hospital.

14. Louise referred to her father-in-law in English, as Father. LB to Louis Bourgeois, November 11, 1938 (LB-1007).

15. Another press clipping: "Goldwater's Son Marries in Paris," October 1938 (LBE-0063). "The marriage of Robert J. Goldwater, son of Dr. S. S. Goldwater, Commissioner of Hospitals, to Miss Louise Bourgeois, of Paris, on September 12th, was announced today by Dr. and Mrs. Goldwater."

16. LB to Louis Bourgeois, November 11, 1938 (LB-1007).

17. LB to Louis Bourgeois, October–November 1938 (LB-1010).

18. Louis Bourgeois to LB, February 3, 1939 (LIB-0015).

19. LB to Louis Bourgeois, October–November 1938 (LB-1010).

20. LB to Louis Bourgeois, November 28, 1938 (LB-1008).

21. LB to Louis Bourgeois, January 17, 1939 (LB-2053).

22. LB to Louis Bourgeois, April 17, 1939 (LB-1015).

23. LB to Louis Bourgeois, October 28, 1938 (LB-1006).

24. LB to Louis Bourgeois, October–November 1938 (LB-1010).

25. Louise was name-dropping a bit; Picasso never did visit America.

26. "Letters to Colette Richarme, 1937–1940," October 8, 1938, in Louise Bourgeois, *Destruction of the Father / Reconstruction of the Father: Writings and Interviews, 1923–1997*, ed. Marie-Laure Bernadac and Hans Ulrich Obrist (Cambridge, MA: MIT Press, and London: Violette, 1998) [hereafter cited as *Destruction*], 32. This indicates how "behind" the two young women were in their knowledge of the avant-garde.

27. "Letters to Colette Richarme, 1937–1940," October 8, 1938, in *Destruction* (French ed.), 32.

28. LB to Louis Bourgeois, January 17, 1939 (LB-2053).

29. "Interview with Robert Storr," c. 1990, in Frances Morris, ed., *Louise Bourgeois*, exh. cat. (London: Tate, 2007), 149.

30. LB to Louis Bourgeois, December 27, 1938 (LB-1009).

31. LB to Louis Bourgeois, December 27, 1938 (LB-1009).

32. LB to Louis Bourgeois, December 27, 1938 (LB-1009).

33. Louise Bourgeois, *The Puritan* (New York: Osiris, 1990). The text was written in 1947 and accompanied by eight abstract engravings in the illustrated edition of 1990.

34. LB to Louis Bourgeois, October 20, 1938 (LB-1005).

35. LB to Louis Bourgeois, November 11, 1938 (LB-1007).

36. LB to Louis Bourgeois, November 11, 1938 (LB-1007).

37. LB to Louis Bourgeois, October–November 1938 (LB-1010).

38. LB to Louis Bourgeois, December 14, 1938 (LB-2052).

39. LB to Louis Bourgeois, December 27, 1938 (LB-1009).

40. LB to Louis Bourgeois, October–November 1938 (LB-1010).

41. Robert wrote to Louis to tell him that Louise was very attached to Antony, for sentimental and financial reasons, and that she cried when she stopped receiving rent payments. RG to Louis Bourgeois, October 28, 1938 (RG-0007).

42. Robert Goldwater, *Primitivism in Modern Painting* (New York: Harper and Brothers, 1938).

43. LB to Louis Bourgeois, October–November 1938 (LB-1010).

44. Louis Carré (1897–1977), a friend of Le Corbusier, antiques and art dealer who specialized in "primitive" art, was an associate of Charles Ratton and organized sales of André Breton and Paul Éluard in 1931. In 1936, he was in New York; the following year he opened a gallery in Paris where he showed Paul Klee, Juan Gris, Le Corbusier, and Picasso. He ran a gallery in New York from 1948 to 1952.

45. LB to Louis Bourgeois, March 31, 1939 (LB-1014).

46. LB to Louis Bourgeois, November 11, 1938 (LB-1007).

47. LB to Louis Bourgeois, November 11, 1938 (LB-1007).

48. Deborah Wye, ed., *Louise Bourgeois: The Complete Prints and Books*, catalogue raisonné (New York: Museum of Modern Art, 2018), cat. no. 1020: *St. Germain* (1938), https://www.moma.org/s/lb/collection_lb/object/object_objid-64784.html. She included the Statue of Liberty as well as the belltower of Saint-Germain-des-Prés, a sign reading *"Les Deux Magots,"* a boat, and a telegraph.

49. LB to Louis Bourgeois, December 27, 1938 (LB-1009).

50. LB to Louis Bourgeois, June 7, 1939 (LB-1018).

51. LB to Louis Bourgeois, March 31, 1939 (LB-1014).

52. LB to Louis Bourgeois, February 6, 1939 (LB-1012).

53. LB to Louis Bourgeois, November 11, 1938 (LB-1007).

54. LB to Louis Bourgeois, November 11, 1938 (LB-1007).

55. Janet married Cuthbert Daniel, with whom she had a son, Francis (who died by suicide). Louise and Robert saw them often. Mary was an actress, lived in Washington, DC, and did not marry. She frequently helped to look after Louise and Robert's adopted son, Michel.

56. LB to Louis Bourgeois, December 27, 1938 (LB-1009). Referring to the 1936 trip, as indicated by a ticket to the British Museum.

57. "I am very sorry Louise had to leave so suddenly, but as you know better than I, because you are there, war seems 90% likely and I believed I was doing the right thing asking her to leave quickly." RG to Louis Bourgeois, October 1938 (RG-0248).

58. LB to Louis Bourgeois, November 28, 1938 (LB-1008).

59. LB to Louis Bourgeois, November 28, 1938 (LB-1008). She wanted to have many children: "Robert who is right by my side tells me to announce that the woman who was at our wedding who was next to you just had her 6th child— He makes fun of me because I admire her a lot." LB to Louis Bourgeois, April 17, 1939 (LB-1015).

60. In her diaries every month she wrote "*Maman garanti*" to indicate the first day of her period.

61. "It is the case of the hysterical woman who cannot procreate because she *is* hysterical." [Emphasis in the original.—Trans.] "Two Conversations with Deborah Wye," 1979 and 1981, in *Destruction*, 125.

62. Jacques de Lacretelle (1888–1985). A novel published in 1922, which won the Prix Femina. In June 1935 (LB-1293), she copied out an excerpt regarding traditional Jewish marriages: "Which nationality will my children be, I do not care [. . .] if they have a soul as tormented as mine, if they suffer as much as I suffered, it does not matter! They will be able to defend themselves they will know how to overcome their hardships."

63. LB to Louis Bourgeois, June 7, 1939 (LB-1018).

64. On Duchamp and Ozenfant, see chapter 5 in this volume.

65. Louis Bourgeois to LB, November 29, 1938 (LIB-0012).

66. "Letters to Richarme," June 11, 1939, in *Destruction*, 34.

67. "Letters to Richarme," June 11, 1939, in *Destruction*, 33.

68. "Letters to Richarme," February 4, 1939, in *Destruction*, 32.

69. LB to Louis Bourgeois, June 7, 1939 (LB 1018).

70. LB to Louis Bourgeois, April 17, 1939 (LB-1015).

71. LB to Louis Bourgeois, April 30, 1939 (LB-1016).

72. LB to Louis Bourgeois, April 17, 1939 (LB-1015).

73. LB to Louis Bourgeois, June 7, 1939 (LB-1018).

74. LB to Louis Bourgeois, April 17, 1939 (LB-1015).

75. LB to Louis Bourgeois, March 31, 1939 (LB-1014).

76. LB to Louis Bourgeois, April 30, 1939 (LB-1016).

77. LB to Louis Bourgeois, April 30, 1939 (LB-1016).

78. LB to Louis Bourgeois, March 10, 1939 (LB-1033).

79. LB to Louis Bourgeois, June 7, 1939 (LB-1018).

80. "Letters to Richarme," June 11, 1939, in *Destruction*, 34.

81. While in Paris she would show some work with Jacques Despierre, Francis Grüber, and André Marchand, as well as at the Galerie Jean Dufresne with other students from the Académie Ranson (July 7–20, 1939 [see exhibition announcement LBE-0016], with Bissière, Le Moal, Pagava, Stahly, and others). "Letters to Richarme," August 6, 1939, in *Destruction* (French ed.), 35.

82. "Letters to Richarme," August 6, 1939, in *Destruction* (French ed.), 36.

83. "Letters to Richarme," August 6, 1939, in *Destruction* (French ed.), 35.

84. "Letters to Richarme," August 6, 1939, in *Destruction* (French ed.), 35.

85. "Letters to Richarme," August 6, 1939, in *Destruction* (French ed.), 36.

86. They went to Le Havre on September 2, then returned to Paris on September 10, staying at the Hôtel Saint-Paul ("full of bedbugs," she wrote in her 1939 diary), then the Hôtel Navigateur. Finally, having received word from Assistance publique, they went to Bordeaux on September 13.

87. Louis Bourgeois to LB, Évian, August 1939 (LIB-0029).

88. "Letters to Richarme," Paris, August 31, 1939, in *Destruction* (French ed.), 37.

89. An orphanage in Margaux. Louise went between September 10 and 13.

90. "Letters to Richarme," January 19, 1940, in *Destruction* (French ed.), 40.

91. "Letters to Richarme," New York, October 3, 1939, in *Destruction* (French ed.), 38.

92. "Letters to Richarme," New York, January 19, 1940, in *Destruction* (French ed.), 40.

93. "We are sending a letter to Bordeaux about Michel we accept to have him come [by] plane." Diary, January 29, 1940.

94. Mrs. Edna McCoy, who was a steward on the boat.

95. "1. sent letter to Assistance Publique Bordeaux, 2. sent all the paperwork to the American consulate in Bordeaux, 3. letter to Marseille company." Diary, February 26, 1940.

96. Headlines from an article in the *New York Times* on May 22, 1940 (LBE-0115) and an unidentified newspaper, May 1940 (LBE-0117).

97. Diary, May 21, 1940.

98. "Letters to Richarme," New York, August 8, 1940, in *Destruction* (French ed.), 41.

99. Diary, September 23, 1940.

100. Diary, July 1, 1940.

101. She would go on to apply to New York University with the hopes of acquiring "the necessary theoretical and experimental foundations so that I will be able to find a useful position in the field of diagnostic testing and remedial care of children." Application draft, loose sheet, c. 1960 (LB-0828), in "Autobiographical Notes," in *Destruction*, 69. She was accepted in 1961, but her studies there were short-lived.

102. Diary, May 25, 1940.

103. Before Alain's birth she referred to him as "la Nicolette."

104. Diary, May 26, 1940.

105. Diary, May 26, 1940.

106. "For two hours he cries *'laisse la porte ouvrir'* [sic] [leave the door open]." Diary, June 2, 1940.

107. Diary, July 11, 1940.

108. In pregnancy, if the cervix begins to shorten or weaken, a cerclage band will be sewn

into and around the cervix to avoid preterm birth. The "ring" she refers to here is this cerclage band. Diary, February 26, 1940.

109. "The most important event in my life was the birth of Jean-Louis. He was born on the 4th of July. He was born early; he was supposed to be born on the 14th of July." "Conversation with Paulo Herkenhoff," in *Louise Bourgeois* (Paris: Phaidon, 2003), 9.

110. Diary, July 4, 1940.

111. Diary, July 7, 1940.

112. Diary, July 11, 1940.

113. "Letters to Richarme," New York, August 8, 1940, in *Destruction* (French ed.), 42.

114. Louis Bourgeois to LB, April 23, 1940 (LIB-0044).

115. Saint Pierre and Miquelon, a French archipelago in the North Atlantic, south of Newfoundland.

116. Louis Bourgeois to LB, February 2, 1940 (LIB-0042).

117. Diary, July 17, 1940.

118. Diary, April 4, 1941.

119. Nickname Louise gave Alain before he was born (when they thought he might be a girl), conjugated in the feminine, as for Michel. Diary, May 11, 1941.

120. Diary, August 8, 1941.

121. Title of a work from 2003.

122. Diary, November 13, 1941.

123. "Letters to Richarme," New York, January 19, 1940, in *Destruction* (French ed.), 37–38.

124. *Cahiers d'art*, no. 7–10 (1935).

125. Small notebook, March 6, 1939 (LB-0381), in "Select Diary Notes, 1939–1944," in *Destruction*, 40. [Underlined in the original.—Trans.]

126. "Letters to Richarme," New York, January 19, 1940, in *Destruction*, 38.

127. LB to Louis Bourgeois, June 7, 1939 (LB-1018).

128. Notebook, February 1940 (LB-1768).

129. Draft of review, typewritten loose sheet, July 1944 (LB-1751).

130. Newspaper founded by Geneviève Tabouis and Henri de Kérillis for French exiles (1942–44); see draft, "Quelques grands noms américains en France: Whistler," typewritten loose sheet, c. 1942 (LB-1438). Louise sent in her article on December 28, 1942, and it was published January 27, 1943 (see her diaries for these dates).

131. Diary, July 12, 1940.

132. Vaclav Vytlacil (1892–1984), painter born in New York to Czech parents. He was Hans Hofmann's assistant, then became a professor and founded the group of American Abstract Artists; Willem de Kooning, Robert Rauschenberg, James Rosenquist, and Cy Twombly were among his students.

133. "Interview with Trevor Rots," May 10, 1990, in *Destruction*, 191.

134. The print *Greetings: Laughing Monster* was used as a greeting card in 1946. Wye, *Complete Prints and Books*, cat. no. 553.1/I, https://www.moma.org/s/lb/collection_lb/object/object_objid-65088.html.

135. The print is titled *Vase of Tears*, c. 1946. Wye, *Complete Prints and Books*, cat. no. 534/III, https://www.moma.org/s/lb/collection_lb/object/object_objid-62502.html.

136. Robert Storr, "Meanings, Materials, and Milieu—Reflections of Recent Work by Louise Bourgeois," *Parkett* 9 (June 1986), reprinted in *Destruction*, 142.

137. *Untitled* (charcoal on paper), 1945.

138. Diary, October 21, 1942.

139. Louis Bourgeois to LB, September 1, 1941 (LIB-0053).

140. Diary, November 20, 1940. [Originally in English except for *"Discours de* Roosevelt" (Roosevelt's speech).—Trans.]

141. Apartment building in New York City constructed in 1869 by Richard Morris Hunt for Rutherford Stuyvesant. See photograph in Robert Storr, *Louise Bourgeois: Intimate Geometries* (New York: Monacelli, 2016), 81.

142. "Letters to Richarme," New York, January 19, 1940, in *Destruction*, 38.

143. Colette Boisseau Richarme Boisseau to LB, May 2–June 11, 1940 (LL-0065).

144. Varian Fry (1907–1967), American journalist sent to Marseille by the Emergency Rescue Committee after the invasion of France, who saved thousands of Jews, anti-Nazi militants, artists, and intellectuals. On his return to New York on September 16, 1941, he tried to raise awareness in America about the fate of European Jewry.

145. This was the piece on Whistler that ran on January 27, 1943, mentioned above.

146. "I come back from Pontigny with Zadkine." Diary, August 9, 1944. "I feel very depressed after Pontigny. It was like a trip to France." Diary, August 10, 1944. The Pontigny meetings, presided over by Jacques Maritain and organized by Jean Wahl and Helen Patch, took place every summer from 1942 to 1944, at Mount Holyoke College in Massachusetts, and brought together French intellectuals in exile.

147. Pierre Lazareff (1907–1972), news publisher, journalist in New York from 1940 to 1944, at La Voix de l'Amérique, a radio service where Breton was briefly employed as a commentator. Louise attempted to be one as well, but Robert Goldwater insisted that she withdraw her application; see Storr, *Louise Bourgeois,* 91.

148. "Interview with Trevor Rots," in *Destruction*, 191.

149. See Emmanuelle Loyer, *Paris à New York* (Paris: Grasset, 2005), 132; and Henri Béhar, *André Breton, le grand indésirable* (Paris: Calmann-Lévy, 1990), 335.

150. Yves Tanguy to André Breton, May 5, 1940, in *André Breton: La beauté convulsive,* exh. cat. (Paris: Centre Pompidou, 1991), 346–47.

151. Who nevertheless stayed briefly at Easton with his wife, Rose, and their two children. See also LB to Paulette Place (LB-1734).

152. He lost his wife in 1944; see diary, September 6, 1944: "Robert goes to Mrs. Chagall's funeral." [Originally in English.—Trans.]

153. See loose sheet, c. 1944 (LB-1170). The Pierre Matisse Gallery, run by Henri Matisse's son, showed French and European artists in New York.

154. Loose sheet, 1944 (LB-1171).

155. Loose sheet, 1944 (LB-1171).

156. Russell Cowles (1887–1979), painter, and his wife, Eleanor, often entertained American and French painters in their home.

157. Diary, February 8–9, 1945.

158. Diary, May 4, 1945. [Originally in English.—Trans.]

159. Loose sheet, 1944 (LB-1168).

160. Diary, January 19, 1948.

161. Diary, August 27, 1944.

162. Diary, May 8, 1946.

163. Diary, May 9, 1946.

164. Diary, May 2, 1946: she noted "paintings of Nevelson, objects in wood." [The phrasing "paintings of Nevelson" is in English.—Trans.]

165. Diary, February 8, 1945.

166. Draft of LB to Paulette Place, c. 1946 (LB-1734).

167. Arts magazine founded in 1941 by Aimé Césaire (1913–2008), his wife, Suzanne (1915–1966), and René Ménil (1907–2004). Judged to be anticolonialist, it was banned by the Vichy regime. Diary, April 30, 1944. [Originally in English.—Trans.]

168. In Robert Storr, *Interviews on Art* (London: Heni, 2017), 35.

169. Diary, May 16, 1944. [Originally in English.—Trans.]

170. André Breton, *Martinique charmeuse de serpents*, illustrated by André Masson (Paris: Le Sagittaire, 1948).

171. Diary, October 12, 1949.

172. Diary, March 12, 1946. "Claude Levi-Strauss structures of popular institutions—every Tuesday 8–9:30." It must also have been the title of a class taught by Claude Lévi-Strauss.

173. Louise did a drawing of their house in Connecticut with figures appearing at the windows, called *Easton House*, 1946 (ink on graph paper). Louise annotated the drawing, writing: "Look for Le Corbusier's books."

174. Le Corbusier's sketches appear on the back of a menu, November 14, 1946 (LL-0179). See also Storr, *Louise Bourgeois*, 88; "in the form of a crow" (*corbeau*) is a play on words (that is, with his nickname, Le Corbu).

175. Diary, February 23, 1943.

176. Diary, March 19–20, 1946.

177. Diary, November 11 and December 10–11, 1946.

178. "Opening of the Italian show at the modern museum. I don't seem to be able to leave the children. on the other hand it is hard to work in the country. There is nothing in the country but what you bring yourself. Is it wise to spend a third of your life in complete solitude [. . .] the children will be happy + secure wherever you are." Diary, June 28, 1949. [Originally in English.—Trans.]

179. Diary, January 30, 1944. [The phrasing "we do not see anyone" in English.—Trans.]

180. Diary, November 28, 1947.

181. "I think my picture is horrible and it makes me very sad." Diary, December 27, 1947. The Whitney show was the *Annual Exhibition of Contemporary American Painting* (December 6, 1947–January 25, 1948). [Originally in English.—Trans.]

182. Diary, August 16, 1947.

183. Bourgeois, "Letter to Alfred H. Barr," April 6, 1942, in *Destruction*, 43.

184. Louise Bourgeois, "Self-Expression Is Sacred and Fatal: Statements," in Christiane Meyer-Thoss, *Louise Bourgeois: Konstruktionen für den freien Fall / Designing for Free Fall* (Zurich: Ammann, 1992), 200.

185. Robert Goldwater, *Primitivism in Modern Art* (New York: Vintage Books, 1966), 220.

186. "Native Talent," *Artforum* 32, no. 5 (1994), reprinted in *Destruction*, 272. [Originally in English. Emphasis in the original.—Trans.]

187. The former was naturalized in 1951 and the latter in 1957.

188. "Self-Expression Is Sacred and Fatal," 201.

189. "In a Strange Way, Things Are Getting Better and Better: Interview with Francesco Bonami," *Flash Art* 27, no. 174 (1994), reprinted in *Destruction*, 268.

190. This was Lydie Sarazin-Levassor (1902–1988), who was neither a peasant nor from Normandy but the first wife of Marcel Duchamp. They married in 1927 on the advice of Francis Picabia so that Duchamp might take care of his financial needs and "settle down." They divorced six months later. See Bernard Marcadé, *Marcel Duchamp* (Paris: Flammarion, 2007), 293–310.

191. Mary Reynolds (1891–1950), war widow, artist, and bookbinder, companion of Marcel Duchamp from 1923 to 1943; she remained in Paris during the Occupation and worked for the Resistance until she left for New York in 1942.

192. "Interview with Douglas Maxwell," *Modern Painters* 6, no. 2 (1993), reprinted in *Destruction*, 241.

193. "Interview with Bonami," reprinted in *Destruction*, 268.

194. "Interview with Bonami," reprinted in *Destruction*, 268.

195. "Conversation with George Melrod," *L'atelier*, no. 182 (October 1994), reprinted in *Destruction*, 270.

196. "Conversation with Melrod," reprinted in *Destruction*, 270.

197. "Conversation with Paulo Herkenhoff," in *Louise Bourgeois* (Paris: Phaidon, 2003), 24.

198. Henry Geldzahler, *Making It New: Essays, Interviews, and Talks* (New York: Turtle Point, 1994), 288.

199. LB to Jean Pelletier (pilot), May 12, 1942 (LB-1723).

200. Katherine Dreier (1877–1952), American artist and philanthropist, friend of Marcel Duchamp, founder of the Société Anonyme.

201. James Johnson Sweeney (1900–1986) was a curator at the Museum of Modern Art in New York from 1935 to 1946, then director of the Solomon R. Guggenheim Museum from 1952 to 1960.

202. Katherine Dreier to LB, March 12, 1945 (LL-0226).

203. A French cultural institute at Columbia University to promote French language, culture, and studies in the United States.

204. See also Peter C. Rhodes to LB, May 8, 1945 (LL-0227), and Jeanie Begg to LB, May 11, 1945 (LL-0230).

205. Exhibition announcement for *Documents France, 1940–1944: Art—Literature—Press of the French Underground*, curated by Louise Bourgeois, Norlyst Gallery, New York, 1945 (LBE-0030).

206. Rahissa Frenkel to LB, November 28, 1940 (LL-0185).

207. Berthe Frenkel to LB, September 3, 1945 (LL-0037), "Rahissa Frenkel [1905] . . . deported from Drancy to Auschwitz around September 28, 1943."

208. Diary, October 25, 1945.

209. Diary, November 19, 1944, in "Select Diary Notes, 1939–1944," in *Destruction*, 42.

210. "Opening of French show 5–8 pm, opening of my show 2–5 pm." Diary, June 4, 1945. [Originally in English.—Trans.]

211. Exhibition announcement for *Paintings by Louise Bourgeois*, Bertha Schaefer Gallery, New York (LBE-0029.02); a drawing titled *Interior* was loaned by Harold English from Los Angeles, who bought it at the Drawing Biennial at the Los Angeles County Museum of History, Science, and Art; see museum director Roland McKinney to LB, April 10, 1945 (LL-0284).

212. Diary, May 1945.

213. Loose sheet, 1944 (LB-1158).

214. Drawings from 1940, remade as two prints: *Self-Portrait* (1990) and *Unaware and Aware* (1997–2003); Wye, *Complete Prints and Books*, cat. no. 545, https://www.moma.org/s/lb/collection_lb/object/object_objid-71579.html.

215. "Natural History," December 1944 (LB-1443), reprinted in *Destruction*, 44. [Originally in English.—Trans.]

216. Diary, January 22, 1944.

217. Loose sheet, 1944 (LB-1179).

218. Loose sheet, 1944 (LB-1142).

219. Exhibition at MoMA, *The Arts in Therapy*, February 3–March 7, 1943. She received an honorary award given to articles not eligible for prizes but noted her disappointment at her failure to fulfill her aim: to use art therapy to treat soldiers. See *Bulletin of the Museum of Modern Art* 10, no. 3 (1943): 7 (LBE-0041).

220. *Art Digest*, June 1, 1945, 31; *Art News*, June 1945, 30, 37.

221. Loose sheet, c. 1945 (LB-1163).

222. Diary, September 18, 1942. [Originally in English.—Trans.]

223. Her high school friend Paulette Mauduit, who had become Paulette Place, having married the art publisher Georges Place, and mother of Jean-Michel Place, who also became a publisher.

224. At first she looked for a French teacher to look after him in the country, see that he went to school, and help him at home. Several letters from 1945 to the teachers' trade association in Paris attest to this. Diary, September 4, 1945.

225. [A long, narrow farmhouse.—Trans.]

226. Draft of LB to Paulette Place, c. 1946 (LB-1734).

227. Georges and Paulette Place to LB, November 24, 1945 (LL-0091). Georges Place was a publisher of art and literature.

228. Stanley William Hayter (1901–1988), British painter and printmaker. Exiled to New York in 1940, he set up his Atelier 17 (founded in Paris in 1933), a workshop where he hosted a number of European and American artists.

229. S. W. Hayter, *New Ways of Gravure* (New York: Pantheon, 1949), (with one hundred illustrations by celebrated artists and printmakers).

230. Diary, January 23, 1949. [Originally in English except for "*angoisse*" (anxiety). —Trans.]

231. Diary, January 24, 1949. [Originally in English.—Trans.]

232. Loose sheet, December 4, 1951 (LB-0458). [Mix of English and French.—Trans.]

233. Louise Bourgeois, *He Disappeared into Complete Silence* (New York: self-published, 1947), reprinted in *Destruction*, 46–49, quotation at 48.

234. Bourgeois, "Self-Expression Is Sacred and Fatal," 178.

235. *Louise Bourgeois*, directed by Camille Guichard (Paris: Terra Luna Films, 1993).

236. Deborah Wye and Carol Smith, *The Prints of Louise Bourgeois*, catalogue raisonné (New York: Museum of Modern Art, 1994), 72, reprinted in *Destruction*, 49.

237. Wye, *Complete Prints and Books*, cat. no. 54: *She Lost It*, https://www.moma.org/s/lb/collection_lb/object/object_objid-59621.html

238. Marius Bewley (1916–1973), Anglo-American literary critic, professor at Rutgers

University, and editor of the *Hudson Review*. Introduction to *He Disappeared into Complete Silence* (New York, 1947), reprinted in Wye, *Complete Prints and Books*, cat. no. 1228, https://www.moma.org/s/lb/collection_lb/object/object_objid-15383.html.

239. Diary, November 25, 1947.

240. Diary, May 9, 1950.

241. Bourgeois, *Puritan*, reprinted in *Destruction*, 51–55.

242. Peggy Guggenheim, *Out of This Century: Confessions of an Art Addict* (1946; reprint, New York: Universe Books, 1987), 259.

243. Diary, December 6, 1949. [Originally in English.—Trans.]

244. Diary, June 27, 1949. [Originally in English.—Trans.]

245. Diary, June 29, 1949. [Originally in English.—Trans.]

246. Diary, February 22, 1949. [Originally in English.—Trans.]

247. Diary, December 2, 1949. [Originally in English.—Trans.]

248. Diary, November 29, 1949.

249. Diary, December 1, 1949.

250. Diary, November 30, 1949.

251. Bourgeois, *Puritan*, reprinted in *Destruction*, 54.

252. Letter to the editor of the *New York Times*, May 28, 1989, reprinted in *Destruction*, 55.

253. "The Passion for Sculpture: A Conversation with Alain Kirili," *Arts* 63, no. 7 (1989): 68–75, reprinted in *Destruction*, 179.

Chapter 4. The Femme Maison

Epigraph: Diary, March 18, 1947, printed as "On Early Paintings," in Louise Bourgeois, *Destruction of the Father / Reconstruction of the Father: Writings and Interviews, 1923–1997*, ed. Marie-Laure Bernadac and Hans Ulrich Obrist (Cambridge, MA: MIT Press, and London: Violette, 1998) [hereafter cited as *Destruction*], 45. [Originally in English except for "*romantique*" (romantic).—Trans.]

1. From October 28 to November 8, 1947, a show that included seventeen paintings.

2. Nemesio Antúnez, text printed on the exhibition announcement. See exhibition announcement for *Louise Bourgeois: Paintings*, Norlyst Gallery, New York (LBE-0017).

3. Nemesio Antúnez (1918–1993), Chilean architect and painter whom Louise met at Hayter's studio in the mid-1940s, and with whom she became very close friends, and even more than friends. Nemesio was married to Inès, had a son, Pablo, and often visited Easton. He was close friends with Roberto Matta, his compatriot. In the 1950s, he worked in Le Corbusier's studio and later had a role in Costa-Gavras's film *State of Siege* (1972). He was named director of the National Museum in Santiago under Allende and played an important role in the Chilean revolution. For Louise, he was a link to South America and political engagement.

4. Loose sheet, c. 1947 (LB-0689), in Philip Larratt-Smith, ed., *Louise Bourgeois: The Return of the Repressed*, 2 vols. (London: Violette, 2012), 2:23.

5. Robert Storr, *Louise Bourgeois: Intimate Geometries* (New York: Monacelli, 2016), 122.

6. "I met him in the elevator and he gave me such a lovely smile, I could not help thinking about this <u>smile</u>." Diary, September 21, 1947. [Originally in English. The word "smile" is underlined in the original.—Trans.]

7. Diary, October 27, 1991. Louise was seven years older than Nemesio.

8. Nemesio Antúnez to Louise Bourgeois [hereafter LB], note on an exhibition announcement, 1986 (LL-0452).

9. Nemesio Antúnez to LB, postcard, January 2, 1984 (LL-0381).

10. Loose sheet, c. 1951–52 (LB-1946). [Originally in English.—Trans.]

11. *"Je découvre les vêtements d'Antúnez: [. . .] veste."* Diary, October 20, 1995.

12. This irritated Louise. She read *Earth and Reveries of Repose* as early as August 10, 1952 (Diary), but later said, "I read [Gaston] Bachelard when I was over seventy-five. If I had read Bachelard before, I would have been a different person, I would not have been divided inside." See Robert Storr, "Meanings, Materials, and Milieu—Reflections of Recent Work by Louise Bourgeois," *Parkett* 9 (June 1986), reprinted in *Destruction*, 142.

13. Gaston Bachelard, *La poétique de l'espace* (Paris: Presses universitaires de France, 1957), 26. [Translation mine.]

14. Shown in January 1938 at the International Surrealist Exhibition in Paris (Galerie des Beaux-Arts, 140, rue du Faubourg-Saint-Honoré).

15. Thomas Kellein, ed., *Louise Bourgeois: La famille*, exh. cat. (Bielefeld, Germany: Kunsthalle, 2006), 24.

16. There is no mention of the surrealists in her notebooks from this time.

17. Interview for Camille Guichard, dir., *Louise Bourgeois* (Paris: Terra Luna Films, 1993).

18. In Jerry Gorovoy and Pandora Tabatabai Asbaghi, eds., *Louise Bourgeois: Blue Days and Pink Days*, exh. cat. (Milan: Fondazione Prada, 1997), 98, reprinted in Frances Morris, "Femme Maison," in *Louise Bourgeois*, ed. Frances Morris, exh. cat. (London: Tate, 2007), 138.

19. Morris, "Femme Maison," 138–42, 142.

20. "Work on the house picture." Diary, June 19, 1944. [Originally in English.—Trans.]

21. Loose sheet, September 1944 (LB-1148).

22. Private collection; see also Storr, *Louise Bourgeois*, 84. Callie was the children's nanny. [Originally in English.—Trans.]

23. See chapter 2 in this volume, featuring the amputees in the Louvre cafeteria.

24. *Art News*, November 1947, 42 (unsigned).

25. From June 12 to July 7, 1945 (see exhibition announcement for *The Women*, Art of This Century, New York, with inscriptions by the artist, LB-1437).

26. The exhibition of 1943—which was Marcel Duchamp's idea—presented work by thirty-one female painters, of which several were surrealists: Jacqueline Lamba, Leonora Carrington, Alice Paalen, Kay Sage, and Isabelle Waldberg. The jury was composed of Max Ernst, André Breton, James Sweeney, Jim Soby, Howard Putzel, Peggy Guggenheim, and Jimmy Ernst. It was because of this show that Max Ernst and Dorothea Tanning met. The show testifies to Guggenheim's daring commitment to, as well as Duchamp's friendly support for, female artists, who were at that time infrequently shown in museums and galleries and were therefore largely invisible in the art world.

27. *She Lost It*, performance at the Fabric Workshop, Philadelphia, on May 12, 1992. See also chapter 10 in this volume.

28. Diary, December 24, 1947. She first showed her wood sculptures in a solo show at the Peridot Gallery in October 1949.

29. Attilio Salemme (1911–1955), American painter, printmaker, and muralist. Several playful photographs, likely taken by LB, show them on the rooftop of the building at 142 East Eighteenth Street, around 1946.

30. Diary, April 8, 1949. They left for San Francisco on April 8, 1949, and returned on April 11.

31. Diary, February 28, 1946.

32. Diary, August 8–9, 1948.

33. Louis Aragon, *La nuit d'exil* (1945), published as "Night of Exile," trans. William Jay Smith, in *Poetry* 67, no. 1 (1945): 21–23, quotation at 23.

34. Deborah Wye, ed., *The Complete Prints and Books,* catalogue raisonné (New York: Museum of Modern Art, 2018), cat. no. 726: *Normandy Landing,* 1994, https://www.moma.org/s /lb/collection_lb/compositions/compositions_id-4514_sov.html.

35. Diary, August 25–26, 1944. [Originally in English.—Trans.]

36. She received a telegram from her father (LIB-0098) with this news on March 16, 1942.

37. Louis Bourgeois to LB, October 26, 1944 (LIB-0055).

38. Louis Bourgeois to LB, May 9, 1945 (LIB-0057).

39. Louis Bourgeois to LB, May 9, 1945 (LIB-0057).

40. Louis Bourgeois to LB, June 8, 1945 (LIB-0058).

41. Louis Bourgeois to LB, July 22, 1945 (LIB-0059).

42. LB wrote in her diary that Pierre obtained a visa on October 31, 1945.

43. LB to Louis Bourgeois, April 24, 1946 (LB-1024)

44. Louis Bourgeois to LB, February 21, 1946 (LIB-0063).

45. Louis Bourgeois to LB, February 21, 1946 (LIB-0063).

46. Louis Bourgeois to LB, May 15, 1946 (LIB-0065).

47. Louis Bourgeois, loose sheet, April 6, 1946 (PB-0023).

48. Draft, Louis Bourgeois to the administrator in charge of patients' personal belongings, June 10, 1946 (PB-0036).

49. Document from the Ville-Évrard asylum, c. 1946 (PB-0008).

50. Statement from the police in La Croix-de-Berny, December 20, 1945 (PB-0018).

51. The letter to his father features a stamp: "Horticulture [illegible] Grand Luxe, P. Bourgeois, 13, avenue d'orléans, Antony Seine," c. 1943 (PB-0078).

52. Pierre Bourgeois to Louis Bourgeois, August 2, 1943 (PB-0093).

53. Louis Bourgeois to LB, November 19, 1947 (LIB-0074).

54. Louis Bourgeois to LB, September 20, 1945 (LIB-0060).

55. Louis Bourgeois to LB, February 21, 1946 (LIB-0063).

56. Louis Bourgeois to LB, September 20, 1945 (LIB-0060).

57. Louis Bourgeois to LB, September 20, 1945 (LIB-0060).

58. A gesture which the ophthalmologist found typically French: "The French are artists in even the most prosaic matters." LB to Louis Bourgeois, April 24, 1946 (LB-1024).

59. LB to Louis Bourgeois, December 19, 1949 (LB-1031).

60. LB to Louis Bourgeois, July 8, 1946 (LB-1035).

61. LB to Louis Bourgeois, July 8, 1946 (LB-1035).

62. LB to Louis Bourgeois, July 8, 1946 (LB-1035).

63. Colette Richarme to LB, July 9, 1945 (LL-0067).

64. Colette Richarme to LB, July 9, 1945 (LL-0067).

65. From June 28 to July 17, 1948.

66. "Easton with Papa. visit to Mr. + Mrs. Prendergast 4 pm, beach 6 pm." Diary, July 21, 1948. Eugénie Prendergast was French. [Originally in English.—Trans.]

67. Diary, July 5, 1948.

68. Diary, July 7, 1948.

69. Diary, July 8, 1948.

70. Rufino Tamayo (1899–1991), Mexican painter and friend of the Goldwaters (and the subject of one of Robert's books, published in 1947). Diary, July 13, 1948.

71. Diary, July 16, 1948.

72. She later recalled his unpleasant behavior during the car ride in Canada. See chapter 5 in this volume.

73. "Toiles de Jouy exhibition [at the] embassy, Leon + Eddie night club." Diary, June 8, 1948.

74. "Self-Expression Is Sacred and Fatal: Statements," in Christiane Meyer-Thoss, *Louise Bourgeois: Konstruktionen für den freien Fall / Designing for Free Fall* (Zurich: Ammann, 1992), 188–89.

75. Diary, January 21, 1974, in "Select Diary Notes, 1960–1979," in *Destruction*, 71. [Originally in English.—Trans.]

76. LB to Louis Bourgeois, December 19, 1949 (LB-1031).

77. LB to Louis Bourgeois, December 19, 1949 (LB-1031).

78. To date, their correspondence includes ninety-four letters from Louis and forty-four letters from LB. Unfortunately, there are no known letters from LB to her father during the period of 1940–45.

79. See LB to Louis Bourgeois, April 24, 1946 (LB-1024). She even read them to her children.

80. Loose sheet, July 14, 1952 (LB-0309). [Capitals in the original.—Trans.]

81. William Rubin, ed., *"Primitivism" in Twentieth Century Art: Affinity of the Tribal and the Modern* (New York: Museum of Modern Art, 1984).

82. One of his students, Teri Wehn-Damish, filmmaker and producer, remembers him with admiration. When at the Institute of Fine Arts, he taught two future feminist art historians who would go on to become famous, Lucy Lippard and Linda Nochlin. They also valued him as a teacher.

83. First published under the title *Primitivism in Modern Painting* in 1938, it was rereleased in 1966 with the help of his son, Jean-Louis Bourgeois, and translated into French by Denise Paulme, though it wouldn't be published (in French) until 1988, by Presses universitaires de France.

84. Alice Goldfarb Marquis, *Alfred H. Barr Jr.: Missionary for the Modern* (Chicago: Contemporary Books, 1989), 267.

Chapter 5. Homesickness

Epigraph: Interview for Camille Guichard, dir., *Louise Bourgeois* (Paris: Terra Luna Films, 1993).

1. Quoted in Michael Brenson, "A Sculptor Comes into Her Own," *New York Times*, October 31, 1982. Cited in Beatriz Colomina, "The Architecture of Trauma," in Jerry Gorovoy and Danielle Tilkin, eds., *Louise Bourgeois: Memory and Architecture*, exh. cat. (Madrid: Museo Nacional, Centro de Arte Reina Sofía, 1999), 38. See also Josef Helfenstein, *Louise Bourgeois: The Early Work*, exh. cat. (Champaign: Krannert Art Museum / University of Illinois Press, 2002), 15.

2. Interview for Camille Guichard, dir., *Louise Bourgeois* (Paris: Terra Luna Films, 1993).

3. Interview for Guichard, *Louise Bourgeois.*

4. In her diary, September 12, 1949, Louise noted, *"trouver titre avec Antúnez"* [to find title with Antúnez].

5. These two works are either no longer extant or their titles were subsequently changed.

6. In the exhibition announcement, Louise called these sculptures *Seventeen Standing Figures in Wood* (LBE-0027.01).

7. An English artist (1904–1990) who lived in Paris, London, and New York. She was also in Peggy Guggenheim's exhibition *The Women* at Art of This Century gallery in 1945.

8. "The Passion for Sculpture: A Conversation with Alain Kirili," *Arts Magazine* 63, no. 7 (1989), reprinted in Louise Bourgeois, *Destruction of the Father / Reconstruction of the Father: Writings and Interviews, 1923–1997,* ed. Marie-Laure Bernadac and Hans Ulrich Obrist (Cambridge, MA: MIT Press, and London: Violette, 1998) [hereafter cited as *Destruction*], 178.

9. "Passion for Sculpture," reprinted in *Destruction*, 178.

10. "Interview with Paulo Herkenhoff," c. 1994, in Frances Morris, ed., *Louise Bourgeois,* exh. cat. (London: Tate, 2007), 207.

11. Diary, September 14, 1950, in "Select Diary Notes, 1949–1954," in *Destruction*, 57. [Originally in English.—Trans.]

12. Bourgeois, "Conversation with Jerry Gorovoy," 1999, quoted in Paulo Herkenhoff, "Quarantania I," in Morris, *Louise Bourgeois*, 234.

13. Herkenhoff, "Quarantania I," 234.

14. This is only one of *The Blind Leading the Blind* sculptures—there were six (now five) versions of this composition, with varying numbers of legs. The version shown at the Peridot Gallery in 1949 as *The Blind Vigils* no longer exists.

15. The painting is also known as *The Parable of the Blind* and is in the collection of the Museo di Capodimonte, Naples, Italy.

16. Interview for Guichard, *Louise Bourgeois.*

17. Photograph later reproduced in Louise Bourgeois, "Child Abuse," *Artforum* 20, no. 4 (1982), reprinted in *Destruction*, 133–35.

18. Guichard, *Louise Bourgeois.*

19. "I wanted to do him as a skyscraper because it is a wonderful American structure, it is the character of New York." Quoted in Paul Gardner, *Louise Bourgeois* (New York: Universe, 1994), 61.

20. "Passion for Sculpture," reprinted in *Destruction*, 185.

21. "Self-Expression Is Sacred and Fatal: Statements," in Christiane Meyer-Thoss, *Louise Bourgeois: Konstruktionen für den freien Fall / Designing for Free Fall* (Zurich: Ammann, 1992), 179.

22. M. S., "Telegraphic Constructions," *Art Digest,* October 1, 1949, 22; M. G., "Louise Bourgeois," *Art News,* October 1949, 46; "In the Village," *New York Sun,* October 14, 1949 (they preferred the drawings over the sculptures).

23. "Louise Bourgeois," *Art News,* October 1950, 48.

24. Stuart Preston, "Modern Masters: Degas, Renoir, Rouault—Young Americans," in *New York Times,* October 9, 1949.

25. Diary, October 9, 1949.

26. See Paul Gardner, "The Discreet Charm of Louise Bourgeois," *Art News,* February 1980, 84, 86.

27. Katherine Brinson, "Femme Volage," in Morris, *Louise Bourgeois,* 144.

28. Draft of LB to Alfred H. Barr, loose sheet, c. 1951 (LB-0684), in *Destruction,* 62–63.

29. Diary, January 11, 1950. [Originally in English.—Trans.]

30. Diary, January 11, 1950. [Originally in English.—Trans.]

31. Diary, January 22, 1950. [Mix of English and French.—Trans.]

32. Diary, March 6, 1950.

33. Diary, March 7, 1950.

34. Diary, June 9, 1950. In April 1952, Barr and his wife, Marga, left for Europe. Louise seemed as enamored as ever: "Passion means death" (diary, June 27, 1952); "Fear no. 6. The person I love does not love me. No solution" (loose sheet, April 24, 1952, LB-0462.) [All originally in English.—Trans.]

35. Diary, May 15, 1950. [Mostly in English.—Trans.]

36. Diary, August 17, 1950. [Originally in English.—Trans.]

37. Jimmy Ernst, Adolph Gottlieb, Robert Motherwell, William Baziotes, Hans Hofmann, Barnett Newman, Clyfford Still, Richard Pousette-Dart, Ad Reinhardt, Jackson Pollock, Mark Rothko, Bradley Walker Tomlin, Willem de Kooning, Hedda Sterne, James Brooks, Weldon Kees, Herbert Ferber, David Smith, Ibram Lassaw, Mary Callery, Day Schnabel, Seymour Lipton, Peter Grippe, Theodore Roszak, David Hare, and LB to Roland L. Redmond, president of the Metropolitan Museum of Art, typewritten loose sheet, June 1, 1950 (LB-1752).

38. With the painter Hedda Sterne and the sculptors Day Schnabel and Mary Callery.

39. The photograph was only of the painters. Louise had already left for France by this date.

40. Louise later referred to this photograph in a letter to Milton Esterow, editor of *Art News:* "The photo is a famous one—but it is a photo of the abstract expressionist painters. We 'Irascibles'—who made Page 1 of The New York Times—were eventually 'pacified' when the Metropolitan gave us a separate show." LB to Esterow, February 2, 1979 (LB-2091). [Originally in English.—Trans.]

41. Hedda Sterne (1910–2011), abstract American painter, born in Bucharest and lived in New York.

42. Hedda Sterne, interviewed by Phyllis Tuchman, December 17, 1985, Archives of American Art.

43. Erick Hawkins (1909–1994) joined Martha Graham's company in 1938; they married in 1948. He left to found his own company in 1951, and they divorced in 1954. Hawkins also worked with Helen Frankenthaler and Robert Motherwell.

44. Erick Hawkins to LB, November 19, 1950 (LL-0186).

45. Loose sheet, November 27, 1951 (LB-2166). Previously part of a document numbered LB-0466, in Philip Larratt-Smith, ed., *Louise Bourgeois: The Return of the Repressed,* 2 vols. (London: Violette, 2012), 2:27. [Originally in English.—Trans.]

46. LB to Erick Hawkins, February 1951 (LB-1761), in *Destruction,* 65.

47. LB to Erick Hawkins, February 1951 (LB-1761), in *Destruction,* 65.

48. Loose sheet, January 15, 1952 (LB-1944). [Originally in English.—Trans.]

49. Robert Storr, *Louise Bourgeois: Intimate Geometries* (New York: Monacelli, 2016), 286–87.

50. He was awarded a Fulbright, a prestigious scholarship for scholars created in 1946 by J. William Fulbright, to fund travel and research for a year.

51. Eleanor Munro, *Originals: American Women Artists* (New York: Simon and Schuster, 1979), reprinted in *Destruction*, 111–12. It is uncertain whether she was actually investigated by McCarthy. There is no trace of it in her diaries and she rarely mentioned it.

52. Alain Bourgeois, interview with the author, New York, May 2014.

53. Diary, October 29, 1950. [Originally in English.—Trans.]

54. Diary, February 5, 1951; they chose the neighborhood for its practical location: "we should live right next to Montparnasse and the Bibliothèque nationale." [Originally in English except for "Bibliothèque nationale."—Trans.] In "Select Diary Notes, 1949–1954," in *Destruction*, 59.

55. Shirley Jaffe (1923–2016) moved to Paris in 1954 and was Louise's tenant from 1955 on. There was a lot to do to prepare it for her: "rue Daguerre let, floor to redo [. . .] chimney broken." Diary, June 26, 1955.

56. Diary, April 18, 1951.

57. Diary, February 5, 1951.

58. Diary, November 22–23, 1950, in *Destruction*, 58–59.

59. Diary, March 21, 1951.

60. Diary, March 23, 1951.

61. Diary, March 23, 1951.

62. Diary, March 24, 1951.

63. Diary, March 24, 1951.

64. Diary, April 2, 1951. [Originally in English.—Trans.]

65. Leleu was a sales representative for an insurance company called La Nationale Vie and the owner of the shop.

66. Diary, April 12, 1951.

67. Her cousin Jacques Bourgeois and his son Édouard. Germaine Martin worked with Louis at the shop on the boulevard Saint-Germain. Nadia Stoka was Louis's partner at that time. Madame Luer was a friend from Nice who went with Louise on the Baltic cruise in July 1932.

68. Death announcement of Louis Bourgeois, April 9–15, 1951 (LIB-0106).

69. Annie Segalen to LB, April 12, 1951 (LL-0093): "My poor dear friend, it's dreadful how suddenly it happened! Last Saturday we spoke of him and you would have told me he was having an operation if it had been a source of concern for you: he must have gone so quickly, and your grief must be that much more violent."

70. Only one mention in a diary entry from March 16, 1951: "bombastic call from Papa who reads us on the phone a letter from his businessman regarding a right of way on the division deed" (which had to do with the draining of water into the sump). [Mix of French and English.—Trans.]

71. Loose sheet, November 14, 1951 (LB-2163). [Originally in English.—Trans.]

72. Loose sheet, January 23, 1952 (LB-0465). [Originally in English.—Trans.]

73. Loose sheet, March 5, 1952 (LB-0461). [Originally in English.—Trans.]

74. Loose sheet, c. 1959 (LB-0231), in Larratt-Smith, *Louise Bourgeois,* 2:98. [The date is a mistake on Louise's part: her father died in 1951.]

75. For example, from Maurice Billaud (a lawyer), Maurice and Jeanne Bourgeois, Betty Chamberlin, Charles Ratton, Henri Torre, Charles and Malina Sterling, and Mr. and Mrs. Van Brabant.

76. Clara Goldwater to LB, April 15, 1951 (GL-0021).

77. Janet Goldwater Daniel to LB, April 15, 1951 (GL-0051).

78. Louise Bourgeois, September 1999, in *Repères,* no. 106, catalog for the exhibition *Francis Bacon: Papes et autres figures* (Galerie Lelong, Paris, December 1999–January 2000), 45.

79. In his will, signed May 7, 1948, Louis left the shop and all his money to Germaine Martin, "the only person, after my dear wife, to have helped me earn it," while also leaving 200,000 francs to Henri Drouin, "as a tribute to our mutual friendship." Nothing for his children, which angered Louise.

80. Diary, July 21–22, 1951. Louise regretted that she hadn't been able to keep any of the tapestries from the shop. However, her friend Paulette Place did manage to keep some of the furniture.

81. Diary, August 2, 1951.

82. Diary, July 1 and 6, 1951.

83. Diary, July 14, 1951.

84. See *Francis Bacon,* 45: "It was an encounter with the man that I have long believed to be one of the great painters of our time."

85. *Francis Bacon,* 47.

86. Diary, August 3, 1951.

87. Diary, September 5, 1951.

88. Diary, September 3, 1951.

89. Diary, September 6, 1951.

90. Diary, November 13, 1951. [Originally in English.—Trans.]

91. Loose sheet, December 2, 1951 (LB-0451). [Originally in English.—Trans.]

92. Diary, November 16, 1951. [Originally in English.—Trans.]

93. Diary, November 20, 1951.

94. Dr. Leonard Cammer (1913–1979), 132 East Seventy-Second Street. She saw him at least nine times between October 24 and December 18, 1951. See loose sheet, December 3, 1951 (LB-0454), for a reference: "After sending my note to Dr. C."

95. She called Lowenfeld ("Dr. L.") on January 2, 1951, and again on January 5.

96. Wilhelm Reich (1897–1957), Austrian doctor and psychiatrist known for his contributions to sexology.

97. Dwight Macdonald (1906–1982), American intellectual and friend of the Goldwaters.

98. Catherine Yarrow (1904–1990), English surrealist artist who lived in Paris, London, and New York.

99. Loose sheet, December 17, 1951 (LB-0455). [Originally in English.—Trans.]

100. Loose sheet, December 31, 1951 (LB-1949). [Originally in English.—Trans.]

101. Diary, May 22, 1952. [Originally in English.—Trans.]

102. The trip had been planned in advance, as indicated by a letter from Robert Goldwater to Jurgis Baltrusaitis dated May 2, 1952, in which he asks him to go to the rue Daguerre to see if Louise's sculptures were in good condition—"we arrive mid-June"—and to find someone

to look after the two boys and to stay with them. Archives of American Art, Robert John Goldwater papers, Series 1: Correspondence, 1934–1973, box 1.

103. James Fitzsimmons, "Art," *Art and Architecture* 70, no. 4 (1953): 35.

104. Fitzsimmons, "Art," 35: "This is very strange, disturbing and rather obsessive work. Improbable images, they have the enigmatic reality of an Easter Island head, of a dolmen on a deserted plane." The sculptures had not yet arrived when Fitzsimmons saw the show, "but the drawings had, and while closely related in feeling to her sculpture, they were also interesting in themselves."

105. Diary, January 15, 1953.

106. Fairfield Porter, "Louise Bourgeois," *Art News,* April 1953, 39.

107. Statement in Belle Krasne, "10 Artists in the Margin," *Design Quarterly* (Minneapolis), no. 30 (1954), 18, as cited in Deborah Wye, *Louise Bourgeois,* exh. cat. (New York: Museum of Modern Art, 1982), 22.

108. "Louise Bourgeois," *Art Digest,* April 1, 1953, 17.

109. Diary, January 29, 1953.

110. Diary, January 29, 1953.

111. Diary, June 11 and 12, 1953.

112. Hans Ulrich Obrist, "Préface," *Destruction* (French ed.), 12.

113. LB in conversation with Jerry Gorovoy, September 5, 1990 (LB-0051).

114. Diary, June 30, 1953.

115. Michel Seuphor (1901–1999), pseudonym of Ferdinand Louis Berckelaers, abstract painter, art critic, and French writer. In 1925, he founded the group Cercle et Carré with Joaquín Torres-García. He visited New York in 1950 and 1951 to write a book about Piet Mondrian. He organized numerous exhibitions and in 1959 published *La sculpture de ce siècle: Dictionnaire de la sculpture moderne* (Neuchâtel, Switzerland: Griffon, 1959), in which Louise's work appeared.

116. Michel Seuphor to LB, September 20, 1951 (LL-0131).

117. Galerie M.A.I. (Meuble, Architecture, Installation) to LB, October 5, 1951 (LL-0133). This letter postpones the exhibition: "It now seems very difficult to hold your exhibition during the month of October."

118. Robert Goldwater [hereafter RG] to Michel Seuphor, December 10, 1951, from notes in the Archives of American Art, Robert John Goldwater papers, Series 4: Writings, 1932–1973, box 3, 241.

119. In a draft letter to her friend Paulette Place: "What interests me above all is to find a gallery in Paris, like Madame Bucher['s]. I have one here, but Paris is Paris." Loose sheet, c. 1945 (LB-1734). Jeanne Bucher was a well-known art dealer and collector in Paris.

120. Michel Seuphor, text written for LB, c. 1953 (LL-0134).

121. Seuphor, text written for LB, c. 1953 (LL-0134).

122. "Robert goes to Facchetti." Diary, July 21, 1953. [Originally in English.—Trans.]

123. Seuphor, *La sculpture de ce siècle.*

124. Diary, September 2, 1953. She may be referring to Seuphor's book on Berto Lardera (1911–1989), published in 1953.

125. RG to LB, July 14, 1953 (RG-0246). [Originally in English except for the word *"étape"* (step), which is also underlined. The word "presence" is underlined in the original as well.—Trans.]

126. RG to LB, July 16, 1953 (RG-0247).

127. RG to LB, July 16, 1953 (RG-0247). [Originally in English.—Trans.]

128. Agenda, August 25, 1953.

129. Agenda, August 31, September 2–3, 1953.

130. Day Schnabel (1905–1991), Austrian painter and sculptor, lived in New York during the war and in Paris in the 1950s. It was through her that Shirley Jaffe rented Louise's studio on the rue Daguerre.

131. Agenda, September 4, 1953.

132. Ludwig Sander and Nancy Ward were also there; see invitation from Willem de Kooning, Elaine de Kooning, Ludwig Sander, Nancy Ward, and Franz Kline to "A Croquet Party at the Red House," Bridgehampton, NY, August 7, 1954 (LBE-0239).

133. Diary, August 10–11, 1955. She even drew the storage boxes she saw at Prouté. [The Galérie Paul Prouté is one of the oldest galleries specializing in prints and drawings, founded in 1876 in Paris.—Trans.].

134. Agenda, July 26, 28, and 29, 1955.

135. Agenda, June 21, 1954: Louise noted that the architect Philip Johnson (1906–2005) and the designer Don Porter wanted to rent the studio in the rue Daguerre.

136. After her marriage to Irving Jaffe, Shirley "moved to Washington, where Mr. Jaffe was the White House correspondent for Agence France-Presse. She attended the Phillips Art School there before moving with her husband to Paris, where he continued working for the news agency and studied sociology at the Sorbonne on the G.I. Bill." Obituary, *New York Times*, October 3, 2016.

137. Seuphor, *La sculpture de ce siècle*, s.v. "Louise Bourgeois."

138. Carola Giedion-Welcker (1893–1979), collector and art historian, author of *Contemporary Sculpture: An Evolution in Volume and Space* (New York: G. Wittenborn, 1955).

139. Located at 114 East Eleventh Street.

140. Diary, February 5, 1954.

141. Agenda, September 19, 1955.

142. Likely the proprietor of a neighboring bookstore.

143. Loose sheet, July 1, 1959 (LB-0439).

144. Loose sheet, c. 1959 (LB-0250).

145. Storr, *Louise Bourgeois*, 290n40.

146. Robert Goldwater, "Sculpture actuelle à New York," *Cimaise* 4, no. 2 (1956): 24–28.

147. Notebook, 1957, 1 (LB-0497). [Mix of French and English.—Trans.]

148. Notebook, 1957, 3 (LB-0497).

149. Notebook, 1957, 28, 29–30 (LB-0497).

150. The building from her childhood, 172, boulevard Saint-Germain.

151. Notebook, 1957, 30 (LB-0497).

152. *Nature in Abstraction*, Whitney Museum of American Art, January 14–March 16, 1958. Including Louise Nevelson, David Smith, David Hare, Isamu Noguchi, and a number of painters. Louise showed *Forêt (Night Garden)* (1953), exhibited with the title *Garden at Night*.

153. A photograph attests to this visit.

154. These names were listed in the "addresses" section of Louise's 1959 agenda.

155. Michel Seuphor, "Le choix d'un critique," *L'œil*, no. 49 (1959): 24–39, 28.

156. Seuphor, "Le choix d'un critique," 28.

157. Seuphor, *La sculpture de ce siècle.*

158. He also mentioned Louise Nevelson's wood assemblages and Day Schnabel.

159. Seuphor, *La sculpture de ce siècle,* 192.

160. Seuphor, *La sculpture de ce siècle,* 241.

161. Michel Ragon, "Art actuel aux États-unis," *Cimaise* 6, no. 3 (1958): 6–30.

162. "My father-in-law rarely spoke about his son and we never knew exactly what was the extent or even the nature of his illness. Has he been informed of Mr. Bourgeois' passing? And how did he react?," draft of RG to Dr. Bergeron, Villejuif, February 5, 1952 (PB-0005).

163. Draft of RG to Dr. Bergeron, Villejuif, February 5, 1952 (PB-0005).

164. Dr. Bergeron to LB, February 9, 1952 (PB-0004).

165. Visitor's pass for Louise to see Pierre Bourgeois, August 25, 1957 (PB-0042). Another visit is mentioned, on August 29 (PB-0043).

166. Alain Bourgeois, interview with the author, May 2014.

167. Loose sheet, February 5, 1952 (LB-0460). [Originally in English.—Trans.]

168. Loose sheet, February 5, 1952 (LB-0460). [Originally in English.—Trans.]

169. "I think of you as my favorite, the one I love. [. . .] I have to get out of here, we must see each other, I have suffered so much without you." Pierre Bourgeois to Alain Bourgeois, August 28, 1957 (PB-0123).

170. Pierre Bourgeois to LB, October 12, 1958 (PB-0120).

171. Pierre Bourgeois to LB, December 17, 1958 (PB-0122).

172. Pierre Bourgeois to LB, c. 1957 (PB-0126).

173. Shirley Jaffe to LB, c. 1957 (LL-0276). [Originally in English.—Trans.] "Today was the first time he mentioned so many names and I asked him to tell me who these people were—a nurse—? Melanie—Henriette, your sister?—he mentioned a pension he was in as a child that was like the hospital—and just right before I left—your father—did I know him? No—he was a terrible man. Very gratuitous reference. Pierre is very sweet and gentle. He told me about a letter he was writing to you—and complaints within to make you help him leave."

174. Shirley Jaffe, interview with the author, May 16, 2016.

175. Villejuif hospital to LB, June 2, 1960 (PB-0002).

176. Henriette Bonnotte to LB, June 1960 (HB-0027).

177. "I discover father's and Pierre's papers all the folders traumatic." Diary, February 5, 1989.

Chapter 6. "The Unconscious Is My Friend"

Epigraph: Loose sheet, c. 1958 (LB-0127): "makes me powerless / makes me into a cop / is a bad dream / is my interest / is my field of study— / is more than I can manage / makes me furious / is a bore / is a nuisance / is a pain in the neck—." [Originally in English.—Trans.]

1. She was in analysis regularly from the 1952 to the mid-1960s, and then occasionally until 1985, when Henry Lowenfeld died. But she repeatedly denied having been in treatment: "I never had an analysis. My friends did and they got worse," Juliet Mitchell, "The Sublime Jealousy of Louise Bourgeois," in *Louise Bourgeois: The Return of the Repressed,* ed. Philip Larratt-Smith, 2 vols. (London: Violette, 2012), 1:47.

2. "Interview with Douglas Maxwell," *Modern Painters,* 6 no. 2 (1993): 38–43, reprinted in Louise Bourgeois, *Destruction of the Father / Reconstruction of the Father: Writings and Interviews,*

1923–1997, ed. Marie-Laure Bernadac and Hans Ulrich Obrist (Cambridge, MA: MIT Press, and London: Violette, 1998) [hereafter cited as *Destruction*], 245.

3. Loose sheet, January 15, 1952 (LB-1944). [Originally in English.—Trans.]

4. Louise Bourgeois, "Freud's Toys," *Artforum* 28, no. 5 (1990): 111–13, reprinted in *Destruction,* 190.

5. Loose sheet, February 8, 1952 (LB-0452). [Originally in English, except for the word *"bercée"* (cradled).—Trans.]

6. Agenda, May 4, 1952. [Originally in English.—Trans.]

7. Loose sheet, February 8, 1952 (LB-0467). [Originally in English.—Trans.]

8. Loose sheet, February 8, 1952 (LB-0467). [Originally in English.—Trans.]

9. Loose sheet, February 8, 1952 (LB-0467). Jacques Bourgeois, her cousin, and Dr. Richiez, with whom she was in love as a young woman. [Originally in English.—Trans.]

10. Loose sheet, February 8, 1952 (LB-0467). [Originally in English.—Trans.]

11. Loose sheet, February 8, 1952 (LB-0467). [Originally in English.—Trans.]

12. Loose sheet, February 8, 1952 (LB-0450). [Originally in English.—Trans.] "He refuses to give decent hours because he feels I am a housewife and have no professional obligations." Loose sheet, February 8, 1952 (LB-0467). [Originally in English.—Trans.]

13. Loose sheet, February 8, 1952 (LB-0467). "Psychoanalysts think that they are gods and yet they have complex [*sic*] like every one else. He thinks that I am pretentious. In fact HE is." [Originally in English; "he" is capped in the original.—Trans.]

14. Agenda, February 12, 1952. [Originally in English.—Trans.]

15. Agenda, June 16, 1952. [Originally in English.—Trans.]

16. Diary, March 6, 1954. [Originally in English.—Trans.]

17. Loose sheet, c. 1957–59 (LB-0436). [Originally in English.—Trans.]

18. Diary, July 18, 1952. [Originally in English.—Trans.]

19. Loose sheet, January 8, 1952 (LB-0453). [Originally in English.—Trans.]

20. John Ferren (1905–1970), American artist who spent time in Paris.

21. Diary, September 28, 1954.

22. Diary, September 29, 1954.

23. Diary, May 24, 1978. [Originally in English.—Trans.]

24. Loose sheet, July 1, 1965 (LB-0731). [Originally in English.—Trans.]

25. Loose sheet, c. 1963 (LB-0366).

26. Yela Lowenfeld (1902–1988), child psychologist.

27. Annie Reich (1902–1971) was a Viennese-born psychoanalyst who immigrated to New York on the eve of the Second World War. She was married to Wilhelm Reich from 1922 to 1933.

28. In William Phillips, *Art and Psychoanalysis* (New York: Criterion Books, 1957). Article written in June 1937 for the Psychoanalytic Society of Vienna, in which Lowenfeld analyzes the case of a woman who resembled Louise, aggressive and timid, who overcame her childhood trauma through sublimation and artistic expression. First published in 1941 in *Psychoanalytic Quarterly.*

29. According to Christopher Turner, "Analysing Louise Bourgeois: Art, Therapy and Freud," *Guardian,* April 6, 2012. During the Cold War, he went so far as to confiscate the letters Otto Fenichel had written to Annie Reich in the 1930s, proof of her Marxist past, so that she wouldn't have any trouble with the American authorities.

30. Loose sheet, November 1, 1954 (LB-0484). [Originally in English.—Trans.]

31. Including Dr. N. Dracoulides, *Psychanalyse de l'artiste et de son œuvre* (BIB-6131); Anton Ehrenzweig, *The Psychoanalysis of Artistic Vision and Hearing: An Introduction to a Theory of Unconscious Perception* (BIB-6044); Sigmund Freud, *Totem and Taboo* (BIB-6272); Clara Thompson, *Psychoanalysis: Evolution and Development, a Review of Theory and Therapy* (BIB-5937); and many, many more.

32. Loose sheet, July 14, 1952 (LB-0309).

33. Loose sheet, c. 1960 (LB-0828), in *Destruction*, 69. [Originally in English.—Trans.]

34. Ronald D. Laing (1927–1989) was a member of the antipsychiatry movement in the United Kingdom. Influenced by Marx, Merleau-Ponty, and Sartre, he was cited by Deleuze and Guattari. He wrote *The Divided Self* in 1960 and *The Politics of the Family and Other Essays* in 1971. The former is in Bourgeois's library (BIB-6159).

35. R. D. Laing, *Knots*, 1970. Louise had an annotated copy of this book in her library (BIB-6133).

36. Eustace Chesser, *Love without Fear: How to Achieve Sex Happiness in Marriage*, 1947 (BIB-5764).

37. Loose sheet, December 4, 1951 (LB-0457). [Originally in English.—Trans.]

38. Loose sheet, February 8, 1952 (LB-0452). [Originally in English.—Trans.]

39. Loose sheet, January 15, 1959 (LB-0257). Two short stories by Jean-Paul Sartre, published in 1939 in the collection *Le mur*.

40. Loose sheet, c. 1959 (LB-0464).

41. Loose sheet, December 2, 1951 (LB-0451): "my parents did not quarrel. They had their relationship very much under control and nothing transpired to the children." [Originally in English.—Trans.]

42. Loose sheet, March 5, 1952 (LB-0461): "The stingyness [*sic*] appeared as the deadly weapon directed against those who refuse to love him [. . .] reassure him or flatter him. You accept me, or I starve you." [Originally in English.—Trans.]

43. Loose sheet, December 2, 1951 (LB-0451): "At the end once I saw her cry." [Originally in English.—Trans.]

44. Diary, April 30, 1992. [Originally in English.—Trans.]

45. Loose sheet, October 17, 1955 (LB-0036): "painful reminiscence [. . .] like a vertigo at the hollow of the stomach + followed by an immediate diarrhea it happens in the digestive track [*sic*] the period cramp is painful but has no visible result." In Larratt-Smith, *Louise Bourgeois*, 2:47. [In English except for the word "*vertige*" (vertigo).—Trans.]

46. Loose sheet, September 13, 1957 (LB-0219).

47. Loose sheet, October 28, 1958 (LB-0266).

48. Diary, April 30, 1992; see also Louise Bourgeois, "Self-Expression Is Sacred and Fatal: Statements," in Christiane Meyer-Thoss, *Louise Bourgeois: Konstruktionen für den freien Fall / Designing for Free Fall* (Zurich: Ammann, 1992), 195.

49. Loose sheet, c. 1958 (LB-0513).

50. Donald Kuspit, "Words as Transitional Objects: Louise Bourgeois's Writings," in Frances Morris, ed., *Louise Bourgeois*, exh. cat. (London: Tate, 2007), 295–301.

51. Loose sheet, May 18, 1936 (LB-1296) [Underlined in the original.—Trans.]; in Morris, *Louise Bourgeois*, 295.

52. Loose sheet, January 15, 1952 (LB-1944): "Give original to L—." [Originally in English.—Trans.]

53. Loose sheet, July 14, 1956 (LB-0437). [Mostly in French.—Trans.]

54. Loose sheet, February 8, 1952 (LB-0467).

55. Diary, February 5, 1954. [In French except for "approved of."—Trans.]

56. Diary, May 12, 1952. [In English except for the word "*taré*" (rocker).—Trans.]

57. Diary, November 5, 1952. "dissect the psychological anatomy of the fathers to make use of them." [Originally in English.—Trans.]

58. Diary, July 1, 1952.

59. Loose sheet, March 5, 1952 (LB-0461).

60. Loose sheet, February 8, 1952 (LB-0450). [Originally in English.—Trans.]

61. Loose sheet, January 23, 1952 (LB-0465). [Originally in English.—Trans.]

62. Loose sheet, April 24, 1952 (LB-0459). [Originally in English.—Trans.]

63. Loose sheet, December 17, 1951 (LB-1947). [In French except for "Later he hated anyone."—Trans.]

64. Loose sheet, November 27, 1951 (LB-2165). Previously part of a document numbered LB-0466, in Larratt-Smith, *Louise Bourgeois*, 2:26, with old document number. [In English except for the word "*poule*" (tramp).—Trans.]

65. Loose sheet, November 27, 1951 (LB-2165).

66. Loose sheet, January 23, 1952 (LB-0465); see also chapter 9 in this volume.

67. Loose sheet, January 23, 1952 (LB-0465).

68. Loose sheet, December 2, 1951 (LB-0451). [Originally in English.—Trans.]

69. Diary, June 1, 1952. [Originally in English.—Trans.]

70. Diary, February 5, 1954. [In French except for "approval."—Trans.]

71. Loose sheet, c. 1961 (LB-0236). [Originally in English.—Trans.]

72. Loose sheet, May 5, 1957 (LB-0223). [Originally in English.—Trans.]

73. Diary, November 17, 1951. [Originally in English.—Trans.]

74. Loose sheet, 1963 (LB-0366): "I consider that my Father is eating at my marriage and I feel guilty about it." [In French except for "guilty about it."—Trans.]

75. Loose sheet, March 18, 1964 (LB-0153). [Mix of French and English.—Trans.]

76. Loose sheet, January 15, 1952 (LB-1944). [Originally in English.—Trans.]

77. Loose sheet, January 15, 1952 (LB-1944). [Mostly in English.—Trans.]

78. Loose sheet, c. 1956 (LB-0237).

79. Diary, June 26, 1952 [Originally in English.—Trans.]; 174, boulevard Saint-Germain, her father's apartment.

80. Loose sheet, April 15, 1958 (LB-0649).

81. Loose sheet, c. 1957 (LB-0269). [In English except for the word "*incestueux*" (incestuous).—Trans.]

82. Loose sheet, December 2, 1951 (LB-0451). [Originally in English.—Trans.]

83. Loose sheet, March 5, 1952 (LB-0461). [Originally in English. *Iphigenia in Aulis* is a play by Euripides in which the father, Agamemnon, wants to sacrifice his daughter to the goddess Artemis so his troops can be successful in their upcoming battle against Troy.—Trans.]

84. Loose sheet, December 2, 1951 (LB-0451). "My mother did not see the danger of excessive emotion[s] because in a way she fell short of them. The way Robert has no sense of drama

and so is not either afraid or prepared for it. It remains a foreign land." [Originally in English.—Trans.]

85. Loose sheet, December 2, 1951 (LB-0451).

86. Loose sheet, December 2, 1951 (LB-0451).

87. Loose sheet, December 2, 1951 (LB-0451). [Originally in English.—Trans.]

88. Loose sheet, February 8, 1952 (LB-0450). [Originally in English.—Trans.]

89. Loose sheet, December 2, 1951 (LB-0451). [Originally in English.—Trans.]

90. Loose sheet, December 2, 1951 (LB-0451). [Originally in English.—Trans.]

91. Loose sheet, November 27, 1951 (LB-2163). [Originally in English.—Trans.] Previously part of a document numbered LB-0466.

92. P. for "penis." Loose sheet, April 15, 1958 (LB-0649): "I am afraid that my mother will abandon me because I am going to steal her husband [. . .] it is certain that if I steal a P. that belongs to her since my father belongs to her she will not be content and she will take her revenge." In Larratt-Smith, *Louise Bourgeois*, 2:78–79.

93. Loose sheet, April 15, 1958 (LB-0649), in Larratt-Smith, *Louise Bourgeois*, 2:78.

94. Loose sheet, c. 1957–59 (LB-0436). [Originally in English.—Trans.]

95. Loose sheet, c. 1964 (LB-0442). [Originally in English.—Trans.]

96. Loose sheet, June 25, 1958 (LB-0444).

97. Loose sheet, c. 1963 (LB-0409). [Originally in English.—Trans.]

98. Loose sheet, October 28, 1958 (LB-0266).

99. Loose sheet, April 15, 1958 (LB-0649).

100. Loose sheet, November 1, 1954 (LB-0484), in Larratt-Smith, *Louise Bourgeois*, 2:43.

101. Diary, March 16, 1975. [Originally in English. The words "refuse" and "need" are underlined in the original.—Trans.]

102. Loose sheet, c. 1959 (LB-0230).

103. Loose sheet, January 15, 1959 (LB-0257), in Larratt-Smith, *Louise Bourgeois*, 2:96.

104. Loose sheet, December 2, 1951 (LB-0451). [Originally in English.—Trans.]

105. Loose sheet, March 18, 1964 (LB-0153). [Originally in English.—Trans.]

106. Loose sheet, October 10, 1958 (LB-0449). [Mix of English and French.—Trans.]

107. Loose sheet, November 15, 1957 (LB-0133). [In English except for the words *"jalousie"* (jealousy) and *"jalouse"* (jealous).—Trans.]

108. Loose sheet, April 24, 1952 (LB-0462). [Originally in English.—Trans.]

109. Diary, November 20, 1951. [Originally in English.—Trans.]

110. Loose sheet, c. 1959 (LB-0530), in Larratt-Smith, *Louise Bourgeois*, 2:106.

111. Loose sheet, c. 1963 (LB-0386).

112. Loose sheet, January 29, 1958 (LB-0272). [Originally in English.—Trans.]

113. Bourgeois, "Self-Expression Is Sacred and Fatal," 177.

114. ["Little Miss Nothing."—Trans.]

115. Diary, March 19, 1986. [Originally in English.—Trans.]

116. Loose sheet, November 27, 1951 (LB-2165). Previously part of a document numbered LB-0466. [In English except for the word *"catholique"* (Catholic).—Trans.]

117. Loose sheet, February 8, 1952 (LB-0450): "It is a bluestocking showing off. No interest is aroused. New break and rejection," she wrote about her love for Lowenfeld. In Larratt-Smith, *Louise Bourgeois*, 2:38. [In English except for *"bas bleu"* (bluestocking).—Trans.]

118. Robert Goldwater [hereafter RG] to Louise Bourgeois [hereafter LB], September 2,

1938 (RG-0002): "they were a little afraid to find you bluestocking, but since you are not it they find you perfect, the family too."

119. Loose sheet, March 5, 1952 (LB-0461): "Why do you play the tearful. So do not weep. You want me to sing." [Mix of English and French.—Trans.]

120. Loose sheet, November 1951 (LB-0466), in Larratt-Smith, *Louise Bourgeois*, 2:25. [Originally in English. LB opens the parentheses but does not close them.—Trans.]

121. Loose sheet, December 17, 1951 (LB-0455). [Originally in English.—Trans.]

122. Loose sheet, April 24, 1952 (LB-0462). [Originally in English.—Trans.]

123. Loose sheet, November 27, 1951 (LB-2166). Previously part of a document numbered LB-0466. [Originally in English.—Trans.]

124. Loose sheet, December 4, 1951 (LB-0458). [In English and French.—Trans.]

125. Loose sheet, c. 1965 (LB-0142): "eternal theme of phallism." ["Eternal theme of" is in French and "phallism," in English, Louise's neologism.—Trans.]

126. Loose sheet, c. 1963 (LB-0366).

127. Diary, February 26, 1954.

128. Karen Horney (1885–1952), German psychoanalyst who immigrated to the United States, author of *Our Inner Conflicts*, 1945. A pioneering feminist, she developed the theory of uterus envy in men to counterbalance penis envy in women.

129. Loose sheet, c. 1959 (LB-0464).

130. Loose sheet, August 17, 1963 (LB-0377): "Castration complex [. . .]. When I used to run away from Brayer, it was all out of shame. I'm ashamed not to be like others (men)." [Mix of French and English.—Trans.]

131. Loose sheet, October 28, 1958 (LB-0266).

132. Loose sheet, c. 1959 (LB-0250), in Larratt-Smith, *Louise Bourgeois,* 2:103. "expressed in my sculpture by the penis, spearhead, knife, sword—to be a woman is to be defenseless. The fears of adolescence reinforce the envy for the father's penis."

133. Loose sheet, c. 1957–60 (LB-0591).

134. Loose sheet, February 5, 1952 (LB-0460). [In English, except for the word *"jalouse"* (jealous).—Trans.]

135. See chapter 1 in this volume.

136. Loose sheet, c. 1959 (LB-0230).

137. Loose sheet, December 17, 1951 (LB-0455). [Originally in English.—Trans.]

138. Diary, March 10, 1954.

139. Loose sheet, June 25, 1958 (LB-0444). [Originally in English.—Trans.]

140. Diary, May 8, 1954. [Originally in English.—Trans.]

141. Diary, August 12, 1991. "Velvet Eyes" is in the title of a piece: *Nature Study (Velvet Eyes)* (1984).

142. Bourgeois, "Self-Expression Is Sacred and Fatal," 196.

143. Loose sheet, c. 1961 (LB-0374).

144. Loose sheet, April 24, 1952 (LB-0462). [Originally in English.—Trans.]

145. Loose sheet, April 24, 1952 (LB-0462). [Originally in English.—Trans.]

146. Loose sheet, December 15, 1951 (LB-1947).

147. "Both Rob[er]t and Alain stand for my mother." Loose sheet, April 15, 1958 (LB-0649), in Larratt-Smith, *Louise Bourgeois,* 2:78. [Originally in English.—Trans.]

148. Loose sheet, December 15, 1951 (LB-1947). [Originally in English.—Trans.]

149. Loose sheet, November 1, 1954 (LB-0484): "I stay in bed after having done my maternal duties the best I could."

150. Loose sheet, December 31, 1951 (LB-1949). Robert and the children must have been celebrating New Year's Eve with their grandparents.

151. Loose sheet, December 31, 1951 (LB-1949). [Originally in English.—Trans.]

152. Diary, April 27, 1953. [Originally in English.—Trans.]

153. Loose sheet, December 31, 1951 (LB-1949). [Originally in English.—Trans.]

154. Diary, June 15, 1952. [Originally in English.—Trans.]

155. Diary, May 8, 1952. [Originally in English.—Trans.]

156. Diary, January 1, 1955. [Originally in English.—Trans.]

157. Diary, March 14, 1955. [In English except for the word "*complexe*" (complex). —Trans.]

158. Loose sheet, c. 1959 (LB-0250), in Larratt-Smith, *Louise Bourgeois*, 2:101. "Refusal to take responsibility for my analysis, for my troubles, for my needs, for my wishes. Always wanting the other one to take care of you. dependency." [Originally in English.—Trans.]

159. Diary, February 3–4, 1953. [Originally in English.—Trans.]

160. Loose sheet, December 2, 1951 (LB-0451). [Originally in English.—Trans.]

161. Loose sheet, October 28, 1958 (LB-0266). [Originally in English.—Trans.]

162. Loose sheet, Autumn 1959 (LB-0228).

163. Loose sheet, April 24, 1952 (LB-0462). [Originally in English.—Trans.]

164. Loose sheet, October 28, 1958 (LB-0266): "Robert will not come out of his room for his fear of my violence excites him."

165. "Psychoanalysis is my religion": LB in conversation with Gorovoy, c. 2007 (LB-2297).

166. Loose sheet, c. 1986 (LB-0506). [Originally in English.—Trans.]

167. Loose sheet, July 14, 1952 (LB-0309). [Mix of English and French.—Trans.]

168. Loose sheet, July 14, 1952 (LB-0309). [Mix of English and French.—Trans.]

169. Bourgeois, "Self-Expression Is Sacred and Fatal," 184.

170. Mitchell, "Sublime Jealousy," 1:52: "she may not have 'had an analysis'; rather, she 'used' it."

171. Mignon Nixon, "L.," in Larratt-Smith, *Louise Bourgeois*, 1:85–95, quotation at 95.

172. Loose sheet, September 13, 1957 (LB-0219). [Originally in English.—Trans.]

173. Conversation between the author and her friend the psychoanalyst and collector Daniel Milman in 2003.

174. Diary, September 11, 1980. [In English except for the word "*inconscient*" (unconscious) in French.—Trans.]

175. Paul Verhaege and Julie De Ganck, "Beyond the Return of the Repressed: Louise Bourgeois's Chthonic Art," in Larratt-Smith, *Louise Bourgeois*, 1:115–125.

176. Figure from Greek mythology who picked up her skirts to reveal her sex and made Demeter laugh.

177. See interview with Xavier Tricot, 1996, in Louise Bourgeois, *Destruction du père / Reconstruction du père: Écrits et entretiens, 1923–2000*, expanded French ed., ed. Marie-Laure Bernadac and Hans Ulrich Obrist (Paris: Daniel Lelong, 2000), 381.

178. Bourgeois, "Self-Expression Is Sacred and Fatal," 195.

179. John Cheim and Jerry Gorovoy, eds., *Louise Bourgeois Drawings* (New York: Robert Miller Gallery, and Paris: Daniel Lelong, 1988), 138.

180. Loose sheet, May 11, 1962 (LB-0511).

181. "Two Conversations with Deborah Wye," 1979 and 1981, in *Destruction*, 129.

Chapter 7. The Organic Refuge

Epigraph: Bourgeois quoted in Frances Morris, ed., *Louise Bourgeois*, exh. cat. (London: Tate, 2007), 166.

1. Loose sheet, c. 1967 (LB-1444), in "Brief Account of Career" in Louise Bourgeois, *Destruction of the Father / Reconstruction of the Father: Writings and Interviews, 1923–1997*, ed. Marie-Laure Bernadac and Hans Ulrich Obrist (Cambridge, MA: MIT Press, and London: Violette, 1998) [hereafter cited as *Destruction*], 77–78. [Originally in English.—Trans.]

2. Loose sheet, c. 1959 (LB-0464). [Mix of English and French.—Trans.]

3. Bourgeois quoted in "William Rubin—Louise Bourgeois: Questions and Answers," previously unpublished notes for Rubin's article "Some Reflections Prompted by the Recent Work of Louise Bourgeois," *Art International* 13, no. 4 (1969): 17–20, in *Destruction*, 81.

4. Interview for Camille Guichard, dir., *Louise Bourgeois* (Paris: Terra Luna Films, 1993).

5. Gaston Bachelard, *The Poetics of Space*, trans. Maria Jolas (Boston: Beacon Press, 1994), 98–99.

6. Bachelard, *Poetics of Space*, 101.

7. Louise Bourgeois, "Self-Expression Is Sacred and Fatal: Statements," in Christiane Meyer-Thoss, *Louise Bourgeois: Konstruktionen für den freien Fall / Designing for Free Fall* (Zurich: Ammann, 1992), 179.

8. Loose sheet, c. 1964 (LB-0165). [In English except for the word *"tordue"* (twisted). —Trans.]

9. Loose sheet, c. 1964 (LB-0165). [Originally in English.—Trans.]

10. Diary, December 21, 1965. [Originally in English.—Trans.]

11. Quoted in "William Rubin—Louise Bourgeois" in *Destruction*, 81.

12. Loose sheet, c. 1965 (LB-0331): "the diseases of the femininity." [Originally in English.—Trans.]

13. Diary, March 12, 1953. [Originally in English.—Trans.]

14. Loose sheet, November 14, 1966 (LB-0654), in Philip Larratt-Smith, ed., *Louise Bourgeois: The Return of the Repressed*, 2 vols. (London: Violette, 2012), 2:156. [Originally in English.—Trans.]

15. Loose sheet, c. March 1964 (LB-0188). [Mostly in French.—Trans.]

16. Loose sheet, c. 1958 (LB-0320).

17. Loose sheet, 1963 (LB-0297).

18. Loose sheet, February 23–27, 1960 (LB-0175). [Mostly in French.—Trans.]

19. Written on the verso of an untitled drawing, c. 1960, in Larratt-Smith, *Louise Bourgeois*, 2:117.

20. Loose sheet, c. 1964 (LB-0372).

21. Loose sheet, c. 1993 (LB-0569), in Larratt-Smith, *Louise Bourgeois*, 2:155, with incorrect date.

22. Loose sheet, March 18, 1964 (LB-0153), in Larratt-Smith, *Louise Bourgeois*, 2:141. [Originally in English.—Trans.]

23. Loose sheet, March–April 1964 (LB-0188), in Larratt-Smith, *Louise Bourgeois*, 2:142. [Mix of French and English.—Trans.]

24. Its second location was on Madison Avenue. "Moving of Erasmus landlord is hard; letter of the law and also ask for 'concessions.'" Diary, February 5, 1960, 4 p.m. [Originally in English—Trans.]. "Robert is critical. We spent all day packing at Erasmus." Diary, February 7, 1960. [Originally in English—Trans.]

25. She received an A in "Evolution of French Theater" but a B– in "Currents of Fifteenth-Century French Painting"!

26. Loose sheet, c. 1960 (LB-0828); see also "Autobiographical Notes" in *Destruction*, 68–69. [Originally in English.—Trans.]

27. Henri Michaux to Louise Bourgeois [hereafter LB], June 12, 1961 (LL-0003).

28. Notebook, c. 1961 (LB-0426): "After reading Michaux, I feel like shouting laughing bursting into laughter. [. . .] The aggression, the word is not pleasing—Michaux but I understand myself / it lives deep down in me"; earlier in the document: "read Strindberg, Michaux, make clouds."

29. "Repellent": Daniel Robbins, "Sculpture by Louise Bourgeois," *Art International* 8, no. 8 (1964): 29–31.

30. Robbins, "Sculpture by Louise Bourgeois," 29.

31. The name of the bird is *couturière* (seamstress), the tailorbird, and not *fée couturière*. That is the artist's invention.

32. Interview for Guichard, *Louise Bourgeois*.

33. In Paola Igliori, *Entrails, Heads and Tails: Photographic Essays and Conversations on the Everyday with Contemporary Artists* (New York: Rizzoli, 1992), [38]n8.

34. Diary, August 7, 1966. [Originally in English.—Trans.]

35. It is also a poetic form with a recurring refrain.

36. Loose sheet, c. 1959 (LB-0630).

37. Loose sheet, January 2, 1961 (LB-0053).

38. Loose sheet, January 2, 1961 (LB-0053).

39. Michael Fried, "New York Letter," *Art International* 8, no. 3 (1964): 58.

40. Daniel Robbins (1932–1995), art historian and curator, close friend of Louise and Robert. Robbins, "Sculpture by Louise Bourgeois."

41. Robbins, "Sculpture by Louise Bourgeois," 29.

42. "William Rubin—Louise Bourgeois," in *Destruction*, 83.

43. "William Rubin—Louise Bourgeois," in *Destruction*, 83.

44. "William Rubin—Louise Bourgeois," in *Destruction*, 84, 85.

45. LB to Robert Goldwater [hereafter RG], April 24, 1965 (LB-1454).

46. LB to RG, April 23, 1965 (LB-1453).

47. LB to RG, April 22, 1965 (LB-1452).

48. LB to RG, April 18, 1965 (LB-1450). "I am here. I am on this [much-discussed] boat," she wrote upon setting out onboard *Le France*.

49. Notebook, 1965 (LB-0771).

50. Notebook, 1965 (LB-0771), 13, 4–5.

51. Loose sheet, c. 1964 (LB-0372).

52. In front of the Luxembourg Gardens; Pons was the bakery and caterer in this road, no doubt a place where Louise and Robert would meet.

53. Notebook, 1965 (LB-0771), 11.

54. Jacqueline Delange (1923–1991), director of the Afrique noire department at the Musée de l'homme from 1960 to 1970; coauthor, with Michel Leiris, of *Afrique noire: La création plastique* (Paris: Gallimard, 1967).

55. Hélène Kamer (b. 1927), African art dealer and wife of Henri Kamer, director of the Kamer Gallery on the boulevard Raspail in Paris and on Madison Avenue in New York, which specialized in African art. Louise met her through Pierre Matisse and Robert Goldwater. After her second marriage, she became Hélène Leloup and opened her own gallery on the quai Malaquais specializing in Dogon sculpture. She socialized with Louise and Robert in New York and Paris. In her 1965 diary, Louise describes Henri's affair and their subsequent separation. She was very affected by it.

56. LB to RG, April 22, 1965 (LB-1452).

57. Notebook, 1965 (LB-0771). Patrick Boulton, whom Louise also called Bolton or P. B. His name appears in the list of men who played an important role in her love life.

58. Loose sheet, c. 1967 (LB-0075).

59. She did, however, tell Robert that she had a date with him: "I have a meeting with Mr. Boulton, 2:45, I don't know what to say." LB to RG, May 11, 1965 (LB-1461).

60. Notebook, 1965 (LB-0771), 27.

61. Notebook, 1965 (LB-0771), 32.

62. Loose sheet, April 1965 (LB-1318). [Originally in English.—Trans.]

63. Notebook, 1965 (LB-0771), 41. [Originally in French; "*ne veux*" (not want) underlined in original.—Trans.]

64. LB to RG, April 22, 1964 (LB-1452), and May 11, 1965 (LB-1461).

65. Notebook, 1965 (LB-0771), 45.

66. LB to RG, April 18, 1965 (LB-1450).

67. Luckily, it was protected by a coating of shellac and enamel. LB to RG, April 23, 1965 (LB-1453).

68. LB to RG, April 23, 1965 (LB-1453).

69. LB to RG, April–May 1965 (LB-1456). Lee Bontecou (1931–2022) was an American artist who was also included in the show at the Rodin Museum.

70. In her copy of the catalog, Louise cut out the picture and put it back in right side up.

71. Henri Zerner (b. 1939), art historian, studied at Columbia and then Harvard. He met Louise in 1958 at her Erasmus bookshop and remained a close friend for many years. Louise would make a mask of his face. See chapter 8 in this volume.

72. This was likely the Polish artist Alina Szapocznikow.

73. LB to RG, May 6, 1965 (LB-1458).

74. LB to RG, May 6, 1965 (LB-1458).

75. LB to RG, April 28, 1965 (LB-1455).

76. John Chamberlain (1927–2011), American sculptor whose work was made from found objects and crushed cars.

77. LB to RG, April 28, 1965 (LB-1455).

78. LB to RG, May 7, 1965 (LB-1459).

79. LB to RG, May 7, 1965 (LB-1459).

80. LB to RG, May 4, 1965 (LB-1457).

81. LB to RG, May 11, 1965 (LB-1460).

82. LB to RG, May 15, 1965 (LB-1462).

83. This was a performance of Aimé Césaire's *Tragédie du roi Christophe*. Michel Leiris was responsible for getting the play performed at the Théâtre de l'Odéon in Paris, in 1965.

84. LB to RG, May 6, 1965 (LB-1458).

85. LB to RG, May 15, 1965 (LB-1462). André Malraux (1901–1976) was a French writer and minister of cultural affairs.

86. LB to RG, May 15, 1965 (LB-1462).

87. LB to RG, May 6, 1965 (LB-1458).

88. LB to RG, May 7, 1965 (LB-1459).

89. LB to RG, May 11, 1965 (LB-1460).

90. LB to RG, May 4, 1965 (LB-1457).

91. LB to RG, May 19, 1965 (LB-1464).

92. "[W]ith the usual plastic dolls and toys glued on this time to women's figures and in color. Strangely, although it is all supposed to be amusing (or so I suppose), no one seemed at all amused." RG to LB, April 25, 1965 (RG-0014). [Originally in English.—Trans.]

93. RG to LB, April 25, 1965 (RG-0014). [Originally in English.—Trans.]

94. "Bruce Barton called, and was surprised to hear you had gone; it was to invite you to a party." RG to LB, April 23, 1965 (RG-0015). [Originally in English.—Trans.]

95. See RG's letters, April–May 1965.

96. "Why did the army classified [*sic*] him 4F 1Y [?]—not local draft board— What will the army say, physical disability, bad mental risk, security risk or more specific[?]" Diary, October 18–24, 1964. [Originally in English.—Trans.]

97. Diary, December 1964 ("dates to remember" page). [Originally in English.—Trans.]

98. Diary, March 15, 1965. [Originally in English.—Trans.]

99. Diary, June 5, 1966. [Originally in English.—Trans.]

100. Diary, January 29, 1966. [Originally in English.—Trans.]

101. LB to RG, May 7, 1965 (LB-1459).

102. Colette Roberts, interview with Louise Bourgeois, 1968, Archives of American Art, Smithsonian Institution.

103. Roberts interview.

104. Xavier Girard, *Louise Bourgeois: Face-à-face* (Paris: Seuil, 2016), 33.

105. Michel Leiris to RG, October 20, 1967 (LL-0180).

106. Diary, June 12, 1966.

107. Lucy R. Lippard, "Eccentric Abstraction," *Art International* 10, no. 9 (1966): 28, 34–40, reprinted in Lippard, *Changing: Essays in Art Criticism* (New York: E. P. Dutton, 1971), 98–111.

108. Lucy R. Lippard, "Eccentric Abstraction," in Frances Morris, ed., *Louise Bourgeois*, exh. cat. (London: Tate, 2007), 114.

109. Lippard, "Eccentric Abstraction" *Art International*, 34.

110. Lippard, "Eccentric Abstraction," *Art International*, 28, 34–40.

111. Vincent Honoré, "*Le regard*," in Morris, *Louise Bourgeois*, 242.

112. Ann Coxon, "Soft Landscape," in Morris, *Louise Bourgeois*, 272.

113. "[T]he [. . .] shapes of my drawing as concave—instead of convex." Notebook, 1965 (LB-0771), 24.

114. Bourgeois, "Self-Expression Is Sacred and Fatal," 180.

115. Observatory built by François Biret at Châtillon, destroyed in 1920 to be replaced by a concrete tower. From the top of it, you can see an immense panorama of Paris and its environs. Bourgeois discussed this place in the 1990s with Paulo Herkenhoff.

116. Loose sheet, c. 1965 (LB-1441), printed as "On the Creative Process" in *Destruction*, 74. [Originally in English.—Trans.]

117. Draft of LB to Henriette Bonnotte, September–October 1967 (LB-1449).

118. Robert left for New York from Pisa on August 26.

119. LB to RG, September 8, 1967 (LB-1476).

120. *Sleep II*, 1967, *Untitled (Sleep)*, 1967, and *Untitled (Sleep II)*, 1968.

121. "*Big Sleep*, because it's not about death, but a little afternoon nap." [Note that this is not an official title.—Trans.] Interview for Guichard, *Louise Bourgeois*.

122. This piece is now in MoMA's collection (object number 250.1983).

123. Bourgeois, quoted in Deborah Wye, *Louise Bourgeois*, exh. cat. (New York: Museum of Modern Art, 1982), 26.

124. LB to RG, September 20, 1967 (LB-1485).

125. "I will kill you a rabbit tomorrow," a worker told her. LB to RG, September 16, 1967 (LB-1483). "The heart is stupid the rabbit not bad." Diary, October 4, 1967.

126. LB to RG, September 16, 1967 (LB-1483).

127. Lorenzo Guerrini (1914–2002), Italian sculptor, took part in the Venice Biennale in 1968 and worked in Pietrasanta.

128. LB to RG, September 2, 1967 (LB-1471).

129. LB to RG, October 2, 1967 (LB-1495).

130. LB to RG, September 22, 1967 (LB-1486).

131. "I find myself rubbing shoulders with a young Japanese man, handsome enough, whom I seduce," written in her diary over a span of entries, July 16–26, 1967, but attributed to "October 5th or 6th, 1967."

132. LB to RG, September 20, 1967 (LB-1485).

133. LB to RG, September 10, 1967 (LB-1478).

134. "I immediately loved Rome—the Pantheon that I see from my window." LB to RG, November 8, 1967 (LB-1515).

135. LB to RG, September 29, 1967 (LB-1493).

136. "I am vague through emptiness [. . .] I suffer from lack of—everything— How can one suffer from an atrocious solitude in the midst of everybody [. . .] nothing appeals to me." Loose sheet, c. 1967 (LB-0075).

137. LB to RG, October 13, 1967 (LB-1503).

138. RG to LB, October 17, 1967 (RG-0071). [Originally in English.—Trans.]

139. "Since you always try to protect me." Draft of LB to RG, c. September 1967 (LB-1446).

140. LB to RG, October 11, 1967 (LB-1501).

141. LB to RG, October 4, 1967 (LB-1496).

142. LB to RG, October 3, 1967 (LB-1495).

143. LB to RG, October 9, 1967 (LB-1500).

144. LB to RG, June 6, 1968 (LB-1526).

145. LB to RG, October 6, 1967 (LB-1497).

146. LB to RG, June 2, 1968 (LB-1523).

147. LB to RG, October 19, 1968 (LB-1585).

148. LB to RG, September 4, 1967 (LB-1473): "your letter included a joke and it is all so serious here that I believe it is what I appreciated most in the whole wide world—a little humor in English or in French."

149. Diary, January 13, 1968. [Mostly in English.—Trans.]

150. Diary, July 21–22, 1967.

151. Diary, June 4, 1967. [Mostly in English.—Trans.] Bourgeois is referring to the Egyptian president Gamal Abdel Nasser's closing of the Gulf of Aqaba to Israeli shipping on May 22, 1967, effectively blockading the Israeli port of Elat. Israel responded on June 5 (the day after Bourgeois's diary entry) with a preemptive strike on an Egyptian air force base, launching the Six-Day War. The UN Security Council issued a call for a ceasefire, which Israel and Jordan immediately accepted; Egypt agreed a day later, and Syria a day after that, on June 10.

152. RG to LB, September 13, 1967 (RG-0043). Robert says the cause was a heart attack, but the actual cause was a cerebral hemorrhage.

153. LB to RG, September 29, 1967 (LB-1493).

154. Jacques Zwobada (1900–1967), French sculptor.

155. LB to RG, September 29, 1967 (LB-1493).

156. Interview for Guichard, *Louise Bourgeois.*

157. Rosalind Krauss, "Portrait of the Artist as Fillette," in Peter Weiermair, ed., *Louise Bourgeois,* exh. cat. (Kilchberg and Zurich, Switzerland: Stemmle, 1995).

158. J. Laplanche and J.-B. Pontalis, *Vocabulaire de la psychanalyse* (Paris: Presses universitaires de France, 1967).

159. Loose sheet, c. 1959 (LB-0464). [Mix of French and English.—Trans.]

160. Krauss, "Fillette," 146.

161. Bourgeois, "Self-Expression Is Sacred and Fatal," 188.

162. Bourgeois, "Self-Expression Is Sacred and Fatal," 181.

163. LB to Albert Elsen, May 20, 1968 (LB-1352), in *Destruction,* 80. [Originally in English.—Trans.]

164. Bourgeois, "Self-Expression Is Sacred and Fatal," 189, 194.

165. Donald Kuspit, *Louise Bourgeois* (New York: Random House, 1988), 68.

166. Bourgeois, "Self-Expression Is Sacred and Fatal," 196.

167. Loose sheet, c. 1959 (LB-0464). [Mix of English and French.—Trans.]

168. Bourgeois, "Self-Expression Is Sacred and Fatal," 182.

169. *Art Now* 1, no. 7 (1969): n.p. (LBE-0042), reprinted as "On *Janus Fleuri*" in *Destruction,* 91.

170. LB to RG, June 2, 1968 (LB-1523).

171. LB to RG, June 5, 1968 (LB-1525).

172. "The *Village drapé* is a name that I don't like and I want to change the name to *Cumul N° I.*" LB to RG, September 21, 1968 (LB-1565).

173. LB to RG, June 3, 1968 (LB-1524).

174. "New materials for molds, glues, etc. make possible a greatly simplified handling of the more traditional materials, and permit a freedom of form that corresponds to ideas for sculpture that I have long had in mind. [...] This can only be done in Italy, because only there is close, daily cooperation with skilled workers possible—and also for reasons of cost." Pro-

gram for Work in Sculpture, most likely part of an application for a Guggenheim grant, c. 1967 (LB-1758), in *Destruction,* 79. [Originally in English.—Trans.]

175. She could be playing on the double meaning of the word "marble"—the material, and the small ball of colored glass. Loose sheet, April 27, 1957 (LB-0141). [Originally in English.—Trans.]

176. LB to RG, September 14, 1967 (LB-1481). [The word "jelled" is in English.—Trans.]

177. *Soft and Apparently Soft Sculpture,* traveling exhibition (October 6, 1968–October 12, 1969) curated by Lippard for the American Federation of Arts, New York, which also included work by Eva Hesse, Bruce Nauman, Keith Sonnier, Richard Serra, Claes Oldenburg, and Yayoi Kusama.

178. This piece is no longer extant.

179. LB to RG, June 24, 1968 (LB-1537).

180. LB to RG, June 15, 1968 (RG-0092). [Originally in English.—Trans.]

181. Louise never managed to spell his name correctly; sometimes she wrote it with a "Y," sometimes with an "H."

182. LB to RG, September 16, 1968 (LB-1561).

183. RG to LB, September 13, 1968 (RG-0108): "You say Ipousteguy is doing the work a little like yours. If it is still figurative, I must say I do not see the connection." [Originally in English.—Trans.]

184. LB to RG, September 21, 1968 (LB-1565).

185. LB to RG, October 19, 1968 (LB-1585).

186. LB to RG, October 2, 1968 (LB-1575).

187. LB to RG, July 3, 1968 (LB-1545).

188. LB to RG, June 1, 1968 (LB-1522).

189. LB to RG, June 7, 1968 (LB-1527).

190. RG to LB, May 27, 1968 (RG-0089). [Originally in English.—Trans.]

191. RG to LB, July 7, 1968 (RG-0097). [Originally in English.—Trans.]

192. French publisher specializing in reprinted avant-garde and surrealist magazines, as well as architecture journals. He created the *Marché de la poésie* festival in 1983.

193. RG to LB, July 9, 1968 (RG-0099). [Originally in English.—Trans.]

194. LB to RG, September 5, 1968 (LB-1551).

195. LB to RG, September 24, 1968 (LB-1569).

196. RG to LB, September 28, 1968 (RG-0118). [Originally in English.—Trans.]

197. "Le chemin parcouru: Interview with Xavier Tricot," 1996, in Louise Bourgeois, *Destruction du père / Reconstruction du père: Écrits et entretiens, 1923–2000,* expanded French ed., ed. Marie-Laure Bernadac and Hans Ulrich Obrist (Paris: Daniel Lelong, 2000), [hereafter cited as *Destruction* (French ed.)] 384.

198. See Albert E. Elsen, *The Partial Figure in Modern Sculpture,* exh. cat. (Baltimore: Baltimore Museum of Art, 1969), 1–2.

199. Loose sheet, February 21, 1965 (LB-0401). [Originally in English.—Trans.]

200. LB to RG, September 16, 1968 (LB-1561).

201. RG to LB, October 5, 1968 (RG-0125): "Did you know that Marcel Duchamp died. He was 81. Apparently just collapsed after dinner in his apartment in Paris." [Originally in English.—Trans.]

202. Diary, May 19, 1968.

203. Diary, October 27, 1968.

204. Diary, June 8, 1968.

205. "Two Conversations with Deborah Wye," 1979 and 1981, in *Destruction*, 128.

206. Colette Roberts (1910–1971), writer, art critic, and art dealer (Grand Central Moderns Gallery). She conducted over a dozen interviews with American artists, including Bourgeois, held at the Archives of American Art.

207. "Well, it was really [Roger] Bissière who taught me the most." Colette Roberts, interview with Louise Bourgeois, 1968, Archives of American Art, Smithsonian Institution.

208. Interview for Guichard, *Louise Bourgeois*.

209. Loose sheet, c. 1959 (LB-0464).

210. Loose sheet, September 23, 1968 (LB-0468). [In French except for "manageable."—Trans.]

211. "Two Conversations," 126.

212. Bourgeois, quoted in Wye, *Louise Bourgeois*, 25.

213. William Rubin, "Some Reflections Prompted by the Recent Work of Louise Bourgeois," *Art International* 13, no. 4 (1969): 17–20.

214. No doubt referring to the exhibition on American sculpture.

215. "William Rubin—Louise Bourgeois," in *Destruction*, 81–86.

216. Rubin, "Some Reflections," 20.

217. Kurt Vonnegut (1922–2007), American writer, published *Cat's Cradle* in 1963 and *Slaughterhouse-Five* in 1969. "The book of Vonnegut was astounding," she wrote. LB to RG, April 21, 1969 (LB-1597).

218. LB to RG, October 1, 1970 (LB-1680).

219. LB to RG, April 29, 1969 (LB-1603).

220. LB to RG, April 21, 1969 (LB-1597).

221. LB to RG, May 3, 1969 (LB-1604). William Agee (1936–2022) was an associate curator at MoMA before becoming director of exhibitions and collections at the Pasadena Art Museum in California.

222. LB to RG, May 9, 1969 (LB-1606).

223. LB to RG, October 1, 1969 (LB-1618). The works today are called *Black II* or *Black III* (also *Bullet* or *Black Worlds*), 1968.

224. LB to RG, October 4, 1969 (LB-1621).

225. LB to RG, November 18, 1969 (LB-1646).

226. LB to RG, November 18, 1969 (LB-1646).

227. Henry Moore (1898–1986), English sculptor.

228. LB to RG, September 22, 1969 (LB-1612).

229. LB to RG, October 31, 1969 (LB-1635).

230. Alina Szapocznikow (1926–1973), Polish artist who moved to Paris in 1963. She was married to Ryszard Stanisławski, director of the Sztuki Museum in Łódź, and then to the graphic artist Roman Cieslewicz. Her work, at the intersection of surrealism, nouveau réalisme (she was close to Pierre Restany), and pop art, is, like Louise's, unique: polyester molds of her belly, her lips, and her breasts and other sexualized, provocative objects; she has been the subject of several important exhibitions (MoMA, Centre Pompidou), which rightly restore her importance as a pioneering artist. Louise had two of her mouth-lamps, which she never took out of the box, and gave her one of her own bronze sculptures (*Sleep*, 1967–68).

231. LB to RG, September 25, 1969 (LB-1615).

232. Frank Gallo (1933–2019), American sculptor who worked with resin.

233. Marisol (1930–2016), American pop artist.

234. LB to RG, October 2, 1969 (LB-1619).

235. LB to RG, October 4, 1969 (LB-1621).

236. LB to RG, October 4, 1969 (LB-1621).

237. See Hélène Gheysens, "Mémoire fragmentaire: Alina Szapocznikow et Louise Bourgeois, 1969–1973," *Notebooks du Musée national d'art moderne,* no. 144 (Summer 2018).

238. Written on the reverse of RG to LB, September 30, 1969 (LB-1335).

239. Maria Papa Rostkowska (1923–2008), Polish sculptor.

240. Loose sheet, December 2, 1951 (LB-0451): "He [Alex] had inherited his father['s] taste and lavishness. [. . .] He had what my father called 'the stone madness' he was a builder, maybe an artist." [Mix of English and French.—Trans.]

241. LB to RG, November 7, 1969 (LB-1638).

242. LB to RG, October 16–17, 1969 (LB-1628): "I intend to examine the 40 contributions of 40 countries + the shorts, documentaries and others."

243. LB to RG, October 20, 1969 (LB-1630).

244. Roman Cieslewicz (1930–1996), Polish artist and graphic designer, husband of Alina Szapocznikow; he wrote Louise a letter (LL-0451) in 1991 when he wanted to sell some sculpture. Louise asked him to create the catalog layout she wanted to make for Robert Goldwater's memorial in 1973. See Gheysens, "Mémoire fragmentaire," which cites a letter from Louise Bourgeois to Roman Cieslewicz, of July 12, 1973 (CLW-107), Institut Mémoires de l'édition contemporaine (Imec), Paris. Nothing came of it or of Louise's project for him to create a calling card for her. See also her other letters to Roman Cieslewicz at Imec.

245. LB to RG, October 20, 1969 (LB-1630).

246. LB to RG, October 18, 1969 (LB-1629).

247. LB to RG, October 25, 1969 (LB-1632).

248. LB to RG, May 9, 1969 (LB-1606).

249. LB to RG, October 16–17, 1969 (LB-1628).

250. LB to RG, November 2, 1969 (LB-1637).

251. RG to LB, November 7, 1969 (RG-0204).

252. LB to RG, November 13, 1969 (LB-1642).

253. LB to RG, September 23, 1969 (LB-1613).

254. LB to RG, October 1, 1969 (LB-1618).

255. LB to RG, November 13, 1969 (LB-1642).

256. Diary, January 11, 1969. [Originally in English.—Trans.]

257. Diary, September 9, 1969. [Originally in English.—Trans.]

258. Diary, September 18, 1969.

259. Diary, October 2, 1969.

Chapter 8. The Destruction of the Father

Epigraph: Quoted in Deborah Wye, *Louise Bourgeois,* exh. cat. (New York: Museum of Modern Art, 1982), 95.

1. Louise Bourgeois, "Self-Expression Is Sacred and Fatal: Statements," in Christiane

Meyer-Thoss, *Louise Bourgeois: Konstruktionen für den freien Fall / Designing for Free Fall* (Zurich: Ammann, 1992), 178

2. Dorothy Seiberling, "The Female View of Erotica," *New York,* February 11, 1974, special issue, "Why Women Are Creating Erotic Art," reprinted in "A Merging of Male and Female" in Louise Bourgeois, *Destruction of the Father / Reconstruction of the Father: Writings and Interviews, 1923–1997,* ed. Marie-Laure Bernadac and Hans Ulrich Obrist (Cambridge, MA: MIT Press, and London: Violette, 1998) [hereafter cited as *Destruction*], 101.

3. *Untitled (Hand),* 1970, wax and fabric.

4. *Mother and Child,* 1970, wax, pins, and needles.

5. And in another, later sculpture, called *Untitled (Hearts),* 1989, rubber and steel.

6. Interview for Camille Guichard, dir., *Louise Bourgeois* (Paris: Terra Luna Films, 1993).

7. Bourgeois inscribed one of the eleven pages of *Paris toujours Paris* (2006): "*Peaux de lapins, chiffons, ferrailles à vendre.*" See also her *Cell* piece, *Peaux de lapins, chiffons, ferrailles à vendre* (2006).

8. Diary, November 26, 1970. [Mostly English with some French.—Trans.]

9. Diary, December 14, 1970. [Originally in English. The word "or" is underlined in the original.—Trans.]

10. Alain Bourgeois, interview with the author, 2018.

11. "Told to Rob[er]t on the phone." Diary, January 28, 1972. [Originally in English. —Trans.]

12. "Sixty-One Questions," 1971, in *Destruction,* 95. This was a questionnaire sent by Alexis Rafael Krasilovsky, a student in Dr. Lenore Weitzman's course "Sociology of the Woman Artist" at Yale University.

13. Diary, March 30, 1970. [In English except for "*pas mal ça*" (bad about this).—Trans.]

14. Diary, March 30, 1970. [Originally in English.—Trans.]

15. Diary, December 7, 1970.

16. "I am tired of France and the French." LB to Dominique Bozo, c. 1979, Dominique Bozo Archives, Bibliothèque Kandinsky, Centre Pompidou.

17. André Chastel (1912–1990), French art historian, specializing in the Italian Renaissance.

18. Director of the Musée national d'art moderne.

19. Critic for *Le Monde* and art historian.

20. Dominique Bozo (1935–1993), young curator at the Musée national d'art moderne, recipient of a Focillon fellowship, bought *Cumul I* (1969) in 1973. He was a close friend of Louise's, and she wrote a piece about him which would be included in the collection published in tribute to him after his death: Louise Bourgeois, "Dominique Bozo: A Possible Portrait," in *Dominique Bozo: Un portrait possible* (Paris: Réunion des musées nationaux, 1994), reprinted in *Destruction,* 286.

21. Erasmus was Louise's shop at 114 East Eleventh Street and then at 922 Madison Avenue at Seventy-Third Street.

22. Henri Zerner, interview with the author, September 13, 2016.

23. Patrice Marandel, curator at the Los Angeles County Museum of Art. Marandel went to the United States in 1967 to do an internship at the Philadelphia Museum of Art and obtained a Focillon fellowship in 1969.

24. Patrice Marandel, interview with the author, New York, October 2016.

25. *Louise Bourgeois: Femme-Maison*, May 3–June 6, 1981.

26. Bourgeois, "Dominique Bozo," 286.

27. In 1979, Louise brought Bozo to Bridgehampton, on Long Island, where she was storing her marbles outside in the grassy dunes. She reminded him of this trip in a letter from 1990: "I associate you with exploring New York." Bozo Archives, Bibliothèque Kandinsky.

28. Françoise Cachin (1936–2011), curator at the Musée national d'art then the Centre Pompidou, and then director of the Musée d'Orsay and eventually director of Musées de France. She was very close friends with Bozo during this time.

29. Isabelle Monod-Fontaine, curator at the Musée national d'art moderne; her husband, Marc, stayed at Louise's place, as attested by a thank-you note, dated September 5, 1975 (LL-0519).

30. "I would very much like to come to Paris with the pieces that remain [from the Hamilton Gallery, 1978]. Do you know of any galleries who like the American school?" N.d., Bozo archive, Bibliothèque Kandinsky.

31. Pietro Cicognani said: "She loved that man." Interview with the author, New York, November, 2016.

32. Bourgeois, "Dominique Bozo," 286.

33. LB to Dominique Bozo, photocopy, June 9, 1976 (LB-2144).

34. Notes handwritten by Jerry Gorovoy, c. 1993, in *François Rouan: Paintings and Drawings 1972–1976*, exh. cat. (New York: Pierre Matisse Gallery, 1976) (LB-2149). [Originally in English.—Trans.]

35. Dominique Bozo to LB, June 15, 1976 (LL-0378).

36. Xavier Fourcade (1926–1987) was a contemporary art dealer who started his own gallery in 1970.

37. LB to Dominique Bozo, Bozo Archives, Bibliothèque Kandinsky.

38. LB to Dominique Bozo, October 10, 1978, Bozo Archives (not inventoried), Bibliothèque Kandinsky.

39. Dominique Bozo to LB, c. 1978 (LL-0511).

40. Louise Bourgeois kept press clippings about him.

41. *Archives Dominique Bozo*, compact disc, Bibliothèque Kandinsky.

42. Pontus Hulten, director of the Musée national d'art moderne from 1977 to 1981.

43. LB to Dominique Bozo, January 7, 1977, Bozo Archives, Bibliothèque Kandinsky.

44. Bourgeois, "Dominique Bozo," reprinted in *Destruction*, 286.

45. See also Xavier Girard, *Louise Bourgeois: Face-à-face* (Paris: Seuil, 2016).

46. Peter Heinrich von Blanckenhagen (1909–1990), professor at the Institute of Fine Arts, specializing in Roman art and mural painting. Louise did his bust in bronze.

47. Peter Agostini (1913–1993), American sculptor, professor at the New York Studio School, Columbia, and Parsons. His work was difficult to classify, called a "puzzle" by critics, because it ranged from realist images of horses to pop objects and also included erotic and sensuous forms that recalled the work of Gaston Lachaise as well as Louise Bourgeois. He was one of Marisol's influences.

48. Diary, July 16, 1970.

49. Adja Yunkers (1900–1983), painter and printmaker, married to Dore Ashton, the curator of the exhibition.

50. Diary, July 19, 1970.

51. "We emphatically condemn the following crimes of the United States government: / War in Southeast Asia / Racism at home and abroad / Unwavering support of fascist governments throughout the world / Suppression of political dissent." Loose sheet, July 16, 1970 (LBE-0232), inserted in Fondation Maeght, *L'art vivant aux États-Unis,* exh. cat. (Saint-Paul-de-Vence, France: Fondation Maeght, 1970) (BIB-6430).

52. "Robert is leaving for Milan." Diary, September 1, 1970.

53. In Deborah Wye and Carol Smith, *The Prints of Louise Bourgeois,* catalogue raisonné (New York: Museum of Modern Art, 1994), 138.

54. LB to Robert Goldwater [hereafter RG], September 10, 1970 (LB-1663). [In French except for "mood."—Trans.]

55. André Schaeffner (1895–1980), French anthropologist and ethnomusicologist.

56. LB to RG, September 14, 1970 (LB-1666): "her friend Pierre Boulez who is in the United States could write a few lines for this new instrument."

57. LB to RG, September 14, 1970 (LB-1666): "The portrait of Peter has been completed I have done the eyes—the cranium is established and unless otherwise indicated it is placed looking up— It could be hanging from a wall or placed on a bronze pole, like the Socrates with a marble base."

58. LB to RG, September 26, 1970 (LB-1676). [The word "respect" is underlined in the original.—Trans.]

59. LB to RG, September 6 and 7, 1970 (LB-1660).

60. LB to RG, October 14, 1970 (LB-1687). [The word "very" is underlined in the original.—Trans.]

61. LB to RG, September 17, 1970 (LB-1668).

62. LB to RG, October 3, 1970 (LB-1682).

63. See also the first part of the video *Feminist Artists Event,* 1974. In another video taken by Louise, we can see Cicognani dressed in a costume with many udders, squatting next to Cosimo, who is draped in fabric next to *Femme couteau.* The Easton Foundation, audio visual recording, c. 1974–75 (AV.00882).

64. LB to RG, October 20, 1970 (LB-1690). "And feel the size of a pea." Reference to the text from 1947 used in the work *She Lost It* (1992) (LB-0833). [Originally in English. —Trans.]

65. LB to RG, October 26, 1970 (LB-1692).

66. LB to RG, October 28, 1970 (LB-1694).

67. LB to RG, September 19, 1970 (LB-1670).

68. Draft of LB to RG, November 1969 (LB-1696).

69. Draft of LB to RG (this letter was not sent, Louise pointed out), c. 1970 (LB-1698).

70. Interview for Guichard, *Louise Bourgeois.*

71. Diary, May 21, 1971. Jean Revol (1929–2012) was a French painter and writer who knew Bachelard. He met Louise in 1966, when he taught art history at Middlebury College in Vermont. He was a member of the American Society of Psychopathology of Expression and taught art to the mentally ill patients at the Hôpital Sainte-Anne in Paris. He sent his books, dedicated to Louise, and did a long interview with her in 1995 that was excerpted in *Le Figaro* (Jean Revol, "Louise Bourgeois: 'Je vais explorer la transcendance,'" *Le Figaro,* June 20, 1995). The exhibition was held at Sonraed Galleries, 141 Prince Street, New York.

72. Press release, May 26, 1971 (with statement by Louise Bourgeois), for *Jean Revol*, Son-raed Galleries, New York, June 5–23, 1971 (LBE-0233). [Originally in English.—Trans.]

73. Diary, July 2–3, 1971. [Mix of French and English.—Trans.]

74. Diary, July 26, 1971. The exact title is *Self-Realization and Self-Defeat* (New York: Grove, 1966); this book was in her library (BIB-3811).

75. Diary, page opposite December 20–26, 1971. [Originally in English.—Trans.]

76. Old hotel for artists and writers in the rue Jacob, near Saint-Germain-des-Prés and the École des beaux-arts.

77. "Robert['s] arm still hurts him, hemorrhages in the upper arm and the lower arm." Diary, February 5, 1967. [Originally in English.—Trans.] Henri Zerner remembers that Robert fainted once in the street and didn't tell Louise about it. Interview with the author, September 13, 2016.

78. Diary, March 24, 1973. [Originally in English.—Trans.]

79. "5AM - Robert dies in his sleep." Diary, March 26, 1973. [Originally in English.—Trans.] That same morning, Patrice Marandel called her to see how she was. She was silent, and then he heard her voice, impersonal, strange: "*Ça va, ça va.*" "And Robert?" he asked. "He is with the children." Marandel was surprised by this reply, and asked: "What is he doing?" She replied, coldly, "He's dead." Interview with the author, New York, October 2016.

80. Robert Goldwater is buried in Cutchogue Cemetery, Long Island.

81. Diary, March 9, 1974. [Originally in English.—Trans.]

82. Diary, May 7, 1973. [Originally in English.—Trans.]

83. For more on the Rothko estate, see the remarks of Paul Gardner, who covered the trial for the press; he tried to interview Louise, who told him, "They killed him," before he could get a word in. Paul Gardner, interview with the author, January 2017.

84. Diary, May 12, 1973. [Originally in English. The word "my" is underlined in the original.—Trans.]

85. Diary, May 12, 1973. [Originally in English.—Trans.]

86. Diary, December 16, 1973.

87. Diary, June 6, 1974. [Mostly in English.—Trans.]

88. Jacqueline Delange, "Robert Goldwater and the African Object," in *Robert Goldwater: A Memorial Exhibition* (New York: Museum of Primitive Art, 1973). The volume also includes tributes from Nelson A. Rockefeller, Gertrud A. Mellon, Douglas Newton, and texts by William Fagg and John Coplans.

89. See also the obituary by Robert Rosenblum in the *New York Times*, April 8, 1973. Rosenblum was Goldwater's student in a modern art class at Queens College.

90. His personal books were not donated and remain in the care of The Easton Foundation.

91. Diary, June 6, 1974. [Originally in English.—Trans.]

92. Diary, June 6, 1974. [Originally in English.—Trans.]

93. Diary, August 19, 1974. [Originally in English.—Trans.]

94. Diary, April 5, 1973. [Originally in English.—Trans.]

95. Joyce Kozloff (born 1942), interview with the author, New York, October 2016. Max Kozloff (1933–2025), her husband, was one of Robert Goldwater's students. He admired him, but he was afraid of him. He remembered student dinners at 347 West Twentieth Street, served by Louise.

96. Diary, June 12, 1974. [The phrase "the inner void" is underlined in the original. —Trans.]

97. Diary, June 14, 1974. [The word *"remplir"* (filling) is double-underlined in the original.—Trans.]

98. Diary, January 12, 1975. [Mostly in English.—Trans.]

99. Diary, August 15, 1974. [Mix of English and French.—Trans.]

100. In my monograph *Louise Bourgeois* (Paris: Flammarion, 1996; rev. ed., 2008), she forbade me to use the words "fetish" and "totem."

101. See also Iris Müller-Westermann, ed., *Louise Bourgeois: I Have Been to Hell and Back*, exh. cat. (Stockholm: Moderna Museet, and Ostfildern, Germany: Hatje Cantz, 2015), 257–67.

102. Ulf Küster, senior curator at Fondation Beyeler, Riehen, Switzerland, is editing a forthcoming volume of Bourgeois-Goldwater letters.

103. Diary, September 5, 1974. She also noted his name and her expenses for July 28 and 29, 1974.

104. "I read Laing *Knots*." Diary, August 10, 1974. [Originally in English.—Trans.] R. D. Laing, *Knots* (New York: Pantheon Books, 1970) (BIB-6133).

105. See Paulo Herkenhoff, "Cannibalism," in Frances Morris, ed., *Louise Bourgeois*, exh. cat. (London: Tate, 2007), 70. Laing, *Knots*, 17.

106. Diary, September 10, 1983. [Originally in English.—Trans.]

107. Chris Kraus, born in 1965, American writer and filmmaker, author of *I Love Dick* and *Aliens and Anorexia* and director of the film *Gravity and Grace*.

108. Chris Kraus, *I Love Dick* (South Pasadena, CA: Semiotext(e), 2006), 241.

109. LB to RG, November 13, 1969 (LB-1642).

110. Epigraph: "Transcendence: Interview with Gary Koepke," *SoHo Journal 1995–1996* (1995), reprinted in *Destruction*, 309.

111. Chryssa (1933–2013), Greek American artist, and Lee Krasner (1908–1984), American painter who was married to Jackson Pollock until his death.

112. Gemeinschaft Deutscher und oesterreichischer Künstlerinnenvereine aller Kunstgattugen (League of Female Artists Associations of All Genres), founded in 1926 in Hamburg by Ida Dehmel.

113. Called *Bringing Home the Evolution*, the photocollage was also mass-produced as a poster in 1978.

114. Elisabeth Lebovici, "Is She? Or Isn't She?," in Morris, *Louise Bourgeois*, 131–36.

115. "Forum: Women in Art," *Arts Magazine*, February 1971, reprinted in *Destruction*, 97; Eva Hesse, Alice Neel, and Nancy Spero also replied.

116. "Sixty-One Questions," 95. [Emphasis in the original.—Trans.]

117. Louise Bourgeois, "Statements from Conversations with Robert Storr," in *Destruction*, 220. [Emphasis in the original.—Trans.]

118. Lebovici, "Is She? Or Isn't She?," 133, 134.

119. This event brought together Janet Sawyer, Pat Mainaridi, Howardena Pindell, Lee Roser, Alice Baber, Faith Ringgold, and Fay Lanzer, among others; it was held at the YMCA on Fifteenth Street in New York; see Bourgeois, "Does Art Have a Gender?," February 16, 1972 (LB-1436), reprinted in *Destruction*, 98.

120. Bourgeois, "Does Art Have a Gender?," in *Destruction*, 99. [Originally in English. —Trans.]

121. "A Merging of Male and Female," *New York Magazine,* February 11, 1974, special issue, "Why Women Are Creating Erotic Art," reprinted in *Destruction,* 101.

122. Participants: Joan Semmel, Ann Sharp, Juanita McNeely, Joan Gluckman, Judith Bernstein, Martha Edelheit. Another round table on the theme of the erotic, moderated by Joan Semmel, was held on January 24, 1975, at the Open Mind (on Greene Street in SoHo).

123. The film is called *Feminist Events and Analysis / Feminist Artists Part II* (1974). Louise Bourgeois Archive, The Easton Foundation, audio visual recording, March 29, 1973 (AV.00943). First part: Louise at home (her dog, her garden, her courtyard). Second part: interview with participants.

124. *Feminist Events and Analysis,* 11:27–13:13 (AV.00943).

125. Louise Bourgeois, "Letter to the Editor," *Art in America* 60, no. 1 (1972): 123, reprinted in *Destruction,* 97.

126. An early, premonitory draft showing an abstract mouth filled with little lumps appeared in her diary on March 4, 1970.

127. Interview for Guichard, *Louise Bourgeois.*

128. Eleanor Munro, *Originals: American Women Artists* (New York: Simon and Schuster, 1979), reprinted in "Statements 1979," in *Destruction,* 115.

129. Diary, February 27, 1975. [Originally in English.—Trans.]

130. Lucy Lippard, "Louise Bourgeois: From the Inside Out," *Artforum* 13, no. 7 (1975): 26–33, reprinted in Lippard, *From the Center: Feminist Essays on Women's Art* (New York: E. P. Dutton, 1976), 238–49.

131. Unpublished transcript of a video clip from *Louise Bourgeois: An Interview,* videotape, 30 min., 40 sec. (Chicago: Video Data Bank, 1975).

132. Transcript of a video clip from *Louise Bourgeois: An Interview;* Diary, May 24, 1978. [Mostly in English.—Trans.]

133. "Renunciation of my father when I turn against him in 1937." Diary, May 24, 1978. [In English except for the word *"Renonciation"* (renunciation).—Trans.]

134. Pietro Cicognani, born in 1954. He studied at the School of Visual Arts, then architecture at Columbia. Today he practices architecture in New York.

135. His maternal grandmother, Elena Stolypine, the princess Wolkonsky, daughter of a prime minister, fled Russia when the revolution broke out. The tragic, romantic stories on Pietro's family tree must have impressed Louise.

136. Pietro Cicognani, interview with the author, New York, November 2016.

137. Transcript of a video clip from *Louise Bourgeois: An Interview.*

138. The letter included three photos of *Cumul* at the Musée national d'art moderne, dated December 4, 1975 (LL-0539).

139. Cicognani interview. According to him, she loved him because he had a job and a family and because he was normal.

140. The young artist told Bourgeois that Baudelaire was buried at Père-Lachaise, in Paris, with his stepfather, whom he hated.

141. Notes by LB on an exhibition announcement for *Sculptors' Drawings,* Fine Arts Building, 105 Hudson Street, New York, May 29–June 8, 1976 (LB-1929): "It was as we were leaving the opening that Pietro said we should get married."

142. Dominique Bozo to LB, June 15, 1976 (LL-0378).

143. LB to Pietro Cicognani, July 12, 1977 (LB-2127).

144. LB to Pietro Cicognani, July 27, 1977 (LB-2128).

145. Pietro Cicognani to LB, July 28, 1977 (LL-0547).

146. "Cosimo passes away 9:30PM. I wrap him in the 'fur blanket' thought he would get well—coughing + trembling + panting did not frighten me—??" Diary, January 13, 1976. [Originally in English.—Trans.]

147. Loose sheet, c. 1977 (LB-1201).

148. Diary, May 2, 1976. [Originally in English.—Trans.]

149. Diary, August 29, 1978. [Mix of French and English.—Trans.]

150. Diary March 17, 1976. [Originally in English.—Trans.]

151. Diary, March 11, 1976. [Originally in English.—Trans.]

152. See Robert Storr, *Louise Bourgeois: Intimate Geometries* (New York: Monacelli, 2016), 286.

153. Interview with Jennifer Dalsimer, April 9, 1986, in Morris, *Louise Bourgeois*, 84.

154. Bourgeois, "Self-Expression Is Sacred and Fatal," 183.

155. Like her student Robbie Tillotson (1949–1987), an artist who worked as a stripper to fund his studies.

156. In Jerry Gorovoy and Pandora Asbaghi, eds., *Louise Bourgeois: Blue Days and Pink Days,* exh. cat. (Milan: Fondazione Prada, 1997), 150.

157. "People Are Talking About . . . Louise Bourgeois," interview with Carter Ratcliff, with photos by Duane Michals, *Vogue,* October 1980, 343, 375–77.

158. Mark Setteducati, interview with the author, New York, 2016.

159. Patricia Hamilton, telephone interview with the author, New York, 2016.

160. Bourgeois, "Self-Expression Is Sacred and Fatal," 182.

161. *Louise Bourgeois, Sculpture, 1941–1953, Plus One New Piece,* September 18–October 13, 1979. The exhibition included thirty-three *Personages* and *Partial Recall* (1979).

162. Louise paid for Suzan to travel to Paris so she could make contacts to further her career as an actress. Louise wrote in her diary that Suzan fell in love with Alex Van Gelder, who would later photograph Louise in old age. Diary, November 16, 1979.

163. From October 28 to December 1, 1979.

164. *Picasso,* Grand Palais, Paris, October 11, 1979–January 7, 1980.

165. Diary, November 24–25, 1979.

166. Diary, November 26, 1979.

167. Diary, December 1–3, 1979. [Originally in English.—Trans.]

168. Diary, December 26, 1979. [Originally in English.—Trans.]

169. December 1, 1978–February 28, 1979.

170. Paul Gardner, "The Discreet Charm of Louise Bourgeois," *Art News,* February 1980, 80–85.

171. Diary, February 8, 1979. [Originally in English. The word "peace" is underlined in the original.—Trans.]

172. Diary, February 22, 1979. [Mostly in English.—Trans.]

173. Diary, August 11–12, 1979.

174. Eleanor Munro, "The Rise of Louise Bourgeois," *Ms.,* July 1979, 65–67, 101–2.

175. "People Are Talking About . . . Louise Bourgeois."

Chapter 9. The Body in Pieces

Epigraph: Louise Bourgeois, "Child Abuse," *Artforum* 20, no. 4 (1982), reprinted in Louise Bourgeois, *Destruction of the Father / Reconstruction of the Father: Writings and Interviews, 1923–1997*, ed. Marie-Laure Bernadac and Hans Ulrich Obrist (Cambridge, MA: MIT Press, and London: Violette, 1998) [hereafter cited as *Destruction*], 134.

1. Max Hutchinson Gallery, March 18–April 19, 1980.

2. This work would be acquired by the Australian National Gallery in Canberra, due to Hutchinson's links to the country—one of Louise's first foreign acquisitions.

3. Deborah Wye met Louise in 1976 and organized a show around her work the following year at the Rose Art Museum at Brandeis University in Waltham, MA. She noticed the paucity of writing on Louise, was driven to do this work, and received a grant for museum professionals from the National Endowment for the Arts in 1978.

4. *The Iconography of Louise Bourgeois*, Max Hutchinson Gallery, September 6–October 11, 1980. Louise showed over thirty paintings from the 1940s, as well as some drawings and prints. The catalog includes a text by Jerry Gorovoy ("The Iconography of Louise Bourgeois") and one by Xavier Girard on *Femme maison* ("Louise Bourgeois: Primary Images").

5. And after her death as well; Gorovoy is the president of The Easton Foundation.

6. Alain Bourgeois, interview with the author, The Easton Foundation, New York, 2015.

7. Diary, January 23, 1981. She also mentions Jerry on January 16 and February 1, 1981.

8. Diary, February 2, 1981.

9. "Jerry [came] for dinner [. . .] I am completely + friendly silent. I let him talk and he talks a lot / wonderful." Diary, November 12, 1985. [Originally in English.—Trans.]

10. "Jerry calls before leaving Janis, nice." Diary, February 25, 1981. [Originally in English.—Trans.] After the Sidney Janis Gallery, which he wouldn't actually leave until 1984, Jerry worked part-time for the Galerie Lelong in New York.

11. The exhibition then toured to Houston, Chicago, and Akron, Ohio.

12. According to Robert Storr, "Louise Bourgeois: Gender and Possession," *Art in America*, April 1983, 128–37, the exhibition was meant to go to the Centre Pompidou in Paris, the Kröller-Muller in Otterlo, The Netherlands, and, in 1984, the Musée de Toulon in France. But these plans did not materialize.

13. "I call Fourcade + break with the gallery because I said that Gill was full of pot (true)." Diary, February 23, 1981. [Originally in English.—Trans.]

14. Robert Miller Gallery showed Joan Mitchell, Alice Neel, and Lee Krasner, among others.

15. "I was terrified by Fourcade." Diary, January 19, 1981. [Originally in English.—Trans.]

16. Diary, April 4, 1980.

17. Diary, June 25, 1984. [Originally in English.—Trans.]

18. Diary, June 22, 1986. [Originally in English.—Trans.]

19. Claire Bourgeois to Louise Bourgeois [hereafter LB], June 19, 1967 (LL-0112).

20. See also Juliet Mitchell, "The Sublime Jealousy of Louise Bourgeois," in Philip Larratt-Smith, ed., *Louise Bourgeois: The Return of the Repressed*, 2 vols. (London: Violette, 2012), 1:47.

21. In her conversations with Deborah Wye, Louise talked about her sister's wooden leg, which was an exaggeration; she had coxotuberculosis with a decalcification in her leg and had

to have her knee operated on. This left her with one leg longer than the other and a limp. See "Two Conversations with Deborah Wye," 1979 and 1981, in *Destruction*, 126.

22. "Two Conversations," 126.

23. Diary, November 16, 1980. [Originally in English.—Trans.]

24. Diary, January 19, 1981. [Originally in English.—Trans.]

25. Diary, November 26, 1985. [Originally in English.—Trans.]

26. Diary, March 28, 1985. The fourth nephew is Francis Daniel, son of Janet, Robert's sister. [Originally in English.—Trans.]

27. Pierre Friloux (1947–2007) was a French actor; in the early 1980s, he won a Fulbright scholarship to go to the United States. He turned to a multidisciplinary, hybrid form of art. Under the Brooklyn Bridge he created a monumental *Vénus Hybride*, a blend of sculpture and video (1988). In 1979, at the Kitchen, he gave a performance: *Vide et au chaud*. Louise must have met him in New York, because he was young, French, and came from the Comédie-Française. This act of abandonment or withdrawal, to which she refers in her journal, is confirmed by a note. Loose sheet, c. 1980 (LB-0792): "I owe an explanation, I owe an explanation to Pierre Friloux for my cruel abandonment." [Mix of French and English. The first "I owe an explanation" is in French and underlined in the original.—Trans.]

28. Diary, May 19, 1980. [Originally in English.—Trans.]

29. Diary, May 19, 1980. [Originally in English.—Trans.] Michael Blackwood (1934–2023), filmmaker, made a number of documentaries about art and artists. He included Louise in two films: *Masters of Modern Sculpture, Part III: The New World*, 1984 (David Smith, Louise Nevelson, and Louise Bourgeois, among others), and *Reclaiming the Body, Feminist Art in America*, 1995. The visit in 1980 was no doubt related to a film on tapestry that Louise wanted him to make. See Dominique Bozo to LB (LL-0509).

30. Diary, February 23, 1979. [Originally in English.—Trans.]

31. Patricia Hamilton, phone conversation with the author, January 2017.

32. Diary, April 26, 1980. [Originally in English.—Trans.]

33. See also her diary: "I use Sadie to interest him. I use my mother to get to D'oelnitz. Robert G., Gert Schiff, Rubin + Varnedoe. My mother tells me: You are a parasite. Call Lowenfeld." Diary, March 18, 1985. [Originally in English.—Trans.]

34. Diary, November 14, 1980. [Originally in English.—Trans.]

35. American writer and journalist Paul Gardner published several important articles about Louise, including "The Discreet Charm of Louise Bourgeois," *Art News*, February 1980, 80–86; "Louise Bourgeois Makes a Sculpture," *Art News*, Summer 1988, 61–67; and "The Houses That Louise Built," *House and Garden*, October 1992, 153–58, 185; as well as a book for the "Universe Series on Women Artists": *Louise Bourgeois* (New York: Universe, 1994). He also, along with Chris Maybach, featured her in a film for the *Art City* series in 1996: *Art City: Making It in Manhattan*.

36. For example, a dinner in 1988 prepared by the photographer Denise Browne Hare. Gardner remembers that Louise arrived in a severe black and white suit and went to the bathroom to change into a pale violet silk blouse, much more glamorous. Interview with the author, New York, October 2016. This dinner was documented in "Is Food Art?," *Contemporanea* 1, no. 4 (1988): 93–97.

37. Diary, January 20, 1980.

38. Diary, February 9, 1980. [Originally in English.—Trans.]

39. A group of feminist performance artists and activists.

40. Janet Fish (b. 1938), American realist painter. Diary, October 10, 1985.

41. *Picasso: A Retrospective*, May 22–September 16, 1980.

42. A young curator at the Musée de Toulon who, on the advice of Dominique Bozo, wanted to do a show around Louise's drawings.

43. Bourgeois, in Xavier Girard, *Louise Bourgeois: Face à face* (Paris: Seuil, 2016), 15.

44. Louise showed *Cumul III/Avenza* (1969), a kind of hollowed-out marble "Cumul" fountain. *Perceiving Modern Sculpture: Selections for the Sighted and Non-Sighted*, July 8–August 22, 1980, Grey Art Gallery, New York University.

45. Girard, "Louise Bourgeois: Primary Images."

46. Bourgeois, in Girard, *Louise Bourgeois* 95–96.

47. Girard, *Louise Bourgeois.*

48. Diary, August 30, 1981. [Originally in English.—Trans.]

49. Diary, September 18, 1981. [In English, except for the phrase *"J'ai peur d'avoir"* (I'm afraid of having); "violence" is double-underlined in the original.—Trans.]

50. Diary, September 19, 1981. [Originally in English.—Trans.]

51. Diary, September 25, 1981.

52. Diary, September 22, 1981. She was referring, respectively, to *Femme maison* (the smaller of two versions) and *Henriette* (both marble). [Mix of English and French.—Trans.]

53. Louise Bourgeois, "Self-Expression Is Sacred and Fatal: Statements," in Christiane Meyer-Thoss, *Louise Bourgeois: Konstruktionen für den freien Fall / Designing for Free Fall* (Zurich: Ammann, 1992), 177.

54. "[Afraid to] slip or trip [. . .] lose your balance stand up straight, [. . .] terrified of moving forward, when Pierre is born." Diary, August 31, 1987. [Mix of French and English.—Trans.] We saw this earlier in a loose sheet from January 1, 1958 (LB-0272): "This question of space is perhaps simply based on the fear of falling— When Pierre was born Maman said— Louise got up and she walked. Maybe I was just afraid to fall at that moment— Vertigo and great fear on balconies (roof at 18th St)." [Originally in English.—Trans.]

55. Diary, July 1, 1982. [Originally in English.—Trans.]

56. Diary, August 26, 1984. [Mix of English and French. (<u>I give you Easton</u> *en toute propriété.*) Underlined in the original.—Trans.]

57. Diary, May 6, 1980. [Mix of English and French.—Trans.]

58. Diary, September 9, 1981. [Originally in English.—Trans.]

59. Diary, October 12, 1981. [Originally in English.—Trans.]

60. Diary, February 9, 1982. This was Louise's wish at the time, but finally a foundation was created with Jerry as its president. [Originally in English. Underlined in the original.—Trans.]

61. Cecile Abish, Blythe Bohnen, Betsy Damon, Martha Edelheit, Jackie Ferrara, April Kingsley, Joyce Kozloff, Lucy Lippard, Mary Miss, Linda Nochlin, Howardena Pindell, Corinne Robins, Dorothy Seiberling, Sylvia Sleigh, Joan Snyder, Nancy Spero, May Stevens, Michelle Stuart, and Barbara Zucker to William Rubin, June 6, 1973 (LL-0214).

62. *From Women's Eyes*, Rose Art Museum, Brandeis University, Waltham, MA, 1977; and *Louise Bourgeois: Matrix / Berkeley 17*, University of California at Berkeley, 1979; see chapter 8 in this volume.

63. Kay Larson, "Women by a Woman," *New York Magazine*, November 22, 1982, 74.

64. Robert Storr, "Meanings, Materials and Milieu—Reflections of Recent Work by Louise Bourgeois," *Parkett* 9 (1986), reprinted in *Destruction,* 144.

65. "Sixty-One Questions," 1971, in *Destruction,* 97. This was a questionnaire sent by Alexis Rafael Krasilovsky, a student in Dr. Lenore Weitzman's course "Sociology of the Woman Artist" at Yale University.

66. Robert Hughes, "A Sense of Female Experience," *Time,* November 22, 1982, 116; Larson, "Women by a Woman," 74, 76.

67. Diary, October 29 and 30, 1981.

68. This important monograph, which Louise so desired, would not appear until 2016; Robert Storr, *Louise Bourgeois: Intimate Geometries* (New York: Monacelli, 2016).

69. "My contract is signed with Bob Storr." Diary, November 20, 1985. [Originally in English.—Trans.] "[A]greement between Robt and me." Diary, December 4, 1985. [Originally in English.—Trans.]

70. Diary, June 18, 1987. [Originally in English.—Trans.]

71. Diary, February 20, 1982. [Originally in English.—Trans.]

72. Called *Partial Recall* (1983), it was made by Gerald Saldo and Laura Tennen with the help of Robert Storr.

73. Diary, May 24, 1982. [Originally in English.—Trans.]

74. Diary, March 19, 1986, in Louise Bourgeois, *Destruction du père / Reconstruction du père: Écrits et entretiens, 1923–2000,* expanded French ed., ed. Marie-Laure Bernadac and Hans Ulrich Obrist (Paris: Daniel Lelong, 2000), 139–40. [Mix of English and French.—Trans.]

75. This was the sculpture entitled *Eyes* (1982), marble.

76. An old photograph that can also be found in Louise Bourgeois, *Album* (New York: Peter Blum, 1994), which elaborates on *Partial Recall* with additional family photographs and a longer text.

77. Ingrid Sischy (1952–2015), art critic, journalist, American author born in South Africa. She worked for *Artforum* (she was the editor-in-chief at the time), the *New Yorker,* Andy Warhol's magazine *Interview,* and finally *Vanity Fair.*

78. "Child Abuse," reprinted in *Destruction,* 133.

79. "Child Abuse," reprinted in *Destruction,* 134.

80. "Child Abuse," reprinted in *Destruction,* 134.

81. "Now do you want me to talk about my personal life . . . I don't like to do that." Bourgeois in "Interview with Susi Bloch," *Art Journal* 35, no. 11 (1976): 370–73, reprinted in *Destruction,* 102–7, quotation at 105.

82. Diary, April 14, 1982. [Originally in English. Capitals in the original.—Trans.]

83. MacDowell Medal Acceptance Speech, August 19, 1990, reprinted in *Destruction,* 198–201.

84. Girard, *Louise Bourgeois,* 72.

85. Diary, July 4, 1983. [Mix of English and French.—Trans.]

86. Award for Outstanding Achievement in the Visual Arts at the National Women's Caucus for Art Conference (1980); Honorary Doctor of Fine Arts Degree at Bard College (1981); elected Fellow of the American Academy of Arts and Sciences, Boston (1981); Honorary Doctor of Fine Arts Degree at the Massachusetts College of Art (1983); member of the American Academy of Arts and Letters, New York (1983); President's Fellows Award from the

Whitney Museum of American Art and Rhode Island School of Design (1984); Honorary Doctor of Fine Arts Degree at the Maryland Institute, College of Art, Baltimore (1984).

87. In Paola Igliori, *Entrails, Heads and Tails: Photographic Essays and Conversations on the Everyday with Contemporary Artists* (New York: Rizzoli, 1992), n.p. [38].

88. Let us recall that the term "nature" at one time designated the male genitals.

89. In Igliori, *Entrails, Heads and Tails*, n.p. [37].

90. Interview for Camille Guichard, dir., *Louise Bourgeois* (Paris: Terra Luna Films, 1993).

91. In Eleanor Munro, *Originals: American Women Artists* (New York: Simon and Schuster, 1979), reprinted as "Statements 1979" in *Destruction*, 115.

92. She made several versions of this sculpture: pink marble, red wax, white porcelain, and blue and red rubber.

93. Storr, "Meanings, Materials and Milieu," reprinted in *Destruction*, 140.

94. Storr, "Meanings, Materials and Milieu," reprinted in *Destruction*, 140.

95. Storr, "Meanings, Materials and Milieu," reprinted in *Destruction*, 145.

96. Diary, May 10, 1984.

97. Loose sheet, October 17, 1955 (LB-0036). [Originally in English.—Trans.]

98. Storr, "Meanings, Materials and Milieu," reprinted in *Destruction*, 140, 142.

99. Diary, February 28, 1985. [Originally in English.—Trans.]

100. Work installed between June and October 1985 on Doris C. Freedman Plaza, Fifth Avenue and Sixtieth Street in New York, sponsored by the Public Art Fund and the Department of Parks and Recreation. This sculpture was bought by the Metropolitan Museum of Art.

101. Interview with the author in *Louise Bourgeois: Pensées-plumes*, exh. cat. (Paris: Centre Pompidou, 1995), reprinted in *Destruction*, 303.

102. Robert Storr writes about these many large eyes alongside Salvador Dalí's set design for Alfred Hitchcock's film *Spellbound* in *Louise Bourgeois*, 387–88.

103. Diary, February 9, 1987; Georges Henri Rivière and Michel Leiris. [Originally in English.—Trans.]

104. See also Philippe Lançon, "Araignée du soir: Louise Bourgeois par Jean Frémon," *Libération*, February 26, 2016. Jean Frémon would subsequently write two books about Louise: *Louise Bourgeois: Femme maison* (Paris: L'Échoppe, 2008); and *Calme-toi, Lison* (Paris: P.O.L., 2016), published in English as *Now, Now, Louison*, trans. Cole Swenson (London: Les Fugitives, 2018).

105. This refers to types of tapestry. Teniers scenes (named after the seventeenth-century Flemish artist David Teniers the Younger) depict genre scenes of people outdoors. Verdure is greenery. Both date to the sixteenth century. Louise notes seeing both types in her diary on February 3, 1985.

106. In this film project on Louise and France, made by Paul Falkenberg (never finished or released), we see her wearing her leopard coat at the Deux Magots with Jerry, going into numbers 172 and 174, boulevard Saint-Germain, visibly moved, and then coming right back out; visiting the *école maternelle* in the rue Saint-Benoît, at the Librairie La Hune (we also see the Lycée Fénelon, but without Louise). The film is part of the Louise Bourgeois Archive at The Easton Foundation (see AV.00066_2).

107. Diary, February 4, 1985. [Originally in English.—Trans.]

108. One scene, shot in the gallery, shows the sculpture set very close to the wall. [Originally in English.—Trans.]

109. Diary, February 6, 1985.

110. Jean-Michel Place, interview with the author, Paris, 2017.

111. Diary, February 7, 1985. [Originally in English.—Trans.]

112. Diary, February 9, 1985. She is most likely signing the photolithographs of *Sheaves* (1984) or *Inner Life* (1985), which were produced in conjunction with the exhibition.

113. Diary, February 9, 1985. [In English, except for the phrase *"la Bonté existe"* (goodness exists).—Trans.]

114. Louise Bourgeois's words, as recalled by Jean-Michel Place in conversation with the author.

115. Alice Bellony-Rewald, "Paris: Louise Bourgeois," *Beaux-arts*, February 1985, 84; Philippe Dagen, "Louise Bourgeois," *Le quotidien de Paris*, February 14, 1985.

116. Pierre Cabanne, "Louise Bourgeois: Sculpteur pour tuer le père," *Le matin de Paris*, February 18, 1985.

117. Geneviève Bréerette, "Les sculptures autobiographiques de Louise Bourgeois," *Le Monde*, March 2, 1985, 15.

118. "There is no doubt that psychoanalysis fits right into this deeply Oedipian symbolism. The sculpture reverses it, little by little." Dagen, "Louise Bourgeois."

119. Galerie Maeght-Lelong, Zurich, April 11–May 1985; *Louise Bourgeois: Nature Study*, Serpentine Gallery, London, May 18–June 23, 1985; "Taking Cover: Interview with Stuart Morgan," *Artscribe*, January 1988, reprinted in *Destruction*, 150–56.

120. Loose sheet, March 7, 1986 (LB-1817). [Originally in English.—Trans.]. Image reproduced in *Destruction*, 138–39.

121. Diary, April 20, 1983. [Originally in English.—Trans.]

122. *Fear Four* is the name of a marble work from 1984; Diary, March 24, 1984.

123. Loose sheet, c. 1986 (LB-0050).

124. *Louise Bourgeois: Drawings, 1939–1987*, Robert Miller Gallery, New York, January 6–30, 1988; *Louise Bourgeois: Works on Paper, 1939–1988*, Museum Overholland, Amsterdam, October 22–December 31, 1988; *Louise Bourgeois: Dessins, 1940–1986*, Galerie Lelong, Paris, February 19–March 25, 1989.

125. "There was identification with both parents." Diary, May 28, 1989.

126. Diary, August 15, 1987. [Originally in English. "Hell" is crossed out and "life" is written underneath it in the original. Capitals in the original.—Trans.]

127. "[O]ne hour early. Sitting in the sun waiting for Jerry on the steps." Diary, April 21, 1984. [Originally in English.—Trans.]

128. Diary, April 2, 1984.

129. Diary, April 21, 1984. [Originally in English.—Trans.]

130. "Working on cleaning the big piece." Diary, February 11, 1985. "[F]rontal piece mean[s] nothing. I need the depth of the pieces: transparence." Diary, February 12, 1985. [Second entry originally in English.—Trans.]

131. Diary, February 25, 1985. This is written under drawings of metal bases labeled "plates from Dean." [Originally in English.—Trans.] She mentions the "Bachelard pieces" again on February 27, 1985 ("Bachelard pieces, 4 or 5 of them").

132. *Louise Bourgeois: Paintings from the 1940s*, Robert Miller Gallery, New York, January 6–31, 1987. Separately, Warhol showed his stitched photographs (it was the last show of his own work that he would attend; he died February 22, 1987). There are several pictures

of them together taken over the course of this evening. Louise and Andy had known each other since the mid-1960s.

133. Diary, August 27, 1984. [Originally in English.—Trans.]

134. Livio Saganic, sculptor and painter, born in Croatia in 1950 and moved to New York in 1964. He studied at the Pratt Institute, then attended Yale's MFA Program, and finally went to Drew University. He saw Louise regularly in the 1980s.

135. Livio Saganic, interview with the author, New York, January 2017.

136. Diary, October 12, 1982. [Originally in English.—Trans.]

137. Diary, August 15, 1983. Louise Neri, art critic.

138. Storr, "Meanings, Materials and Milieu," reprinted in *Destruction*, 144–45.

139. Cooper and Kraus produced theatrical performances together, for instance *Scenes from an Almost Socialist Marriage,* in which Suzan played the role of the mother. Bourgeois designed the poster advertising the event (see LBE-0225).

140. Sylvère Lotringer (1938–2021), French philosopher, literary critic, professor at Columbia University, then at the European Graduate School in Saas-Fee, founder of the journal *Semiotext(e)*.

141. Chris Kraus, *I Love Dick* (South Pasadena, CA: Semiotext(e), 2007), 180. It's not clear which Tenth Street show this is, whether Louise ever went with Rauschenberg to his opening, or whether she was even there.

142. Kraus, *I Love Dick,* 180.

143. American writer born in 1938, author of *American Mythologies* (1992).

144. Diary, December 15, 1985. [Originally in English.—Trans.] In the end, Chris Kraus did not carry the pregnancy to term.

145. Diary, May 29, 1985. [Jerzy Grotowski and Tadeusz Kantor were leading directors in experimental theater; Grotowski wrote the classic text *Towards a Poor Theatre* (1968). —Trans.]

146. Louise played the role of the Cousin. A photograph shows her at the center of a group that included Beverly Pepper, Françoise Gilot, Jack Youngerman, and Red Grooms. David Hockney and Marisol were also part of the group. See program for Ubu Repertory Theater, *Catch Desire by the Tail,* Solomon R. Guggenheim Museum, New York, October 25 and 26, 1984 (LBE-0234).

147. She would return to this theme when she worked on the Marguerite Duras project; see chapter 10 in this volume.

148. Louise read Roland Barthes's *Fragments d'un discours amoureux* in 1977. Loose sheet, c. 1977 (LB-1201): "Roland Barthes essay on Istanbul, on ⌊Pierre⌋ Loti, *A Lover's Discourse: Fragments.*" [Originally in English.—Trans.]

149. In Meyer-Thoss, *Louise Bourgeois,* 124–25.

150. Diary, June 27, 1989. [Mix of English and French.—Trans.]

151. On July 30, 1984, she noted: "J. Lacan—*The Seminar,* 1973. *The Four Fundamental Concepts of Psychoanalysis* (Seuil)." *The Four Fundamental Concepts of Psychoanalysis* is a book based on a seminar given by Jacques Lacan in 1964. The book was originally published in French in 1973 by Seuil.

152. *Qu'est ce que la sculpture moderne?,* Centre Georges Pompidou, Musée national d'art moderne, Paris, July 3–October 13, 1986.

153. See also Robert Hughes's article in *Time*, September 1, 1986, cited in Storr, *Louise Bourgeois*, 489.

154. Donald Kuspit, *Louise Bourgeois* (New York: Random House, 1988).

155. Diary, February 15, 1987. [Mix of English and French. The word "sacred" is underlined in the original.—Trans.]

156. Diary, June 3, 1987. [Originally in English. The words "kill myself" are underlined in the original.—Trans.]

157. "The Passion for Sculpture: A Conversation with Alain Kirili," *Arts* 63, no. 7 (1989): 68–75, reprinted in *Destruction*, 176–85.

158. Storr, "Meanings, Materials and Milieu," reprinted in *Destruction*, 142.

159. Bourgeois, "Self-Expression Is Sacred and Fatal," 179.

160. Chris Maybach and Paul Gardner, dirs., *Art City: Making It in Manhattan* (Los Angeles: Twelve Films, 1996).

161. See also Jacques Soulillou, *Impunité de l'art* (Paris: Seuil, 1995), 133. Bourgeois had two copies (BIB-6818 and BIB-7173).

162. Diary, March 28, 1986.

163. Diary, March 28, 1986.

164. *Les magiciens de la terre*, Centre Pompidou, La Villette, May 16–August 15, 1989, commissioned by Jean-Hubert Martin, director of the Musée national d'art moderne.

165. Bourgeois, "Self-Expression Is Sacred and Fatal," 183.

166. Storr, "Meanings, Materials and Milieu," reprinted in *Destruction*, 143.

167. As well as *Gathering Wool* (1990), which presented an open structure with balls of wood in front of it.

168. Diary, December 20, 1989.

169. *Louise Bourgeois: Works on Paper, 1939–1988*, Museum Overholland, Amsterdam, October 22–December 31, 1988. The drawings had previously been shown at the Robert Miller Gallery, New York, January 6–30, 1988.

170. Diary, October 6, 1988 (written before she left). [Originally in English. The words "embarrassed" and "fear of success" are underlined in the original.—Trans.]

171. *Louise Bourgeois: Dessins, 1940–1986*, Galerie Lelong, Paris, February 19–March 25, 1989.

172. In 1992, they would be transferred from the Cabinet d'art graphique du Musée national d'art moderne to the Centre Pompidou.

173. Diary, February 13, 1989. [Originally in English.—Trans.]

174. Louise Bourgeois, "Acceptance Speech: CAA Achievement Award," February 15, 1989, reprinted in *Destruction*, 174.

175. Diary, February 17, 1988. [Mix of English and French.—Trans.]

176. Diary, September 27, 1987. [Originally in English.—Trans.]

177. Diary, December 5, 1987. [In English except for "*équilibré*" (balanced). The word "truth" is underlined in the original.—Trans.]

Chapter 10. Becoming a "Star"

Epigraph: Louise Bourgeois, "Artist's Statement," Carnegie International, Pittsburgh, 1991, in *Louise Bourgeois: The Locus of Memory, Works, 1982–1993*, exh. cat. (New York: Brooklyn Museum and Harry N. Abrams, 1994), 25, 41, reprinted in "On Cells" in Louise Bourgeois,

Destruction of the Father / Reconstruction of the Father: Writings and Interviews, 1923–1997, ed. Marie-Laure Bernadac and Hans Ulrich Obrist (Cambridge, MA: MIT Press, and London: Violette, 1998) [hereafter cited as *Destruction*], 205.

1. For Marion Cajori and Amei Wallach, dirs., *Louise Bourgeois: The Spider, the Mistress, and the Tangerine* (New York: Art Kaleidoscope Foundation and Zeitgeist Films, 2008).

2. After working in several different jobs, such as school bus driver and production assistant for Woody Allen's films.

3. Setteducati was Louise Bourgeois's former student and first assistant. Louise was being awarded an Honorary Doctorate at Yale University at the same time as B. B. King and former president Gerald Ford. Setteducati drove Louise, Jean-Louis, and Alain. Michel slipped discreetly in on his own. Mark Setteducati, interview with the author, The Easton Foundation, New York, January 27, 2017.

4. Information confirmed by letters sent between Robert and Louise, who were frequently worried about Michel's instability.

5. In the end, there would be no advisory board. After Louise's death, several people were named to advise the foundation: Deborah Wye, Robert Storr, and Paulo Herkenhoff. But it would be led by Jerry Gorovoy, Jean-Louis, and Alain Bourgeois.

6. Diary, January 22, 1990.

7. Diary, February 14, 1992.

8. "<u>Dean</u> becomes the headquarters of the foundation and the property of the said foundation? The purpose of the meeting is <u>to inform</u> the trustees of the state of things. No voting is necessary. [. . .] Louise is giving 475 to the found[ation]." Diary, August 7, 1990. [In English except for *"siège"* (headquarters). "Dean" and "to inform" are underlined in the original.—Trans.]

9. Diary, August 20, 1990. All of Louise's archives are housed at The Easton Foundation.

10. Diary, March 28, 1993. [Originally in English.—Trans.]

11. Diary, October 20, 1992. Claire never actually received the cabinets. Two years later she used them in the *Cell* titled *Red Rooms (Parents)*.

12. French artist (born 1956), daughter of Iannis and Françoise Xenakis, married to David Klatzmann; during a visit to New York in 1989, she went to see Louise.

13. Diary, July 15, 1993. [Mix of English and French.—Trans.]

14. Alex Bourgeois, Alain's son and Louise's grandson.

15. Wendy Williams, who at that time worked at the Robert Miller Gallery and later was Louise's studio manager, played go-between for Louise and Alex. "Wendy is the confidant between Alex + me." Diary, June 14, 1991. [Originally in English.—Trans.]

16. Diary, August 8–9, 1991. [Originally in English.—Trans.]

17. Loose sheet, August 3, 1995 (LB-0781). [Originally in English.—Trans.]

18. Diary, October 9, 1990. [Mix of English and French.—Trans.]

19. Diary, July 16, 1990.

20. Diary, August 8, 1990. [Originally in English.—Trans.]

21. *Louise Bourgeois: A Retrospective Exhibition,* organized by Peter Weiermair, Frankfurter Kunstverein, Germany, December 3, 1989–January 28, 1990.

22. Located at this time in a wing of the Musée Saint-Pierre, Musée des beaux-arts.

23. Thierry Raspail, preface to *Louise Bourgeois,* exh. cat. (Lyon: Musée Saint-Pierre art contemporain, 1990), 7 (exhibition dates, July 5–August 20, 1990).

24. Diary, June 17, 1990.

25. Caroline Schmulde, "Louise Bourgeois," *Art Press,* October 1990.

26. *Galeries Magazine,* June–July 1990, 95–103, 140.

27. Michael Brenson, "For Louise Bourgeois at 79, Honor in Her Homeland at Last," *New York Times,* August 6, 1990.

28. "I returned to Cannes in 1990 after an exhibition I'd been having at the Musée d'art contemporain in Lyon. We revisited Le Cannet and went back to the Hôtel de Grande-Bretagne, which made me realize that buildings and places can be peripheral too. When I was a child, the Hôtel de Grande-Bretagne was a three-star hotel. I think by the 1940s there was no further demand for it," she told Hans Ulrich Obrist, explaining that the hotel had been destroyed to make way for a "much less salubrious" establishment. "Interview with Obrist," in *Destruction,* 290.

29. Diary, July 2, 1990 (but no doubt this was actually written on July 8, after Lyon.) [Originally in English.—Trans.]

30. Diary, July 14, 1990.

31. Diary, November 5, 1990.

32. Diary, November 5, 1990.

33. Loose sheet, c. 1961 (LB-0103).

34. Loose sheet, c. 1960 (LB-0222).

35. Diary, November 8, 1990.

36. Exhibition curated by Mark Francis and Lynne Cooke at the Carnegie Museum of Art, Pittsburgh, October 19, 1991–February 16, 1992.

37. Directly referring to her mother's illness.

38. Tadeusz Kantor (1915–1990) and Jerzy Grotowski (1933–1999), Polish theater directors whose work Louise saw in New York in the 1980s.

39. Louise Bourgeois on *Cell (Glass Spheres and Hands)* in "Mortal Elements: Pat Steir Talks with Louise Bourgeois," *Artforum* 32, no. 1 (1993), reprinted in *Destruction,* 237.

40. *New York Times* survey: "My favorite smell. Smell of the garden after the rain. I have always worn Shalimar." Diary, October 24, 1992. [Originally in English.—Trans.]

41. Loose sheet, June 21, 1994 (LB-0551).

42. Diary, February 4, 1997. [Mix of French and English.—Trans.]

43. Peter Blum, art dealer and publisher based in New York.

44. "All my subjects are contemporary. Opening MoMA 6:30 P.M., *Dislocations* dinner at 8 P.M." Diary, in both LB's and Jerry Gorovoy's handwriting. October 16, 1991. [Mix of French and English.—Trans.]

45. According to Storr, Nauman said, smiling, "You've gotta watch out for that woman," when he saw *Twosome* in *Dislocations.* Like Bourgeois, Nauman was included in the exhibition *Eccentric Abstraction* in 1966. See Robert Storr, *Louise Bourgeois: Intimate Geometries* (New York: Monacelli, 2016), 510.

46. Christian Leigh, "The Earrings of Madame B . . . : Louise Bourgeois and the Reciprocal Terrain of the Uncanny," in *Louise Bourgeois: The Locus of Memory, Works 1982–1993,* exh. cat. (New York: Brooklyn Museum, 1994), 65.

47. Interview for Camille Guichard, dir., *Louise Bourgeois* (Paris: Terra Luna Films, 1993).

48. Interview for Guichard, *Louise Bourgeois.* This work was positioned right at the entrance to the exhibition *Féminin-masculin: Le sexe de l'art,* Centre Pompidou, Paris, 1995.

49. In *Dislocations,* exh. cat. (New York: Museum of Modern Art, 1991), 37.

50. Louise Bourgeois, interview with the author, in *Louise Bourgeois: Pensées-plumes*, exh. cat. (Paris: Centre Pompidou, 1995), reprinted in *Destruction*, 303.

51. From July 1 to August 27, 1992, Louise showed *Janus fleuri* (1968), *Fée couturière* (1963), *Rabbit* (1970), *Confrontation* (1978), *Cell V* (1991), and *Le défi* (1991), alongside work by Joseph Beuys (1921–1986).

52. Louise notes in her diary that Christiane Meyer-Thoss said that Beuys and Bourgeois had liberated twentieth-century sculpture. Diary, October 25, 1989.

53. Diary, July 23, 1992.

54. "Shop on Atlantic avenue / Michel's dream / fulfillment of an absence." Diary, February 25, 1991.

55. Diary, June 21, 1991. [Originally: *"la sculpture de Michel doit être érigée,"* meaning somewhat vague.—Trans.]

56. "Alain, you can retire. Jerry will take care of you." Diary, December 20, 1991. [Originally in English.—Trans.]

57. Diary, December 20, 1991. [Mix of French and English.—Trans.]

58. Diary, January 2, 1992. [Mix of French and English.—Trans.]

59. Diary, May 7, 1994. [Originally in English.—Trans.]

60. Carollee Pelos, photographer, married to Jean-Louis Bourgeois, died of cancer.

61. Diary, December 5, 1991.

62. Louise made two sculptures to benefit amfAR, the Foundation for AIDS Research: *Mannequin Head, Male and Female* (1993), and a small pink rubber object that is part phallus, part breasts for Act Up's *Art Box* of multiples in 1994.

63. Diary, January 28, 1992. [Originally in English.—Trans.]

64. Bourgeois, "On Cells," reprinted in *Destruction*, 208.

65. Suzanne Pagé and Béatrice Parent, "Interview with Louise Bourgeois," in *Louise Bourgeois*, exh. cat. (Paris: Musée d'art moderne de la Ville de Paris, 1995), 15.

66. Diary, May 3, 1992. "1929 Lycée Fénelon: infirmary: the cold shiver at the appearance of blood." [Mix of English and French.—Trans.]

67. Diary, April 30, 1992. [Originally in English.—Trans.]

68. Diary, March 1, 1994. We also see this anagram in her drawings of this period.

69. Diary, August 21, 1991. [In English except for the word *"merde"* (shit).—Trans.]

70. Diary, October 15, 1991.

71. Diary, March 26, 1992. [Originally in English.—Trans.]

72. Louise Bourgeois, notes on *Precious Liquids* shared with the Musée national d'art moderne de la Ville de Paris, Centre Pompidou, Paris, after they acquired the work on November 5, 1992. [Originally in English.—Trans.]

73. Bourgeois, notes on *Precious Liquids*.

74. Bourgeois, notes on *Precious Liquids*.

75. "George Lapcik has to take the water tower down says the insurance man, what kind of policy do we have?" Diary, November 29, 1991. George Lapcik was Louise Bourgeois's welder. This is before the piece was conceived but was the impetus for creating it (the water tower had to be dismantled from the roof). [Originally in English.—Trans.]

76. The acquisition was proposed by the author, who was then a curator in the Cabinet d'art graphique at the Musée national d'art moderne and who had been deeply impressed by

what she saw at *Documenta*. By autumn, she suggested an exhibition of drawings by Louise Bourgeois.

77. President of the Centre Pompidou and director of the Musée national d'art moderne; see Dominique Bozo's account of this trip in *Un possible portrait* (Paris: Réunion des Musées Nationaux / Centre Pompidou, 1993), 189.

78. Diary, September 18, 1992. [Originally in English.—Trans.]

79. "[Jacques] Doucet, bad father, [Robert] Storr bad father, all the critics are bad fathers." Diary, January 27, 1996.

80. Donald Kuspit, *Louise Bourgeois* (New York: Random House, 1988), 52.

81. Louise Bourgeois, "Freud's Toys," *Artforum* 28, no. 5 (1990): 111–13, written to coincide with the exhibition *The Sigmund Freud Antiquities: Fragments from a Buried Past*, University Art Museum of the State University of New York, Binghampton, New York, February 9–March 23, 1990, reprinted in *Destruction*, 186–90.

82. Bourgeois, "Freud's Toys," reprinted in *Destruction*, 186.

83. Bourgeois, "Freud's Toys," reprinted in *Destruction*, 188. She does point out, however, that the worm is a symbol of rebirth.

84. Bourgeois, "Freud's Toys," reprinted in *Destruction*, 189.

85. Bourgeois, "Freud's Toys," reprinted in *Destruction*, 190. [Emphasis in the original.—Trans.]

86. Bourgeois, "Freud's Toys," reprinted in *Destruction*, 190.

87. "Gaston Lachaise, Père Lachaise." Diary, July 8, 1999.

88. Louise Bourgeois, "Obsession," *Artforum* 30 no. 8 (1992), reprinted in *Destruction*, 211–14.

89. Bourgeois, "Obsession," reprinted in *Destruction*, 213.

90. Bourgeois, "Obsession," reprinted in *Destruction*, 214.

91. Bourgeois, "Obsession," reprinted in *Destruction*, 213.

92. Louise Bourgeois, "Native Talent," *Artforum* 32, no. 5 (1994): 73–81, written to coincide with *Joan Miró*, Museum of Modern Art, New York, October 17, 1993–January 11, 1994, reprinted in *Destruction*, 271–74.

93. Bourgeois, "Native Talent," reprinted in *Destruction*, 273.

94. Bourgeois, "Native Talent," reprinted in *Destruction*, 274. [Emphasis in the original.—Trans.]

95. Exhibition from June 13–October 10. Included were *Cell (Choisy)*, 1990–93; *Cell (Arch of Hysteria)*, 1992–93; *Cell (Eyes and Mirrors)*, 1989–93; and *Cell (Glass Spheres and Hands)*, 1990–93.

96. She had Georges Didi-Huberman's book *L'invention de l'hystérie* (Paris: Macula, 1982), which Hans Ulrich Obrist gave to her and which can still be found in her library.

97. "A Conversation with Bernard Marcadé" for Guichard, *Louise Bourgeois*, in *Destruction*, 249.

98. "Conversation with Marcadé," 252.

99. "Conversation with Marcadé," 250.

100. Bourgeois, "On Cells," reprinted in *Destruction*, 207.

101. Interview for Guichard, *Louise Bourgeois*.

102. The theater was inaugurated on October 7, 1972.

103. Louise Bourgeois, *Album* (New York: Peter Blum, 1994), reprinted in *Destruction*, 285.

104. Louise Bourgeois in March Dachy, ed., *Et nous changent le monde*, exh. cat. (Lyon:

Biennale d'art contemporain, 1993), reprinted as "On *Cell (You Better Grow Up)*" in *Destruction*, 232–33.

105. These two last *Cells*—*Cell (Three White Marble Spheres)* and *Cell (You Better Grow Up)*, both 1993—were not shown in Venice.

106. It was awarded that year to Robert Wilson for sculpture and Richard Hamilton and Antoni Tàpies for painting; Germany won best pavilion; and there were special mentions for Louise Bourgeois, Ilya Kabakov, Joseph Kosuth, and Jean-Pierre Raynaud.

107. "'Fuck them!' she shouted into the receiver and hung up." Storr, *Louise Bourgeois*, 524.

108. Diary, June 13, 1993. [Originally in English.—Trans.]

109. Interview with Nigel Finch, 1993, in "Arena," in *Destruction*, 262.

110. Guichard, *Louise Bourgeois*.

111. At this time he oversaw the collection "Contemporains" at Flammarion and worked with the author on this book proposal.

112. Initially, the interviewer was Robert Storr.

113. Interview for Guichard, *Louise Bourgeois*.

114. "Conversation with Marcadé," 251.

115. Nigel Finch (1949–1995), British filmmaker who had a large impact on the development of queer British cinema. He made several documentaries for the BBC's *Arena*, including *Chelsea Hotel, Robert Mapplethorpe, Kenneth Anger*, and *Louise Bourgeois* in 1994. He died of AIDS in 1995.

116. Diary, May 9, 1993. [In French except for "argument."—Trans.]

117. Interview with Finch, 259.

118. Chris Maybach and Paul Gardner, dirs., *Art City: Making It in Manhattan* (Los Angeles: Twelve Films, 1996).

119. Marion Cajori and Amei Wallach, dirs., *The Spider, the Mistress, and the Tangerine* (New York: Art Kaleidoscope Foundation and Zeitgeist Films, 2008).

120. Performance to celebrate the fifteenth anniversary of the Fabric Workshop and Museum, in honor of Louise Bourgeois and Anne d'Harnoncourt.

121. The couple was played by Christina Roberts and Virgil Marti.

122. Louise Bourgeois, *The Puritan* (New York: Osiris Editions, 1990).

123. Diary, June 20, 1991. [Originally in English. The word "never" is underlined in the original.—Trans.]

124. Diary, November 10, 1990. [In French; the word "*journal*" (diary) is underlined in the original.—Trans.]

125. Louise Bourgeois, *The Insomnia Drawings* (Zurich: Daros Collection, 2000), 6; see also "Insomnia Drawings" in *Destruction*, 340.

126. "Louise is a little glossary-maker making the definitions clearer and clearer: trying every possible metaphor." Diary, June 4, 1990. [Mix of English and French.—Trans.]

127. Diary, January 22, 1993. [Somewhat untranslatable wordplay on "*fer*" (iron) and "*faire*" (make).—Trans.]

128. Diary, January 21, 1993.

129. Diary, July 17, 1991.

130. Diary, August 21, 1991.

131. See also Brigitte Cornand, *Les expressions consacrées*, 2004, unreleased film. This is a short excerpt from Brigitte's archive, shown in an exhibition in Sète, France.

132. "Taking Cover: Interview with Stuart Morgan" reprinted in *Destruction*, 155.

133. Hans Ulrich Obrist, "Préface," *Destruction* (French ed.), 12.

134. Diary, December 3, 1991.

135. Diary, February 15, 1996 (*Seamstress Mistress Distress Stress*, 1997, is the title of one of Louise's "pole" pieces; the phrase is welded on its base).

136. Hans Ulrich Obrist gave her this book in 1994.

137. "Lacan's controlled trance, he plays with words, thinks through words, language; [. . .] clichés. The demystification of Lacan." Diary, December 6, 1991.

138. "Lacan's <u>writings are transcripts</u> and are not to be read." Diary, July 31, 1994. [Originally in English. Underlined in the original.—Trans.]

139. LB in conversation with Jerry Gorovoy, September 5, 1990 (LB-0051). [Originally in English.—Trans.]

140. LB in conversation with Gorovoy, September 5, 1990 (LB-0051). "Lacan fights with Jewish psychoanalysis. [. . .] He stole from the Jewish men and gave everything his love + compassion to Jewish woman. . . . He was analyzed by 3 Jewish doctors." [Originally in English.—Trans.]

141. LB in conversation with Gorovoy, September 5, 1990 (LB-0051). [Originally in English.—Trans.]

142. Notebook, 1994 (LB-0830), 27. [Originally in English. Strikethrough in the original.—Trans.]

143. Interview with Jerry Gorovoy, The Easton Foundation, New York, 2017.

144. Bourgeois made a few works on paper that show Ophelia in the water or bound to the young man who is rescuing her. *Hamlet and Ophelia* (1996) was created as a benefit print for the Brooklyn Academy of Music.

145. In Marie-Laure Bernadac, "The Insomnia Drawings of Louise Bourgeois," in Louise Bourgeois, *The Insomnia Drawings* (Zurich: Daros Collection, 2000), 12.

146. Drawing with the inscription "Hayter's nightmare" in memory of her work at Hayter's printmaking studio, Atelier 17. Bourgeois, *Insomnia Drawings*, 65v.

147. Bourgeois, *Insomnia Drawings*, 136v.

148. Diary, October 9, 1994.

149. Bourgeois, *Insomnia Drawings*, 16.

150. "The year of the French": "Interview with Vincent Katz," *Print Collector's Newsletter* 26, no. 3 (1995): 90, reprinted in *Destruction*, 320.

151. Among the many people who came to see her during the 1990s were Catherine Flohic, for an issue of her journal *Ninety*, in 1994; Maria Fluxà, who curated an exhibition in Palma de Mallorca and published some prints; as well as many photographers, including Nan Goldin, Brigitte Lacombe, Jacqueline Salmon, Dominique Nabokov, and Jean-François Jaussaud, who asked for his negatives back (after Louise had reviewed them) and found that Bourgeois had censored some of the images.

152. She went with her husband, David Klatzmann, researcher and doctor, who also went frequently to see Louise.

153. Mâkhi Xenakis, *Louise Bourgeois: The Blind Leading the Blind* (Arles, France: Actes Sud and London: Galerie Lelong, 2008). She also published *Louise, sauvez-moi! Conversations avec Louise Bourgeois, 1988–2009* (Arles, France: Actes Sud, 2018).

154. Diary, November 14, 1991.

155. "Pagé objects to the show at the Pompidou. [. . .] Bozo does not manipulate Pagé (Philip Morris wants a commitment before) delay the drawings show at Pompidou." Diary, December 1, 1992. [Originally in English.—Trans.]

156. Marie-Laure Bernadac, *Louise Bourgeois* (Paris: Flammarion, 1995; rev. ed., 2006).

157. *Féminin-masculin: Le sexe de l'art*, Centre Pompidou, Paris, October 17, 1995–January 11, 1996.

158. Diary, June 1, 1994. [Originally in English.—Trans.]

159. *Féminin-masculin: Le sexe de l'art*, exh. cat. (Paris: Centre Georges Pompidou, 1995), 122–23. [Bonnotte: a kind of expensive French potato as well as her sister's married name; good grade; haggle/quibble; turd; slang for a person from Paris; he talks, she chats [. . .] he cooks, she messes about in the kitchen; the amigo's wife is a female amigo; the camelette is the wife of the camel.—Trans.]

160. "Bernard is working on the rap Tango" and "*C'est Ça, C'est Ça*, Rap Brigitte, Ramuntcho Matta." Diary, April 7 and 10, 1995.

161. Jacques Soulillou, *L'impunité de l'art* (Paris: Seuil, 1995).

162. Diary, September 3, 1993.

163. Jacques Soulillou and André Magnin, *Contemporary Art of Africa* (New York: Harry N. Abrams, 1996).

164. "Though I have never been to the marketplace, I find it strangely exhilarating that curious tourists and locals can find sculpture for sale among the fleshy, smooth-skinned fruit and raw vegetables." Bourgeois in Soulillou and Magnin, *Contemporary Art of Africa*, 54.

165. She was being awarded the Medal of Honor from the Center for French Civilization and Culture at NYU.

166. *Louise Bourgeois: Sculptures, environnements, dessins, 1938–1995*. This exhibition was an extension of *The Locus of Memory* (itself an extension of the 1993 Venice Biennale), which was shown at the Brooklyn Museum in 1993.

167. Curator at the Fonds national d'art contemporain.

168. Rainer Mason was a curator in the graphic art department of Musée Rath in Geneva and was in charge of contemporary acquisitions for the Chalcographie du Louvre. The work was called *Lacs de montagne* (1997). Deborah Wye, ed., *Louise Bourgeois: The Complete Prints and Books*, catalogue raisonné (New York: Museum of Modern Art, 2018), cat. no. 553/XIII https://www.moma.org/s/lb/collection_lb/object/object_objid-84134.html.

169. Louise had seen an episode of Bernard Pivot's *Apostrophes* on Marguerite Duras, which intrigued her; she discussed it with Jean Frémon, who brought her some books. They discussed *Ah! Ernesto*. (Information provided by Jean Frémon.) *Louise Bourgeois: Dessins pour Duras*, March 9–April 23, 1995: "Intense work for Duras at the Vieux-Colombier." Diary, February 17, 1995. Two of Duras's plays were performed, *Le shaga* (for which she invented a language) and *Le square*.

170. *Untitled (Hommage à Duras)*, 1995. These wooden panels came from Louise's Brooklyn studio, which had once been a garment factory. One of the panels is an old paper cutter.

171. There are two works with the title *Untitled (Hommage à Duras)*, 1995, one of which is steel.

172. Diary, November 20, 1994.

173. In October 1993, Mâkhi Xenakis gave her a copy of *Écrire* (Paris: Gallimard, 1993) (BIB-6051). Louise underlined every instance of the word "ça" in pencil in the first few chapters. She also owned *L'amant de la Chine du Nord* (Paris: Gallimard, 1991) (BIB-0649).

174. Notes in Marguerite Duras, *La pluie d'été* (BIB-6123).

175. Notes in Marguerite Duras, *Le square* (BIB-6050).

176. Diary, June 11, 1994.

177. Notebook, 1994 (LB-0830), 23. [Underlined in the original.—Trans.]

178. Louise Bourgeois, "Self-Expression Is Sacred and Fatal," in Christiane Meyer-Thoss, *Louise Bourgeois: Konstruktionen für den freien Fall / Designing for Free Fall* (Zurich: Ammann, 1992), 178.

179. Stuart Morgan wrote several books and articles about her, including the catalog for the Serpentine Gallery show in 1985.

180. Stuart Morgan, "Le corps en morceaux," *Beaux-arts,* June 1992, 80–89.

181. Epigraph: "July Memos and Birthday Reminders." Diary, July 1994.

182. Inscription on the back of *Spider* (1994, crayon on paper).

183. *Ode à ma mère,* illustrated book with nine drypoint prints (Paris: Solstice, 1995), reprinted in *Destruction,* 321–29.

184. Loose sheet, c. 1986 (LB-0050).

185. Bourgeois, "Self-Expression Is Sacred and Fatal," 185.

186. Diary, May 21, 1995.

187. *Ode à ma mère,* reprinted in *Destruction,* 329.

188. They are nearly the same as those in *Partial Recall* (1983), with additional text.

189. Loose sheet, c. 1958 (LB-0146).

190. "The fashion system": Paulo Herkenhoff gave Louise a copy of this book by Roland Barthes in 1996 (BIB-5783).

191. Some of these handkerchiefs (1995–96) were shown at the Pièce unique gallery in Paris, then at CAPC—Musée d'art contemporain in Bordeaux, 1998.

192. *Untitled (I Have Been to Hell and Back),* 1996, embroidered handkerchief. "I have been to hell and back. And let me tell you, it was wonderful." She also wrote this in her diary on February 12, 1996.

193. Paulo Herkenhoff, "Louise Bourgeois, Femme-Temps," in Jerry Gorovoy and Pandora Tabatabai Asbaghi, eds., *Louise Bourgeois: Blue Days and Pink Days,* exh. cat. (Milan: Fondazione Prada, 1997), 268.

194. Diary, July 11, 1972.

195. *Louise Bourgeois: New Work,* Cheim & Read, New York, November 20, 2001–January 5, 2002.

196. Gorovoy and Asbaghi, *Louise Bourgeois,* 254.

197. Gorovoy and Asbaghi, *Louise Bourgeois,* 256.

198. Diary, July 30, 1990.

199. *Louise Bourgeois,* XXIIIrd International São Paulo Biennial, Brazil, October 5–December 15, 1996.

200. *Louise Bourgeois: Sculpture,* Centro Cultural Banco do Brazil, Rio de Janeiro, February 27–April 6, 1997; *The Drawings of Louise Bourgeois,* Centro Cultural da Light, April 10–May 11, 1997.

201. *He Disappeared into Complete Silence* (1947), reprinted in *Destruction,* 48.

202. *Untitled* (1943), ink and pencil on gray paper.

203. Diary, August 18, 1997. Cited by Paulo Herkenhoff, "Cannibalism," in Frances Morris, ed., *Louise Bourgeois,* exh. cat. (London: Tate, 2007), 70.

204. Loose sheet, 1959 (LB-0230).

205. Interview with Deborah Wye and Marsha Pels, July 2, 1979, in Herkenhoff, "Cannibalism," 70.

206. "[A] vow made is forgotten, and remains operative, unconsciously operative, and it can be denied and procrastinated until death, then it is absorbed by your children + continue[s] to eat its way through generation[s]." Diary, August 19, 1991. [Originally in English. —Trans.] No doubt she was referring to the vow of chastity she took so her mother wouldn't die. See chapter 1 in this volume.

207. Diary, June 27, 1991.

208. Diary, May 10, 1984.

209. Diary, May 10, 1997.

210. Diary, September 2, 1994. [Underlined in the original.—Trans.]

211. Diary, September 3, 1994.

212. *Premises: Invested Spaces in Visual Arts and Architecture from France, 1958–1998*, Centre Pompidou, Paris, October 13, 1998–January 11, 1999.

213. *Francis Bacon, Louise Bourgeois, Franz Xaver Messerschmidt: A Juxtaposition of Three Artists*, Cheim & Read Gallery, New York, November 18–December 31, 1998.

214. Francis Bacon, *Repères*, no. 106, September 1999; *Francis Bacon: Papes et autres figures, Peintures de la Succession*, exh. cat. (Paris: Galerie Lelong, 1999); for excerpts from this article, see *Destruction* (French ed.), 387–89.

215. This and preceding quotations in *Francis Bacon: Papes et autres figures*, 47.

216. The same year, she also received the Præmium Imperiale from Japan—not being able to go herself, she sent Jean-Louis—as well as other prizes and honorific medals.

217. *Louise Bourgeois, Memory and Architecture*, Museo Nacional Centro de Arte Reina Sofía, Madrid, November 16, 1999–February 14, 2000.

218. Director and curator at the Tate Modern, at the time.

219. Meyer-Thoss, *Louise Bourgeois*.

220. Kuspit, *Louise Bourgeois*.

221. Henry Geldzahler (1935–1994), curator at the Metropolitan Museum of Art. "Louise Bourgeois," *Interview*, March 1992, 98–103, reprinted in *Making It: Essays, Interviews and Talks* (New York: Mariner Books, 1996).

222. Douglas Maxwell, interview published in *Modern Painters* 6, no. 2 (1993): 38–43.

223. Obrist did a number of interviews with artists and interviewed Louise in January 1995; published in *Destruction*, 287–92.

224. Diary, December 10, 1994. We hear the criticism and disdain in her voice when she writes: "Each visit from Rob[er]t Storr who finished his book is a federal case." Notebook, September 7, 1994 (LB-0830), 21v. [Mix of English and French.—Trans.]

225. Diary, October 13, 1997. [Mix of English and French.—Trans.]

226. Diary, December 22, 1995 (written on the page for December 15, 1995). [Mix of English and French.—Trans.]

227. Diary, March 7, 1996. [Mix of English and French.—Trans.]

228. Loose sheet, c. March 1990 (LB-0047), [In French except for "spinning around," which is in English.—Trans.] Full English translation in "Panic" in Morris, *Louise Bourgeois*, 200.

229. Loose sheet, c. March 1990 (LB-0047).

230. Loose sheet, c. 1964 (LB-0379).

231. Diary, August 27, 1993.

232. Diary, January 9, 1994. [Mix of French and English.—Trans.]

233. Diary, June 8, 1996.

234. Diary, August 20, 1996.

235. Guidelines for participants in Louise's Sunday salons, composed by Louise.

236. Diary, June 27, 1999.

237. Pouran Esrafily, Iranian filmmaker, filmed the Sunday salons from 1999 to 2007 and made the short film *Abandon* in 1998.

238. Diary, December 2, 1996. [Mix of English and French.—Trans.]

239. Diary, June 12, 1991.

240. Loose sheet, August 3, 1995 (LB-0781).

241. Diary, November 23, 1999.

242. Diary, September 9, 1997. [Originally in English.—Trans.]

243. Diary, March 29, 1990.

244. Diary, April 3, 1999. [Mix of French and English.—Trans.]

245. Diary, September 2, 1999.

246. Diary, November 15, 1993. [Mix of French and English.—Trans.]

247. "My memory is moth eaten." Inscription on *When Did This Happen?* (2007), a series of five etchings with hand additions; also featured on loose sheet, June 21, 1994 (LB-0551).

248. Diary, August 10, 1999. ["Au feu les pompiers" is a well-known children's song in France.—Trans.]

249. "Lady in Waiting: everything is in order. I can wait. I do not mind waiting. State of equilibrium (stable), the tools are in order." Diary, August 12, 1990. [Mix of English and French. Underlined in the original.—Trans.]

250. *Lady in Waiting* (2003), tapestry, thread, stainless steel, steel, wood, and glass.

251. Loose sheet, c. December 1996 (LB-0760): "The Map of Tendre—concerning: Matthew, Phyllis, Ann Laure Lyon and the Sunday visitors. [. . .] Rosamonde, Brigitte, Gardner, Grace Glueck, Marie-Laure, the friends, old or new."

252. The Carte du Tendre, or Map of Tendre, as it's sometimes called in English, is a map to the country of love, invented by the seventeenth-century *précieuses*.

Chapter 11. Petite Maman

Epigraph: *Untitled* (2006), fabric, fabric collage, and embroidered text; see Philip Larratt-Smith, ed., *Louise Bourgeois: Petite Maman* (Mexico City: Museo del Palacio de Bellas Artes, 2014), 39.

1. Frances Morris had already shown Louise's work in the exhibition *Rites of Passage: Art for the End of the Century*, Tate Modern, London, June 15–September 3, 1995, organized in collaboration with Stuart Morgan. Afterward, she curated *Louise Bourgeois: Stitches in Time*, Irish Museum of Modern Art, Dublin, 2002.

2. The three towers were acquired by Château La Coste, near Aix-en-Provence, France, for permanent installation in a building designed by architect Jean Nouvel.

3. This addition was made at the request of Nicholas Serota, director of the Tate Modern, who also wanted to show a spider.

4. Louise Bourgeois, written February 28, 2000, for the presentation of her work at the Tate Modern, reprinted in Louise Bourgeois, *Destruction du père / Reconstruction du père: Écrits*

et entretiens, 1923–2000, expanded French ed., ed. Marie-Laure Bernadac and Hans Ulrich Obrist (Paris: Daniel Lelong, 2000) [hereafter cited as *Destruction* (French ed.)], 390.

5. It was also the title of an exhibition curated by Thomas Kellein, *Louise Bourgeois: La famille,* Kunsthalle Bielefeld, Germany, March 12–June 5, 2006.

6. In "Interview with Esther Harriet," 1989, in "Family," in Frances Morris, ed., *Louise Bourgeois,* exh. cat. (London: Tate, 2007),127.

7. In *Louise Bourgeois: La famille,* exh. cat. (Cologne: König, 2006), 161, reprinted in *Destruction* (French ed.), 315.

8. *A View from the Outside: Louise Bourgeois, the Reticent Child,* Sigmund Freud Museum, Vienna, November 25, 2003–February 29, 2004.

9. The artist's words, which were included in the Sigmund Freud Museum exhibition.

10. "*Incestuelle*" and not "incestuous," to borrow Paul-Claude Racamier's distinction in *L'inceste et l'incestuel* (Paris: Dunod, 1995).

11. She is referring to Louis Malle's film *Le souffle au cœur* (1971), which tells the story of the incestuous relationship between a mother and her son.

12. A series of seventy-six drawings, also titled *Tous les cinque* but depicting five red circles nested inside each other, were shown as well.

13. "Central Intelligence Agency CIA," she wrote on the back of one of the forty-nine drawings she made while the Democratic National Convention was in session in July 2004. On the back of another drawing from the series, she wrote "D.N.C." (Democratic National Committee).

14. *Untitled* (1998), red ink and pencil; see Morris, *Louise Bourgeois,* 294.

15. See Linda Nochlin, "Old Age Style: Late Louise Bourgeois," in Morris, *Louise Bourgeois,* 195.

16. Louise Bourgeois (Paris, 1563–1636), midwife and writer who delivered all of Marie de Médicis's children, including Louis XIII, and was the first woman to publish a childbirth manual. Book and information provided by Peter Blum.

17. Work illustrated by the print triptych *The Reticent Child* (2004). Deborah Wye, ed., *Louise Bourgeois: The Complete Prints and Books,* catalogue raisonné (New York: Museum of Modern Art, 2018), cat. no. 560, https://www.moma.org/s/lb/collection_lb/object/object_objid -193131.html. See also cat. no. 612–615: Recueil des Secrets de Louyse Bourgeois https://www .moma.org/s/lb/collection_lb/object/object_objid-128382.html.

18. See chapter 5 in this volume.

19. These large red gouaches were first shown in an exhibition curated by Philip Larratt-Smith, *Louise Bourgeois: Nature Study,* Inverleith House, Royal Botanical Gardens, Edinburgh, May 3–July 6, 2008.

20. She began making these heads in 1998 and continued making them until 2009.

21. "Basement sale, all the clothes belonging to five people (the family)!! Everything must go!" Diary, July 7, 2000.

22. Loose sheet, c. 1995 (LB-0782).

23. Written on an undated drawing; see Morris, *Louise Bourgeois,* 187.

24. Diary, January 11, 2001.

25. *Ode à la Bièvre* (2002), n.p.

26. A street that runs into the boulevard Saint-Germain; the Café de Flore is found at this

intersection. That is where she attended nursery school and went to a restaurant called Le Petit Saint-Benoît with her father.

27. Where she married Robert Goldwater in 1938.

28. Jean Sablon (1906–1994), popular French singer; the song is from 1947.

29. Maurice Chevalier (1888–1972), French singer; the song is from 1939.

30. Brigitte Cornand, dir., *C'est le murmure de l'eau qui chante* (Paris: Films du Siamois, 2002).

31. See the drawing *What Is the Shape of This Song* (2002), which was used for the cover of the brochure published for the exhibition *Le jour, la nuit, le jour,* Palais de Tokyo, October 7, 2002–April 6, 2003.

32. Diary, January 6, 2001.

33. *A View from the Outside: Louise Bourgeois, the Reticent Child.*

34. *Louise Bourgeois,* White Cube, London, February 4–March 1, 2003.

35. *Louise Bourgeois, New Work,* Hauser & Wirth Colnaghi, London, October 10–November 17, 2007.

36. *Louise Bourgeois: Echo,* Cheim & Read, New York, September 9–November 1, 2008.

37. The title of this work is *Self-Portrait* (2009); it was shown at the gallery during the exhibition *Louise Bourgeois,* September 17–December 12, 2009.

38. This is one of ten sets; some have only twenty sheets, one has thirty, and two sets have forty.

39. For a time, she worked in both formats at once and was always glad to work with both printers. She made more experimental work with Benjamin Shiff in her later years, but Felix Harlan remained a trusted friend and continued to print on fabric for her until the very end.

40. Produced by Benjamin Shiff, who organized the handmade paper, platemaking, and printing and returned the printed compositions to Bourgeois for her hand additions.

41. Loose sheet, c. 1959 (LB-0768), in Philip Larratt-Smith, ed., *Louise Bourgeois: The Return of the Repressed,* 2 vols. (London: Violette, 2012), 2:115.

42. Loose sheet, c. 1990 (LB-0554), in Larratt-Smith, *Louise Bourgeois,* 2:179. [Mix of French and English.—Trans.]

43. Inspired by the original text from c. 1961; see Notebook (LB-0426). [Originally in English.—Trans.]

44. Roni Horn (born 1955), American artist and writer.

45. Roni Horn, *Wonderwater: Alice Offshore,* 4 vols. (Göttingen, Germany: Steidl, and London: Thames and Hudson, 2004), with contributions by Louise Bourgeois, Anne Carson, Hélène Cixous, and John Waters.

46. Examples include Melanie Klein, Donald Winnicott, Otto Rank, Karen Horney, Sigmund and Anna Freud, and her new friend the psychoanalyst Daniel Milman. For writers, she included Balzac, Baudelaire, Sand, Zola, and Flaubert. Horn, *Wonderwater,* 1:8–9, annotated by Louise Bourgeois.

47. Tracey Emin (born 1963) is a British artist who won the Turner Prize in 1999 and represented Great Britain at the Venice Biennale in 2007.

48. Gary Indiana (1950–2024), American writer and filmmaker.

49. In 2005, Louise made *Father and Son,* a fountain at the entry to the Olympic Sculpture Park at the Seattle Art Museum. Her last large-scale project, *The Damned, the Possessed, and the Beloved* (2007–10), made in collaboration with the Swiss architect Peter Zumthor (born 1943),

was inaugurated on June 23, 2011, at the Steilneset Memorial in Vardø, Norway—and it was also her last *Cell*, after *Cell* (*The Last Climb*), from 2008. Steilneset is a memorial to those executed during the witch trials of the seventeenth century.

50. Diary, January 10, 2001.

51. "Art is my religion." Diary, December 5, 1987. [Originally in English.—Trans.]

52. Part of Jean-Claude Meyer's private property but open to the public by appointment and on certain days.

53. Loose sheet, c. 1990 (LB-0512), written on the back of a postcard with the artist's print of a child in the middle of a double profile: *Self-Portrait,* 1990. See "Gratitude" in Morris, *Louise Bourgeois,* 153. [Mix of French and English.—Trans.]

54. Diary, February 28, 2003.

55. Bourgeois, "On Beauty: A Conversation with Bill Beckley," 1997–98, in Bill Beckley, ed., *Uncontrollable Beauty: Toward a New Aesthetic* (New York: Allworth, 2001), reprinted in *Destruction,* 361.

56. Diary, May 1, 1983, in *Destruction,* 130 (misdated April 30, 1983). [Originally in English.—Trans.]

57. Diary, October 7, 1951. [Originally in English.—Trans.]

58. Diary, September 12, 1993.

59. *Louise Bourgeois,* retrospective exhibition organized by Frances Morris, Marie-Laure Bernadac, and Jonas Storsve, at the Tate Modern, London, October 10, 2007–January 20, 2008, then at the Centre Pompidou, Paris, New York's Guggenheim Museum, the Museum of Contemporary Art, Los Angeles, and the Hirshhorn Museum and Sculpture Garden, Washington, DC.

60. Nadine Satiat, *Au miroir de Louise* (Paris: Flammarion, 2014). She also wrote a biography of Gertrude Stein.

61. Three large prints with hand additions, three small prints on fabric, a gouache on paper, and the sixteen-part mixed-media fabric suite *Eugénie Grandet.*

62. Diary, October 7, 1994. [In French except for "be informed."—Trans.]

63. Diary, February 24, 1996.

64. Loose sheet, c. 1993 (LB-0105). See also Louise Bourgeois, *Moi, Eugénie Grandet,* preface by Jean Frémon (Paris: Gallimard, 2010).

65. Loose sheet, c. 1968 (LB-0046), in Larratt-Smith, *Louise Bourgeois,* 2:167.

66. Loose sheet, August 3, 1995 (LB-0781).

67. Loose sheet, c. 1988 (LB-0829).

68. Diary, November 18, 2001. Translates to "The word pity calms me." She also used this phrase in prints on fabric.

69. Loose sheet, March 1986 (LB-0507). [In English, except the last line is in French.—Trans.]

70. Brigitte Cornand, *Grabigouji: À Louise Bourgeois, mon amie,* photography by Brigitte Cornand (Paris: Dilecta, 2011).

71. *C'est le murmure de l'eau qui chante* (Paris: Les Films du Siamois and Centre Georges Pompidou, 2002); *La rivière gentille* (Paris: Les Films du Siamois and Centre Georges Pompidou, 2007).

72. Diary, February 10, 1992.

73. Diary, August 13, 2001.

74. Diary, April 20, 2002. [Lines from "Oh, What a Beautiful Mornin'," from *Oklahoma!* (1943), music by Richard Rodgers, lyrics by Oscar Hammerstein II.—Trans.]

75. Alex Van Gelder, *Mumbling Beauty: Louise Bourgeois,* with texts by Hans Ulrich Obrist and Alex Van Gelder (London: Thames and Hudson, 2015). Louise met Alex Van Gelder in 1970 in Paris with Suzan Cooper. At that time he was a dealer in African art.

76. Edward Said, *On Late Style* (New York: Random House, 2006).

77. See Pablo Picasso, *Le jeune peintre*, 1972, Musée Picasso, Paris.

78. In Paola Igliori, *Entrails, Heads and Tails: Photographic Essays and Conversations on the Everyday with Contemporary Artists* (New York: Rizzoli, 1992), n.p. [41].

79. Notebook, 1965 (LB-0771), 27. [Mix of French and English.—Trans.]

80. Her family and a few close friends.

81. She had planned to place a granite version of *Le Trani Episode* (according to Jerry Gorovoy in 2017). Michel shares Robert's plot.

82. Loose sheet, c. 2008 (LB-0516). [Originally in English.—Trans.]

83. "I have been to Hell and back. And let me tell you, it was wonderful," *Untitled* (1996), embroidered handkerchief; see also Diary, February 12, 1996. [Originally in English. —Trans.]

SELECTED BIBLIOGRAPHY

Writings by the Artist

Album. New York: Peter Blum, 1994. Illustrated book with sixty-nine photolithographs.

"Child Abuse." *Artforum* 20, no. 4 (1982): 40–47 and cover.

Francis Bacon: Papes et autres figures—Peintures de la Succession. With Antonio Saura and David Sylvester. Exh. cat. Paris: Galerie Lelong, 1999.

"Freud's Toys." *Artforum* 28, no. 5 (1990): 111–13.

He Disappeared into Complete Silence. New York: self-published, 1947; expanded 2nd ed., New York: Museum of Modern Art, 2005. Illustrated book with nine engravings.

Homely Girl: A Life. With Arthur Miller. New York: Peter Blum, 1992.

"Native Talent." *Artforum* 32, no. 5 (1994): 73.

"Obsession." *Artforum* 30, no. 8 (1992): 85–87.

Ode à la Bièvre. Limited ed. New York: Zucker Art Books, 2007. Illustrated book with digital prints and screenprint.

Ode à ma mère. Paris: Solstice, 1995. Illustrated book with nine engravings.

The Puritan. New York: Osiris, 1990. Illustrated book with eight engravings, text from 1947.

"Tender Compulsions." *World Art,* February 1995, 108.

Published Interviews, Books, and Articles

Bal, Mieke. *Louise Bourgeois' Spider: The Architecture of Art-Writing.* Chicago: University of Chicago Press, 2001.

Bernadac, Marie-Laure. *Louise Bourgeois.* Paris: Flammarion, 1996. Rev. ed., 2006.

Bernadac, Marie-Laure, and Elisabeth Bronfen. *Louise Bourgeois: The Insomnia Drawings.* Zurich: Daros; in collaboration with New York: Peter Blum, and Zurich: Scalo, 2000.

Bloch, Susi. "An Interview with Louise Bourgeois." *Art Journal* 35, no. 4 (1976): 370–73.

Bonami, Francesco. "Louise Bourgeois: In a Strange Way, Things Are Getting Better and Better." *Flash Art* 27, no. 174 (1994): 36–39.

Bourgeois, Louise. *Deconstruction of the Father / Reconstruction of the Father: Writings and Interviews, 1923–1997.* Edited by Marie-Laure Bernadac and Hans Ulrich Obrist. Cambridge, MA: MIT Press, and London: Violette, 1998.

Bourgeois, Louise. *Destruction du père / Reconstruction du père: Écrits et entretiens, 1923–2000.* Expanded French ed. Edited by Marie-Laure Bernadac and Hans Ulrich Obrist. Paris: Daniel Lelong, 2000.

Caux, Jacqueline. *Tissée, tendue au fil des jours, la toile de Louise Bourgeois.* Paris: Seuil, 2003.

Clair, Jean. "Five Notes on the Work of Louise Bourgeois." In *Francis Bacon, Louise Bourgeois, Franz Xaver Messerschmidt.* Exh. cat. New York: Cheim & Read, 1998.

Cooke, Lynne, and Mark Francis. *Carnegie International 21.* Exh. cat. Pittsburgh, PA: Carnegie Museum of Art, 1991.

Crone, Rainer, and Petrus Graf Schaesberg. *Louise Bourgeois: The Secret of the Cells.* Munich: Prestel, 1998; rev. ed., 2008.

Frémon, Jean. *Louise Bourgeois, femme maison.* Paris: L'Échoppe, 2013.

Frémon, Jean. *Now, Now, Louison.* Trans. Cole Swenson. London: Les Fugitives, 2018.

Gardner, Paul. *Louise Bourgeois.* New York: Universe, 1994.

Gibson, Ann. "Louise Bourgeois and Retroactive Politics of Gender." *Art Journal* 53, no. 4 (1994): 44–47.

Girard, Xavier. *Louise Bourgeois: Face à face.* Paris: Seuil, 2016.

Glick, Geoffrey. *Louise Bourgeois: The Institute.* New York: New York University's Institute of Fine Arts, 2005.

Goldwater, Robert. *What Is Modern Sculpture?* New York: Museum of Modern Art, 1969.

Herkenhoff, Paulo, Allan Schwartzman, and Robert Storr. *Louise Bourgeois.* London: Phaidon, 2003.

Horn, Roni. *Wonderwater (Alice Offshore).* 4 vols. Göttingen, Germany: Steidl, 2004.

Igliori, Paola. *Entrails, Heads and Tails: Photographic Essays and Conversations on the Everyday with Contemporary Artists.* New York: Rizzoli, 1992.

"Interview with Douglas Maxwell." *Modern Painters* 6, no. 2 (1993): 38–43.

Kaplan, Cheryl. "Cut in Two: A Conversation between Louise Bourgeois and Cheryl Kaplan." *Deutsche Bank Magazine,* no. 24 (2004).

Kirili, Alain. "The Passion for Sculpture: A Conversation with Louise Bourgeois." *Arts Magazine* 63, no. 7 (1989): 68–75.

Krauss, Rosalind. "Louise Bourgeois: Portrait of the Artist as *Fillette.*" In *Bachelors.* Cambridge, MA: MIT Press, 1999.

Kuspit, Donald. *Louise Bourgeois.* New York: Random House, 1988.

Larratt-Smith, Philip, ed. *Louise Bourgeois: The Return of The Repressed* (vol. 1) and *Louise Bourgeois: Psychoanalytic Writings* (vol. 2). London: Violette, 2012.

Lippard, Lucy R. "The Blind Leading the Blind." *Bulletin of the Detroit Institute of the Arts,* Spring 1981, 24–29.

Lippard, Lucy R. "Louise Bourgeois: From the Inside Out." In *From the Center: Feminist Essays on Women's Art* (New York: Dutton, 1976). Orig. publ. in *Artforum* 13, no. 7 (1975): 26–33.

Lippard, Lucy R. *Overlay: Contemporary Art and the Art of Prehistory.* New York: Pantheon, 1983.

Meyer-Thoss, Christiane. "I Am a Woman with No Secrets." *Parkett* 27 (1991): 37–43.

Meyer-Thoss, Christiane. *Louise Bourgeois: Konstruktionen für den freien Fall / Designing for Free Fall.* Zurich: Ammann, 1992.

Miller, Lynn F., and Sally S. Swenson. *Lives and Works: Talks with Women Artists*. London: Scarecrow, 1981.

Moore, Allison. *In the Margins: Nineteen Interviews*. Minneapolis, MN: Montgomery Glasoe Fine Art Gallery, 1995.

Nixon, Mignon. *Fantastic Reality: Louise Bourgeois and a Story of Modern Art*. Cambridge, MA: MIT Press, 2005.

Pearlstein, Philip. "The Private Myth." *Art News* 60, no. 5 (1961): 42–45, 61–62.

Pels, Marsha. "Louise Bourgeois: In a Search for Gravity." *Art International* 23 (October 1979): 46–54.

Pollock, Griselda. "Old Bones and Cocktail Dresses: Louise Bourgeois and the Question of Age." *Oxford Art Journal* 22, no. 2 (1999): 71–100.

Rubin, William. "Some Reflections Prompted by the Recent Work of Louise Bourgeois." *Art International* 13, no. 4 (1969): 17–20.

Samoyault, Tiphaine. *La main négative*. Paris: Argol, 2008.

Satiat, Nadine. *Au miroir de Louise: Essai sur l'artiste Louise Bourgeois*. Paris: Flammarion, 2014.

Seiberling, Dorothy. "The Female View of Erotica." *New York Magazine*, February 11, 1974, 56.

Steir, Pat. "Mortal Elements: Pat Steir Talks with Louise Bourgeois." *Artforum* 32, no. 1 (1993): 86–87.

Storr, Robert. *Louise Bourgeois: Intimate Geometries*. New York: Monacelli, 2016.

Storr, Robert. "Meanings, Materials and Milieu: Reflections of Recent Work by Louise Bourgeois." *Parkett* 9 (1986): 82–85.

"Transcendence: Interview with Gary Koepke." *SoHo Journal, 1995–1996* (1995).

Xenakis, Mâkhi. *Louise Bourgeois: The Blind Leading the Blind*. Arles, France: Actes Sud, and London: Galerie Lelong, 2008).

Xenakis, Mâkhi. *Louise, sauvez-moi! Conversations avec Louise Bourgeois, 1988–2009*. Arles, France: Actes Sud, 2018.

Solo Exhibition Catalogs

1964 Robbins, Daniel. *Drawings by Louise Bourgeois*. New York: Rose Fried Gallery.

1978 Wye, Deborah. *Matrix / Berkeley 17: Louise Bourgeois*. Berkeley, CA: University Art Museum.

1980 Gorovoy, Jerry. *The Iconography of Louise Bourgeois*. New York: Max Hutchinson Gallery.

1981 Marandel, Patrice. *Louise Bourgeois: Femme Maison*. Chicago: Renaissance Society of the University of Chicago.

1982 Pincus-Witten, Robert. *Bourgeois Truth*. New York: Robert Miller Gallery.
      Wye, Deborah. *Louise Bourgeois*. New York: Museum of Modern Art.

1985 Bourgeois, Louise, and Stuart Morgan. *Louise Bourgeois*. London: Serpentine Gallery.
      Frémon, Jean. *Louise Bourgeois: Rétrospective, 1947–1984*. Paris: Galerie Maeght-Lelong.
      Frémon, Jean, and Robert Storr. *Louise Bourgeois: Retrospektive, 1947–1984*. Zurich: Galerie Maeght-Lelong.

1986 Gorovoy, Jerry. *Louise Bourgeois*. New York: Robert Miller Gallery.

1987 Morgan, Stuart. *Louise Bourgeois*. Cincinnati, OH: Taft Museum.

1988 Cheim, John and Jerry Gorovoy, eds. *Louise Bourgeois Drawings*. New York: Robert Miller Gallery, and Paris: Daniel Lelong.

Louise Bourgeois: Works on Paper. Amsterdam: Museum Overholland.

1989 Geldzahler, Henry. *Louise Bourgeois*. Bridgehampton, NY: Dia Art Foundation.

Meyer-Thoss, Christiane. *Louise Bourgeois: 100 Zeichnungen, 1919–1989*. Zurich: Galerie Lelong.

1990 *Louise Bourgeois*. Lyon, France: Musée Saint-Pierre art contemporain.

Morgan, Stuart. *Louise Bourgeois. Recent Work, 1984–1989*. London: Riverside Studios.

1991 *Louise Bourgeois: L'œuvre gravée*. Zurich: Galerie Lelong.

1992 *Louise Bourgeois*. Milwaukee, WI: Milwaukee Art Museum.

1993 Kotik, Charlotta. *Louise Bourgeois. Recent Work*. New York: Brooklyn Museum for the United States Pavillon, Forty-Fifth Venice Biennale.

Louise Bourgeois. Milan: Galerie Karsten Greve.

Louise Bourgeois. Denver, CO: Ginny Williams Family Foundation.

Murillo, Jorge Garcia. *Louise Bourgeois*. San Pedro, Mexico: Galeria Ramis Barquet.

1994 Emont Scott, Deborah. *Louise Bourgeois: Sculptures and Drawings*. Kansas City, MO: Nelson-Atkins Museum of Art.

Haenlein, Carl, ed. *Louise Bourgeois: Skulpturen und Installationen*. Hanover, Germany: Kestner Gesellschaft.

Kotik, Charlotta, Terrie Sultan, and Christian Leigh. *Louise Bourgeois: The Locus of Memory; Works, 1982–1993*. New York: Brooklyn Museum of Art, and Washington, DC: Corcoran Gallery of Art.

Louise Bourgeois: Drawings and Early Sculptures, Sculptures and Installations. Cologne, Germany: Galerie Karsten Greve.

Louise Bourgeois: The Red Rooms. New York: Peter Blum-Blumarts, 1994.

Strick, Jeremy. *Louise Bourgeois: The Personages*. Saint Louis, MO: Saint Louis Art Museum.

Wye, Deborah, and Carol Smith. *The Prints of Louise Bourgeois*, catalogue raisonné. New York: Museum of Modern Art.

1995 Bernadac, Marie-Laure, ed. *Louise Bourgeois: Pensées-plumes*. Paris: Centre Georges Pompidou.

Bourgeois, Louise, and Lawrence Rinder. *Louise Bourgeois: Drawings and Observations*. Berkeley, CA: University Art Museum.

Cole, Ian. *Louise Bourgeois. Sculpture/The Prints of Louise Bourgeois*. Oxford: Museum of Modern Art.

Louise Bourgeois. Bourges, France: Galerie La Box / École nationale des beaux-arts de Bourges.

Louise Bourgeois. Fukuoka City, Japan: Mitsubishi-Jisho Artium, with the cooperation of MoMA Contemporary.

Louise Bourgeois. Seville, Spain: Centro Andaluz de arte contemporàneo.

Louise Bourgeois. Sydney: Museum of Contemporary Art.

Louise Bourgeois: An Exhibition of Sculpture. Oxford: Museum of Modern Art.

Marshall, Richard D., and Paulo Herkenhoff. *Esculturas de Louise Bourgeois: La elegancia de la ironía.* Monterrey, Mexico: Museo de Arte Contemporaneo de Monterrey.

Pagé, Suzanne, and Béatrice Parant, eds. *Louise Bourgeois: Sculptures, environnements, dessins, 1938–1995.* Paris: Musée d'art moderne de la Ville de Paris and La Tempête.

Pernoud, Emmanuel. *Louise Bourgeois: Estampes.* Paris: Bibliothèque nationale de France.

Smith, Jason, and Robert Storr. *Louise Bourgeois.* Melbourne: National Gallery of Victoria.

Weiermair, Peter, ed. *Louise Bourgeois.* Kilchberg and Zurich, Switzerland: Stemmle.

1996 Diego, Estrella de. *Louise Bourgeois.* Madrid: Galeria Soledad Lorenzo.

Louise Bourgeois. Brussels: Xavier Hufkens Gallery.

Louise Bourgeois. Mexico City: Museo Rufino Tamayo.

Louise Bourgeois: The Forties and Fifties. Westford, CT: Joseloff Gallery, Harry Jack Gray Center, University of Hartford.

Louise Bourgeois: Sculptures and Objects. Salzburg, Austria: Rupertinum.

Red Rooms: Louise Bourgeois. Zurich: Hauser & Wirth.

Zdenek, Felix. *Louise Bourgeois der Ort des Gedächtnisses: Skulpturen, Environments und Zeichnungen, 1946–1995.* Hamburg: Deichtorhallen Hamburg; Paris: La Tempête.

1997 Amano, Taro. *Louise Bourgeois: Homesickness.* Yokohama, Japan: Yokohama Museum of Art.

Gorovoy, Jerry, and Pandora Tabatabai Asbaghi, eds. *Louise Bourgeois: Blue Days and Pink Days.* Milan: Fondazione Prada.

Herkenhoff, Paulo. *Louise Bourgeois: Sculpture.* Rio de Janiero: Centro Cultural Banco do Brazil.

Herkenhoff, Paulo, and Angelica de Moraes. *Louise Bourgeois: Desenhos/Drawings.* Rio de Janeiro: Centro Cultural Light.

Louise Bourgeois. Chicago: Arts Club of Chicago, 1997.

Louise Bourgeois. Cologne: Galerie Karsten Greve.

Louise Bourgeois: Drawings. Chicago: Rhona Hoffman Gallery.

Louise Bourgeois: Ode à ma mère. Cincinnati, OH: Contemporary Arts Center.

Louise Bourgeois: Recent Drawings. Paris: Galerie Karsten Greve.

1998 Bernadac, Marie-Laure, ed. *Louise Bourgeois: Œuvres récentes / Recent Works.* Bordeaux. CAPC Musée d'art contemporain; Lisbon: Centro Cultural de Belém; Malmö, Sweden: Malmö Konsthall; and London: Serpentine Gallery.

Louise Bourgeois: Topiary. New York: Whitney Museum of American Art.

Waterfall, Ann. "*Sacred and Fatal*": The Art of Louise Bourgeois. Raleigh, NC: Museum of Art.

1999 Catoir, Barbara, and Mary Jane Jacob. *Louise Bourgeois.* Cologne: Galerie Karsten Greve.

Gorovoy, Jerry, and Danielle Tilkin, eds. *Louise Bourgeois: Memoria y arquitectura / Memory and Architecture.* Madrid: Museo Nacional, Centro de Arte Reina Sofía.

Kellein, Thomas. *Louise Bourgeois,* vol. 1, *Sculpturen, 1994–1998,* and vol. 2, *Die Zeichnungen, 1996–1998.* Bielefeld, Germany: Kunsthalle Bielefeld.

Louise Bourgeois: Metamorfosis and Other Work on Paper. New York: Galerie Lelong.

Smith, Carol. *Louise Bourgeois Prints, 1989–1998*. Lynchburg, VA: Museum of Art, Randolph-Macon Woman's College.

2000 Kang, Seung-Wan, Mihwa Park, and Bernard Marcadé. *Louise Bourgeois: The Space of Memory*. Kyunggi-Do, South Korea: National Museum of Contemporary Art.

Louise Bourgeois. Athens: Kappatos Gallery.

Louise Bourgeois: Handkerchiefs. Venice: Fondazione Bevilacqua La Masa.

Louise Bourgeois: Neue Arbeiten / Recent Works. Zurich: Hauser & Wirth.

Louise Bourgeois: Works on Paper. Milan: Galerie Karsten Greve.

Morris, Frances, ed. *Louise Bourgeois (The Unilever Series)*. London: Tate Modern.

2001 Cheim, John, and Thomas Whitridge, eds. *Louise Bourgeois: New Work*. New York: Cheim & Read.

Lévy, Sophie. *Louise Bourgeois: Livres illustrés*. Giverny, France: Musée d'art américain.

Louise Bourgeois. Bilbao, Spain: Museo Guggenheim.

Pincus-Witten, Robert. *Louise Bourgeois: The Personages*. New York: C & M Arts.

Suzuki, Sarah J. *Louise Bourgeois: Illustrated Books*. New York: Miriam and Ira D. Wallach Art Gallery, Columbia University.

Sylvester, Julie, ed. *Louise Bourgeois at the Hermitage*. St. Petersburg: Hermitage Museum.

2002 Aliaga, Juan Vicente. *Louise Bourgeois*. Madrid: Galeria Soledad Lorenzo.

Louise Bourgeois: Le jour la nuit le jour. Paris: Palais de Tokyo.

Helfenstein, Josef. *Louise Bourgeois: The Early Work*. Champaign, IL: Krannert Art Museum; Madison, WI: Art Center; and Aspen, CO: Aspen Art Museum.

Louise Bourgeois. Provincetown, MA: Fine Arts Work Center in Provincetown.

Louise Bourgeois: Recent Sculptures and Drawings. Trans. Allison Plath-Moseley. Luxembourg City: Galerie Beaumontpublic.

Louise Bourgeois: Recent Work. Paris: Galerie Karsten Greve.

Pérez-Ratton, Virginia, and Paulo Herkenhoff. *Louise Bourgeois: Childhood*. San José, Costa Rica: Fundación Ars Teor Etica.

Schneider, Eckhard, ed. *Louise Bourgeois: Drawings and Sculpture / Zeichnungen und Skulpturen*. Bregenz, Austria: Kunsthaus Bregenz.

Unterdörfer, Michaela. *Louise Bourgeois: Works in Marble / Marmorarbeiten*. Zurich: Hauser & Wirth.

2003 Becker, Kathrin, Antje Weitzel, and Valeria Schulte-Fishchedick, eds. *Louise Bourgeois: Intime Abstraktionen*. Berlin: Akademie der Künste.

Louise Bourgeois. Cologne: Galerie Karsten Greve.

Louise Bourgeois. London: White Cube.

Louise Bourgeois: La sage-femme. Arrecife Lanzarote, Canary Islands: Museo internacional de arte contemporáneo (MIAC).

Morawinska, Agnieszka. *Louise Bourgeois: Geometry of Desire*. Warsaw: Zacheta Gallery of Art.

Morris, Frances. *Louise Bourgeois: Stitches in Time*. Dublin: Irish Museum of Modern Art; and North Miami, FL: Museum of Contemporary Art.

Tøjner, Paul Erik, and Penelope Vending. *Louise Bourgeois: Life as Art*. Humlebæk, Denmark: Louisiana Museum of Modern Art.

2004 De Braekeleer, Catherine, *Louise Bourgeois: Prints and Illustrated Books*. La Louvière, Belgium: Centre de la gravure et de l'image imprimée.

Keller, Eva, Malin Regula, and Robert Storr. *Louise Bourgeois: Emotions Abstracted: Werke / Works, 1941–2000*. Zurich: Daros.

Louise Bourgeois. Yokosuka, Japan: Akira Ikeda Gallery Muranchi.

Lyon-Wall, Scott. *Louise Bourgeois: The Reticent Child*. New York: Cheim & Read.

2005 Aguiló, Magdalena, and Antoni Boix. *Louise Bourgeois: Repairs in the Sky*. Palma de Majorca, Spain: Fundació Pilar i Joan Miró.

Herkenhoff, Paulo. *Louise Bourgeois: Selected Prints, 1989–2005*. London: Marlborough Graphics Gallery.

Larratt-Smith, Philip. *Louise Bourgeois: One and Others*. Havana, Cuba: Wifredo Lam Center.

Larratt-Smith, Philip, Gerald Matt, and Peter Weiermair. *Louise Bourgeois: Aller-Retour, Zeichnungen und Skulpturen / Drawings and Sculptures*. Vienna: Kunsthalle.

Nixon, Mignon. *Louise Bourgeois*. Seoul: Kukje Gallery.

Thompson, Cynthia. *Louise Bourgeois: Topiary, the Art of Improving Nature*. Memphis, TN: Memphis College of Art.

2006 Kellein, Thomas, ed. *Louise Bourgeois: La famille*. Bielefeld, Germany: Kunsthalle Bielefeld.

Stoops, Susan L. *Louise Bourgeois: The Woven Child (in Context)*. Worcester, MA: Worcester Art Museum.

2007 Morris, Frances, ed. *Louise Bourgeois*. London: Tate.

2008 Bernadac, Marie-Laure, and Jonas Storsve. *Louise Bourgeois*. Paris: Centre Pompidou.

Echo, New York: Cheim & Read.

Nesbitt, Paul, and Philip Larratt-Smith. *Nature Study*, Edinburgh: Inverleith House Gallery.

2010 Celant, Germano. *Louise Bourgeois: The Fabric Works*, Venice: Fondazione Vedova; Milan: Skira.

Louise Bourgeois: Moi, Eugénie Grandet. With a preface by Jean Frémon. Paris: Gallimard.

2011 Küster, Ulf. *Louise Bourgeois*. Berlin: Hatje Cantz.

2012 Larratt-Smith, Philip. *Louise Bourgeois: Conscious and Unconscious*. Doha: Qatar Museum Authority / Bloomsbury Qatar Foundation.

Tilkin, Danielle. *Louise Bourgeois: "HONNI soit QUI mal y pense."* Madrid: La Casa Encendida / Skira.

2014 Larratt-Smith, Philip. *Louise Bourgeois, petite maman*. Mexico City: Museo del Palacio de Bellas Artes.

2015 Lorz, Julienne, ed. *Louise Bourgeois: Structures of Existence: The Cells*. Munich: Haus der Kunst and Prestel.

Müller-Westermann, Iris. *Louise Bourgeois: I Have Been to Hell and Back*. Stockholm: Moderna Museet and Berlin: Hatje Cantz.

2016 Mitchell, Juliet. *Louise Bourgeois: Autobiographical Prints*. London: Hayward.

2017 Landau, Suzanne. *Louise Bourgeois: Twosome*. Tel Aviv: Tel Aviv Museum of Art.

Wye, Deborah. *Louise Bourgeois, an Unfolding Portrait*. New York: Museum of Modern Art.

2018   Rales, Emily Wei, and Ali Nemerov, eds. *Louise Bourgeois: To Unravel a Torment.* Potomac, MD: Glenstone Museum.

Wye, Deborah, ed. *Louise Bourgeois: The Complete Prints and Books.* Catalogue raisonné. New York: Museum of Modern Art. See http://www.moma.org/bourgeoisprints.

2019   Larratt-Smith, Philip, ed. *Louise Bourgeois: The Eternal Thread.* Beijing: Song Art Museum.

2020   Larratt-Smith, Philip, and Juliet Mitchell. *Louise Bourgeois: Freud's Daughter.* New York: Jewish Museum; and New Haven: Yale University Press.

2022   Davies, Clare, and Briony Fer. *Louise Bourgeois: Paintings.* New York: Metropolitan Museum of Art.

Rugoff, Ralph, ed. *The Woven Child.* London: Hayward.

2023   Paton, Justin, ed. *Louise Bourgeois: Has the Day Invaded the Night or Has the Night Invaded the Day?* Sydney: Art Gallery of New South Wales.

Rollig, Stella, Sabine Fellner, and Johanna Hofer, eds. *Louise Bourgeois: Persistent Antagonism.* Cologne: Verlag der Buchhandlung Walther and Franz König.

2024   Larratt-Smith, Philip, Geraldine Leardi, and Chloé Perrone, eds. *Louise Bourgeois: Unconscious Memories.* Rome: Galleria Borghese.

Tsubaki, Reiko, and Manabu Yahagi, eds. *Louise Bourgeois: I Have Been to Hell and Back. And Let Me Tell You, It Was Wonderful.* Tokyo: Mori Art Museum.

Audio and Film Recordings

Alexander, Alexander, dir. *Les Mains de Paris.* Film. Nero-Film AG, 1934. Preserved and restored by CNC, Paris.

Bernier, Rosamond, prod. *Louise Bourgeois at Close Quarters.* Film. New York: Metropolitan Museum of Art, and Kultur International Films, 1995.

Bernier, Rosamond, prod. *The Many Faces of Louise Bourgeois.* Film. New York: Metropolitan Museum of Art, 2002.

Bourgeois, Louise. *C'est le murmure de l'eau qui chante: Songs.* Compact disc. Paris: Brigitte Cornand, Les Films du Siamois, 2002.

Bourgeois, Louise. *Otte.* Music by Satch Hoyt and Ramuntcho Matta. Compact disc. Paris: Brigitte Cornand, Les Films du Siamois, 1995.

Cornand, Brigitte, dir. *Chère Louise.* Film. Paris: Les Films du Siamois, with support from Canal+, 1995.

Cornand, Brigitte, dir. *La rivière gentille.* Film. Paris: Les Films du Siamois, with support from Harvestworks and The Easton Foundation, 2007.

Cornand, Brigitte, dir. *Louise Bourgeois: C'est le murmure de l'eau qui chante.* Film. Paris: Les Films du Siamois, 2002.

Cornand, Brigitte, dir. *Louise Bourgeois: Mes travaux en cours 1*2*3.* Film. Paris: Les Films du Siamois, with support from CAPC de Bordeaux and the Maison Yves Saint-Laurent, Paris, 1998–99.

Falkenberg, Paul, dir. *Louise Bourgeois in Paris.* Film footage, 1985. Courtesy the Louise Bourgeois Archive / The Easton Foundation, New York.

Finch, Nigel, dir. *Louise Bourgeois: No Trespassing.* Film. London: Arena Films, BBC, 1994.

Guichard, Camille, dir. *Louise Bourgeois*. Film. Paris: Terra Luna Films and Centre Pompidou, 1993.

LoSchiavo, Theresa, dir. *Louise Bourgeois: A Banquet / A Fashion Show of Body Parts*. Filmed at the Hamilton Gallery of Contemporary Art, New York, 1978.

Louise Bourgeois. Interview conducted by Lyn Blumenthal and Kate Horsfield, School of Visual Arts, New York. Produced by Video Data Bank, School of the Art Institute of Chicago. September 1975.

Louise Bourgeois: Partial Recall. Film. New York: Museum of Modern Art, 1983.

Maybach, Chris, and Paul Gardner, dirs. *Art City: Making It in Manhattan*. Film. Los Angeles: Twelve Films, 1996.

Tschinkel, Paul, prod. *Louise Bourgeois*. Film. New York: ART, 1987.

Wallach, Amei, and Marion Cajori, dirs. *Louise Bourgeois: The Spider, the Mistress, and the Tangerine*. Film. New York: Art Kaleidoscope Foundation and Zeitgeist Films, 2008.

Page 12 bottom: © The Easton Foundation / Licensed by VAGA at Artists Rights Society (ARS), New York / Photo: Rafael Lobato

Page 14: © The Easton Foundation / Licensed by VAGA at Artists Rights Society (ARS), New York / Photo: Allan Finkelman

Page 15 top: Art: © The Easton Foundation / Licensed by VAGA at Artists Rights Society (ARS), New York / Photo: Peter Moore, © Northwestern University

Page 16: *Louise Bourgeois*, 1982. © Robert Mapplethorpe Foundation. Used with permission

Gallery 3

Page 1 bottom: Art: © The Easton Foundation / Licensed by VAGA at Artists Rights Society (ARS), New York / Photo: © Inge Morath

Page 2 top: © The Easton Foundation / Licensed by VAGA at Artists Rights Society (ARS), New York / Photo: Katherine Keller

Page 2 bottom: © The Easton Foundation / Licensed by VAGA at Artists Rights Society (ARS), New York / Photo: Christopher Burke

Page 3: © The Easton Foundation / Licensed by VAGA at Artists Rights Society (ARS), New York / Photo: Rafael Lobato

Page 4 top: Art: © The Easton Foundation / Licensed by VAGA at Artists Rights Society (ARS), New York / Photo: © Inge Morath

Photo 4 bottom: © The Easton Foundation / Licensed by VAGA at Artists Rights Society (ARS), New York / Photo: Peter Bellamy

Page 5 top: © The Easton Foundation / Licensed by VAGA at Artists Rights Society (ARS), New York / Photo: Beth Phillips

Page 5 bottom: © The Easton Foundation / Licensed by VAGA at Artists Rights Society (ARS), New York / Photo: Frédéric Delpech

Page 6: © The Easton Foundation / Licensed by VAGA at Artists Rights Society (ARS), New York / Photo: Peter Bellamy

Page 7: Art: © The Easton Foundation / Licensed by VAGA at Artists Rights Society (ARS), New York / Photo: Vera Isler-Leiner, © Artists Rights Society (ARS), NY/ProLitteris, Zurich

Page 8: © The Easton Foundation / Licensed by VAGA at Artists Rights Society (ARS), New York / Photo: Beth Phillips

Page 10: © The Easton Foundation / Licensed by VAGA at Artists Rights Society (ARS), New York / Photo: Christopher Burke

Page 11: © The Easton Foundation / Licensed by VAGA at Artists Rights Society (ARS), New York / Photo: Pouran Esrafily

Page 12: © The Easton Foundation / Licensed by VAGA at Artists Rights Society (ARS), New York / Photo: Christopher Burke

Page 13: © The Easton Foundation / Licensed by VAGA at Artists Rights Society (ARS), New York / Photo: Christopher Burke

Page 14: © The Easton Foundation / Licensed by VAGA at Artists Rights Society (ARS), New York / Photo: Christopher Burke

Page 15: Art: © The Easton Foundation / Licensed by VAGA at Artists Rights Society (ARS), New York / Photo: © Alex Van Gelder

Page 16: © The Easton Foundation / Licensed by VAGA at Artists Rights Society (ARS), New York / Photo: Christopher Burke

INDEX

———